D1289407

Law School Publications

of

WEST PUBLISHING COMPANY

St. Paul, Minnesota 55102

ADMINISTRATIVE LAW

Davis' Cases, 592 pages, 1959.
Davis Text, 617 pages, 1959.
Davis' Cases, Text and Problems, 2nd Ed., 609 pages, 1965.
Merrill's Cases, 720 pages, 1954.

ADMIRALTY

Healy and Currie's Cases and Materials on Admiralty, 872 pages, 1965.

AGENCY

Seavey and Hall's Cases, 431 pages, 1956.
Seavey's Studies, 451 pages, 1949.
Seavey's Text, 329 pages, 1964.
See Agency-Partnership.

AGENCY PARTNERSHIP

Seavey, Reuschlein & Hall's Cases, 599 pages, 1962.
Steffen's Cases, 3rd Ed., 733 pages, 1969.

BANKRUPTCY

MacLachlan's Text, 500 pages, 1956.
See Creditors' Rights.

BILLS AND NOTES

Aigler and Steinheimer's Cases, 670 pages, 1962.
Britton's Text, 2nd Ed., 794 pages, 1961.
See Commercial Transactions.

COMMERCIAL TRANSACTIONS

Speidel, Summers and White's Teaching Materials, 1144 pages, 1969.

COMMON LAW PLEADING

Koffler and Reppy on Common Law Pleading, 663 pages, 1969.
McBaine's Cases, Introduction to Civil Procedure, 399 pages, 1950.
Shipman's Text, 3rd Ed., 644 pages, 1923.

COMMUNITY PROPERTY

Burby's Cases, 4th Ed., 342 pages, 1955.
Huie's Texas Cases on Marital Property Rights, 681 pages, 1966.
Verrall and Sammis' Cases on California Community Property, 358 pages, 1966.

CONFLICT OF LAWS

Cramton and Currie's Cases—Comments—Questions, 915 pages, 1968.
Ehrenzweig's Text, 824 pages, 1962.
Ehrenzweig's Conflicts in a Nutshell, 2nd Ed., 392 pages, 1970.
Ehrenzweig and Louisell's Jurisdiction in a Nutshell, 2nd Ed., 315 pages, 1968.
Goodrich's Text, 4th Ed., 483 pages, 1964.
Scoles and Weintraub's Cases, 956 pages, 1967.
Selected Readings, 1151 pages, 1956.
Stumberg's Cases, 499 pages, 1956.

CONSTITUTIONAL LAW

Lockhart, Kamisar and Choper's Cases — Comments — Questions, 3rd Ed., 1,487 pages, 1970.
Lockhart, Kamisar and Choper's Cases and Materials on The American Constitution, 3rd Ed., 1970.
Selected Essays, 971 pages, 1963.
See Constitutional Rights and Liberties.

CONSTITUTIONAL RIGHTS & LIBERTIES

Lockhart, Kamisar and Choper's Cases and Materials on Constitutional Rights and Liberties, 3rd Ed., 1970.

CONSUMER CREDIT

Kripke's Cases, 454 pages, 1970.
Young's Cases on Consumer Credit. Pamphlet reprint from Dodyk, et al. Law and Poverty, 115 pages, 1969.

LAW SCHOOL PUBLICATIONS — Continued

CONTRACTS

Calamari & Perillo's Text, 621 pages, 1970.

Corbin's Cases, 3rd Ed., 1381 pages, 1947. 1953 Supplement, 36 pages.

Corbin's Text, Student Edition, 1224 pages, 1952.

Fuller and Braucher's Cases, 907 pages, 1964.

Simpson's Cases, 592 pages, 1956.

Simpson's Text, 2nd Ed., 510 pages, 1965.

CORPORATIONS

Henn's Text, 2nd Ed., 956 pages, 1970.

Stevens and Henn's Statutes, Cases and Materials on Corporations and Other Business Enterprises, 1448 pages, 1965.

Stevens and Henn's Practice Projects Supplement, 81 pages, 1965.

CREDIT TRANSACTIONS

Maxwell & Riesenfeld's California Cases on Security Transactions, 371 pages, 1957.

Maxwell & Riesenfeld's Supplement, 68 pages, 1963.

Sturges' Cases, 4th Ed., 599 pages, 1955.

Young's Cases on Consumer Credit. Pamphlet reprint from Dodyk, et al. Law and Poverty, 115 pages, 1969.

CREDITORS' RIGHTS

Riesenfeld's Cases on Creditors' Remedies and Debtors' Protection, 669 pages, 1967.

Riesenfeld's Statutory Supplement.

CRIMINAL LAW

Hall & Glueck's Cases, 2d Ed., 699 pages, 1958.

Miller's Text, 649 pages, 1934.

Stumberg's Texas Cases, 505 pages, 1954.

Stumberg and Maloney's Texas Cases Supplement, 117 pages, 1965.

CRIMINAL PROCEDURE

Hall, Kamisar, LaFave and Israel's Materials on Modern Criminal Procedure, 3rd Ed., 1456 pages, 1969.

Hall, Kamisar, LaFave and Israel's Materials on Basic Criminal Procedure, 3rd Ed., 617 pages, 1969.

Hall, Kamisar, LaFave and Israel's 1970 Criminal Procedure Supplement.

DAMAGES

Crane's Cases, 3rd Ed., 337 pages, 1955.

McCormick's Text, 811 pages, 1935.

DICTIONARIES

Black's, one volume.

Bouvier's, two volumes.

DOMESTIC RELATIONS

Clark's Cases, 870 pages, 1965.

Clark's Text, 754 pages, 1968.

Madden's Text, 748 pp., 1931.

Paulsen's Cases on Family Law and Poverty Pamphlet, reprint from Dodyk, et al. Law and Poverty, 266 pages, 1969.

DRUGS AND DRUGGISTS

Arthur's Text, 4th Ed., 399 pp., 1955.

ENGINEERING LAW

Simpson & Dillavou's Text, 4th Ed., 506 pages, 1958.

Sweet's Legal Aspects of Architecture, Engineering and the Construction Process, about 927 pages, 1970.

EQUITY

Cook's Cases, 4th Ed., 1192 pp., 1948.

McClintock's Text, 2nd Ed., 643 pages, 1948.

Van Hecke's Cases on Equitable Remedies, 651 pages, 1959.

See Remedies.

EVIDENCE

Cleary and Strong's Cases, 967 pages, 1969.

McCormick's Cases, 3rd Ed., 663 pages, 1956.

McCormick's Text, 774 pages, 1954.

Rothstein's Evidence in a Nutshell, 406 pages, 1970.

Selected Writings, 1232 pages, 1957.

FEDERAL ANTI-TRUST LAWS

Oppenheim's Cases on Robinson-Patman Act, Pamphlet, 295 pages, 1967.

Oppenheim and Weston's Cases, 3rd Ed., 952 pages, 1968.

Oppenheim and Weston's Supplement, 1970.

FEDERAL ESTATE AND GIFT TAXATION

See Taxation.

FEDERAL INCOME TAXATION

See Taxation.

FEDERAL JURISDICTION AND PROCEDURE

Bunn's U. S. Courts, Text, 5th Ed., 408 pages, 1949.

Currie's Cases on Federal Courts, 823 pages, 1968.

Ehrenzweig and Louisell's Jurisdiction in a Nutshell, 2nd Ed., 315 pages, 1968.

Forrester, Currier and Moye's Cases, 2nd Ed., 933 pages, 1970.

Wright's Text, 2nd Ed., 745 pages, 1970.

FUTURE INTERESTS

Gulliver's Cases, 624 pages, 1959.
Powell's Cases, 3rd Ed., 1961.
Simes Text, 2nd Ed., 355 pages, 1966.
See Wills, Intestate Succession, Trusts,
Gifts and Future Interests.

GRATUITOUS TRANSFERS

See Wills.

HOUSING AND URBAN DEVELOPMENT

Berger's Cases on Housing, Pamphlet
reprint from Dodyk, et al. Law and
Poverty, 277 pages, 1969.
Krasnowiecki's Cases, 697 pages, 1969.
Krasnowiecki's Statutory Supplement
1969.

INSURANCE

Keeton's Basic Insurance Law, 655
pages, 1960.
Keeton's Insurance Law and Torts Supplement (Compensation Systems),
56 pages, 1969.
Vance's Text, 3rd Ed., 1290 pages, 1951.

INTERNATIONAL BUSINESS

Ebb's Cases, 885 pages, 1964.
Ebb's 1968 Supplement.

INTERNATIONAL LAW

Friedmann, Lissitzyn and Pugh's Cases,
1,205 pages, 1969.

INTRODUCTION TO LAW

Fryer and Orentlicher's Cases and Ma-
terials on Legal Method and Legal
System, 1,043 pages, 1967.
Kimball's Historical Introduction to Le-
gal System, 610 pages, 1966.
Smith's Cases on Development of Legal
Institutions, 757 pages, 1965.
See Legal Method.

JURISPRUDENCE

Wu's Cases, 719 pages, 1958.

LABOR LAW

Handler & Hays' Cases, 4th Ed., 916
pages, 1963.
Sovern's Cases on Racial Discrimination in Employment, Pamphlet reprint
from Dodyk et al. Law and Poverty,
188 pages, 1969.

LAND USE

Beuscher and Wright's Cases on Land
Use, 788 pages, 1969.

LEGAL BIBLIOGRAPHY

Cohen's Legal Research in a Nutshell,
233 pages, 1968.
How To Find The Law, with Special
Chapters on Legal Writing, 6th Ed.,
313 pages, 1965.
How To Find The Law Student Problem
Book.

LEGAL ETHICS

Pirsig's Cases on Professional Responsibility, 2nd Ed., 447 pages, 1970.
Selected Readings Legal Profession, 565
pages, 1962.

LEGAL HISTORY

Kimball's Historical Introduction to Le-
gal System, 610 pages, 1966.
Radin's Text, 612 pages, 1936.
Smith's Cases on Development of Legal
Institutions, 757 pages, 1965.

LEGAL INTERVIEWING AND COUNSEL-
ING

Freeman's Cases, 253 pages, 1964.

LEGAL METHOD—LEGAL SYSTEM

Fryer and Orentlicher's Cases & Materials, 1043 pages, 1966.
See Introduction to Law.

LEGAL WRITING STYLE

Weihofen's Text, 323 pages, 1961.
See Legal Bibliography.

LOCAL GOVERNMENT LAW

Michelman and Sandalow's Materials
on Government in Urban Areas, 1216
pages, 1970.
Stason and Kauper's Cases, 3rd Ed.,
692 pages, 1959.

LEGISLATION

Nutting, Elliott and Dickerson's Cases
4th Ed., 631 pages, 1969.

MASS COMMUNICATION LAW

Gillmor and Barron's Cases and Comment, 853 pages, 1969.

MORTGAGES

Osborne's Cases Secured Transactions,
559 pages, 1967.
Osborne's Cases on Property Security,
2nd Ed., 725 pages, 1954.
Osborne's Text, 2nd Ed., 805 pages,
1970.
Sturges' Cases Credit Transactions, 4th
Ed., 599 pages, 1955.

MUNICIPAL CORPORATIONS

Michelman and Sandalow's Materials on Government in Urban Areas, 1216 pages, 1970.

Stason and Kauper's Cases, 3rd Ed., 692 pages, 1959.

See Local Government Law.

NATURAL RESOURCES

Trelease, Bloomenthal and Geraud's Cases and Materials on Natural Resources, 1131 pages, 1965.

OFFICE PRACTICE

A.B.A. Lawyer's Handbook, 557 pages, 1962.

See Legal Interviewing and Counseling.

OIL AND GAS

Huie, Walker and Woodward's Cases, 848 pages, 1960.

See Natural Resources.

PARTNERSHIP

Crane and Bromberg's Text, 695 pages, 1968.

See Agency-Partnership.

PERSONAL PROPERTY

Aigler, Smith and Tefft's Cases on Property, 2 Vols., 1339 pages, 1960.

Bigelow's Cases, 3rd Ed., 507 pages, 1942.

Fryer's Readings, 3rd Ed., 1184 pages, 1938.

PLEADING AND PROCEDURE

Brown, Karlen, Meisenholder, Stevens, and Vestal's Cases and Materials on Procedure Before Trial, 784 pages, 1968.

Clark's Cases, Modern Pleading, 1042 pages, 1952.

Clark's Text, 2nd Ed., 874 pages, 1947.

Cleary's Cases on Pleading, 2d Ed., 434 pages, 1958.

Cound, Friedenthal and Miller's Cases on Civil Procedure, 1075 pages, 1968.

Cound, Friedenthal and Miller's Cases on Pleading, Discovery and Joinder, 643 pages, 1968.

Cound, Friedenthal and Miller's Civil Procedure Supplement, 1970.

Ehrenzweig and Louisell's Jurisdiction in a Nutshell, 2nd Ed., 315 pages, 1968.

Elliott & Karlen's Cases, 441 pages, 1961.

Hodges, Jones and Elliott's Cases on Texas Trial and Appellate Procedure, 623 pages, 1965.

PLEADING AND PROCEDURE—Cont'd

Hodges, Jones, Elliott and Thode's Texas Judicial Process Prior to Trial, 935 pages, 1966.

Karlen's Cases on Trials and Appeals, 436 pages, 1961.

McBaine's Cases, Introduction to Civil Procedure, 399 pages, 1950.

POVERTY LAW

Dodyk, Sovern, Berger, Young and Paulsen's Cases on Law and Poverty, 1,234 pages, 1969.

Dodyk's Cases on Income Maintenance, Pamphlet reprint from Dodyk, et al. Law and Poverty, 379 pages, 1969.

REAL PROPERTY

Aigler, Smith & Tefft's Cases on Property, 2 Vols., 1339 pages, 1960.

Berger's Cases on Housing, Pamphlet reprint from Dodyk, et al. Law and Poverty, 277 pages, 1969.

Browder, Cunningham & Julin's Basic Property Law, 1209 pages, 1966.

Burby's Text, 3rd Ed., 490 Pages, 1965.

Jacobs' Cases Landlord and Tenant, 2nd Ed., 815 pages, 1941.

Moynihan's Introduction, 254 pages, 1962.

Phipps' Titles in a Nutshell—The Calculus of Interests, 277 pages, 1968.

Smith's Survey, 398 pages, 1956.

See Housing and Urban Development.

REMEDIES

Cribbet's Cases on Judicial Remedies, 762 pages, 1954.

Wright's Cases, 498 pages, 1955.

York and Bauman's Cases, 1271 pages, 1967.

RESTITUTION

Thurston's Cases, 964 pages, 1940.

See Remedies.

REVIEW MATERIALS

Ballantine's Problems.

Burby's Law Refreshers.

Nutshell Series.

Smith Reviews.

SALES

McCurdy's Cases, 480 pages, 1959.

Nordstrom's Text, about 565 pages, 1970.

Nordstrom and Lattin's Problems and Materials on Sales and Secured Transactions, 809 pages, 1968.

Vold's Text, 2nd Ed., 611 pages, 1959.

See Commercial Transactions.

SECURED TRANSACTIONS

See Commercial Transactions.
See Sales.

SURETYSHIP AND GUARANTY

Osborne's Cases, 221 pages, 1966.
Simpson's Text, 569 pages, 1950.
Simpson's Cases, 538 pages, 1942.
Sturges' Cases Credit Transactions, 4th Ed., 599 pages, 1955.

TAXATION

Chommie's Text on Federal Income Taxation, 742 pages, 1968.
Chommie's Supplement, 1970.
Hellerstein's Cases on State and Local Taxation, 3rd Ed., 741 pages, 1969.
Kragen & McNulty's Cases on Federal Income Taxation, 1,182 pages, 1970.
Lowndes & Kramer's Text on Federal Estate and Gift Taxes, 2nd Ed., 951 pages, 1962.
Rice's Problems and Materials in Federal Estate & Gift Taxation, 504 pages, 1966.
Rice's Problems and Materials in Federal Income Taxation, 623 pages, 1967.

TORTS

Green, Pedrick, Rahl, Thode, Hawkins and Smith's Cases, 1311 pages, 1968.
Green, Pedrick, Rahl, Thode, Hawkins and Smith's Cases on Injuries to Relations, 466 pages, 1968.
Hepburn's Cases, 3rd Ed., 540 pages, 1954.
Keeton's Insurance Law and Torts Supplement (Compensation Systems), 56 pages, 1969.
Prosser's Text, 3rd Ed., 1238 pages, 1964.
Seavey, Keeton and Keeton's Cases, 2nd Ed., 1055 pages, 1964.
Seavey, Keeton and Keeton's Supplement, 1970.

TRADE REGULATION

See Federal Anti-Trust Laws.
See Unfair Trade Practices.

TRUSTS

Bogert's Text, 4th Ed., 528 pages, 1963.
Powell's Cases, Trusts and Wills, 639 pages, 1960.
Smith's Survey, 167 pages, 1949.
See Wills, Intestate Succession, Trusts, Gifts and Future Interests.

UNFAIR TRADE PRACTICES

Oppenheim's Cases, 783 pages, 1965.
Oppenheim and Weston's Supplement.
Oppenheim's Robinson-Patman Act Pamphlet, 295 pages, 1967.

WATER LAW

Trelease's Cases, 364 pages, 1967.

WILLS

Atkinson's Text, 2nd Ed., 975 pages, 1953.
Turrentine's Cases, 2nd Ed., 483 pages, 1962.
See Wills, Intestate Succession, Trusts, Gifts and Future Interests.

WILLS, INTESTATE SUCCESSION, TRUSTS, GIFTS AND FUTURE INTERESTS

Gulliver, Clark, Lusky and Murphy's Cases and Materials on Gratuitous Transfers: Wills, Intestate Succession, Trusts, Gifts and Future Interests, 1017 pages, 1967.

WORKMEN'S COMPENSATION

Malone and Plant's Cases, 622 pages, 1963.

HANDBOOK

OF THE LAW OF

SALES

By

ROBERT J. NORDSTROM

Professor of Law, Ohio State University

Columbus, Ohio

HORNBOOK SERIES

ST. PAUL, MINN.

WEST PUBLISHING CO.

1970

Nordstrom Law of Sales **HB**

To Avis

•

IX

ACKNOWLEDGMENTS

The author gratefully acknowledges the assistance received in the preparation of this text. Special thanks go to Professors Albert L. Clovis (Ohio State) and Ernest Gellhorn (Duke) for their helpful comments on various sections of the manuscript. Benjamin T. Chinni, Joseph J. Cox (both of Ohio State), and Dale B. Ramerman (Duke), as research assistants, accepted the task of checking footnotes and cite-checking cases and statutes. They also read the manuscript, indicating places where it could be improved to aid the reader.

Several people typed various portions of the manuscript. Those who were most directly involved were Bunny Haffke, Gwendolyn Lane, Susan Mayer, and Kathryn Nordstrom. The assistance of Mrs. Walter Paulin is gratefully acknowledged. Her assignment of secretarial time to this project made its performance much easier than it otherwise would have been.

The author is also indebted to those hundreds of students, both at Duke and Ohio State, who have taken the course in Sales. They suggested several interpretations of the Uniform Commercial Code which could not have occurred to any one person no matter how often he read the Code. Many of those interpretations are included in this text.

ROBERT J. NORDSTROM

Columbus, Ohio
July, 1970

*

SUMMARY OF CONTENTS

SUMMARY OF CONTENTS

TABLE OF CONTENTS

TABLE OF CONTENTS

CHAPTER II. COVERAGE OF ARTICLE 2—Continued

B. SUBJECT MATTER WITHIN ARTICLE 2

CHAPTER III. FORMATION AND INTERPRETATION OF A CONTRACT FOR SALE

A. FORMALITIES

1. The Statute of Frauds

2. The Effect of a Seal

B. FORMATION OF A CONTRACT FOR SALE

TABLE OF CONTENTS

CHAPTER III. FORMATION AND INTERPRETATION OF A CONTRACT FOR SALE—Continued

C. TERMS OF A CONTRACT FOR SALE

D. INTERPRETATION OF A CONTRACT FOR SALE

CHAPTER IV. WARRANTIES OF THE SELLER

A. INTRODUCTION

B. WARRANTY OF TITLE

TABLE OF CONTENTS

CHAPTER IV. WARRANTIES OF THE SELLER—Continued

C. WARRANTIES OF QUALITY

1. Introduction

TABLE OF CONTENTS

CHAPTER V. PERFORMANCE OF THE SALES CONTRACT

A. INTRODUCTION

B. PERFORMANCE OBLIGATIONS OF THE SELLER

1. Warranty and Tender Obligations

2. Limitations on the Perfect Tender Rule

3. Excuse from Performance

C. PERFORMANCE OBLIGATIONS OF THE BUYER

1. Acceptance and Payment

TABLE OF CONTENTS

CHAPTER V. PERFORMANCE OF THE SALES CONTRACT—Continued

C. PERFORMANCE OBLIGATIONS OF THE BUYER—Cont'd

2. Right of Inspection

CHAPTER VI. TITLE, INSURABLE INTEREST, AND RISK OF LOSS

A. TITLE TO GOODS

B. INSURABLE INTEREST

C. RISK OF LOSS

CHAPTER VII. REMEDIES

A. INTRODUCTION

TABLE OF CONTENTS

CHAPTER VII. REMEDIES—Continued

B. SELLER IN DEFAULT

1. The Buyer's Courses of Action

2. The Buyer's Monetary Recoveries

3. The Buyer's Right to the Goods

C. BUYER IN DEFAULT

1. The Seller's Courses of Action

2. The Seller's Control of the Goods

TABLE OF CONTENTS

CHAPTER VII. REMEDIES—Continued

C. BUYER IN DEFAULT—Continued

2. The Seller's Control of the Goods—Continued

3. The Seller's Monetary Recoveries

D. PROTECTION OF THE RESTITUTION INTEREST

E. LIMITATION OF ACTIONS

†

HANDBOOK
ON THE
LAW OF SALES

CHAPTER I

INTRODUCTION TO THE
UNIFORM COMMERCIAL CODE

Analysis

Sec.
1. Scope of this Text.
2. History of the Code.
3. Repeal of the Uniform Sales Act and Statutes Affecting Commercial Transactions.
4. Uniformity of the Code.
5. Construing the Code.
6. Use of the Code Comments.

§ 1. Scope of this Text

Every book written about law necessarily has a limited scope; else there would be no place to begin and no place to end. This text is no exception. The law applicable to sales is based on the general law of contracts, finds some of its concepts in the law of property, involves statutes, ordinances and the control exercised by consumer groups aimed at maintaining and improving the quality of goods, assumes a knowledge of remedies, and draws from such diverse fields of human knowledge as (to name but a few) medicine, engineering, accounting, chemistry, and psychology. Any complete treatise on sales would require volumes to explore all of these areas of knowledge, relating them to the central theme, as well as more volumes explaining the business practices underlying the transactions. This book does not purport to undertake such a monumental task.

This text outlines the basic law of the United States relating to the sale of goods. It does not cover the legal rules applicable to international sales, although from time to time some mention will be made of transactions between buyers and sellers in different countries. Also, this book does not detail or expound economic theories about the movement of goods in commerce, although a complete omission of such theories would not only be foolish—it would be impossible. Nor is this a book about the history of commercial law—beginning with the Romans and moving through principles of English common law, the law merchant, the English Sale of Goods Act, and the Uniform Sales Act. However, once again these influences on our commercial law will not be ignored whenever they aid in interpreting present law.

Narrowing its scope even further, this text deals primarily with Article 2 of the Uniform Commercial Code. As expected, this Article cannot be treated in a vacuum; its relation to other Articles of the Code will be presented. Yet, through all of this moving back and forth through history, economic theories, and the interrelation of a complex code, the direction of this book remains fairly narrow—to present in textual fashion the current law of the United States applicable to the sale of goods. It is written for the law student and for the lawyer who is not yet a commercial law "expert."

§ 2. History of the Code

The Uniform Commercial Code is a product of approximately twenty years of hard work by a number of dedicated people.[1] This work began around the mid-forties (although legal historians may with justification select an earlier date) [2] and falls into two stages. First, there was the drafting followed by study, analysis, and more drafting. All of the drafting was sponsored by the National Conference of Commissioners on Uniform State Laws and by the American Law Institute. The most comprehensive study was that of the New York Law Revision Commission which concentrated its attention on the 1952 Official Text of the Code.[3] There were in addition many scholarly articles

1. There is a concise history of the Uniform Commercial Code in Malcolm, *The Uniform Commercial Code in the United States*, 12 Int'l & Comp.L.Q. 226 (1963). There is also a short history of the Code (and a listing of the names of those who worked on the Code) in the introductory Comment to the 1962 Official Text.

2. One earlier date that could be selected is 1938 when the Merchants Association of the City of New York sponsored a proposal for the drafting of a federal sales act to govern interstate sales. Responding to this proposal, the National Conference of Commissioners on Uniform State Laws undertook a revision of the Uniform Sales Act. Two years later the National Conference broadened the undertaking

to include a complete commercial code. Malcolm, *The Uniform Commercial Code in the United States*, 12 Int'l & Comp.L.Q. 226, 229 (1963).

3. The report of the New York Law Revision Commission was made in 1956. The Commission, after considering the arguments for and against codification of the law, concluded that "the preponderance is in favor of careful and foresighted codification of all or major parts of commercial law" but believed that "the Uniform Commercial Code is not satisfactory in its present form and cannot be made satisfactory without comprehensive reexamination and revision in the light of all critical comment obtainable." 1956 N.Y.Law Rev.Comm'n Rep. 67–68. In addition to the 1956 report volume

written by both practicing and teaching lawyers examining separate portions of the Code. One of the results of these analyses was the adoption of two further drafts of the Code: the 1958 and the 1962 Official Texts. The 1962 draft is the current text. It is the one which has served as the model for the legislation adopted by the states, either as their original legislation or as amendments to prior adoptions of the Code. It is also the one which will be used as the basis for discussion in this book.

The second stage in the history of the Code is found in the Code's adoption in 49 states, the District of Columbia, and the Virgin Islands. In the main, this stage was a product of the 1960's with the last state's Code having become effective on March 31, 1968.[4] Only Louisiana remains without the Code. Thus, in roughly twenty years the Uniform Commercial Code grew from little more than an idea to a comprehensive code enacted by all but one state in the United States.

It would, however, be erroneous to believe that the process of study and amendment is now closed. Although the bulk of the Code has worked extremely well in its application to commerce, there remain isolated sections which will not produce the legal results intended by the drafters or by the legislatures. These must be amended. Also, despite the foresight which the drafters evidenced, there will inevitably be changes in commercial practices which will require additions to and changes in the 1962 Official Text. Accordingly, the two sponsoring organizations have established a Permanent Editorial Board for the Uniform Commercial Code. This Board reviews state changes in the Code's official text and recommends whether those changes should be uniformly adopted. In addition the Board recommends amendments whenever new commercial practices have rendered provisions of the Code obsolete or new provisions desirable, court decisions have cast doubt on the intended interpretation of some section, some provision has been proved unworkable, or for any other reason a provision "obviously requires amendment." [5] This process should aid in attaining the goal of uniform legislation and provide a periodic review of commercial law in the United States.

there are two volumes devoted to the Commission's hearings (1954) and three to its study (1955) of the Code.

4. The first state in which the Code became effective was Pennsylvania. Thus far, Mississippi has the distinction of being the last state in which the Code became effective.

5. Uniform Commercial Code XIV. The statute is hereinafter cited as UCC. Unless otherwise noted, all references to the UCC are to the 1962 Official Text.

§ 3.   Repeal of the Uniform Sales Act and Statutes Affecting Commercial Transactions

The Uniform Commercial Code replaces many statutes which once controlled the legal aspects of commercial transactions.   The Code specifically repeals the Uniform Sales Act, the Uniform Negotiable Instruments Act, the Uniform Warehouse Receipts Act, the Uniform Stock Transfer Act, the Uniform Conditional Sales Act, and the Uniform Trust Receipts Act.[6]   Also repealed are statutes relating to bank collections, bulk sales, chattel mortgages, conditional sales, factor's liens, farm storage of grain and similar acts, and assignment of accounts receivable.[7]   Of primary importance to the subject of sales is the repeal of the Uniform Sales Act.

The Uniform Sales Act was drafted by Professor Samuel Williston, who used as his model the English Sale of Goods Act (1893).   The National Commissioners on Uniform State Laws approved the Uniform Sales Act in 1906, and this Act was adopted between 1907 and 1941 in 36 states and the District of Columbia.   Even though now repealed in every jurisdiction, the Uniform Sales Act had a strong impact on Article 2 of the Code.   Many of the Act's ideas were reproduced in Article 2.   An understanding of Article 2 requires a knowledge of why its sections are written the way they are; this, in turn, necessitates a familiarity of the Uniform Sales Act.[8]   This book will draw from that history whenever it is believed that history will make the current law more understandable.

Prior to the adoption of the Uniform Commercial Code, each state had a series of statutes affecting the various security devices used whenever the lender or seller desired to create a security interest in personal property.   The form of security device chosen could be of prime importance to the validity of the security interest; and the selection of a conditional sale contract when the "proper" document was a chattel mortgage could invalidate the security interest.[9]   Statutes

---

6.   UCC § 10–102.

7.   *Id.*   The applicable statutes are to be inserted by the legislature since these vary from state to state.

8.   The most authoritative pre-Code treatment of the law of sales is S. Williston, Sales (rev.ed.1948).

9.   *E. g.,* Oliver v. Electrical Prod. Consol., 59 Wash.2d 276, 367 P.2d 618 (1961), which involved a conditional sale of the personalty used in the operation of a hotel.   The contract provided that any after-acquired property

was also to become the property of the seller.   A priority problem arose as to the after-acquired property, with the conditional vendor competing with a judgment creditor of the conditional vendee.   After stating that an after-acquired property clause was valid when included in a chattel mortgage, the court continued:

"The conditional sale contract is a device recognized by statute to protect the seller of personal property which is to be paid for in installments although possession is delivered to the conditional vendee. . . . The seller must be the *actual owner* of the

relating to these arrangements as well as to pledges, trust receipts, field warehousing, and accounts receivable—varying from state to state —created a maze which defied all but the expert in the choice of the proper form of security and the proper office in which to record the chosen form. The penalty for failure to predict what the courts would decide several months or years later when the transaction was called into question was the loss of the security interest in the collateral.[10] This could be a staggering financial blow to the lender or seller who then found himself sharing ratably with all other unsecured creditors.

Since this text is limited to the sale of goods and does not include an extensive consideration of the use of goods as security for the extension of credit, neither pre-Code statutes affecting secured transactions nor Article 9 of the Code will be examined in any detail. There are, nevertheless, instances in which Articles 2 and 9 overlap (*e. g.*, section 2–403(4)). It is, therefore, necessary to understand that the maze of pre-Code statutes has been replaced by a single security interest which is comprehensively covered by Article 9 of the Code.[11]

§ 4.   Uniformity of the Code

Commercial transactions are planned transactions, creating reasonable expectations in the parties thereto. Commercial law needs a substantial degree of predictability so that these expectations will not be frustrated. The widespread adoption of the Code should provide that predictability. Interstate transactions can be planned with considerable certainty as to their validity and results. Even with intrastate transactions, the similarity in the origin of the Code makes decisions from sister states relevant in construing the local Code, promoting uniformity among the states.[12] Further, since the Code reflects sound

---

property sold in order to retain title. A genuine sale is the indispensable prerequisite. Because the respondents never owned the property, it was impossible for them to retain title to such property." *Id.* at 278–79, 367 P. 2d at 620. See also Hughbanks, Inc. v. Gourley, 12 Wash.2d 44, 120 P.2d 523 (1941), which did not involve an after-acquired property clause.

10. There was a complete loss of the security interest in the collateral if bankruptcy intervened and if the trustee could find one creditor as to whom the security interest was voidable. *In re* Plonta, 311 F.2d 44 (6th Cir. 1962), applying the rule of the famous case of Moore v. Bay, 284 U.S. 4, 52 S.Ct. 3, 76 L.Ed. 133 (1931). The problem is discussed in J. MacLachlan,

Bankruptcy § 284 (1956), and in Kennedy, *The Trustee in Bankruptcy as a Secured Creditor Under the Uniform Commercial Code*, 65 Mich.L.Rev. 1419 (1967).

11. UCC § 9–102. The best textual source for comparison of the Code with pre-Code law is I & II G. Gilmore, Security Interests in Personal Property (1965).

12. "Parenthetically, it should also be noted that the policy of the New Jersey Legislature in adopting the Uniform Commercial Code is that the courts of this State are to consciously attempt to give the Code a uniform interpretation not only as between our courts but also with those of other states wherever possible. N.J.S. 12A:1–

business practices, the rules applied will not be unjust to the business-man or the novice, to the merchant or the consumer. This predicta-bility, uniformity, and justice make the Code a worthy addition to commercial law.

Some of the uniformity of the *Uniform* Commercial Code is, how-ever, illusory. Legislatures have not simply adopted the Code. Every state version varies from the 1962 Official Text. Most of the variations are minor in their general impact on commercial transactions.[13] Even so, they cannot be ignored in planning a sale or a secured transaction with connections in another state. Unfortunately, a few of the varia-tions are of considerable significance.[14] As long as local changes re-main—and the chances are good that complete uniformity in statutory language will never be attained—a part of the predictability and sta-bility important in commercial transactions is lost. In their place are substituted local policies which the legislature of that particular state believed to be of greater importance than uniformity between states.

Also, the Code is not as comprehensive as might first appear. It is not intended to cover all of the law of commerce; the drafters inten-tionally omitted certain legal problems from the scope of the Code. For example, the Code does not regulate consumer credit connected with the sale of goods "on time";[15] another uniform act has been recom-

---

102(2) (c). Therefore sister-state in-terpretations of the Code are more than mere persuasive authority." A. J. Armstrong Co. v. Janburt Embroi-dery Corp., 97 N.J.Super. 246, 259, 234 A.2d 737, 744 (Sup.Ct.1967).

13. Listing an example of a "minor" deviation in a local Code is an act of foolhardiness because it is possible that the deviation chosen will, on some occasion, be the basis of distinguishing that Code from the official text. Nevertheless, the addition of the sen-tence "The Secretary of the Common-wealth shall not be required to index the statement according to the name of the secured party" to UCC § 9–403 (4) would appear to fall in the "minor variation" classification. See Pa. Stats. Tit. 12A § 9–403(4) (Supp.1969). Perhaps the least significant varia-tions are those found in the differing filing fees that states require under Article 9. See UCC § 9–407.

14. Instances of significant changes in the official text of Article 2 of the Code will appear throughout this vol-ume. One example of a significant change in Article 9 is found in Ohio's reversal of a part of the priorities

established when a security interest in fixtures is competing with an interest in the real estate. *Compare* UCC § 9–313 *with* Ohio Rev.Code Ann. § 1309.32 (Page Supp.1968). On the other hand, Iowa's Code states that "Nothing in this Act governs the priority between a security interest in goods which are or are to become fixtures and the claims of any person who has an in-terest in the real estate." Iowa Code Ann. § 554.9313 (1967). In addition to state-inspired changes, the 1962 Offi-cial Text provides for alternative solu-tions to some problems. *E. g.,* UCC § 6–106.

15. The retail installment sales act is one of the principal state statutes de-signed to control this type of credit. These statutes often regulate the con-tents of the form used in the trans-action and the finance charges which can be charged. See Warren, *Regu-lation of Finance Charges in Retail Installment Sales,* 68 Yale L.J. 839 (1959). One comprehensive retail in-stallment sales act was enacted by Massachusetts in 1966 and is contained in Mass.Gen.Laws Ann. ch. 255D (1968). That the Code does not repeal these statutes is made clear by UCC

mended for that purpose.[16] There is no attempt to give uniformity to the many motor vehicle title registration acts [17] or to regulate assignment of wages as security for the sale of goods.[18] There were a variety of reasons for carving these and other areas out of the scope of the Uniform Commercial Code. In some instances the drafters feared that local policies as to these matters were so strong and so varied that an attempt to incorporate a uniform answer into this Code would jeopardize the chances of its adoption. In other instances other groups were at work on a uniform law and deference was given to their labors. Time, too, must have been a factor in determining just what could be covered in the Code. If every commercial problem were to be covered and agreement reached among the drafters on all of those problems, the drafting time would have been extended for many more years. The result is that there are several areas of the law affecting the commercial transaction which are not touched by the Code. These remain the subjects of local policies and, until further uniform legislation is proposed and adopted, these omissions dilute the appearance of uniformity originally given by a Uniform Commercial Code.

This discussion is not intended as a criticism of the job done by the drafters or by the legislatures. Competing arguments had to be reconciled and decisions had to be reached. The resulting product, despite a few shortcomings (some of which will be noted in the following pages), is an excellent code—one on which further uniform legislation can be built in future years. Rather, the limits of the Code were included simply to serve as a caution: there are places where the state Codes are not uniform and there are areas of commercial law not reached by the Code. To these extents, the appearance first given by the title of the *Uniform Commercial* Code becomes an illusion.

---

§§ 2–102, 9–102, 9–203(2) and by the Comment to UCC § 9–101.

16. See the Uniform Consumer Credit Code approved by the National Commissioners on Uniform State Laws in 1968. As of the date this text was written no state as yet had an opportunity to adopt this code. For an analysis of the Uniform Consumer Credit Code, see Symposium, *Consumer Credit Reform*, 33 Law & Contemp.Prob. 639 (1968).

17. UCC § 9–302(3) (b).

18. UCC § 9–104(d). UCC § 9–104 lists several other transactions which are excluded from the coverage of Article 9. UCC § 2–102 concludes by stating that Article 2 (Sales) "does not apply to any transaction which although in the form of an unconditional contract to sell or present sale is intended to operate only as a security transaction nor does this Article impair or repeal any statute regulating sales to consumers, farmers or other specified classes of buyers."

§ 5. Construing the Code

Construing the Uniform Commercial Code requires a strange kind of double-mindedness. At the same moment the same section must be read both narrowly and broadly.

The Code is a group of statutes, and statutes must be read precisely. It is often tempting to paraphrase a statute and to say that a certain section *really* means this or that. The difficulty with paraphrasing is that the "this or that" is very often an inaccurate generalization, and is not what the section "means," let alone what it *really* means. For example, section 2–703 begins: "Where the buyer wrongfully rejects or revokes acceptance of goods or fails to make a payment due on or before delivery or repudiates with respect to a part or the whole . . . ." [19] It certainly is not accurate to say that what this phrase really means is: "When the buyer defaults . . . ." The first word is not "when"; the first word is "where." The first word does not pick a point in time but introduces a series of conditions the occurrence of any one of which will trigger the operation of section 2–703. This is true of many of the Code sections in Article 2. Rather than stating sweeping generalizations of law (like the lump title concept under the Uniform Sales Act), many sections of Article 2 state that if certain specific facts occur or fail to occur, certain specific results will follow. [20]

Nor would it be accurate to say that the introductory phrase of section 2–703 really means that "where the buyer is in default," certain results follow. Section 2–703 does not use the word "default." Instead, it selects four events—each of which may be a default, but all of which do not add up to all of the possible defaults which a buyer may commit—and lists those events with precision. It is only when one of those events occurs that section 2–703 is applicable. Thus, the only way to state what section 2–703 *really* means is to quote the section verbatim.

The Code, however, is more than a group of statutes; it is a code. As such, it expresses several discernible policies. Sometimes these policies are expressed in specific Code sections. [21] Other times they emerge only from a reading of several parts of the Code and from an understanding of the business background from which those parts were written. A search for Code policies often results in reading broadly the same section that in the above paragraph was recommended for close and narrow reading. It is this double-mindedness that is required in construing the Code.

---

19. UCC § 2–703 is discussed in §§ 139–45 *infra*.

20. Part 5 of Article 2 contains a number of sections of this type. See UCC §§ 2–503(2)–(5), 2–504, 2–505, 2–507 through 2–510, and 2–512.

21. Several policies are stated in UCC §§ 1–102(2) and 1–106.

§ 6. Use of the Code Comments

Each section of the Uniform Commercial Code is followed by a Comment. These Comments, which vary in length from a single sentence to several pages, contain information about prior uniform statutory provisions dealing with the subject matter of that particular Code section, the changes, if any, made in these prior provisions, and the purposes of the Code section or of the changes. From time to time courts refer to these as the "Official Comments" as if they were the legislative history in the state which has adopted the Code.[22] This, of course, is not true.

The Comments were not drafted or enacted by the legislatures;[23] they were drafted by the committees which worked on the various Articles of the Code. Thus, the Comments are not "legislative history" in the sense of being a record of the committee deliberations at the time the Code was being considered in the state legislature. It would seem, therefore, that the Comments are not entitled even to the weight which the court gives to legislative records when the court is attempting to find the "meaning" of a statute.

The early history of the Code further complicates the role which, in theory, the Comments should play in interpreting the Code. Prior to 1957 the Code contained a paragraph (f) under section 1–102(3) which read:

> (f) The Comments of the National Conference of Commissioners on Uniform State Laws and the American Law Institute may be consulted in the construction and application of this Act but if text and comment conflict, text controls.

This paragraph was statutory authorization for the Comments and a clear mandate for their use. In 1956 this paragraph was removed with the explanation that the older Comments were out of date and it was not known when the new ones could be prepared.[24] Although revised Comments were prepared, no new paragraph similar to section 1–102 (3)(f) has been introduced into the Code. An argument could, therefore, be made that the Comments ought to have no effect at all; that they are not legislation; that they are not legislative history; and that the deletion of section 1–102(3)(f) indicated that the Comments were no longer even to be consulted in the construction of the Code.

Such an argument should fail. First, it ignores the stated reason for the removal of section 1–102(3)(f). There was no dissatisfaction

---

22. Park County Implement Co. v. Craig, 397 P.2d 800, 802–03, (Wyo. 1964).

23. Miller v. Preitz, 422 Pa. 383, 393, 221 A.2d 320, 325 (1966), *overruled* *on another point*, Kassab v. Central Soya, 432 Pa. 217, 246 A.2d 848 (1968).

24. 1956 Recommendations of the Editorial Board for the Uniform Commercial Code 3.

with the process of consulting the Comments; they were only temporarily out of date. It does, however, suggest that there may still be places where all vestiges of Comments to prior versions of the Code may not have been removed, and that the Comments need to be studied carefully to be certain that they reflect the present Code.

Second, the argument ignores the role which the drafters believe ought to be given to the Comments. The introductory Comment to the Code states:

> This comment and those which follow are the Comments of the National Conference of Commissioners on Uniform State Laws and the American Law Institute. Uniformity throughout American jurisdictions is one of the main objectives of this Code; and that objective cannot be obtained without substantial uniformity of construction. To aid in uniform construction these Comments set forth the purpose of various provisions of this Act to promote uniformity, to aid in viewing the Act as an integrated whole, and to safeguard against misconstruction.[25]

Of course, to the extent that Comments are to be ignored, both the explanatory note appended to the 1956 deletion of section 1–102(3)(f) and the introductory Comment to the Code must also be ignored.

There is, however, a third (and undoubtedly the most persuasive) reason why it would be erroneous to conclude that the Comments will not affect court decisions.[26] There is a wealth of material in the Comments; that material was before the legislatures when the Code was adopted; and that material should not be overlooked as a source of Code construction. The Comments often explain why certain statutory language was chosen, what policies were sought to be adopted or rejected, and how the section under consideration harmonizes with other parts of the Code. This material is just too valuable to be ignored.[27]

Nevertheless, it must be remembered that the Comments are not the legislation. The difficulty is not that the Comments will be ignored

---

25. UCC at 1.

26. "The 'Official Comments' of the Code are, of course, not binding on a federal court which is in the process of exercising its equitable discretion in a reclamation proceeding. But, they are powerful dicta for the Code is 'well on its way to becoming a truly national law of commerce,' and is, therefore, as we have noted, a most appropriate source of federal law." *In re* Yale Express System, Inc., 370 F.2d 433, 437 (2d Cir. 1966). For a later opinion in the same case, see 384 F.2d 990 (2d Cir. 1967).

27. "Although fully realizing that the official comments appearing as part of the Uniform Commercial Code are not direct authority for the construction to be placed upon a section of the code, nevertheless they are persuasive and represent the opinion of the National Conference of Commissioners on Uniform State Laws and the American Law Institute. The purpose of the comments is to explain the provisions of the code itself, in an effort to promote uniformity of interpretation." Burchett v. Allied Concord Financial Corp., 74 N.M. 575, 578, 396 P.2d 186, 188 (1964).

by lawyers and courts; [28] the difficulty is that they will be relied upon in preference to a close study of the Code. On many occasions the Comments are written in a more readable form than is the Code. Why try to puzzle out the legalistic language of the Code when the Comments state more clearly what was intended? The answer is easy to give, but may be hard to follow: the Code is the legislation; the Comments are not. The Comments suggest a construction (but only *a* construction) of statutory language, form a basis for double-checking a construction already arrived at, refer to other sections which might otherwise be overlooked, and are an extremely valuable tool to aid in statutory construction. When the Code and the Comments conflict, however, the Comments must be rejected. [29]

---

28. The following statement was made by Professor Llewellyn during a discussion before the New York Law Revision Commission during its study of the 1952 version of the Code which contained the Code provision that the Comments "may be consulted in the construction and application" of the Code: "It does not say 'shall control.' It quite deliberately says 'may be consulted'—just that and nothing more. As Learned Hand put it in this discussion—and nobody could put it better—'Well, what this comes to is to say that we may do what we shall do anyway.' " 1954 N.Y.Law Rev. Comm'n Rep. (vol. 1) 175.

29. Zinni v. One Township Line Corp., 36 Pa.D. & C.2d 297 (C.P.1965). On the Code question involved in this case (whether Article 6 applied to the sale of a restaurant), see Nichols v. Acers Co., 415 S.W.2d 683 (Tex.Civ.App. 1967); Levy v. Paul, 207 Va. 100, 147 S.E.2d 722 (1966).

CHAPTER II
COVERAGE OF ARTICLE 2

Analysis

A. THE CODE AND CHOICE OF LAW

1. Introduction

A. THE CODE AND CHOICE OF LAW

1. INTRODUCTION

§ 7. Application of the Code in Space [1]

When suit is brought on a commercial transaction with multistate connections, a decision may have to be made as to what law should govern the transaction. Should it be the law of the forum, the law specified by the parties in the contract, the law of the place where the contract was made or where it was to be performed, or some other law?

---

1. Substantial parts of this portion of the text appeared originally in Nordstrom and Ramerman, *The Uniform Commercial Code and the Choice of Law*, 1969 Duke L.J. 623. Reprinting is with permission of the Duke Law Journal.

The Code contains six sections specifically designed to aid in the solution of these problems. The basic section is contained in Article 1 as 1–105 and establishes three rules:

1. For five factual patterns—transactions controlled by Code provisions dealing with rights of creditors against goods sold, bank deposits and collections, bulk transfers, investments securities, and secured transactions—the law of a particular jurisdiction is to be applied by all states.[2] In general, these are situations in which a third party is likely to become involved and in which a type of situs law can reasonably be selected as the controlling law.

2. Aside from these situations, the Code provides that the parties to a transaction are free, with some limitations, to choose which system of law will govern their rights and duties.

3. If the parties fail to choose the applicable law and if the transaction is not one of the five mentioned above, the Code of the forum state is to be applied to transactions bearing an appropriate relation to the forum state.

It is the latter two rules, as set forth in section 1–105(1), which cause difficulties of construction and application:

> Except as provided hereafter in this section, when a transaction bears a *reasonable relation* to this state and also to another state or nation the parties may agree that the law either of this state or of such other state or nation shall govern their rights and duties. Failing such agreement this Act applies to transactions bearing an *appropriate relation* to this state.[3]

The problems created by this provision, its relation to traditional conflict of laws rules, and suggested solutions are discussed in the following sections of this text.

§ 8. Importance of Choice of Law Under a Uniform Code

Before examining the Code's choice of law rules, consideration should be given as to why choice of law is important under a uniform code. Since 51 jurisdictions now have the Code, what difference does it make whether the Code of State A or the Code of State B applies? The results should be the same, and only the theoretician concerns himself with which system of law is used when the results under all systems are identical.

One answer is that many transactions will have connections with foreign countries, and some disputes arising out of these international

---

2. UCC § 1–105(2).   3. Emphasis supplied.

transactions will be litigated in a court in the United States.   The chances are good that those foreign countries will not have adopted the Code, and a statutory choice of law rule—especially one which gives the parties an opportunity of selecting applicable law—can have great practical utility.   The parties to an international commercial transaction can select applicable law and, if a dispute is litigated in a Code state, the selected law will be used by the court.[4]

Further, the Codes as adopted have not been uniform.   Most states have discovered policies which they thought should be changed to reflect local considerations.   As time goes on, courts will find others.   Interpretations of uniformly drafted sections will be disparate.   Therefore, even with interstate transactions the Code which is applied to determine substantive rights can be determinative of the results, and party autonomy can give a certainty to those who care to plan their transactions with possible disputes in mind.[5]

2. PARTY AUTONOMY

§ 9. Theoretical Objections to Party Autonomy

There is no substantial dissent from the proposition that the parties to a contract ought to be (and are) free to select the system of law which will be used to aid in the *interpretation* of the language which they use.   After all, the parties could have written into their contract the detailed principles of law of the selected state, and the court would have accepted the parties' agreement as a guide to the meaning of the language chosen.   There is no good reason why those same parties should not be able to make a general reference to that system of law,

4. E. Gerli & Co. v. Cunard S.S. Co., 48 F.2d 115 (2d Cir. 1931).

5. The differing legislative and judicial treatment given to the privity problem is one area of substantive law in which the choice of law question can be determinative of the results in a particular case.   See §§ 90–91 *infra*. Examples of other areas include all instances in which courts interpret the local Code differently from an interpretation given by some other state. Statutory differences include: (1) the omission by Mississippi of UCC § 2–316, Miss.Code 1942 § 41A (Spec.UCC Supp.1969); (2) the omission of UCC § 2–302 by California, West's Ann.Cal. Commercial Code, § 2–302, and North Carolina, N.C.Gen.Stat. § 25–2–302 (1965); (3) the increase by Oklahoma in the statutory period in UCC § 2–725 to five years, Okl.Stat.Ann.12A, § 2–725 (1963); (4) the provision in the Colorado Code that the four-year period of limitations may not be varied by agreement, Colo.Rev.Stat.Ann. § 155–2–725 (1963); and (5) the provision in the Massachusetts Code providing that there are no implied warranties in contracts to sell human blood, blood plasma, or other human tissues or organs from a blood bank or reservoir of such tissues and organs, Mass.Gen.Laws Ann. ch. 106, § 2–316 (5) (Supp.1968).   These are cited as illustrative, and not as limiting the number of instances in which choice of law can determine the results of the case.

thus incorporating that system into their agreement.[6] The Comments to section 1–105 recognize this privilege:

> But an agreement as to choice of law may sometime take effect as a shorthand expression of the intent of the parties as to matters governed by their agreement, even though the transaction has no significant contact with the jurisdiction chosen.[7]

The privilege of parties, however, to select the system of law which will govern the *validity* of their agreement—as distinguished from matters of interpretation—has met with considerable resistance both from courts and writers.[8] The theoretical objection to this privilege has been stated in terms of the inability of parties to legislate for themselves. Judge Learned Hand expressed it this way: "People cannot by agreement substitute the law of another place; they may of course incorporate any provisions they wish into their agreements—a statute like anything else—and when they do, courts will try to make sense out of the whole, so far as they can. But an agreement is not a contract, except as the law says it shall be, and to try to make it one is to pull on one's bootstraps. Some law must impose the obligation, and the parties have nothing whatever to do with that; no more than with whether their acts are torts or crimes." [9]

The analogy to bootstraps gives the argument a surface appeal but should not hide the assumption which has formed the basis of the argument against the use of party-selected law to measure the validity of the agreement. That assumption is disclosed in the last sentence quoted from Learned Hand: for every commercial transaction with multistate contacts, one of these contacts (such as the place of making or performance) *dictates* the application of some system of law to deter-

6. Ringling Bros.–Barnum & Bailey Combined Shows, Inc. v. Olvera, 119 F.2d 584 (9th Cir. 1941); People v. Globe & Rutgers Fire Ins. Co., 96 Cal. App.2d 571, 216 P.2d 64 (1950); Burns v. Burns, 190 N.Y. 211, 82 N.E. 1107 (1907); and cases cited in H. Goodrich, Conflict of Laws 219–20 (4th ed. revised by Professor E. Scoles 1964). *But see* Owens v. Hagenbeck-Wallace Shows Co., 58 R.I. 162, 192 A. 158 (1937).

7. UCC § 1–105, Comment 1.

8. *E. g.*, Oceanic Steam Nav. Co. v. Corcoran, 9 F.2d 724 (2d Cir. 1925); Johnston v. Commercial Travelers Mut. Accident Ass'n, 242 S.C. 387, 131 S.E.2d 91 (1963); Lorenzen, *Validity and Effects of Contracts in the Con-*

flict of Laws, 30 Yale L.J. 565, 655 (1921); Szold, *Comments on Tentative Draft No. 6 of the Restatement (Second), Conflict of Laws—Contracts*, 76 Harv.L.Rev. 1524 (1963); Weintraub, *The Contracts Proposals of the Second Restatement of Conflict of Laws—a Critique*, 46 Iowa L.Rev. 713 (1961). See also Freund, *Analysis of Conflicts of Law Provisions of Section 1–105*, 1955 N.Y.Law Rev.Comm'n Rep. (vol. 1) 175, 179–81; Comment, *Conflict of Laws: "Party Autonomy" in Contracts*, 57 Colum.L.Rev. 553 (1957).

9. E. Gerli & Co. v. Cunard S.S. Co., 48 F.2d 115, 117 (2d Cir. 1931). *Cf.* H. Goodrich, Conflict of Laws 326 (3d ed. 1949). See also H. Goodrich, Conflict of Laws 212–16 (4th ed. 1964).

mine the validity of that transaction, and the parties have no power
to make this choice for the courts. If this assumption is granted, it
follows that the parties do not have the power to choose applicable law,
and party autonomy can be discarded as theoretically unsound. Without this assumption, however, the "theoretical" difficulties disappear.
If either the law of the forum or the law of the state which would otherwise govern the validity of the agreement recognizes the privilege of
party autonomy, then the parties can agree as to applicable law without pulling "on one's bootstraps." No longer is there anything theoretically unsound about measuring validity by the chosen law.[10] Instead
the problem becomes: ought the law, as a matter of policy, recognize
party autonomy in determining which system of law will be used to
measure the validity of an agreement?

The Code has answered this question affirmatively. Writers may
continue to object to the answer,[11] but the answer remains.[12] It is now
permissible, within the limitations imposed in the Code, for parties to a
commercial transaction to agree as to the law which "shall govern their
rights and duties." The wise use of this privilege will allow those parties to plan their transaction and give them a certainty which before
was only an illusion.[13]

---

10. Siegelman v. Cunard White Star, Ltd., 221 F.2d 189 (2d Cir. 1955); Duskin v. Pennsylvania-Central Airlines Corp., 167 F.2d 727 (6th Cir. 1948), *cert. denied* 335 U.S. 829, 69 S.Ct. 56, 93 L.Ed. 382 (1948); Ringling Bros.-Barnum & Bailey Combined Shows, Inc. v. Olvera, 119 F.2d 584 (9th Cir. 1941). The most telling attack on the place of making test appears in W. Cook, The Logical and Legal Bases of the Conflict of Laws 389–432 (1942). This chapter was originally published in 32 Ill.L.Rev. 899 (1938) and in 34 Ill.L.Rev. 423 (1939) under the title *"Contracts" and the Conflict of Laws: "Intention" of the Parties.*

11. Szold, *Comments on Tentative Draft No. 6 of the Restatement (Second), Conflict of Laws—Contracts,* 76 Harv.L.Rev. 1524 (1963); Weintraub, *The Contracts Proposals of the Second Restatement of Conflict of Laws—a Critique,* 46 Iowa L.Rev. 713 (1961).

12. Professor Weintraub has attacked the wisdom of party autonomy but recognizes that "section 1–105(1) is *fait accompli,* and tilting at windmills, although good artery-flushing exercise, is somewhat discouraging, especially when, as here, the windmills show no sign of weakening." Weintraub, *Choice of Law for Products Liability: the Impact of the Uniform Commercial Code and Recent Developments in Conflicts Analysis,* 44 Texas L.Rev. 1429, 1434 (1966). See also, Weintraub, *Choice of Law in Contract,* 54 Iowa L.Rev. 399 (1968).

13. Many writers have joined several courts in supporting party autonomy in choosing the applicable law, subject to varying limitations. Among these are Braucher, *Impromptu Remarks,* 76 Harv.L.Rev. 1718 (1963); Ehrenzweig, *Adhesion Contracts in the Conflict of Laws,* 53 Colum.L.Rev. 1072 (1953); Tuchler, *Boundaries to Party Autonomy in the Uniform Commercial Code: A Radical View,* 11 St. Louis L.J. 180 (1967); Yntema, *Contract and Conflict of Laws: "Autonomy" in Choice of Law in the United States,* 1 N.Y.L.F. 46 (1955).

§ 10. Limitations on Party Autonomy—The Reasonable Relation Test

There are several limitations on the privilege of selecting applicable law. The first of these is the "reasonable relation" test. The Code permits parties to select the law which will govern their rights and duties provided that their transaction bears a "reasonable relation" to the state or nation whose law is selected.[14] The inference is that if the parties choose the law of some state which has no reasonable relation to the transaction, that choice will not be recognized.[15] There appear to be no theoretical objections to allowing the parties complete freedom of choice as to applicable law,[16] just as they may bargain over any other term of their agreement. Nevertheless, the Code clearly limits their choice, perhaps to protect courts from having to apply a bizarre foreign law chosen by caprice. Such fears would seem to be misplaced, however, for given the financial implications of a commercial transaction, few contracting parties are apt to agree that their rights and duties are to be governed by a law which has no connection with their transaction.[17] Further, these "built-in" limitations do not protect courts from being confronted with unfamiliar law in those instances in which the transaction does bear a reasonable relation to a foreign country.

Most of the cases in which courts will be called upon to consider the reasonable relation test of section 1–105 will be fairly easy to decide.[18] The situations in which parties tend to agree upon applicable law are those in which the contacts are divided, roughly equally, between two or more jurisdictions. In such a case, the parties' choice of law should be upheld if the only challenge is that the connection is not reasonable. There will, however, be a few cases, as measured by the total number of disputes, in which the state or nation whose law is chosen will have only a minimal connection with the facts of the trans-

14. UCC § 1–105(1).

15. *Cf.* Associates Discount Corp. v. Palmer, 47 N.J. 183, 219 A.2d 858 (1966).

16. Practical objections to an unfettered rule allowing party autonomy are suggested in W. Cook, Logical and Legal Bases of the Conflict of Laws 412–18 (1942).

17. "The forum will not apply the chosen law to determine issues the parties could not have determined by explicit agreement directed to the particular issue if the parties had no reasonable basis for choosing this law.

The forum will not, for example, apply a foreign law which has been chosen by the parties in the spirit of adventure or to provide mental exercise for the judge. Contracts are entered into for serious purposes and rarely, if ever, will the parties choose a law without good reason for doing so." Restatement (Second) of Conflict of Laws § 187, comment *f* at 191 (Proposed Official Draft, 1968).

18. *E. g.,* Old Colony Trust Co. v. Penrose Industrial Corp., 280 F.Supp. 698, 711 (E.D.Pa.), *aff'd* 398 F.2d 310 (3d Cir. 1968). *See* A. S. Rampell, Inc. v. Hyster Co., 3 N.Y.2d 369, 165 N.Y.S. 2d 475, 144 N.E.2d 371 (1957).

action: for example, it may be only the domicile of one or both of the parties, the place from which the offer was made, the place from which the goods were shipped, the principal place of business of one or both of the parties,[19] or the situs of the property sold. The question will then become whether any one of these contacts satisfies the "reasonable relation" test of 1–105.

With respect to this requirement the Comment to section 1–105 states, in necessarily vague terms, that "[i]n general, the test of 'reasonable relation' is similar to that laid down by the Supreme Court in *Seeman v. Philadelphia Warehouse Co.,* 274 U.S. 403, 47 S.Ct. 626, 71 L.Ed. 1123 (1927). Ordinarily the law chosen must be that of a jurisdiction where a significant enough portion of the making or performance of the contract is to occur or occurs."[20] No one, not even the drafters of 1–105, could detail all of the factors which, in every case, will constitute a reasonable relation. However, the last quoted sentence, which at first appears only to substitute "significant" in place of "reasonable," may provide a guideline to aid in solving those cases in which it is asserted that the law chosen by the parties is not reasonably related to the transaction. That sentence states that the law chosen by the parties will meet the test of reasonableness if a significant *portion* of *either* the making or the performance is to occur or occurs in the chosen jurisdiction. The entire commercial transaction is to be divided into its principal components, formation and performance, and only a *portion* of either of these components must be significant. Consequently, even though the contact relied upon in choosing applicable law could be classified as insignificant when measured against all of the contacts involved in the entire commercial transaction in dispute, nevertheless, that single contact may be significant when measured against the isolated facts of the contract's making or the facts of its performance, and thus sufficient under section 1–105 to justify choosing the law of that state.

The *Seeman* case cited in the Comment involved the question of which state's usury statute was to govern a loan transaction between a New York borrower and a Pennsylvania lender. Although the loan agreement did not contain a choice of law clause, the parties signed the notes and arranged for performance in Pennsylvania, evidently for the purpose of having that state's usury laws control (and uphold) the agreement. The Supreme Court, in applying the law apparently intended by the parties, stated that the commercial loan would be upheld if the loan was valid either at the place of making or at the place of

---

19. Siegelman v. Cunard White Star, Ltd., 221 F.2d 189 (2d Cir. 1955); Born **v. Norwegian** America Line, Inc., 173 F.Supp. 33 (S.D.N.Y.1959).

20. UCC § 1–105, Comment 1.

performance. The Court added this limitation: "[T]he parties must act in good faith. . . . The effect of the qualification is merely to prevent the evasion or avoidance at will of the usury law otherwise applicable, by the parties' entering into the contract or stipulating for its performance at a place which has no normal relation to the transaction and to whose law they would not otherwise be subject." [21]

When the Comment reference to *Seeman* is combined with the statutory policy favoring party autonomy, the result is that the parties' choice should be upheld unless the transaction lacks a *normal* connection with the state whose law was selected. Only when it is shown that the contact did not occur in the normal course of the transaction, but was contrived to validate the parties' choice of governing law, should the relation be held unreasonable; in other cases, the clause should be upheld.[22] Courts should guard against combining notions of sovereignty in choice of law with the flexibility of the Code's "reasonable relation" test to strike down the selected law—leaving the parties with an uncertainty which the Code was designed to eliminate.

§ 11.   Limitations on Party Autonomy—Contact with the Forum

One apparently simple case may cause difficulty under the peculiar wording of section 1–105: "when a transaction bears a reasonable relation to this state *and also* to another state or nation the parties may agree that the law either of this state or of such other state or nation shall govern their rights and duties." Difficulties may arise if the transaction has no connection with the forum state but does have contacts with one or more other states. In such a case should the forum give effect to the choice of law agreement, or should it hold that the agreement is invalid simply because there was no reasonable relation to the forum? [23]

---

21. 274 U.S. at 408, 47 S.Ct. at 627. Although the *Seeman* case did not involve an explicit choice of law clause, it has been frequently cited by cases in which the validity of such a clause is in issue. *See, e. g.,* Consol. Jewelers, Inc. v. Standard Fin. Corp., 325 F.2d 31 (6th Cir. 1963); Merchants' & Manufacturers' Sec. Co. v. Johnson, 69 F.2d 940 (8th Cir. 1934); Ury v. Jewelers Acceptance Corp., 227 Cal. App.2d 11, 38 Cal.Rptr. 376 (1964).

22. See Restatement (Second) of Conflict of Laws § 187, comment *f* (Proposed Official Draft, 1968). Other readings of UCC § 1–105 are suggested in Tuchler, *Boundaries to Party Autonomy in the Uniform Commercial Code: A Radical View,* 11 St. Louis L.J. 180 (1967).

The transaction may have no factual contact with the chosen law; yet the choice may be upheld on the basis of the familiarity of the parties with that law. Vita Food Prod. Inc. v. Unus Shipping Co., [1939] A.C. 277 (P.C.) (Nova Scotia).

23. Another alternative is open to the courts. It may dismiss the case under a doctrine of *forum non conveniens.* Such dismissal should rest on the lack of any significant contact with the forum and could be applied to sales cases under the same tests as used for actions generally. Gulf Oil Corp. v. Gilbert, 330 U.S. 501, 67 S.Ct. 839, 91

The answer clearly ought to be that the agreement is effective. In such a situation the forum has no interest in the outcome of the litigation; no local policy is called into play since, by hypothesis, the forum has no reasonable connection with the transaction and is providing only a situs for the suit.[24] Moreover, the Code expresses a policy favoring party autonomy. If the chosen law is from a jurisdiction which has a reasonable connection with the facts of the transaction, the clause should be upheld although for this case the Code is inartfully drafted.[25] In short, section 1–105 ought to be read as Comment 1 to that section suggests:

> Subsection (1) states affirmatively the right of the parties to a multi-state transaction or a transaction involving foreign trade to choose their own law. That right is subject to the firm rules stated in the six sections listed in subsection (2), and is limited to jurisdictions to which the transaction bears a "reasonable relation."

§ 12. Limitations on Party Autonomy—Miscellaneous Limitations

There are other limitations on party autonomy—other than that the transaction must have a reasonable relation to the chosen law—which will be read into section 1–105 by the courts. These limitations include:

1. RIGHTS OF THIRD PARTIES

Although the parties may agree as to the law which will govern their rights and duties, they may not bind third parties to the transaction. This limitation on party autonomy is exemplified in some of the exceptions contained in subsection (2) of section 1–105. One such exception is found in section 2–402 which provides that situs law is to be used to determine the rights of creditors of a seller who has retained

L.Ed. 1055 (1947); Kamas State Bank v. American Sur. Co., 285 F.Supp. 430 (W.D.Mo.1967).

Federal courts may transfer "any civil action to any other district or division where it might have been brought" under 28 U.S.C.A. § 1404(a) (1964). For the applicable law in that situation, see Van Dusen v. Barrack, 376 U.S. 612, 84 S.Ct. 805 (1949). See also Norwood v. Kirkpatrick, 349 U.S. 29, 75 S.Ct. 544, 99 L.Ed. 789 (1955) (power of federal courts under § 1404 is broader than the doctrine of *forum non conveniens*).

24. For a Code case involving a situation where the forum had no connection with the transaction (but in which there was no express agreement as to applicable law) see Associates Discount Corp. v. Cary, 47 Misc.2d 369, 262 N.Y.S.2d 646 (Civ.Ct.1965).

25. A similar result could be reached through an application of the doctrine of renvoi. The local court could refer to the law of that state whose law was chosen by the parties as the "appropriate" law under the second sentence of UCC § 1–105(1), and then apply the whole Code of that state—including its version of UCC § 1–105(1)—to uphold the parties' choice. Application of choice of law rules of another state is recognized in UCC §§ 1–105(2) and 9–103.

possession of sold goods. Here third parties to the sale, the creditors, have intervened, and any choice of law rule agreed upon in the seller-buyer contract will have no impact on those third parties.

A case involving this third-party limitation on party autonomy is *Industrial Packaging Products Co. v. Fort Pitt Packaging International Incorporated,*[26] in which Fort Pitt assigned to a lender all payments due or to become due under a contract which Fort Pitt had with the United States. The contract of assignment contained a clause providing that the "agreement and performance thereof shall in all respects be governed by and in accordance with the laws of the state of New York." The Supreme Court of Pennsylvania stated that this clause was binding as between the parties but held that the rights of creditors of Fort Pitt were not affected by the agreement as to applicable law. "Otherwise, it would be possible for two parties to render nugatory as to third parties an act of Assembly passed for the benefit of such third parties."[27] The result of this case can be explained either on the basis that Article 9 transactions are expressly exempted from section 1–105[28] or on the language of section 1–105(1): the *parties* may agree as to the system of law which will govern *their* rights and duties. There is no statutory authority which allows the parties to an agreement to select a law which will govern the rights of third parties.

2. AGREEMENT OF THE PARTIES

There is one word in 1–105(1) which could cause some difficulties of interpretation. That word is "agree"; the parties may *agree* on the law which is to govern their rights and duties. Without a doubt this allows the parties, within the limitations discussed, to include in their commercial contract a clause expressly choosing a system of law.

The question, however, is whether "agree" is also broad enough to include an implied choice of law agreement. That is, suppose that a sales contract without an express choice of law clause was "made" in State B but had a preponderance of its factual contacts with State A. Suppose further that litigation involving this contract arose in State B and that State B would say that, since the contract was "made" there, the transaction had an appropriate relation to State B—and was about to apply its version of the Code.[29] How effective would the following argument be?

The Code, in section 1–105, states that the parties may "agree" as to the applicable law. While the word "agree" is

26. 399 Pa. 643, 161 A.2d 19 (1960).

27. *Id.* at 647, 161 A.2d at 21.

28. UCC §§ 1–105(2), 9–102, 9–103.

29. See the second sentence in UCC § 1–105(1).

not defined, "agreement" is defined in section 1–201(3) to include the bargain of the parties from the language used "or by implication from other circumstances." Here an agreement as to applicable law should be implied from the circumstances—those circumstances being the preponderance of contacts with State A—and the law of State A should be applied under the first sentence of section 1–105(1) rather than the law of State B under the second sentence.[30]

Even though there is nothing in the history of section 1–105 which would indicate that the drafters of the Code intended that the word "agree" in section 1–105 was to include anything beyond the usual express choice of law clause, there is nothing in the language of the Code which makes the above argument unreasonable. Indeed, the reference in the Comments to the *Seeman*[31] case could be used to support the argument because, in *Seeman,* there was no choice of law clause. Nevertheless, the Comments cite that case as an example of what is meant by a "reasonable relation."

What ought a court do when faced with this argument? Perhaps the best way of answering the argument is to hold that the laws of State A should not be applied under the party autonomy sentence of section 1–105 but should be applied under the appropriate relation test of section 1–105. This interpretation of the second sentence of section 1–105 is expanded below.[32] If, however, the court does not accept the suggested interpretation of "appropriate relation," the finding of an implied agreement under the first sentence of section 1–105 can be employed to reach a sensible result in the area of choice of law in commercial transactions: the application of the most appropriate law for the transaction, considering the problem presented to the court.

---

30. Considerable support for this argument can be obtained from pre-Code cases which justified their choice of law rules on the basis that the law applied was the law intended by the parties. The intent in these cases was implied from the facts. Examples include Lauritzen v. Larsen, 345 U.S. 571, 73 S.Ct. 921, 97 L.Ed. 1254 (1953); Pinney v. Nelson, 183 U.S. 144, 22 S.Ct. 52, 46 L.Ed. 125 (1901); Pritchard v. Norton, 106 U.S. 124, 1 S.Ct. 102, 27 L.Ed. 104 (1882); Grand v. Livingston, 4 App.Div. 589, 38 N.Y.S. 490 (1896), aff'd 158 N.Y. 688, 53 N.E. 1125 (1899). Further, the more recent "grouping of contacts" approach to choice of law can be explained on a presumed intent (or agreement) basis. Auten v. Auten, 308 N.Y. 155, 124 N.E. 2d 99 (1954); Baffin Land Corp. v. Monticello Motor Inn, Inc., 70 Wash.2d 893, 425 P.2d 623 (1967). Finally, this argument can be buttressed by the approach of Chinchilla v. Foreign Tankship Corp., 195 Misc. 895, 91 N.Y.S. 2d 213 (City Ct.1949), *modified* 197 Misc. 1058, 97 N.Y.S.2d 835 (App.T. 1950), aff'd 278 App.Div. 556, 102 N.Y. S.2d 438 (1951), which can be read as applying the law impliedly agreed upon by the parties.

31. Seeman v. Philadelphia Warehouse Co., 274 U.S. 403, 47 S.Ct. 626, 71 L. Ed. 1123 (1927). See also Green v. Northwestern Trust Co., 128 Minn. 30, 150 N.W. 229 (1914). *But see* Lyles v. Union Planters Nat. Bank, 239 Ark. 739, 393 S.W.2d 867 (1965), which assumed that an express agreement was needed under UCC § 1–105.

32. § 19 *infra*.

3. Unconscionable Clauses

In its ideal form the principle of freedom of contract presupposes two parties of approximately equal bargaining strength dickering about the purchase and sale of property or services. The difficulty, of course, is that the American market often bears little resemblance to the theoretical model. It may be that one of the parties is in such a superior bargaining position that he can dictate the price on a take-it-or-leave-it basis.[33] His position and the use of mass-produced contract forms may also foreclose an opportunity by the other party to negotiate any of the terms of the deal.[34] In such a case there is no freedom to dicker; the only freedom is either to enter into an agreement for the property or the services, or not to enter into such an agreement. Additionally, if the price, property, or services are thought by one of the parties to be essential to his well-being, even the freedom to refuse to contract becomes an illusion. Beyond agreements forced by the party with the superior bargaining position, other activities may disrupt the agreement process. Fraud, duress, mistake, undue influence, or unfair advantage upset notions of agreement.

The line between allowable pressure and forbidden overreaching is a difficult one to draw. Nevertheless, the courts have drawn the line.[35] Using doctrines of contract interpretation, inadequacy of consideration, fraud, mistake, sharp bargain, and duress, courts have attempted to preserve maximum freedom of contract without allowing parties to destroy the process of agreement. The nature of the problem prevents the framing of fixed rules and requires courts to proceed on a case-by-case basis, working with general principles of what a consensual transaction ought to be.

The choice of law clauses in an agreement are no exception. To the extent that they have been *agreed upon* by the parties, the Code commands their enforcement. However, the court must not abdicate its task of determining whether the parties have *agreed*. A choice of law clause reproduced in the fine print of a take-it-or-leave-it document may, like other clauses in the same document, properly be held not to have been the product of the agreement of the parties. Given such a conclusion, the choice of law clause ought not be enforced.

The Code contains the bases for policing party autonomy in choice of law. One basis has already been suggested: the parties must *agree*

33. Ehrenzweig, *Adhesion Contracts in the Conflict of Laws*, 53 Colum.L.Rev. 1072 (1953).

34. Henningsen v. Bloomfield Motors, Inc., 32 N.J. 358, 161 A.2d 69 (1960), discussed in § 92 *infra*. Schuchman,

Consumer Credit by Adhesion Contracts, 35 Temp.L.Q. 125, 281 (1962).

35. Dawson, *Economic Duress—An Essay in Perspective*, 45 Mich.L.Rev. 253 (1947).

on the applicable law.[36] Something short of agreement will not suffice. This does not mean that the clause must have been discussed or that the complaining party must actually have read the clause. It means only that the court must be convinced that this clause was fairly enough obtained so that it ought to become a part of the total legal obligations of the parties.[37] This calls into play the usual doctrines of contract formation by which all provisions of the document are tested.

Another Code section which can be used to police party autonomy is section 1–103. That section cuts across the entire Code. It reads:

> Unless displaced by the particular provisions of this Act, the principles of law and equity, including the law merchant and the law relative to capacity to contract, principal and agent, estoppel, fraud, misrepresentation, duress, coercion, mistake, bankruptcy, or other validating or invalidating cause shall supplement its provisions.

Section 1–203, imposing an obligation of good faith in the performance of every Code contract, can also be used to strengthen an argument under section 1–103.

For sales transactions the controversial section on unconscionability (section 2–302) can form another base from which to test the enforceability of a choice of law clause. This section, which gives the court the power to refuse to enforce any clause which it finds to be unconscionable, is examined in detail later in this text.[38] The ideas expressed there are equally applicable to choice of law clause.

---

36. UCC § 1–105(1).

37. "Agreement" is defined in UCC § 1–201(3); "contract" is defined in UCC § 1–201(11). See § 47 *infra*.

38. § 44 *infra*. There have been no reported cases in which the court has been asked to strike a choice of law clause on the basis that the clause or its method or procurement was unconscionable. There is, however, nothing unique about these clauses, and general doctrines of unconscionability developed in other contexts should apply to agreements as to applicable law. The leading case is Williams v. Walker-Thomas Furniture Co., 121 U. S.App.D.C. 315, 350 F.2d 445 (1965). Other cases which have applied this section include American Home Improvement, Inc. v. MacIver, 105 N.H. 435, 201 A.2d 886 (1964) (court found that writing did not comply with local retail installment act and also that contract was unenforceable because buyers "were paying $1,609 for goods and services valued at far less");

Toker v. Perl, 103 N.J.Super. 500, 247 A.2d 701 (L.Div.1968) (court found contract was induced by fraud and also that price paid for goods was exorbitant) case was affirmed on first basis in 108 N.J.Super. 129, 260 A.2d 244 (App.Div.1970); Zabriskie Chevrolet, Inc. v. Smith, 99 N.J.Super. 441, 240 A.2d 195 (L.Div.1968) (disclaimer of warranty clause held unenforceable, one ground being that the clause violated UCC § 2–302); Frostifresh Corp. v. Reynoso, 52 Misc.2d 26, 274 N.Y.S. 2d 757 (Dist.Ct.1966), *rev'd in part* 54 Misc.2d 119, 281 N.Y.S.2d 964 (App.Div. 1967) (sales techniques and price made contract unconsionable, and price term was rewritten by court). The *Williams* and *American Home* cases are analyzed in Leff, *Unconscionability and the Code—The Emperor's New Clause*, 115 U.Pa.L.Rev. 485 (1967). In Paragon Homes, Inc. v. Carter, 56 Misc.2d 463, 288 N.Y.S.2d 817, *aff'd* 30 A.D.2d 1052, 295 N.Y.S.2d 606 (1968), the court held unconscionable a clause by which the parties (a Maine corpora-

The combined impact of these sections of the Code places a limit on the power of parties to select their applicable law—a limit which was called "unconscionable clauses" at the beginning of this discussion. To the extent that these printed choice of law clauses are ignored by courts, certainty and predictability are lost. An attorney cannot simply look at a written document and advise whether the courts will apply the chosen law. He must inquire into the factual background from which the writing emerged. Even then he will on occasion be called upon to predict whether the court will find the clause to be unconscionable, and he may predict incorrectly. Nevertheless, courts believe (and properly so) that the expectation interest of a party who has overreached in obtaining a signature on a written document is simply not worthy of protection, and at this point certainty must give way to other values.

4. Public Policy of the Forum

One limitation courts should not place on choice of law clauses in commercial transactions is the long-recognized principle that the public policies of the forum are not to be overriden by the application of foreign law.[39] The proposed Restatement (Second) of Conflicts of Laws expands this public policy exception by providing that the law chosen by the parties will be used to determine the validity of a contract unless (among other things) "application of the chosen law would be contrary to a fundamental policy of the state which would be the state of the governing law in the absence of an effective choice by the parties."[40]

The Code contains no public policy exception to party autonomy in choosing applicable law, and none should be read in by the courts. It may well be that for the general area of conflict of laws some restrictions are needed on allowing parties to contract out from under local policies, but no such exception is required in commercial law where states have almost unanimously agreed on the basic Code policies. Although local Code variations have occurred which could be decisive in a particular case, these variations do not express some fundamental policy, "some deep-rooted tradition of the common weal,"[41] which should override legislative approval of the Code in general or of the doctrine of party autonomy in specific. There is no longer room in

tion and a Massachusetts resident) agreed to submit to the jurisdiction of a New York court.

39. Restatement of Conflict of Laws § 612 (1934).

40. Restatement (Second) of Conflict of Laws § 187 (Proposed Official Draft

1968). There is little direct authority on the application of public policy to strike a choice of law clause. The only case found bearing on this problem is Fricke v. Isbrandtsen Co., 151 F.Supp. 465 (S.D.N.Y.1957).

41. Loucks v. Standard Oil Co., 224 N. Y. 99, 111, 120 N.E. 198, 202 (1918).

commercial law for a notion that because the rules applied to a particular problem vary in their detail, those details express some principle of strong local policy negating the parties' own choice of law.[42]

3. APPROPRIATE RELATION TEST

§ 13. History of the Choice of Law Clause—Purpose of the Drafters

The drafters of the Uniform Commercial Code believed that it might take several years, or even decades, before there would be anything approaching unanimous acceptance of the Code. It is now apparent that they overestimated the period of time that would elapse between the Code's promulgation and its adoption by the state legislatures, but for a period of about five years during and following the study of the New York Law Revision Commission it appeared that the Code might never receive approval except from a handful of states.

Nevertheless, the drafters firmly believed that the Code was a marked improvement over prior law and ought to be applied to as many transactions as possible.[43] One way to accomplish this result was to seek further adoptions; this they did through amendments designed to meet justified criticisms which had been raised. Another way was to have the adopted Codes applied to as many commercial transactions as could constitutionally be reached. To secure this widespread application of adopted Codes, the drafters selected a choice of law rule which provided that a forum with the Code should apply the Code to determine the rights and duties of the parties in all transactions in which there was at least a minimal connection between the forum state and the transaction.[44] The drafters were helped by the fact that the

42. *Cf.* Hughes v. Fetter, 341 U.S. 609, 71 S.Ct. 980, 95 L.Ed. 1212 (1951); Oltarsh v. Aetna Ins. Co., 15 N.Y.2d 111, 256 N.Y.S.2d 577, 204 N.E.2d 622 (1965); Intercontinental Hotels Corp. (Puerto Rico) v. Golden, 15 N.Y.2d 9, 254 N.Y.S.2d 527, 203 N.E.2d 210 (1964).

43. Although the Comments to the 1952 Code did not expressly state that this was the reason for adopting a forum-oriented rule, this motive was acknowledged in the 1958 and 1962 Comments: "Application of the Code in such circumstances may be justified by its comprehensiveness, by the policy of uniformity, and by the fact that it is in large part a reformulation and restatement of the law merchant and of the understanding of a business community which transcends state and even national boundaries." UCC § 1–

105, Comment 3. Professor Goodrich denied that a forum-oriented rule was selected because of a "primitive view that a state will resolve all legal problems with foreign contacts solely according to its own laws because it deems its law the best or most enlightened." Goodrich, *Conflicts Niceties & Commercial Necessities*, 1952 Wis.L.Rev. 199, 202. He suggested, the explanation, not incompatible with that set out in the text, that the rule was adopted to insure that the law of a single state governed the entire transaction. *Id.* at 202. This was not the case under pre-Code law. *See* Restatement of Conflict of Laws §§ 332, 358 (1934).

44. *Cf.* Weintraub, *Choice of Law in Contract*, 54 Iowa L.Rev. 399, 418 (1968); Weintraub, *Choice of Law for Products Liability: The Impact of the*

Supreme Court had not developed sweeping constitutional principles affecting choice of law—even though the Court undoubtedly has the power to do so under the due process and the full faith and credit clauses of the Constitution.[45]

Such a Code section would, of course, have no direct impact in courts of states which had not adopted the Code; those states would remain free to apply their common law notions and to refer sales questions to the law of the place of making, the place of performance, the intended law, the place with the most significant contacts, or whatever constitutional rule they chose to develop. However, if the Code were to be adopted in those states having a sizeable number of commercial transactions, the choice of law section would result in Code-established policies controlling the outcome of a significant portion of this country's commerce.

§ 14. History of the Choice of Law Clause—The 1952 Official Draft

The choice of law provision in the 1952 version of the Code contained six subsections. One provided for party autonomy, under certain limitations, in selecting applicable law. The other subsections each specified certain minimal contacts with the Code state which, if found to exist, would provide a basis for applying the Code to a transaction with interstate connections in those instances in which the parties had not or could not agree on applicable law. For example, Article 2 on Sales was to be used to determine the rights and duties of the parties if:

1. The contract was made in the state, *or*
2. The offer was made in the state, *or*
3. The acceptance occurred in the state, *or*
4. The contract was to be performed or completed wholly within the state, *or*
5. The contract was to be performed or completed in part within the state, *or*
6. The contract related to or involved goods "which are to be or are in fact delivered, shipped or received" within the state, *or*
7. The contract involved "a bill of lading, warehouse receipt or other document of title which is to be or is in fact issued, delivered, sent or received" within the state, *or*

Uniform Commercial Code & Recent Developments in Conflicts Analysis, 44 Texas L.Rev. 1429, 1436–37 (1966).

45. *See* A. Ehrenzweig, Conflict of Laws 28–32 (1962); G. Stumberg, Principles of Conflict of Laws 51–65 (3d ed. 1963). Both cite and discuss the leading cases involving the Supreme Court's attitude on developing choice of law rules; in addition, Professor Ehrenzweig has included a comprehensive list of law review discussions of this subject.

8. The contract "is an application or agreement for a credit made, sent or received within this state, or involves a credit issued in this state or under which drafts are to be presented in this state or confirmation or advice of which is sent or received within this state, or involves any negotiation within this state of a draft drawn under a credit," *or*

9. The transaction occurred within the state.

Since these phrases were connected with an "or", the existence of any one would suffice to make the local Code applicable to the sales transaction. In this way the Uniform Commercial Code would reach out and affect sales with only a minimal contact with a Code state— provided that the suit was brought in the Code state and that section 1–105 as drafted was constitutional.

§ 15.   History of the Choice of Law Clause—Objections to the 1952 Draft

There were immediate objections to the 1952 draft of section 1– 105.[46] Some attacked the policy which formed the basis for 1–105; others challenged the constitutionality of the section. To understand these objections it must be recalled that courts had long been deciding cases under the shadow of a vested rights theory [47] which included a set

---

46.   One of the earliest objections to the pre-1952 drafts came from a number of teachers of conflict of laws who met in 1949 and passed a resolution which stated that UCC § 1–105 (in both forms which they reviewed) "is unwise and should be omitted from the Code." This resolution is reproduced in Rheinstein, *Conflict of Laws in the Uniform Commercial Code*, 16 Law & Contemp. Prob. 114, 115 (1951).

47.   There have been a number of theories advanced as to why a court refers to some system of law other than its own to determine the rights of litigants now before the forum court. These are discussed in H. Goodrich, Conflict of Laws 6–8 (4th ed. 1964), and in G. Stumberg, Principles of Conflict of Laws 5–15 (3d ed. 1963). See also A. Ehrenzweig, Conflict of Laws 347–68 (1962). One of these theories has been called the "vested rights" approach: rights were acquired in the territory of some sovereignty and the forum simply enforces those rights. This theory of conflict of laws was the basis of Professor Joseph Beale's treatise, Conflict of Laws (1935), and of the Restatement of Conflict of Laws

(1934). The vested rights theory, under the leadership of Mr. Justice Holmes, became the basis of many court opinions. Examples of Holmes' opinions include Mutual Life Ins. Co. v. Liebing, 259 U.S. 209, 42 S.Ct. 467, 66 L.Ed. 900 (1922); Slater v. Mexican Nat. R.R., 194 U.S. 120, 24 S.Ct. 581, 48 L.Ed. 900 (1904). The most devastating attack on the vested rights theory came from Professor Walter Wheeler Cook in a series of articles between 1919 and 1942. These articles are collected and supplemented in his treatise, W. Cook, The Logical and Legal Bases of the Conflict of Laws 20–22, 41–46 (1942). More recent scholars who have joined in the search for some theoretical undergirding for conflict of laws include Professors Ehrenzweig (whose treatise is cited *supra* this note) and Currie. See *e. g.*, Currie, *Notes on Methods and Objectives in the Conflict of Laws*, 1959 Duke L.J. 171 at 178. During the last 75 years a number of excellent minds have considered the troublesome problem of when and why to refer to foreign law. In addition to those already mentioned, the list includes such scholars as David Cavers, Elliott

of "rules" to determine which law should be applied to determine the validity of a contract—rules like "place of making," [48] "place of performance," [49] "intended law," [50] and "lex loci contractus." [51] It is true that some courts had discarded these slogans and were talking about "the place with the most significant contacts" as the jurisdiction whose laws should govern the outcome of a case,[52] but the Code's 1952 test was strikingly different from any of these tests. Section 1–105 did not suggest application of the *most* significant law or even the law of the jurisdiction where the rights had vested; it required the court to apply local law if any one of the minimal contacts was found.[53]

The 1952 Code test could result in the most open type of forum shopping. If the outcome of a case would differ under the Code and non-Code law, the choice of the forum for the suit could determine which substantive law would be applied. For example, an offer for an open price agreement might be made from a buyer in a Code state and accepted by a seller in a non-Code state with performance scheduled for the non-Code state. Adoption of either the place of making or place of performance test would result in the agreement being held unenforceable if the non-Code law followed the usual common law rules on illusory promises.[54] Yet, if the suit could somehow be brought in the Code state, the 1952 version of section 1–105 would command application of the Code, and the agreement could be held enforceable.[55]

Cheatham, Moffat Hancock, Robert Leflar, Ernest Lorenzen, Willis Reese, and Hessel Yntema. No answer satisfactory to the courts, however, has as yet been suggested. See D. Cavers, The Choice-of-Law Process 1–18, 59–87 (1965); A. von Mehren and D. Trautman, The Law of Multistate Problems 24–79 (1965); and Symposium, *New Trends in the Conflict of Laws*, 28 Law & Contemp.Prob. 673–869 (1963).

48. "The general rule is that the validity of a contract is to be determined by the law of the state in which it is made; if it is valid there, it is deemed valid everywhere . . . ." Milliken v. Pratt, 125 Mass. 374, 375 (1878).

49. R. Leflar, Conflict of Laws 232 (1959).

50. Pritchard v. Norton, 106 U.S. 124, 129, 1 S.Ct. 102, 105, 27 L.Ed. 104 (1882). *See* 2 E. Rabel, Conflict of Laws 376 (2d ed. 1960); Cook, *"Contracts" and the Conflict of Laws: "Intention" of the Parties*, 32 Ill.L. Rev. 899 (1938), 34 Ill.L.Rev. 423 (1939).

51. Pritchard v. Norton, 106 U.S. 124, 1 S.Ct. 102, 27 L.Ed. 104 (1882).

52. Bowles v. Zimmer Mfg. Co., 277 F. 2d 868 (7th Cir. 1960); Global Commerce Corp. v. Clark–Babbitt Industries Inc., 239 F.2d 716 (2d Cir. 1956); W. H. Barber Co. v. Hughes, 223 Ind. 570, 63 N.E.2d 417 (1945); Auten v. Auten, 308 N.Y. 155, 124 N.E.2d 99 (1954); Peterson v. Warren, 31 Wis.2d 547, 143 N.W.2d 560 (1966), *overruled on another point* Allen v. Ross, 38 Wis. 2d 209, 156 N.W.2d 434 (1968).

53. § 7 *supra.*

54. *E. g.*, Weston Paper Mfg. Co. v. Downing Box Co., 293 F. 725 (7th Cir. 1923), in which the agreement provided that the price shall "be fixed by the seller . . . which price shall be the seller's market price then existing under this seller's standard form of quarterly price fixing contract." The court held that the agreement was unenforceable. *But see* Moore v. Shell Oil Co., 139 Or. 72, 6 P.2d 216 (1931).

55. UCC § 2–305, discussed in § 38 *infra.*

There were many who thought that promotion of forum shopping was bad on policy grounds, without ever getting to the question of whether section 1–105 was constitutional.[56] These writers recommended that section 1–105 be changed or deleted.[57]

There was, however, another basis for attacking the detailed provisions of the 1952 version of section 1–105: this section, in its attempt to make the Code applicable to transactions having only the slightest factual connection with the Code forum, may have violated the due process clause of the fourteenth amendment. The scholars who urged this position were forced to state their argument in terms of probabilities rather than certainties. During the early part of this century the Supreme Court appeared ready to use the due process clause, and perhaps even the full faith and credit clause, to forge sweeping choice of law rules which would have to be followed by state courts.[58] In the late '30s and early '40s, however, this trend was reversed. Except for a few isolated cases,[59] the Supreme Court stopped accepting choice of law cases and by default allowed states to develop their own conflicts rules.[60]

The principal case on which those who attacked the 1952 version of section 1–105 rested their arguments was one which was decided during the time the Supreme Court appeared to be developing a national body of choice law principles—*Home Insurance Co. v. Dick*.[61] In that

---

56. Stumberg, *Commercial Paper and the Conflict of Laws*, 6 Vand.L.Rev. 489, 504 (1953). The use of choice of law rules to prevent the accident of the forum from determining the outcome of the litigation has been expressed in several non-contract cases as well. *E. g.*, Lauritzen v. Larsen, 345 U.S. 571, 73 S.Ct. 921, 97 L.Ed. 1254 (1953). *See generally* Linn v. Employers Reinsurance Corp., 392 Pa. 58, 139 A.2d 638 (1958); Goodrich, *Public Policy in the Law of Conflicts*, 36 W. Va.L.Q. 156 (1930).

57. Rheinstein, *Conflict of Laws in the Uniform Commercial Code*, 16 Law & Contemp.Prob. 114, 128 (1951).

58. Hartford Accident & Indem. Co. v. Delta & Pine Land Co., 292 U.S. 143, 54 S.Ct. 634, 78 L.Ed. 1178 (1934); New York Life Ins. Co. v. Dodge, 246 U.S. 357, 38 S.Ct. 337, 62 L.Ed. 772 (1918); New York Life Ins. Co. v. Head, 234 U.S. 149, 34 S.Ct. 879, 58 L.Ed. 1259 (1914); Allgeyer v. Louisiana, 165 U.S. 578, 17 S.Ct. 427, 41 L.Ed. 832 (1897).

59. Hughes v. Fetter, 341 U.S. 609, 71 S.Ct. 980, 95 L.Ed. 1212 (1951); Order of United Commercial Travelers of America v. Wolfe, 331 U.S. 586, 67 S.Ct. 1355, 91 L.Ed. 1687 (1947). A classification is suggested in the dissenting opinion of Mr. Justice Frankfurter in Carroll v. Lanza, 349 U.S. 408, 414, 75 S.Ct. 804, 808, 99 L.Ed. 1183 (1955). *See* Leflar, *Constitutional Limits on Free Choice of Law*, 28 Law & Contemp. Prob. 706 (1963).

60. With the cases cited in note 58, compare State Farm Mut. Auto. Ins. Co. v. Duel, 324 U.S. 154, 65 S.Ct. 573, 89 L.Ed. 812 (1945); Hoopeston Canning Co. v. Cullen, 318 U.S. 313, 63 S.Ct. 602, 87 L.Ed. 777 (1943); and Osborn v. Ozlin, 310 U.S. 53, 60 S.Ct. 758, 84 L.Ed. 1074 (1940). There are excellent discussions in A. von Mehren and D. Trautman, The Law of Multistate Problems 1247–58 (1965); Jackson, *Full Faith and Credit—The Lawyer's Clause of the Constitution*, 45 Colum.L.Rev. 1 (1945).

61. 281 U.S. 397, 50 S.Ct. 338 (1930).

case the Supreme Court emphasized the absence of contacts between the forum state, Texas, and the transaction, specifically discounted the fact that the forum was the residence of the plaintiff, and overturned the state court's application of forum law. According to the Court, "Texas was, therefore, without power to affect the terms of contracts so made. Its attempt to impose a greater obligation than that agreed upon and to seize property in payment of the imposed obligation violates the guaranty against deprivation of property without due process of law." [62]

From this case it was argued that "the Court has never relinquished all controls over state choice of law and there are indications that the court will not allow the application of its own law by a state which does not have an interest regarded as sufficient by the Court." [63] To the extent that this analysis of the due process clause is correct, the 1952 version of section 1–105 was in grave constitutional doubt.

Other scholars defended section 1–105, both on its policy and as to its validity under the Constitution. On policy grounds they argued that there was need for one law to apply to an entire transaction and that that law ought to be the Code. Such law, based in large part on a "reformulation and restatement of the law merchant and of the understanding of a business community which transcends state and even national boundaries," [64] was supposed to promote simplicity and facilitate commerce. [65] The Code's policies were to be preferred over non-Code doctrines, and the commercial transaction ought to be subject to one law rather than a myriad of confusing and overlapping laws. [66] Of course, there was also the question as to just how *Dick* and the other cases of that era ought to be read. Had they been impliedly overruled by later decisions which appeared to return to the state the determination of choice of law rules? Was *Dick*, even if not impliedly overruled, to be read as holding that application of forum law was forbidden when the ONLY connection with the forum was that the suit was brought there? If this narrow reading was to be given *Dick*, section 1–105 would survive an attack under the due process clause because the Code required something more than that the suit be brought in the forum as a prerequisite to Code application. No one could be sure

62. *Id.* at 408, 50 S.Ct. at 341.

63. Rheinstein, *Conflict of Laws in the Uniform Commercial Code*, 16 Law & Contemp. Prob. 114, 120 (1951).

64. UCC § 1–105, Comment 3.

65. Goodrich, *Conflicts Niceties and Commercial Necessities*, 1952 Wis.L. Rev. 199, 202.

66. The Restatement of Conflict of Laws (1934) states that different laws govern different elements of the contract: questions of validity by the place of making (§ 332); questions of performance by the place of performance (§ 358).

how these questions would be answered; arguments were necessarily stated in terms of probabilities.[67]

These arguments were never resolved. In 1956 the New York Law Revision Commission joined with those who were attacking section 1–105. It concluded that the policy of one law applying to the entire transaction had not been effected by the Code and that attempts "to apply law of the forum enacting the Code to a transaction having only a remote connection with that jurisdiction raise constitutional questions of due process." [68] The Commission recommended that section 1–105 be deleted from the Code.[69] The drafters did not, however, delete section 1–105. Instead, the 1958 version of the Code included a new draft of section 1–105—a version which retained party autonomy in selection of applicable law but which rewrote the necessary connections with the Code state if the parties had not selected a law to be applied.

§ 16. History of the Choice of Law Clause—Impact on the Present Draft

There are two reasons for including this historical summary of section 1–105. First, the evolution of the section is helpful in interpreting the meaning of the present language. In the 1952 text the drafters were attempting to reach as many transactions for Code applications as they could. It is arguable that the "appropriate relation" test of the present section 1–105 is nothing more than a generic term for the more specific details of the 1952 version. On the other hand a reasonable argument can be made that the drafters were concerned about the criticisms which had been directed toward their 1952 draft and intended to require a closer connection between the facts and the Code jurisdiction than had been true under the 1952 draft.[70] If so, the present version is particularly vague as to just how much "closer" this connection must be.[71] A third, and most likely, explanation is that the

---

67. Comment, *The Uniform Commercial Code and Conflict of Laws*, 9 Am.J. Comp.L. 458 (1960). Cases which cast doubt on whether the *Dick* case is still the law include Crider v. Zurich Ins. Co., 380 U.S. 39, 85 S.Ct. 769, 13 L.Ed.2d 641 (1965), *on remand* 348 F. 2d 211 (5th Cir. 1965), *cert. denied* 382 U.S. 1000, 86 S.Ct. 586, 15 L.Ed.2d 487 (1966); Clay v. Sun Ins. Office, Ltd., 377 U.S. 179, 84 S.Ct. 1197, 12 L.Ed.2d 229 (1964).

68. 1956 N.Y.Law Rev.Comm'n Rep. 34.

69. 1956 N.Y.Law Rev.Comm'n Rep. 34– 35. A report of the Commission's

study appears in 1955 N.Y.Law Rev. Comm'n Rep. (vol. 1) 175–200.

70. Cullen, *Conflict of Laws Problems Under the Uniform Commercial Code*, 48 Ky.L.J. 417, 425 (1960); Reese, *The Uniform Commercial Code and its Application in the Non-Code States*, 15 Baylor L.Rev. 291, 301 (1963).

71. "Where there is no agreement as to the governing law, the Act is applicable to any transaction having an 'appropriate' relation to any state which enacts it. Of course the Act applies to any transaction which takes place in its entirety in a state which has enact-

drafters intended to affirm the party autonomy concept and to leave to the courts the task of deciding choice of law problems on a case-by-case basis whenever the parties have not selected the law to govern their rights and duties.

These arguments lead to a second reason for including the history of section 1–105. To the extent that courts construe the present version of section 1–105 as broadly as was commanded by the 1952 version, the same policy and the same constitutional arguments are again presented. The material discussed in the prior section would then be directly relevant to the present Code text.[72]

§ 17. The Appropriate Relation Test—Problem of Code Construction

When the parties have not agreed as to the law which will govern their rights and duties, the Code applies "to transactions bearing an appropriate relation to this state." Such a terse legislative command to the forum court attempting to solve a choice of law problem leaves many difficulties. Among these are:

1. What is an "appropriate relation" ? Does it differ from the "reasonable relation" which had to be found before the parties could select their applicable law? If so (and the usual presumption is that a difference was intended when different language is used in the same section of a statute), does an "appropriate relation" require more or less connection with the state than does a "reasonable relation" ? [73]

2. Once some meaning is given to appropriate relation, the court is told to apply the local Code. Suppose, however, that the court finds that the transaction bears a minimal but appropriate relation to the forum but is much more closely connected with another Code state and that the Codes differ as to the solution of the problem presented. Does the test of section 1–105 require that the forum court (State A) apply its own Code even though, had this dispute been presented to any other state court in the United States, the State A Code would not have been applied?

---

ed the Act. But the mere fact that suit is brought in a state does not make it appropriate to apply the substantive law of that state. Cases where a relation to the enacting state is not 'appropriate' include, for example, those where the parties have clearly contracted on the basis of some other law, as where the law of the place of contracting and the law of the place of contemplated performance are the same and are contrary to the law under the Code." UCC § 1–105, Comment 2.

72. § 15 *supra*.

73. UCC § 1–105, Comment 3, indicates that the question of what is an "appropriate" relation is left to judicial decision, but urges application of forum (Code) law because of the Code's comprehensiveness, a policy of uniformity, and the fact that the Code restates the law merchant and the understanding of the business community. Then follows a curious reference directing that the courts *compare* Global Commerce Corp. v. Clark-Babbit Industries, Inc., 239 F.2d 716 (2d Cir. 1956). That case refused to apply forum law under any of the newer choice of law tests. *Id.* at 719.

3.   On the other hand, what is a forum court to do if it determines that the transaction does not bear an appropriate relation to the forum? The local Code dictates what to do only if such a relation is found with the forum.   It is silent as to what should be done if the forum is completely disinterested in this case.[74]   Should the forum, providing that it decides not to dismiss the case under some variation of the *forum nom conveniens* doctrine, return to the pre-Code choice of law rules, or should it attempt to seek out and to apply the policies underlying the selection of the "appropriate relation" test of section 1–105? [75]

§ 18.   The Appropriate Relation Test—Comments and Present Cases

Little assistance as to the scope of an appropriate relation or the connection between the 1952 and present rules is found in the Comments, which merely state that the determination of "what relation is 'appropriate' is left to judicial decision," while reiterating that courts deciding cases under the Code are not bound by pre-Code conflicts cases.[76]   The only relations excluded by the Comments as "not appropriate" are those in which the forum's sole contact is its status as forum, and where the parties clearly contracted with reference to some other law—for example, where the law of the places of contracting and performance are the same but contrary to forum law.

Thus far appellate courts have not been required to consider the full meaning of an "appropriate relation."   In *Skinner v. Tober Foreign Motors, Incorporated,*[77] the seller of an airplane was a Massachusetts corporation with its principal place of business in Massachusetts.   Both negotiation and execution of the contract took place in Massachusetts, and delivery was made in that state.   Shortly thereafter the airplane developed engine trouble, and the buyers, being financially unable to keep up the payments and at the same time repair or replace the engine, offered to return the airplane in cancellation of the agreement.   Instead, the seller orally agreed to reduce the monthly payments so that the buyers could proceed with the repairs.   While the buyers, residents of Connecticut, were meeting their obligations under the oral agreement—but in default of the written agreement—the seller took the airplane from Connecticut (where it was kept) and returned it to

74.   In Associates Discount Corp. v. Cary, 47 Misc.2d 369, 262 N.Y.S.2d 646 (Civ.Ct.1965), New York was the place of suit with the facts touching Massachusetts and Washington, D.C. The court referred to Massachusetts law, probably relying on UCC § 9–103, but rephrased UCC § 1–105 by stating that "the code would apply to all transactions bearing an 'appropriate relation' to the state where it was in force." *Id.* at 373, 262 N.Y.S.2d at 650.

75.   There is a penetrating analysis of this problem in Currie, *The Disinterested Third State*, 28 Law & Contemp. Prob. 754 (1963).

76.   UCC § 1–105, Comment 3.

77.   345 Mass. 429, 187 N.E.2d 669 (1963).

Massachusetts. The buyers brought suit against the seller in a Massachusetts court, seeking equitable replevin or damages. Affirming an award of damages for the buyers, the court pointed out that there was no evidence as to where the oral modification was made and held that Massachusetts law applied because the transaction bore an appropriate relation to that state. Since the Code (then effective in Massachusetts but not in Connecticut) dispensed with the requirement of consideration to support a contractual modification, the buyers were entitled to recovery.

In *Park County Implement Co. v. Craig*,[78] the only transactional connection with the non-Code state was that the buyer took delivery of the goods there. All other contacts were with the Code state (Wyoming), including the residence of the parties, the place where the goods were ordered, and the place to which the goods were taken after delivery. The seller sued the buyer in Wyoming for the price after the goods had been destroyed by fire. The court held that the transaction bore an appropriate relation to Wyoming and that the Wyoming Code determined whether there had been an acceptance of the goods. The relation to the non-Code state was described as "minor." [79]

§ 19. The Appropriate Relation Test—A Suggested Interpretation

The basic reason for including a forum-oriented choice of law rule in the Code—the maximization of the number of commercial transactions which would be subject to the Code's policies [80]—assumes that only a few states have adopted the Code and that most of the cases tried in a Code state will involve some factual connections with non-Code states. Today, however, all but one of the states have adopted the Code, and there is no longer a tug-of-war between the enlightened answers of the Code and the older answers it displaced. Except in international transactions, almost all commercial choice of law problems will arise between Code states; the goal which motivated the selection of the forum-oriented choice of law rule, the wide-spread use of the Code in solving commercial problems, has been achieved through legislative acceptance of the Code. The choice of law problem continues, nevertheless, in those areas in which the adopted statutes or their interpretations differ.

78.   397 P.2d 800 (Wyo.1964).

79.   *Id.* at 802. Other Code cases include Silver v. The Sloop Silver Cloud, 259 F.Supp. 187 (S.D.N.Y.1966) (place of making, delivery, and payment); Lyles v. Union Planters Nat. Bank, 239 Ark. 738, 393 S.W.2d 867 (1965);

Atlas Credit Corp. v. Dolbow, 193 Pa. Super. 649, 165 A.2d 704 (1960) (applying 1952 text of Code).

80.   Comment, *The Uniform Commercial Code and Conflict of Laws*, 9 Am.J. Comp.L. 458, 467 (1960).

Fortunately, the test chosen by the drafters, that the relation must be appropriate, gives the courts freedom to develop rational choice of law rules and apply them to commercial transactions. The advantages of this flexibility are apparent, for a relation which was *appropriate* when the problem was whether to apply a newly drafted comprehensive code or the law of a non-Code state does not necessarily continue to be *appropriate* when all states involved have the same basic legislation. In the first type of case, a court could justify finding an overriding policy supporting Code application because it represented a "reformulation and restatement of the law merchant and of the understanding of a business community which transcends state and even national boundaries." [81] In short, the Code could have been applied simply because it came the closest to protecting the justified expectations of the businessmen involved. However, that reason disappears once all states have the Code, and the court is free to develop further choice of law policies to refine the process which it began in cases like *Skinner* and *Park County*.[82]

Although it is not possible to review all the policies which can be promoted through choice of law rules, it should be suggested at this point that section 1–105 is flexible enough to reach at least these goals in cases presenting choice of law problems: [83]

1. *Separate the true conflicts cases from the false ones.* In some interstate transactions there is no conflict among the laws involved— even though the language of the Code sections involved differs. These transactions are sometimes called false conflict cases; on the surface there appears to be a conflict in the applicable rules, but upon analysis of the policies which those rules seek to serve the conflict disappears.

For example, suppose that State A has adopted the 1962 official version of section 2–318 which extends warranties to the family, household, and guests (in the home) of the buyer, but has refused to accept the invitation of the Comments to increase the number of persons within the protected class. There may be many reasons for such a limited view of section 2–318; one such reason could be grounded on a policy supporting manufacturing and promoting business within State A. That is, manufacturers ought to be attracted to the state because they know that sales made within that state carry a type of a built-in limit on liability. Suppose, however, that State B has amended its

81. UCC § 1–105, Comment 3.

82. § 18 *supra*.

83. Weintraub, *The Contracts Proposal of the Second Restatement of Conflict of Laws—A Critique*, 46 Iowa L.Rev. 713, 713–719 (1961). These considera-

tions were originally set out in Cheatham and Reese, *Choice of the Applicable Law*, 52 Colum.L.Rev. 959 (1952). See also Currie, *Notes on Methods and Objectives in the Conflict of Laws*, 1959 Duke L.J. 171; Traynor, *Is this Conflict Really Necessary?*, 37 Texas L.Rev. 657 (1959).

version of section 2–318 to extend warranties to persons who might reasonably be expected to be affected by the goods—even though they are not within the family, household, or guest classification adopted in State A. Here the policy could be that of insuring that injured persons, including at least State B's residents, will have funds to pay doctor and hospital bills and will not become charges upon the welfare taxes of State B.[84]

Suppose that, with the law and policies as described in the prior paragraph, an automobile was manufactured in State B and was sold to Buyer in State B. Buyer and his employer (both residents of State B) attended a convention in State A where the employer—while a passenger in Buyer's car—was injured because of a defective part in the automobile. Under these facts, a court could reasonably conclude that there is no conflict in the policies underlying the different versions of section 2–318.[85] Since the car was not manufactured in State A, State A's policy of promoting State A manufacturing will not be harmed by extending the warranty protection to the employer; State B's policy of providing added protection to its citizens through warranty protection will be advanced by applying State B's version of the Code. Thus, if this problem is presented to a court in State A, that court ought to use the "appropriate relation" test to sort out the policies underlying the sections of the Codes which appear to be in conflict and, in a proper case, determine that it is not *appropriate* to apply State A's version of section 2–318 because the *relation* of the parties to State A under these facts does not present a case in which the policies of State A law have any concern. Furthermore, this result should not be altered despite the fact that Buyer may have mailed the purchase order from State A while Buyer was on a State A vacation, the automobile was delivered from State B to Buyer while he was temporarily in State A, or because Buyer had arranged for credit with a State A bank—all contacts with State A, any one of which would have required application of State A's Code under the 1952 version of section 1–105.[86]

2. *Provide a rational basis for the solution of the true conflicts case.* A so-called "true" conflicts case can be presented by returning to the assumed automobile purchase case of the prior paragraphs but reversing the states of the purchase and the injury. Had Buyer pur-

84. *See* Currie, *Survival of Actions: Adjudication versus Automation in the Conflict of Laws,* 10 Stan.L.Rev. 205 (1958).

85. This type of analysis is used on the problem of the applicable statute of frauds in Bernkrant v. Fowler, 55 Cal.2d 588, 12 Cal.Rptr. 266, 360 P.2d 906 (1961). For a case raising the privity problem in a sale of an automobile, but involving a purchase before the Code was effective in either jurisdiction, see McCrossin v. Hicks Chevrolet, Inc., 248 A.2d 917 (D.C.App. 1969).

86. § 14 *supra.*

chased the automobile in State A from a State A manufacturer and had the injury to the employer occurred while the parties were in State B, State A's policy of promoting manufacturing by limiting the number of persons who can recover for defects in the goods collides with State B's policy of providing compensation for injured plaintiffs—especially if the employer and Buyer are residents of State B. It is this kind of case which is now being subjected to critical analysis by judges and by writers.[87] No single solution has as yet been agreed upon by the courts, nor is one suggested in this book. All that is urged here is that the "appropriate relation" test is sufficiently broad to enable the courts of Code states to continue their development of choice of law principles and not feel bound to apply forum law in a commercial transaction simply because they find a minimum contact between the facts of the transaction and the forum. For example, to the extent that the forum court believes that true conflicts cases ought to be solved by reference to the law of the state with the most significant connection with the transaction, only a slight wrench of Code language is required to classify this connection as the "appropriate relation" and to apply that policy to a Code transaction within Section 1–105(1).[88]

3. *To the extent possible, minimize the impact which the accident of the forum has in determining the outcome of the litigation.* Certainty and predictability in commercial transactions are worthy goals. As long as forum law is applied simply because the forum has some minimal contact with the underlying transaction, a degree of certainty and predictability in counseling will be lost. On some occasions this loss is totally unnecessary. For example, in the false conflicts case discussed under 1, above, it was concluded that the assumed policies indicated that it was not appropriate for the forum to apply its version

---

87. See A. von Mehren and D. Trautman, The Law of Multistate Problems, 76–79 (1965), and the reference to the articles by Professor Currie, especially Currie, *The Constitution and the Choice of Law: Governmental Interests and the Judicial Function*, 26 U. Chi.L.Rev. 9 (1958). *See also* Baade, *Counter-Revolution or Alliance for Progress? Reflections on Reading Cavers, The Choice-of-Law Process*, 46 Texas L.Rev. 141 (1967); A. Ehrenzweig, Conflict of Laws 309–26, 347–54 (1962); D. Cavers, The Choice-of-Law Process (1965). For a "true" conflicts case in torts, *see* Kilberg v. Northeast Airlines, Inc., 9 N.Y.2d 34, 211 N.Y.S.2d 133, 172 N.E.2d 526 (1961).

88. Associates Discount Corp. v. Cary, 47 Misc.2d 369, 262 N.Y.S.2d 646 (Civ. Ct.1965), may provide that wrench although the decision probably rests on UCC § 9–103. The statement in the text may be supported by the suggestions made in Ideal Structures Corp. v. Levine Huntsville Development Corp., 396 F.2d 917, 921–23 (5th Cir. 1968). Unfortunately, the court in this non-Code case was not free to pursue the suggestion since it was bound by the state choice of law rule. Klaxon Co. v. Stentor Electric Mfg. Co., 313 U.S. 487, 61 S.Ct. 1020, 85 L.Ed. 1477 (1941). The approach suggested in the text was adopted in General Elec. Credit Corp. v. R. A. Heintz Constr. Co., 302 F.Supp. 958 (D.Or. 1969), and by dictum in Griffith v. United Air Lines, Inc., 416 Pa. 1, 203 A.2d 796 (1964), n. 17.

of the Code in framing a rule of decision for the litigation between the automobile manufacturer and the employer. Such a conclusion is negative in its impact; it says only that the forum Code should not be applied. It is now suggested that the forum court should go further and frame a rule of decision patterned after that version of the Code whose policies will be promoted by the solution of the legal problems presented by the factual pattern involved in the litigation—in the assumed case, this would be the law of State B. Such application minimizes the importance of the forum without sacrificing any local policy. Likewise, the suggested reading of section 1–105(1) in the true conflicts case (see 2, above) insulates a commercial transaction from the happenstance of the forum to the same extent that the forum's general choice of law rules seek this goal.

Admittedly, this suggested interpretation of the appropriate relation test of section 1–105(1) takes some liberty with the terse command of the Code. However, section 1–105 was drafted for situations in which it was assumed that only a few states had the Code, and the drafters desired that its comprehensive restatement of the law merchant have the widest possible application. Now that this application has been obtained through wide adoption of the Code, the "appropriate relation" test can take on new meaning, lose its forum-oriented direction, and promote rational choice of law results.[89]

89. Forum law was applied, but only because it was the place where the last material act occurred. Roto-Lith, Ltd. v. F. P. Bartlett & Co., 297 F.2d 497 (1st Cir. 1962); McCrossin v. Hicks Chevrolet, Inc., 248 A.2d 917 (D.C.App. 1969).

The conclusion that the drafters intended to state a forum-oriented rule only during the time that the Code was effective in a few jurisdictions is supported by the terse command of UCC § 1–105: "Failing such agreement this Act applies to transactions bearing an appropriate relation to this state." No express provision was made for the case in which there existed no appropriate relation to the forum. Should a court which is a disinterested forum, providing it decides not to dismiss the case under some variation of the *forum non conveniens* doctrine, (1) return to pre-Code choice of law rules resting on place of making or place of performance or whatever, or (2) seek out and apply the policies underlying the appropriate relation test? Only the second alternative is reasonable. The drafters were expressing a desire that the *appropriate* law be applied. Now that nearly all of the states have the Code, the appropriate law need not be tied to the forum. Such a reading of UCC § 1–105 is also supported by its Comment 2: "Where there is no agreement as to the governing law, the Act [not *this* version of the Act] is applicable to any transaction having an 'appropriate' relation to any state which enacts it." See also D. Cavers, The Choice-of-Law Process 233–40 (1965).

B. SUBJECT MATTER WITHIN ARTICLE 2

§ 20. Scope of Article 2

The basic scope section of Article 2 is found in section 2–102. That section is divided into two parts—the first is affirmative, indicating the reach of Article 2; the second is negative, listing transactions to which Article 2 has no application.

The affirmative scope section is extremely short: "Unless the context otherwise requires, this Article applies to transactions in goods . . . ." If the scope section stopped with only this affirmative statement, some transactions in goods would be brought into Article 2 which were not intended to be covered. For example, a loan of money secured by goods could be considered a *transaction* in goods; also all of the statutes regulating consumer sales (like retail installment sales acts) might be held to involve a *transaction* in goods. Unless these relationships were excluded from Article 2, the framers of the Code could have found that statutes affecting these dealings had been repealed. Since this was not their intention,[90] a negative scope statement was included in section 2–102: Article 2 "does not apply to any transaction which although in the form of an unconditional contract to sell or present sale is intended to operate only as a security transaction nor does this Article impair or repeal any statute regulating sales to consumers, farmers or other specified classes of buyers." In construing the first half of this statement the word "only" needs to be underscored. A transaction in goods may be both a sale and the creation of a security interest—as when a seller sells goods to a buyer, reserving a security interest in those goods for the balance of the unpaid purchase price. Article 9 applies to that part of the transaction which involves the creation and perfection of the security interest, but Article 2 applies to that portion which involves the sale from the seller to the buyer.[91]

Two words in the affirmative scope statement need to be considered. These are: what is a *transaction* and what are *goods*? These questions are considered in the following sections.

---

90. Article 9 does repeal pre-Code security statutes. See UCC § 9–102 implemented through UCC § 10–102. The Code does not, however, supersede regulatory legislation such as small loan acts or retail installment sales acts. UCC § 9–101, Comment. The Commissioners on Uniform State Laws have approved a Uniform Consumer Credit Code to cover many of the regulatory functions specifically disclaimed by the Uniform Commercial Code. See Symposium, *Consumer Credit Reform*, 33 Law & Contemp. Prob. 639–785 (1968); Jordan and Warren, *A Proposed Uniform Code for Consumer Credit*, 8 B.C.Ind. & Comm. L.Rev. 441 (1967).

91. Associates Discount Corp. v. Palmer, 47 N.J. 183, 219 A.2d 858 (1966); UCC § 2–102, Comment.

§ 21. Meaning of "Transaction"

Although "transaction" is not defined in the Code, it is clear that Article 2 applies both to contracts for the sale of goods and to the sale of goods.[92] Any doubts about this can be quickly dispelled by a cursory reading of the sections within Article 2. Nearly every section contains some reference to a sale,[93] a contract for sale,[94] or to a seller [95] or a buyer.[96] Both "buyer" and "seller" are defined in terms of either a sale or a contract for the sale of goods.[97] Further, section 2–101 states that this "Article shall be known and may be cited as Uniform Commercial Code—Sales."

The problem is not whether the word "transactions" includes sales and contracts for sale; it clearly does. The question is whether it is also broad enough to embrace relationships which fall short of a contract to sell—that is, relationships which do not result in the passing of title from a seller to a buyer for a price.[98] Does Article 2 reach such transactions as gifts, bailments, and leases of goods? Consider the following situations:

Case # 1. Ben was visiting the local county fair. The day was hot; Ben was thirsty. Ben stopped by a local soft drink stand and, when he was informed that the vendor had just run out of soft drinks, Ben asked for and was given a cup of water. Ben paid nothing for the water—which was polluted and caused Ben to become extremely ill. Ought Ben's rights against the donor of the water be determined by Article 2? [99]

92. These terms are defined in UCC § 2–106(1).

93. *E. g.*, UCC § 2–402.

94. The implied warranty of merchantability is an example. UCC § 2–314. According to a computer index of Articles 1 and 2, the terms "contract for sale" and "contracts for sale" appear 52 times in those Articles. In addition, contract (or contracts) to sell appears in UCC §§ 2–105, 2–106, 2–107, and 2–706.

95. According to a computer index, the word "seller" (or "seller's") is used 200 times in Articles 1 and 2. Most appropriate to this discussion are the remedies given by Article 2. These are limited to a *seller*. *E. g.*, UCC § 2–703.

96. The computer index lists 197 times that the word "buyer" (or "buyer's") is used in Articles 1 and 2. See the use in UCC § 2–711. The number of

times the key words are used in Code is mentioned in this and the prior two footnotes only to indicate the impact of the concept of sale on Articles 1 and 2.

97. UCC § 2–103.

98. This is the definition of "sale" in UCC § 2–106(1).

99. *See* Yochem v. Gloria, Inc., 134 Ohio St. 427, 17 N.E.2d 731 (1938), where the water was served with a meal. The court was able to find a "definitely established custom for restaurants and hotels to supply their customers with water for drinking purposes with each meal . . .." *Id.* at 429, 17 N.E.2d at 733. In Wentzel v. Berliner, 204 So.2d 905 (Fla.Dist.Ct. App.1967), *cert. denied* 212 So.2d 871 (1968), defendant's services were donated, but the court found he was not a vendor. Holding for the defendant, the court said that "before the doctrine of implied warranty of fitness

Case # 2. Patient visited Dentist's office to have a tooth filled. While Dentist was administering a local anesthetic, the hypodermic needle broke just below Patient's gum line. Because of the peculiar way in which the needle was lodged, a very painful operation was required to remove the broken piece of metal. It has now been determined that a defect in the needle (and not any negligence of Dentist) was the cause of the break. Although it does not require much imagination to say that Dentist sold the anesthetic to Patient, it is much more difficult to find that Dentist sold the needle to Patient—especially if the needle involved was to be re-used on other patients. Ought Patient's rights against Dentist be determined by Article 2? [1]

Case # 3. Salesman was required by his employer to visit customers in a distant city. Salesman flew to the city and rented an automobile from U-Drive-It Co. The automobile had defective brakes and Salesman was injured when the brakes failed to stop the automobile at the bottom of a steep hill. Ought Salesman's rights against U-Drive-It be determined by Article 2? [2]

In all of these cases there has been no sale of the goods involved. In the first there was a gift; in the second the goods were used in connection with a sale of other goods and services; in the third the goods were only leased. Nevertheless, in each case it is arguable that there was a *transaction* in goods and that Article 2 should apply to the relationship between the parties. Many legal problems arising out of breach of warranty in the sale of products are considered later in this text,[3] but since the problems here can be broader than a consideration of warranties, a few general comments about the scope of the Code should be made at this point.

First, there is statutory difficulty in trying to apply the Code directly to cases in which there is no sale or contract for sale. Even though "transaction" is read broadly to include more situations than contracts and sales, the precise Code sections involved in the solution of the problem probably will be limited to contracts and to sales. For example, one of the sections which would be involved in each of the

---

is applicable, there must be something more than mere voluntary activity on the part of the defendant." *Id.* at 906.

1. *See* Magrine v. Krasnica, 94 N.J. Super. 228, 227 A.2d 539 (Hudson County Ct.1967), *aff'd sub nom.* Magrine v. Spector, 100 N.J.Super. 223, 241 A.2d 637 (App.Div.1968), *aff'd per curiam,* 53 N.J. 259, 250 A.2d 129 (1969), holding for the dentist. If this case is followed, the patient must rely upon the sale of the needle to the dentist and sue his seller for breach of warranty, overcoming the argument of privity. See UCC § 2–318. In the alternative a suit could be based upon the doctrine found in Restatement (Second) of Torts § 402A (1965). See § 54 *infra.*

2. This is a slight variation of Cintrone v. Hertz Truck Leasing & Rental Service, 45 N.J. 434, 212 A.2d 769 (1965), in which the Code was referred to although no sale was involved.

3. § 54 et seq. *infra.*

above cases is section 2–314—the implied warranty of merchantability. That section begins:

> Unless excluded or modified (Section 2–316), a warranty that the goods shall be merchantable is implied in a contract for their sale if the seller is a merchant with respect to goods of that kind.

Therefore, even if "transaction" in section 2–102 is given a broad application reaching well beyond sales and contracts for sale, there is no express Code basis for finding a warranty of merchantability in non-sales cases.[4] The same construction can be given to other sections dealing with warranties of quality.[5]

Second, all that should be concluded from the above paragraphs, however, is that several specific sections of Article 2 (and these extend beyond the sections on warranties) are expressly applicable to sales and contracts for sale; it should not be concluded that these sections cannot be used to shape the rights and duties of parties to non-sales cases.[6] Recall that each question following the three hypothetical cases was framed in terms of whether the Code ought to be used. Those questions should be answered affirmatively if the policies underlying the Code decision to imply a warranty (or to require whatever is involved in the particular problem) are similar to the policies underlying the solution to the non-sales problem now before the court.

The Code is more than an isolated statute adopted by a few states; it is a comprehensive treatment of commercial law enacted by more than 50 legislatures. It expresses several discernible policies regarding commercial transactions. Although many sections are built on the concept of contracts for sale, a sale has neither form nor substance. A sale is a concept created by lawyers and courts to aid them in reaching a sensible solution to a dispute among parties to a transaction gone awry. When a sale is involved Code warranties can be applied to the transaction; however, when a sale is not involved, the court ought not conclude (as some courts have) that because of this fact alone no warranty is involved.[7] Instead the court should search for the reasons why the legislature thought that warranties should be attached to a

---

4. McKone v. Ralph's Wonder Market, Inc., 27 Mass.App.Dec. 159 (1963).

5. *See* Cheshire v. Southampton Hospital Ass'n, 53 Misc.2d 355, 278 N.Y. S.2d 531 (Sup.Ct.1967). UCC § 2–313 deals with express warranties by "the seller"; UCC § 2–315 creates the basis for an implied warranty of fitness for purpose and speaks of "seller" and "buyer."

6. See Farnsworth, *Implied Warranties of Quality in Non-Sales Cases*, 57 Colum.L.Rev. 653 (1957).

7. "The acts of the hospital being a service and not a sale do not give rise to an action for breach of implied warranty." Koenig v. Milwaukee Blood Center, Inc., 23 Wis.2d 324, 330, 127 N.W.2d 50, 53 (1964). This type of logic should be disapproved. Dodd v. Wilson, [1946] 2 All E.R. 691 (K.B.).

sale, and determine whether similar reasons exist for implying a warranty in the non-sales transaction. If it finds the reasons to be similar, the Code ought to be used to shape the rights and duties of the parties to the non-sales transaction.

The third hypothetical serves as a good example of this approach. Some of the reasons warranties are implied in the sale of goods include an impetus for making a safer product, protection of the public from injuries arising out of the manufacture and use of a defective product, and the spreading of losses on a broad base. Those policies are also applicable to leases of goods. In fact, there is probably more reason for implying warranties in leases than in sales. A lessee of an automobile is less apt to have that automobile checked by a mechanic than would a purchaser of the same automobile. The lessee accepts and drives the automobile as delivered to him. Therefore, to the extent that the policies underlying a lease are similar to those found in a sale, the lessor of goods should be held at least to the same warranties as are found in the Code.[8] One way to describe this process is to state that the Code is being applied "by analogy" in the same way as courts have long used cases from related areas of the law as a basis for decision. The use of the word "transaction" in section 1–102 invites courts to use the Code in this manner.[9]

Third, a court which does not want to accept the Code's invitation for broad coverage can turn to the closely related doctrine of absolute liability which is now finding its way into cases and determine the rights and duties of the parties under this doctrine—a doctrine which is closely related to the results required by Article 2. This doctrine is discussed in a later chapter dealing with products liability.[10]

§ 22. Meaning of "Goods"

Article 2 applies to transactions in *goods*. The definition of goods is found in section 2–105(1):

> "Goods" means all things (including specially manufactured goods) which are movable at the time of identifica-

---

8. Sawyer v. Pioneer Leasing Corp., 244 Ark. 943, 428 S.W.2d 46 (1968); Cintrone v. Hertz Truck Leasing & Rental Service, 45 N.J. 434, 212 A.2d 769 (1965); Hertz Commercial Leasing Corp. v. Transportation Credit Clearing House, 59 Misc.2d 226, 298 N.Y.S.2d 392 (Civ.Ct.1969).

9. Transatlantic Financing Corp. v. United States, 124 U.S.App.D.C. 183, 363 F.2d 312 (1966); Newmark v. Gimbel's Inc., 102 N.J.Super. 279, 246 A.

2d 11 (App.Div.1968) *aff'd* 54 N.J. 585, 258 A.2d 697 (1969) (relying also on doctrine of strict liability in tort); UCC § 2–105, Comment 1, and UCC § 2–313, Comment 2. The Code can also be used by analogy in a lease transaction to strike inconspicuous disclaimer clauses. Sawyer v. Pioneer Leasing Corp., 244 Ark. 943, 428 S.W.2d 46 (1968). *Cf.* Victor v. Barzaleski, 19 Pa.D. & C.2d 698 (C.P.1959).

10. §§ 54, 64–92 *infra*.

tion to the contract for sale other than the money in which the price is to be paid, investment securities (Article 8) and things in action. "Goods" also includes the unborn young of animals and growing crops and other identified things attached to realty as described in the section on goods to be severed from realty (Section 2–105).

The basic portion of this definition is found in the opening phrase. To be goods the items involved must fall within a category of items called *things*, those things must be *movable*, and the movability must occur at the time those things are *identified to the contract*. Then follow three exclusions (probably out of an abundance of caution) [11] and two classes of inclusions. The drafters wanted to be certain that unborn animals could be the subject of contracts covered by Article 2, and they needed a reference to section 2–107. This, then, is the pivotal section around which Article 2 of the Code operates.

The words chosen in section 2–105 could conceivably create difficulty for the courts. There is no Code definition of "things," and the word has no single accepted pre-Code meaning.[12] Nevertheless, the entire scope of Article 2 centers on undefined "things." Also, what is movable and what is immovable may well depend on how hard someone is willing to work on the project of moving. Even Blackacre can be moved in the sense that much of the dirt, gravel, water, and minerals that comprise the "thing" called Blackacre can be transported to another location. The concept of movability has long puzzled scholars who have attempted to assign some precision to its use.[13] In short, it is possible to stare so long at the words of section 2–105 that they lose

---

11. There was probably little chance that "things in action" would have been held to be goods. 1 S. Williston, Sales § 67 (rev. ed. 1948). However, the definition of goods in the Uniform Sales Act excluded things in action, and the exclusion was continued into the Code. Uniform Sales Act § 76; *cf. Id.* § 4. Likewise, the exclusion of the money in which the price is to be paid was probably not needed but it, too, had its antecedents in § 76 of the Uniform Sales Act. A somewhat similar definition of goods is found in UCC § 9–105(1) (f), but the exclusion there is for "money" rather than "the money in which the price is to be paid." Courts have, however, construed UCC § 9–105(1) (f) similar to UCC § 2–105. Zuke v. St. Johns Community Bank, 387 F.2d 118 (8th Cir. 1968); *In re* Atlanta Times, Inc., 259 F.Supp. 820 (N.D.Ga.1966), *aff'd sub nom.*

Sanders v. National Acceptance Co. of America, 383 F.2d 606 (5th Cir. 1967). The inclusion of a reference to specially manufactured goods makes it clear that courts are not to follow an old line of cases which held that contracts relating to items to be specially manufactured were not contracts for the sale of goods. *See* Cooke v. Millard, 65 N.Y. 352 (1875). On the comparison of the definitions of goods under Articles 2 and 9, see I G. Gilmore, Security Interests in Personal Property § 12.2 (1965).

12. *Compare* Western Union Tel. Co. v. Bush, 191 Ark. 1085, 89 S.W.2d 723 (1935), *with* Gayer v. Whelan, 59 Cal. App.2d 255, 138 P.2d 763 (1943).

13. The movable-immovable distinction is sometimes used in conflict of laws. J. Falconbridge, Conflict of Laws 506–

any content and become little more than a blur of ink on a printed page.

When the purpose of Article 2 is kept in mind, however, the definition of "goods" has as much meaning as can be expected from any group of words. Article 2 is designed to codify and restate a portion of the law applicable to the movement of items of property [14] in commerce. This Article sets forth certain principles applicable to warranties, risk of loss, form and formation of the contract, performance, breach, and remedies. The key to an understanding of "goods" lies in this understanding of what Article 2 attempts to do. Combining the Code's purpose with the exception for things in action, the words of section 2–105 lose much of their obscurity. The drafters were concerned with items of tangible property which were portable at the time they were set aside for their transfer, items which normally flow in commerce. These items may be as easily carried as a can of soup or a piece of gum; they may be as bulky as a bulldozer or a large machine; but they all are *things* and they are *movable* at the time they were *identified* to the contract for sale.

The difficulty is that courts have on occasion lost sight of the purpose of the scope section and have read the definition of "goods" as approaching a string of meaningless words. For example, in suits involving polluted blood several courts have stated that the supplying of blood by a hospital to a patient is a service rather than a sale of goods. Apparently on this basis, they denied warranty coverage to the recipient of the blood.[15] In a different type of case, a plaintiff alleged that she suffered injury when she had her hair tinted in a beauty par-

---

13 (2d ed. 1954). However, many writings use the term "movable" as interchangeable with "personal property." See G. Cheshire, Private International Law 406–09 (7th ed. 1965); Restatement of Conflict of Laws §§ 255–310 (1934), in which the topic heading is "movables" but the sections refer to "chattels." Gilmore states that "movable" was used to distinguish real from personal property. 1 G. Gilmore, Security Interests in Personal Property § 12.2 at 369 (1965). Thus, the definition of goods may mean only that goods are things which can be classified as chattels at the time of identification—hardly a helpful definition.

14. The author could think of only one word better than "items of property." That word was "goods." This is the problem faced by the drafters of the Code, who did all that could be ex-

pected of them in stating the scope of Article 2.

15. The leading case denying warranty protection is Perlmutter v. Beth David Hosp., 308 N.Y. 100, 123 N.E.2d 792 (1954), discussed in § 80 *infra*. The theory of the case was that the service function predominated and the transaction was, therefore, not a sale of the blood within the Uniform Sales Act. See also Lovett v. Emory University, Inc., 116 Ga.App. 277, 156 S.E. 2d 923 (1967), and cases cited therein. Courts disagree as to whether there is a sale by the blood bank which supplied the blood to the hospital. Community Blood Bank, Inc. v. Russell, 196 So.2d 115 (Fla.1967), holding there is a sale; Balkowitsch v. Minneapolis War Memorial Blood Bank, Inc., 270 Minn. 151, 132 N.W.2d 805 (1965), denying a sale.

lor.[16] She filed a suit for breach of warranty against the beauty parlor, the supplier of the hair color product, and the manufacturer of the hair color product. In upholding a demurrer filed by all defendants, the court stated that the "issue reduces itself to the simple one of whether or not the use of the products involved in the course of the beauty treatment amounts to a sale or a contract for the sale of goods under the pertinent sections of the code." [17] The court found that "obviously" the plaintiff received a service—that is, a beauty treatment—and had not purchased goods. Therefore, the plaintiff's reliance on a Code warranty was misplaced.

Such approaches to the Code ought to be rejected. The blood and the hair coloring were things which were movable at the time of identification to the contract—even though services played an important role in their ultimate use. Services always play an important role in the use of goods, whether it is the service of transforming the raw materials into some usable product or the service of distributing the usable product to a point where it can be easily obtained by the consumer. The section 2–105(1) definition should not be used to deny Code application simply because an added service is required to inject or apply the product.

There will be cases in which it will be important to determine whether what was sold was goods or services; [18] however, this decision ought to be made on the basis of the impact of the Code and the policies involved—such as disclaimers and charitable immunity [19]—and not on a sterile reading of a definition. It is extremely difficult to find such policies when the subject of the transaction is a preparation for the hair. Fortunately, other courts have analyzed the problem as something more than the application of a definition to a set of facts and have applied the Code to the goods involved, even though services play a predominant part in the entire transaction.[20]

16. Epstein v. Giannattasio, 25 Conn. Supp. 109, 197 A.2d 342 (C.P.1963).

17. *Id.* at 110–11, 197 A.2d at 343.

18. Aegis Productions, Inc. v. Arriflex Corp. of America, 25 A.D.2d 639, 268 N.Y.S.2d 185 (1966). A contract with an architect to draw sketches is an agreement for services. Gerber v. Weinstein, 6 N.J.Misc. 284, 141 A. 3 (Sup.Ct.1928). Likewise, a contract with a painter to paint a picture is a contract for services rather than for a sale of goods. National Historic Shrines Foundation, Inc. v. Dali, 4 UCC Rep. 71 (N.Y.Sup.Ct.1967).

19. The doctrine of (partial) charitable immunity may be the basis for the blood cases discussed above. Forrest v. Red Cross Hosp., Inc., 265 S.W.2d 80 (Ky.1954); § 80 *infra.* Otherwise, it is difficult to distingish these cases from such decisions as Vlases v. Montgomery Ward & Co., 377 F.2d 846 (3d Cir. 1967), and Parke-Davis & Co. v. Stromsdot, 411 F.2d 1390 (8th Cir. 1969).

20. Warner Motors, Inc. v. Chrysler Motors Corp., 5 UCC Rep. 365 (U.S. Dist.Ct.E.D.Pa.1968); Newmark v. Gimbel's Inc., 102 N.J.Super. 279, 246 A.2d 11 (App.Div.1968) *aff'd* 54 N.J.

The definition of "goods" excludes money in which the "price is to be paid." This exclusion undoubtedly refers to the money used as a medium of payment. Thus, when money (such as foreign money or even a coin collection) is the subject of the sale, the exception found in section 2–105 should have no application.[21] Also excluded from the definition of goods are investment securities and things in action.

The definition of goods is continued in section 2–107, a section in which the drafters were concerned about where realty ends and goods begin. Three principles form the basis of that section:

1.   Certain materials affixed to the real estate are to be considered goods if they are to be severed by the seller. These include "timber, minerals or the like or a structure or its materials." By implication it is assumed that if the buyer is to remove these materials, the subject matter of the contract is not goods—but is still to be classed as realty. There is good reason for requiring severance by the seller in the case of minerals or even structures. A lease of land ought not be converted into a contract for the sale of goods even though the lessee in possession is given the privilege of removing a part of the realty—such as its gravel, coal, or oil. Lawyers have too long thought of such an arrangement as a lease with all the attendant duties of recording determined under real estate statutes. There simply was no good policy reason for changing the prior law. Why timber was included in this list is another question. If the transaction is a lease of the land with a right in the lessee to remove the timber, the situation is so similar to the mineral case that it was reasonable to treat both cases the same and to classify them as within the local law affecting real estate.[22] However, if a logger has a contract with the land owner to enter the premises and cut and remove the standing timber, there seems little reason to exempt the transaction from Code coverage.[23] Yet this is the result of the Code except in those states which have deleted the reference in section 2–107(1) to timber.[24]

585, 258 A.2d 697 (1969). There is no reason why the Code ought not be applied to the portion of the transaction which affects goods. Foster v. Colorado Radio Corp., 381 F.2d 222 (10th Cir. 1967). Cases are collected in Annot., 17 A.L.R.3d 1010 (1968).

21.   See discussion in footnote 11 of this section and UCC Comment 1.

22.   Newton v. Allen, 220 Ga. 681, 141 S.E.2d 417 (1965), where there was a lease of timber for turpentine.

23.   1955 N.Y.Law Rev. Comm'n Rep. (vol. 1) 365.

24.   Alabama, Arizona, California, Maine, and Oregon have deleted "timber" from UCC § 2–107(1). All of these states except Alabama have added to UCC § 2–107(2) the words "or of timber to be cut" immediately preceding "is a contract." This should assure that the situation discussed in the text would be subject to Article 2. Alabama may have accomplished the same result through its definition of timber, as added in UCC § 9–105(1) (j).

2.   Certain other materials affixed to the real estate are to be considered goods irrespective of whether the seller or the buyer is to remove them from the realty.   These include growing crops and other things attached to the realty if (a) they are sold "apart" from the realty, (b) they are capable of severance without material harm to the realty, and (c) they do not fall within the kinds of material listed in 1, above.   Unless all three of these conditions are met, the implication is that the items involved are not goods but remain real estate.

Some of this language may cause difficulty.   There was probably no reason to separate growing crops from "other things attached to realty"—a phrase sufficiently broad to include growing crops.   However, the drafters undoubtedly thought that growing crops clearly could be removed without materially harming the realty and wanted to emphasize the fact that crops now growing on the land could be the subject matter of an Article 2 contract for sale even though they were not movable within the section 2–105 test of goods.[25]   Indeed, the growing crops can even be the subject matter of a present sale if proper identification is made.[26]   This emphasis by the drafters should not be read to exclude from Article 2 a contract for the sale of a crop not yet planted or sown—for example, a contract for the sale of 5,000 bushels of wheat to be harvested within twelve months.   Such a contract would fall within the scope of section 2–105 (the wheat is a "thing" which would be movable at the time it was to be identified to the contract), but no interest in the wheat would pass until the wheat was both existing and identified to the contract.[27]

Whether removal will result in material harm is a question of fact for the trier of fact.   Close distinctions as to just when a particular harm has become a material harm will have to be drawn, but the test is harm to the real estate and not to the things attached to the realty.[28]

---

25.   The pre-Code distinction between *fructus industriales* and *fructus naturales* is rejected.   *See In re* Buchanan, 24 F.2d 553 (W.D.Pa.1928);   Twin Falls Bank & Trust Co. v. Weinberg, 44 Idaho 332, 257 P. 31 (1927);   Sparrow v. Pond, 49 Minn. 412, 52 N.W. 36 (1892);   1 S. Williston, Sales §§ 61, 62 (rev. ed. 1948).

26.   UCC § 2–107(2).   This is not true with timber, minerals, or structures. Until severed, a present sale of these items is only a contract to sell, unless the sale is also effective as a transfer of an interest in land.   UCC § 2–107(1).

27.   UCC § 2–105(2).   There is difficulty in fitting growing crops and unborn young of animals into the Code's definitional scheme.   When goods are *identified* is determined by UCC § 2–501 where a twelve-month limitation is placed on growing crops and unborn animals.   However, despite UCC § 2–105, Comment 5, UCC § 2–501 is written primarily to determine when a buyer obtains an insurable interest and a special property so he can use UCC § 2–502.   Thus, it may be that the drafters did not intend to deny Code application to contracts for the sale of crops (or animals to be born) more than twelve months after the contract is made—any more than a contract to produce goods two, three, or more years in the future is exempt from the Code.

28.   *Cf.* UCC § 9–313(5).

3. Rights of third parties are protected if they comply with the real estate laws of the jurisdiction involved. The Code also makes clear that which otherwise ought to have been clear: contracts for the sale of things attached to the real estate—even though they may involve goods under the above discussions—may be executed and recorded as documents transferring an interest in land, and thereby acquire whatever protection is accorded to such transfers.[29]

29. UCC § 2–107(3).

CHAPTER III

FORMATION AND INTERPRETATION OF A CONTRACT FOR SALE

Analysis

A. FORMALITIES

1. The Statute of Frauds

2. The Effect of a Seal

B. FORMATION OF A CONTRACT FOR SALE

C. TERMS OF A CONTRACT FOR SALE

D. INTERPRETATION OF A CONTRACT FOR SALE

A. FORMALITIES

1. THE STATUTE OF FRAUDS

§ 23. The Basic Rule

The statute of frauds for Article 2 is contained in section 2–201. That section continues several principles which were common to prior statutes of frauds relating to the sale of goods. These are:

1.   The statute must be satisfied only if the goods are sold for a certain minimum price, or more. This minimum price is set by the Code at five hundred dollars.[1] Contracts by which goods are sold for less than five hundred dollars may be enforced even though oral.

2.   The principal method of satisfying the statute is by a writing.

3.   This writing must be signed "by the party against whom enforcement is sought or by his authorized agent or broker."[2] There is no requirement in the Code that the agent or broker have this authorization in writing.

---

1.   The Uniform Sales Act § 4 also established $500 as the minimum amount but referred to *value*, rather than the Code's *price*. Even under the Code the price (value) of any services promised by the buyer will have to be considered in determining whether UCC § 2–201 is applicable. See UCC § 2–304(1). Evidently the need for a minimum price as a condition to the application of a statute of frauds rests on the notion that for "small" contracts parties do not tend to rely upon writings; however, for "large" contracts parties either do or should require writings. Further, there is less chance that a person will perjure himself to fabricate a "small" deal; the potential rewards are not worth the risks. This need for a writing for agreements over a stated minimum is not shared by all countries. In 1954 the British Parliament repealed the statute of frauds provisions in the Sale of Goods Act. Law Reform (Enforcement of Contracts) Act of 1954, 2 & 3 Eliz. 2, c. 34 § 2.

The $500 limit is applicable, under UCC § 2–201(1), to *a* contract for the sale of goods. This requires a determination that the goods involved were purchased under a single contract rather than a series of contracts. Pre-Code cases are collected in 1 S. Williston, Sales § 70 (rev. ed. 1948). For a discussion of the meaning of "goods," see § 22 *supra.*

2.   UCC § 2–201(1). Graulich Caterer Inc. v. Hans Holterbosch, Inc., 101 N.J.Super. 61, 243 A.2d 253 (App.Div. 1968); Whirlpool Corp. v. Regis Leasing Corp., 29 A.D.2d 395, 288 N.Y.S.2d 337 (1968).

4. The terms "writing" and "signed" are given a broad meaning. Writing is not limited to handwriting; it includes printing, typewriting, and any other intentional reduction to tangible form.[3] Signing is not limited to the manual reproduction of a person's name with a fountain pen on a sheet of paper; it includes any symbol executed or adopted by a party with the present intention to authenticate a writing.[4] A combination of these definitions presents all sorts of possibilities. The writing may be pencilled doodles on a scratch pad lying on the desk of the seller or the buyer, or it may conceivably even be a motion picture, a television tape, or a recording of a telephone conversation; the signing may be some mark on the paper or tape box, or it could be the company's name printed on top of a letterhead or on the scratch pad. Perhaps problems like these will someday be presented to a court, but arguments that the statute of frauds is satisfied will be afterthoughts in an attempt to make enforceable an agreement for which there is no document or exchange of documents. Certainly, reliance on these forms of writings and signings in planning a transaction would be an act of foolhardiness. It is clear, however, that the normal exchange of completed order and acknowledgement forms is sufficient and, if they are signed, will comply with the writing requirement of the statute of frauds in Article 2.[5]

5. The quantity of goods sold must be contained in the writing.

6. A provision is included for satisfying the statute by paying for the goods or by receiving and accepting them.[6]

While the Code and pre-Code statutes of frauds are similar in many ways, there are some marked changes between the statute of frauds found in Article 2 and those which preceded it.[7] With but few exceptions, these differences have tended to increase the number of factual situations in which the contract may be enforced even though there is no compliance with the basic rule set out in section 2–201(1). These differences and the writing requirement are discussed in the following sections of this text.

3. UCC § 1–201(46).

4. UCC § 1–201(39). The problem is whether the symbol was used with the intention of authenticating the writing. Benedict v. Lebowitz, 346 F. 2d 120 (2d Cir. 1965).

5. The Code does not change the burden of pleading the statute of frauds, Evans Implement Co. v. Thomas Industries, Inc., 117 Ga.App. 279, 160 S.E.2d 462 (1968); but a demurrer has been held not to be the proper pleading to raise the statute even though the complaint shows on its face that the facts are within the statute of frauds, Garrison v. Piatt, 113 Ga.App. 94, 147 S.E.2d 374 (1966). See, however, pre-Code cases reaching contrary result in 2 A. Corbin, Contracts § 318 (1950).

6. UCC § 2–201(3) (c). Pre-Code law is discussed in 1 S. Williston, Sales §§ 53 et seq. (rev. ed. 1948).

7. The Code contains other statutes of frauds. *E. g.*, UCC §§ 1–206, 8–319, and 9–203.

§ 24. Contents of the Writing

When planning a commercial transaction involving any substantial sum of money there are usually many good reasons, other than satisfying the statute of frauds, for preparing a memorandum of the agreement reached by the parties and for having the parties sign that memorandum. Memories are faulty, especially when a considerable length of time intervenes between the agreement and the dispute. Parties on occasion may honestly recall two different accounts of their negotiations and the agreement reached. If they can be shown a signed document which covers the point in dispute, the chances are excellent that the dispute will be resolved quickly and without litigation.

This section of the text necessarily takes a different approach in presenting the need for a signed writing. Instead of listing reasons why a detailed memorandum of agreement is desirable, this section considers the narrow question of how little the parties may write and still satisfy Article 2's statute of frauds.[8] In considering this question, the position of the parties should be kept in mind. One is claiming that the parties had an agreement which the other is not performing, or has not performed, as he promised. The claimant is met with a defense that does not go to the merits of dispute—that is, he is met with the defense that there is no signed writing sufficient to allow the claimant to proceed with his lawsuit. If the defense is successful, the merits will never be considered.[9] However, if the defense fails, this does not mean that the claimant will win his case; it means only that the statute of frauds has been removed as a bar, and the claimant will be allowed to attempt to prove the contract, the breach, and the loss alleged.[10] This point merits emphasis because some courts appear to believe that unless the statute of frauds can be used to keep out oral testimony of the transaction, the claimant will necessarily prevail in his version of the dispute.

8. The statute of frauds has had a long history in Anglo-American law. The first statute was enacted in England in 1677, 29 Car. II, c. 3, and copied by many states in this country. Section 17 of the English statute applied to sales of goods. The Uniform Sales Act contained a statute of frauds applicable to goods and choses in action. Uniform Sales Act § 4. In the main, however, the study of prior statutes of frauds has been a study of case law rather than a close reading of the statute, in large part because the statute is susceptible of causing as many frauds as it prevents. 2 A. Corbin, Contracts § 275 (1950).

9. "[C]ourts are very slow to apply the statute of frauds where by so doing instead of preventing a fraud its application will have the effect to work a fraud." Piper v. Fosher, 121 Ind. 407, 410, 23 N.E. 269, 270 (1889). See also Rupp v. Hill, 149 Colo. 48, 367 P. 2d 746 (1962).

10. American Parts Co., Inc. v. American Arbitration Ass'n, 8 Mich.App. 156, 154 N.W.2d 5 (1967); Harry Rubin & Sons, Inc. v. Consolidated Pipe Co. of America, 396 Pa. 506, 153 A.2d 472 (1959).

This belief was expressed in several pre-Code cases construing the statute of frauds in the Uniform Sales Act which required "some note or memorandum in writing of the contract or sale." [11] It was easy to emphasize the "of the contract or sale" language and to conclude that the note or memorandum had to come close to mirroring the agreement between the parties. In testing the sufficiency of the memorandum, courts were called upon to decide whether it was necessary that the essential elements of a contract be found in the writing. Was the memorandum sufficient if it failed to state the price, the consideration (if different from the price), the subject matter bought and sold, the quantity of goods, or the parties to the transaction? What was the effect of misstating a term of the agreement or omitting an item now claimed to be a part of the "deal"? Many pre-Code courts concluded that the memorandum must state the *essential elements* of the agreement—that is, it had to be a memorandum *of the contract*—or the statute of frauds barred the claimant from even presenting his version of the dispute.[12]

This approach to the statute of frauds is now history. Besides the necessity of a signing, Article 2 lists only two requirements which the contents of the writing must meet. First, the writing must state the quantity of goods involved in the contract. Second, it must be sufficient to indicate that a contract for sale has been made between the parties.[13] Beyond the quantity term there is no requirement that the writing satisfy the court that the *terms* of the contract for sale are as

---

11. Uniform Sales Act § 4.

12. "Generally speaking, a memorandum is sufficient if it sets forth with reasonable certainty the names of the parties to the contract, a description of the goods to which the contract relates and the essential terms and conditions constituting the oral contract, including the consideration." R. H. Lindsay Co. v. Greager, 204 F.2d 129, 131 (10th Cir.), *cert. denied* 346 U.S. 828, 74 S.Ct. 50, 98 L.Ed. 353 (1953). Bauer v. Victory Catering Co., 101 N.J. L. 364, 128 A. 262 (Ct.Err. & App. 1925); Webster v. Harris, 189 Or. 671, 222 P.2d 644 (1950); S. T. Edwards & Co. v. Shawano Milk Prods. Co., 211 Wis. 378, 247 N.W. 465 (1933). *See* 2 A. Corbin, Contracts §§ 467–97 (1950); 1 S. Williston, Sales §§ 100–10 (rev. ed. 1948); Restatement of Contracts § 207 (1932).

13. UCC § 2–201(1). This portion of the Code could be read to require that the agreement precede the writing—that is, that the writing must indicate *at the time of the writing* that a contract for sale *has been* made. Harry Rubin & Sons, Inc. v. Consolidated Pipe Co. of America, 396 Pa. 506, 153 A.2d 472 (1959). This would change the pre-Code law in some states. Uniform Sales Act § 4; Kohn & Baer v. I. Ariowitsch Co., 181 App.Div. 415, 168 N.Y.S. 909 (1918). A better reading of the Code, however, is that the writing must indicate *at the time of the trial* that a contract for sale *has been* made. Under this construction of UCC § 2–201, writings which precede the agreement (like a written order for goods, later accepted) could satisfy the statute of frauds if other evidence (like a written acceptance) substantiates the existence of a contract. There is no requirement that the writing be delivered to the claimant. *See* UCC § 2–207, Comment 7.

now claimed. Price need not be stated,[14] no one needs to be named as the buyer or seller, the names of both parties need not appear in the writing, the time for performance may be omitted, claimed warranties and disclaimers need not be included, the method of delivery need not be stated, and so on. All that the writing must contain is a statement of the quantity of goods involved [15] and enough to indicate that the parties did make a contract for sale. This does not mean that a scratch pad with the words "1,000 bushels of wheat, Sam Seller" will necessarily satisfy the statute of frauds in a suit brought by Ben Byer against Sam Seller for failure to deliver 1,000 bushels of wheat. If that is all the court has before it, the court could conclude that this writing, although containing a quantity and signed by the party to be charged, is not sufficient to indicate that a contract was made between Byer and Seller for the sale of wheat.[16] However, if this piece of paper is a part of other documentation which does indicate to the court that a contract was made between these parties, the statute of frauds has been satisfied and Byer will be allowed to introduce oral evidence of the contract —up to 1,000 bushels of wheat.[17]

Article 2, therefore, relaxes the pre-Code requirements relating to the details needed in a writing introduced to satisfy the statute of frauds. It is of course possible for a court to return to pre-Code law by holding that there has been no indication of a contract for sale unless the writing contains substantially all of the details of that contract.

14. Julian C. Cohen Salvage Corp. v. Eastern Elec. Sales Co., 205 Pa.Super. 26, 206 A.2d 331 (1965), *aff'g* 34 Pa.D. & C.2d 705 (C.P.1963); UCC § 2–201, Comment 1. Failure to set a price in the agreement may once have been fatal to establishing a contract, Gordon v. Pelahatchie Broiler Hatchery, 220 Miss. 722, 71 So.2d 769 (1954) (reported as Gordon v. Fechtel in the Southern Reporter), but not under the Code. UCC § 2–305 and § 38 *infra*.

15. The quantity may be stated in terms of requirements. Graulich Caterer Inc. v. Hans Holterbosch, Inc., 101 N.J.Super. 61, 243 A.2d 253 (App. Div.1968). The purpose of signing is not important. Crawford v. Obrecht, 171 Md. 562, 189 A. 809 (1937).

16. Where the writing did not indicate the goods sold, it was held incomplete in Oswald v. Allen, 285 F.Supp. 488 (S.D. N.Y.1968), but an alternative basis for the decision was that there was no agreement as to subject matter sold. The decision was affirmed in 417 F.2d 43 (2d Cir. 1969). Where

the memorandum indicated that the agreement was tentative, there was no compliance with UCC § 2–201. Arcuri v. Weiss, 198 Pa.Super. 506, 608, 184 A.2d 24 (1962).

17. Julian C. Cohen Salvage Corp. v. Eastern Elec. Sales Co., 205 Pa.Super. 26, 206 A.2d 331 (1965), *aff'g* 34 Pa.D. & C.2d 705 (C.P.1963); 2 A. Corbin, Contracts § 507 (1950).

Code courts have not yet been faced with the problem of whether a memorandum which incorrectly states the quantity agreed upon can be reformed to state the correct quantity. Comment 1 to UCC § 2–201 can be read to suggest that reformation is contrary to the policy of the Code's statute of frauds. If the elements of reformation are present, however, there is no sound reason why the statute of frauds ought to deny its application. See the arguments made and cases cited in Palmer, *Reformation and the Statute of Frauds*, 65 Mich.L.Rev. 421 (1967). *But see* Donald Friedman & Co. v. Newman, 255 N.Y. 340, 174 N.E. 703 (1931).

While this approach to Article 2 could arguably fit within the first sentence of section 2–201(1), it ignores the Comments [18] and would be contrary to the second sentence of that section:

> A writing is not insufficient because it omits or incorrectly states a term agreed upon but the contract is not enforceable under this paragraph beyond the quantity of goods shown in such writing.[19]

§ 25.　Exceptions to the Basic Writing Requirement—The Purpose of Section 2–201

Section 2–201 contains four exceptions to the basic writing requirement of subsection (1). These involve:

1. Writings signed by the claimant.[20]
2. Specially manufactured goods.
3. Admissions in court.
4. Performance by one of the parties.[21]

The reasons for including these exceptions are apparent on a close reading of the entire section.

First, section 2–201 is based upon the idea that a court should be assured that in substantial cases (that is, those involving $500 or more) there is a contract between the parties, and this assurance ought to be found in something other than the oral testimony of the claimant.[22] The fear is that the claimant will use perjured testimony to fabricate the details of a supposed agreement and will recover damages for an alleged breach.[23] Such activity is a fraud not only on the other party to the suit but also on the court which listens to the perjury and uses

---

18. UCC § 2–201, Comment 1.

19. UCC § 2–201(1). The relaxation of common law rules relating to formation of the contract support the position taken in the text. See §§ 32–40 *infra.*

20. UCC § 2–201(2).

21. UCC § 2–201(3).

22. Whether there should be a statute of frauds applicable to the sale of goods is another question. Perhaps about the best that can be said is that, after living with such a statute for three hundred years, lawyers have come to accept the writing requirement as an act of faith rather than as a product of reason. There is a feeling that the need for a writing somehow eliminates fraudulent claims from ripening into damage judgments, protects the judge and jury from having to listen to perjured testimony, makes businessmen more business-like, and generally makes the world a tidier place in which to live. If lawyers have expected these results (or any one of them) from the statute of frauds, they have been sadly disappointed. See the excellent discussion in 2 A. Corbin, Contracts § 275 (1950).

23. The statute of frauds becomes a convenient tool for deciding cases against the plaintiff when the court is convinced that the alleged oral agreement never existed. E. g., General Overseas Corp. v. Republic Pictures Int'l Corp., 74 F.Supp. 698 (S.D.N.Y. 1947).

its power to compel the payment of damages. If, however, there is evidence other than the oral testimony produced by the claimant and his witnesses which gives the court that needed assurance, the chances of fraudulent claims are materially reduced. That evidence can be a writing signed by the party to be charged or it can be the four instances set out above, under the safeguards of subsections (2) and (3) of section 2–201.

Second, no one argues that fabricated agreements resting on perjured testimony ought to be enforced by a court; but if a writing signed by the party to be charged were the only method of satisfying the statute of frauds, evidence of oral agreements which were in fact entered into becomes inadmissible just because the requisite writing is not available. Thus, if there was an agreement between the parties, application of the writing requirement would frustrate the expectation interests of people who relied on the oral contractual word of others— interests which are justified by the business practices in this country. Such a statute of frauds could well perpetrate more frauds than it prevents, especially if some faith is placed in the ability of the trier of facts to sort out liars from those who are telling the truth.[24]

The last two subsections of section 2–201 respond to these two policies: the fear of liability based upon perjury and the desire to protect expectation interests which have arisen from oral agreements. In each subsection the court is directed to consider certain evidence which indicates that a contract was entered into between the parties. In section 2–201(2) that evidence is an unanswered writing signed by the claimant which confirms the contract and is "sufficient to indicate that a contract for sale has been made between the parties," but application is limited to merchants. In section 2–201(3) that evidence is of one of three kinds: a substantial commitment in the procurement or manufacture of goods not suitable for sale to others in the course of the seller's business, admissions in court by the party against whom enforcement is sought, and performance by payment or by receipt and acceptance. In each of these cases there is reason to believe that some agreement does exist between the parties, and that reason rests on facts outside the oral testimony of the parties. Further, whenever possible the enforcement is limited to the quantity shown by those external facts.

24. Whether the requirement of a writing prevents creation of contractual liability through perjured testimony is open to serious question. Professor Corbin asserts that a memorandum, if lost or destroyed, may be proved by oral testimony. 2 A. Corbin, Contracts § 275 (1950). A person setting out to fabricate evidence of a contract would probably not hesitate to fabricate evidence of a writing, now lost.

Compliance with section 2–201(2) or (3) has the same legal effect as if there had been a writing which complied with the test of section 2–201(1). The statute of frauds is removed as a defense and the claimant is allowed to attempt to prove the existence of an agreement. Once again it should be emphasized that satisfaction of the statute of frauds does not mean that the claimant will be successful in his suit. He bears the burden of proving the agreement; he has not met that burden by eliminating the statute of frauds from his case.[25] The following sections of this text discuss the application of sections 2–201(2) and (3).

§ 26. Exceptions to the Basic Writing Requirement—Writings Signed by the Party Seeking to Enforce the Contract

Prior to the adoption of the Code the only type of a writing which would satisfy the statute of frauds for the sale of goods was a writing signed by the party against whom enforcement was being pressed.[26] No special problems were presented when both parties had signed because no matter which one was seeking to enforce the underlying agreement, there was a signing by the other party which removed the statute of frauds as a defense. The difficulty arose when only one signature appeared on the memorandum. Now the underlying agreement could be enforced against the signer but not against the one who had failed to sign the writing.[27] Such a result could perhaps be rationalized, but justification was extremely difficult. The non-signer of an executory agreement could sit back and await the day set for performance. If the agreement turned out to be profitable for him, he could secure judicial enforcement of the other's promise; if, however, the agreement turned out to be unprofitable, he could use the statute of frauds to shield himself from liability. In short, the non-signer could "play the market" and take whatever action was economically beneficial to him.

Article 2 introduces a new concept into the statute of frauds and partially changes the pre-Code rule for non-signers of memoranda. Subsection (2) of section 2–201 provides:

> Between merchants if within a reasonable time a writing
> in confirmation of the contract and sufficient against the

---

25. § 24 *supra*.

26. Uniform Sales Act § 4.

27. Bresky v. Rosenberg, 256 Mass. 66, 152 N.E. 347 (1926); Carter, Macy & Co. v. Matthews, 220 App.Div. 679, 222 N.Y.S. 472 (1927), *aff'd* 247 N.Y. 532, 161 N.E. 171 (1928) (probably a sufficient writing by both parties if measured by Code standards); Franklin Sugar Ref. Co. v. John, 279 Pa. 104, 123 A. 685 (1924); Franklin Sugar Ref. Co. v. Kane Milling & Grocery Co., 278 Pa. 105, 122 A. 231 (1923).

sender is received and the party receiving it has reason to know its contents, it satisfies the requirements of subsection (1) against such party unless written notice of objection to its contents is given within ten days after it is received.

No longer can a merchant refuse to answer his mail, secure in the belief that because he has not placed his signature on a writing he will be able to rely successfully on the statute of frauds. The qualifications placed on this subsection merit consideration.

First, the subsection applies only when the transaction is between merchants.[28] Both the seller and buyer must be merchants; if either is a non-merchant, a writing signed only by the claimant will not suffice. "Merchant" is defined in section 2–104 to include two classes of persons: a person who deals in goods of the kind involved and a person who holds himself out as having, or is chargeable with, knowledge or skill "peculiar to the practices or goods involved in the transaction."[29] The second portion of this definition will make section 2–201(2) applicable to nearly every one in business because businessmen have knowledge of the "practices" involved—namely that of answering mail.[30] Therefore, all merchants, when acting in their business capacity, are called upon to object to spurious confirmations which they receive from other merchants—or else lose the benefit of the statute of frauds.[31]

Second, the subsection requires that the writing (a) be in confirmation of the contract and (b) be sufficient against the sender. These are the qualitative standards of section 2–201(2), designed to indicate what must be stated in the document. The second standard

---

28. The term "between merchants" is defined in UCC § 2–104(3).

29. UCC § 2–104(1); § 33 *infra*.

30. UCC § 2–104, Comment 2. This Comment suggests that many non-businesses (such as universities) will also fall within this definition of merchant because they do hold themselves out as having knowledge of the practice of answering mail. Nevertheless, one court has held that a farmer is not a merchant for the purpose of UCC § 2–201(2). Cook Grains, Inc. v. Fallis, 239 Ark. 962, 395 S.W.2d 555 (1965).

31. There is a problem as to how far the "merchant" definition will be applied. Even a private person has knowledge of the practice of answering mail; it may be, however, that he does not "hold himself out" as having this knowledge—but neither do businessmen. Nevertheless, the Comments

suggest that "a lawyer or bank president buying fishing tackle for his own use is not a merchant." UCC § 2–104, Comment 2.

One type of case which is not, but ought to be, within UCC § 2–201(2) is that in which a merchant and a non-merchant have entered into an oral agreement, but the only writing is one signed by the non-merchant. It is hard to believe that the drafters intended to allow the merchant, at the expense of the non-merchant, to speculate on the market and to use the statute of frauds as a shield to liability if it turned out to be economically desirable for the merchant to renege on the oral agreement. This type of case must have been overlooked by the drafters, probably because it is so rare. Yet this use of the statute of frauds would appear possible because of the opening reference to transactions *between* merchants.

(sufficient against the sender) requires the court to refer back to subsection (1), assume that the sender was being sued, and determine whether the writing involved would prevent the sender from relying successfully on the statute of frauds. It would if the writing states a quantity of goods, is signed by the sender, and indicates that a contract for sale has been made between the parties.[32] The first requirement of section 2–201(2) (confirmation of the contract) may require that the writing be more detailed than the minimum which would satisfy subsection (1). This conclusion is based on the language, *confirmation* of *the* contract, in contrast to the somewhat looser test of section 2–201 (1): *indication* of *a* contract. The reason for the added standard in subsection (2) is apparent. A writing in a particular case might be ambiguous yet sufficiently clear to satisfy the statute of frauds if its author were being sued, but not clear enough to alert the businessman who received it that its author was claiming that he had a contract with the recipient.[33] Such an ambiguous document ought not, and does not, meet the qualitative test of section 2–201(2).

Third, the writing must be received within a reasonable time. Therefore, if the writing arrives unreasonably late, it may be ignored without concern that the defense of the statute of frauds will be lost. Read this way, the "reasonable time" requirement of section 2–201(2) sounds like many of the other reasonable time requirements which have crept into our law, and this familiarity with the concept makes it sound eminently fair. The difficulty with subsection (2), however, is that it states only one of the events against which a reasonable time is to be measured. The Code says that the writing must be received within a reasonable time, but does not expressly answer the question: within a reasonable time of what? All sorts of constructions of section 2–201(2) are possible,[34] but the one which was most probably meant by the drafters is that the writing must be received within a reason-

---

32. § 24 *supra.*

33. The memorandum, although using the word "order" rather than "contract," was held to be sufficient in Harry Rubin & Sons, Inc. v. Consolidated Pipe Co. of America, 396 Pa. 506, 153 A.2d 472 (1959). For an example of an insufficient memorandum, see John H. Wickersham Engineering & Constr. Co. v. Arbutus Steel Co., 58 Lanc.L.Rev. 164 (Pa.C.P.1962). For a writing which the court thought did not indicate that a contract had been made, see Oswald v. Allen, 417 F.2d 43 (2d Cir. 1969); Arcuri v. Weiss, 198 Pa.Super. 506, 608, 184 A.2d 24 (1962).

34. For example, one construction that might be placed on UCC § 2–201(2) is that the writing must be received within a reasonable time after the party learns that the other party does not intend to perform the oral agreement. Up until that moment, the non-defaulter expects that the agreement will be performed and it is only after he has learned of the breach that those expectations appear frustrated. The difficulty with this construction is that it would allow all oral agreements to be enforced if the non-defaulter receives proper legal advice, and this does not appear to come within the intention of a statute of frauds like the one set out in UCC § 2–201.

able time after the alleged making of the oral agreement.[35]   In the normal case the plaintiff will allege that he and the defendant (both merchants) entered into an oral agreement for the purchase and sale of a certain quantity of specific goods, that so many days later plaintiff sent to defendant a written document which satisfied the substantive and signing requirements of section 2–201(2), and that this document was received by defendant within a certain number of days after it was sent.[36]   The problem facing the trier of facts under these allegations is whether the writing was received within a reasonable time after the making of the alleged oral agreement.   If it was, the statute of frauds will be no defense; if it was not, the statute of frauds will be a defense.[37]

While this might be the "normal" case and the orderly presentation which was envisioned by the drafters of the Code, all kinds of variations are possible which will challenge any single interpretation of the reasonable time test.   For example, the only writing may be a purchase order which preceded any negotiations by the parties, and the buyer may allege that this order was later orally accepted by the seller.   Such a writing was not in *confirmation* of the contract; neither was it sent a reasonable time *after* the oral agreement.[38]   On the other hand, the only writing may be an acknowledgment sent by the seller who now claims that the buyer placed an oral order with seller who could not at that moment promise delivery but, after checking his stock, found that he could provide the ordered goods, and sent the acknowledgment form which was received by the buyer.   Such a writing —coming at the time of contract—could be viewed as a *confirmation,* but may have difficulty in meeting the reasonable time *after* the oral agreement test.   Courts could rely on the mailbox rule [39] or the lan-

---

35.   John H. Wickersham Engineering & Constr. Co. v. Arbutus Steel Co., 58 Lanc.L.Rev. 164 (Pa.C.P.1962).

36.   *E. g.,* Associated Hardware Supply Co. v. Big Wheel Dist. Co., 355 F.2d 114 (3d Cir. 1965).

37.   This statement assumes that the only basis of relying on the statute of frauds is the one being examined in the text: whether the writing was received within a reasonable time after the making of the oral agreement. There may be other reasons why Article 2's statute of frauds is not applicable.   For example, the contract may be one of services rather than of goods, National Historic Shrines Foundation, Inc. v. Dali, 4 UCC Rep. 71 (N.Y.Sup.Ct.1967), the recipient of the writing may have objected in writing within the allowable ten-day per-

iod, or the statute of frauds may not have been properly raised.   Skinner v. Tober Foreign Motors, Inc., 345 Mass. 429, 187 N.E.2d 669 (1963).

38.   UCC § 2–204(2) might be helpful to the claimant in some cases falling within the pattern suggested by the text, but is of no aid under the precise facts involved.   That Code section removes the common law necessity of finding a moment of contract formation, but it does not change the moment of contracting if one exists under the facts.

A reading of the Code which requires the written memorandum to come at the time of or after the oral agreement may change pre-Code law.   1 S. Williston, Sales § 106 (rev. ed. 1948).

39.   Adams v. Lindsell, 1 B. & Ald. 681, 106 Eng.Rep. 250 (K.B.1818).   Under

guage of other Code sections [40] to find that the seller's acknowledgment did satisfy section 2–201(2); this could mean that the seller's form is sufficient but the buyer's form is not. Such a position might be hard to explain to businessmen.

This interpretation of section 2–201(2)—that the writing must be received a reasonable time after the oral agreement—could also cause trial problems. Suppose that a court has before it the "normal" case: that is, one in which the writing came after the alleged oral agreement but the issue is whether the writing was received within a reasonable time after that agreement. Suppose further that the defendant denies the making of the agreement and asserts that, even if made, the writing was not received within a reasonable time. How does the trial proceed? The trier of fact may have to hear evidence of the oral agreement to determine whether a reasonable time had elapsed between its making and the receipt of the writing. This would make relevant all of the same evidence which the Code makes irrelevant if the statute of frauds is applicable, and the case may be decided in favor of the plaintiff on the credibility of the evidence rather than on the time issue isolated by the Code.[41]

No single solution can be given to the many problems which cluster on the edges of the statute of frauds. In large part the inability to produce such a solution rests on the fact that an understanding of any statute of frauds has always rested more on a study of case law than on the ability to parse the sentences of the statute. This will continue to be so under the Code. A court faced with any of these problems should remember that the Code has relaxed many of the requirements of the prior statute of frauds applicable to the sale of goods; a court ought not thwart this attempt by clinging to notions of prior law. However, the Code has not repealed the statute of frauds. Some evidence outside the oral testimony of the parties is required and, unless that evidence exists, the oral testimony should be excluded. Solutions to the more difficult Code problems will be

---

this doctrine it could be argued that the contract was made when the acknowledgment was dropped in the mailbox and that the writing was received by the buyer within a reasonable time (that is, the course of mail) thereafter. Kirkhof Mfg. Corp. v. Sem-Torq, Inc., 312 F.2d 578 (6th Cir. 1963) (in which a buyer used the mails to accept offer); Morrison v. Thoelke, 155 So.2d 889 (Fla.Ct.App.1963) (involving real estate but containing a discussion of the mailbox rule). See citation of cases and analysis of rule in 1 A. Corbin, Contracts § 78 (1963).

40. UCC § 2–204(2).

41. It has been suggested that one way to avoid the problem in the text is to require the writing to recite the date of the alleged oral agreement. Comment, *An Anatomy of Sections 2–201 and 2–202 of the Uniform Commercial Code*, 4 B.C.Ind. & Com.L.Rev. 381 (1963). However, the written date was not required in John H. Wickersham Eng'r & Constr. Co. v. Arbutus Steel Co., 58 Lanc.L.Rev. 164 (Pa.C.P.1962).

found by measuring the facts of each case against these goals—rather than by a careful definition of one or two words found within the statute of frauds.

Fourth, the writing must be received by the party against whom enforcement is sought. Although there is no separate definition of the word "received," there are two related definitions [42] which leave little doubt as to the intention of the drafters: the confirmation must be duly delivered to the other party's place of business and, if the recipient has more than one place of business, to the one from which the oral negotiations took place.[43] It is not necessary to show that the proprietor or president of the entity against which enforcement is sought ever held the document in his hand because the time of receipt will be measured as if the organization involved had used due diligence in getting the document to the appropriate person.[44] However, evidence only that the writing was sent will not suffice—except when the means of sending are sufficient to create a presumption of delivery and that presumption is not rebutted.

Fifth, the recipient must have reason to know the contents of the writing. It is not necessary that the recipient actually have read the document or, if he did read it, that he understood it. All that must be proved is that someone within the addressee's organization received the document and that, in the normal course of business, the document should have been brought to the addressee's attention.[45]

If these five qualifications have been met, the writing will satisfy the statute of frauds (even though the person against whom enforcement of the contract is sought has signed nothing) unless "written notice of objection to its [the writing's] contents is given within ten days after it is received." This final clause gives the recipient a chance to retain his statute of frauds defense even though he has received a document which otherwise complies with section 2–201(2). The recipient is not required to make sure that the objection is received; posting a properly-addressed and stamped letter will amount to the giving of notice.[46] Nevertheless, there are problems which

---

42. UCC §§ 2–103(1) (c) and 1–201(26). *Cf.* UCC § 1–201(38).

The use of the phrase "received and accepted" in UCC § 2–201(3) (c) does not compel a different reading of the word "received" in UCC § 2–201(2). "Acceptance" has a Code meaning over and beyond the taking of physical possession. UCC § 2–606. § 142 *infra.*

43. If the recipient directed the confirmation be sent to a particular office, delivery to that office should also suffice. UCC § 1–201(26).

44. UCC § 1–201(27).

45. *Id.*

46. UCC §§ 1–201(26) and 1–201(38). However, UCC § 2–201(2) requires the notice given to be written. Thus, although an oral notice might comply with UCC § 1–201(26), it would not amount to a sufficient UCC § 2–201 (2) objection.

might arise. The recipient must give his objections within ten days; the Code contains no indication as to how this time is to be computed.[47] Further, in a particular case the court may be called upon to determine whether the answer which was given can properly be classed as an "objection to its contents." This requires a construction of the language chosen in the notice, but as long as that language reasonably informs the sender of the section 2–201(2) document that its recipient denies that the parties ever reached agreement, the notice should be held sufficient.

In prior sections of this text it has been asserted that compliance with the statute of frauds does not mean that the party asserting the contract will win the lawsuit. That party retains the burden of persuading the trier of fact that there was an oral contract between the parties.[48] However, whenever the statute of frauds is satisfied by a writing, that writing will affect the terms of any contract which is enforced by the court. Clearly the drafters intended that the contract not be enforceable beyond the quantity term stated in the writing. Beyond this obvious limitation, section 2–207 might operate to make the terms of the writing an addition to the oral agreement, thus expanding the scope of the oral agreement. This problem is discussed in a later section of this text.[49]

§ 27. Exceptions to the Basic Writing Requirement—Specially Manufactured Goods, Admissions in Court, and Partial Performance

Three subsections of section 2–201(3) provide other ways to satisfy the statute of frauds found in Article 2. These relate to:

1. *Specially manufactured goods.* If a writing were the only method of satisfying Article 2's statute of frauds, there would be a number of cases in which the parties would be forced to suffer a serious economic loss even though the court was reasonably certain that an oral agreement had in fact been entered into by these parties. One such case is presented when the seller proves that he made commitments to manufacture or procure goods which he cannot readily resell to others, and further proves (without relying on the oral agreement)

---

47. Statutes in some states may aid in making this determination. An example is Ohio Rev.Code § 1.14 (Page 1969).

48. To this extent Cook Grains, Inc. v. Fallis, 239 Ark. 962, 395 S.W.2d 555 (1965) is inaccurate when it says (after quoting UCC § 2–201): "Thus, it will be seen that under the statute, if appellee is a merchant he would be liable on the alleged contract because he did not, within ten days, give written notice that he rejected it." *Id.* at 963, 395 S.W.2d at 556.

49. § 37 *infra.*

that the circumstances of the transaction are such that those goods were for the buyer. If there was an oral agreement between the parties, the use of the statute of frauds to prevent recovery by such a seller would require him to bear the losses incurred when he could not resell at anything near the contract price; but if there was no oral agreement between the parties, the use of seller's commitments to satisfy the statute of frauds allows presentation of a perjured claim and a possible damage recovery against the buyer. At this point legislatures have been justifiably impressed by the fact that the chances are good that a seller will not incur commitments for goods not readily resalable in order to fabricate a claim against this buyer.[50]

Both the Uniform Sales Act and the Code contain provisions designed to guard the seller against economic loss when he relies on an oral agreement and to protect the buyer from fabricated claims. Section 2–201(3)(a) of the Code provides that the statute of frauds is satisfied if (1) the goods are to be specially manufactured[51] for the buyer;[52] (2) the goods are not suitable for sale to others in the ordinary course of the seller's business; (3) before repudiation[53] by the buyer, the seller has made a substantial beginning of their manufacture or commitments for their procurement; and (4) the circumstances reasonably indicate that the goods are for the buyer.[54] This fourth

---

50. When the seller seeks to satisfy the statute of frauds by showing that he has begun manufacturing goods (or has made commitments to procure goods) which are suitable for sale in the course of his business, the primary safeguard of the statute is not met. No longer is there evidence outside the oral agreement that the goods are for this buyer. *See* Golden Eagle Milling Co. v. Old Homestead Bakery, 59 Cal.App. 541, 211 P. 56 (1922). To allow the seller to avoid the statute in such cases would effectively repeal the statute of frauds for sellers, but retain it for buyers. Further, when the goods are readily resalable, the loss in reliance on an oral agreement is not as severe. True, the seller may have lost a profit he otherwise would have made, but the possibility of perjured claims outweighs the goal of full compensation for losses arising out of a breach.

51. When goods are *specially* manufactured is not always easy to determine, especially when it is shown that the seller could comply with the alleged oral agreement by altering existing goods. If the alteration is substantial so that the goods are not readily salable to others, courts have held that the manufacture is special. Erving Paper Mills v. Hudson-Sharp Mach. Co., 332 F.2d 674 (7th Cir.), *cert. denied* 379 U.S. 946, 85 S.Ct. 440, 13 L. Ed.2d 544 (1964). Ericsson Mfg. Co. v. Caille Bros. Co., 195 Mich. 545, 162 N.W. 81 (1917).

52. The statute requires that the goods *are to be* specially manufactured for the buyer. Thus, goods already manufactured are not within UCC § 2–201 (3)(a)—no matter how special was their manufacture. 2 A. Corbin, Contracts § 477 (1950).

53. The statutory language is "before notice of repudiation is received." UCC § 2–201(3)(a). See UCC § 1–201 (26). If the notice of repudiation is written, it may satisfy the writing requirements of UCC § 2–201(1), and the agreement can be enforced against the repudiator on that basis. *E. g.,* Roth Shoe Co. v. Zager & Blessing, 195 Iowa 1238, 193 N.W. 546 (1923). Other cases are collected in 1 S. Williston, Sales § 106 n. 10 (rev. ed. 1948).

54. The Uniform Sales Act contained a similar provision for specially manu-

requirement can be used to guard against fraudulent claims by the seller; the goods must be for the buyer, not some third party, and the circumstances must reasonably indicate this fact. Beyond this, however, all that section 2–201(3)(a) says is that the statute of frauds is satisfied. The seller must still prove that there was an agreement between the parties.

The type of case which readily falls within this subsection is one in which a jeweler has engraved the buyer's unique family crest on a set of expensive silverware pursuant to what the jeweler claims was an oral agreement with the buyer to purchase the completed set for a price in excess of $500. In such a case the engraved silver would not be suitable for sale to others (who wants someone else's family crest on an expensive set of silver?) and the connection between the buyer and this crest should satisfy the fourth requirement of section 2–201 (3)(a).[55]

Other cases will be more difficult. For example, suppose that a plaintiff seller is suing on an oral purchase agreement for a price of $500 or more and is urging that his reliance on that agreement satisfies section 2–201(3)(a). The additional facts involved are, alternatively:

a. Plaintiff is a tailor; defendant is a 6' 7" basketball player; the oral agreement was for three suits; and the plaintiff had cut the material for all three suits before the defendant repudiated.

b. Plaintiff is a department store; defendant is a home owner; the oral agreement was for custom-made draperies to be made out of a little used kind of silk which had to be specially ordered; the windows in defendant's home were not of the ordinary size; and the draperies were cut and sewn before the defendant repudiated.

c. Plaintiff is a rug company; defendant is the owner of a new store about to open; the oral agreement was for 2,500 square yards

---

factured goods, and pre-Code cases may be helpful in interpreting UCC § 2–201(3)(a). There are, however, important differences in the two statutes which must be remembered in reading pre-Code cases. Under the Sales Act the goods had to be manufactured *by the seller*; no reliance had to be shown; repudiation prior to reliance did not affect the applicability of the statute; and there was no express requirement that the circumstances reasonably indicate that the goods are for the buyer. Uniform Sales Act § 4(2). The requirement of manufacture by the seller did not preclude manufacture by employees of the seller. E. G. Lumber Co. v. New York

Bondstone Corp., 15 Misc.2d 985, 179 N.Y.S.2d 45 (App.Div.1958).

55. If the crest could be removed without considerable expense or harm, the silverware could be sold to others in the course of business. *See* Erving Paper Mills v. Hudson-Sharp Mach. Co., 332 F.2d 674 (7th Cir.) *cert. denied* 379 U.S. 946, 85 S.Ct. 440, 13 L.Ed.2d 544 (1964). In Bauer v. Victory Catering Co., 101 N.J.L. 364, 128 A. 262 (Sup.Ct.1925), the engraving from $8,000 worth of silverware could be removed at a cost of $650; the court held that the contract was not enforceable but did not discuss § 4(2) of the Uniform Sales Act.

of a specially dyed and brightly colored carpeting; the carpeting material had been ordered before the defendant repudicated; and the carpeting (because of its color) could not be returned to the factory except at a substantial loss.[56]

The most serious evidentiary problem facing the plaintiff in these cases is to show that the circumstances "reasonably indicate that the goods are for the buyer." [57] This must be shown without relying on the oral agreement because the problem is whether the circumstances of the case will allow the admission of evidence of that oral agreement. While such circumstances can be found for the set of silverware, it becomes increasingly difficult with the new suits (how many 6' 7" men live in this community?), the drapery material (how oddly shaped are these windows?), and the carpeting (what is there about this color to connect this carpeting with this buyer?).

Assuming that the four elements listed above can be shown, the emphasis of section 2–201 on the quantity term should not be ignored. Enforcement of the agreement (if proved by the seller) should be limited to the quantity for which a substantial beginning or commitment is shown. The agreement between the tailor and the basketball player might have been for five suits, but there is nothing in the work

---

56. One Code problem these cases present is whether any of these items are suitable for sale to others in the ordinary course of the seller's business. On this question pre-Code cases can be helpful. Holding that the goods were not suitable for sale to others are Franklin Research & Dev. Corp. v. Swift Elec. Supply Co., 340 F.2d 439 (2d Cir. 1964) (light fixtures for a shopping center); Erving Paper Mills v. Hudson-Sharp Mach. Co., 332 F.2d 674 (7th Cir.), cert. denied 379 U.S. 946, 85 S.Ct. 440, 13 L.Ed.2d 544 (1964) (packaging machine); Canister Co. v. National Can Corp., 63 F.Supp. 361 (D.C.Del.1945) (metal ends for paint cans designed by buyer); Roth Shoe Co. v. Zager & Blessing, 195 Iowa 1238, 193 N.W. 546 (1923) (shoes of odd sizes for "special trade" with the buyer's name stamped in shoes); M. K. Smith Corp. v. Ellis, 257 Mass. 269, 153 N.E. 548 (1926) (special cider tank); Brooks v. Stone, 256 Mass. 167, 152 N.E. 59 (1926) (carpeting cut for buyer's office); In re Gies' Estate, 160 Mich. 502, 125 N.W. 420 (1910) (monogrammed dishes, but question was whether dishes were "goods"); Schneider v. Lezinsky, 162 N.Y.S. 769 (App.T.1917) (suit of clothes cut and sewn from cloth).

Holding that the goods were suitable for sale to others are Saco-Lowell Shops v. Clinton Mills Co., 277 F. 349 (1st Cir. 1921) (machinery); Berman Stores Co. v. Hirsh, 240 N.Y. 209, 148 N.E. 212 (1925) (2,250 suits of clothes).

Holding that the problem is a question for the jury are Adams v. Cohen, 242 Mass. 17, 136 N.E. 183 (1922); Ludke Elec. Co. v. Vicksbury Towing Co., 240 Miss. 495, 127 So.2d 851 (1961); and that the seller bears the burden of proving that specially manufactured goods are not salable to others is Erving Paper Mills v. Hudson-Sharp Mach. Co., 332 F.2d 674 (7th Cir.), cert. denied 379 U.S. 946, 85 S.Ct. 440, 13 L.Ed.2d 544 (1964).

57. Pre-Code cases are of no direct aid in interpreting the meaning of these words because the Uniform Sales Act contained no such express requirement. Many of the cases in the prior note, however, were concerned with the general problem of whether these goods were in fact ordered by the buyer. To that extent they may be helpful under the Code.

done by the tailor to show this. His work on three suits should not allow him to recover damages for anything beyond those three suits. In short, the reliance interest under section 2–201(3)(a) should supply the quantity term beyond which enforcement will not be allowed.[58]

2. *Admission in court.* A pleading signed by a party and alleging the oral contract would satisfy the writing requirement of 2–201(1). However, oral admissions in court will likewise assure the trier of facts that some contract was entered into by the parties. Thus, section 2–201(3)(b) provides that any admission in court will suffice to satisfy the statute of frauds,[59] but not beyond the quantity admitted.[60] There is no requirement that the admission be in the action now pending; admission in some other suit should suffice to satisfy the statute of frauds in this action.

3. *Partial or full performance.* Under the Uniform Sales Act, part performance by either the seller or the buyer satisfied the statute of frauds.[61] The difficulty with such a rule was that part performance was no indication of how many items had been the subject matter of the oral agreement. A delivery of four new stoves to an owner of an apartment complex did not indicate whether the oral agreement had been for four, forty, four hundred (or some other number of) new stoves. There was, therefore, a chance of perjury and presentation of fabricated claims.

The Code has partially changed this rule. The statute of frauds in Article 2 is satisfied under section 2–201(3)(c) "with respect to goods for which payment has been made and accepted or which have been received and accepted." The delivery of four stoves falls within the second portion of this statute providing the stoves have been accepted by the buyer.[62] The statute of frauds has been satisfied for the goods received and accepted—but no more. Thus, the parties will be allowed to introduce evidence of the oral agreement and, if the existence of the agreement is proved, recovery will be allowed for the four

---

58. The Code's insertion of a reliance requirement will prevent a buyer from successfully using UCC § 2–201(3)(a) prior to the time of the seller's substantial reliance. After that, there is no reason why the buyer should not be able to use this subsection if he wants to enforce the oral agreement. See Erving Paper Mills v. Hudson-Sharp Mach. Co., 332 F.2d 674 (7th Cir.), *cert. denied* 379 U.S. 946, 85 S. Ct. 440, 13 L.Ed.2d 544 (1964).

59. *In re* Particle Reduction Corp., 60 Berks.L.J. 65 (Pa.Dist.Ct.1968).

60. A demurrer is not an admission for the purpose of UCC § 2–201(3)(b). Beter v. Helman, 41 Westm.L.J. 7 (Pa. C.P.1958). In Garrison v. Piatt, 113 Ga.App. 94, 147 S.E.2d 374 (1966), it was held that a demurrer was not the proper method of raising the statute of frauds question.

61. Uniform Sales Act § 4(1).

62. *See* Motors Ins. Corp. v. Safeco Ins. Co. of America, 412 S.W.2d 584 (Ky. 1967). "Acceptance" is defined in UCC § 2–606.

stoves.[63] Likewise, if the buyer has paid for four stoves not yet delivered and if the seller has accepted the payment, the statute of frauds has been satisfied for the quantity of four—but no more. Either of these actions (receipt or payment, plus acceptance) indicates that some type of deal existed between the parties, and the chances of perjured testimony establishing a false claim are less than the harm that would result if a writing were required to enforce the underlying oral agreement. If either party has fully performed, the entire return promise—even though oral—becomes enforceable.

The change made by the Code is emphasized by the Comments: " 'Partial performance' as a substitute for the required memorandum can validate the contract only for the goods which have been accepted or for which payment has been made and accepted." [64] Under the Uniform Sales Act partial performance allowed enforcement of the entire oral agreement as established by the claimant; [65] under the Code partial performance allows enforcement only as to the quantity received and accepted or as to the amount paid and accepted. While this change will restrict the possibility of fraudulent claims, it will create two additional problems for judicial interpretation.

The first deals with the difficulty of apportioning the contractual performances.[66] This subsection of the statute of frauds contemplates an oral agreement requiring the seller to deliver a certain number of goods for a price per unit or for a total price. If all of the goods have been received and accepted by the buyer or if the entire price has been paid by the buyer and accepted by the seller, there is no need to apportion the return contractual performance required by the oral agreement. Full delivery would require payment of the entire price; payment of the entire price would make the oral agreement enforceable with respect to all of the goods. Where, however, only a part of the goods called for by the oral agreement has been received and accepted or where only a part of the price established by the oral agreement has been made and accepted, a decision must be reached as to whether the full return performance called for by the contract can be apportioned to the part performance. If it can, that portion of the oral agreement is enforceable and a remedy will lie for the failure to perform the

63. Clark Grave Vault Co. v. Mealtime Foods, Inc., 11 Leb.County L.J. 441 (Pa.C.P.1967).

64. UCC § 2–201, Comment 2.

65. Uniform Sales Act § 4(1).

66. Apportionment is suggested by the Comments. See UCC § 2–201, Comment 2. The problem of apportionment is highlighted by UCC § 2–201 (3) (c), but can exist whenever the court enforces an agreement for less than the quantity orally agreed upon by the parties. Thus, all of the subsections of UCC § 2–201 can raise the difficulty discussed in the text.

apportionable part. Thus, if the retail price of a certain brand of stove is two hundred dollars, an oral agreement to purchase six stoves at a total price of twelve hundred dollars could be apportioned so that receipt and acceptance of four of those stoves would give the seller a remedy under section 2–709 to recover eight hundred dollars. Likewise, a partial payment of eight hundred dollars would give the buyer a cause of action for damages under section 2–713 (or, under appropriate facts, for specific performance or replevin under section 2–716) for the failure to deliver four of the six stoves.

There will be cases in which no "just apportionment" [67] can be made between the full performance called for by the oral agreement and the partial performance which occurred. For example, the price set by the oral agreement may have reflected a quantity discount which the seller was willing to give only because the buyer had agreed to purchase a large number of the goods involved but which the seller would not have been willing to give for the small number which were received and accepted by the buyer. In such a case there is no price agreement with respect to the goods delivered, and no contract to be enforced under the command of section 2–201(3)(c). Nevertheless, since the part performance was not intended as a gift, it should not be left with the party who happened to receive it. Concepts of restitution provide the closest analogy from which ideas can be drawn to resolve this problem. These concepts are discussed in a later section of this text.[68]

The other problem arises when the oral agreement alleged by the buyer is for one item and the buyer has paid only a part of the total purchase price. Literally there are no goods for which payment has been made and accepted; the down payment cannot be apportioned for part of a single item. One case has read section 2–201(3)(c) in this way and has refused to enforce the oral agreement.[69] However, the receipt of money by a seller is evidence of some kind of economic relationship between the parties and, if the seller is a retailer of goods, the

---

67. This phrase is suggested by Comment 2 to UCC § 2–201 where the drafters indicate what should be done if just apportionment can be made. No suggestion is made as to what should be done in instances where apportionment of the contract price is not "just."

68. § 29 *infra.*

69. Williamson v. Martz, 11 Pa. D. & C.2d 33 (1956). The text may not do justice to the result of a case like *Williamson.* When a seller sells different kinds or styles of goods, the part payment is not referable to any specific item of goods. Admission of oral evidence can result in perjured claims—but so could the introduction of oral evidence when the buyer alleges full payment, and the Code specifically approves the admission of evidence in such a situation. All of which emphasizes two points: (1) what a court does with the statute of frauds depends upon its trust in the trier of facts; and (2) generalizations about the statute of frauds are, by and large, worthless.

probabilities are that the contract was for the sale of at least one item. The use of the statute of frauds to prevent the buyer from introducing evidence of an oral agreement for the sale of one item results in the buyer's losing the value of his bargain even though the court can be reasonably certain that some contract did in fact exist between the parties. There is, therefore, justification for judicial construction of section 2–201(3)(c) which holds that part payment satisfies the statute of frauds for one item of goods sold by the seller and, if buyer can satisfy the trier of fact that an oral agreement was entered into by these parties for one specific item of goods, that oral agreement will be enforced for the goods and at the price shown. This result also has judicial approval.[70]

§ 28.   Other Statutes Requiring a Writing for a Contract for the Sale of Goods

In any particular state, section 2–201 may not be the only statute which requires some kind of a writing to make a contract for the sale of goods enforceable. Legislatures have provided additional writing requirements for some types of sales, and these must be complied with to avoid the penalty provided by these statutes. For example, retail sales to consumers in which the seller is extending credit have been a favorite subject of legislation designed to protect the consumer from an overreaching seller.[71] These statutes contain a requirement of a fairly detailed writing regarding the financial terms of the sale and credit, including in some states a written indication of the percentage which the finance charge bears to the principal balance.[72] A formula is provided by which this percentage figure must be computed, and this figure must be included in the writing. Additionally, the size of type is sometimes specified in the statute.

This is not the place to examine these statutes. It is sufficient to note that they exist and to caution that, for sales of goods falling within these special statutes, a writing requirement in addition to that found in section 2–201 is required.[73]

---

70. Starr v. Freeport Dodge, Inc., 54 Misc.2d 271, 282 N.Y.S.2d 58 (Dist.Ct. 1967).

71. Some of these statutes are collected and discussed in B. Curran, Trends in Consumer Credit Legislation (1965); E. McAlister, Retail Instalment Credit; Growth and Legislation (1964). See also § 2.302 of the Uniform Consumer Credit Code approved by the National Conference of Commissioners on Uniform State Laws.

72. *E. g.,* Mass.Gen.Laws Ann. ch. 255D, § 9 (1968).

73. The Consumer Credit Protection Act, 82 Stat. 146 (1968), 15 U.S.C.A. §§ 1601–77 (1969), 18 U.S.C.A. §§ 891–96 (1969), will also affect the writing requirements for some installment sales.

§ 29.   Unenforceable Contracts—Protection of the Restitution Interest

The Uniform Commercial Code will present restitutionary problems not faced under the Uniform Sales Act. Under that Act part payment or partial delivery took the factual pattern out from under the operation of the statute of frauds and allowed enforcement of the entire contract.[74] Courts could protect the expectation interests of the parties without separating the restitution interests for special analysis.

Under the Code, however, there will be times in which one of the parties to an oral agreement will have partially performed but be unable to enforce the agreement because there was no compliance with section 2–201. In these cases the statute of frauds prevents protection of the expected gains because of the following language of 2–201(1): "a contract for the sale of goods for the price of $500 or more is not enforceable by way of action or defense . . .." Nevertheless, the fact remains that one party has transferred a portion of his assets to the other party and received nothing in return. If the court refuses all relief, the transferee will have been enriched—unjustly—at the expense of the transferor. The statute of frauds does not command that the enrichment be left with the transferee; requiring a return of the enrichment is not an *enforcement* of the contract, either by way of action or defense. Thus, courts should and will require that the enrichment be returned to the transferor.[75] This much is easy. The difficult part will be that of measuring the enrichment.

One type of partial performance can occur when the buyer has paid a portion of the purchase price under conditions in which the price paid cannot be justly apportioned to any part of the goods.[76] Unless some other subsection of section 2–201 is applicable, the oral agreement cannot be enforced against an unwilling seller, and the buyer cannot get any part of the goods contracted for. It seems clear that in such a case the seller should be required to return the money he has received, thereby preventing his unjust enrichment.[77] Two dif-

---

74. Uniform Sales Act § 4(1); 2 A. Corbin, Contracts §§ 482–96 (1950).

Because the restitution problems considered by the text could not arise under the Uniform Sales Act, most of the cases cited in this section of the text must deal with contracts other than for the sale of goods. Restitutionary remedies for cases involving goods have, prior to the Code, been granted on the basis that the statute of frauds is satisfied. 2 A. Corbin, Contracts § 326 (1950).

75. *But see* Restatement of Contracts § 355(3), (4) (1932). Other restitution problems are discussed in §§ 183–84 *infra*.

76. § 27 *supra*.

77. Mitchell v. Land, 355 P.2d 682 (Alaska 1960); Triplett v. Knight, 309 Ky. 349, 217 S.W.2d 802 (1949); Duck v. Quality Custom Homes, Inc., 242 Md. 609, 220 A.2d 143 (1966) (quantum meruit recovery may also include value of services rendered); Shopneck

ficulties stand in the buyer's path. First, how does the court know that the money was paid on an unperformed contract rather than for some other purpose, such as payment of a prior debt or even made as a gift? The only way it can know is by listening to the evidence of the oral agreement. Introduction of this evidence is permissible under the Code because it is not admitted to *enforce* the contract, and does not fall within the prohibition of section 2–201(1). Therefore, the oral agreement is relevant evidence to determine how the seller came into possession of money once belonging to the buyer.

Second, how should the enrichment of the seller be measured if the court finds that the partially performing buyer was in default of the oral agreement?[78] Courts have disagreed as to how this question should be answered in areas outside the Code's coverage. The majority has refused the defaulting buyer any recovery, evidently on the theory that it is not "just and equitable" that a party in default should be allowed restitution for his down payments.[79] A few courts, however, have rejected the notion that the buyer's default should be used as a basis for punishing the buyer beyond the damages suffered by the seller and have allowed the buyer to recover the amount of his payments less the seller's damages.[80] These cases are effectively awarding the seller his expected gain under the contract even though the statute of frauds is not satisfied. That gain is the amount of damages which is subtracted from the down payment, and the seller is allowed to retain that sum of money even though he could not successfully have brought an action to recover these damages had the buyer not made his down payment. Still other courts have awarded the buyer a return of his entire part payment together with interest, irrespective of the fact that the buyer had defaulted on his oral promise to the seller.[81] If this question arises under the Code, the last group of cases should

---

v. Rosenbloom, 326 Mass. 81, 93 N.E. 2d 227 (1950); Arjay Inv. Co. v. Kohlmetz, 9 Wis.2d 535, 101 N.W.2d 700 (1960).

78. UCC § 2–718 is not applicable to the problem discussed in the text because that section assumes the existence of an enforceable agreement. See § 184 *infra*.

79. Noel v. Dumont Builders, Inc., 178 Cal.App.2d 691, 3 Cal.Rptr. 220 (1960); Watkins v. Wells, 303 Ky. 728, 198 S. W.2d 662 (1946); Phelan v. Carey, 222 Minn. 1, 23 N.W.2d 10 (1946) (a check was used as the medium of payment); Burford v. Bridwell, 199 Okl. 245, 185 P.2d 216 (1947) (payment made from escrow); Schweiter v. Halsey, 57

Wash.2d 707, 359 P.2d 821 (1961). *See* 2 A. Corbin, Contracts §§ 332–34 (1950).

80. Stuesser v. Ebel, 19 Wis.2d 591, 120 N.W.2d 679 (1963); Arnold v. Conklin, 145 N.Y.S.2d 507 (Suffolk City Ct. 1955) (vendor failed to prove any damage).

81. Rush v. Autry, 210 Ga. 732, 82 S.E. 2d 866 (1954); Reedy v. Ebsen, 60 S.D. 1, 242 N.W. 592, *aff'd on rehearing*, 61 S.D. 54, 245 N.W. 908 (1932); Brandeis v. Neustradtl, 13 Wis. 142 (1860) (alternative holding; contains a detailed discussion of effect of the wording of the statute of frauds on vendee's ability to recover down payment). Cases are collected in Annot., 169 A.L.R. 187 (1947).

be followed because the Code expressly makes the oral agreement unenforceable either "by way of action or defense." However, the chances of this kind of case arising under the Code are slight. The buyer's suit for a return of his partial payment will often allege the existence of the oral agreement—at least to show how the money being sued for came into the seller's possession. This admission in court will satisfy section 2–201(3)(b), make the agreement enforceable against the buyer, and allow a court to award the seller damages suffered by any buyer's default.

The other type of partial performance can occur when the seller has delivered a portion of the goods under conditions in which the goods delivered cannot be justly apportioned to the price.[82] In such a case there is no contract price for the goods which the buyer has received. The contract price was set for a mass of goods, not for the portion delivered, and the price of the goods received is not a mathematical division of the entire consideration. The problems here are much the same as those discussed in the prior paragraph. In the seller's suit for unjust enrichment, evidence of the oral agreement ought to be admitted to determine whether a just apportionment can be worked out.[83] If it can, the rights and duties of the parties will be determined on the basis of section 2–201(3)(c). If it cannot, the court faces the unenviable task of determining the best method of preventing the buyer's unjust enrichment. In some cases this may require the buyer to return the goods received.[84] However, if those goods have depreciated in value since received, a return to the seller will not disgorge all of buyer's benefit. About the best a court can do is to require the buyer to pay the market price of the goods received,[85] in effect restoring the parties to the same financial position they were in prior to the oral agreement.[86] The resulting award may

---

82. This problem was outlined in the discussion of partial performance as a method of satisfying Article 2's statute of frauds. See § 27 *supra*.

83. The oral agreement is also evidence of value. Bennett Leasing Co. v. Ellison, 15 Utah 2d 72, 387 P.2d 246 (1963).

84. "It is a well settled principle of law that one who has rendered services or transferred property under a contract voidable under the statute of frauds may recover the property or the value of such services or property . . . ." Martin v. Martin, 122 Ind. App. 241, 244, 103 N.E.2d 905, 906 (1952). 2 A. Corbin, Contracts §§ 323–24 (1950). The Restatement indicates

that the defendant can extinguish plaintiff's right to value restitution by tendering the property prior to suit if specific restitution will place the plaintiff in substantially the same position he was in prior to suit. Restatement of Contracts § 355(2) (1932).

85. Consolidated Prod. Co. v. Blue Valley Creamery Co., 97 F.2d 23 (8th Cir.), *cert. denied* 305 U.S. 629, 59 S.Ct. 93, 83 L.Ed. 403 (1938); Crowe v. Baumann, 196 F. 965 (N.D. N.Y. 1912); Sparkman v. Triplett, 292 Ky. 569, 167 S.W.2d 323 (1942); Bennett Leasing Co. v. Ellison, 15 Utah 2d 72, 387 P.2d 246 (1963).

86. With standard price items, the task of determining their "market price" is

bear little resemblance to the oral agreement, but by hypothesis the case is one in which there is no method of apportioning the contract price for the goods received. For this limited type of case it may be that the result under the Uniform Sales Act was preferable to the one commanded by the Code.

§ 30.   Estoppel and the Statute of Frauds

This text has suggested that a study of the statute of frauds is primarily a study of case law rather than a careful analysis of the structure of the sentences of any particular statute. The reason for the importance of case law is obvious. The writing requirement is designed to prevent fraud through the presentation of fabricated claims resting on perjured testimony. If the parties did enter into an oral agreement, however, one of the parties may have relied on that agreement and suffered substantial losses which cannot be recovered if the defaulting party is allowed to use the statute of frauds as a shield to liability. The statute of frauds, designed to prevent fraud, can become the cause of fraud.[87]

It is in this area that case law has become important. In all jurisdictions courts to varying degrees have enforced oral agreements

relatively easy. On some occasions, however, a determination of the market price of property can be extremely difficult. Some of the problems are explored in 5 A. Corbin, Contracts §§ 1112–15 (1964); Krauskopf, *Solving Statute of Frauds Problems,* 20 Ohio St.L.J. 237 (1959); Jeanblanc, *Restitution Under the Statute of Frauds: Measurement of the Legal Benefit Unjustly Retained,* 15 Mo.L. Rev. 1 (1950). One of the problems discussed by these authors is the effect of the contract price on measurement of value. *Compare* Dreidlein v. Manger, 69 Mont. 155, 220 P. 1107 (1923) *with* McGilchrist v. F. W. Woolworth Co., 138 Or. 679, 7 P.2d 982 (1932). This problem has several facets under UCC § 2–201 of the Code. If the value sought is less than the total contract price, proration of the contract price (as suggested in Spinney v. Hill, 81 Minn. 316, 322, 84 N.W. 116, 117 (1900)) is impossible once the court has determined that apportionment is not possible under UCC § 2–201(3) (c). If the value sought exceeds the contract price for total performance by the seller, the effect of the contract price as a limit on value recovery is a problem which challenges the theoreti-

cal assumptions on which our remedial system is based. Allowing a seller more than the contract price means that the buyer pays more than he would have paid for full performance; denying such a recovery is enforcing the price term of the oral agreement— contrary to UCC § 2–201(1). One way to solve the dilemma is to admit the oral contract price as an admission against interest, F. Woodward, Quasi-Contracts § 104 (1913), but this is not much more than a poor disguise for enforcing the oral agreement. A Code solution can be found if the seller must (or does) admit the contract in pleading his restitutionary cause of action. UCC § 2–201(3) (b). Beyond these cases, some authorities can be found in the above-cited texts and law review articles, and in Palmer, *The Contract Price as a Limit on Restitution for Defendant's Breach,* 20 Ohio St.L.J. 264 (1959).

87.   "[T]he statute of frauds was enacted to prevent fraud, not to foster or encourage it . . . ." Hazen v. Garey, 168 Kan. 349, 359, 212 P.2d 288, 295 (1949). Similar statements can be found in many of the other cases cited in this section.

when they believe that application of the writing requirement would work an injustice to the relying party. That injustice must be more than loss of the hoped-for gain which would have accrued under the oral agreement; [88] it must be a loss or hardship resulting from the reliance.[89] The relief comes through the use of estoppel.[90] The defaulting party who caused the loss, or who has received an unjust gain from the oral agreement, is estopped from pleading the requirement of a writing. Since estoppel is not defined in the statute, cases must be studied to determine the extent of the doctrine in any particular jurisdiction.

The classic statement of estoppel contains six requirements. These requirements have been summarized thus:

The classic statement of estoppel contains six requirements. These requirements have been summarized by many courts and text writers, but the following quotation is representative:

> (1) Words or conduct by the party against whom the estoppel is alleged amounting to a misrepresentation or concealment of material facts; (2) the party against whom the estoppel is alleged must have knowledge, either actual or implied, at the time the representations were made, that they were untrue; (3) the truth respecting the representations so made must be unknown to the party claiming the benefit of the estoppel at the time they were made and at the time they were acted on by him; (4) the party estopped must intend or expect that his conduct or representations will be acted on by the party asserting the estoppel or by the public generally; (5) the representations or conduct must have been relied and acted on by the party claiming the benefit of the estoppel; and (6) the party claiming the benefit of the estoppel must have so acted, because of such representations or conduct, that he would be prejudiced if the first party is permitted to deny the truth thereof.[91]

The most difficult portion of this definition for the relying party to prove is the requirement that a *fact* be misrepresented or concealed. Most often all that is involved is an exchange of *promises* and, unless a court is willing to hold that a promise represents a present and con-

88. Coastwise Petroleum Co. v. Standard Oil Co., 179 Md. 337, 19 A.2d 180 (1941).

89. Wilk v. Vencill, 30 Cal.2d 104, 180 P.2d 351 (1947); Beers v. Pusey, 389 Pa. 117, 132 A.2d 346 (1957).

90. One other area where this doctrine has had a significant impact on the statute of frauds is the enforcement of oral contracts to convey realty, where the vendee has partly performed the agreement. See 2 A. Corbin, Contracts §§ 420–43 (1950), for citation of cases and discussion of principles.

91. Lowenberg v. Booth, 330 Ill. 548, 555–56, 162 N.E. 191, 195 (1928). These elements are discussed, in Summers, *The Doctrine of Estoppel Applied to the Statute of Frauds*, 79 U.Pa.L.Rev. 440 (1931).

tinuing state of mind to perform, reliance on the promise will not amount to an estoppel even though a financial loss has accrued.[92]

Other courts have liberalized the definition of estoppel. For example, in *Monarco v. Lo Greco*[93] Mr. Justice Traynor stated:

> The doctrine of estoppel to assert the statute of frauds has been consistently applied by the courts of this state to prevent fraud that would result from refusal to enforce oral contracts in certain circumstances. Such fraud may inhere in the unconscionable injury that would result from denying enforcement of the contract after one party has been induced by the other seriously to change his position in reliance on the contract . . . or in the unjust enrichment that would result if a party who has received the benefits of the other's performance were allowed to rely upon the statute.[94]

The emphasis here is not placed on the need for finding that a *fact* has been misrepresented. What must be shown is that unconscionable injury or unjust gain resulted from reliance on an oral contract.[95]

The Uniform Commercial Code recognizes the justness of the above statement from *Monarco v. Lo Greco*. To the extent that the seller has relied on an oral agreement to purchase specially manufactured goods not suitable for sale to others and to the extent that the seller (before repudiation and under circumstances reasonably indicating that the goods are for the buyer) has made either a substantial beginning of their manufacture or commitments for their procurement, the oral agreement will be enforced.[96] This is nothing more than an example of a situation in which reliance has induced a financially harmful change of position. For this case the Code will control and the doctrine of estoppel will not have to be used.[97]

---

92. Ozier v. Haines, 411 Ill. 160, 103 N.E.2d 485 (1952).

93. 35 Cal.2d 621, 220 P.2d 737 (1950).

94. *Id.* at 624, 220 P.2d at 739–40. That case also rejected the notion that an estoppel arises only out of a representation that a writing is not needed or that the statute will not be relied upon. As to this last point, see Wilk v. Vencill, 30 Cal.2d 104, 180 P.2d 351 (1947) (involving realty; prejudice shown); Starkey v. Galloway, 119 Ind. App. 287, 84 N.E.2d 731 (1949) (involving personalty; no prejudice shown). The result of the last case would probably be changed by the Code on the basis of the admission in court. UCC § 2–201(3) (b).

95. Mosekian v. Davis Canning Co., 229 Cal.App.2d 118, 40 Cal.Rptr. 157 (1964). See also Note, *Part Performance, Estoppel and the California Statute of Frauds*, 3 Stan.L.Rev. 281 (1951).

96. UCC § 2–201(3) (a). This subsection is discussed in § 27 *supra*.

97. Some pre-Code cases which relied on estoppel can now rely on UCC § 2–201(3) (a). *Cf.* Irving Tier Co. v. Griffin, 244 Cal.App.2d 852, 53 Cal. Rptr. 469 (1966). The same doctrine is applied to an oral lease by which the lessor remodels premises to fit the lessee's needs. Artcraft Specialty Co. v. Center Woodland Realty Co., 40 Ohio App. 125, 178 N.E.2d 213 (1931).

There are, however, other kinds of cases which are not covered by the Code's statute of frauds. The reliance by the seller may not amount to a "beginning of their manufacture" or a commitment for the "procurement" of the goods. Section 2–201(3)(a) would be no help to such a seller. On the other hand, the reliance may be by the buyer. He may have changed his manufacturing process, cut off other sources of goods, or entered into contracts for remodeling his store. Such reliance is no less real than a seller's under section 2–201(3)(a) and in some cases may cause exactly the same kind of loss envisioned by that subsection: the money spent in reliance on the oral agreement will be lost unless the agreement is enforced.[98]

Code courts face a choice in these reliance cases which fall outside the express terms of section 2–201. They can refuse all relief on the basis that a careful reading of the Code indicates that the kind of reliance involved is not within any of the exceptions to section 2–201 (1), or they can grant relief on the basis of case law if the facts fall within their notion of estoppel. The latter approach is to be preferred because no statute of frauds yet drafted, including those contained in the Uniform Commercial Code, has been able to anticipate every combination of facts which requires decision. All that the legislature can do is provide the basis for solving the typical cases and leave to courts the difficult task of reaching a just decision for the unanticipated factual pattern. The doctrine of estoppel has been used, and should continue to be used, when the statute of frauds will cause serious injury to a relying party.[99]

2. THE EFFECT OF A SEAL

§ 31. Seals

The seal has long been waging a losing battle to retain the position it once held in common law history. The Code continues the onslaught:

> The affixing of a seal to a writing evidencing a contract for sale or an offer to buy or sell goods does not constitute the writing a sealed instrument and the law with respect to sealed instruments does not apply to such a contract or offer.[1]

---

98. Examples of buyer's reliance include Union Packing Co. v. Cariboo Land & Cattle Co., 191 F.2d 814 (9th Cir. 1951), *cert. denied* 342 U.S. 909, 72 S.Ct. 303, 96 L.Ed. 680 (1952) (cattle); Mosekian v. Davis Canning Co., 229 Cal.App.2d 118, 40 Cal.Rptr. 157 (1964) (peach crop); Hazen v. Garey, 168 Kan. 349, 212 P.2d 288 (1949) (right to manufacture and sell patented goods; not "goods" within Code).

99. The unjust enrichment cases mentioned in the quotation from Monarco v. Lo Greco, 35 Cal.2d 621, 220 P.2d 737 (1950), can be brought within the doctrine of estoppel or handled through principles of restitution, whichever reaches the fairer result. See § 29 *supra.*

1. UCC § 2–203.

This section, drafted more clearly than many of its pre-Code predecessors, states as plainly as it can be stated that affixing a seal to a writing which evidences an Article 2 contract or offer is a waste of time. A blob of wax, a scrawl, the word "seal," or the initials "L.S." will not bring a contract within a local statute of limitations applicable to "sealed instruments"—for the simple reason that the Code states that the instrument evidencing the contract is not a sealed instrument.[2] Instead, any controversy for breach of an Article 2 contract falls within the four-year period prescribed by the Code.

Nevertheless, some of the effects which a seal once had can be obtained through appropriate draftsmanship. For example, the seal was once sufficient to make an offer irrevocable. A merchant can accomplish this result under the Code for a period of time up to three months by choosing language which gives assurance that the offer will remain open.[3] There is no need to require that a seal be affixed to such an offer, and the Code quite properly makes the seal inoperative.

B. FORMATION OF A CONTRACT FOR SALE

§ 32. Application of General Contract Principles to Code Cases

The law of sales is a branch of the more general law of contracts. Therefore, rules of law applicable to contracts generally are applicable to contracts for the sale of goods unless those rules have been displaced by the Code.

The Uniform Sales Act changed very little of the general law of contracts. In one sense, the Code continues this pattern. When measured against contract principles relating to offer, acceptance, consideration, breach, conditions, assignment, third party beneficiaries, frustration, remedies, and so on, the Code makes but few changes in this great bulk of the law. However, as compared to the number of changes made by the Uniform Sales Act, the Code has made several significant modifications of contract law. These modifications occur in areas in which the drafters believed that the common law development of contract principles did not comport with better commercial practices and needs. This portion of the text contains a discussion of the Code sections which change (or codify) general contract law.

The basic Code provision is contained in section 1–103:

Unless displaced by the particular provisions of this Act, the principles of law and equity, including the law merchant

2. Associates Discount Corp. v. Palmer, 47 N.J. 183, 219 A.2d 858 (1966). The Code also abrogates the common law rule that a principal is not a party to a contract executed by his agent under seal. Commonwealth Bank & Trust Co. v. Keech, 201 Pa.Super. 285, 192 A.2d 133 (1963).

3. UCC § 2–205. See § 33 infra.

and the law relative to capacity to contract, principal and agent, estoppel, fraud, misrepresentation, duress, coercion, mistake, bankruptcy, or other validating or invalidating cause shall supplement its provisions.

The part of this Code section specifically applicable to this chapter of the text would be: "Unless displaced by the particular provisions of this Act, the principles of law and equity, including . . . validating or invalidating cause shall supplement its provisions." All principles of law or of equity which either validate or invalidate a transaction are brought into the Code by section 1–103.[4] The Comments indicate the breadth intended by the draftsmen. " 'Validating' as used here in conjunction with 'invalidating' is not intended as a narrow word confined to original validation, but extends to cover any factor which at any time or in any manner renders or helps to render valid any right or transaction." [5]

The result is that the Code, like the Uniform Sales Act which it replaced, rests firmly on a foundation of general contract law. It is only in those instances in which some section of the Code has displaced the general law that the Code commands a different result.

§ 33. Firm Offers

According to common law dogma an offer is revocable even though the offeror has stated that the offer is irrevocable or that the offer is to remain open for a given period of time. This result was thought to follow from the nature of offers: an offer is a promise committing the offeror to the stated terms when and if the offeree accepts either by performing the requested act or making the requested return promise. The offer, however, falls short of being a contract, and it is contracts which create enforceable promises.[6] Since the offer "by its nature" is not a contract, it can be recalled at the whim of the offeror. In compelling cases the common law found ways around this dogma, but the exceptions produced cumbersome rules, artificial dis-

---

4. UCC § 1–103 was used to abolish vertical privity in Pennsylvania. Finding that UCC § 2–318 does not cover problems of vertical privity (manufacturer to consumer), the court concluded that UCC § 1–103 required application of general principles of law. Kassab v. Central Soya, 432 Pa. 217, 246 A.2d 848, 856 (1968), *overruling* Miller v. Preitz, 422 Pa. 383, 221 A.2d 320 (1966). The word "including" in UCC § 1–103 merits special mention. The listing which follows is only an example of the principles which are applicable to Code cases. The mandate of UCC

§ 1–103 is that legal and equitable principles, in general, continue to be Code principles unless displaced by a particular Code provision.

5. UCC § 1–103, Comment 1.

6. Roth v. Moeller, 185 Cal. 415, 197 P. 62 (1921); Night Commander Lighting Co. v. Brown, 213 Mich. 214, 181 N.W. 979 (1921); Bancroft v. Martin, 144 Miss. 384, 109 So. 859 (1926); Krohn-Fechheimer Co. v. Palmer, 282 Mo. 82, 221 S.W. 353 (1920).

tinctions,[7] and sometimes required a search for expected reliance through the doctrine of promissory estoppel.[8]

The Code's approach is much cleaner. Merchants can make firm offers, subject to certain stated limitations. By a "firm" offer the Code means that during the term that the offer is assured to be open, the offeror may not recall the offer on the ground that he received no consideration for it. During the stated period of time the offeree has the power to accept the offer, thus turning the relationship into that of contract, even though the offeror has attempted to revoke. The Code section which accomplishes this results is as follows:

> An offer by a merchant to buy or sell goods in a signed writing which by its terms gives assurance that it will be held open is not revocable, for lack of consideration, during the time stated or if no time is stated for a reasonable time, but in no event may such period of irrevocability exceed three months; but any such term of assurance on a form supplied by the offeree must be separately signed by the offeror.[9]

An analysis of this section (2–205) indicates its scope. First, there must be an *offer*. Preliminary negotiations or a quotation of prices not rising to the level of commitment will not suffice. Since "offer" is not defined by the Code, common law cases remain relevant in determining whether the document involved contains only a request for further negotiations or whether it indicates that the signer is willing to deal on the terms stated if and when they are accepted by the other party.[10] Section 2–205 goes on to require an assurance that the offer will remain open; therefore, the distinction between preliminary negotiation and an offer will ordinarily not be as critical as it was under pre-Code law. Merchants do not often assure that their preliminary negotiations will remain firm, unless those negotiations qualify as offers.

Second, the offer must be made by a *merchant*. Non-merchants are not covered by section 2–205; their offers remain subject to pre-Code common law rules. This limitation on 2–205 was included because of a belief that merchants could be fairly held to a standard of reliability when they make firm offers even though unsupported by consideration. "Merchant" is a defined Code term,[11] and the definition

---

7. *See* 1 A. Corbin, Contracts §§ 43–44 (1963).

8. Schultz, *The Firm Offer Puzzle: A Study of Business Practice in the Construction Industry*, 19 U.Chi.L.Rev. 237 (1951).

9. UCC § 2–205.

10. Metropolitan Convoy Corp. v. Chrysler Corp., —— Del. ——, 208 A.2d 519 (1965); Fairmount Glass Works v. Crunden-Martin Wooden Ware Co., 106 Ky. 659, 51 S.W. 196 (1899); Buffalo Pressed Steel Co. v. Kirwan, 138 Md. 60, 113 A. 628 (1921); Courteen Seed Co. v. Abraham, 129 Or. 427, 275 P. 684 (1929).

11. UCC § 2–104(1).

has been discussed earlier in this text.[12] It was there suggested that the Code includes two classes of persons as "merchants"; it is perhaps more accurate, however, to accept three groups of people within the definition (although the last two can easily be grouped together):

1. Persons who deal in goods of the kind involved; or

2. Persons who hold themselves out as having knowledge or skill peculiar to the practices or goods involved; or

3. Persons to whom this knowledge or skill (as to the practices or goods) may be attributed because of their employment of someone who by his occupation holds himself out as having this knowledge or skill.

The last two categories may, on some occasions, be broader than the first by including more people as "merchants" than would be covered by a definition limited solely to persons who deal in goods of the kind involved in the transaction. For example, a person who does not deal in a particular kind of goods may, nevertheless, hold himself out as having knowledge regarding those goods—or he may have hired someone who represents that he has such knowledge. Further, the last two categories include "practices" as well as "goods." Under section 2–205 the practice is that of making offers (or perhaps firm offers). Therefore, this definition of "merchants" brings into the firm offer section many persons who might not be merchants if the definition were limited to a requirement that the person *deal* in the involved goods. Section 2–205 adopts the broad concept of merchant, but before the section is applicable the signer of the document must be acting in his mercantile capacity in making the offer.[13]

Third, the merchant's offer must be *to buy or to sell goods*.[14] Section 2–205 limits its application to Article 2 of the Code. For other Code transactions the common law rules, as modified by other applicable statutes, would control.[15]

Fourth, the offer must be contained in a *signed writing*. An oral offer will not suffice, even if the price of the goods involved is less than $500.[16] Thus, section 2–205 has its own built-in statute of frauds. There is no question but that the writing must be signed by the offeror, although the Code's language is only that there must be a "signed"

12. § 26 *supra*.

13. UCC § 2–104, Comment 2.

14. This requirement may negate the broad definition of merchant suggested in UCC § 2–104, Comment 2. If the offer must be one to buy or to sell goods, the merchant involved will generally be a person dealing in goods of that kind. *See* UCC § 2–104.

15. *But see* Wilmington Trust Co. v. Coulter, 41 Del. 548, 200 A.2d 441, 452 (1964).

16. *Cf.* UCC § 2–201.

writing—without indicating who must do the signing. All that is involved is an offer, not a contract. While either or both parties may sign a writing which evidences a contract, it is the offeror who signs an offer. Indeed, if the irrevocability clause is contained in a form which was prepared by the offeree, that clause must be separately signed by the offeror.[17]

Whether the offer has been "signed" will usually cause no difficulties. If the offer was prepared by the offeror, his signature—or that of some agent of the offeror—at the bottom of the paper is sufficient. There undoubtedly will be cases, however, in which the offeror has used a rubber stamp in place of a handwritten signature or has forgotten to write his name on the paper before the paper was delivered to the offeree. In these cases, the Code's definition of "signed" will be helpful: "any symbol executed or adopted by a party with present intention to authenticate a writing." [18] The stamp clearly complies with this requirement. The typed name at the bottom of the paper could also suffice even though the offeror did not take a pen and write his name under or above the typing.[19] The test is intention to authenticate; the symbol may be anything. The Comments suggest that the printed letterhead could also amount to a signing.[20] However, when the form has been supplied by the offeree, the intention to authenticate must be applied to the clause containing the firm offer. Such an offeree ought to require a handwritten signature beside the clause or, at the least, the handwritten initials of the offeror; but an "O.K." or even a check mark will satisfy the Code if the requisite intent can be shown.

Finally, the writing must contain a term which gives *assurance* that the offer will be kept open. A written offer to supply goods at a stated price does not comply with section 2–205, even though made and signed by a merchant, unless a clause in the writing gives assurance to the offeree that the offer will remain open for acceptance.[21] The term may be for a specific time period, or it may contain no stated time period at all. Thus, such statements as "this offer to remain firm until midnight of January 16," or "this offer to remain open" comply with the assurance requirement of section 2–205. In the latter case a reasonable time will be implied,[22] but in neither case can the period

17. See the last clause of UCC § 2–205.

18. UCC § 1–201(39).

19. Benedict v. Lebowitz, 346 F.2d 120 (2d Cir. 1965) (financing statement). As to the content of the signature, see *In re* Excel Stores, Inc., 341 F.2d 961 (2d Cir. 1965).

20. UCC § 1–201, Comment 39.

21. E. A. Coronis Associates v. M. Gordon Constr. Co., 90 N.J.Super. 69, 216 A.2d 246 (App.Div.1966).

22. However, no offeror should leave the assurance open without a stated time limit. The implication of a "reasonable time" leaves the situation too am-

exceed three months. Thus, a written assurance that an offer will remain open for six months is limited by section 2–205 to a three-month period of irrevocability.[23]

If these five conditions are met, the offer is not revocable *for lack of consideration*. During the time of assurance, up to three months, an attempt by the offeror to withdraw his offer because it was unsupported by consideration is unavailing. The offeree may accept and convert the offer into a contract, thereby opening remedies for breach if the offeror refuses to perform. In this way, expectations of those who deal with a merchant are protected when they rely on offers which have been made "firm" by the merchant-offeror.

The portion of section 2–205 which is apt to be overlooked are the four words, "for lack of consideration." The offeror of the section 2–205 firm offer may no longer withdraw that offer prior to its acceptance simply because the offeree did not give consideration to keep the offer open. This is all section 2–205 covers. Section 2–205 does not make firm offers irrevocable against all invalidating causes. Thus, a firm offer obtained by fraud or duress will be revocable prior to acceptance just as the completed contract arising out of the fraud or duress could be avoided later. Likewise, a firm offer which is based upon a mistake remains revocable prior to acceptance to the same extent that an agreement resting on the same mistake could be rescinded.[24] These invalidating causes fall outside the command of 2–205, but are made applicable to the firm offer either by section 2–302 or section 1–103.

One Code case has suggested the possibility that section 2–205 may preclude the application of the doctrine of promissory estoppel to an offer which does not comply with the requirements of section 2–205.[25] The basis of such a suggestion must be something like this:

biguous for prediction. Further, a date when the offer terminates should be stated, not a time period. *See* Caldwell v. Cline, 109 W.Va. 553, 156 S.E. 55 (1930).

23. After the three-month period the offeror may revoke on the basis that no consideration has been given for the offer. The revocation must be communicated to be effective. Larson v. Superior Auto Parts, Inc., 275 Wis. 261, 81 N.W.2d 505 (1957). This communication may come from a third party as well as from the offeror. Dickinson v. Dodds, L.R. 2 Ch. 463 (1876). If the offeror does not revoke, the offer may be accepted by the offeree within the time period stated in the offer even though the Code three-month period has elapsed.

24. M. F. Kemper Constr. Co. v. Los Angeles, 37 Cal.2d 696, 235 P.2d 7 (1951); Geremia v. Boyarsky, 107 Conn. 387, 140 A. 749 (1928). Cases are collected in Annot., 52 A.L.R.2d 792 (1957).

25. In E. A. Coronis Associates v. M. Gordon Constr. Co., 90 N.J.Super. 69, 80, 216 A.2d 246, 253 (App.Div.1966), the court remarked (in footnote 2): "We do not consider whether the existence of section 2–205 of the Uniform Commercial Code precludes reliance on an offer not conforming to its provisions."

the Code has indicated how merchants can make their offers firm; that method requires compliance with section 2–205; the section 2–205 method is exclusive; and all other methods are repealed by the Code. Several factual patterns can present this problem. For example, an offeror may make an offer on which he reasonably could expect the offeree to rely. That offer can assure the offeree that it will remain firm for six months, or it could contain no term of assurance at all. If the offeree does rely upon such an offer to his substantial economic detriment, there is non-Code authority that the offeror is estopped from revoking his offer even though the acceptance comes after the attempted revocation.[26] Section 2–205 should not be read to prevent further development of this doctrine of promissory estoppel and its application to contracts for the sale of goods.[27] Section 2–205 is aimed at one problem: the revocation of firm offers on the basis that there was no consideration given. The Code does not deal with revocation of offers for which consideration has been given or for which a substitute for consideration is present. Since these problems are not covered by the Code, there has been no displacement of the common law principles which, in a particular jurisdiction, could either validate or invalidate such a transaction. Therefore, section 1–103 is directly applicable and the doctrine of promissory estoppel can continue development in Article 2 cases, consistent with its common law pattern.[28]

§ 34. The Deviant Acceptance—Unilateral and Bilateral Contracts

The common law drew a distinction between offers for unilateral and bilateral contracts.[29] In an offer for a unilateral contract the offeror has requested an act; such an offer is to be accepted by performing the act, not by promising that the act will be done.[30] In an

---

26. Travelers Indem. Co. v. Holman, 330 F.2d 142 (5th Cir. 1964); Drennan v. Star Paving Co., 51 Cal.2d 409, 333 P.2d 757 (1958); Restatement of Contracts § 90 (1932). There is authority that the doctrine of promissory estoppel does not apply to offers for commercial transactions, Friedman v. Tappan Dev. Corp., 22 N.J. 523, 126 A.2d 646 (1956), or to offers which contemplate a return promise, James Baird Co. v. Gimbel Bros., 64 F.2d 344 (2d Cir. 1933). See also Litterio & Co. v. Glassman Constr. Co., 115 U.S. App.D.C. 335, 319 F.2d 736 (D.C.Cir. 1963); Petty v. Gindy Mfg. Corp., 17 Utah 2d 32, 404 P.2d 30 (1965); Hilton v. Alexander & Baldwin, Inc., 66 Wash.2d 30, 400 P.2d 772 (1965).

27. E. A. Coronis Associates v. M. Gordon Constr. Co., 90 N.J.Super. 69, 216 A.2d 246 (App.Div.1966).

28. For a more complete discussion of the enforcement of promises based on reliance, including a criticism of the use of the "promissory estoppel" description, see 1A A. Corbin, Contracts §§ 193–209 (1963).

29. Typical language is contained in Martindell v. Fiduciary Counsel, Inc., 131 N.J.Eq. 523, 26 A.2d 171 (Ch. 1942), aff'd 133 N.J.Eq. 408, 30 A.2d 281 (Ct.Err. & App.1943). The subject is discussed in 1 A. Corbin, Contracts §§ 21, 65 (1963).

30. Rehm-Zeiher Co. v. F. G. Walker Co., 156 Ky. 6, 160 S.W. 777 (1913); Williams v. Emerson-Brantingham Implement Co., 198 S.W. 425 (Mo.App. 1917); Restatement of Contracts § 52 (1932). Performance of the requested act forms a contract even though the offeror could have withdrawn the of-

offer for a bilateral contract the offeror has requested a promise; such an offer is to be accepted by making the promise, not by commencing to perform the act.[31] In some situations the distinction between these two types of acceptance may be important to the offeror. If so, the parties ought to be left free to make their bargain. However, in many cases the distinction becomes artificial. In cases involving the sale of goods, the buyer and seller are looking forward to performance—the buyer to receipt of the goods, and the seller to receipt of the purchase price. The fact that the buyer's purchase order may be of the type which lawyers would classify as an offer for a unilateral contract ("Please ship at once") is of no significance to many buyers. One phrase, rather than the other, may have been the result of how an employee happened to fill out the forms that day, or of which pad of printed order forms the purchasing department bought six months ago. What the buyer wanted was the goods. Yet under the common law, the seller's immediate promise to ship would not have been an acceptance of an order requesting shipment, and an actual shipment would not have been an acceptance of an order requesting a promise to ship. The result of the common law was that, unless the seller did exactly what was requested, the buyer was free to refuse the goods for any reason—such as a change in the buyer's needs or an unexpected decline in prices.[32]

The Code has changed a part of the common law rule by providing that an offer to buy goods for prompt or current shipment is to be construed as inviting acceptance "either by a prompt promise to ship or by the prompt or current shipment of conforming or non-conforming goods . . . ."[33] Therefore, an offer phrased in terms of a prompt or current shipment can be accepted by a promise to ship promptly or currently,[34] and a contract results even though the seller has not as yet performed the requested act.[35] If the seller follows his promise with a shipment which complies with the terms of the con-

fer prior to the acceptance. Lasswell v. Anderson, 127 Wash. 591, 221 P. 300 (1923). As to the effect of partial performance of a requested act, see Restatement of Contracts § 45 (1932).

31. White v. Corlies, 46 N.Y. 467 (1871); but the promise may be inferred from the acts of performance. Calo, Inc. v. AMF Pinspotters, Inc., 31 Ill.App.2d 2, 176 N.E.2d 1 (1961); Albright v. Stegeman Motor Car Co., 168 Wis. 557, 170 N.W. 951 (1919).

32. Barber-Greene Co. v. M. F. Dollard, Jr., Inc., 239 App.Div. 655, 269 N.Y.S.

211 (1934), *aff'd* 267 N.Y. 545, 196 N.E. 571 (1935); Nierenberg Corp. v. C. Haedke & Co., 236 N.Y.S.2d 389 (Sup. Ct.1962).

33. UCC § 2–206(1) (b).

34. Mailing of an acknowledgment can be an acceptance. Roto-Lith, Ltd. v. F. P. Bartlett & Co., Inc., 297 F.2d 497 (1st Cir. 1962).

35. *E. g.*, McAden v. Craig, 222 N.C. 497, 24 S.E.2d 1 (1943).

tract, the buyer will be in default of his contractual promise to accept and pay for the goods—even though he may have tried to revoke his order after the seller's promise was made but before the shipment. Likewise, the seller's failure to ship following such a promise would be a default for which the buyer could recover damages.

Timely shipment of conforming goods in response to an order to ship specified goods will also result in a contract. This does not change the common law; the seller has performed the requested act. The Code, however, goes on to state that a shipment of nonconforming goods will also amount to an acceptance.[36] Thus, if a buyer orders a shipment of goods of a specified quality (e. g., #10 aluminum wood screws) and the seller ships goods of a different quality (e. g., #10 steel wood screws), the shipment of the nonconforming goods is an acceptance of the buyer's order. The result is a contract; the problem centers on the terms of that contract. Is it a contract for the delivery of aluminum screws or of steel screws? Are contractual obligations of these parties to be based upon the requirements stated in the buyer's order or upon the quality of the nonconforming goods which the seller shipped? Although the Code is open to a construction which would create obligations based upon the seller's deviant delivery,[37] neither the intention of the drafters nor the purpose of this section can support such a construction.[38] The shipment of the nonconforming goods forms a contract based upon the buyer's offer and is, at the same time, a default which opens remedies for the buyer.[39] The Code adds a significant exception: "but such a shipment of non-conforming goods does not constitute an acceptance if the seller seasonably notifies the buyer that the shipment is offered only as an accommodation

36.   UCC § 2–206(1) (b).

37.   That argument would be as follows: UCC § 2–206(1) (b) states that an "offer to buy goods for prompt or current shipment shall be construed as inviting acceptance . . . by the prompt or current shipment of . . . nonconforming goods"; thus, UCC § 2–206(1) (b) requires a construction of offers which allows delivery of nonconforming goods as an alternative performance (as when the offeree has an option as to which goods he wishes to deliver); and since seller performed the nonconforming goods alternative, there has been performance—not breach. See discussion of alternative contracts in 5 A. Corbin, Contracts § 1087 (1964).

38.   The argument in the prior footnote leads to the conclusion that a seller can change the buyer's order to whatever the seller cares to send, and obligate the buyer to purchase what has been sent. Such a conclusion is contrary to the law of contracts and was not intended by the drafters. See 1955 New York Law Rev. Comm'n Rep. (vol. 1) 623–24.

39.   Seller might have an opportunity to cure the nonconforming tender. See UCC § 2–508 and § 105 infra.

When the act requested by the buyer is shipment, and the seller responds by moving the goods out of his factory or warehouse, a problem can arise as to the point in time that the goods have been "shipped." The following are helpful in reaching a decision in particular cases: UCC §§ 2–204, 2–206 (2), and 2–504; UCC § 2–206, Comment 2; Williams v. Emerson-Brantingham Implement Co., 198 S.W. 425

to the buyer." [40]   When the seller received the order for aluminum screws, discovered that he had none in stock, but believed that the buyer might be willing to accept steel screws, the seller could send those steel screws without having the shipment amount to an acceptance and breach—if the proper notice was sent to the buyer.

The Code section which establishes this rule as to the construction of the buyer's offer begins: "Unless otherwise unambiguously indicated by the language or circumstances," the rule of construction discussed above is to be applied to the buyer's order.   Therefore, the buyer may "unambiguously" indicate in his offer that what he wants is a shipment —not a promise to ship.   If he does so indicate, the seller's promise to ship is not an acceptance and no contract results until the requested act (shipment) is performed; but the indication must be *unambiguous*. It is not enough to state "ship at once" or the like.[41]   There must be some expression or some circumstance which makes the offer different from the usual or ordinary offer.   The buyer is free to bargain for an act if this is what he wants, but the fact that he wants the act rather than a promise must be shown without any ambiguity.

§ 35.   Necessity to Notify Offeror That Offeree has Commenced Performance

When the offer requires or allows the offeree to perform an act and the act requires a period of time for its performance, application of common law notions of offer and acceptance would compel the conclusion that there is no acceptance until the offeree has completed the requested performance.[42]   Until acceptance (that is, until the act is completely performed) the offeror could, according to the dogma of judicial decisions, withdraw his offer without contractual liability for damages suffered by the offeree.   This left the offeree in an awkward position: a promise to perform was not an acceptance because an act (not a promise) was requested, and until the performance was complete the offeree was incurring expenses which would be recoverable only if the offeror did not change his mind and revoke the offer.   Non-Code law attempted to correct this inequity in two ways.   First, it provided that reliance on certain kinds of promises made the promises binding.[43]

(Mo.App.1917).   UCC § 2–206(2) is discussed in § 35 *infra*.

40.   UCC § 2–206(1) (b).

41.   UCC § 2–206, Comment 2.

42.   See § 34 *supra*.   The classic overstatement of this principle is contained in Wormser, *The True Conception of Unilateral Contracts*, 26 Yale L.J. 136 (1916).   With this, contrast Llewellyn, *On Our Case Law of Contract: Offer and Acceptance*, 48 Yale L.J. 1, 779 (1938, 1939), and Wormser's recantation in Wormser, *Book Review*, 3 J.Legal Ed. 145, 146 (1950).

43.   Restatement of Contracts § 90 (1932).   A slightly revised version appears in Restatement (Second) of Contracts § 90 (Tent. Draft No. 2, 1965).

Second, it stated that when reliance on an offer for a unilateral contract had gone so far as to become a part of the consideration requested (that is, had gone beyond the preparation for performance stage and had entered the performance stage), the offeror would be bound by his promise providing that the offeree completed his performance within the time limits of the offer.[44]

Application of these two rules can, in turn, cause justifiable doubts in the mind of the offeror. In some instances, he has no way of knowing whether the offeree is performing the requested act. Thus, the offeror might believe that the offeree had decided not to accept, make arrangements for the goods from some other source, and then learn that the offeree is performing—with the result that the offeror is now bound to two contracts. This possibility is especially applicable to purchases of goods where the goods must be manufactured, and a considerable time delay is involved.[45]

One answer could be that the offeror has put himself in this position, and should pay the consequences. Had he asked for a promise to deliver rather than for a delivery, the offeror would have the assurance which he lacked because of the manner in which he framed his order. This response to the plight of the buyer who has requested an act has legal rationality, but avoids the commercial realities of buyers who do not consult attorneys every time they make purchases. Thus, the Code has rejected strict application of this legal rationale and has substituted the principles which come closer to reflecting the probable intention of businessmen.

First, "an offer to make a contract shall be construed as inviting acceptance in any manner and by any medium reasonable in the circumstances."[46] The "by any medium" language allows telegraphic acceptances of written offers, or letter answers to telegraphic offers—if reasonable under the circumstances.[47] It also is general enough to

---

44. Restatement of Contracts § 45 (1932). This section is expanded and clarified in Restatement (Second) of Contracts § 45 (Tent. Draft No. 1, 1964).

45. See the opinions in Crook v. Cowan, 64 N.C. 743 (1870).

46. UCC § 2–206(1) (a).

47. The textual statement is based upon Comment 1 to UCC § 2–206, and states what has undoubtedly been the law of contracts for decades. The Comment reference ("Former technical rules as to acceptance, such as requiring that telegraphic offers be accepted by tele-graphed acceptance, etc., are rejected. . . .") is an elliptical statement which may hide its intention. Pre-Code law did not require that a telegraphic offer be accepted by telegram. What was required was that the offer be accepted before it lapsed or was revoked. A telegraphic offer might indicate the need for a quick answer, and the offer was open for only a short time. The Comment is probably referring to the famous "mailbox rule" of Adams v. Lindsell, 1 B. & Ald. 681, 106 Eng.Rep. 250 (K.B.1818), which made the acceptance effective when posted, as against lapse or an overtaking revocation. Byrne & Co. v. Leon Van Tienhoven & Co., 5 C.P.D.

encompass new media of communication as they develop. The language which is important to this section of the text, however, is that which construes offers as inviting acceptance "in any manner" reasonable in the circumstances. A specific example of the impact of this rule of construction has been discussed in the prior section of this text. A more general statement of its impact is that the offeree need not respond by doing an act or by making a promise just because the offer is framed in terms of unilateral or bilateral contract. He may do whichever is later determined to have been a reasonable course of action. Thus, in a particular case commencement of the performance requested may be a reasonable method of accepting the offer, protecting the offeree who has relied on the offer.

Second, the Code provides that where "the beginning of a requested performance is a reasonable mode of acceptance an offeror who is not notified of acceptance within a reasonable time may treat the offer as having lapsed before acceptance." [48] This subsection responds to the problems facing a buyer who has ordered goods but has not heard from the seller and does not know whether the seller has begun performance. Such a buyer may treat his offer as having lapsed, and a lapsed offer cannot create contractual obligations by a later acceptance.[49] The result of these rules is that the offeree who relies on an offer by beginning performance is protected provided that he takes the business-like step of notifying his offeror that he is performing the contract.

This is the Code's commercial response to business situations in which the transaction has not been planned by an attorney. Nevertheless, attorneys should not often rely on these sections of the Code in contract formation. Too much is left open to the later determination of reasonableness. Instead, attorneys planning transactions for their clients ought to accept the Code's invitation and spell out clearly what will amount to an acceptance of the specific offer made, including whether notice of acceptance is necessary to form legal obligations.[50]

---

344 (1880). The offeree must, however, have had the implied authority to use the mails as a method of acceptance before the mailbox rule is effective. Henthorn v. Fraser, [1892] 2 Ch. 27. All kinds of difficulties arise as to when the offeree had "authority" to use the mails or a telegram. Stephen M. Weld & Co. v. Victory Mfg. Co., 205 F. 770 (D.N.C.1913); Lucas v. Western Union Telegraph Co., 131 Iowa 669, 109 N.W. 191 (1906). However, the method of communication was immaterial if the acceptance arrived before the offer lapsed or was revoked. Therefore, the Comment must mean that the drafters intended to retain the mailbox rule (see also the "sent" in UCC § 2–207(1) and the definition of "send" in UCC § 1–201(38)), but make the choice of the offeree's method of communication rest on reasonableness.

48. UCC § 2–206(2).

49. Restatement of Contracts § 35(1)(b) (1932).

50. UCC § 2–206 rules apply only if a different result is not "otherwise unambiguously indicated."

§ 36. The Deviant Acceptance—The "Battle of Forms"—Common Law Background

The common law of offer and acceptance was clear. "To constitute a contract the acceptance of the offer must be absolute and identical with the terms of the offer. If one offers another to do a definite thing, and that other person accepts conditionally or introduces a new term into the acceptance, his answer is either a mere expression of willingness to treat or it is in effect a counter proposal . . . . To bind the parties, an acceptance must be in exact conformity with the proposal. A qualified acceptance does not constitute a contract." [51] This requirement that the acceptance mirror the offer before a contract is formed worked without serious defects as long as parties negotiated each individual agreement. However, with the introduction of the printed form serious defects in the system became apparent. Parties who thought they had a contract discovered that, because of a minor deviation between their communications, they had no enforceable agreement.[52]

Sales transactions are initiated in countless ways. The seller may telephone the buyer about an item which he is selling or the buyer may call the seller for information and quotations. Salesmen spend their lives attempting to interest prospective purchasers in various products. Purchasing agents are continually seeking the most economical and reliable source of goods. Generally, however, these contacts are merely preliminary negotiations, falling short of reaching a binding agreement for the sale and purchase of goods. It is the buyer who usually takes the first step which has any legal significance in reaching a contract. The buyer sends to the seller a printed order form on which have been typed a description of the goods, the quantity desired, and often the price of those goods.[53] This form was most probably prepared for the buyer by his attorney and pads of this form were printed so that the buyer did not have to stop and consult with his attorney before each order of goods. The buyer's attorney has therefore prepared a general form which will work reasonably well for the bulk of the buyer's purchases. Most probably the attorney did not have this particular pur-

51. Cohn v. Penn Beverage Co., 313 Pa. 349, 352, 169 A. 768, 769, (1934). See also Restatement of Contracts § 60 (1932). Cases are collected in 1 A. Corbin, Contracts § 82 (1963).

52. F. W. Berk & Co. v. Derecktor, 301 N.Y. 110, 92 N.E.2d 914 (1950), may be such a case—the offeree had used the words "subject to" in describing his acceptance. The classic case is Poel v. Brunswick-Balke-Collender Co., 216 N.Y. 310, 110 N.E. 619 (1915).

53. The order may have been sent without prior conversations between the parties, but more often the purchase order follows an oral agreement—usually over the telephone—as a confirmation of that agreement. See 1 W. Hawkland, A Transactional Guide to the Uniform Commercial Code 25–27 (1964).

chase in mind when the form was drafted. The attorney, however, did want to protect the buyer against all kinds of contingencies and the order form reflects this desire. It is, in short, a buyer-oriented document.

When the seller receives the purchase order, he may take that action which is requested by the form—usually that of signing and returning the order to the buyer. If the seller takes this requested action, there is, unless the buyer has made his promise illusory, a binding agreement between the seller and the buyer under any view of the law of contracts and the contract terms are those stated in the purchase order. This is, of course, the hope of the buyer's attorney. More often, however, the seller has been advised by his attorney not to sign and return the purchase order. Instead, the seller files that order and returns to the buyer a form drafted for him (the seller). This document (an acknowledgment of order) repeats the quantity and price of the goods, but there the similarity ends. The seller's attorney was equally diligent in protecting his client; thus, the seller's form varies materially from the offer which was received. In answer to the buyer's offer the seller has returned a seller-oriented form and under the common law no contract has resulted. At best, there is a counter-offer which the buyer can accept or reject. Usually, though, the buyer files the acknowledgment of his order and awaits the goods.[54]

Fortunately, business has survived the lack of a binding agreement in most sales. The goods are usually shipped, the price paid, and the file closed. There are, however, those troublesome cases in which one of the parties wants to renege on his deal or in which the goods have been destroyed in transit. There are also those cases in which the buyer discovers (after the goods have been shipped and the price paid) that the goods were not up to the quality which the buyer expected and the buyer wants to recover damages caused by the defects. It was at this point that many buyers and sellers discovered that they had no contract and no right to pursue a remedy. Thus, in those cases in which the existence of a contract was important, the battle of the printed forms prevented the creation of that contract, or postponed its creation until the buyer took the goods.[55] Taking the goods could then be viewed as an acceptance of seller's counter-offer, binding the buyer to the seller's terms.[56]

54. See *In re* Doughboy Indus., Inc., 17 A.D.2d 216, 233 N.Y.S.2d 488 (1962), for a factual example of the statement in the text.

55. There is much to be said for the use of standardized forms, and it has been well and concisely said in Llewel-lyn, *Book Review*, 52 Harv.L.Rev. 700 (1939).

56. Cage v. Black, 97 Ark. 613, 134 S.W. 942 (1911), is an example of this principle without the use of printed forms. An example involving the use of forms is Roto-Lith, Ltd. v. F. P. Bartlett & Co., Inc., 297 F.2d 497 (1st Cir. 1962).

§ 37. The Deviant Acceptance—The "Battle of Forms"—The Code's Answer

The Code's answer to the problems created when the acceptance does not mirror the offer is contained in section 2–207:

(1) A definite and seasonable expression of acceptance or a written confirmation which is sent within a reasonable time operates as an acceptance even though it states terms additional to or different from those offered or agreed upon, unless acceptance is expressly made conditional on assent to the additional or different terms.

(2) The additional terms are to be construed as proposals for addition to the contract. Between merchants such terms become part of the contract unless:

(a) the offer expressly limits acceptance to the terms of the offer;

(b) they materially alter it; or

(c) notification of objection to them has already been given or is given within a reasonable time after notice of them is received.

(3) Conduct by both parties which recognizes the existence of a contract is sufficient to establish a contract for sale although the writings of the parties do not otherwise establish a contract. In such case the terms of the particular contract consist of those terms on which the writings of the parties agree, together with any supplementary terms incorporated under any other provisions of this Act.

Unfortunately, this section is not a model of clarity. The drafters were undoubtedly attempting to change the common law answer to the effect which is to be given to the deviant response to an offer.[57] The extent to which they were successful turns on how courts will respond to the language which was chosen. Consider the following hypothetical situations and the Code problems which they raise:

Case # 1. Assume that a buyer and a seller were located in distant cities. They had never before dealt with each other; they knew each other only by their business reputations. The buyer desired to purchase 1,000 units of a certain kind of goods manufactured by the seller, and initiated the buying process by completing and mailing to the seller a printed order form. This form contained a number of printed clauses on its front and back but also had several blank spaces

---

57. § 34 *supra.*

in which the buyer typed the name of the seller, a description of the goods desired, the quantity and price of those goods, and the date and method of their delivery.

Two days later this order form was delivered at the seller's factory. At that point in time the buyer's order had undoubtedly become an "offer." Notice that this classification of "offer" is a legal conclusion which indicates that the words used by the buyer can reasonably be understood as committing the buyer to the terms stated on his order form if the seller takes whatever action is necessary to classify as an "acceptance." [58] Assume that the seller immediately responded by filing the buyer's order form, shipping the goods, and mailing to the buyer a printed acknowledgment. This acknowledgment contained a number of printed clauses but also had enough blank spaces so that the seller could type in the necessary information about the goods, their price, and their delivery. In this particular case the seller completed his acknowledgment with precisely the same information about the goods as was typed on the buyer's order form. This acknowledgment arrived at the buyer's place of business and was filed in a box for "incoming goods." A comparison of the two forms would show: (1) that the seller's acknowledgment has a printed clause limiting warranties as to the quality of these goods, while the buyer's form has a printed clause expanding the warranty of quality; and (2) that the seller's acknowledgment has a printed clause which requires that the parties submit any dispute to a panel of arbitrators, while the buyer's order form is silent on this subject. The buyer received the goods two days later. Is there a contract between the buyer and the seller? If so, what are its terms?

Case # 2. Assume the same facts as are set out in Case #1 except that these forms were exchanged after the buyer and seller had orally agreed on the telephone as to the kind and number of goods which were to be delivered, their price, and the date and method of their delivery. Is there a contract? If so, what are its terms?

The Comments indicate that the drafters intended section 2–207 to cover both of these situations. The problem examined here is what the Code does to answer the questions posed after each of the two cases.

---

58. "An offer is an expression by one party of his assent to certain definite terms, provided that the other party involved in the bargaining transaction will likewise express his assent to the identically same terms. An offer looks forward to an agreement—to mutual expression of assent." Quoted approvingly in Calo, Inc. v. AMF Pinspotters, Inc., 31 Ill.App.2d 2, 8, 176 N.E.2d 1, 4–5 (1961). This is the common law definition, partially changed by UCC §§ 2–206 and 2–207. The definition in the text reflects this change by not requiring that the person receiving the commitment (or promise) assent to *exactly* the same terms, only that he take whatever action is required by the Code.

First, as to Case #1: the Code states that a "definite and seasonable expression of acceptance . . . which is sent within a reasonable time operates as an acceptance . . .."[59] Since the seller's acknowledgment was sent within a reasonable time,[60] it appears that the seller has accepted the buyer's offer, and that there is a contract (offer and acceptance) between the two parties. However, this conclusion can be reached only if two different meanings are given to the word "acceptance" the first two times that word is used in section 2–207 (1). The second time the word is used (operates as an acceptance) "acceptance" refers to a legal conclusion—the offeree-seller has sent a response which is sufficient to convert the buyer's "offer" (also a legal conclusion) into a contract. This use of "acceptance" is its normal legal meaning in the law of contracts. However, the first time the word is used (definite and seasonable expression of acceptance) the reference cannot be to a legal conclusion, or there would be no purpose for section 2–207(1). A statute is not needed to indicate that an acceptance turns an offer into a binding promise. "Acceptance" as it is first used in section 2–207(1) refers not to the legal conclusion but to the facts upon which the conclusion is based. In Case #1 these facts center in the seller's acknowledgment which expressed agreement as to the quantity and kind of goods to be sold, their price, their time and method of delivery, and such other points as were similar in the two printed forms.[61] Thus, section 2–207(1) is to be read as stating that a definite and seasonable *response* to an offer operates as an *acceptance* binding the parties to a contract "even though it [the response] states terms additional to or different from those offered or agreed upon . . .."

This, however, is not the complete meaning of section 2–207(1). There are some responses to offers that should not be considered "expressions of acceptance." For example, if the seller in Case #1 had completed his acknowledgment form by inserting the description of a kind of goods different from those ordered by the buyer, the response would be insufficient to express acceptance. The kind of response which was contemplated by the Code is one which expresses assent to the principal terms of the offer, although it differs from or adds to some of the terms.[62] The drafters did not mean that any re-

---

59. UCC § 2–207(1).

60. For a discussion of a similar Code phrase, see § 26 *supra.*

61. The sending of the goods could also be viewed as a definite and seasonable expression of acceptance, as is later argued in the text. However,

finding acceptance in the act of shipment does not fit neatly within the statute which views the acceptance as some act which states terms. See UCC § 2–207(1). But shipment would fall within UCC § 2–207(3), discussed later in this section of the text.

62. UCC § 2–207, Comment 1.

sponse would amount to an acceptance; this was their purpose in including the phrase: "even though it states terms additional to or different from those offered or agreed upon . . .." They did not contemplate that a complete disparity between the buyer's offer and the seller's response would create a contract.[63] This need for agreement on the principal points of the transaction probably caused the drafters to select the word "acceptance" the first time it was used in section 2–207 (1).

One more idea must be explored before Case #1 can be answered: the response expressing assent operates as an acceptance of what? One answer might be that the response is an acceptance (in the legal sense) of those portions of the offer with which it agrees.[64] Under this reading of section 2–207 the terms of the contract would consist of (a) those terms which were the same in both forms, (b) the additional terms of the response which became a part of the contract under section 2–207(2), and (c) possibly those supplementary portions of the Code and general contract law (such as implied warranties) as would be made a part of a contract of sale where the parties have been silent as to the subject.[65] There are difficulties with this reading. The parties have not been silent. One or both have said something about the subject. If the offer alone contains the controversial statement, it should at least have as much chance of becoming a part of the contract as if the statement had been a part of the response.[66] If the two forms speak to the subject but say conflicting things, this reading of the Code would ignore what both have said and substitute either a vacuum or a Code provision which may or may not be anything like what either party had in mind.

On occasion there is justification for this approach to contract terms. The writings may be sketchy or the seller's response may have clearly indicated that he was not accepting the buyer's offer (and the buyer may have been just as adamant that he would not deal on the

---

63. When goods are shipped, as in Case #1, before the buyer has had an opportunity to receive the acknowledgment, a shipment of nonconforming goods could result in a contract under UCC § 2–206. See discussion in § 34 *supra.*

64. This reading is suggested by UCC § 2–207, Comment 6. That Comment, however, is concerned with "confirming" forms—probably situations where the forms confirm a prior dickered deal. In such a situation neither form initiates the contract and there is no outstanding offer to accept. See Case #2 *infra* this section. See also Weeks,

"Battle of the Forms" Under the Uniform Commercial Code, 52 Ill.Bar.J. 660, 665–66 (1964).

65. "Possibly" because UCC §§ 2–207 (1) and (2) make no provisions for supplementary terms. *See* UCC § 2–207(3).

66. This result can be accomplished by rephrasing the answer to the question posed in the text: the response is an acceptance of those portions of the offer with which the response expresses no disagreement. A standard clause in the response would soon make these tests indistinguishable.

seller's terms). Nevertheless, these parties may have gone ahead and bought and sold goods, only to have some controversy which requires judicial solution. In this situation the best that can be done is to see where the writings agreed and to supplement that agreement with Code provisions. Section 2–207(3) provides this solution for these cases and, at the same time, presents the principal difficulty in construing section 2–207(1) as suggested above. If section 2–207(1) is read to mean that the seller has accepted only those provisions of the offer with which the seller agrees (or with which he has not expressly disagreed), subsection (1) is little more than a repetition of subsection (3). There is no reason to assume that the drafters tried to say the same thing in two different ways in the same Code section.

The purpose of section 2–207(1) is quite different. It is designed to aid in the solution of those cases in which the offeree has indicated a willingness to accept—as by shipping the goods before assuring himself that the buyer knows that they will be shipped on terms other than those contained in the offer. In those cases the expression of acceptance operates as an acceptance *of the entire offer*. Of course, the contents of the offer will be judged as with any other document. Ambiguous language will be treated like ambiguous language, small print hidden in a maze of fine print will be ignored, and unconscionable provisions can be dealt with in a forthright fashion; but when the terms of the offer are finally sifted out and a determination is made as to what a reasonable offeree would have understood from the form which was received, these are the terms which are "accepted" under section 2–207(1). Therefore, a partial answer to Case #1 can now be suggested. There is a contract between the buyer and seller, and the terms are those contained in the buyer's order form.

The result is a contract on the terms of the buyer's order with the seller's additional and different terms remaining outside the contractual obligations. What happens to these terms? No further mention is made in the Code of those terms that are "different"; evidently they remain in limbo to be accepted by the Case #1 buyer only if he desires to have them become a part of the parties' obligations. However, section 2–207(2) picks up the "additional" terms. These become proposals (offers?) for additions to the contract, and between merchants they do become a part of the contract unless one of the three conditions listed in section 2–207(2) is satisfied. Assuming that the buyer and seller in Case #1 are merchants,[67] it is first necessary to decide whether the two changes in the seller's acknowledgment form are *different* from the buyer's order or whether they are *additional* to

---

67. The merchant concept of the Code is discussed in § 33 *supra*.

it. A quick look at the forms might lead to the conclusion that the limitation of warranties is "different" because it contradicts an express term of the buyer's order, while the arbitration clause is "additional" to the buyer's order because the order is silent as to the method of settling disputes.

It may be that this is the way courts will decide whether the extra terms are additional or different. However, such a distinction makes little commercial sense. When the buyer's attorney prepared the order form, he may well have realized that a failure to include an arbitration clause would mean that any disputes would be resolved by the judicial system. Whether he consciously realized this or not, it is clear that implied in the buyer's order was the proposition that disputes would be solved by courts, rather than by arbitrators. Thus, one way to look at both of the extra clauses in the seller's acknowledgment is that they are different from the buyer's terms; it is equally possible to look at those clauses as additional to the agreement of the parties.[68] The distinction between "different from" and "additional to" disappears—just as it did for the drafters when they wrote the Comments.[69]

The suggested solution to Case #1, therefore, is that there is a contract between these parties. The extra terms proposed by the seller are "additional terms" under section 2-207(2), and become a part of the contract (since the buyer and seller are merchants) unless they materially alter the contract which has been formed. Since both of these clauses would materially alter the contract, they are not a part of the terms of the agreement which the court will enforce.[70] In short, the resulting Case #1 contract is found in the buyer's order plus those parts of the acknowledgment which concur with the order.

Such a result is, of course, foreign to the common law lawyer and will be resisted by courts steeped in the common law tradition.[71] Yet, this is the result which the Code commands, and there are sound policy reasons for the Code's solution. The common law tradition was that there was no contract when the seller sent his acknowledgement be-

---

68. See *In re* Doughboy Indus., Inc., 17 A.D.2d 216, 233 N.Y.S.2d 488 (1962).

69. *See* UCC § 2-207, Comment 3.

70. The limitation of warranties is a material alteration under Roto-Lith, Ltd. v. F. P. Bartlett & Co., Inc., 297 F.2d 497 (1st Cir. 1962). There is a question as to whether an arbitration clause is a material alteration. *Compare In re* Doughboy Indus., Inc., 17 A.D.2d 216, 233 N.Y.S.2d 488 (1962),

with American Parts Co. v. American Arbitration Ass'n, 8 Mich.App. 156, 154 N.W.2d 5 (1967), where such a problem was held to be a question of fact.

71. The resistance is evident in Roto-Lith, Ltd. v. F. P. Bartlett & Co., Inc., 297 F.2d 497 (1st Cir. 1962). *See also* Construction Aggregates Corp. v. Hewitt-Robins, Inc., 404 F.2d 505 (7th Cir.), *cert. denied* 395 U.S. 921, 89 S.Ct. 1774, 23 L.Ed.2d 238 (1969).

cause it was only a counter-offer. Thus, during the time that the goods were being shipped, neither party was bound and the buyer could renege for any reason sufficient to him.[72] The Code creates a contract at a much earlier stage in the transaction, conforming to the expectations of businessmen. Further, in selecting the offer (the order in Case #1) as the controlling document for determining the basic terms of the contract, the Code has not left the offeree helpless. He may check the offer when it arrives and determine whether he wants to deal on that basis. If not, he may notify the offeror and tell him the only terms on which he (the offeree) will deal. This may mean that the goods cannot be shipped quite as fast as they could at common law, but the framers of any rule of law relating to contract formation face a choice as to which of the conflicting documents forms the terms of the resulting contract. At common law, the seller's acknowledgment was most often the controlling document because it amounted to a counter-offer which the buyer accepted when he took the goods. The Code rejects the notion that goods during shipment are only a part of a counter-offer and that a buyer should be forced to take the goods or to ship them back depending on what terms he wants in his contract. The Code accepts a more sensible solution by recognizing that if the Case #1 seller wants to enter into a deal by shipping the goods before the terms are worked out to his (the seller's) satisfaction, he may do so—but on the terms of the only document which triggered the shipment of those goods: the buyer's order form.

Case #2 is harder to solve under the language of the Code, but it is clear that the drafters intended that section 2–207 apply to such a problem.[73] In Case #2 the parties have an oral agreement which is enforceable if the statute of frauds has been satisfied. They then exchanged forms with conflicting clauses. The applicable language from section 2–207 is: "a written confirmation which is sent within a reasonable time operates as an acceptance even though it states terms additional to or different from those offered or agreed upon . . .." How can the confirmation be viewed as an "acceptance" of anything? The oral conversation resulted in an offer and an acceptance, a contract. There is nothing to accept or reject. Thus, the Code language is even harder to fit into the facts of Case #2.

Evidently the drafters had in mind that the oral agreement would be sketchy at best. Price, quantity, delivery—these are the principal items dealt with on the telephone. These are the terms that are important to businessmen who are looking forward to performance. The confirmation, in the form of a written order or acknowledgment, often proposes terms which are "additional to" the principal part of

72. § 34 *supra*.   73. UCC § 2–207, Comment 1.

the parties' agreement, even though they cannot technically be viewed as an acceptance of an outstanding offer. Thus, the drafters intended that the same tests suggested for the answer to Case #1 be applied to Case #2 whenever such application makes sense.

There will be times, however, in which only one confirmation is sent [74] or in which the confirmations cross in the mails. In some of these cases it will be difficult to determine just what is an "additional term." In those cases, section 2–207(3) may be ideally suited for sorting out the terms of the contract.[75] The contract will then consist of the terms agreed on, supplemented by additional terms implied by the Code.

If this were all there was to section 2–207, the "battle of forms" would at least be partially solved. Reasonable people might disagree as to the wisdom of the solution; but a solution there would be. The difficulty is that the drafters did not stop at this point. They added two provisos:

1. The offeree's response is an acceptance of the offer even though it contains additional or different terms, "unless acceptance is expressly made conditional on assent to the additional or different terms." [76] Such Code language could be interpreted to allow the seller in Case #1 to include in his acknowledgment a printed statement that his acceptance is conditioned on the buyer's assent to any deviant terms in the acknowledgment, and that assent is shown by a failure to object. If such a clause is given effect, there has been no acceptance (in the legal sense of that word), and no contract has resulted from the exchange of forms.

2. The additional terms become a part of the contract between merchants unless, among other things, "the offer expressly limits acceptance to the terms of the offer." [77] This subsection apparently allows the Case #1 buyer to have a clause printed in his order form to the effect that any acceptance must be in terms of the offer made. If this clause is given effect, the seller's additional terms will not become a part of the resulting contract—no matter how minor their impact.[78]

---

74. Tidewater Lumber Co. v. Maryland Lumber Co., 3 UCC Rep. 351 (N.Y.Sup. Ct.1966).

75. American Parts Co. v. American Arbitration Ass'n, 8 Mich.App. 156, 154 N.W.2d 5 (1967); UCC § 2–207, Comment 6.

76. UCC § 2–207(1).

77. UCC § 2–207(2) (a).

78. Even without such a clause, UCC § 2–207(2) (c) may be used to show objection to terms in the seller's form which conflict with terms in the buyer's form, UCC § 2–207, Comment 6.

The result is obvious. To the extent that the courts allow these printed clauses to control contract formation the battle of forms will still rage. There will be no contract while the goods are in shipment and the buyer will have the option to accept or reject the goods on arrival but, should he accept, the contract will be on the seller's terms. Such a result is not required by the Code. The courts can use the word "expressly" in section 2–207 to look beyond the printed forms to see whether, in fact, the parties did deal on the basis of their forms. Notice that in Case #1 the seller shipped the goods at about the same time he sent out his acknowledgment. He was willing to deal and, although his form stated that the deal was to be on his terms, such a seller has not *expressly* made his assent conditional on the buyer's assent to the additional or different terms contained in the acknowledgment.[79]

In some cases the best result will be found by use of subsection (3). When the writings which were exchanged result in no contract but the conduct of the parties shows that they recognized the existence of a contract, the court can gather the terms from those parts of the writings in which there is agreement and add supplementary provisions under the Code. The buyer will lose his extended warranty; the seller will lose his disclaimer. In their place will be substituted the implied warranty of merchantability and perhaps the implied warranty of fitness for purpose. These fall short of the intentions of both parties as that intention is found from the forms they used, but may be the most equitable result in cases in which the parties deal with each other, paying little heed to the forms which their attorneys had so carefully drafted for them.

C. TERMS OF A CONTRACT FOR SALE

§ 38. Open Price Agreements

There are occasions in which businessmen find it to their mutual advantage to enter into agreements which they intend to be binding but which do not fix the price of the goods bought and sold. Most often these agreements involve goods to be delivered at some future date, and neither is willing at this point in time to fix a price. The seller desires to be assured of a market for the goods he is manufacturing of distributing; the buyer wants to be assured that he will have a source of supply for those goods. Price is of secondary importance.

---

79. "The theme of section 2–207 is that tidy draftsmanship or clausemanship may not end the inquiry." American Parts Co. v. American Arbitration Ass'n, 8 Mich.App. 156, 175, 154 N.W. 2d 5, 15 (1967). For suggestions as to drafting clauses for buyers' and sellers' forms, see Note, *Contract Draftsmanship Under Article Two of the Uniform Commercial Code*, 112 U.Pa. L.Rev. 564, 567–72 (1964).

This kind of an agreement caused difficulties at common law.[80] If nothing was said as to price, there was no agreement as to one of the principal terms of the transaction. If the parties had agreed to set a mutually satisfactory price, there was nothing more than an agreement to agree at some future time; until the future agreement became a reality, there was no defignite commitment which the courts could enforce.[81] If the parties had agreed that one of them could fix the price, some courts concluded that he could set an unreasonable price and that his promise was illusory; [82] in effect, he could perform or not as he saw fit simply by the price which he could later determine. Of course, these conclusions were not inevitable. Courts could have interpreted these agreements regarding price in the way they were intended: as creating a firm market at a reasonable price, with the reasonableness being determined at some future date.[83]

The Code brings the law into line with the expectations of business-men. An agreement of the parties does not fail to become a contract (that is, does not fail to create legal obligation) simply because the price is not set at the time of the agreement.[84] On the other hand, every open price agreement is not a contract. There are instances in which the parties have reached a tentative agreement which they intend to be binding only after the price has been fixed. In those cases, there is no contract until the condition is met—that is until there is an agreement as to price.[85] Therefore, the Code provides that the parties "if they so intend" [86] can conclude a contract even though the price is not set by their agreement. The same section of the Code (2–305)

---

80. Prosser, *Open Price in Contracts for the Sale of Goods*, 16 Minn.L.Rev. 733 (1932).

81. Sun Printing & Publishing Ass'n v. Remington Paper & Power Co., 235 N.Y. 338, 139 N.E. 470 (1923).

82. Weston Paper Mfg. Co. v. Downing Box Co., 293 F. 725 (7th Cir. 1923).

83. *See* 1 A. Corbin, Contracts §§ 97, 98 (1963). Parties worked out devices to make the agreement definite as to price but still sufficiently open to protect against swings in the market. Such devices included reference to some outside price list, Eastern Rolling Mill Co. v. Michlovitz, 157 Md. 51, 145 A. 378 (1929), and reference to arbitrators if the parties fail to agree. Texas Co. v. Z. & M. Independent Oil Co., 156 F.2d 862 (2d Cir. 1946). More courageous courts have implied a reasonable price. See 5A A. Corbin, Contracts § 1174 (1964).

84. UCC § 2–305. A contract for a basic price *plus extras* is within UCC § 2–305. Silver v. The Sloop Silver Cloud, 259 F.Supp. 187 (S.D.N.Y.1966).

85. An example is contained in Comment 4 to UCC § 2–305: the sale of a particular painting at a price to be fixed by a trusted expert, and the chosen expert fails to set the price. See UCC § 2–305(4). Any goods the buyer has received must be returned or, if unable to be returned, must be paid for at their reasonable value; the seller must return any portion of the price paid. Thus, this subsection recognizes that there is no contract between the parties where (1) they intend not to be bound until the price is fixed and (2) the price is not fixed. *See* Interstate Plywood Sales Co. v. Interstate Container Corp., 331 F.2d 449 (9th Cir. 1964). Compare § 183 *infra*.

86. UCC § 2–305(1).

sets out rules as to how the price is to be determined. In summary these rules are:

1.   If the agreement allows one of the parties to set the price, this means that that party may set the price but he must do so *in good faith*.[87] For non-merchants, good faith means honesty in fact,[88] but open price terms are uncommon among buyers and sellers who are not merchants. For the merchant, good faith "means honesty in fact and the observance of reasonable commercial standards of fair dealing in the trade."[89] In most instances the "good faith" requirement translates into a price which is the market price of those goods at the time specified in the contract.

2.   If nothing is said as to price, the agreement is to be construed as setting a reasonable price at the time for delivery.[90]

3.   If the price is to be fixed by agreement of the parties and they fail to agree, the agreement is to be construed as setting a reasonable price at the time for delivery.[91]

4.   If "the price is to be fixed in terms of some agreed market or other standard as set or recorded by a third person or agency and it is not so set or recorded," the agreement is to be construed as setting a reasonable price at the time for delivery.[92] An example of the operation of this section is an agreement which sets the price of future goods as a certain percentage of the price recorded in a trade publication. That publication may be taken off the market after agreement is reached and before the time for delivery has arrived, or a change in editorial policy may have withdrawn the price recording feature from the publication. Even so, the agreement does not fail; the price is set as a reasonable price.

5.   "When a price left to be fixed otherwise than by agreement of the parties fails to be fixed through fault of one party the other may at his option treat the contract as cancelled or himself fix a reasonable price."[93] This subsection applies to the situations involved in rules 1, 2, and 4 above. Thus, if the contract gives the seller the power to set the price of the goods to be sold and if the seller refuses

87.   UCC § 2–305(2).

88.   UCC § 1–201(19).

89.   UCC § 2–103(1) (b).

90.   UCC § 2–305(1) (a); American Sand & Gravel, Inc. v. Clark & Fray Constr. Co., 2 Conn.Cir. 284, 198 A.2d 68 (1963).

91.   UCC § 2–305(1) (b); Sylvia Coal Co. v. Mercury Coal & Coke Co., 151

W.Va. 818, 156 S.E.2d 1 (1967). Prices quoted in market news report are evidence of reasonable price. Lamberta v. Smiling Jim Potato Co., 25 Agri. Dec. 1181, 3 UCC Rep. 981 (U.S. Dept. of Agriculture, 1966).

92.   UCC § 2–305(1) (c).

93.   UCC § 2–305(3).

to set the price (or if he sets a price otherwise than in good faith), the buyer may either cancel—retaining any remedy for breach—or fix a reasonable price.[94] Notice the difference in the prices which could be set under such an agreement: the seller's obligation is to fix the price "in good faith"; failure to do so allows the buyer to fix a "reasonable price." In theory these are different tests. In practice, the reasonableness of the price set by the seller will have a strong bearing on whether he has acted in good faith.[95] Thus, the rules are probably not as far apart as they may at first seem.

§ 39. Open Terms Other Than Price

There are a number of Code sections, other than the one dealing with open price contracts, which supply content to incomplete agreements. Many of these sections are discussed later in this text. Some, however, can be conveniently grouped under two hypothetical cases.

Case # 1. Seller manufactures men's shoes; buyer owns and operates a large chain of retail stores which sells men's shoes. Two weeks ago buyer and seller agreed as follows: seller promised to sell to buyer 10,000 pairs of shoes and buyer promised to pay to seller $55,000 for the shoes. The two parties signed a writing which was sufficient to satisfy the statute of frauds but which contained only the terms set out above. This is the first time that this buyer and seller have dealt with each other, and there are no trade customs which affect any portion of this transaction.

It is readily admitted that Case #1 is, indeed, "hypothetical." The more normal case would involve a writing (or writings) which would fill out many terms of the basic agreement reached in Case #1. Such a writing would probably contain terms on whether the goods are to be delivered at one time or in installments, the time and place of delivery, credit terms (if any), as well as other details applicable to this transaction. However, Case #1—with its skeletal agreement —was chosen as a basis for presenting several Code sections which give content to the parties' agreement.

Most of the sections applicable to Case #1 begin with the familiar "unless otherwise agreed," the following rules are to apply. The Code, therefore, leaves the parties free to work out their own agreement. This agreement need not be entirely in writing; to the extent that the parol evidence rule is not violated, evidence of oral agreements is

---

94. The statement in the text assumes the existence of a contract—that is, that the parties intended to conclude a contract. UCC §§ 2–305(1) and (4). Whether they "intended" a contract will undoubtedly be determined by common law rules. Euclid Engineering Corp. v. Illinois Power Co., 79 Ill. App.2d 145, 223 N.E.2d 409 (1967); 1 A. Corbin, Contracts § 34 (1963).

95. UCC § 2–305, Comment 3.

admissible to supplement the writing.[96] Also, usage of trade can give content to language used by the parties.[97] It is only when a term is left open that the Code steps in to supply a meaning for the parties. This is the type of situation imagined in Case #1: the parties have worked out only the minimum elements of the entire sale. The solutions for the open terms, unless otherwise agreed, are:

1. All of the goods are to be delivered at one time, not in several lots.[98]

2. The buyer has the option of selecting the assortment of the goods; the seller has the option of determining the specifications or arrangements relating to shipment.[99]

3. The seller has a reasonable time to make delivery.[1] Indeed, when the contract calls for any act without specifying a time for its performance, the Code provides that act must be performed within a reasonable time.

4. The place for delivery of goods in a noncommercial sale and for those occasional commercial sales where no means or place of delivery was agreed upon is determined by the following rules: *Rule #1*, if the contract is for the sale of identified goods and if the parties know the location of those goods, that location is the place of delivery; and *Rule #2*, if Rule #1 is not applicable, the seller's place of business (or, if he has no place of business, his residence) is the place of delivery.[2] These rules would not be applicable to Case #1 if the agreement can be interpreted as requiring or authorizing the seller to ship the goods to the buyer.

5. If the agreement authorizes the seller to send the goods to the buyer (and the location of buyer and seller in distant cities could amount to this authorization), the seller may use documents of title and ship under reservation.[3]

6. Payment of the price is due on receipt of the goods,[4] subject to the buyer's right to inspect and this inspection may be after the goods have arrived if they are shipped to the buyer,[5] "but where the

---

96. See § 53 *infra*.

97. See § 52 *infra*.

98. UCC § 2–307.

99. UCC § 2–311(2).

1. UCC § 2–309(1).

2. UCC § 2–308.

3. UCC § 2–310(b). The delivery problems are discussed in §§ 97–102, *infra*.

4. UCC §§ 2–301, 2–310(a), 2–507. "Tender" is defined in UCC § 2–503(1). The seller's tender must be at a reasonable hour and kept available reasonably long enough for the buyer to take possession. UCC § 2–503(1) (a). See §§ 96–99 *infra*.

5. UCC § 2–513. See also UCC § 2–310 (b). Inspection may be waived in the contract. UCC §§ 2–512, 2–513(3).

circumstances give either party the right to make or demand delivery in lots the price if it can be apportioned may be demanded for each lot." [6]

Applying these rules to Case #1, the seller is obligated to deliver the 10,000 pairs of shoes at one time; he may ship them to the buyer under reservation; and the buyer is obligated to pay for them after they have been inspected or the right to inspection has been waived. Payment may be by check unless the seller demands cash.[7] The Code has filled these terms into the skeletal agreement which the parties entered into concerning the sale and purchase of shoes.

Case # 2. Assume the same basic factual pattern as in Case #1: a contract for the sale and purchase of 10,000 pairs of shoes at a total price of $55,000. Assume further that the agreement between the parties gave the buyer the option of choosing sizes and colors.

In addition to the terms filled out by the prior discussion, the Code gives content to the term which allows one of the parties to fill in the particulars of the agreement.[8] The specifications by that party (the buyer in Case #2) "must be made in good faith and within limits set by commercial reasonableness." [9] Further, where the specifications are not seasonably made and materially affect the other party's performance (as they possibly would when the buyer fails to select the sizes and colors of the shoes he wants), the other party may have any remedies given by the Code and (a) is excused for the resulting delay in his performance and (b) may perform in some reasonable manner or treat the failure to specify as a breach.[10]

The result of these rules can be summarized thus: The parties are free to work out the terms of their own contract. As long as those terms fall within the boundaries of conscionability and fair dealing, the courts will enforce those terms. However, failure to agree on each and every term will not result in an unenforceable agreement. The Code fleshes out the skeletal contract by providing terms which the drafters thought would most probably be in the minds of the parties. Most agreements will contain more terms than the ones

---

6. UCC § 2–307.

7. UCC § 2–511. If cash is demanded by the seller, the buyer has a reasonable time to procure the cash. UCC § 2–511(2) ; § 112 *infra.*

8. "An agreement for sale which is otherwise sufficiently definite (subsection (3) of Section 2–204) to be a contract is not made invalid by the fact that it leaves particulars of performance to be specified by one of the par-

ties." UCC § 2–311(1). As was indicated in § 38 *supra,* the parties must have intended to make a contract before their agreement will be enforced. Luis Hirsch Y S.A. v. Rosenblatt Casing Co., 418 F.2d 1300 (2d Cir. 1969). There must also be "a reasonably certain basis for giving an appropriate remedy." UCC § 2–204(3).

9. UCC § 2–311(1).

10. UCC § 2–311(3).

imagined in this section of the text; for these, only one or two terms will be added by the Code. Nevertheless, even with agreements as abbreviated as those contained in Cases #1 and #2, the Code provides sufficient certainty so that standards are available against which performance can be measured.

There is another "open" term which the Code attempts to "close." Whether it was successful can be determined only after some difficult problems have been resolved by case law. There are agreements which call for successive performances but contain no duration term. For example, in Case #1 the agreement might have been open as to the total number of shoes to be bought and sold, but have provided only that the seller agreed to sell, and the buyer to buy, 1,000 pairs of shoes each month for $5.50 a pair. Such an agreement is open as to how long buyer and seller are required to deal with each other, thereby creating a problem as to whether there was ever a mutuality of obligation.[11] The Code resolves this difficulty by providing that such an agreement "is valid for a reasonable time"—thus making the agreement a contract at its inception—and adds "but unless otherwise agreed may be terminated at any time by either party." [12] The buyer and seller in this variation on Case #1 have, therefore, a contract for the purchase and sale of shoes at a stated price and this contract creates obligations for a reasonable time, but the contract is subject to the right of either party to terminate at any time—presumably even though a reasonable time has not yet elapsed. At this point the Code appears first to have given parties a right (that is, a right to the contractual obligations for a reasonable time) and then to have taken this right from them through termination.[13]

Application of this section of the Code could work a serious economic hardship upon some terminated parties. A buyer, in reliance on his agreement with the seller, may have invested considerable sums of money in the expectation that this money will be recouped out of the profits to be made from the sale of these shoes over a reasonable period of time.[14] Abrupt termination may result in these expenditures being almost worthless to the buyer; yet the Code states

11. *E. g.*, Meadows v. Radio Indus., Inc., 222 F.2d 347 (7th Cir. 1955); Joliet Bottling Co. v. Joliet Citizens' Brewing Co., 254 Ill. 215, 98 N.E. 263 (1912); Fuchs v. Standard Thermometer Co., 178 Mich. 37, 144 N.W. 484 (1913).

12. UCC § 2–309(2).

13. *E. g.*, Weilersbacher v. Pittsburgh Brewing Co., 421 Pa. 118, 218 A.2d 806 (1966).

14. Such a buyer could have insisted upon a term contract, but the disparity of bargaining power may make this suggestion impractical. C. Robert Ingram, Inc. v. Chrysler Corp., 256 F.2d 684 (10th Cir. 1958); Motor Car Supply Co. v. General Household Util. Co., 80 F.2d 167 (4th Cir. 1935).

that the agreement may be terminated *at any time.* Does this section mean the seller may use his right of termination irrespective of the economic losses which result to the buyer? Certainly the Code can be read to reach such a result.[15] However, Code ideas of good and bad faith [16] together with its ideas of unconscionability [17] dictate a different answer. Although neither of these sections fits precisely the problem of abrupt termination, their underlying philosophies indicate that courts should police contract termination in the same manner as they police the formation and the performance of contracts. When the terminated party has reasonably relied on a contract of indefinite duration and when the impact on the terminated party of an abrupt termination is out of proportion to the benefit (or need) gained by the terminating party, courts should limit the seemingly unlimited right of termination. This limitation can come through the ideas of good faith and unconscionability already mentioned, or through the section of the Code which provides:

> Termination of a contract by one party except on the happening of an agreed event requires that reasonable notification be received by the other party and an agreement dispensing with notification is invalid if its operation would be unconscionable.[18]

Although notice of termination may be made *at any time*, that notice must pick a date of termination which is reasonable—considering the facts of the case involved.[19] If expenditures have been minimal and substitute goods can be quickly acquired, termination may be at once even though the terminated party complains that he will lose expected profits. Also, if the terminated party's losses are balanced by the terminating party's gains through termination, there is no

---

15. The leading pre-Code case was Bushwick-Decatur Motors, Inc. v. Ford Motor Co., 116 F.2d 675 (2d Cir. 1940). A Code case is Weilersbacher v. Pittsburgh Brewing Co., 421 Pa. 118, 218 A. 2d 806 (1966).

16. UCC § 1–203. The problem with using this section is that good faith is imposed on the "performance or enforcement" of the contract. It should not, however, take much ingenuity to conclude that exercise of a termination **right** is a *performance* of the entire contractual obligation and must be exercised in good faith. Tele-Controls, Inc. v. Ford Indus., Inc., 388 F.2d 48 (7th Cir. 1967).

17. UCC § 2–302. The problem with using this section is that it limits un-

conscionability to the time the contract was made. Termination clauses may be conscionable at that moment of time although unconscionable at the time of exercise. Sinkoff Beverage Co. v. Jos. Schlitz Brewing Co., 51 Misc.2d 446, 273 N.Y.S.2d 364 (Sup.Ct.1966). There is, however, no reason why predictable future events cannot be used to measure the agreement's conscionability when made, especially in view of UCC § 2–309(3) which measures one kind of termination unconscionability as of the time of its "operation." *See also* UCC § 2–719(3) discussed in § 103, *infra.*

18. UCC § 2–309(3).

19. Mastrian v. William Freihofer Baking Co., 45 Pa.D. & C.2d 237 (C.P.1968).

reason to delay the effective date of the termination. However, when the losses to the terminated party are greater than the other party's benefit (including avoided losses), the Code does not require that the absolute right to abrupt termination be lodged in the control of one of the parties to the contract.[20] In short, the open duration term is filled in by the Code, but only within bounds of reasonableness.

§ 40. Output, Requirements, and Exclusive Dealing Agreements

Subsection (1) of section 2–306 states:

> A term which measures the quantity by the output of the seller or the requirements of the buyer means such actual output or requirements as may occur in good faith, except that no quantity unreasonably disproportionate to any stated estimate or in the absence of a stated estimate to any normal or otherwise comparable prior output or requirements may be tendered or demanded.

While this subsection does not expressly make output and requirements agreements enforceable as contracts, the implication of validity is clear. The theoretical difficulty with these agreements has been that they border on being illusory. An agreement by a buyer to purchase from the seller all of a certain goods that he "requires" could be read to leave the buyer with a choice as to whether he wishes to require any goods at all; likewise, an agreement by which a seller agrees to sell all of his "output" to a buyer could be read to leave the seller free to control his output. Read thus, these agreements appear to leave one of the parties free to perform or not to perform as he sees fit.[21] There are, however, good commercial reasons for these agreements and recent common law courts have with unanimity found ways to uphold both output and requirements agreements if the only objection to their enforceability is that they are too indefinite.[22] The Code assumes the existence of the general common law rule validating output and requirements agreements and contains two rules of construction which further remove them from the claim that they are too indefinite to enforce. At the same time the Code gives some

20. See the excellent discussion of the problems involved in terminating franchise agreements in Gellhorn, *Limitations on Contract Termination Rights—Franchise Cancellations*, 1967 Duke L.J. 465.

21. American Trading Co. v. National Fibre & Insulation Co., 31 Del. 258, 114 A. 67 (1921).

22. Imperial Ref. Co. v. Kanotex Ref. Co., 29 F.2d 193 (8th Cir. 1928) (output contract); Oldershaw v. Kingsbaker Bros. Co., 53 Cal.App. 667, 200 P. 729 (1921) (output contract); Minnesota Lumber Co. v. Whitebreast Coal Co., 160 Ill. 85, 43 N.E. 774 (1895) (requirements contract); Mantell v. International Plastic Harmonica Corp., 141 N.J.Eq. 379, 55 A.2d 250 (Ct.Err. & App.1947) (output contract).

guidance to courts which are called upon to police these agreements. Quite naturally, this guidance cannot be in the form of specific amounts of goods which can be tendered or demanded; the parties to the agreement did not phrase their obligations in terms of specific amounts, and the Code does not attempt to dictate contract terms. The Code provides:

First, the measure of the quantity involved must be determined "in good faith." [23] The buyer in a requirements agreement or the seller in an output agreement is not free, with an uncontrolled discretion, to determine the quantity of goods which can be demanded or tendered under the agreement.[24] An example of a type of agreement in which one of the parties has an uncontrolled discretion would be one in which the buyer can order as much of a specified quantity of goods "as he wants." Such an agreement—absent any peculiar circumstances requiring a different construction of these words—leaves the buyer free to buy or not to buy at his discretion.[25] Such an "agreement" lacks mutuality of obligation, and amounts to no more than an offer by the seller which would become a contract with each order from the buyer, but which could be revoked by the seller at any time prior to acceptance.[26] The Code does not attempt to change this common law rule. However, an agreement by which the seller will sell and the buyer will buy all (or a stated portion) of the buyer's requirements does not leave the buyer free to order or not at his discretion. If the buyer has requirements, he is obliged to purchase those from the seller. Further, section 2–306 states that the buyer must exercise good faith in determining his requirements. The non-merchant must act with honesty in fact; [27] the merchant must meet this same test and, in addition, "is required to operate his plant or

23. The obligation of good faith was implied in pre-Code cases. William C. Atwater & Co. v. Terminal Coal Corp., 115 F.2d 887 (1st Cir. 1940); New York Central Iron Works v. U. S. Radiator Co., 174 N.Y. 331, 66 N.E. 967 (1903).

24. Lima Locomotive Mach. Co. v. National Steel Castings Co., 155 F. 77 (6th Cir. 1907).

25. Willard, Sutherland & Co. v. United States, 262 U.S. 489, 43 S.Ct. 592, 67 L.Ed. 1086 (1923); Wickham & Burton Coal Co. v. Farmers' Lumber Co., 189 Iowa 1183, 179 N.W. 417 (1920); Bailey v. Austrian, 19 Minn. 465 (1873). A seller may also reserve so much discretion that he has no obligation to deliver. If so, no contract results. Morrow v. Southern Express Co., 101 Ga. 810, 28 S.E. 998 (1897).

26. Nat Nal Service Stations, Inc. v. Wolf, 304 N.Y. 332, 107 N.E.2d 473 (1952). There are those inevitable problems of interpreting the language of the agreement to determine whether the parties have limited their freedom to buy from or sell to others. These problems will continue under the Code. E. g., Pittsburgh Plate Glass Co. v. H. Neuer Glass Co., 253 F. 161 (6th Cir. 1918); Ehrenworth v. Stuhmer & Co., 229 N.Y. 210, 128 N.E. 108 (1920). Cf. Oscar Schlegel Mfg. Co. v. Peter Cooper's Glue Factory, 231 N.Y. 459, 132 N.E. 148 (1921) (agreement not enforced, but probably the buyer was not buying "in good faith"; under the Code, this case could be decided on basis that orders greatly exceeded prior requirements).

27. UCC § 1–201(19).

conduct his business . . . according to commercial standards of fair dealing in the trade so that his . . . requirements will approximate a reasonably foreseeable figure." [28] The same test must be met by a seller under an output agreement.

Second, the Code provides a center around which the quantity is to be determined. The buyer cannot demand (thus the seller is not obligated to deliver) nor can the seller tender (thus the buyer is not obligated to take) any quantity which is "unreasonably disproportionate" to any estimate which the parties have stated or to any comparable prior requirements or output, if no estimate was stated. Thus, if a seller has agreed to deliver all of the buyer's requirements of a certain product and if the buyer has been ordering approximately 100 units each month, the seller would not be obligated to deliver 900 units in one month even though the buyer could prove that 900 units were "required" for his business.[29] Which prior period is "comparable" is a question of fact depending upon the nature of the business involved, but the Code does not require that the comparable period chosen be one in which these parties were dealing with each other. If this is the first output or requirements contract between these parties and if no estimate is stated, the Code allows *any* normal or comparable period involving the seller's output or the buyer's requirements to be used in measuring the obligations under such an agreement.

Even though the output and requirements agreements are made sufficiently definite enough for enforcement, difficult problems of determining the obligations under these agreements arise whenever there is an unexpected shift in the demand for or the price of the goods involved. In these instances, businessmen may look for ways to change their production schedules, altering their output (if a seller) or their requirements (if a buyer).

Attempts to increase or decrease "requirements" will promote disputes between the parties, some of which will call for judicial intervention. While these problems are not new to the Code,[30] the Code's "unreasonably disproportionate" test will provide a tool which, when combined with the requirement of good faith, will allow courts to

---

28. UCC § 2–306, Comment 2. See also UCC § 2–103(1) (b). A Code case involving the problems of this section is Gruschus v. C. R. Davis Contracting Co., 75 N.M. 649, 409 P.2d 500 (1965). The court held that "good faith" was a question of fact. For a later opinion, see 77 N.M. 614, 426 P.2d 589 (1967).

29. Massachusetts Gas & Elec. Light Supply Corp. v. V–M Corp., 387 F.2d 605 (1st Cir. 1967).

30. *See* Oscar Schlegel Mfg. Co. v. Peter Cooper's Glue Factory, 231 N.Y. 459, 132 N.E. 148 (1921).

police these disputes.[31] In an attempt to give further guidance in the solution of these problems the Comments provide:

> Reasonable elasticity in the requirements is expressly envisaged by this section and good faith variations from prior requirements are permitted even when the variation may be such as to result in discontinuance. A shut-down by a requirements buyer for lack of orders might be permissible when a shut-down merely to curtail losses would not. The essential test is whether the party is acting in good faith. Similarly, a sudden expansion of the plant by which requirements are to be measured would not be included within the scope of the contract as made but normal expansion undertaken in good faith would be within the scope of this section. One of the factors in an expansion situation would be whether the market price had risen greatly in a case in which the requirements contract contained a fixed price.[32]

The Code also provides that a lawful agreement which results in an exclusive dealing in goods imposes, unless otherwise agreed, "an obligation by the seller to use best efforts to supply the goods and by the buyer to use best efforts to promote their sale." [33] This requirement is a specific application of the general doctrine of good faith which the Code imposes on parties to an agreement.

A complete discussion of whether an output, requirements, or other exclusive dealing arrangement is "lawful" under section 2–306 is beyond the scope of this text. Their legality may depend upon the application of federal or state antitrust laws. A sale or lease of "commodities" in interstate commerce on condition that the purchaser or lessee agrees not to deal in competing commodities (exclusive dealing, requirements, and tying arrangements) is specifically proscribed by Section 3 of the Clayton Act "where the effect . . . may be to substantially lessen competition or tend to create a monopoly in any line of commerce." [34] Such arrangements, as well as output contracts, may also violate the Sherman Act [35] and the Federal Trade

---

31. Where the amount of goods delivered and accepted was unreasonably disproportionate to the estimate in seller's proposal (but not mentioned in buyer's acceptance), seller was entitled to extra compensation at the contract rate for the amount delivered in excess of the estimate. Romine, Inc. v. Savannah Steel Co., Inc., 117 Ga. App. 353, 160 S.E.2d 659 (1968).

32. UCC § 2–306, Comment 2. Good faith does not require that there be

requirements. *E. g.*, HML Corp. v. General Foods Corp., 365 F.2d 77 (3d Cir. 1966).

33. UCC § 2–306(2).

34. 38 Stat. 731 (1914), 15 U.S.C.A. § 14 (1964).

35. 26 Stat. 209 (1890), 15 U.S.C.A. §§ 1, 2 (1964).

Commission Act.[36] The Code recognizes that these statutes may affect these contracts by providing that only "lawful" agreements have the effect stated in the Code.

§ 41. Sale on Approval—Sale or Return

There are occasions in which a manufacturer or distributor consigns goods to a retailer. Although the consignment looks forward to a sale, there is no sale until the terms of the consignment are met. Consider the following factual pattern:

A manufacturer of electronic equipment has developed a small electronic desk calculator. These calculators are expensive, and it is not yet known whether they will sell in sufficient numbers to make their production profitable. The manufacturer would, however, like to place these calculators with retailers to learn what market does exist.

One method of distributing these calculators to retailers is by direct cash sales. This would require substantial investments by retailers for a product which may not sell; thus, their reluctance to invest in the full cost of these calculators is understandable. An alternative would be for the manufacturer to extend credit to the retailers for the total purchase price, taking a security interest in the calculators and filing financing statements in the appropriate state offices. Although the sale on credit obviates the necessity of a single large investment by the retailers, it still obligates the retailers to make the purchase and eventually to pay the price—obligations which retailers may be unwilling to assume with an item which may not be marketable.

The compromise has been the consignment—an agreement by which possession of goods is transferred but title is retained until the transferee sells the goods to some third party. In this agreement there is no sale at the time of transfer, and the transferee may return the goods even though they conform to the contract description. In short, this is either a *sale or a return*.

A similar arrangement is employed by retailers who sometimes deliver goods to customers "on approval." Again, there is no sale at the time possession is transferred. The sale does not occur until the customer approves, and he may disapprove (and return the goods) even though the goods conform to the contract. This arrangement is called a *sale on approval.*

36. 38 Stat. 721 (1914), 15 U.S.C.A. § 45 (1964). *See generally* Tampa Elec. Co. v. Nashville Coal Co., 365 U.S. 320, 81 S.Ct. 623, 5 L.Ed.2d 580 (1961); Day, *Exclusive Dealing, Tying and Reciprocity—A Reappraisal*, 29 Ohio St.L.J. 538 (1968).

The Code has two sections (2–326 and 2–327) which deal with these agreements. Section 2–326 defines the sale on approval and the sale or return, and then states some of the results of each of these arrangements. The definition is straight-forward: if the delivered goods may be returned by the transferee even though the goods conform to the contract, the transaction is:

(a) a "sale on approval" if the goods are delivered primarily for use, and

(b) a "sale or return" if the goods are delivered primarily for resale.[37]

One of the problems created by the sale on approval and by the sale or return is the effect of these transactions on creditors of the parties involved. Suppose that the manufacturer of the desk calculators decided to consign ten of these units to a specific retailer. This retailer now appears to be the owner of the calculators—that is, he has possession of them, they contain no tags indicating ownership by someone else, and there is no filed record of any third party's interest in them. To allow the manufacturer to recapture those calculators (on the theory that he is the bailor-owner) could be unfair to creditors who advanced credit to the retailer on the strength of the retailer's apparent ownership. In recognition of this potential misuse of the sale or return, the Code provides:

> Except as provided in subsection (3), goods held on approval are not subject to the claims of the buyer's creditors until acceptance; goods held on sale or return are subject to such claims while in the buyer's possession.[38]

This is the last reference in section 2–326 to the sale on approval: goods subject to such a transaction are not subject to the claims of the transferee's creditors. As soon as there has been an "approval," the sale takes place—probably on credit—title and risk of loss pass to the buyer,[39] and the goods do become subject to the claims of the buyer's creditors. This does not mean that those claims are necessarily superior to those of the seller. The seller ought to prevail

---

37. UCC § 2–326(1).

38. UCC § 2–326(2).

39. UCC § 2–327(1) (a). Subsections (b) and (c) state other incidents of the sale on approval: acceptance occurs on a failure to give the seller season-able notice of an election to return the goods, but use in accordance with the agreement is not acceptance (contrast UCC § 2–606, applicable to a regular sale); acceptance of part is acceptance of the whole of the goods (contrast UCC § 2–601); and return is at the seller's risk and expense.

over the buyer's creditors if the seller has complied with the provisions of Article 9 [40] or if he can bring the case within the application of section 2–702.[41]

Although section 2–326 is not drafted as tightly as it could have been, its purpose with regard to sale or return goods seems clear: if those goods are delivered to a person (1) who maintains a place of business, (2) at which he deals in goods of the kind involved, and (3) if that place of business is under a name other than the name of the transferor, "then" (that is, if the three conditions are met) the transaction is a "sale or return" with respect to the "claims of creditors of the person conducting the business." [42] Reading this conclusion into the subsection quoted in full above, this means that those goods are subject to the claims of the transferee's creditors. This result follows irrespective of whether the terms of the agreement between the transferor and the transferee reserve title to the transferor or contain such phrases as "on consignment" or "on memorandum." [43] Thus, the "sale or return" features of an agreement cannot be changed by any language of the agreement if the transferee may without liability return conforming goods to the transferor.

Section 2–326(3) goes on to state that the subsection is not applicable if the person making delivery does one of three things: [44]

(a) complies with an applicable law providing for a consignor's interest or the like to be evidenced by a sign,[45] or

(b) establishes that the person conducting the business is generally known by his creditors to be substantially engaged in selling the goods of others,[46] or

(c) complies with the filing provisions of the Article on Secured Transactions (Article 9).

40. In most instances, sale or return goods will be inventory (UCC § 9–109 (4)) for which a financing statement must be filed (UCC § 9–302). The place of filing is determined by UCC § 9–401; the priority of the security interests is determined by UCC § 9–312. If the consignment is intended as security for credit extended, a security interest subject to Article 9 has been created. See UCC §§ 1–201 (37) and 9–102(2).

41. §§ 165–71 *infra*.

42. UCC § 2–326(3).

43. *In re* Murta, Appleton Co., 2 UCC Rep. 620 (U.S.Dist.Ct.E.D.Pa.1964); General Elec. Co. v. Pettingill Supply Co., 347 Mass. 631, 199 N.E.2d 326 (1964).

44. This section of the Code does not deal with the right to return nonconforming goods. UCC § 2–326, Comment 1.

45. It is not enough to put signs on the property; there must be an applicable consignment statute providing for signs. *In re* Levy, 3 UCC Rep. 291 (U.S.Dist.Ct.E.D.Pa.1965); *In re* Downtown Drug Store, Inc., 3 UCC Rep. 27 (U.S.Dist.Ct.E.D.Pa.1965); Vonins, Inc. v. Raff, 101 N.J.Super. 172, 243 A.2d 836 (App.Div.1968).

46. Vonins, Inc. v. Raff, 101 N.J.Super. 172, 243 A.2d 836 (App.Div.1968).

Certainly, no seller planning a sale or return ought to rely on trying to establish the first two facts. Signs are easily removed; what is generally known to creditors becomes difficult to prove, especially when those same creditors are competing for priority. Thus, filing is the only safe alternative. The other two alternatives are available, however, in situations in which the seller has not filed. The purpose of providing these three exceptions to section 2–326 is clear: in each (signs, general knowledge, or filing) creditors of the transferee know or should know that the goods are not the transferee's.

The result of failing to comply with any of these alternatives is that the sale or return goods are subject to the claims of the transferee's creditors while the goods are in the transferee's possession. Thus far, most of the cases have presented situations in which a trustee in bankruptcy (or assignee for the benefit of creditors) has used this section in an effort to obtain priority as to the goods, leaving the noncomplying seller with an unsecured claim against the transferee's estate.[47] Such a use comports with the express language of the statute, but can often result in increasing the size of the bankrupt estate at the expense of the transferor and for the benefit of creditors who did not in fact rely on the buyer's ownership of the goods involved. Such a result may be justified when the seller is a merchant—as in the case of the manufacturer or distributor attempting to market the new desk calculators—but becomes questionable when a consumer has left goods with a retailer to be sold on a commission basis. The consumer knows little of filing, signs, or the general knowledge of creditors. Unless a creditor of the retailer has specifically relied on the retailer's possession of these goods, there seems no reason to prefer the creditor over the the consumer.[48] One case has reached this result but without adequate discussion.[49]

The phrase "subject to the claims of creditors" is broader than the bankruptcy cases which have thus far found their way to the courts. Creditors may rely on the transferee's indicia of ownership and perfect a security interest in the sale or return goods while they are in the possession of the transferee. If the seller cannot establish

---

47. *In re* Bankston, 3 UCC Rep. 345 (U.S.Dist.Ct.N.D.Ga.1966); *In re* Griffin, 1 UCC Rep. 492 (U.S.Dist.Ct. W.D.Pa.1960); Guardian Discount Co. v. Settles, 114 Ga.App. 418, 151 S.E. 2d 530 (1966) (trover); *In re* Mincow Bag Co., 29 A.D.2d 400, 288 N.Y.S.2d 364 (1968), *aff'd* 24 N.Y.2d 776, 300 N.Y.S.2d 115, 248 N.E.2d 26 (1969); 4A Collier, Bankruptcy ¶ 70.62A[7.4] (14th ed. 1969).

48. Specific reliance here should be the extension of credit and the taking of a security interest in the goods while in the possession of the retailer. See Article 9 of the Uniform Commercial Code.

49. Allgeier v. Campisi, 117 Ga.App. 105, 159 S.E.2d 458 (1968). *Cf.* McDonald v. Peoples Auto. Loan & Fin. Corp., 115 Ga.App. 483, 154 S.E.2d 886 (1967), where the transferor was a wholesaler.

any of the three alternatives, the secured claim of the creditors ought to be protected under the language of section 2–326 and the scope of Article 9.

Section 2–326 contains a final subsection:

> Any "or return" term of a contract for sale is to be treated as a separate contract for sale within the statute of frauds section of this Article (Section 2–201) and as contradicting the sale aspect of the contract within the provisions of this Article on parol or extrinsic evidence (Section 2–202).[50]

The sale or return contract is different from the sale on approval in that with the former the goods are held at the transferee's risk until their return to the seller. Further, the transferee is not required to accept all of the goods if he accepts any part of them. The nature of the sale or return is that any unsold goods may be returned providing the option to return is exercised seasonably.[51]

§ 42. Auction Sales

Special rules are provided by Article 2 for the sale by auction.[52] These rules apply to all auction sales involving goods whether or not the auction is being used to foreclose a security interest in the goods.[53]

There are two kinds of auction sales: with reserve and without reserve. These terms refer to whether the seller has reserved the privilege of withdrawing the goods after a bid has been made, but before the hammer has fallen.

"With reserve" auctions. Auctions are "with reserve unless the goods are in explicit terms put up without reserve."[54] Thus, a statement that an item is to be sold to the highest bidder does not prevent the seller from withdrawing the goods during the bidding. In auctions "with reserve" the goods may be withdrawn at any time—even though there are outstanding bids—until the auctioneer announces that the sale is complete. If the goods are withdrawn, there is no contract with the bidder who made the highest bid, and such bidder has no claim for damages based upon breach of contract.[55]

"Without reserve" auctions. In an auction "without reserve" the item cannot be withdrawn after the call for bids unless no bid is

---

50. UCC § 2–326(4).

51. UCC § 2–327(2).

52. UCC § 2–328.

53. UCC § 9–504(1).

54. UCC § 2–328(3). "In a sale by auction if goods are put up in lots each lot is the subject of a separate sale." UCC § 2–328(1).

55. Drew v. John Deere Co., 19 A.D.2d 308, 241 N.Y.S.2d 267 (1963).

made within a reasonable time, but there is no requirement that the goods be "put up" for bids by the auctioneer.[56]

In both types of auctions the bidder may withdraw his bid prior to the auctioneer's announcement that the sale has been completed. However, "a bidder's retraction does not revive any previous bid." [57]

The auction sale for any item terminates with the fall of the hammer or in any other customary manner. At that time title and risk of loss pass to the buyer.[58] If a bid is made while the hammer is falling, the auctioneer may ignore the bid made while the hammer was falling and declare the goods sold to the prior bidder, or he may reopen the bidding. If he reopens the bidding, the bid which was made while the hammer was falling becomes the high bid, the prior bid is discharged, and the auction proceeds from that point.[59]

This section also contains a provision dealing with the effect of a sale in which the seller has forced up the price, either by personally bidding at the sale or by procuring a bid in his behalf. That section provides:

> If the auctioneer knowingly receives a bid on the seller's behalf or the seller makes or procures such a bid, and notice has not been given that liberty for such bidding is reserved, the buyer may at his option avoid the sale or take the goods at the price of the last good faith bid prior to the completion of the sale. This subsection shall not apply to any bid at a forced sale.[60]

§ 43. Modification and Waiver

In the normal sales transaction the parties conclude their negotiations with a signed writing, an exchange of memoranda, or perhaps a handshake. If their oral negotiations or writings have created an enforceable agreement—that is, a contract—the court, in the event of a dispute, must interpret the parties' language to determine the obligations which were created by the terms of the agreement.[61] The basic assumption of this approach to contract formation is that the terms become set as of the time of the contract and, even though the Code relaxes the requirement that the exact moment that the contract was made be determined,[62] nevertheless there is some point in

---

56. UCC § 2–328, Comment 2.

57. UCC § 2–328(3).

58. Diefenbach v. Gorney, 93 Ill.App. 2d 51, 234 N.E.2d 813 (1968).

59. UCC § 2–328(2).

60. UCC § 2–328(4).

61. See §§ 46–53 *infra*.

62. UCC § 2–204(2). Perhaps the "basis of the bargain" test of UCC § 2–313 also expands the time during which statements, descriptions, models, and

time when the bargain has been struck and the terms have created rights and obligations.

There are occasions, however, in which the parties attempt to modify the terms of their contract at some time subsequent to its formation. This attempt created conceptual difficulties for pre-Code courts: the rights and duties had already been fixed by the contract; to alter these rights and duties required some new consideration.[63] The Code has eliminated this requirement by providing: "An agreement modifying a contract within this Article needs no consideration to be binding." [64] The contract must be "within this Article"—that is, must be for the sale of goods. The sale may also include the creation of a security interest within Article 9 and still be a sale within Article 2,[65] but modification of transactions not falling within Article 2 are not expressly covered by this section of the Code—except as courts believe that the section states a principle of general law.

There is good reason for the Code's relaxation of the consideration requirement for modifications. Consideration is the tool by which courts sort out those promises which ought to be enforced from those which do not merit intervention of the legal system—those which rest on an exchange or are followed by an anticipated substantial reliance [66] from those which appear to be no more than a promise to make a gift. This search may have validity when the problem is one of original contract formation, but once the parties have reached the contract stage, promises to forgo a right are normally made with an understanding of the consequences. Enforcement is not apt to create surprise, is not apt to leave businessmen thinking that someone has received something for nothing. Thus, the drafters of the Code eliminated the requirement of consideration when parties agree to a modification of an existing contract.[67]

samples become express warranties. See § 67 *infra.*

63. Rexite Casting Co. v. Midwest Mower Corp., 267 S.W.2d 327 (Mo.Ct.App. 1954); Moffitt v. Hieby, 149 Tex. 161, 229 S.W.2d 1005 (1950). These cases involved a change in price. For a case involving an allegation of an added warranty after the sale, see Connell v. Diamond T. Truck Co., 88 N.H. 316, 188 A. 463 (1936). Cases on this point are so numerous that adding citations has been described as being like "carrying coals to New Castle." Lingenfelder v. Wainwright Brewing Co., 103 Mo. 578, 593, 15 S.W. 844, 848 (1891). Cases are collected in Note, 39 Cornell L.Q. 114 (1953).

64. UCC § 2–209(1). *See also* UCC § 3–605(1) (b). If the waiver or renunciation is in writing and is signed and delivered by the aggrieved party, UCC § 1–107 allows a claim arising out of breach to be discharged without consideration.

65. Asco Mining Co. v. Gross Contracting Co., 3 UCC Rep. 293 (Pa.C.P. 1965).

66. Goodman v. Dicker, 83 U.S.App.D.C. 353, 169 F.2d 684 (1948).

67. Lunsford v. Wilson, 113 Ga.App. 602, 149 S.E.2d 515 (1966); Skinner v. Tober Foreign Motors, Inc., 345 Mass. 429, 187 N.E.2d 669 (1963).

Elimination of the requirement of consideration does not, however, eliminate the need to police carefully agreements to modify a contract. There are situations in which the existence of the contract increases the bargaining power of one of the parties and, if he uses this power to extract a new agreement, that new agreement ought not be enforced by the courts.[68] For example, a buyer who has concluded a long-term requirements contract may have so re-arranged the operation of his business that it would be expensive for him to secure goods from another source if this seller refuses to supply those requirements. Such a seller may be tempted to use his increased bargaining power to extract an increase in price, arguing later that all that was accomplished was a "modification" for which no new consideration was needed. Pre-Code law would classify such tactics as duress; the Code's Comments indicate that such a modification would fail because of the doctrine of good faith imposed by the Code.[69] Further, even a technical consideration will not support a modification made in bad faith.

Even though the drafters intended to give parties more freedom in adjusting their contractual rights and duties, they hedged this freedom in situations involving oral modifications so that modifications could not "be conjured up by oral testimony."[70] The fear that liars may win lawsuits produced two rules which may result in the exclusion of testimony of modifications which were in fact made. These rules are contained in subsections (2) and (3) of section 2–209:

> (2) A signed agreement which excludes modification or rescission except by a signed writing cannot be otherwise modified or rescinded, but except as between merchants such a requirement on a form supplied by the merchant must be separately signed by the other party.

> (3) The requirements of the statute of frauds section of this Article (Section 2–201) must be satisfied if the contract as modified is within its provisions.

The probable result of the first rule is that many printed forms will contain a no-modification-unless-in-writing clause. While the consumer will be protected unless such a clause is brought to his attention for his signature, these clauses will have their impact in contracts between merchants. A court will be able to point to the printed form and tell the party who has alleged an oral modification of the written agreement that if his argument "were to prevail, contractual

---

68. Alaska Packer's Ass'n v. Domenico, 117 F. 99 (9th Cir. 1902), is an example in a case involving a contract for services.

69. UCC § 2–209, Comment 2.

70. UCC § 2–209, Comment 3.

obligations would become phantoms, solemn obligations would run like pressed quicksilver, and the whole edifice of business would rest on sand dunes supporting pillars of rubber and floors of turf. Chaos would envelop the commercial world." [71]

The second rule is more general, operating even when there is no signed agreement excluding oral modification. In general, the idea of requiring the *modified contract* to be in writing sounds as fair as that of requiring the original agreement to be in writing whenever the price of the goods is $500 or more. In the easy case this would mean that evidence could be introduced to show that the original agreement to buy and sell goods for $600 (presumably in writing) was modified later to reduce the price to $450, but not show a reduction to $550. The first modified contract is under the dollar limits of section 2–201; the second is not. There are, however, difficulties lurking in this second rule.

Suppose that the first agreement to buy and sell goods for $600 had been oral and that none of the provisions of the Code's statute of frauds had been satisfied. Such an agreement would not be enforceable "by way of action or defense." Thus, if the seller sought to enforce the agreement, the statute would be a defense for the buyer. Nevertheless, suppose that the seller has begun a suit for damages allegedly caused by the buyer's failure to perform the oral agreement. The statute poses a dilemma for the buyer's attorney if the buyer states that, following the original agreement, the parties orally modified the price to $550 and that the buyer would like to make the purchase at that price, but the seller has refused to deliver except for $600. Pleading the modification might amount to an admission of the original agreement—making that enforceable; but, since the modification was also oral, the $550 agreement could not be enforced unless the seller was cooperative and admitted the making of that agreement—a quality which the buyer's attorney ought not ascribe to the seller at the time defenses are being asserted. The result of pleading the modification, therefore, could be that the court will be required to enforce an agreement which the parties displaced with a later modification, solely because the buyer attempted to present the entire transaction to the court. Failure to plead the oral modification appears at first to be the safest course for the buyer (he would not then run the risk of having admitted the $600 oral agreement), but at the pleading stage of the suit the buyer's attorney may not know whether the seller can satisfy the statute by facts other than a writing. If it turns out that the seller has such facts, the failure to plead the modification might later pre-

71. C.I.T. Corp. v. Jonnet, 419 Pa. 435, 438, 214 A.2d 620, 622 (1965).

vent the buyer from attempting to show the $550 oral agreement. Again, the result would be that the court would be required to enforce an agreement which did not represent the entire transaction between the parties.

Next, suppose that the first agreement was in writing, but that the modification to $550 was oral. Nevertheless, the statute of frauds can be "satisfied" by showing that the goods were delivered and accepted *after* the oral modification.[72] The drafter's purpose of securing a writing has been frustrated in those cases in which the oral modification comes between the time of the first agreement and the delivery of the goods, but if the oral modification comes after delivery, evidence of the modification is not admissible—unless the statute of frauds can be satisfied by the other party's admission in court.[73]

Finally, the modifications suggested above assume that the change by the parties was in the total price of the goods. Modifications, however, may occur as to any one of a number of other terms in the contract. Warranties may be increased or limited, delivery schedules may be delayed, or payment dates may be extended. All of these later agreements, if oral, will not be enforceable by way of action or defense if the total price of the goods is $500 or more. The original written agreement is enforced without the court's ever hearing any evidence of the modification. From this discussion at least this much can be gleaned: *all* modifications of existing contracts should be reduced to writing to obviate the uncertainties of section 2–209.

Clearly, not all parties will heed this advice. They will continue to deal on the telephone and not stop to think that the modification which they just made ought to be written to be enforced. Up to this point the Code has built an almost impenetrable barrier to their ability to prove the oral modification. Only the small cases (those under $500), and perhaps a few others by mistake, have slipped through that barrier. However, subsections (4) and (5) of section 2–209 do a quick about-face, and that which was taken away under the prior two rules may be given back to the party who failed to secure a writing evidencing the modification:

> (4) Although an attempt at modification or rescission does not satisfy the requirements of subsection (2) or (3) it can operate as a waiver.

> (5) A party who has made a waiver affecting an executory portion of the contract may retract the waiver by reasonable notification received by the other party that strict

---

72. UCC § 2–201(3) (c).

73. UCC § 2–201(3) (b). Compare UCC § 1–107.

performance will be required of any term waiver, unless the retraction would be unjust in view of a material change of position in reliance on the waiver.

The Code does not define "waiver," and waiver is a sufficiently ambiguous word [74] so that courts can admit evidence of almost any alleged oral modification to see whether that evidence—although not sufficient to operate as a modification in and of itself—will "operate as a waiver." The Code does not state what it is that is being waived. Is it the substantive contract term—the $600 figure? Or is it the term preventing oral modifications and the statute of frauds which are being waived? The Comments read as if the second meaning is the one intended by the drafters.[75] If so, the chaos which is about to envelop the business world appears to rest on the pleader. If he pleads only oral modification, evidence of the alleged agreement is excluded; if he adds an allegation of waiver, the evidence is admitted.[76] Such is the stuff out of which section 2–209 is made.

Nevertheless, there is a purpose to section 2–209. It is the same purpose which underlies all statutes of frauds. Liars ought not win through perjured testimony, but the existence of a writing should not prevent the court from seeking out the truth. The parties and the court are cautioned about the need for a writing to support oral modifications, but if the court is convinced that one of the parties has freely relinquished a known right, he will not be allowed to recapture that right by showing an earlier writing. The concept of "waiver" is sufficiently flexible to allow a court to justify its decisions whenever a signed writing has allegedly been modified by a later oral agreement.[77]

---

74. Contrast Globe Mut. Life Ins. Co. v. Wolff, 95 U.S. 326, 333, 24 L.Ed. 387, 390 (1877) (the "doctrine of waiver . . . is only another name for the doctrine of estoppel"), with Hayes v. Manning, 263 Mo. 1, 45, 172 S.W. 897, 907 (1914) (quoting "estoppel *in pais* has connections in no wise akin to waiver"). Some courts require consideration for waiver, Smith v. Minneapolis Threshing Mach. Co., 89 Okl. 156, 214 P. 178 (1923), while others do not, Champion Spark Plug Co. v. Automobile Sundries Co., 273 F. 74 (2d Cir. 1921). The result is that there is no one meaning for the word "waiver" because of the many tasks it is asked to solve. Certainly, consideration ought not be required for a UCC § 2–209 waiver, except in those rare instances in which one party attempts to "waive" the entire consideration due from the other party—thereby turning a contractual promise into a gift promise. Waiver under UCC § 2–209 ought to be found when the oral modification is one which would have been enforced had it been the original agreement and when the court finds that the oral modification was in fact entered into without concern by the parties for the printed forms or the Code's statute of frauds.

75. UCC § 2–209, Comment 4.

76. C.I.T. Corp. v. Jonnet, 419 Pa. 435, 214 A.2d 620 (1965).

77. Nor would the parol evidence rule, which applies to prior or contemporaneous agreements, prevent the introduction of evidence of the later oral modification. *See* UCC § 2–202.

§ 44.   Unconscionable Contracts and Unconscionable Terms

One of the most controversial sections of Article 2 is section 2–302 dealing with unconscionable contracts and unconscionable clauses in a contract:

(1) If the court as a matter of law finds the contract or any clause of the contract to have been unconscionable at the time it was made the court may refuse to enforce the contract, or it may enforce the remainder of the contract without the unconscionable clause, or it may so limit the application of any unconscionable clause as to avoid any unconscionable result.

(2) When it is claimed or appears to the court that the contract or any clause thereof may be unconscionable the parties shall be afforded a reasonable opportunity to present evidence as to its commercial setting, purpose and effect to aid the court in making the determination.

Summarizing the principal points in this section: whether the contract or clause is unconscionable is to be determined as of the time the contract was made;[78] unconscionability is to be determined as a matter of law, not as a question of fact for the jury, but evidence is admissible to show the commercial setting, purpose, and effect of the contract or clause;[79] the court is not limited to the single remedy of refusal to enforce the entire agreement, but may in an appropriate case strike the clause which is unconscionable or limit the clause to

---

78. Thus, a change in price between the date of the contract and the time of delivery will not make the price clause unconscionable. UCC § 2–302 is not to be used to change an agreement solely because that agreement causes hardship on one of the parties. See cases cited in footnote 87 *infra* this section. There are instances, however, in which special types of unconscionability may be measured at some date after the agreement is reached. UCC § 2–309(3) discussed in § 39 *supra* and UCC § 2–719(3) discussed in § 103 *infra*.

California and North Carolina did not adopt UCC § 2–302 when they enacted the Code.

79. This section will present problems for the trial lawyer and judge. Once unconscionability is claimed and the judge believes that the clause may be unconscionable, evidence is admissible to aid the court in reaching a decision.

Dow Corning Corp. v. Capitol Aviation, Inc., 411 F.2d 622 (7th Cir. 1969); *In re* Elkins-Dell Mfg. Co., 253 F.Supp. 864 (E.D.Pa.1966); E. F. Lynch, Inc. v. Piccirilli, 28 Mass.App.Dec. 49 (1964); Central Budget Corp. v. Sanchez, 53 Misc.2d 620, 279 N.Y.S.2d 391 (Civ.Ct. 1967). Supposedly this evidence will be received outside the hearing of the jury, because conscionability is a matter of law for the court to decide. However, the evidence presented may convince the judge that the clause is conscionable but the jury, which did not hear the evidence, may adjust its verdict to reflect its notions of fair play—and the adjustment may not have been made if it, too, could have heard the evidence. Moreover, this section is silent as to who bears the burden of proof, and no appellate case has as yet discussed the problem at any length.

avoid an unconscionable result. Thus, through section 2–302 courts are given the express authority to remake, modify, or rescind sales agreements.

The existence of this authority did not originate with the Code. Courts have long policed agreements under vague standards of fairness, only the policing was done through diverse principles of law which defied systematic study. Rules of interpretation and construction, manipulation of the doctrines of assent, application of public policy, measurement of the adequacy of the consideration, and findings of duress, overreaching, and sharp practice—all of these, as well as other doctrines, were called into play to reach a sensible result in the case before the court.[80] Now, the policing can be overt and, since the problem is one of law for the court, the decisions will result in precedents in which the standard of fairness—once vague—can be examined and refined.

The Code does not define "unconscionability," nor is it suggested that such a definition ought to be attempted.[81] The strength of this clause lies in the belief that courts can solve problems of unconscionability on a case-by-case basis rather than through some tight definition of terms. The Comments (which can be criticized both as to content and sentence structure) give some idea of what the drafters had in mind:

> The basic test is whether, in the light of the general commercial background and the commercial needs of the particular trade or case, the clauses involved are so one-sided as to be unconscionable under the circumstances existing at the time of the making of the contract. . . . The principle is one of the prevention of oppression and unfair surprise . . . and not of disturbance of allocation of risks because of superior bargaining power.[82]

The Comment sentences can easily be criticized. Superior bargaining power tends to produce one-sided agreements, and what help is it to be told that the basic test of unconscionability is whether the clauses "are so one-sided as to be unconscionable"? Little is gained in defining a word in terms of itself. Yet, through the words chosen,

---

80. Many of these ideas appear in the pre-Code case of Henningsen v. Bloomfield Motors, Inc., 32 N.J. 358, 161 A.2d 69 (1960), discussed in § 92 *infra*. See also Henry v. W. S. Reichenbach & Son, 45 Pa.D. & C.2d 171 (C.P.1968), a Code case which relied on rules of interpretation rather than on UCC § 2–302.

81. For a critical analysis of UCC § 2–302—and one considerably different from that of this text—see Leff, *Unconscionability and the Code—the Emperor's New Clause*, 115 U.Pa.L. Rev. 485 (1967).

82. UCC § 2–302, Comment 1.

certain ideas emerge. Those ideas center on the two concepts suggested by the Comments: (1) unfair surprise and (2) oppression.[83]

Unfair surprise. This branch of unconscionability will have its greatest impact on situations involving the form contract, although it is by no means limited to the form contract. A typical case might contain these facts:

A buyer has succumbed to an intensive advertising campaign and has decided that he needs a specific item of consumer goods. The buyer visited several retail stores to compare prices on the item involved, and was finally ready to make the purchase. He and the salesman may have dickered as to the color, price, and terms of payment, but at last an agreement was reached. The buyer and seller made a "deal"—they agreed upon the product, its price, and the terms of payment. At this point the seller submitted to the buyer a printed document containing two pages of carefully drafted clauses, designed to protect the seller. The buyer affixed his signature on the appropriate line and received the product. Later the product proved to be defective, but the buyer's claims were met by the seller's reliance on a printed clause which absolved the seller from liability for any defect in the goods.

Such a buyer is surprised to find these clauses in the writing which he signed. His deal had nothing to do with the printed document. In effect, it is as if the parties had made two contracts: one was hammered out through negotiation or was, at the least, clearly understood by both even if presented by one party on a take-it-or-leave-it basis; the other contract was the printed form which the buyer signed to get the product or the financing.[84] It is the second contract at which the doctrine of unfair surprise is aimed. The resulting total agreement ought not unfairly surprise the buyer as he considers the transaction which he completed. To say to the buyer that he is bound by the printed clause because he ought to have read what he signed is to ignore the commercial realities of the sale and purchase of consumer goods. On the other hand, to say to the seller that the buyer is bound by nothing that he signs unless he has read each clause places too great a strain on the certainty which ought to accompany commercial transactions. The answer lies, as it did before the Code, between these two extremes. The parties are free to contract and their contract may be evidenced by printed forms which turn out to surprise one of the parties, but the Code states that the resulting agreement must not be unconscionable—the surprise must not be *unfair*.

---

83. *In re* Elkins-Dell Mfg. Co., 253 F.Supp. 864, 871 (E.D.Pa.1966).

84. Llewellyn, Common Law Tradition 370–71 (1960).

Many factors go into the determination of whether an unfair surprise is involved. These factors include the relation of the parties, whether the seller sought out the customer or whether the customer sought out the seller, the sales techniques involved, whether all form contracts in this industry contain the same clause thereby preventing this buyer from shopping for better terms, and how unexpected the clause is in this type of transaction.[85] Such an approach emphasizes the surprise to the party claiming unconscionability, but it is equally possible to view the "unfair surprise" branch of unconscionability by looking at the expectations of the party resisting the claim of unconscionability (the seller in the assumed case): when the transaction was consummated and the names had been affixed to the writing, did the party who is now asserting that the clause settles the dispute have a *reasonable* expectation that this clause was understood as as a part of the agreement? If not, the clause should not be enforced; if so, the clause is a part of the contract unless it is oppressive.[86]

Oppression. Even though both parties understood the exact terms of the agreement, the resulting agreement may be so oppressive on one of the parties that it ought not be enforced. Such a notion does violence to the symmetry of the doctrine of freedom of contract, but courts have long allowed legislation to prescribe limits within which parties are free to bargain. The idea of unconscionability is nothing more than a statutory recognition of doctrines courts have applied in assuring that parties have in fact had a *freedom* to contract:

---

85. Frostifresh Corp. v. Reynoso, 52 Misc.2d 26, 274 N.Y.S.2d 757 (Dist.Ct. 1966), *rev'd on amount of recovery* 54 Misc.2d 119, 281 N.Y.S.2d 964 (App.T. 1967); *In re* New York v. ITM, Inc., 52 Misc.2d 39, 275 N.Y.S.2d 774 (Sup.Ct. 1966); Henningsen v. Bloomfield Motors, Inc., 32 N.J. 358, 161 A.2d 69 (1960).

86. A New York bank inserted a waiver-of-jury clause in its signature cards and on monthly statements. The Civil Court held the clause unenforceable, relying in part on UCC § 2–302 and the ideas of unfair surprise. David v. Manufacturers Hanover Trust Co., 55 Misc.2d 1080, 287 N.Y.S.2d 503 (Civ.Ct. 1968). This decision was reversed by Appellate Term when the court concluded that the clause was sufficiently clear—hence, no surprise. 59 Misc.2d 248, 298 N.Y.S.2d 847 (App.T.1969). Neither opinion considered whether such a clause was oppressive, even if not surprising.

The Appellate Term in *David* did not discuss UCC § 2–302. It concluded that public policy imposes no limitation on freedom of contract between a bank and its depositor. The three cases cited are not persuasive. In one case the court construed the agreement so that it did not absolve the bank for the loss. Isler v. National Park Bank, 239 N.Y. 462, 147 N.E. 66 (1925). The other two involved stop payment orders which the bank overlooked. Gaita v. Windsor Bank, 251 N.Y. 152, 167 N.E. 203 (1929); Seldowitz v. Manufacturer's Trust Co., 34 Misc.2d 111, 202 N.Y.S.2d 129 (App.T.1960). The Code's answer to these two cases is UCC §§ 4–103(1) and 4–403. 1955 N.Y.Law Rev. Comm'n Rep. (vol. 2) 1501–09. The UCC § 2–302 aspects of *David* can be explained on the basis that the case did not involve a transaction in goods. UCC § 2–102(1). If these waiver-of-jury clauses become popular in sales agreements, the problem of their Code conscionability will be squarely presented.

a party with the superior bargaining position may not use that position to force a contract which is oppressive on the other party.

Again, care must be used in application of this doctrine. The Code does not suggest that courts should remake agreements simply because one party finds that he made a bad or foolish deal. That one party now wishes that he had bargained for a different price or included (or limited) a clause in the agreement does not make the resulting agreement unconscionable.[87] The test is much harder to meet. The agreement must have crossed from the arena of allowable pressure into the fact of oppression.

Many of the factors which were appropriate to a determination of unfair surprise are relevant to a decision as to whether the resulting agreement was oppressive. Did the seller seek out the customer or did the customer seek out the seller? Did the sales techniques (or the purchase techniques of a buyer in a situation in which the buyer has the superior bargaining position) border on fraud and duress? Did the complaining party have a choice as to terms in making this agreement?[88] Returning to the suggested test for the unfair-surprise unconscionability, and modifying it only slightly: when the transaction was consummated and the names had been affixed to the writing, did the party who is now asserting that the clause settles the dispute have a *justifiable* expectation that this clause would be enforced by a court?[89]

The best known unconscionability case arose in the District of Columbia before the Code became applicable in that jurisdiction. Nevertheless, a majority of the court relied in part on section 2–303 to reach its decision. In *Williams v. Walker-Thomas Furniture Co.*[90] the retailer sold consumer goods and took a security interest in the goods. The agreement between the retailer and customer contained an "add-on" provision which consolidated all unpaid installment sales made by this retailer to this customer so that a security interest was retained in all items sold until the entire account was paid. The customer defaulted and the retailer sought to replevy everything purchased during the past five years, although the total payments left a balance due of less than the purchase price of the last item purchased.

---

87. *In re* Elkins-Dell Mfg. Co., 253 F.Supp. 864 (E.D.Pa.1966). *See* Romine, Inc. v. Savannah Steel Co., 117 Ga.App. 353, 160 S.E.2d 659 (1968); Hernandez v. S. I. C. Fin. Co., 79 N.M. 673, 448 P.2d 474 (1968).

88. **Delta Air** Lines, Inc. v. Douglas Aircraft Co., 238 Cal.App.2d 95, 47 Cal. Rptr. 518 (1965).

89. In dictum, it has been stated that a specific disclaimer of liability will not be effective if the goods are worthless. Vlases v. Montgomery Ward & Co., 377 F.2d 846, 850 (3d Cir. 1967).

90. 121 U.S.App.D.C. 315, 350 F.2d 445 (1965).

The customer claimed that the contract was unconscionable. In holding that the trial court had the power to determine whether this agreement was in fact unconscionable, the court stated:

> Unconscionability has generally been recognized to include an absence of meaningful choice on the part of one of the parties together with contract terms which are unreasonably favorable to the other party. Whether a meaningful choice is present in a particular case can only be determined by consideration of all the circumstances surrounding the transaction. In many cases the meaningfulness of the choice is negated by a gross inequality of bargaining power. The manner in which the contract was entered is also relevant to this consideration.[91]

At this point the court is concerned about oppression—even though the party knew the terms, there was no meaningful choice. The court went on to cross over to ideas of unfair surprise:

> Did each party to the contract, considering his obvious education or lack of it, have a reasonable opportunity to understand the terms of the contract, or were the important terms hidden in a maze of fine print and minimized by deceptive sales practices? . . . In such a case the usual rule that the terms of the agreement are not to be questioned should be abandoned and the court should consider whether the terms of the contract are so unfair that enforcement should be withheld.[92]

This text has not attempted to define the point at which conscionability ends and unconscionability begins. Any such attempt would fail because too many combinations of facts are possible. Often fraud or some type of duress will accompany the unconscionability,[93] but neither fraud nor duress is necessary for the application of section 2–302. When the unconscionability affects the price agreed upon, courts are willing to remake the price or rescind the contract.[94] Like-

---

91. *Id.* at 449.

92. *Id.* at 449–50. This case is discussed in Skilton and Helstad, *Protection of the Installment Buyer of Goods Under the Uniform Commercial Code*, 65 Mich.L.Rev. 1465, 1476–82 (1967).

93. Toker v. Perl, 103 N.J.Super. 500, 247 A.2d 701 (L.Div.1968), *aff'd* 108 N.J.Super. 129, 260 A.2d 244 (App.Div. 1970).

94. American Home Improvement, Inc. v. MacIver, 105 N.H. 435, 201 A.2d 886

(1964); Toker v. Perl, 103 N.J. Super. 500, 247 A.2d 701 (L.Div.1968) *aff'd* 108 N.J.Super. 129, 260 A.2d 244 (App.Div.1970); Frostifresh Corp. v. Reynoso, 52 Misc.2d 26, 274 N.Y.S.2d 757 (Dist.Ct.1966), *rev'd on question of amount of recovery* 54 Misc.2d 119, 281 N.Y.S.2d 964 (App.T.1967); Jones v. Star Credit Corp., 59 Misc.2d 189, 298 N.Y.S.2d 264 (Sup.Ct.1969); *In re* New York v. ITM, Inc., 52 Misc.2d 39, 275 N.Y.S.2d 774 (Sup.Ct.1966); Central Budget Corp. v. Sanchez, 53 Misc.2d 620, 279 N.Y.S.2d 391 (Civ.Ct.1967) (case sent back to determine commercial setting). However punitive dam-

wise, if other terms are the product of unconscionability, they will be remade or stricken.[95] There may be some who will view these decisions with alarm, claiming that they destroy the certainty which contracts are intended to promote. Nevertheless, the single most important impression gained from a reading of the section 2–302 cases decided thus far is this: this section of the Code is not being used to reach unexpected results—that is, to impair obligations which would have been enforced under pre-Code law.[96] Courts have not used section 2–302 to remake obligations on any broad-scale basis. Quite the contrary, parties remain free within broad notions of conscionability to make their own deals, and the results reached in Code cases would in all probability have been reached by pre-Code law.[97] The big difference is that the pre-Code decisions would have had to follow a more tortuous path to reach these results.

ages are not available just because the agreement is unconscionable. Pearson v. National Budgeting Systems, Inc., 31 A.D.2d 792, 297 N.Y.S.2d 59 (1969).

95. One company put a clause in its home improvement contracts by which the homeowner submitted to the jurisdiction of the New York courts. A series of decisions held this clause unconscionable. Paragon Homes, Inc. v. Carter, 56 Misc.2d 463, 288 N.Y.S.2d 817, aff'd mem. 30 A.D.2d 1052, 295 N.Y.S.2d 606 (1968); Paragon Homes of New England, Inc. v. Langlois, 4 UCC Rep. 16 (N.Y.Sup.Ct.1967); Paragon Homes of Midwest, Inc. v. Grace, 4 UCC Rep. 19 (N.Y.Sup.Ct.1967).

It has been argued that UCC § 2–302 has no application to disclaimers of warranties. The basis of this argument is that UCC § 2–316 spells out the requirements for a valid disclaimer, and when these are satisfied the disclaimer will be upheld. This position should not be accepted by courts. UCC § 2–316 sets the procedural safeguards—takes the surprise out of a disclaimer —but has nothing to do with how oppressive the clause may be. Courts are applying UCC § 2–302 to disclaimers. E. g., Vlases v. Montgomery Ward & Co., 377 F.2d 846, 850 (3d Cir. 1967) (dictum). For a discussion of the application of UCC § 2–302 to a limitation of remedies, see Wilson Trading Corp. v. David Ferguson, Ltd., 23 N.Y.2d 398, 244 N.E.2d 685, 297 N.Y.S.2d 108 (1968).

Whether UCC § 2–302 applies to other Articles of the Code has not yet been adequately considered by the courts. Denying the application of UCC § 2–302 to Article 9 transactions which did not involve a sale: In re Advance Printing & Litho Co., 277 F.Supp. 101 (W.D.Pa.1967), aff'd per curiam 387 F.2d 952 (3d Cir. 1967); Hernandez v. S. I. C. Fin. Co., 79 N.M. 673, 448 P.2d 474 (1968). Applying the section to commercial paper problems: Unico v. Owen, 50 N.J. 101, 232 A.2d 405 (1967).

96. The only hesitation in making this statement arises from the *Williams* case, a pre-Code case. Putting aside the facts that one of the customers was a widow, living on relief (known to the retailer), and had just purchased a stereo for $515—facts which have nothing to do with the add-on clause—there is nothing oppressive about the deal. All of the customer's goods could have been used to secure the extension of credit. See UCC §§ 9–204(3) and (4).

97. One use of UCC § 2–302 may result in more agreements being enforced than under pre-Code law. To the extent that one term in the agreement is unconscionable, that term can be eliminated from the agreement by the court. If the dispute does not involve that clause, the resulting agreement could be enforced, contrary to the approach in Campbell Soup Co. v. Wentz, 172 F.2d 80 (3d Cir. 1948).

§ 45.   Assignment and Delegation

The early common law viewed a contract as creating a personal relationship between the contracting parties—a relationship that was too personal to permit some third person to intrude through notions of assignment or delegation. Commercial realities, however, gradually eroded this doctrine until it was replaced by a substantial body of law supporting assignment and delegation. Section 2–210 of the Code accepts this later common law development.

Section 2–210 is based upon a fundamental idea in the law of contracts: an agreement which is enforceable as a contract creates certain rights and duties. These rights and duties are correlative—that is, one party's right corresponds to the other party's duty. For example, when a seller has agreed to sell goods to a buyer who has agreed to pay the price, the seller has a *right* to the price and a *duty* to deliver the goods; the buyer has a correlative *duty* to pay the price and a correlative *right* to the goods. (If the contract is unilateral, as where the seller has shipped the goods in exchange for the buyer's promise to pay the price, the buyer has the *duty* to pay and the seller has a *right* to the price.) Assignment and delegation operate on these rights and duties, not on the entire contract

The Code rules are:

As to delegation. Certain contractual duties may be delegated,[98] but no duty may be assigned.[99] The difference between delegation and assignment is not just an exercise in rhetoric; the difference carries substantial legal consequences. The basic idea of an assignment is that of transfer: whatever the assignor once owned and included within the terms of the transfer is now owned by the assignee. An effective assignment terminates ownership rights in the assignor and creates those rights in the assignee.[1] A delegation, however, does not free the delegator from his performance obligations. In that sense there has been no transfer of duties. If performance is not forthcoming in accordance with the contract, the delegator is liable for default of the original contract.[2] The basic idea of delegation is that of authorizing a third party to render the contractual performance.

---

98. UCC § 2–210(1). The Code does not purport to be a complete statement of the law of assignment and delegation; rather it only clarifies certain aspects of the topic. UCC § 2–210, Comment 7.

99. UCC § 2–210(1); Crane Ice Cream Co. v. Terminal Freezing & Heating Co., 147 Md. 588, 128 A. 280 (1925).

1. National Motor Serv. Co. v. Walters, 85 Idaho 349, 379 P.2d 643 (1963).

However, the obligor's defenses against the assignor are, in general, preserved in any suit by the assignee, and payment to the assignor prior to notification of assignment discharges the debt. 4 A. Corbin, Contracts §§ 892–905 (1951). *See also* UCC § 9–318.

2. UCC § 2–210(1); Davidson v. Madison Corp., 257 N.Y. 120, 177 N.E. 393 (1931).

Often the delegation is accomplished by a contract which creates a second liability making the delegatee also liable for the nonperformance. This liability runs to the delegator according to the terms of the contract delegating the duty, and—if the delegation contract amounted to a third party beneficiary contract—the liability of the delegatee also runs to the obligee under the original contract.[3] Section 2–210(5) completes the protection afforded the nondelegating party by allowing him to demand assurances from the delegatee without prejudicing any rights against the delegator

The result of the differences between assignment and delegation can be summarized by the cryptic statement that *rights* may be assigned and *duties* may be delegated. Such a statement contains at least a half-truth. It emphasizes the legal conclusion that contractual duties cannot be discharged by the unilateral activity of the obligor. The delegation may, of course, be accompanied by an agreement between the original contracting parties, and this agreement may relieve the delegator from his duties to perform. The original contract may be discharged just as any contractual obligation may be discharged, but the basic rule remains. The delegation itself cannot relieve the delegator of his performance obligations.

The difficulty with the statement that rights may be assigned and duties delegated is that it overstates the law. There are some rights which cannot be assigned and there are some duties which may not be delegated. As to duties the Code language is: "A party may perform his duty through a delegate unless otherwise agreed or unless the other party has a substantial interest in having his original promisor perform or control the acts required by the contract." [4] Thus, the agreement between the parties may prevent delegation. Likewise, the nature of the obligation may be such that delegation is prohibited. An example of this latter type of case could include a transaction in which the buyer has contracted to receive the seller's continuing control of the quality of the goods. If the delegation would result in seller's loss of interest in that quality, an attempted delegation by the seller would be prohibited by the Code.[5]

---

3. An "acceptance" of an assignment of a contract or rights under a contract is to be construed as a promise by the "assignee" to perform the duties—unless language or circumstances indicate the contrary. This promise may be enforced by the assignor or by the other party to the original contract. UCC § 2–210(4). *Cf.* Langel v. Betz, 250 N.Y. 159, 164 N.E. 890 (1928) (real estate).

4. UCC § 2–210(1).

5. The general law of delegation is discussed in British Waggon Co. & Parkgate Waggon Co. v. Lea & Co., 5 Q.B.D. 149 (1880).

As to assignment. The Code's basic rule is that all rights of the buyer and the seller are assignable. Four exceptions are listed in section 2–210(2), but if none of these exceptions is applicable, the buyer may freely assign his right to the goods and the seller his right to the price. These exceptions are:

(1) Where the assignment "would materially change the duty of the other party." [6] One party to a contract cannot materially change the duties of the other party by assigning his rights. An attempt to do so is void. An assignment of the buyer's rights under a requirements contract might be such a case. The assignee's requirements could differ from those of his assignor and materially change the seller's delivery duties. [7] However, to the extent that the section on requirements contract has substituted an objective standard for the quantity, the rights under some of these agreements may have become assignable. [8]

(2) Where the assignment would "increase materially the burden of risk imposed on him by his contract." [9] The Code is not clear as to who the "him" is in this section, but it undoubtedly refers to the other party to the contract (the one not making the assignment). A type of case which might fall within this prohibition is one in which the contract gives the buyer control over the quality of the goods to be manufactured by the seller. Here an assignment by the buyer would substitute a new person with different demands as to quality, changing the risks assumed by the seller. [10]

(3) Where the assignment would "impair materially his chance of obtaining the return performance." [11] Once again, the "his" ought to be read as referring to the nonassigning party. A seller who has a continuing obligation in regard to goods already delivered under a contract by which the buyer is to pay at least a part of the price at future dates may present an example of a case in which the seller may not assign his contractual right to payment. Such an assignment may diminish the seller's interest in continuing his performance, thereby modifying the buyer's contractual rights. [12]

6. UCC § 2–210(2).

7. Crane Ice Cream Co. v. Terminal Freezing & Heating Co., 147 Md. 588, 128 A. 280 (1925).

8. UCC § 2–306, discussed in § 40 *supra*.

9. UCC § 2–210(2).

10. *Accord,* Jetter v. Scollan, 48 Misc. 546, 96 N.Y.S. 274 (App.T.1905), *aff'd mem.* 114 App.Div. 902, 100 N.Y.S. 1122 (1906).

11. UCC § 2–210(2).

12. Paper Products Mach. Co. v. Safepack Mills, 239 Mass. 114, 131 N.E. 288 (1921) (assignment by a licensor). *See also* Goldschmidt & Loewenick, Inc. v. Diamond State Fibre Co., 186 App.Div. 688, 174 N.Y.S. 800, (1919) *appeal dismissed,* 230 N.Y. 621, 130 N.E. 918 (1921).

Each of the three examples discussed above has suggested situations which might possibly fit within the Code's nonassignable rights. No firm position can be taken as to any of these examples until further facts are explored because the Code requires a *material* change, increase, or impairment.

(4) Where the assignment is contrary to the agreement of the parties.[13] Section 2–210(2)—the section which establishes the Code's rule favoring assignment—begins with the familiar "unless otherwise agreed" language. These three words afford the parties with an apparent option: if they wish, they may agree that no rights arising out of their contract can be assigned, or they may agree that certain rights are—while others are not—assignable. True, they must "agree" in the sense that the clause prohibiting assignment must be the bargain of the parties in fact [14] and, unless circumstances indicate the contrary, a clause which bars an assignment of "the contract" (rather than rights under the contract) will be construed as barring only the delegation of duties,[15] but the "unless otherwise agreed" language *apparently* allows the parties a contractual freedom to make rights as personal as they were under the common law.

This appearance of contractual freedom disappears in large part on a further reading of other parts of the Code. Section 2–210(2) adds:

> A right to damages for breach of the whole contract or a right arising out of the assignor's due performance of his entire obligation can be assigned despite agreement otherwise.

The breach must be of the *whole* contract; the performance must be of the *entire* obligation. If either of these events occurs, the clause which prohibited assignment will be given no effect. There is commercial justification for this position. When there has been a default in the whole contract or when one of the parties has performed fully, there is no continuing contractual relationship and no good business reason for enforcing a clause which makes the right to performance personal. For example, if the buyer has defaulted by wrongfully rejecting a tender of the conforming goods, there is no commercial reason for holding that the seller cannot assign his damage action against the buyer—even though the seller-buyer contract contained an agreement that the seller could not assign his rights. Also, if the seller has delivered all of the goods called for by the contract and the buyer has accepted them, there is no commercial reason for hold-

---

13. UCC § 2–210(2). As to whether this agreement may be modified orally, see C. I. T. Corp. v. Jonnet, 419 Pa. 435, 214 A.2d 620 (1965), and § 43 *supra*.

14. UCC § 1–201(3); § 47 *infra*.

15. UCC § 2–210(3).

ing that the seller cannot assign his right to the price. An argument by the buyer that he was willing to subject himself to the collection procedures of the seller, but not those of some unknown third party, is not substantial enough to override the Code's policy of free assignability.

There is another Code section applicable to attempts by the buyer to make the seller's right to payment non-assignable. This is section 9–318(4):

> A term in any contract between an account debtor and an assignor which prohibits assignment of an account or contract right to which they are parties is ineffective.

This section appears in Article 9—the Article which provides a comprehensive scheme for the regulation of financing arrangements using personal property and fixtures as collateral for credit. The definition of "account debtor" includes a buyer of goods [16] and the reference to both an account and a contract right [17] makes ineffective a clause prohibiting assignment even though the Article 9 seller has performed only a portion (or even none) of his contractual obligations—contrary to the inference drawn from section 2–210(2).

The Comment attempt to harmonize these two sections is inadequate.[18] Not only is it difficult to determine just what assignments of accounts and contract rights fall within Article 9,[19] but to allow the validity of the prohibition clause to turn on the nature of the transaction between the assignor and his assignee leaves the buyer in an awkward position. He cannot predict the validity of the pro-

---

16. UCC § 9–105(1) (a).

17. " 'Account' means any right to payment for goods sold or delivered or for services rendered which is not evidenced by an instrument or chattel paper. 'Contract right' means any right to payment under a contract not yet earned by performance and not evidenced by an instrument or chattel paper." UCC § 9–106.

18. Comment 3 to UCC § 2–210 begins by repeating the idea of the last sentence of UCC § 2–210(2), tying to the "account" definition in Article 9. The Comment statement is accurate but it misses the difficult problem of what will be done with assignments of "accounts" which arise out of due performance which is less than an entire performance. The last sentence of Comment 3 is inaccurate. UCC § 2–210 (2) does cover "contract rights" in its

opening mandate: "*all* rights of either seller or buyer can be assigned." If the drafters wanted one rule for sales which did not involve assignment financing and another rule for sales resulting in assignment financing, they chose (in the last sentence of UCC § 2–210(2)) a cumbersome method of expressing that thought. Comment 4 to UCC § 9–318 is the better treatment of the subject.

19. Sales of accounts and contract rights are subject to Article 9. UCC § 9–102(1) (b). However, non-financing sales are exempted by UCC § 9–104(f). There are difficult questions of construction under this last section. For example, when is an assignment "for the purpose of collection only"? More important, when does an assignment cease being for the purpose of collection *only* and start being for some other purpose also?

hibition clause at the time of contracting, and he must later determine whether the assignment did in fact fall within the scope of Article 9. Despite the Comments it appears that these two sections (2–210(2) and 9–318(4)) were drafted by different groups for different purposes —and unfortunately were never harmonized. It is, therefore, impossible to suggest the scope of the fourth exception to the Code rule of free assignment of rights. About the best that can be done is to relate that the Code says that the basic rule of assignability is subject to a contrary agreement of the parties, provides in Article 2 a limited exception to the parties' freedom of contract (an exception applicable to both buyers and sellers), but adds an extremely broad exception in Article 9 when a seller wishes to assign his contractual right to payment in face of a clause prohibiting assignment.[20]

D. INTERPRETATION OF A CONTRACT FOR SALE

§ 46. Problems of Interpretation

Thousands of pages of judicial opinions have been devoted to the tasks (a) of interpreting the words which the parties used in reaching their agreement and (b) of construing that agreement, as interpreted, to determine its legal effect. That these tasks are difficult cannot be denied.[21] English words, even though used precisely, lack precision.[22] Further, many sales agreements result from an exchange of forms which contain broadly drafted clauses couched in vague and general language. The court must, if possible, extract a meaning from these words so that it can determine the scope of the promises exchanged. The process of interpretation takes time and, if it is explained to the litigants, requires many pages in judicial opinions.

The source of the difficulties, however, is deeper. Interpretation is the process of determining the meaning of words; yet the pre-Code cases have not agreed on *whose* meaning is important in interpreting the words of an agreement. The surface answer is appealingly simple: the courts should give those words the meaning attributed to them by the parties to the agreement.[23] To the extent that the parties do have a common meaning, such an answer is quite proper. The dif-

---

20. Since UCC § 9–318(4) applies only to "account debtors", that section would not expand the buyer's rights of assignment in face of a clause prohibiting assignment of rights. Such a buyer is limited to UCC § 2–210(2).

21. *E. g.*, Chastain & Blass Real Estate & Ins., Inc. v. Davis, 280 Ala. 489, 195 So.2d 782 (1967); Daman v. Walton Lumber Co., 53 Wash.2d 747, 337 P.2d 37 (1959).

22. Hurst v. Lake & Co., 141 Or. 306, 310, 16 P.2d 627, 629 (1932). There are many books which discuss the "softness" of the English language. One of the best is C. Ogden & I. Richards, The Meaning of Meaning (10th ed. 1952).

23. Romine, Inc. v. Savannah Steel Co., 117 Ga.App. 353, 160 S.E.2d 659 (1968).

ficulty arises in those cases in which *the parties* did not have *a* common meaning. To the promisor the words conveyed one idea; to the promisee they meant something quite different. When meanings differ, whose interpretation is to be preferred? [24]

An attempt to solve this question has been expressed in several subsidiary rules of interpretation. Thus, cases indicate that words should be construed "against" the draftsman, that written words have priority over printed words, that certain words have a plain or clear meaning and the signer is bound by that meaning, and so on. Court opinions repeat these "rules" seemingly without concern over the fact that the rules often overlap, produce conflicting results, and do little to advance a rational solution of interpretation problems.[25]

There is a related doctrine in the law of contracts which has increased the difficulties of determining whose meaning is important. That doctrine, called the theory of objective mutual assent, was colorfully expressed by Judge Learned Hand in these words:

> A contract has, strictly speaking, nothing to do with the personal, or individual, intent of the parties. . . . If . . . it were proved by twenty bishops that either party, when he used the words, intended something else than the usual meaning which the law imposes upon them, he would still be held, unless there were some mutual mistake, or something else of the sort.[26]

Much can be said in support of this idea of contract formation. The older theory that a subjective "meeting of the minds" was necessary

24. The question posed in the text should be answered by reference to the purpose of contract law—the enforcement of the justified expectations of the parties. If expectations differ because different meanings are ascribed to the words used, but if one party (A) knows or has reason to know the meaning ascribed by the other party (B) at the time agreement was reached, the expectations of A are not "justified," those of B are "justified," and B's meaning is the only meaning which is material. Sun Oil Co. v. Dalzell Towing Co., 55 F.2d 63 (2d Cir.), *aff'd* 287 U.S. 291, 53 S.Ct. 135, 77 L.Ed. 311 (1932); Dickey v. Hurd, 33 F.2d 415 (1st Cir. 1929); Cage v. Black, 97 Ark. 613, 134 S.W. 942 (1911) (the buyer knew the seller's meaning of the critical word involved when the buyer accepted the goods, and the court found no contract prior to that time); Cargill Commission Co. v. Mowery, 99 Kan. 389, 161 P. 634 (1916), 162 P. 313 (1917). If, on the other hand, the meanings of A and B differ and both are justified in ascribing their meanings to the words used, there is no agreement on that term. This is the famous case of Raffles v. Wichelhaus, 2 H. & C. 906, 159 Eng.Rep. 375 (Ex. 1864), in which there were two ships named "Peerless" and each party reasonably meant a "Peerless" different from the other. See also Stong v. Lane, 66 Minn. 94, 68 N.W. 765 (1896); Farnsworth, *"Meaning" in the Law of Contracts*, 76 Yale L.J. 939 (1967).

25. Bristol v. Cornell Univ., 237 App. Div. 771, 263 N.Y.S. 386 (1933). For a collection of cases, see 3 A. Corbin, Contracts §§ 545-52 (1960).

26. Hotchkiss v. National City Bank, 200 F. 287, 293 (S.D.N.Y.1911), *aff'd* 201 F. 664 (2d Cir. 1912), *aff'd* 231 U.S. 50, 34 S.Ct. 20, 58 L.Ed. 115 (1913).

to form a contract could lead to inequities whenever one party was reasonably misled by the other into believing that they had agreed and that the terms of that agreement were those as understood by the misled party. One way to prevent those inequities was to emphasize that the theory of contract formation was that of objective mutual assent and to hold the misleading party to contractual liability based upon the reasonable understanding of the other party to the transaction.[27]

The quotation from Judge Hand may be read to go further and to deny the materiality of a mutual understanding when it does exist. That reading rests on the notion that words have an objective, or usual, meaning to a disinterested third party, and the law will impose that meaning on the parties irrespective of their understanding when they used those words.[28] The problem of interpretation thus becomes a peculiar blend of what is meant by the word "meaning." In some instances it is the promisor's meaning that is important; in others it is the promisee's; in still others it is both of their understandings; and in some cases the meaning of the parties, even though the same, must give way to that "usual meaning which the law imposes upon them." The most famous dictum expressing this last idea comes from an early opinion by Mr. Justice Holmes: "It would open too great risks if evidence were admissible to show that when they said five hundred feet they agreed that it should mean one hundred inches, or that Bunker Hill Monument should signify the Old South Church."[29] Evidently the risks referred to are that, if the evidence is admitted, one party will be able to change the agreement which was in fact entered into (five hundred feet) to one that was never considered by the parties (one hundred inches). Perhaps these risks are not as great as imagined if it is remembered that the party seeking to show the agreement for one hundred inches would have to present extremely convincing evidence before he could persuade the trier of facts that the agreement was for something different from the five hundred feet which had been written by the parties. Nevertheless, a court which purports to follow the above-quoted dictum faces the added problem

27. Hugo v. Erickson, 110 Neb. 602, 194 N.W. 723 (1923); Restatement of Contracts § 505 (1932).

28. *See generally* Minmar Builders, Inc. v. Beltway Excavators, Inc., 246 A.2d 784 (D.C.App.1968). For a case which probably did make a contract for the parties which was different from their meaning, see American Sumatra Tobacco Corp. v. Willis, 170 F.2d 215 (5th Cir. 1948). See also the majority opinion and Mr. Justice Traynor's answer in Laux v. Freed, 53 Cal.2d 512, 348 P.2d 873 (1960).

29. Goode v. Riley, 153 Mass. 585, 586, 28 N.E. 228 (1891). The idea is repeated (but limited to oral declarations and agreements) in Holmes, *Theory of Legal Interpretation*, 12 Harv.L.Rev. 417, 421 (1899).

of sorting out those words which are plain and clear from those which are ambiguous or vague.[30]

The idea which has caused the greatest judicial difficulty in interpreting agreements is the faith which has been placed on the written, as opposed to the oral, words of the parties. This faith finds its most vocal expression in the parol evidence rule. This rule provides in substance that once the parties to an agreement have adopted a writing as a complete embodiment of their agreement, evidence of prior understandings or agreements will not be admitted to add to or to vary the unambiguous language contained in the writing.[31] Countless cases have applied this rule in what appears to be an extremely inflexible manner.[32] First, they search to determine whether the writing is an "integration" of prior understandings, and one of the tests adopted to reach this decision is whether the document is facially integrated—that is, whether the document looks to the court as if it is complete enough to be an "integration." [33] Second, these courts decide whether the evidence sought to be introduced adds to or varies the writing. Finally, they decide if the writing is "unambiguous." If each of these searches results in an affirmative answer, the evidence is excluded.[34]

The principles behind the parol evidence rule (like those underlying the statement from Judge Hand) are worth retaining, but not in the literal form in which they have been stated. The essential task is that of determining *the* agreement between these parties.[35] Agree-

---

30. *E. g.*, Smith v. Bear, 237 F.2d 79 (2d Cir. 1956); and the protracted litigation in Inman Mfg. Co. v. American Cereal Co., 133 Iowa 71, 110 N.W. 287 (1907) (the same case is reported in 124 Iowa 737, 100 N.W. 860 (1904); 142 Iowa 558, 119 N.W. 722 (1909); 155 Iowa 651, 136 N.W. 932 (1912)). There is a delightful discussion of this point in Chafee, *The Disorderly Conduct of Words*, 41 Colum.L.Rev. 381 (1941).

31. Hathaway v. Ray's Motor Sales, Inc., 127 Vt. 279, 247 A.2d 512 (1968). A discussion of the parol evidence rule can be found in the cases cited in the remaining notes in this section and in 3 A. Corbin, Contracts §§ 573 et seq. (1960); 4 S. Williston, Contracts §§ 600 et seq. (3d ed. 1961); and 9 J. Wigmore, Evidence §§ 2400 et seq. (3d ed. 1940).

32. *E. g.*, American Sumatra Tobacco Corp. v. Willis, 170 F.2d 215 (5th Cir.

1948); J. B. Colt & Co. v. Clay, 216 Ky. 782, 288 S.W. 745 (1926).

33. Spurgeon v. Buchter, 192 Cal.App. 2d 198, 13 Cal.Rptr. 354 (1961); Thompson v. Libby, 34 Minn. 374, 26 N.W. 1 (1885). Many other tests have been used. They are discussed in § 53 *infra*.

34. The parol evidence rule does not prevent the introduction of oral evidence to show that there was no contract. Barnsdall Ref. Corp. v. Birnamwood Oil Co., 92 F.2d 817 (7th Cir. 1937) (misrepresentation); Burrowes Corp. v. Read, 151 Me. 92, 116 A.2d 127 (1955) (oral condition precedent); White Showers, Inc. v. Fischer, 278 Mich. 32, 270 N.W. 205 (1936) (oral condition precedent).

35. See the excellent discussion of the parol evidence rule in Zell v. American Seating Co., 138 F.2d 641 (2d Cir. 1943), *rev'd* 322 U.S. 709, 64 S.Ct. 1053, 88 L.Ed. 1552 (1944). Other cases which state that the parol evidence

ments can be rescinded; understandings can be changed. If the parties intend to rescind prior agreements and to change past understandings by the execution of a new agreement, they may do so—and the prior agreements and understandings no longer have any legal effect. They have no effect because they are no longer a part of *the* agreement between these parties, and they are not material to any issue before the court. In such a case the evidence should be excluded, just as should all immaterial evidence. However, if the parties did not intend to rescind or change their prior agreements by adopting this writing, evidence of those prior agreements as well as of the circumstances which surrounded the writing should be admitted so that the court can determine *the* agreement entered into by these parties.[36]

Many of the pre-Code cases applying the parol evidence rule in what appears to be an inflexible manner may, however, be expressing another function of the rule: the evidence sought to be introduced is excluded because it is not believable. The written words of the parties ought to be given great weight in determining what the parties meant by their agreement. The party who seeks to prove that their private understanding was different from the usual meaning attached to their later-written words bears the burden of proving that understanding. In many cases he cannot meet this burden. His evidence just does not fall within the bounds of what reasonable men can believe. It is much easier for the court to tell him that he loses his case because of some immutable principle of law than that his testimony was not believable. Many cases applying the parol evidence rule can be explained on this basis.[37]

The following pages of this text will discuss the problems of interpreting contractual language under the Code. It may appear at first that the Code has changed many of the rules set out above. However, these pre-Code rules were presented out of the context of the entire law of contract interpretation. Other doctrines cut across these rules and allow admission of prior agreements and understandings, if material to the case. For example, even though the parties have used

rule defines the limits of the contract include Warinner v. Nugent, 362 Mo. 233, 240 S.W.2d 941 (1951); Charles A. Burton, Inc. v. Durkee, 158 Ohio St. 313, 109 N.E.2d 265 (1952); Barber v. Rochester, 52 Wash.2d 691, 328 P.2d 711 (1958).

36. For the pre-Code effect of a clause which provides that the writing supersedes prior oral agreements, *compare* R. G. Varner Steel Prods., Inc. v. Puterbaugh, 233 Ark. 953, 349 S.W.2d 805 (1961), *with* International Milling Co. v. Hachmeister, Inc., 380 Pa. 407, 110 A.2d 186 (1955). This problem under the Code is discussed in §§ 53, 69 *infra*.

37. 3 A. Corbin, Contracts § 542 (1960). For a similar problem under the statute of frauds, see Julian C. Cohen Salvage Corp. v. Eastern Elec. Sales Co., 205 Pa.Super. 26, 206 A.2d 331 (1965).

words which would be unambiguous to a reasonable outsider, one of the parties may show that he mistakenly attached an unusual meaning to those words, and have the resulting apparent agreement rescinded—at least if the other party had reason to know that a mistake had been made.[38] In a proper case reformation is also available to make the writing conform to the prior agreement or understandings of the parties, even though oral.[39] Further, if the customs of that particular trade may ascribe an unusual meaning to the words, the trade custom may be introduced to aid in the interpretation.[40] It may be that the parties used these words on several other occasions and interpreted them to mean that which one party is now claiming they mean; this evidence is admissible to show the understanding of the parties when they used the words in this agreement.[41] It may even be that the parties adopted a private code; courts have admitted evidence of this code.[42] In short, the whole pattern of pre-Code law has not been as harsh as the discussion of the separate rules would indicate. In this sense the Code's interpretation rules are not a striking departure from the prior sales law.

§ 47. Distinction between "Agreement" and "Contract"

The Code's approach to the problem of interpretation begins with its distinction between the fact of agreement and the concept of contract. Agreement is defined as follows:

> "Agreement" means the bargain of the parties in fact as found in their language or by implication from other circumstances including course of dealing or usage of trade or course of performance as provided in this Act . . . .[43]

38. Bell v. Carroll, 212 Ky. 231, 278 S. W. 541 (1925). Compare this case to the discussion of the "plain meaning" of words, *supra* this section.

39. Cases are discussed in Palmer, *Reformation and the Parol Evidence Rule*, 65 Mich.L.Rev. 833 (1967). See also Palmer, *Reformation and the Statute of Frauds*, 65 Mich.L.Rev. 421 (1967). The possibility of reformation at law is suggested by Whipple v. Brown Bros. Co., 225 N.Y. 237, 121 N. E. 748 (1919).

For an interplay of the rules discussed in this section, see Smith v. Bear, 237 F.2d 79 (2d Cir. 1956). In New York Life Ins. Co. v. Rak, 30 Ill.App.2d 86, 173 N.E.2d 603 (1961), the court reformed the policy to conform to the application. On appeal the decision was affirmed on the basis of interpretation of the policy and of the application for the policy. 24 Ill.2d 128, 180 N.E.2d 470 (1962).

40. Walker v. Syms, 118 Mich. 183, 76 N.W. 320 (1898); Soutier v. Kellerman, 18 Mo. 509 (1853); Hurst v. Lake & Co., 141 Or. 306, 16 P.2d 627 (1932).

41. 3 A. Corbin, Contracts § 558 (1960). Circumstances surrounding the formation of the contract are admissible. Georgiades v. Glickman, 272 Wis. 257, 75 N.W.2d 573 (1956).

42. Morrison v. Wilson, 30 Cal. 344 (1866); Cargill Commission Co. v. Mowery, 99 Kan. 389, 161 P. 634 (1916), 162 P. 313 (1917). Cases are collected in 9 J. Wigmore, Evidence §§ 2462–63 (3d ed. 1940).

43. UCC § 1–201(3).

On the other hand, contract is defined as:

> "Contract" means the total legal obligation which results from the parties' agreement as affected by this Act and any other applicable rules of law.[44]

Agreement is the word used by the Code to describe what the parties do; *contract* is the word used by the Code to describe what the law does about what the parties have done. The parties negotiate through oral conversations, printed forms, exchanged memoranda, inflections of the voice, a wave of the hand, or a nod of the head. The words or acts that they used may have a special meaning to them because they have used them before or because the trade to which they belong attaches a special meaning to them. The parties do not enter into a contract; they reach a bargain. That bargain is the Code's "agreement." The next step is to decide what legal obligations arise from their agreement. If the agreement lacks consideration, results from fraud or unconscionability, or is the product of a mistake, a court may conclude that there are no legal obligations—that there is no "contract." If, however, the agreement contains the required elements of "contract," a court will award some remedy which reflects the obligation of the parties to perform their promises.

This distinction has many practical impacts. One arises in this area of interpretation. Each of the Code sections which establish principles of interpretation makes some reference to the agreement of the parties.[45] These references focus attention on what the parties did—on the meaning that they gave their words or acts, not on some meaning forced on them because the words they chose have a "usual" dictionary meaning.

Any doubts about this are resolved by a careful reading of the definition of agreement. It is the *bargain in fact* which is important. Although bargain is not defined, it carries with it the notion of coming to terms, and it is this on which the idea of agreement centers. Further, it is the bargain *of the parties* which is essential. If they understood that their words (or their action or silence) had a certain meaning, that understanding is their agreement. The fact that some third person would have interpreted what they did to have a different meaning does not change the bargain of these parties. Finally, all relevant evidence of bargain is a part of their agreement. Language, course of dealing, course of performance, trade usage—these are examples of the totality of experience which give meaning to the parties' bargain.

Once the court determines the bargain in fact of the parties, it then must determine the legal obligations resulting from that bargain.

---

44. UCC § 1–201(11).

45. UCC §§ 1–205, 2–202, 2–208, and 2–209.

On some occasions this means deciding whether warranties are to be implied, who bears the risk of loss for goods destroyed in transit, or whether the buyer is obliged to tender cash on delivery of the goods. Whatever the question may be, the answer could well turn on interpreting what the parties said or did when they entered into their agreement. The Code's approach is to move from agreement through interpretation to contract. Stated in another way, the Code recognizes that a distinction is to be drawn between what the parties did, on the one side, and what the law ought to do about what the parties did, on the other. This distinction is first found in the difference between an "agreement" and a "contract"—a difference which is assumed in the following sections of this text.

§ 48. "Meaning" Under the Code

The Code, read with the general law of contracts, will determine what evidence can be introduced to interpret the agreement of the parties. Some types of evidence are clearly admissible. For example, a writing which purports to set forth some or all of the terms of the agreement will be considered by the court in interpreting that agreement. Nothing which is said in the following pages should be considered to be an objection to the use of such evidence. Words chosen by the parties and deliberately reduced to a writing are excellent evidence of what they intended. That writing ought to be considered by the court when it is trying to determine the scope and content of their agreement. The problem, however, has not been whether the writing is admissible; it clearly is. Instead the problem has been whether the writing is to be considered as the sole evidence of the agreement.

Pre-Code law on this problem has already been discussed.[46] The Code, capturing the mainstream of the prior law, establishes certain principles to aid the court in interpreting the agreement of the parties. In general, these principles favor the admission of evidence extrinsic to any writing that may be involved so long as that evidence is material to the problem before the court.[47] The problem is one of

---

46. § 46 *supra.*

47. Some writers have suggested that the Code liberalizes pre-Code law by allowing the introduction of more evidence of the parties' intent than would have been admitted under prior law. While this may be an acceptable shorthand method of evaluating Code changes, it may convey unintended meanings because of the ambiguities in such words as "strict" or "liberal." 3 A. Corbin, Contracts § 533 (1960). A more accurate way to describe what the Code does is to state that the Code recognizes that the entire bargain of the parties forms their agreement, and evidence of that bargain must be admitted to show the agreement. *See* UCC § 1–201(3). The Code rejects the idea found in many pre-Code cases that certain words have a plain meaning, and that the meaning is to be imposed on the parties. UCC § 2–202, Comment 1(b); UCC § 1–205, Comment 1. Whether this is more "liberal" than pre-Code law is now immaterial to the commercial lawyer.

determining the meaning of the words and acts used by the parties in reaching an agreement, and any evidence which aids the court in determining that meaning ought to be admitted. This process involves consideration of at least these two questions:

First, whose meaning is important under the law of contracts? This question must be answered because, until it is answered, there is no way of measuring whether the proffered evidence is in fact relevant to the issue of interpretation. This text has already suggested how this question ought to be answered. First and foremost, the law of contracts is concerned with the common meaning of the parties.[48] If the parties meant the same thing by a word or an act, that common meaning is their agreement and ought to be enforced by the court. Stated in Code terms, their common meaning has become their "contract." There will, however, be times in which the parties did not have a common meaning when they used the words of their agreement. In such a situation, the law has several alternatives. As an original proposition it could have said that there is to be no contract unless both parties were thinking the same thing at the same time—that is, unless there was a "meeting of the minds."[49] If this ever was the law, it has long since been discarded. There can be a contract even though there is no common meaning. A footnote to this text has suggested that one of the primary purposes of contracts is the enforcement of justified expectations.[50] Therefore, when two parties to a transaction (call them parties A and B) have ascribed different meanings to the same word or act but to the extent that A knows or has reason to know the meaning ascribed by B at the time of their negotiations, it is B's meaning that is worthy of protection—that is, it is B's meaning and expectations that are "justified"—but A's meaning is not. A shorthand expression of this conclusion is to state that when meanings differ there still may be a contract, and in the case suggested above the meaning that is relevant is the meaning given by B.[51]

Second, what evidence is relevant in this process of interpretation? There can, of course, be no complete listing of all of the kinds of evidence which will aid the court in determining the meaning of con-

---

48. § 46 *supra.*

49. For a period in the history of the law of contracts, this might have been an accurate summary of judicial opinions. *E. g.,* Cooke v. Oxley, 3 T.R. 653, 100 Eng.Rep. 785 (K.B.1790). Many vestiges of such an approach remain in our law today, among them the famous "mail-box rule" of Adams v. Lindsell, 1 B. & Ald. 681, 106 Eng. Rep. 250 (K.B.1818).

50. See discussion and cases cited in § 46 n. 24 *supra.*

51. A more detailed analysis of this problem can be found in Farnsworth, *"Meaning" in the Law of Contracts,* 76 Yale L.J. 939 (1967).

tractual language. The variation in factual patterns is too great for such categorization. However, the Code does two things which bear upon the answer to this second question:

1. The Code incorporates the general law of contracts.[52] Commercial law in many respects is nothing more than a specialized branch of the law of contracts. Some contract rules have been codified by the Code; others have been modified or changed; but when the Code is silent about a problem, the general contract rules of the particular jurisdiction may be consulted for a solution. This is true with problems of interpretation.[53] One way of expressing the interpretation problem is this: what is the total legal obligation of the parties resulting from their agreement? They used certain words, or they remained silent about certain problems, or one party said something as they moved along the path toward an agreement. The court's job is to determine what legal obligations were created by what the parties did. The Code's answer to this problem is that " '[c]ontract' means the total legal obligation which results from the parties' agreement as affected by this Act *and any other applicable rules of law.*"[54] Therefore, unless the Code has changed some rule of general contract law, those rules are applicable to aid in the interpretation of the parties' agreement.

2. Although commercial law is a specialized branch of contract law, there are instances in which the Code sets out specific rules which may vary the common law of contracts in some jurisdictions. These instances occur for problems which the drafters recognized and for which they wanted a specific and uniform answer. Some of these special rules will affect the interpretation of agreements. One type has already been discussed: that is, the Code has adopted special rules relating to the formation of contracts.[55] An example is the Code treatment of the "battle of the forms." It is now possible for *the contract* to consist of obligations proposed by one of the parties but never

---

52. UCC §§ 1–103 and 1–201(11).

53. Thus, Code courts will continue to apply such "rules" as: writings are to be construed against the party who chose the words, Peacock & Peacock, Inc. v. Stuyvesant Ins. Co., 332 F.2d 499 (8th Cir. 1964); Alabama-Tennessee Natural Gas Co. v. City of Huntsville, 275 Ala. 184, 153 So.2d 619 (1963); Smith v. Russ, 184 Kan. 773, 339 P.2d 286 (1959); Massachusetts Turnpike Authority v. Perini Corp., 349 Mass. 448, 208 N.E.2d 807 (1965); Page v. Lyle H. Hall, Inc., 125 Vt. 275, 214 A.2d 459 (1965); specific

words control over general language, Marshall v. Patzman, 81 Ariz. 367, 306 P.2d 287 (1957); Schlosser v. Van Dusseldorp, 251 Iowa 521, 101 N.W.2d 715 (1960); Garrett v. Hart, 250 Miss. 822, 168 So.2d 497 (1964); and that written words control over that which is printed, Bartlett & Co. Grain v. Merchants Co., 323 F.2d 501 (5th Cir. 1963); *In re* Couch's Estate, 170 Neb. 518, 103 N.W.2d 274 (1960); Mailey v. Rubin, 388 Pa. 75, 130 A.2d 182 (1957).

54. UCC § 1–201(11).

55. § 32 *supra.*

specifically accepted by the other.[56] Rules such as this affect the scope of agreement and may bear upon the parties' obligations.

There are, however, three sources of extrinsic evidence specifically recognized by the Code: trade usage, course of dealing, and course of performance. Evidence of these is admissible to interpret the words used by the parties in reaching their agreement. The Code sections applicable to these sources of contract interpretation are considered in the following sections.

§ 49.   Principles of Interpretation

The Code establishes a hierarchy of probative values for various types of evidence used in interpreting agreements. These are:

First, the express terms of the agreement and any course of performance, course of dealing, and usage of the trade are to be construed as consistent with each other "whenever reasonable." [57] This is the Code's mandate to consider all of the revelant evidence of the parties' meaning, and to attempt to construe this evidence as consistent. The reason is clear: most of the time the parties have in fact bargained from the background of their trade, their prior dealings, and their prior performance, and have selected the terms of their agreement in light of this background. The court ought to consider these terms as they were used by the parties.

Second, there will be times that the parties intend to change the obligations which would otherwise arise from the way they have been performing their contract, from the way they have been dealing with each other, or from those obligations suggested by the usages of their trade. The Code makes it clear that they may do so.[58] Further, since the problem of the parties' intention may arise as a matter of interpretation of a writing, the Code goes on to state that whenever it is "unreasonable" to construe the writing as consistent with course of performance, course of dealing, and usage of the trade, the terms of the writing shall control.[59]

Third, the Code establishes a hierarchy of probative values among the extrinsic evidence which is admissible. Reading two sections to-

---

56. UCC § 2-207.

57. This conclusion is drawn from two Code sections. UCC § 1-205(4) dealing with course of dealing and usage of trade, and UCC § 2-208(2) dealing with course of performance. An argument can be made that UCC § 2-208 applies only to contracts for sale since it is contained in Article 2—Sales. UCC § 2-102 and Universal C.I.T. Credit Corp. v. Middlesboro Motor Sales, Inc., 424 S.W.2d 409, 411 (Ky. 1968). However, since UCC § 2-208 finds its basis in common law, courts will undoubtedly apply the concept of UCC § 2-208 to other Articles of the Code. *In re* Bengtson, 40 Conn.Bar J. 57 (U.S.Dist.Ct.D.Conn.1965).

58. *See* UCC § 1-201(3); Koreska v. United Cargo Corp., 23 A.D.2d 37, 734, 258 N.Y.S.2d 432 (1965).

59. UCC §§ 1-205(4), 2-208(2).

gether, the Code makes: (a) course of performance controlling over both course of dealing and usage of trade; and (b) course of dealing controlling over usage of trade.[60] Thus, if a writing is to be interpreted by reference to course of performance, course of dealing, and usage of trade, and if these produce conflicting meanings of the words used, the Code commands that the interpretation given follow the hierarchy set out above.

These "rules" of interpretation appear to establish a system by which the meaning of each agreement can quickly be tested. Apparently all that must be done is to follow these rules and the court will have before it the relevant evidence material to a determination of the meaning of the agreement. Life is not that simple. Determination of meaning is not that easy. A course of dealing may be "strong" (that is, it may have occurred over many months under agreements precisely the same as the one involved) or it may be extremely "weak" (that is, the prior conduct may consist of but a few acts and, as compared to the terms of the present writing, may be on the edge of being ambiguous). On the other hand, the usage of trade may be ancient and well-known, even codified, or it may be only emerging and still bordering on the amorphous. Is the Code to be read to mean that the clear trade usage must bow to a doubtful course of performance? Only if these "rules" of interpretation are read with a rigidity which they were never intended to have could this question be answered affirmatively.

The Code ought not be read with this inflexibility. The Code establishes certain principles to aid the court in finding meaning. In general, these principles are designed to increase the amount of admissible evidence extrinsic to the writing, but those principles are not rigid rules because the slightest change in the background of a particular agreement can have a profound impact on the meaning of certain words used. The Code should be read with its purpose firmly in mind. In interpreting agreements the Code requires that the words used be put in the context of their use. Consider how the parties have dealt with each other in the past; is there a sequence of conduct which aids in interpreting the words used in this agreement? This sequence of conduct may relate to this very agreement or to other agreements between these parties. Does the trade in which they are engaged have usages which give meaning to the words used? If either of these questions is answered affirmatively, the court should interpret the parties' agreement as consistent with this extrinsic evidence. If the extrinsic evidence is conflicting, that which is most closely connected with these parties and with this agrement should be given the greatest

---

60. UCC §§ 1–205(4), 2–208(2).

weight. Therefore, course of performance is more apt to point toward the parties' meaning than is a more general course of dealing; in turn, a course of dealing will usually be of greater impact than a usage in the trade. The court cannot, however, escape a balancing or weighing function as it considers this extrinsic evidence.[61] Nevertheless, it must be recognized that, while what parties have done in the past is some evidence of what they intended to do under this agreement, that evidence does not control their present intention and does not bind them to go on acting as thy did in the past. They may agree to change their past relationships and to substitute new agreements. Likewise, they may agree not to be bound by the usages of their trade. When the court believes that this was their intention, it can hold that the attempt to construe the writing with prior dealings and trade usages is "unreasonable," and find the meaning [62] in the express terms of the writing; or it can hold that the new agreement makes evidence of the prior dealings or trade usage immaterial. It is this way that the Code's "rules" of interpretation should be read.

§ 50.   Course of Performance

The idea that a course of performance may be used to aid in interpreting an agreement is not new. "Practical construction by uniform and unquestioned acts from the outset, especially when continued for a long period of time, is entitled to great, if not controlling weight, for it shows how the parties who made the contract understood it. If they do not know what they meant, who can know?" [63]

The Code states the idea in these terms:

> Where the contract for sale involves repeated occasions for performance by either party with knowledge of the nature of the performance and opportunity for objection to it by the other, any course of performance accepted or acquiesced in without objection shall be relevant to determine the meaning of the agreement.[64]

Before this section is applicable, the contract must call for more than one performance—"repeated occasions for performance" is the Code language. No specific number of performances are required. It could be as many as one hundred, or a thousand, or even more; it

---

61. 3 A. Corbin, Contracts § 542A (1960).

62. UCC § 2–208(2).

63. Carthage Tissue Paper Mills v. Village of Carthage, 200 N.Y. 1, 14, 93 N.E. 60, 64 (1910). There are hundreds of other cases which contain language roughly equivalent to that quoted, as any digest or contracts text will attest. Many are cited in 3 A. Corbin, Contracts § 558 (1960), where the author admits that the cases are "so numerous as to be impossible of full citation here."

64. UCC § 2–208(1).

could be as few as two, although some courts may read the word "repeated" to mean "several" or even "many." Probably no harm will be done by this reading because the fewer the performances under an agreement the more unlikely it is that those performances will have built up a *course* of performance. In any event, the statute is clear that any course of performance which the other party accepts or acquiesces in without an objection [65] "shall be relevant to determine the meaning of the agreement." The evidence is admissible. Whether it will be accepted as controlling the meaning of the writing is a problem for the trier of fact, but the longer the course of performance the better are the changes that the trier of fact will find that the words meant what the parties did.

There will be times in which what the parties have done could be viewed as inconsistent with what they wrote. For example, the writing may call for several deliveries at a price f. o. b. buyer's city, but for the first ten deliveries the seller charged, and the buyer paid, the price f. o. b. seller's city. What is the price which must be paid for the eleventh delivery?

The first subsection of section 2–208 indicates that this past course of performance (the demand by the seller for payment, f. o. b. seller's point, and the buyer's payment according to the seller's demand) is relevant to determine the "meaning" of the agreement. The buyer may have a factual defense: his payment of the larger amount was a mistake and that he was not acquiescing in such an interpretation of the agreement. The buyer may also have a Code argument: the "meaning" of the writing is unambiguous and the course of performance is not reasonably consistent with the words of the writing.[66] The term f. o. b. buyer's point means just that and

---

65. The course of performance must be "accepted or acquiesced in without objection" by the recipient of the performance. UCC § 2–208(1). Thus, unilateral acts by one party will not suffice to create a favorable interpretation for him. Andrews v. St. Louis Joint Stock Land Bank, 107 F.2d 462 (8th Cir.), *cert. denied* 309 U.S. 667, 60 S.Ct. 592, 84 L.Ed. 1014 (1939); Davis v. Kramer Bros. Freight Lines, Inc., 361 Mich. 371, 105 N.W.2d 29 (1960). However, the Code does not require that the recipient expressly agree to the performances as received; it is sufficient that he acquiesces without objection. *See* W. J. Howard & Sons v. Meyer, 367 Mich. 300, 116 N.W.2d 752 (1962) (a non-Code case).

66. Many non-Code cases have stated that the course of performance—or "practical construction," as it was often called—was admissible only if the writing was ambiguous. *E. g.*, Fowler v. Pennsylvania Tire Co., 326 F.2d 526 (5th Cir. 1964); Minnesota Mut. Life Ins. Co. v. Wright, 312 F.2d 655 (8th Cir. 1963); Pekovich v. Coughlin, 258 F.2d 191 (9th Cir. 1958); Coe v. Zwetchkenbaum, 89 R.I. 358, 153 A.2d 517 (1959). This text has already commented on the idea that some language is so unambiguous that the dictionary meaning should be applied irrespective of the intention of the parties. § 46 *supra*. Interestingly, some courts have allowed the conduct of the parties to show the ambiguity, thus reach-

under no reasonable construction can it be construed to mean f. o. b. seller's point. The buyer would then rely on the second subsection of section 2–208 which states that whenever it is unreasonable to construe the express terms of an agreement as consistent with the course of performance, "express terms shall control course of performance."

There are two Code answers to the buyer's last argument. First, there is no term in a writing that has such a plain meaning that it precludes a party from showing how the parties in fact used the term. Course of performance is one method of showing the meaning attributed to the term by the parties. Once that evidence is admitted (and believed), the words written by the parties have the meaning which the parties attributed to those words, and therefore there is no inconsistency between the words and course of performance.[67] Such an answer may, however, be unacceptable to those courts which continue to believe (in spite of the Code) that words do have a plain meaning which can be ascertained by reading the latest edition of a dictionary. Perhaps for this reason the Code gives a second answer to the buyer's argument:

> Subject to the provisions of the next section on modification and waiver, such course of performance shall be relevant to show a waiver or modification of any term inconsistent with such course of performance.[68]

Even though there is an "inconsistency" between the writing and the course of performance, the course of performance may amount to either a waiver or a modification of the writing. The Code section on modification and waiver is discussed elsewhere in this text,[69] but the following points should be summarized. The Code rejects the notion that just because the parties have entered into a "contract" something magical has occurred which prevents any change of that contract without all of the elements of a new contract. The Code's concept of contract is that of a continuing relationship between the parties, a relationship which can be changed by them as they move from the negotiation stage through to complete performance. No consideration need be given for the modification or the waiver,[70] but one of

---

ing sensible results while clinging to old case language. Crestview Cemetery Ass'n v. Dieden, 54 Cal.2d 744, 8 Cal.Rptr. 427, 356 P.2d 171 (1960); Bullough v. Sims, 16 Utah 2d 304, 400 P.2d 20 (1965).

67. UCC § 2–208 does not require an ambiguity in the writing as a condition to the admissibility of course of performance. See especially UCC § 1–205, Comment 1; UCC § 2–208,

Comment 2. The latter Comment states: "Under this section a course of performance is always relevant to determine the meaning of the agreement."

68. UCC § 2–208(3).

69. § 43 *supra*.

70. UCC § 2–209(1).

the parties is protected from spurious claims of modification by the requirement that the statute of frauds must be satisfied if the contract *as modified* is within the terms of the statute.[71]

The result of the Code's emphasis on course of performance is to strengthen its philosophy that the agreement which ought to be enforced is the agreement which the parties in fact entered into. The writing is evidence of that agreement; so is what the parties did under the words of that writing. Neither is conclusive. Evidence of both is to be admitted and the court is called upon to use its best judgment to ascertain the meaning of what the parties did. Whether this is done under the guise of interpreting words or modifying the writing makes little difference to the final result.[72]

§ 51. Course of Dealing

In addition to evidence of course of performance, evidence of course of dealing is also admissible to interpret an agreement. "Course of dealing" is defined in these words:

> A course of dealing is a sequence of previous conduct between the parties to a particular transaction which is fairly to be regarded as establishing a common basis of understanding for interpreting their expressions and other conduct.[73]

The difference between course of performance and course of dealing centers on the time in the transaction that the conduct occurs. A sequence of conduct prior to the particular agreement involved is a "course of dealing." A sequence of conduct after the particular agreement is entered into and occurring under that agreement is a "course of performance." [74] Since both are admissible, there will often be little reason to distinguish between them. Both rest on the notion that how parties have acted is relevant in determining what they meant when they used the words of their agreement. However, since course of dealing is more remote to the particular agreement involved than is the course of their performance, the Code provides that if there should be a conflict between these two sequences of conduct, course of performance (the more closely related sequence) is to control over course of conduct.[75] Thus, in cases of conflict it is necessary to distinguish between the two.

A sequence of previous conduct is a "course of dealing" if it "is fairly to be regarded as establishing a common basis of understanding for interpreting" the expression of the parties. Consider the following

---

71. UCC § 2–209(3).

72. *See* 3 A. Corbin, Contracts § 558 (1960).

73. UCC § 1–205(1).

74. § 50 *supra.*

75. UCC § 2–208(2).

example. Suppose that the seller and buyer have dealt with each other for a period of years. Each contract of sale between them has been represented by a writing which was silent as to the place the goods are to be delivered. Under the Code it is clear that, unless the parties have otherwise agreed, the place for delivery of goods is the seller's place of business.[76] Thus, the Code has filled in the contract term which the parties omitted. However, suppose that in each of the prior transactions between the buyer and the seller, the seller has delivered the goods to the buyer. Suppose further that these two parties have entered into another agreement for the purchase and sale of the same goods and that this agreement is also represented by a writing, silent as to the place of delivery. Is the seller now obligated to deliver the goods to the buyer, or may he rely on the Code's statement as to place of delivery and tell the buyer to come and pick up the goods?[77] The Code's answer is clear. The sequence of previous conduct between these parties—even though it relates to other contracts for other deliveries—is admissible to interpret (probably to supplement)[78] this writing and, if believed by the trier of fact, forms an agreement as to the place of delivery. This, of course, does not mean that the parties are bound by their prior conduct if they wish to change it for this particular agreement. They may provide in their present writing that, although the seller has in the past delivered the goods to the buyer, in this case the buyer will be obligated to pick up the goods at the seller's place of business. Such an agreement would control the prior course of dealing because no longer could the prior dealing establish a common basis for the buyer's belief that the agreement required the seller to deliver the goods involved.

Care must be taken not to place too great an emphasis on course of dealing. All the Code does is to make the evidence admissible and, if found to be controlling, to give meaning to and to supplement or qualify the terms of the agreement. The course of dealing may be found clearly to exist, but not to be controlling as to the question presented under the present writing. For example, the prior deliveries by the seller in the assumed case may all have been "small." The present agreement may involve a "large" delivery. In such a case, a court could find that the course of dealing between this buyer and seller cannot fairly be regarded as establishing a "common basis of understanding" for interpreting this particular writing—that is, one calling for a different kind of delivery.[79]

---

76. UCC § 2–308(a).

77. See In re Bengtson, 40 Conn.Bar J. 57 (U.S.Dist.Ct.D.Conn.1965); Dovax Fabrics, Inc. v. G. & A. Delivery Corp., 4 UCC Rep. 492 (N.Y.Civ.Ct.1967).

78. UCC § 1–205(3).

79. See Skeels v. Universal C.I.T. Credit Corp., 335 F.2d 846 (3d Cir. 1964).

The prior section of this text indicated that a course of performance could operate not only as a basis for interpreting the words of a writing but also, in a proper case, as a modification or a waiver. This is not true for a course of dealing. By definition a course of dealing occurs prior to the transaction now involved in the dispute— the Code language is "sequence of *previous* conduct." Modification and waiver are *subsequent* conduct—that is, conduct subsequent to the agreement. Therefore, a course of dealing cannot be used to support either a modification of the present agreement or a waiver of its terms.

§ 52. Usage of Trade

The third type of extrinsic evidence which the Code specifically makes admissible is evidence of trade usage. This term is defined as follows:

> A usage of trade is any practice or method of dealing having such regularity of observance in a place, vocation or trade as to justify an expectation that it will be observed with respect to the transaction in question.[80]

The basic idea is the same as it is for course of dealing.[81] Words of agreement are not to be read out of the context of the parties' agreement. A course of dealing between the parties can give content and meaning to the words they used. Likewise, a trade usage (as above defined) can have the same effect.

Perhaps the most important part of the definition is the emphasis placed on justified expectations. One of the primary reasons for enforcing promises is to protect the justified expectations of those to whom the promises were made.[82] Therefore, if one member of a trade makes a promise to another member of the same trade, general contract law [83] (and now the Code) requires that the promisee's justified expectations arising out of that promise be enforced. To the extent that this particular trade has a practice which is so regularly observed and followed as to create in the promisee a justified expectation that the promisor had that practice in mind when he made his promise, the trade practice ought to—and does under the Code—become a part of the agreement between these parties.[84]

---

80. UCC § 1–205(2).

81. § 51 *supra.*

82. See discussion in § 48 *supra.*

83. 3 A. Corbin, Contracts §§ 555–57 (1960).

84. *E. g.,* Robinson v. United States, 80 U.S. (13 Wall.) 363 (1871).

An example of the proper application of a trade usage can be found in *Hurst v. W. J. Lake & Co.*,[85] a pre-Code case in which the parties agreed in writing that if the subject matter of the sale (horse meat scraps) analyzed "less than 50% of protein," the price was to be reduced $5.00 a ton. The seller delivered nearly 350 tons of horse meat; of those, 140 tons contained between 49.53% and 49.96% protein. The seller demanded full price for those 140 tons but the buyer paid only the full price less the $5.00 per ton discount. In a suit by the seller for the balance due the court reversed a judgment which had been entered for the buyer on the pleadings, relying on an allegation by the seller that there was a usage in the trade in which the parties were engaged that "a protein content of not less than 49.5 per cent was equal to and the same as a content of 50 per cent protein." The same result should be reached under the Code. If the seller can prove the trade usage, he is entitled to the full price for the 140 tons of horse meat delivered and accepted.[86]

One part of *Hurst* has special significance for another Code problem. The Code provides that the terms of an agreement and a usage of trade are to be construed as consistent whenever reasonable; but whenever such a construction is unreasonable, the express terms control the trade usage.[87] The argument made in *Hurst* was that when the parties used the term "50% of protein" they rejected the trade usage. In Code terms the argument will be that the express written term (50% or more) controls the trade usage (49.5% or more) because it is unreasonable to construe the two as consistent. The court's answer was:

> We believe that it is safe to assume, in the absence of evidence to the contrary, that when tradesmen employ trade terms they attach to them their trade significance. If, when they write their trade terms into their contracts, they mean to strip the terms of their special significance and demote them to their common import, it would seem reasonable to believe that they would so state in their agreement. Otherwise, they would refrain from using the trade term and express themselves in other language.[88]

In discussing the above case, this text stated: "If the seller can prove the trade usage, he is entitled to the full price for the 140 tons of horse meat delivered and accepted." Certainly this conclusion cannot rest solely on the definition of trade usage. All that definition does is to indicate what the Code classifies as a usage of trade. The

85. 141 Or. 306, 16 P.2d 627 (1932).

86. UCC § 2–709.

87. UCC § 1–205(4).

88. Hurst v. W. J. Lake & Co., 141 Or. 306, 317–18, 16 P.2d 627, 631.

impact of a trade usage is contained in another Code subsection—and it is on the basis of this subsection that the above conclusion was reached:

> A course of dealing between parties and any usage of trade in the vocation or trade in which they are engaged or of which they are or should be aware give particular meaning to and supplement or qualify terms of an agreement.[89]

This subsection applies to "any usage of trade." The definition of this term has already been set out, but only part has been emphasized. The prior discussion has emphasized what might be called the merchant notion of trade usage—practices in a vocation or trade. The definition is, however, broader. Usage of trade also includes any practice or method of dealing which has a sufficient regularity of observance *in a place* so as to create justified expectations that those practices or methods of dealing will be followed in this particular transaction. This part of the definition may conceivably include non-merchants who are dealing *at a place* with common practices. Since they are not members of a vocation or trade, section 1–205(3)—quoted above—makes this type of trade usage controlling only if the parties "are or should be aware" of these common practices or methods of dealing with each other.

The usage of trade may be employed for three purposes. It may give a particular meaning to the terms of an agreement (as was done with the case involving a discount for horse meat with less than 50% of protein); it may supplement the terms of an agreement; or it may qualify the terms of an agreement. The drafters intended that course of dealing and trade usage could be used well beyond the normal interpretation-of-language problems. They can be used to add obligations and rights not covered by the writing,[90] and they can be used to qualify obligations and rights spelled out in the writing.[91] Therefore, when a course of dealing between parties and a usage of the trade in which they are engaged have created a justified expectation that a particular notice would be given the defendant, the requirement of notice was added to the written agreement even though the writing contained a clause waiving all notices and a provision that the defendant's liability was absolute and unconditional.[92] The court found

---

89. UCC § 1–205(3).

90. Provident Tradesmens Bank & Trust Co. v. Pemberton, 196 Pa.Super. 180, 173 A.2d 780, *aff'g* 24 Pa.D. & C.2d 720 (1961).

91. Valley Nat'l Bank v. Babylon Chrysler-Plymouth, Inc., 53 Misc.2d 1029, 280 N.Y.S.2d 786 (Sup.Ct.), *aff'd* 28 A.D.2d 1092, 284 N.Y.S.2d 849 (1967).

92. Provident Tradesmens Bank & Trust Co. v. Pemberton, 196 Pa.Super. 180, 173 A.2d 780 (1961).

that those written provisions applied to the text of the agreement and not to the trade usage "which is binding on the parties irrespective of" the text of their writing.

In making this last statement the court may have gone too far, depending on facts which are not presented in the opinion. As this text has developed, it is possible to agree that usages of the trade will not apply—and such an agreement is effective.[93] Perhaps all the court meant to say was that the evidence in that case did not dispel the commercial presumption that the parties were bargaining from the background of their past dealings and the usages of their trade. If so, there can be no quarrel with its conclusion.

There are other points in connection with trade usage which merit at least a brief mention. The existence and the scope of a trade usage must be proved as any other fact, but if a written trade code is involved, the court (that is, the judge) is to interpret the code.[94] The usage of trade at the place of performance is to be used in interpreting the agreement relating to that part of the performance.[95] Finally, the Code guards against unfair surprise by providing that evidence of trade usage is not admissible unless and until sufficient notice has been given to the other party.[96]

Evidence of trade usage, course of dealing, and course of performance (as these are defined by the Code) is admissible to interpret writings which evidence agreements under the Code. The Code has rejected any notion that words have but one meaning and that that meaning is to be imposed on the parties irrespective of how they meant those words. While this creates an uncertainty in commercial law—uncertainty in the sense that a lawyer cannot take a written agreement and his copy of a new unabridged dictionary, lay them side-by-side, and tell his client just what the agreement "means"—the Code's approach is eminently sound in that it directs the court to ascertain as best it can, and from all material evidence, just what these parties meant by the words they used.[97] Properly used, these tools can aid in attaining the primary goal of contract law: the enforcement of the justified expectations of the parties.

---

93. Martin v. Ben P. Eubank Lumber Co., 395 S.W.2d 385 (Ky.1965), may be such a case, but the suggestion in the opinion that evidence of trade usage and course of dealing is to be limited to ambiguities in the contract should be rejected. *See* Annawan Mills Inc. v. Northeastern Fibers Co., 26 Mass.App.Dec. 115 (1963).

94. UCC § 1–205(2).

95. UCC § 1–205(5).

96. UCC § 1–205(6).

97. The Comments suggest that the trade usage, to be recognized under the Code must be "currently observed by the great majority of decent dealers, even though dissidents ready to cut corners do not agree." UCC § 1–205, Comment 5. Further, unconscionable trade usages are as ineffective as any other unconscionable clauses in the contract, UCC § 2–302, but the presumption is that the trade usage is reasonable. UCC § 1–205, Comment 6.

§ 53.   The Code's Parol Evidence Rule

Before analyzing the Code's parol evidence rule, the nature of the problem which that rule seeks to solve should be understood. The problem arises when the parties to a sales transaction are involved in some type of dispute. For example, the buyer may be claiming that the seller made certain warranties which were not fulfilled, or the seller may be claiming that the buyer agreed to pay on delivery but now is demanding credit. One of the parties to the dispute has advanced a writing which he claims supports his position. The other admits the existence of the writing and may also admit that he signed it, but claims that the parties had a prior oral agreement which supports his position. One party is relying on the words written on a piece of paper; the other is relying on words which he asserts formed the basis of an oral agreement entered into before the writing was signed. It is at this point that the parol evidence rule comes into play. The holder of the writing responds by urging that his writing prevents the trier of fact from even listening to any evidence of a prior agreement (written or oral) and, for that matter, to any evidence of a contemporaneous oral agreement.[98]

There are substantial reasons to support the argument of the party who advances the writing as the sole evidence of agreement on the point in dispute. Opening a writing to evidence of other agreements (especially oral ones) creates uncertainty in the enforcement of contracts. How can a party rely on a writing if that writing is subject to being changed through oral testimony of prior understandings? This text has argued on other occasions that certainty is a worthwhile goal in commercial transactions. It is no less so here. The desire for certainty, however, ought not outweigh the attempt to ascertain the agreement that the parties in fact made. The purpose of contract law is not to obtain certainty, as such, but to enforce the justified expectations of the parties. To the extent that the prior or contemporaneous agreement was not intended to be changed by the writing, reliance on the writing does not create the type of expectation interest which is worthy of court protection.[99] Evidence of these agreements, although oral, ought to be admitted despite the existence of the writing.

Another reason to deny the admission of evidence of prior and contemporaneous oral agreements is based on the fear that one of the parties will, through perjury, be able to change the agreement

---

98. The pre-Code parol evidence rule is introduced in § 46 *supra*. Cases and texts are cited in that section.

99. Goble v. Dotson, 203 Cal.App.2d 272, 21 Cal.Rptr. 769 (1962); Golden Gate Corp. v. Barrington College, 98 R.I. 35, 199 A.2d 586 (1964).

expressed in the writing. The parties may well have agreed that the writing expressed their final agreement as to the entire transaction, or as to the problem involved in the dispute which has now arisen, but in retrospect one of them may wish to change that agreement (and the writing) by imagining a prior or contemporaneous understanding beneficial to his position in the dispute. By perjured testimony he may be able to convince the trier of fact that such an agreement did exist, thereby destroying the justified expectations of the party who was relying on the writing.[1] Strict application of a rule which prevents a court from listening to testimony of prior understandings will, of course, prevent such a rogue from winning his case through perjury. This is as it should be. However, suppose that the prior agreement was in fact entered into and that the parties did not intend to change that prior agreement when they signed the writing. In such a case "the agreement" between these parties is a combination of what is contained in the writing and what was orally agreed upon before they signed the writing. A blanket prohibition against admission of testimony relating to that prior agreement would prevent proof of the entire agreement and allow the party with the writing to win the case by showing only a portion—the written portion—of the entire agreement.[2]

Courts should always guard against perjury, but the fear of possible perjury should not be allowed to overshadow the attempt to do justice in each case. Justice in sales cases requires the court, at a minimum, to determine what agreement the parties in fact entered into. This means that the judge must listen to the evidence of the alleged prior agreement or of the contemporaneous oral agreement, and decide whether that evidence—if believed by the trier of fact— would be material to the problem before the court. It is not material if the writing superseded the prior or contemporaneous agreement. It is material if the writing did not have this effect and if the agreement relates to an issue in the case. If the judge decides that the evidence is material, that evidence should then be presented to the trier of fact to decide if it is credible. The person who advances the prior or contemporaneous agreement will properly have a difficult time convincing the trier of fact that his version of the entire agreement is the correct one—especially when that version varies substantially from the writing—but the law ought not to say to him that his task is so difficult that he will not even be allowed to try.[3]

---

1. Hoffman v. Late, 222 Ark. 395, 396–97, 260 S.W.2d 446, 447 (1953).

2. Pitcairn v. Philip Hiss Co., 125 F. 110 (3d Cir. 1903).

3. The judge may also refuse to allow the trier of fact to consider the oral evidence if the judge is convinced that reasonable people could not believe the evidence. This function of

These are the problems which the parol evidence rule seeks to solve. A party should not be allowed to lie and thereby win a lawsuit; but neither should a party be allowed to win by keeping the court from hearing the entire agreement which was entered into. Parties ought to be able to rely on written records of agreements; but that reliance is misplaced when they understood that the written record was to be supplemented by their prior understandings. In short, what the parol evidence rule seeks to do is to determine *the contract* between these parties. To the extent that the parties intended their writing to displace their prior understandings, those prior understandings are no longer material to the dispute before the court—and evidence of them should be excluded.[4] To the extent that the parties intended that their agreement was to consist of both the writing and their prior understandings, the prior understandings are material, and evidence of them should be admitted. Once admitted, the trier of fact faces the task of determining whether the evidence is credible.

The above paragraphs express the philosophy underlying the Code's parol evidence rule. Because this section[5] merits careful analysis, it is set out in full:

> Terms with respect to which the confirmatory memoranda of the parties agree or which are otherwise set forth in a writing intended by the parties as a final expression of their agreement with respect to such terms as are included therein may not be contradicted by evidence of any prior agreement or of a contemporaneous oral agreement but may be explained or supplemented
>
> (a) by course of dealing or usage of trade (Section 1–205) or by course of performance (Section 2–208); and
>
> (b) by evidence of consistent additional terms unless the court finds the writing to have been intended also as a complete and exclusive statement of the terms of the agreement.

This section contains two basic thoughts. The first is negative: prior agreements and contemporaneous oral agreements may not be used to contradict certain writings. The second is positive: these writings may, however, be explained or supplemented by certain types of evidence listed in the two subsections. The Code's parol evidence rule can, therefore, be viewed as two rules and the analysis in this text will proceed from this basis.

the parol evidence rule is considered in the last paragraph of this section of the text.

4. For a good statement of the rule, see *In re* Estate of Gains, 15 Cal.2d 255, 264–65, 100 P.2d 1055, 1060 (1940).

5. UCC § 2–202.

THE NEGATIVE RULE

Evidence extrinsic to a writing will be admitted unless the court finds that three conditions exist:

1. *The writing is either (a) confirmatory memoranda which agree as to the term in dispute or (b) a writing intended by the parties as a final expression of agreement as to the term in dispute.* Thus, not all writings will prevent the introduction of evidence of prior agreements or of contemporaneous oral agreements. A memorandum sent by one party or a proposed formulation of the agreement will not exclude such evidence.

The "confirmatory memoranda" requirement suggests several ideas. First, there must be more than one memorandum. The implication is that each party must have sent at least one memorandum.[6] Further, these memoranda must agree on the term which is now in dispute. The memoranda may agree on many points but if neither (or only one) contains the term being challenged, the writings do not satisfy the "memoranda" requirement.[7] Finally, the memoranda must confirm the prior oral agreement.

If there are no confirmatory memoranda which agree, the only other type of a writing which will satisfy the Code's parol evidence rule is one which is "intended by the parties as a final expression of their agreement with respect to such terms as are included therein." Each of the words in this requirement assumes importance. The "writing" undoubtedly need not be a single document or piece of paper (although either could suffice); several documents taken together by the parties will, in appropriate cases, satisfy the need for "a writing." [8] The principal factor in determining whether the writing is appropriate

---

6. The parol evidence rule must be distinguished from the statute of frauds. The Code statute of frauds requires a writing, or a substitute, for contracts for the sale of goods at a price of $500 or more. The parol evidence rule never requires a writing, but states only what effect a writing which the parties chose to adopt will have on prior or contemporaneous understandings. A single memorandum will satisfy the statute of frauds if signed by the party to be charged, and may satisfy the statute of frauds if the non-signer is sought to be charged. UCC §§ 2–201(1) and (2). However, a single memorandum adopted by only one party will never satisfy the writing requirement for the parol evidence rule. UCC § 2–202.

7. UCC § 2–207 may present a case which may form an exception to the textual statement. Suppose a buyer sends a confirmatory memorandum of an oral contract to purchase goods. Thereafter, seller sends his confirmatory memorandum, but inserts an additional term. If seller and buyer are merchants, the additional term will "become part of the contract" unless one of the conditions of UCC § 2–207(2) is met. This additional term could be considered as agreed upon, and thus satisfy the memoranda requirement of UCC § 2–202.

8. Stern & Co. v. State Loan & Fin. Corp., 238 F.Supp. 901 (D.Del.1965); General Equip. v. Bible Press, Inc., 10 Mich.App. 665, 160 N.W.2d 370 (1968).

for the application of the parol evidence rule is whether the *parties* (both of them) intended that writing to be the final expression of the agreement in regard to the terms in dispute.[9] It is not enough that one party intended finality; they both must have this intention. Before excluding the evidence, the judge must find either that both parties subjectively had this intention or that the one now relying on the writing had a reasonable belief that the other also intended the writing to have finality as to the terms in dispute.[10] The example often found in decided cases is the printed form contract which was presented to a consumer-buyer on a take-it-or-leave-it basis, and which contained a statement that the writing is the final and complete agreement of the parties and that there have been no oral representations or promises beyond those contained in the writing. If the consumer-buyer signed the writing under conditions in which it was clear to the retailer-seller that the buyer did not have or take time to read the fine print, did not realize the clause was included in the form, or did not understand its significance, there is no writing *intended*—subjectively or objectively—by the *parties* to have the requisite finality regarding prior oral promises.[11] In such a case the printed clause should not bar evidence of prior agreements even though a term in the writing is being contradicted. The writing involved does not meet the first Code requirement for the operation of the parol evidence rule.

2. *The extrinsic evidence contradicts a term of the writing.* The prohibition is against contradiction. With one exception, to be discussed under the positive rule of this Code section, there is no prohibi-

---

9. Hull-Dobbs, Inc. v. Mallicoat, 57 Tenn.App. 100, 415 S.W.2d 344 (1966).

10. The Code is not clear in UCC § 2–202 as to the division of duties between the judge and the jury. However, the statement in the text appears to be the intention of the drafters especially in view of UCC § 2–202(b) which states that the *court* (which Comment 3 says means the judge) is to decide whether the parties intended the writing to be the complete and exclusive statement of the terms of the agreement. That problem is similar to the one considered in the text. This reading of UCC § 2–202 would further mean that the judge ought to decide whether the confirmatory memoranda *agree* as to the term in dispute. Pre-Code law on this question was not clear. See 9 J. Wigmore, Evidence § 2430 (3d ed. 1940); McCormick, *The Parol Evidence Rule as a Procedural Device for Control of the Jury*, 41 Yale L.J. 365 (1932).

11. UCC § 2–202(b). *See* Leveridge v. Notaras, 433 P.2d 935 (Okl.1967), where court found such a writing to be ambiguous because of a handwritten note in the margin dealing with "30 day warranty," and admitted parol evidence of the warranty. Admission was clearly proper under these facts, but a better Code reason for admission would have been that the buyer did not intend the printed form to be a final expression of the entire agreement or of the warranty terms—and seller had no reason to believe that buyer intended finality be given the writing. *Cf.* Green Chev. Co. v. Kemp, 241 Ark. 62, 406 S.W.2d 142 (1966) (but court suggested that buyer waited too long to reject or revoke acceptance); and HML Corp. v. General Foods Corp., 365 F.2d 77 (3d Cir. 1966) (where the court thought the particular agreement would have been included if it had been made).

tion against the use of evidence of prior agreements or contemporaneous oral agreements to explain or supplement a writing. The line between contradiction and explanation is not easy to draw. Nevertheless, the Code rejects the idea that language has a single meaning arising out of rules of law, rather than the meaning which the commercial context supports.[12] To the extent that prior agreements have given the written words a commercial context, those agreements ought to be admitted in evidence even though it first appears that the writing is being "contradicted."[13]

Perhaps the most important word in the Code's parol evidence rule is "terms." The Code rejects the assumption that because a writing is intended to be final on some matters, it is to be taken as final on all matters agreed upon.[14] This rejection is accomplished through the use of the word "terms." It is only the *terms* in the writing which may not be contradicted by prior agreements or contemporaneous oral agreements. If the writing is silent on the particular matter in dispute, extrinsic evidence is to be freely admitted— unless the court goes on to find that the writing was also intended to be the complete and exclusive statement of all of the terms of the agreement. Therefore, the definition of the word "terms" becomes crucial to an understanding of the Code's parol evidence rule. Is this word to be construed so that extrinsic evidence is barred whenever the general subject of that extrinsic evidence is mentioned in the writing, or does this word mean that the precise subject must be included before the extrinsic evidence is barred?

To illustrate, consider the following hypothetical problems:

Case # 1. Buyer sued Seller for damages caused when the brakes on the automobile which Buyer had bought from Seller failed to operate properly. Buyer and Seller had signed a writing which said nothing about brakes, did not disclaim warranties of quality, but did contain a warranty of title. Buyer, however, wants to introduce into evidence an oral statement allegedly made by Seller (prior to the execution of the writing) warranting that the brakes were in excellent shape and good for another 10,000 miles. Seller objects to the introduction of this oral statement on the basis of the parol evidence rule.

---

12. UCC § 2–202, Comment 1(b).

13. Webb & Sons v. Hamilton, 30 A. D.2d 597, 290 N.Y.S.2d 122 (1968). Evidence of prior agreement is admissible to show that the promise to pay $5,000 "from the jobs now under construction" meant "from the profits of jobs now under construction." Parol evidence did not contradict writing. *Cf.* Eskimo Pie Corp. v. Whitelawn Dairies, Inc., 284 F.Supp. 987 (S.D. N.Y.1968) (pre-Code case).

14. UCC § 2–202, Comment 1(a).

Case # 2. Buyer and Seller exchanged memoranda confirming a telephone conversation in which Seller agreed to sell to Buyer certain goods for "$35.00 per hundredweight." The memoranda agreed as to the price. Buyer is now claiming that Seller agreed, during the telephone conversation, to give Buyer a 2% discount for payments made within 10 days of the invoice date. Seller claims that the parol evidence rule prevents this statement from being considered.

There were several pre-Code methods of introducing evidence of prior agreements. In the first example, above, Seller's statement may have been more than a promise about the brakes; it may have been a fraudulent misrepresentation or it may have been a condition precedent to the contractual obligations. If it was either of these, common law tradition supports its admissibility. In the second example above, the discount alleged may also be a trade custom. If so, both the prior law and the Code allow the evidence to be considered by the court.[15] Further, in a proper case a writing will be reformed to conform to a prior oral agreement. These "exceptions" to the parol evidence rule have already been discussed.[16] When needed, these "exceptions" can be used by the courts to admit the extrinsic evidence. One court has already held that fraudulent statements are not precluded by the Code, although the Code's parol evidence rule is not expressly conditioned on the absence of fraud.[17] The court relied on pre-Code law and on section 1–103—which brings into the Code all validating and invalidating causes unless displaced by a particular Code provision—to support its admission of the parol evidence. This type of reasoning will allow courts to bring all pre-Code exceptions into the Code parol evidence rule.

There is, however, a much more direct method of analyzing these problems—one that is more consistent with the language of the Code. Assuming that the court does not find that the writings in these hypothetical cases were intended to be a complete and exclusive statement of all of the terms of the parties' agreements, the Code states that the evidence will be admitted unless the proffered evidence contradicts a *term* in the writing. In Case #2 there is a price term, but there is no term dealing with discounts. Is the Code word "terms" to be read narrowly—that is, to mean that the precise subject matter (discount) must be included in the writing—or is it to be read broadly so that any reference to the topic of price or consideration precludes evidence of prior agreements and contemporaneous oral agreements on the same broad subject matter? The same problem exists in Case #1. There are no warranties of quality in the writing, nor is there a disclaimer of

---

15. UCC § 2–202(a).

16. §§ 50–52 *supra*.

17. Associated Hardware Supply Co. v. Big Wheel Distrib. Co., 355 F.2d 114 (3d Cir. 1965).

such warranties.[18] Thus, it appears that there is no "term" which is being contradicted by the proffered evidence. However, there is a warranty of title. Is "term" to be read to prevent this extrinsic evidence from being considered by the court because the broad subject of warranties is mentioned in the writing? [19]

Unfortunately, the Code is not clear in its answer. The definition of "term" indicates that it is "that portion of an agreement which relates to a particular matter." [20] "Agreement" is defined as the "bargain of the parties in fact as found in their language or by implication from other circumstances." [21] Combining these definitions, a "term" becomes a particular matter in the parties' bargain. Emphasis on "particular" suggests that the precise matter must be mentioned (the discount or the warranty of quality) before the oral evidence is excluded, but the Code is far from decisive on this problem. To date, courts have not been required to focus on this problem.

The logic underlying the parol evidence rule favors a narrow construction of "terms"—that is, favors excluding parol evidence only if the precise matter was mentioned in the writing (again, unless the court finds that the parties intended to rescind all prior understandings when they signed the writing).[22] The court is dealing with what is admittedly an incomplete writing; the parties did not intend to integrate their entire agreement. Thus, any part of their agreement which is not directly contradicted is material, remembering that the closer the alleged oral agreement comes to contradicting a term in the writing the more difficult it will be for the proponent to convince the trier of fact that such an agreement did exist.[23]

Nevertheless, even if the court in the first case does construe the Code's "terms" broadly to include any mention of warranties and finds that the warranty of title in the supposed sale of the automobile is such a *warranty term*, the oral evidence of the warranty of the brakes should still be admitted. The second requirement for the application of the negative parol evidence rule is that the extrinsic evidence must *contradict* a term of the writing. The proffered evidence is material and in no way contradicts the warranty term in the writing. Extrinsic evidence is not inadmissible when it adds to or supplements a term.[24]

---

18. Disclaimers and the parol evidence rule are discussed in § 69 *infra.*

19. For a pre-Code case raising this problem, see Rogers v. Zielinski, 92 R.I. 479, 170 A.2d 294 (1961).

20. UCC § 1-201(42).

21. UCC § 1-201(3). See § 47 *supra.*

22. UCC § 2-202(b).

23. Hunt Foods & Indus., Inc. v. Doliner, 26 A.D.2d 41, 270 N.Y.S.2d 937 (1966).

24. Webb & Sons v. Hamilton, 30 A. D.2d 597, 290 N.Y.S.2d 122 (1968).

3. *The proffered evidence is of a prior agreement or of a contemporaneous oral agreement.* Prior agreements, whether written or oral, are excluded if the first two requirements of the Code's parol evidence rule are met. The prior written agreement, like the oral, may be integrated into a later written term. If it is so integrated, the past agreement—regardless of its form—is no longer a part of the parties' contract and should be excluded as immaterial. However, only oral contemporaneous agreements are excluded, evidently on the principle that if many documents are signed or adopted at the same time, the court should consider all of these documents in determining the agreement of the parties.

Under no version of the parol evidence rule are subsequent agreements rendered inadmissible. If such an agreement is oral, it may be excluded because it fails to comply with the statute of frauds,[25] but parties cannot integrate future understandings into a present writing. The parol evidence rule seeks only to determine the parties' agreement as of the time of the writing. Parties may later change this agreement without concern over the parol evidence rule.

THE POSITIVE RULE

The Code could have concluded the parol evidence rule with the provisions already discussed, but to make clear the kind of evidence which will be admitted the drafters included two subsections as to evidence which could be used to explain or supplement the writing. These are:

1. *Evidence of course of dealing, usage of trade, or course of performance will be admitted.* The meaning of these terms has already been discussed.[26] Evidence of each is clearly admissible even under the negative portion of the Code's parol evidence rule. None of them is a prior or contemporaneous *agreement.* Each is a series of events which gives meaning and content to the words used by the parties when they entered into their oral or written agreement, and each can be used to explain or supplement a writing. Courts admit this type of extrinsic evidence even though the writing contains words or figures which appear unambiguous until the extrinsic evidence is admitted.[27] To negate course of dealing, usage of trade or course of performance the writing must clearly express the intention to reach this result; certainly, the fact that the court finds that the writing was intended to

25. UCC § 2–209(3) ; § 43 *supra.*

26. §§ 50–52 *supra.*

27. Hurst v. Lake & Co., 141 Or. 306, 16 P.2d 627 (1932).

be a complete and exclusive statement of the agreement is not sufficient to exclude any evidence of this type.[28]

2. *Evidence of consistent additional terms will be admitted.* Because the writing is final as to some terms of the agreement (for example, price, subject matter, and warranties), this does not mean that it is final as to all matters agreed upon. Therefore, terms which add to the agreement expressed in the writing are admissible so long as they are "consistent"—that is, do not contradict the writing. This is nothing more than a positive restatement of the negative aspect of the parol evidence rule, already discussed. The Code, however, adds a significant condition to this portion of the rule: the consistent additional terms will be admitted "unless the court finds the writing to have been intended also as a complete and exclusive statement of the terms of the agreement."[29] This addition is consistent with the theory of the parol evidence rule presented above. If the parties intended that the writing was to be the final embodiment of all they had agreed upon up to the time of the writing and that all prior understandings were rescinded if not contained in the writing, the writing has become the sole evidence of their agreement and all of their prior agreements—whether consistent, contradictory, explanatory, or supplemental—are inadmissible because they show nothing which is material to a determination of *the contract* of these parties.

The sentence structure of this Code subsection makes it clear that the party who is seeking to keep out evidence of (prior or contemporaneous) consistent additional terms bears the burden of convincing the court of the writing's finality. The evidence is to be admitted *unless* the court is convinced that the writing was intended as a complete and exclusive statement of the terms of their agreement. Pre-Code law disagreed as to how this finality should be determined. In some cases, finality was to be determined by looking at the writing to see if it appeared on its face to be complete.[30] One way to make this determination was to see if there was a clause saying that the writing was complete,[31] but such a clause was not essential to a determination of completeness. In other cases, finality was determined by ascertaining whether the particular element involved in the suit was dealt with

---

28. The fact that the writing was intended as complete and exclusive bars only additional terms of agreement, not course of dealing, course of performance, or trade usage. See UCC § 2–202(b), and Comment 2. *Cf.* General Elec. Co. v. United States Dynamics, Inc., 403 F.2d 933 (1st Cir. 1968).

29. UCC § 2–202(b).

30. Spurgeon v. Buchter, 192 Cal.App. 2d 198, 13 Cal.Rptr. 354 (1961); Thompson v. Libby, 34 Minn. 374, 26 N.W. 1 (1885).

31. J. B. Colt & Co. v. Clay, 216 Ky. 782, 288 S.W. 745 (1926); Valley Refrigeration Co. v. Lange Co., 242 Wis. 466, 8 N.W.2d 294 (1943).

by the writing.[32] Other tests were also suggested.[33] The Code's emphasis on the necessity for the parties to have intended finality leaves many problems unsolved, but it should effectively change the "facially complete" test in those states which had used it prior to the Code. The document says nothing about the intention of the parties when they signed it. Evidence of the circumstances of the signing is needed to determine whether the parties either subjectively or objectively intended to rescind past agreements when they signed the writing.

The Comments suggest that this final Code subsection is to be used to keep out evidence which is not reasonably credible. "If the additional terms are such that, if agreed upon, they would certainly have been included in the document in the view of the court, then evidence of their alleged making must be kept from the trier of fact."[34] This secondary function of the parol evidence rule was discussed in a prior section of this text.[35] There is nothing improper about using the parol evidence rule for this purpose, but the court should be aware that a different function is being served by this use. The normal operation of the rule is that of deciding what facts are material to a determination of the contract between the parties; whether those facts are credible becomes an issue for the trier of fact. The secondary operation of the rule is to take from the trier of fact those statements (although material if true) which the court is convinced could not be believed by reasonable men.[36]

---

32. Shelton Yacht & Cabana Club, Inc. v. Suto, 150 Conn. 251, 188 A.2d 493 (1963); Salzman v. Maldaver, 315 Mich. 403, 24 N.W.2d 161 (1946); Rogers v. Zielinski, 92 R.I. 479, 170 A.2d 294 (1961).

33. These include: (1) If parties would normally include this agreement in the writing, the prior agreement was integrated. O'Brien v. O'Brien, 362 Pa. 66, 66 A.2d 309 (1949). (2) If the agreement is collateral to the writing, the agreement is not integrated. Lefforge v. Rogers, 419 P.2d 625 (Wyo.1966).

34. UCC § 2–202, Comment 3.

35. § 46 *supra*.

36. The litigation in Hunt Foods & Industries, Inc. v. Doliner, 49 Misc.2d 246, 267 N.Y.S.2d 364 (Sup.Ct.), *rev'd* 26 A.D.2d 41, 270 N.Y.S.2d 937 (1966), is an example of the disagreement as to whether the evidence was believable. See also Eskimo Pie Corp. v. Whitelawn Dairies, Inc., 284 F.Supp. 987 (S.D.N.Y.1968); Whirlpool Corp. v. Regis Leasing Corp., 29 A.D.2d 395, 288 N.Y.S.2d 337 (1968).

CHAPTER IV

WARRANTIES OF THE SELLER

Analysis

A. INTRODUCTION

D. LIMITATIONS ON AND EXCLUSION OF WARRANTIES

E. PERSONS PROTECTED

A. INTRODUCTION

§ 54. Historical Analysis of Product Liability Cases

The seller has many obligations under a contract for the sale of goods, but the ones which have created the largest number of legal problems are those dealing with his obligations as to the quality of the goods sold. The nineteenth century American tradition was that of *caveat emptor*—let the buyer beware. A sprawling country with vast resources and a faith in rugged individualism promoted the idea that if each person was left alone to make his own advantage or disadvantage, society as a whole would benefit. Close distinctions between latent and patent defects were drawn,[1] but there was something American about the horse trade in which both the seller and the buyer tried to get the better of each other.[2]

The American tradition is illustrated in *Seixas v. Woods*,[3] a New York case decided in 1804. Wood was shipped from New Providence under an invoice listing the wood as brazilleto. The agent for the seller advertised the wood as brazilleto and so described it in the bill of sale to the buyer. The delivered wood turned out to be peachum—evidently of less value than brazilleto. The buyer sought to return the peachum and to recover his purchase price. A refusal by the agent prompted a law suit in which the buyer sought to recover the price he had paid.

Today this would be a "clear case"—the buyer would be allowed to recover at the least those damages measured by the difference between the value of brazilleto and the value of peachum. If the buyer acted quickly enough and gave the proper notice, he could (instead of recovering difference-money damages) return the wood and receive a

---

1. Hoe v. Sanborn, 21 N.Y. 552 (1860).

2. Paddock v. Strobridge, 29 Vt. 470 (1857). Generally, see Hamilton, *The Ancient Maxim Caveat Emptor*, 40 Yale L.J. 1133 (1931). Early English law did not imply a warranty of title unless the seller fraudulently concealed his lack of title. 1 S. Williston, Sales § 217 (rev. ed. 1948).

3. 2 Caines (N.Y.) 48 (1804).

refund of the price plus damages. Even in 1804 this was described as a "clear case" by one of the judges, but it was a "clear case for the defendant." A majority of the court agreed. The buyer kept his peachum; the agent retained the price.

A look at history will place both this case and the current law of product liability in perspective. Reports of warranty cases had begun to appear by the fourteenth century, and these cases had their origin in forms of action which today lawyers would classify as tort.[4] To say that the fourteenth century warranty action was tortious in nature is to read a lot of modern thinking back into the writs which lawyers used without concern as to whether contract or tort was involved. In fact, the beginnings of assumpsit (contract) were only vaguely emerging at the time these warranty cases were being decided. More than a hundred years would pass before assumpsit would split from the great common law writ of trespass on the case and become a separate writ.[5] Nevertheless, the flavor of these early cases can be gathered from this quotation: "If a man sells me seed and warrants it good, and it is bad, or warrants that it is seed of a certain county, and it is not, I shall have action of deceit." [6] The action was based not on the promise but on the injury caused by the wrongful act. True, the act was wrongful because of the promise—and today we could so analyze the problem—but it was the wrongful act which was the basis of the action in the early common law.[7]

When assumpsit became a recognized form of action, an alternative basis for warranty was presented. The promise could be the gist of the cause of action. That alternative bases existed is shown by *Seixas v. Woods*, already discussed, in which the seller's agent sold peachum wood under an affirmation of fact that the wood was brazilleto. The court refused to allow the buyer to recover his price, with one judge saying, "From an examination of the decisions in courts of common law, I can find no case where an action has been sustained under similar circumstances: an express warranty, or some fraud in the sale, are deemed indispensably necessary to be shown." [8] An earlier case is *Chandelor v. Lopus*,[9] a famous English decision which helped shape American law of warranty for over two hundred years. In *Chandelor* a buyer sued a goldsmith in trespass on the case alleging that the gold-

4. Ames, *The History of Assumpsit*, 2 Harv.L.Rev. 1, 8 (1888).

5. T. Plucknett, A Concise History of the Common Law 637–46 (5th ed. 1956).

6. Y.B. 11 Ed. IV. Trin. pl. 10. Quoted in 3 W. Holdsworth, History of English Law 430–31 (3d ed. 1923).

7. See, e. g., *Humber Ferry Case*, 22 Ass. 94 (no. 41) (1348), discussed in T. Plucknett, A Concise History of the Common Law 470 (5th ed. 1956).

8. 2 Caines (N.Y.) 48, 52 (1804).

9. 3 Cro.Jac. 4, 79 Eng.Rep. 3 (Ex. 1603).

smith had sold a stone to the buyer for one hundred pounds, affirming it to be a bezoar stone. (A bezoar is thus defined: "any of various concretions found chiefly in the alimentary organs of ruminants and formerly believed to possess magical properties.") [10] In fact the stone was not a bezoar. The buyer had a verdict, but error was brought in the Exchequer Chamber "because the declaration contains not matter sufficient to charge defendant, *viz*, that he warranted it to be a bezoar-stone, or he knew that it was not a bezoar-stone; for it may be, he was ignorant whether it was a bezoar-stone or not." The judgment was reversed.

> [H]eld, that for this cause it was error: for the bare affirmance that it was a bezoar-stone, without warranting it to be so, is no cause of action: and although he knew it to be no bezoar-stone, it is not material; for every one in selling his wares will affirm that his wares are good, or the horse which he sells is sound; yet if he does not warrant them to be so, it is no cause of action, and the warranty ought to be made at the same time of the sale.[11]

Since no warranty was alleged, the declaration failed.

This decision contains the language of *caveat emptor* which was picked up by *Seixas* and hundreds of other American cases. This decision also shows the division between approaches in fraud (tort) and warranty (contract). Evidently there was only one way to make a warranty, and that was by an express promise which contained the word "warrant"—or some word close thereto.

There are, therefore, several ways to analyze the facts of a case in which the buyer is claiming that the quality of the goods was not what was agreed upon at the time of the sale. The three most commonly used are:

1. *Contract liability through warranty.* In *Seixas v. Woods* the advertisement, the negotiations, and the bill of sale all described the wood as brazilleto. The difficulty with an analysis in contract is that there was no promise that the wood was brazilleto. The failure to use the magic words of promise prevented recovery by the buyer in *Seixas* and *Lopus* as well as in some twentieth century cases.[12] However, both the Uniform Sales Act [13] and the Uniform Commercial Code [14] provide that affirmations of fact and descriptions can give rise to war-

---

10. Webster's Seventh New Collegiate Dictionary (1967).

11. 3 Cro.Jac. 4, 79 Eng.Rep. 3, 4 (Ex. 1603).

12. Heilbut v. Buckleton, [1913] A.C. 30. See Williston, *Representation and*

Warranty in Sales.—Heilbut v. Buckleton, 27 Harv.L. Rev. 1 (1913).

13. Uniform Sales Act, §§ 12, 14.

14. UCC § 2–313(1).

ranties. Certainly, the advertisement, the negotiations, and the bill of sale affirmed the fact that the wood was brazilleto and, in addition, described the wood as brazilleto. Since the seller's statements became at least a part of the basis of the bargain, modern law would hold that there was a warranty that the wood delivered would be brazilleto. Delivery of peachum was a default by the seller, and the buyer could today recover the price he had paid plus damages caused by the fact that the goods delivered were not as warranted.[15]

2. *Rescission based upon mistake.* Both the buyer and the seller assumed that the wood involved was brazilleto and they entered into their agreement on the basis of this assumption. That assumption, basic to their deal, turned out to be false. The warranty analysis, above, fastened attention on the seller's expressions of his belief. By fastening attention on the belief of both parties, a court can conclude that the agreement rested on mutual mistake and rescind the transaction, allowing the buyer to recover the purchase price which he paid.[16] Principles of mistake, therefore, complement Code warranty remedies based upon ideas of cancellation. Principles of mistake, however, do not complement Code warranty remedies based upon ideas of affirmance. Suppose that the buyer in *Seixas v. Woods* had sued the seller for damages based upon the difference between the value of the promised wood (brazilleto) and the value of the delivered wood (peachum). If the seller were allowed to rely on the doctrine of mutual mistake, the seller could defeat the damage action by rescinding the agreement out of which the warranty arose. Thus, when a buyer is seeking damages, ideas of mistake conflict with the protection given by a warranty. Quite properly, courts have worked out solutions to these cases on the basis of warranty, but principles of mistake remain on the outer edges of sales law and can be used to handle the harder cases.[17]

3. *Liability through concepts of tort.* One type of tort liability begins with an analysis similar to that of warranty liability: the advertisements, the negotiations, and the bill of sale all described the wood as brazilleto. These descriptions, the buyer would urge, amounted to a representation as to the quality of the wood. The *Seixas* court thought it was necessary for the buyer to show that the seller knew that these

---

15. UCC § 2–711(1).

16. Smith v. Zimbalist, 2 Cal.App.2d 324, 38 P.2d 170 (1934). In this case the buyer defeated an action for the price but did not ask for a return of prepayments. If he had, the following cases indicate that the request would have been granted following proper restitution. California Steel Prods. Co. v. Wadlow, 58 Ariz. 69, 118 P.2d 67 (1941); International Harvester Co. v. Tjentland, 181 Iowa 940, 165 N.W. 180 (1917). Compare §§ 143, 146 *infra.*

17. Dadourian Export Corp. v. United States, 291 F.2d 178 (2d Cir. 1961).

representations were false at the time he made them; [18] there is authority today that misrepresentations negligently made will suffice for damages [19] and even that an innocent misrepresentation will allow rescission. [20]

The principal tort remedy for injuries caused by defective goods centers not on fraud and deceit, but on principles of negligence (with or without res ipsa loquitur) and strict liability. A change in the facts of *Seixas* will illustrate these principles. Suppose that the buyer in that case had ordered from the seller a ladder to be made out of brazilleto wood, and suppose further that brazilleto is a hard wood known for its sturdiness. (The author has no idea whether this is a fact, but the assumption will be made for the purpose of presenting the tort theory of recovery.) The delivered ladder was, however, made of peachum— which it will be assumed is a soft wood not known for its sturdiness. While the buyer was using the ladder, the rung on which he was standing broke (because it was made of peachum), and the buyer fell— suffering serious personal injuries.

This factual pattern, presenting injury to person and property, can be analyzed through concepts of warranties made at the time of the sale. Relaxation of the requirement that certain words had to be used before a warranty existed [21] made sales law a popular theory for product liability cases. The reason was obvious: if a warranty could be shown, recovery was simplified because knowledge of the falsity of a misrepresentation or negligence in the manufacture of the product did not have to be shown. All that the injured party was required to prove was the warranty and its breach. [22] Because of this, sales law for a time was used almost exclusively to solve product liability problems.

The law of sales, however, had other difficulties—primarily that of a need for privity. Sales law implied contract and a contract is a consensual relationship between people. How could someone who was

18. This became the rule of Derry v. Peek, 14 A.C. 337 (1889), overruled in Hedley Byrne & Co. v. Heller & Partners, [1964] A.C. 465, 2 All Eng.Rep. 575.

19. Mullen v. Eastern Trust & Banking Co., 108 Me. 498, 81 A. 948 (1911); Sult v. Scandrett, 119 Mont. 570, 178 P.2d 405 (1947); Brown v. Underwriters at Lloyd's, 53 Wash.2d 142, 332 P.2d 228 (1958).

20. Joslyn v. Cadillac Automobile Co., 177 F. 863 (6th Cir. 1910); Henry v.

Kopf, 104 Conn. 73, 131 A. 412 (1925); Montgomery Door & Sash Co. v. Atlantic Lumber Co., 206 Mass. 144, 92 N. E. 71 (1910); Seneca Wire & Mfg. Co. v. A. B. Leach & Co., 247 N.Y. 1, 159 N.E. 700 (1928); Lanners v. Whitney, 247 Or. 223, 428 P.2d 398 (1967) (Code case).

21. UCC § 2–313(2). This section conforms to pre-Code law. 1 S. Williston, Sales §§ 196–203 (rev. ed. 1948).

22. 1 S. Williston, Sales § 197 (rev. ed. 1948).

not a party to the contract possibly have a cause of action on the contract?[23] The lawyer's classification system produced an impasse.

Contractual privity was not a problem of tort law, so injured buyers turned to negligence when they were suing a remote seller, and remote sellers became more common in an economy based on mass-produced goods. *Thomas v. Winchester,*[24] and *Huset v. J. I. Case Threshing Co.*[25] led the way, but the best known case accepting the tort analysis is *MacPherson v. Buick Motor Co.,*[26] where the purchaser of an automobile was allowed to recover damages (on a theory of negligence) from the manufacturer of the automobile for injuries sustained when a wheel collapsed. Negligence, however, is difficult to prove—especially when the facts of manufacture are known only to the defendant. Res ipsa loquitur was some help to plaintiffs, but the pressure mounted for courts to accept a principle of strict liability.

That step was taken by California in *Greenman v. Yuba Power Products, Inc.,*[27] in which the user of a power drill was injured by a defect in the construction of the drill. Suit was brought against both the retailer and the manufacturer of the drill. The principal defense advanced by the manufacturer was that the injured party had not given notice of his injuries within a reasonable time as required by the Uniform Sales Act.[28] The court held that such notice was not needed, and assigned two reasons. First, before the drill was purchased the injured party had studied a brochure prepared by the manufacturer; this brochure contained misrepresentations as to the drill; and the notice provisions of the Sales Act do not apply to misrepresentations. Second, a "manufacturer is strictly liable in tort when an article he places on the market, knowing that it is to be used without inspection for defects, proves to have a defect that causes injury to a human being."[29] Other states have followed *Greenman's* lead.[30] The doctrine of strict liability is summarized in two sections of the *Restatement (Second) of Torts.* The first sets out the rule thus:

23. Winterbottom v. Wright, 10 M. & W. 109, 152 Eng.Rep. 402 (Ex. 1842). Privity under the Code is discussed in §§ 90–92 *infra.*

24. 6 N.Y. 397 (1852).

25. 120 F. 865 (8th Cir. 1903).

26. 217 N.Y. 382, 111 N.E. 1050 (1916).

27. 59 Cal.2d 57, 377 P.2d 897, 27 Cal. Rptr. 697 (1962). See also Vandermark v. Ford Motor Co., 61 Cal.2d 256, 391 P.2d 168, 37 Cal.Rptr. 896 (1964).

28. For the Code's notice requirements, see UCC §§ 2–602, 2–607, 2–608.

29. 59 Cal.2d at 62, 27 Cal.Rptr. at 700, 377 P.2d at 900.

30. *E. g.,* Dealers Transp. Co. v. Battery Distrib. Co., 402 S.W.2d 441 (Ky. 1965); McCormack v. Hankscraft Co., 278 Minn. 322, 154 N.W.2d 488 (1967), 281 Minn. 571, 161 N.W.2d 523 (1968); Santor v. A & M Karagheusian, Inc., 44 N.J. 52, 207 A.2d 305 (1965); Lonzrick v. Republic Steel Corp., 6 Ohio St.2d 227, 218 N.E.2d

(1) One who sells any product in a defective condition unreasonably dangerous to the user or consumer or to his property is subject to liability for physical harm thereby caused to the ultimate user or consumer, or to his property, if

>   (a) the seller is engaged in the business of selling such a product, and

>   (b) it is expected to and does reach the user or consumer without substantial change in the condition in which it is sold.

(2) The rule stated in Subsection (1) applies although

>   (a) the seller has exercised all possible care in the preparation and sale of his product, and

>   (b) the user or consumer has not bought the product from or entered into any contractual relation with the seller.[31]

The second section complements the one already quoted by providing a basis for recovery when misrepresentation is involved. That section of the *Restatement (Second) of Torts* provides:

>   One engaged in the business of selling chattels who, by advertising, labels, or otherwise, makes to the public a misrepresentation of material fact concerning the character or quality of a chattel sold by him is subject to liability for physical harm to a consumer of the chattel caused by justifiable reliance upon the misrepresentation, even though

>   (a) it is not made fraudulently or negligently, and

>   (b) the consumer has not bought the chattel from or entered into any contractual relation with the seller.[32]

Many of the ideas contained in this latter provision parallel those found in warranty liability under the Code.[33]

There were two reasons for beginning this chapter with the case of *Seixas v. Woods*. First, it shows the tradition from which the American law of sales began. The buyer was required to look out for his own interests; failure to do so left him with only himself to blame.

185 (1966); Olney v. Beaman Bottling Co., 220 Tenn. 459, 418 S.W.2d 430 (1967). *Cf.*, Stubblefield v. Johnson-Fagg, Inc., 379 F.2d 270 (10th Cir. 1967).

31. Restatement (Second) of Torts § 402A (1965). See Prosser, *The Fall of the Citadel (Strict Liability to the Consumer)*, 50 Minn.L. Rev. 791 (1966).

32. Restatement (Second) of Torts § 402B (1965).

33. See Rapson, *Products Liability Under Parallel Doctrines: Contrasts Between the Uniform Commercial Code and Strict Liability in Tort*, 19 Rutgers L.Rev. 692 (1965).

As the court remarked: "The agent of the plaintiffs, who made the purchase, was present at the delivery of the wood; and the defect now complained of was within the reach of his observation and judgment, had he bestowed proper attention." [34] Could not the seller also have ascertained the defect if he had bestowed the proper attention? Why select the buyer as the one who must inspect as he buys? The court's answer was: "I see no injustice or inconvenience resulting from this doctrine, but, on the contrary, think it best calculated to excite the caution and attention which all prudent men ought to observe in making their contracts." [35] Of course, the judge did not mean that *all* prudent men ought to be excited into exercising caution when they enter into contracts. What he meant was that all prudent *buyers* ought to exercise caution; sellers would be lulled into the security of non-caution and inattention by the doctrine of *Seixas v. Woods*. Nevertheless, this is the tradition from which American commercial law began. *Seixas* was overruled approximately 75 years later,[36] but its vestiges remained. How far the Uniform Sales Act and the Uniform Commercial Code have been successful in eradicating the early tradition of *caveat emptor* is the subject of this chapter.

The second reason for beginning this chapter with *Seixas* is that it suggests the alternative analyses available in dealing with problems of product liability. The court considered both fraud (tort) and contract principles. Over 150 years of case law would lead readers of the court opinions to believe that the liability question ought to turn on whether the rights of the parties are to be shaped under principles of tort or contract law.[37] On the surface this dispute may sound reasonable, but only because it is the kind of issue which is familiar to the lawyer. The difficulty with such a dispute is that it does not correspond to anything which has existence outside of the courtroom. Lawyers have created the concepts of "tort" and of "contract." Such

34. 2 Caines (N.Y.) 48, 54 (1804).

35. *Id.*

36. White v. Miller, 71 N.Y. 118 (1877), 78 N.Y. 393 (1879).

37. Clary v. Fifth Ave. Chrysler Center, Inc., 454 P.2d 244 (Alaska 1969); Bailey v. Montgomery Ward & Co., 6 Ariz. App. 213, 431 P.2d 108 (1967); Rossignol v. Danbury School of Aeronautics, Inc., 154 Conn. 549, 227 A.2d 418 (1967); McCormack v. Hankscraft Co., 278 Minn. 322, 154 N.W.2d 488 (1967), 281 Minn. 571, 161 N.W.2d 523 (1968); Lonzrick v. Republic Steel Corp. 6 Ohio St.2d 227, 218 N.E.2d 185 (1966); Dippel v. Sciano, 37 Wis. 2d 443, 155 N.W.2d 55 (1967). The *Lonzrick* case upheld a petition on the basis that it stated a cause of action in tort based upon breach of warranty. Recent cases continue the search for ways of reconciling strict liability and warranty. See Seely v. White Motor Co., 63 Cal.2d 9, 45 Cal.Rptr. 17, 403 P.2d 145 (1965); State *ex rel.* Western Seed Prod. Corp. v. Campbell, 250 Or. 262, 442 P.2d 215 (1968), *cert. denied* 393 U.S. 1093, 89 S.Ct. 862, 21 L.Ed.2d 784 (1969). Some, however, are ready to obliterate any distinction based upon classification of the facts. Kassab v. Central Soya, 432 Pa. 217, 246 A.2d 848 (1968).

a creation may have been needed to reach socially desirable results, but this does not hide the fact that torts and contracts are only legal concepts. What was important to the buyer when he bought the ladder in the hypothetical case was that the law protected his exclusive right to control the use of that ladder; what is important to him now is that he was injured using the ladder and incurred expenses in an attempt to heal those injuries. He cares little about "torts" or "contracts." His concern is whether he will be compensated for his injuries. A dispute over classification can obscure the primary issues and, in turn, promote litigation. Those primary issues center on a decision as to shifting of risks and a determination of where those risks should be placed. This general problem can be subdivided into at least three questions:

1. Which parties in the chain of distribution ought to be liable? The answer to this question involves not only the problem of privity —a doctrine that is all but dead—but also a consideration of whether the retailer should be liable when he does not know of the defect and could not have learned of it with reasonable care. It is assumed that the retailer should be liable because he was the "seller" and because he is usually available for service of process. Further, he can pass this liability back up the chain of distribution by some type of third-party action or separate suit (with or without a vouching-in procedure). However, are there good reasons to retain retailer liability in these cases now that judicial jurisdiction can be easily obtained in most states over nonresident defendants? [38]

2. For what kinds of defects ought the parties be liable? The broken brake rivet and the poisoned food present easy cases, but what of the automobile whose general design is for beauty rather than safety? Does this make the automobile "defective"? [39] And what of the product which is safe for a large percentage of the population but harmful to those with an allergy? Should this product be considered "defective" as to those few people? [40]

3. To whom ought this liability extend? Here some courts rely on notions of privity or of whether it was reasonable for the seller to expect that this person would use the product. Should these concepts be retained in an economy in which the manufacturer is advertising so that its product will reach the largest market possible? [41]

---

38. Tate v. Renault, Inc., 278 F.Supp. 457 (E.D.Tenn.1967), *aff'd* 402 F.2d 795 (6th Cir. 1968); Fayette v. Volkswagen of America, Inc., 273 F.Supp. 323 (W.D.Tenn.1967); Henry v. John W. Eshelman & Sons, 99 R.I. 518, 209 A.2d 46 (1965).

39. See Larsen v. General Motors Corp., 391 F.2d 495 (8th Cir. 1968), commented upon in 28 Md.L.Rev. 386 (1968).

40. Howard v. Avon Prods., Inc., 155 Colo. 444, 395 P.2d 1007 (1964).

41. On occasion, a manufacturer advertises its product only to a small seg-

These questions are not easily answered; however, it should be clear that the answers should not come woodenly from a classification of the facts as either tort or contract. Each merits careful consideration, keeping in mind the results which will follow from a decision of liability (or of no liability). The doctrine of "let the buyer beware" is all but dead; it ought not be assumed that the only alternative is "let the seller beware."

Nevertheless, many court opinions continue this search for proper classification. This text, dealing as it does with the Code, will examine the warranty bases of liability, leaving most of the tort cases for analysis in other sources. There will, however, be occasions in which this text will cross the contract-tort line and suggest at least partial answers to the questions posed.[42]

§ 55. Overview of the Code Warranty Provisions

Article 2 contains several sections dealing with the warranties of a seller. This text will analyze these sections in detail. This analysis proceeds against the following general Code pattern of warranties.

First, the seller warrants certain things about the title to the goods sold. Generally, this is a warranty that the title is good, the transfer rightful, and that there are no outstanding security interests or liens which are unknown to the buyer.[43] This assures a buyer that if his title does fail, either wholly or partially, he has a cause of action against his seller.

Second, there are three sections defining the scope of the warranties of quality. The first sets the basis for the express warranties that accompany a sale. These arise from affirmations of fact, promises, descriptions, samples, or models.[44] The next two establish the implied warranties—warranties that accompany a sale just be-

---

ment of the public. For example, a manufacturer of cosmetics makes and advertises some of its products to be used only by professionals. When a non-professional applies the product, one court held that the manufacturer was not liable in tort to the person injured. Helene Curtis Indus., Inc. v. Pruitt, 385 F.2d 841 (5th Cir. 1967), *cert. denied* 391 U.S. 913, 88 S.Ct. 1806, 20 L.Ed.2d 652 (1968).

42. Contract and tort law are not the only tools by which an attempt is made to assure consumer protection. Perhaps the strongest force in obtaining quality products is the pride of the manufacturer in his product. History has shown, however, that this

force is not sufficient by itself. Federal and state legislation specifically regulating some types of manufacturers supplement the Code's provisions. See, *e. g.*, Federal Food, Drug, and Cosmetic Act, 52 Stat. 1040 (1938), 21 U.S.C.A. §§ 301 et seq. (1966); Federal Trade Commission Act, 38 Stat. 717 (1914) 15 U.S.C.A. § 41 et seq. (1963). In addition, consumer frauds sections have been established by the Attorneys-General of many states. In short, contract and tort law should be viewed as but one of several methods of assuring consumer protection.

43. UCC § 2–312.

44. UCC § 2–313.

cause it is a sale: the implied warranty of merchantability [45] and the implied warranty of fitness for purpose.[46] The first applies only to merchants who deal in goods of the kind sold; the second applies to merchants and non-merchants, but only if the seller has reason to know the particular purpose for which the goods will be used and that the buyer is relying on the seller's skill or judgment to select or furnish suitable goods. These sections assure the buyer that if the goods are below the contractual standard of quality, he will have an action against the seller for breach of warranty.

Third, these warranties are not limited to the immediate buyer. They extend, according to the 1962 version of the Code, to a limited class of persons connected with the buyer.[47] This class is greatly expanded in the 1966 recommendations of the Permanent Editorial Board for the Uniform Commercial Code and in several states which have amended the third party beneficiary section of the Code.[48]

Fourth, warranties can be excluded.[49] Express warranties are excluded by not making them; implied warranties may be excluded by specific language and, when excluded by a writing, in such a place and manner as to be "conspicuous." It is, therefore, still possible under the Code for sellers to limit their contractual liability—but they must do so under conditions which make it reasonable for the court to conclude that the exclusion or modification of warranties was understood by the buyer. Similarly, the warranty of title may be excluded.[50]

Fifth, the parties may agree to expand or to limit remedies available for default,[51] and this agreement is binding on the parties except that where circumstances "cause an exclusive or limited remedy to fail of its essential purpose, remedy may be had as provided in this Act."[52] These sections allowing the parties to exclude warranties or limit remedies support ideas of freedom of contract (a merchant can sell goods "as is" or limit remedies for breach of warranty to return and repair); however, cutting across this entire contractual relationship, including contract formation, are the ideas of good faith [53] and conscionability.[54] An unconscionable exclusion or limitation will fall just as will any other clause in the agreement.[55]

---

45. UCC § 2–314.

46. UCC § 2–315.

47. UCC § 2–318.

48. § 90 *infra.*

49. UCC § 2–316.

50. UCC § 2–312(2).

51. UCC § 2–719(1).

52. UCC § 2–719(2).

53. UCC § 1–203.

54. UCC § 2–302.

55. An argument can be made that the unconscionability section does not apply to those sections of the Code, like

The following sections of this text discuss these warranties of the seller. At times the results will be contrasted to recoveries based upon tort. However, the principal emphasis will be placed on the Code and its attempt to assure buyers that they will receive title to quality goods, or be compensated for their losses.

B. WARRANTY OF TITLE

§ 56. The Basic Code Section

The basic title warranty of the Code is contained in section 2–312 (1). This section provides:

> (1) Subject to subsection (2) there is in a contract for sale a warranty by the seller that
>
> > (a) the title conveyed shall be good, and its transfer rightful; and
> >
> > (b) the goods shall be delivered free from any security interest or other lien or encumbrance of which the buyer at the time of contracting has no knowledge.[56]

Subsection (2) provides instances in which the warranty may be excluded or modified, and will be discussed later in this text.[57] The present discussion relates to the scope of the title warranty.

Section 2–312(1) will be the one most often relied upon by the parties to determine the transactions in which there is a warranty of title and to define the extent of that warranty. It need not, however, be the exclusive subsection for these determinations. In an appropriate case, section 2–313—dealing with express warranties—could also be used. If the seller affirms his ownership, promises that he is or will at the time of sale be the owner, or if he describes the goods as belonging to him, there is a warranty that the "goods shall conform"[58] to the affirmation, promise, or description—providing that the affirmation, promise, or description was a part of the basis of the bargain between the parties. The "goods shall conform" language is primarily directed toward quality, but could be read to include statements relating to ownership of those goods. In most instances it will not be necessary to rely upon section 2–313; section 2–312

UCC § 2–316, which provide specific details to guide the actions of buyers and sellers. This argument is discussed in § 44, note 95 *supra*.

56. **UCC § 2–312(1).** The Code's warranty exists irrespective of possession in the seller. *Cf.* Robinson v. Rice, 20 Mo. 229, 235 (1855).

57. § 60 *infra*.

58. UCC § 2–313(1). Yattaw v. Onorato, 66 R.I. 76, 17 A.2d 430 (1941).

will suffice for the buyer. Nevertheless, the two sections can be used to buttress each other and to support buyer's claim of breach.

§ 57. Changes from the Uniform Sales Act

Under the Uniform Sales Act the warranty of title was described as an "implied warranty on the part of the seller." [59] The Code has eliminated this reference to an "implied warranty" by providing that *there is in a contract for sale* a warranty by the seller relating to title. The title warranty is not described as being either implied or express; it is simply *in* the contract unless, of course, the parties have excluded or modified it. The importance of this change is that a general disclaimer of implied warranties will not exclude the title warranty. The exclusion must relate directly to title.[60]

The reason that the Code takes this approach is understandable. When parties agree to exclude "all implied warranties" from their sale, they are most probably thinking of promises as to the quality of the goods—not as to whether the seller had title. When the buyer buys goods "as is" or "with all faults," he tends to think of the dents, mars, or scratches, and understands that he is buying in spite of these defects; he is not apt to consider that one of the "faults" may be that the seller does not own the item involved. It is, therefore, the Code's position that a general exclusion of warranties does not exclude a warranty of title. Exclusion of the title warranty must be more direct and must call attention to the fact that the seller may or may not have title.[61]

The Uniform Sales Act also drew a distinction between a sale and a contract to sell. With the sale there was an implied warranty that the seller *has* a right to sell; with a contract to sell there was an implied warranty that the seller *will have* a right to sell at the time the *property* is to pass.[62] Since property could pass in advance of the time of delivery if the parties so intended,[63] there were instances in which the title warranty could be breached even though the seller was not obligated to deliver them until a future date.

The Code's obligation is that the title *shall be* good—evidently referring to the "time and place at which the seller completes his per-

---

59. Uniform Sales Act § 13.

60. UCC § 2–312, Comment 6.

61. § 60 *infra*.

62. "In a contract to sell or a sale, unless the contrary intention appears, there is—

"(1) An implied warranty on the part of the seller that in the case of a sale he has a right to sell the goods, and that in the case of a contract to sell he will have a right to sell the goods at the time the property is to pass. . . . ." Uniform Sales Act § 13.

63. Uniform Sales Act, §§ 18, 19.

formance with reference to the physical delivery of the goods." [64] This appears to change the scope of the warranty of title in some contracts for the sale of goods to be delivered in the future. Under the Uniform Sales Act as soon as property passed the warranty of title was breached if the seller did not then have the right to sell; under the Code there is no breach until the seller completes his performance. Thus, in a shipment contract, the warranty is that the seller's title shall be good at the time of shipment. This could leave the buyer in an awkward position if he learns that goods which the seller has promised to deliver six months from now are owned by a third party. True, he realizes now that if the seller does not acquire the ownership within the six months, the buyer will have a cause of action against the seller; but since there is no present breach, the buyer is not free to treat the agreement as cancelled. Such a buyer could not safely make present arrangements for substitute goods as he could under the language of the Uniform Sales Act.

The difference between the Sales Act and the Code as to this point is probably more apparent than real. While there is no default in the warranty of title, the failure of the seller to have title to goods scheduled for future delivery could present reasonable grounds for the buyer's believing that the seller cannot perform on the future date. These grounds for insecurity would allow the buyer to demand assurances of the seller's performance (such as a showing of how he will obtain the title, or a bond against default, or whatever else is commercially reasonable under the particular facts) and, if the assurances were not forthcoming, the buyer could suspend his performance and eventually treat the failure to give assurances as a repudiation.[65] Thus, the Code protects such a buyer through the adequate assurance section rather than through the section on warranty of title. This method of protection is preferable to that given by the Uniform Sales Act since it ties repudiation to reasonable grounds for insecurity rather than to the sole fact that the seller may not have had title the moment the property passed to the buyer.

There is one major change in the Code's title warranty from that found in the Uniform Sales Act. Under the Sales Act there was an "implied warranty that the buyer shall have and enjoy quiet possession of the goods as against any lawful claims existing at the time of the sale." [66] This warranty was dropped by the Code. Interference with quiet possession is one method of proving that the title which was conveyed was not "good," but there is no separate default when quiet

---

64. UCC § 2–401(2). There is no Code distinction between a sale and a contract for sale. UCC § 2–106(1).

65. UCC § 2–609.

66. Uniform Sales Act, § 13(2). *See* 1 S. Williston, Sales § 221 (rev. ed. 1948).

possession is disturbed. The principal effect of this change will be to shorten the period of time in which suits for breach of title warranty can be tried. Under the Code the title warranty is breached, if at all, on conveyance, and the four-year period runs from that date—not from the date on which the buyer's quiet possession was disturbed.[67]

§ 58. Warranty That the Title shall be Good and the Transfer Rightful

The first Code warranty of title is that "the title shall be good, and its transfer rightful." [68] This takes the place of the "right to sell" language of the Uniform Sales Act.

The meaning of "and its transfer rightful" is obscure. The Comment reference to this portion of the warranty only repeats the Code language, but the drafting of section 2–312 makes it clear that rightfulness of the transfer is in addition to the quality of the title conveyed. Not only must the title be good, but the transfer must be rightful. Evidently the drafters had in mind a situation in which the title was good but in which the seller had some agreement with a third party which made any transfer of the title wrongful. If this agreement destroyed the goodness of the title, the "transfer rightful" language is redundant; the title warranty was breached because the title conveyed was not "good." If this agreement did not destroy the goodness of the title in the buyer, it is difficult to understand why the drafters thought that a default in that agreement should also be a default in the title warranty with the buyer. Perhaps what they had in mind was a case in which it is not clear whether the agreement with the third party restricting the right of transfer amounted to a defect in title. In such a case, litigation would be needed to determine the quality of the title; and the buyer purchased goods—not a lawsuit.[69] This reading of section 2–312 would allow the buyer to claim immediately that the title warranty was breached. Such a buyer could cancel the contract of sale, recover his purchase price plus allowable damages, and leave the seller and the third party to determine their rights and obligations.

The principal title warranty is that the title shall be *good*. In the usual case the seller will have the unfettered right to sell and will pass his title to the buyer. The buyer will receive the goods, free from any third party's claim and there will be no default in the warranty. At

---

67. UCC § 2–725. Omitting the quiet possession warranty may have the effect of changing cases like First Nat'l Bank v. Associates Inv. Co., 140 Ind. App. 394, 221 N.E.2d 684 (1966), in which it was held that harassment of the buyer was a basis for rescission although the buyer's title was good.

One question will be whether the obligation of good faith can be used to support the buyer's right to quiet enjoyment. UCC § 1–203.

68. UCC § 2–312(1) (a).

69. UCC § 2–312, Comment 1.

the other extreme there will be a few cases in which the seller had no title, as when he has purchased from a thief. In this situation, the buyer will receive no title [70] and the seller will have defaulted in his title warranty. These cases are clear. The difficult cases are those in which some third party has presented a claim to the goods, and there is a genuine dispute as to the validity of that claim. If the third party is correct in his claim, the title will fail and there will be a clear default in seller's warranty; but if the third party fails to establish his claim, it will then be apparent that the title was originally *good*. Is the Code to be construed so that there is a default in the title warranty only if the third party has a claim which as a matter of hindsight turns out to be well-founded? Certainly such a construction of section 2–312 is possible.[71] However, "good" title is not a term of art, having a fixed meaning in the law of property. Further, such a reading places the buyer in a most awkward position in regard to facts with which he is in no way connected.

Consider the following example:

A buyer purchased a valuable painting from his neighbor. During a party at buyer's house one of the guests exclaimed that the painting belonged to him, that he had taken it to a small gallery to be cleaned, and that when he returned to pick up the painting he found only an empty building. The guest demanded the painting, but the buyer resisted temporarily until he had had an opportunity to consult with his neighbor. The neighbor told both the guest and the buyer that he had visited that gallery and had purchased the painting from several which were on sale, that he had no idea that it belonged to anyone other than the owner of the gallery, that he paid full value for it, and that he has a bill of sale to prove the truth of his statements.

These facts create the problem of determining whether the neighbor did acquire the title of the guest. Although the details of this problem are examined at another place in this text,[72] it is sufficient now simply to indicate the problems which could arise under section 2–403, which provides:

> Any entrusting of possession of goods to a merchant who deals in goods of that kind gives him power to transfer all rights of the entruster to a buyer in ordinary course of business.[73]

Before the buyer can determine the quality of his title, he must answer such questions as: did the guest "entrust" the painting to the gallery?

---

70. UCC § 2–403(1). See also 2 S. Williston, Sales § 311 (rev. ed. 1948) The buyer bears the burden of proving lack of title. Wujnovich v. Colcord, 105 N.H. 451, 202 A.2d 484 (1964).

71. *But see* UCC § 2–312, Comment 1.

72. § 170 *infra.*

73. UCC § 2–403(2).

Is the gallery owner a merchant who deals in goods of that kind? Is a gallery which shows and cleans paintings a merchant with respect to the *sale* of paintings? Did the neighbor buy in the ordinary course of business? [74] The answers to some of these questions involve a determination of fact for which the buyer now has only the word of the guest and the neighbor. Others involve interpretation of the Code. It may turn out, after protracted litigation, that the neighbor did acquire the guest's title when he purchased the painting at the gallery and that this title was transferred to the buyer, or it may turn out that the neighbor did not meet the criteria of section 2–403—and that he did not acquire the guest's title. In either event, the decision may be months or even years away. The problem for the buyer at the present moment of time is whether there has been a default by the neighbor-seller of his warranty that the title conveyed shall be *good*. Is the title sufficiently clouded by the claim of the guest so that the buyer ought to be able to cancel the sale, return the painting to the neighbor (his seller), and allow the neighbor to spend the time and money in determining whether his title was in fact good?

The answer to this question ought to be in the affirmative—the neighbor-seller should be the one to bear these expenses and inconveniences. The buyer did not purchase a lawsuit. He purchased a painting. The title to which he is entitled ought to be one that is free from colorable claims which existed at the time he purchased—even if the seller did not know of the claims. If the buyer did not receive this quality of a title (that is, one free from colorable claims), there is a default in the warranty of good title. This default gives the buyer the option (a) of cancelling the sale and recovering the price he paid (plus damages) or (b) of defending the suit brought by the third party and recovering damages from the seller at the conclusion of that suit. If the buyer elected to defend and was successful in the litigation with the third party, those damages will be limited to the cost of defending the title; if the third party was successful and recaptured the goods or recovered their value, the buyer's damages will be increased by the value of the goods lost.[75]

---

74. Some of the difficulties facing such a buyer are illustrated in Universal C. I. T. Credit Corp. v. Middlesboro Motor Sales, Inc., 424 S.W.2d 409 (Ky. 1968) (conditional sale); Atlas Auto Rental Corp. v. Weisberg, 54 Misc.2d 168, 281 N.Y.S.2d 400 (Civ.Ct.1967) (theft); Linwood Harvestore, Inc. v. Cannon, 427 Pa. 434, 235 A.2d 377 (1967) (bailment).

75. Gaito v. Hoffman, 5 UCC Rep. 1056 (N.Y.Sup.Ct.1968). The seller, in turn, is entitled to recover his losses from the person who sold the goods to the seller—if that contract for sale contained a warranty of title. Such recovery will include, in addition to the judgment which seller had to pay, any additional expenses (such as attorney fees) necessarily incurred in defense of the seller's title. When sued by his buyer, the seller should implead his seller (if allowed in local practice) or use the Code's vouching-in procedure. UCC § 2-607(5). *See* Pinney v. Geraghty, 209 App.Div. 630, 205 N.Y.S. 645 (1924).

It is not every third-party claim, however, which should be considered a default in the warranty of title. Spurious title claims can be made by anyone at any time. The seller of goods is not warranting against these kinds of claims being pressed. The Code tried to separate the spurious claim by limiting the warranty to a *good* title and a *rightful* transfer. The title is good and the transfer rightful even though an unfounded claim is presented. The title ought not be considered good and the transfer ought not be rightful if the third party's claim is colorable. This leaves an area for judicial discretion (when a claim is no longer spurious but has become colorable); however, that discretion is needed here just as it is with a determination of the quality of the goods sold.

§ 59. Warranty Against Security Interests, Liens, and Encumbrances

The second Code warranty of title is set forth in these words: "the goods shall be delivered free from any security interest or other lien or encumbrance of which the buyer at the time of contracting has no knowledge." [76] The reference to security interests is primarily a reference to Article 9 of the Code. Prior to the Code these interests would have been called a chattel mortgage, a conditional sale, a bailment lease, a trust receipt, a factor's lien, or whatever local name was given to an agreement by which one party was given an interest (sometimes title) in personal property to secure the payment of money. A typical example with consumer goods would be the purchase by conditional sale in which the retailer retained title to the goods until the purchase price was paid. [77] An example with a manufacturer's inventory would be the trust receipt or the factor's lien by which the financer was given title to or a lien on the inventory until the amount borrowed was paid. [78]

The Code does not contain a seller's warranty that the goods are free from a security interest while they are in the possession of the seller—only that the goods are *delivered* free from a security interest.

---

76. UCC § 2–312(1) (b). This is similar to the implied warranty under Uniform Sales Act § 13(3).

77. *In re* Plonta, 311 F.2d 44 (6th Cir. 1962).

78. Examples of factor's liens include *In re* Summit Hardware, Inc., 302 F.2d 397 (6th Cir.), *appeal dismissed sub nom.* Foote v. Schwemler, 371 U.S. 882, 83 S.Ct. 154, 9 L.Ed.2d 118 (1962); *In re* Freeman, 294 F.2d 126 (3d Cir. 1961); Perkins v. Lakeport Nat'l Bank, 13 F.Supp. 898 (D.N.H.1955). Examples of cases involving trust receipts include *In re* Crosstown Motors, Inc., 272 F.2d 224 (7th Cir. 1959), *cert. denied sub nom.* Commercial Credit Corp. v. Allen, 363 U.S. 811, 80 S.Ct. 1246, 4 L.Ed.2d 1152 (1960) (automobiles); Coin Machine Acceptance Corp. v. O'Donnell, 192 F.2d 773 (4th Cir. 1951) (coin machines). Field warehousing could also be used for some types of inventory. Barry v. Lawrence Warehouse Co., 190 F.2d 433 (9th Cir. 1951).

Thus, if there are some security interests which are terminated in the goods at the time of the delivery, there would be no default in the warranty of title even though the goods were subject to a security interest while they were held by the seller. The Code contains several examples of this situation. The one most likely to occur with the sale of goods is detailed in section 9–307. Certain buyers of inventory, equipment, and consumer goods take free of a security interest even though that security interest was perfected and enforceable against the seller.[79] It is, therefore, necessary to consult Article 9 to determine whether the goods are *delivered* free from a security interest before it can be determined whether there was a default in this branch of the title warranty.[80]

Since Article 9 covers all contractual agreements which prior to the Code would have created a lien or encumbrance on goods to secure the payment of an obligation,[81] the further reference in section 2–312 (1)(b) to "lien or encumbrance" will have reference only to non-contractual arrangements. Examples would include an outstanding levy or attachment, a mechanic's lien, or a lien arising out of the operation of some local law. Again, the warranty is that the goods be *delivered* free from these claims. If the lien or encumbrance was terminated at the time of delivery, there would be no default.[82]

This title warranty extends only to those security interests, liens, and encumbrances which were not actually known to the buyer at the time of contracting.[83] Thus, a buyer who buys goods subject to an outstanding claim cannot successfully contend that the seller has defaulted on his title warranty. Presumably, such a buyer considered the value of the outstanding claim in determining the price to be paid the seller; to allow such a buyer a further reduction in the price would result in a windfall to him.

There may be times in which a buyer is presented with a claim of an outstanding security interest, lien, or encumbrance, and in which it is not clear whether this claim is enforceable against the buyer. Only costly litigation will determine whether the buyer has taken free from those claims. These situations will require an interpretation of section 2–312(1)(b). Does this section mean that the warranty has been

---

79. UCC § 9–307.

80. A security interest in goods is also lost if the secured party authorized a sale of the goods. UCC § 9–306(2). If there is an outstanding security interest, buyer may cancel the sale and recover the purchase price paid. Kruger v. Bibi, 3 UCC Rep. 1132 (N.Y. Sup.Ct.1967).

81. UCC § 9–102(1) and (2).

82. *See, e. g.,* the statutes discussed in Decker v. Aurora Motors, Inc., 409 P.2d 603 (Alaska, 1966).

83. See the definition of "knowledge" in UCC § 1–201 (25).

breached only if, following the litigation, it turns out that the buyer took subject to the outstanding claim—or should this section be read to mean that the existence of an unknown but colorable claim (whether security interest, lien, or encumbrance) is sufficient to amount to a default even though the buyer might have prevailed had he defended the claim? Unless the answer can be drawn out of the general obligation of good faith,[84] the Code does not answer this question. The general problem was discussed in the prior section of this text and will not be repeated. However, a buyer faced with this problem ought to consider arguing that his title was not *good* (because of the outstanding claim), and that the default falls under subsection (a). Here the Comment language becomes pertinent:

> Subsection (1) makes provision for a buyer's basic needs in respect to a title which he in good faith expects to acquire by his purchase, namely, that he receives a good, clean title transferred to him also in a rightful manner so that he will not be exposed to a lawsuit in order to protect it.[85]

§ 60. Modification or Exclusion of Title Warranties

The Code warranties of title can be modified or excluded in only one of two ways:

1. *By specific language.* If the parties desire to modify or exclude a warranty of title from their sale, they may do so by the language of their agreement.[86] The seller may, for example, state in the contract for sale that the seller is not warranting title to the goods sold. If the buyer knows or has reason to know of the statement, the exclusion becomes part of their agreement (presumably affecting the price the buyer was willing to pay), and the seller has not warranted his title to the goods. If title later fails, such a buyer would have no action against the seller for any damages incurred.

The Code requires that the exclusion or modification be by "specific language." A general exclusion of all warranties from the sale is not sufficient to exclude the title warranty. The reason for the Code's insistence on a specific reference to title rests on the assumption that language which only generally refers to an exclusion of warranties is most apt to be understood by the buyer as referring to the quality of—and not the title to—the goods purchased. Before language in the contract for sale negates a warranty of title, that language must be specific enough reasonably to call the buyer's attention to the fact that the buyer is losing all or a part of his title warranty.

---

84. UCC § 1–203.

85. UCC § 2–312, Comment 1.

86. UCC § 2–312(2).

2. *By certain circumstances.* Title warranties can be excluded or modified "by circumstances which give the buyer reason to know that the person selling does not claim title in himself or that he is purporting to sell only such right or title as he or a third person may have." [87] Whether these circumstances exist is a question of fact to be determined by the trier of fact, but the Comments state that sales by sheriffs, executors, foreclosing lienors "and persons similarly situated" do not give rise to personal obligations if title does fail.[88] These people are purporting to sell only the rights of some third person (the judgment debtor or the decedent) and a buyer at such a sale has reason to know this fact. Such a buyer could attempt to obtain an express warranty of title; whether he would be successful in this attempt is another matter.

Even though there is no warranty of title because the buyer has reason to know that the person selling is purporting to sell only such rights as a third person may have, consideration should be given to the possibility of a quantum meruit claim based upon mistake. For example, suppose that a judgment creditor has caused the sheriff to levy execution on goods which the judgment creditor believes are owned by the judgment debtor. When those goods are sold at an execution sale, it is clear that there is no Code warranty of title running from the sheriff to the purchaser; further, there is probably no warranty of title made by the judgment creditor since he is purporting to sell only such rights in the property as the judgment debtor might have. Suppose that after the purchaser has paid the price and received possession of the goods, it turns out that the goods were owned by someone other than the judgment debtor—and that the owner has reclaimed his goods. The purchaser has paid the price of the goods but has received nothing in return. Such a purchaser, although he has no warranty of title, may nevertheless urge that the sale was made on the basis of a mutual mistake; that is, both the judgment creditor and the purchaser assumed that the judgment debtor was the owner of the goods, that they were mistaken in this basic assumption, and that their mutual mistake is a ground for rescinding the sale. Such a claim presents several equitable reasons to support its acceptance. Unless there is some judicial intervention, the debtor will have paid his debt to the judgment creditor from money obtained by the execution purchaser. One solution is to revive the judgment debt and to subrogate the purchaser to the judg-

---

87. UCC § 2–312(2).

88. UCC § 2–312, Comment 5. The insurance company which purchased an automobile from its insured and resold to the plaintiff was not excluded from the title warranty under UCC § 2–312. John St. Auto Wrecking v. Motors Ins. Corp., 56 Misc.2d 232, 288 N.Y.S.2d 281 (Dist.Ct.1968).

ment creditor's claims against the judgment debtor.[89] This has its drawbacks as far as the purchaser is concerned because he now finds himself trying to recover from someone who had difficulty in paying the original claim, and the chances are good that the debtor will have as much difficulty in paying the purchaser. Another solution is to rescind the sale and allow the purchaser to recover the price which he paid and which eventually was used to pay off the judgment creditor's claim.[90] The theoretical difficulty with this solution is that it effectively inserts a warranty of title—in face of Code language denying the warranty—to the extent of allowing rescission, although not damages for any fancied goodness of the purchase. The final solution would be to apply the doctrine of *caveat emptor* and to leave the purchaser in the unhappy position already mentioned—that is, of having paid off the judgment debtor's debt and having received nothing in return. Apparently, most pre-Code cases reached this result.[91]

There are difficulties with each of these solutions. However, the second solution (allowing rescission and quantum meruit) appears to reach the preferable result. It should be remembered that it was the judgment creditor who selected the property to be sold and who instigated this particular sale. Had the purchaser discovered the debtor's lack of ownership after his bid but before he actually paid the price, he would not have been compelled to carry out his agreement to buy.[92] The fact that the owner waited until the price had been paid ought not change the result. In short, the preferable solution in this type of case is to allow rescission based upon mistake—even though it effectively inserts a warranty of title for the limited purpose of recovering the price paid—but not to allow the purchaser damages for any losses because the property was worth in excess of the purchase price.[93]

Care must be taken not to misread a part of this exclusionary section. It can be argued with force that every seller purports to sell

89. Russell v. Sarkeys, 286 F.2d 736 (5th Cir. 1961); Muir v. Berkshire, 52 Ind. 149 (1875). Subrogation ought to be given to encourage bidding at the judicial sale. Wilson v. Brown, 82 Ind. 471 (1882).

90. Stonerook v. Wisner, 171 Iowa 109, 153 N.W. 351 (1915); Dresser v. Kronberg, 108 Maine 423, 81 A. 487 (1911) (suggesting the judgment creditor would then be entitled to a new execution). *See also* Schwinger v. Hickok, 53 N.Y. 280 (1873), where the creditor knew the sale was void.

91. Copper Belle Mining Co. v. Gleeson, 14 Ariz. 548, 134 P. 285 (1913); Milam v. Adams, 216 Ga. 440, 117 S.E.2d 343 (1960); Tetrault v. Ingraham, 54 Mont. 524, 171 P. 1148 (1918) (but suggesting that judgment is revived for the benefit of the purchaser). Cases are collected in Annot., 68 A.L.R. 659 (1930).

92. Pittsburgh Plate Glass Co. v. Forbes, 258 N.C. 426, 128 S.E.2d 875 (1963).

93. The drafters intended the Code to be neutral on the problem of restitution. UCC § 2–312, Comment 5.

only the title which *he*—and not some third party—has.[94] This reading of the Code would eliminate the warranty of title from nearly every sale. This, of course, was not the intention of the drafters, and the exclusion section of 2–312 need not be read this broadly. A more accurate understanding of this language can be obtained by emphasizing the word "purporting"—there is no warranty of title when the buyer has reason to know that the seller is *purporting* to sell only such title as he has. The idea to be conveyed is that the seller has told the buyer that the seller does not know whether he is the owner of the goods but that he is willing to transfer whatever title it turns out later that the seller had. In this sense, this portion of the section allows the seller to give a quitclaim bill of sale if he makes clear to the buyer that this is what is involved.

§ 61. Damages for Breach of Title Warranty

The damage problem for breach of a title warranty can be illustrated through a hypothetical factual pattern introduced in a prior section.[95] There it was assumed that a seller sold buyer a painting which was claimed by a third party. The prior discussion centered on whether the seller had defaulted in his warranty of title. Both pre-Code law and the Code define the scope of the warranty but, strangely, neither is clear as to the measure of the buyer's damages should the seller default in his title obligations. The damage problem is created when the price paid varies from the value of the goods which, in turn, fluctuates between the date of delivery and the time of dispossession. Suppose, for example, that the buyer paid $5,000 for the painting at a time when it was "worth" $7,000, but when the third party successfully asserted his ownership claim the painting had increased in value so that it was "worth" $10,000.

Three possible measures of recovery are presented by these facts: (1) the price the buyer paid; (2) the value of the goods at the time the buyer accepted them; and (3) the value of the goods at the time the buyer was dispossessed of the goods. Policy grounds can be found to support any one of these solutions. The strange part is that neither the Uniform Sales Act nor the Code specifically responded by adopting a measure of recovery for a default in the title warranty.

Pre-Code law is not difficult to summarize, but little aid is gained from the summary.[96] There was probably no dissent from the proposi-

---

94. See UCC § 2–312(2), quoted *supra* this section in text to footnote 87.

95. § 58 *supra*.

96. Cases are collected in Annot., 13 A.L.R.2d 1372, 1374–78 (1950). *See also*

Annot., 13 A.L.R.3d 875 (1967). Whether lost profits are recoverable depends on their foreseeability. Wentworth & Irwin, Inc. v. Sears, 153 Or. 201, 56 P.2d 324 (1936).

tion that a buyer could, if he desired, rescind the sale because of the title failure and recover the purchase price paid, usually with interest. In the hypothetical this theory would award the buyer a minimum of $5,000 (the price paid) even though the goods might have been worth only $4,000 and have declined in value after the date of the sale. There are no good policy reasons for allowing the seller to retain a portion of the purchase price when no title was conveyed.[97] The division came when the buyer sought to recover more than the price he paid. Some courts limited the buyer to the price paid (as is usually done with real estate); others allowed him the value of the goods at the time of the sale; and still others granted the buyer the value of the goods at the time that he was dispossessed.[98]

Faced with this diversion of opinion, the drafters could have been expected to have recommended a Code section settling on a uniform rule of damages for breach of title warranty. However, they either ignored the question or left the problem to be solved by the Code's general damage sections. Unfortunately, these sections are either too general to be of specific aid or were drafted for the situation in which the breach was one of tender or of the warranted quality of the goods. Such sections do not fit neatly the problem of measuring recovery when the defect is in title. Nevertheless, there are several Code sections which a buyer can urge in solving the title-damage problem. These are considered below.

The buyer's general index of damages is contained in section 2–711. Those remedies are conditioned on the occurrence of one of four triggering events, and the only ones applicable to title defects would be rightful rejection or justifiable revocation of acceptance. A buyer can reject goods "if the goods or the tender of delivery fail in any respect to conform to the contract."[99] Do the *goods* or their *tender* fail to conform when the defect is in title? There are statutory difficulties in reaching an affirmative answer to this question. An argument can be made that the reference to "goods" is to their quality and the reference to "tender" is to the mechanics of making the goods available to the buyer.[1] However, such a reading overlooks the commercial practicalities of the situation. No matter how high the quality of the goods and no matter how formal the delivery, the buyer does

97. For cases involving a claimed deduction for the value of the use of the goods, see Park Circle Motor Co. v. Willis, 201 Md. 104, 92 A.2d 757 (1952), *rearg. denied* 201 Md. 104, 94 A.2d 443 (1953); Davis v. Gonzales, 235 S.W.2d 221 (Tex.Civ.App.1950); Peregrine v. West Seattle State Bank, 120 Wash. 653, 208 P. 35 (1922).

98. 3 S. Williston, Sales § 615a (rev. ed. 1948); Annot., 13 A.L.R.2d 1372 (1950).

99. UCC § 2–601.

1. As to tender, see UCC § 2–503.

not have goods which *conform* to the contract if he receives less than the warranted title.[2] He is harmed as much by a worthless title as he is by worthless goods. Therefore, failure of title in any respect ought to allow the buyer to reject.[3]

The buyer who has rightfully rejected can always recover any part of the price he paid. This measure is a part of section 2–711(3) which allows price recovery as the minimum. In addition, a rejecting buyer has a choice as to additional damages. First, he can "cover" and have damages measured by the cost of the cover contract less the contract price.[4] Second, he can elect not to "cover" and have damages measured under section 2–713 by the difference between the market price at the time the buyer learned of the breach and the contract price.[5] In either case the buyer is also entitled to any incidental and consequential damages suffered less expenses saved as a result of seller's default.[6]

Both of these recoveries give the buyer a value recovery if that value exceeds the price paid. Under cover the value is the cost of the substitute contract which must be entered into without unreasonable delay. Under section 2–713 the value is determined as of the time the buyer "learned of the breach." While this phrase causes trouble with anticipatory breaches,[7] it opens the possibility of a determination of value at a date subsequent to the delivery of the goods. However, since rejection must occur reasonably soon after the tender or the delivery,[8] the time differential will be important only for goods with a wide swing in price over a short time. Otherwise, both cover and section 2–713 damages produce a value recovery for the buyer measured as of the time the seller delivered the goods.

If the title defect is not discovered until the buyer has accepted (thereby precluding rejection),[9] there is still the possibility that the buyer can revoke his acceptance, recover so much of the price as he has paid, and additionally either cover or have damages under section 2–713. These damages would be computed in the same manner as if the buyer had rejected, except that revocation of acceptance can occur

---

2. UCC § 2–503(1) requires "conforming" goods for a proper tender. Goods are "conforming" when they are in accordance with the contract. UCC § 2–106 (2). It does not take much ingenuity to conclude that goods are not in accordance with the contract when their warranted title fails, but the Code is not as clear as it could be.

3. The buyer's courses of action on default of the seller are considered in detail in §§ 139–45 *infra.*

4. UCC § 2–712; § 147 *infra.*

5. § 148 *infra.*

6. One court allowed the buyer to recover the finance charges which he paid. Riggs Motor Co. v. Archer, 240 S.W.2d 75 (Ky.1951).

7. § 149 *infra.*

8. UCC § 2–602(1); § 141 *infra.*

9. UCC § 2–607(2).

at a time later than would have been allowed for rejection. Revocation of acceptance can occur at any time after delivery providing it is "within a reasonable time after the buyer discovers or should have discovered" the defect.[10] When the defect is in the goods' title, this reasonable time could be construed to be months or years after delivery.[11] Thus, the cover damages (2–712) or the section 2–713 damages could conceivably be used to shift to the seller losses measured by the value of the goods at the time the buyer was dispossessed—or even shortly thereafter.[12] However, a court which believes these damages to be unduly burdensome to the seller can control its decision by manipulating the "reasonable time" for revocation of acceptance. Reaching damage results by this type of manipulation is unfortunate because it obscures analysis of the factors involved in determining what the measure of damages ought to be for breach of the title warranty.

The Code section which contains language most nearly applicable to the title problem is section 2–714:

> (1) Where the buyer has accepted goods and given notification (subsection (3) of Section 2–607) he may recover as damages for any non-conformity of tender the loss resulting in the ordinary course of events from the seller's breach as determined in any manner which is reasonable.

> (2) The measure of damages for breach of warranty is the difference at the time and place of acceptance between the value of the goods accepted and the value they would have had if they had been as warranted, unless special circumstances show proximate damages of a different amount.

> (3) In a proper case any incidental and consequential damages under the next section may also be recovered.

As pointed out later in this text, this section applies when the buyer has accepted the goods and the time for revocation of acceptance has elapsed.[13] Therefore, this section could be used to determine damages for breach of a title warranty (1) if the court concludes that rejection and revocation of acceptance are not proper alternatives for title cases or (2) if these alternatives would normally be available but the time for revocation of acceptance elapsed before the buyer gave the appropriate notice of the revocation.

---

10. UCC § 2–608(2); Campbell v. Pollack, 101 R.I. 223, 221 A.2d 615 (1966). § 143 *infra*.

11. There is, however, a four-year statute of limitations. UCC § 2–725.

12. For a case involving pre-Code facts but reaching the result suggested by the text, see Menzel v. List, 24 N.Y.2d 91, 246 N.E.2d 742, 298 N.Y.S.2d 979 (1969).

13. § 150 *infra*.

Conceivably a title defect creates a "non-conformity of tender" under subsection (1), but the measure of damages outlined there is of no help in resolving the pre-Code conflict in decisions. More likely, a title defect should be considered as falling within subsection (2). Indeed, the language of this section ("breach of warranty," which could include the title warranty) could be read as establishing the exclusive measure for cases involving title defects. However, this is not the exclusive damage section for defects in the warranted quality, and there is no reason to believe that the drafters intended it as the sole measure for breaches of the title warranty.

Section 2–714(2) is helpful in that it resolves the time at which value is important—the date of acceptance. This will be shortly after delivery of the goods. If the section 2–714 formula produces an amount less than the price paid, the recovery should be the price paid, but section 2–714 (written for breach of the quality warranties) fails to take this minimum recovery into account when title fails.

The result of this resumé of the Code is that no one Code section deals specifically with the damages recoverable when title fails. Each comes close but, written from the background of damages for inferior quality or defective tender, each misses the mark of a definitive answer. Further, all present varying times for selecting value—the problem which plagued pre-Code courts.

Perhaps the proper conclusion from this view of the Code is that no remedial section should be applied and the problem ought to be referred to section 1–106. Section 1–106(2) provides that any Code right or obligation is enforceable by action unless some provision limits the effect of that right or obligation. The obligation to deliver a good title free from security interests, liens, or encumbrances thus becomes enforceable even though no specific section details the buyer's damages. Section 1–106 goes on to state that the "remedies provided by this Act shall be liberally administered to the end that the aggrieved party may be put in as good a position as if the other party had fully performed." [14] Such a rule supports value recovery, not limiting the buyer to the price he paid, but fails to indicate the time when the buyer ought to be placed in the same position as if the seller had performed. Should it be the time of delivery or the time of dispossession—or at some intermediate time?

This survey of remedies supports the following conclusions when the seller has defaulted in his title warranty:

14. UCC § 1–106(1). Use of UCC § 1–106 may lose consequential damages for the buyer.

1.   The buyer will always recover at least the price he paid.   To this recovery will be added incidental and consequential damages and from this recovery will be subtracted expenses saved as a consequence of the default.[15]

2.   The Code generally supports an additional recovery based on the value of the goods.[16]

3.   However, the Code is not clear as to the time when the value should be determined.   On this question the pre-Code conflict will probably continue.   Fortunately, most goods (unlike realty or investment securities) do not increase in value as time elapses.   Thus, value recovery as of the date of delivery, or shortly thereafter, will solve the great bulk of disputes.

When the title does not fail completely but is subject to an outstanding lien or security interest, the problem of damages is more quickly solved.   In this instance the buyer is compensated by payment of the dollar value of the lien or security interest,[17] together with costs. This result has been reached under the Code.[18]

§ 62. Warranties Against Infringement

Section 2–312 contains a separate subsection dealing with warranties against infringement.[19]   There is, therefore, no need to attempt to force these cases within the usual warranty of title.

The warranties are of two kinds.   First, there is the warranty of the seller-merchant.   If the seller is a merchant who deals in goods of the kind involved and selects them from his normal stock, he warrants that the goods are delivered free from any rightful claim by a third person "by way of infringement or the like."[20]   In addition to

---

15.   This was stated to be the "normal damages for breach of warranty of title. . . ." John St. Auto Wrecking v. Motors Ins. Co., 56 Misc.2d 232, 288 N.Y.S.2d 281 (Dist.Ct.1968).

16.   Value recovery was allowed a buyer even though value exceeded price. The court relied on UCC § 2–714. Miles v. Lyon, 6 UCC Rep. 659 (Mass.App.Div. 1969).

17.   Where buyer purchased the outstanding title, the price paid was used to measure recovery. Field v. Jones, 8 So.2d 711 (La.Ct.App.1942). For a case in which there was only a partial failure of title, see Hoffman v. Chamberlain, 40 N.J. Eq. 663, 5 A. 150 (Ct.Err. & App.1885). Where the seller gave assurances that the lien would be dis-

charged and waived further payments by the buyer until "they had matters straightened out" but later repossessed the goods without discharging the lien, the seller is liable for the market value of the goods less the buyer's secured indebtedness. Seymour v. W. S. Boyd Sales Co., 257 N.C. 603, 127 S.E.2d 265 (1962).

18.   Gaito v. Hoffman, 5 UCC Rep. 1056 (N.Y.Sup.Ct.1968) (damages awarded to cover cost of removing security interest plus attorney fees).

19.   UCC § 2–312(3).

20.   "This section rejects the cases which recognize the principle that infringements violate the warranty of title but deny the buyer a remedy un-

trademark violations, a rightful claim by way of patent or trademark would amount to a default in this warranty. Non-merchants do not make this warranty.

Second, there is the warranty of the buyer. On some occasions the buyer furnishes the seller with plans and specifications for goods which the buyer has contracted to have the seller manufacture. In these situations the seller is not warranting that the final product will be free from infringement claims. To the contrary, such a buyer is obligated to hold his seller harmless against any claim arising out of a compliance with the furnished specifications.

C. WARRANTIES OF QUALITY

1. INTRODUCTION

§ 63. Scope of Warranties of Quality

There are three sections of the Code which deal with the creation of warranties in a sale of goods. These are: section 2–313 (express warranties); 2–314 (implied warranty of merchantability); and 2–315 (implied warranty of fitness for purpose). Several other sections bear upon the impact of these warranties. Among these are: sections 2–316 (exclusion or modification of warranties); 2–317 (cumulation and conflict of warranties); and 2–318 (third party beneficiaries of warranties). The remaining portions of this chapter will discuss these Code sections and their relationship to problems of product liability.

Product liability cases are among the most frequently litigated factual patterns in current American law. One reason for this frequency in litigation has already been suggested: the legal system has been too concerned about classification rather than careful analysis of the policies involved.[21] As doctrines of strict liability in tort and warranty liability in sales begin to merge, this concern over classification will have less importance—and properly so. Nevertheless, the number of disputes involving potential liability for a defective product will probably continue. Mass production of fairly complicated goods capable of causing injury results in distributing huge quantities of these goods among the American public. Since quality control devices

less he has been expressly prevented from using the goods. Under this Article 'eviction' is not a necessary condition to the buyer's remedy since the buyer's remedy arises immediately upon receipt of notice of infringement; it is merely one way of establishing the fact of breach." UCC § 2–312, Comment 4.

21. § 54 *supra.* See Seely v. White Motor Co., 63 Cal.2d 9, 403 P.2d 145, 45 Cal.Rptr. 17 (1965).

are limited by the economic realities of a profit-oriented system and by the scientific knowledge of the manufacturer, defective products will continue to reach the consumer. Further, misuse of complicated goods by the user will create disputes as to whether the goods were in fact "defective" when purchased by the ultimate consumer.[22] As has already been mentioned, this text concentrates on the Code's solution to problems arising out of goods which are claimed to be defective.

The discussion which follows should be read against the background out of which it arises: neither warranties nor strict liability creates an absolute liability on the part of sellers. They are not insurers of the safety of the products which they sell.[23] Both theories require that the product be defective—under the Code this defectiveness is measured against the contractual obligations of the seller; the *Restatement* (*Second*) *of Torts* adds that the defective condition must be *unreasonably* dangerous to the user or his property.[24] Further, the defective condition must cause the loss involved. Therefore, even though this text will emphasize the extent to which the Code has created seller-liability, this approach is taken because of the change which has been made in the doctrine of *caveat emptor* and not to suggest that sellers have become insurers in relation to goods they have sold.

2. EXPRESS WARRANTIES

§ 64. Overview of Express Warranties

Section 2–313 states that express warranties can be created in any one of four ways: by the affirmation of a fact, by a promise, by a description, or by a sample or model. Before there is an express warranty, two other conditions must be met:

1. In cases of an affirmation of fact or the making of a promise, the affirmation or promise must be made by the seller to the buyer and relate to the goods. No such condition is stated for the other two methods of making an express warranty.

2. In all instances, the affirmation, promise, description, or sample or model must be "a part of the basis of the bargain."

22. *Olin Mathieson Chemical Corp. v. Moushon*, 93 Ill.App.2d 280, 235 N.E.2d 263 (1968).

23. *Gossett v. Chrysler Corp.*, 359 F.2d 84 (6th Cir. 1966); *Campo v. Scofield*, 301 N.Y. 468, 95 N.E.2d 802 (1950);

Lonzrick v. Republic Steel Corp., 6 Ohio St.2d 227, 218 N.E.2d 185 (1966). *See also* § 82 *infra*.

24. Restatement (Second) of Torts § 402A (1965).

If these conditions are met, there is an express warranty that the goods shall conform to the affirmation, promise, description, sample, or model —depending on which is involved in the case. It is not necessary that the seller use such words as "warrant" or "guarantee"; nor must the seller have a specific intention to make a warranty.

Out of an abundance of caution the Code goes on to state that certain types of "puffing" or sales talk will not rise to the level of warranty. The seller may continue to affirm the value of his goods or state his opinion or commendation of the goods without having made a warranty. The specific language of the Code (section 2–313) is set out below:

> (1) Express warranties by the seller are created as follows:
>
>> (a) Any affirmation of fact or promise made by the seller to the buyer which relates to the goods and becomes part of the basis of the bargain creates an express warranty that the goods shall conform to the affirmation or promise.
>>
>> (b) Any description of the goods which is made part of the basis of the bargain creates an express warranty that the goods shall conform to the description.
>>
>> (c) Any sample or model which is made part of the basis of the bargain creates an express warranty that the whole of the goods shall conform to the sample or model.
>
> (2) It is not necessary to the creation of an express warranty that the seller use formal words such as "warrant" or "guarantee" or that he have a specific intention to make a warranty, but an affirmation merely of the value of the goods or a statement purporting to be merely the seller's opinion or commendation of the goods does not create a warranty.

A reading of appellate opinions in product liability cases indicates that not enough imaginative thought has gone into possible uses of section 2–313. True, there are some cases in which the buyer buys "as is" and "with all faults."[25] True, also, there are auction sales of unopened boxes in which the buyer takes the complete risk as to what is inside. These cases, however, are few and far between. In the great bulk of cases the seller, sometime during the negotiation, has said something about the product he intends to sell. At the least he will have placed the item into its general category of all of the goods available

---

25. UCC § 2–316(3). Even this language will not exclude express warranties made by the seller. UCC § 2–313, Comment 4.

in the world. For example, he will have called his item a car, a bottle of aspirin, a calculator, a typewriter, or whatever it is. He may have made these statements either orally or in writing. His written statements may have been on an acknowledgment form, in a leaflet, or in a magazine advertisement [26]—but these statements become express warranties if they are a part of the basis of the bargain between the parties. Even in the supermarket sale in which the clerk only handles the product before ringing up the purchase, the labels will have described the goods or made some affirmation of fact about them.[27] At the other extreme there are sales in which the description was extremely detailed. A seller of a machine may have included a book of specifications as to the size and power of the motor, the tolerances within which the machine operates, and the speed of certain of its parts. A seller of a television set or a radio may have included a schematic showing how the receiver was supposed to have been wired. Each of these, if a part of the basis of the bargain, will become an express warranty that the goods conform to the specifications or to the schematic.

When the machine fails to conform to the specifications, it is quickly seen that an express warranty has been breached.[28] Only a little more imagination is needed when the description is more general. Calling an item of goods a "car" implies certain physical attributes about that item: that it is a certain shape and perhaps even of a certain size. If the sale is not of a toy, the word "car" further implies that this item will serve as a means of transportation. If it turns out that the item has no engine at all, the description as a "car" is false—and the express warranty has been breached. However, if everything is in working order except the windshield wipers, the warranty that the item is a "car" has probably not been breached. At some point between the automobile body without an engine and an automobile body with all of the accessories except windshield wipers, a no-car has become a car. This leaves for decision instances in which there were no spark plugs, there were spark plugs but they were inoperative, the tires were worn smooth, or the steering linkage was defective. Are items which otherwise look like cars properly classified as "cars" if they have some

---

26. Randy Knitwear, Inc. v. American Cyanamid Co., 11 N.Y.2d 5, 181 N.E.2d 399, 226 N.Y.S.2d 363 (1962); Rogers v. Toni Home Permanent Co., 167 Ohio St. 244, 147 N.E.2d 612 (1958). As to the need for reliance on the advertisement, see §§ 66–68 *infra*. Annot., 75 A.L.R.2d 112, 128–33 (1961).

27. An alternative basis of warranty liability can be based on UCC § 2–314 (2) (f).

28. City Mach. & Mfg. Co. v. A. & A. Machinery Corp., 4 UCC Rep. 461 (U.S. Dist.Ct.E.D.N.Y.1967).

or all of these defects? [29] The answer will turn on the circumstances of each case, but the basic thought remains: each sale should be examined carefully for statements and descriptions which were a part of the negotiations. These statements and descriptions should be interpreted from the background of the parties as a reasonable buyer would have understood them.[30] On many occasions they will become express warranties and form the basis for a solution of the controversy between these parties.

§ 65. Affirmation of Fact or a Promise

An express warranty may be created by either an affirmation of fact or a promise. This portion of section 2–313 is drawn directly from the Uniform Sales Act.[31] Thus, pre-Code cases dealing with the definition of "affirmation of fact" and "promise" are relevant to the Code.

Since both an affirmation of fact and a promise can create an express warranty, it makes no difference whether the seller says, "I promise you that this coal contains no more than 10% ash," or if he says, "This coal contains no more than 10% ash." If either of these statements becomes a part of the basis of the bargain between the seller and the buyer, an express warranty that the coal contains 10% ash, or less, has been created. As has already been pointed out, the meaning of the warranty is open to interpretation (if the delivered coal contains 10.5% ash, has the warranty been breached?),[32] but the form in which the seller made his statement—whether as an affirmation of a fact or as a promise—makes no difference as far as express warranties are concerned. Parties who are bargaining do not distinguish between affirmations and promises when both cover the same subject matter. Thus, a statement by the seller that the "seller warrants the goods to be sound and healthy at the time of shipment"[33] is as much a basis for a warranty as if the seller had said, "The goods are sound and healthy at the time of shipment." Likewise, when a patient has taken a prescription to a drug store and the druggist, instead of filling the prescription, hands the patient a packaged drug and says, "This is the same thing,"[34] there is as much a basis for a

29. Denna v. Chrysler Corp., 1 Ohio App.2d 582, 206 N.E.2d 221 (1964); Basta v. Riviello, 66 Lack.J. 77 (Pa.C. P.1965). See § 75 *infra*.

30. § 48 *supra*. See also the interpretation of "good" in Newmark v. Gimbel's, Inc., 102 N.J.Super. 279, 246 A.2d 11 (App.Div.1968), *aff'd* 54 N.J. 585, 258 A.2d 697 (1969).

31. Uniform Sales Act § 12.

32. §§ 50–52 *supra*.

33. Vandenberg v. Siter, 204 Pa.Super. 392, 204 A.2d 494 (1964).

34. Jacobs Pharmacy Co. v. Gipson, 116 Ga.App. 760, 159 S.E.2d 171 (1967).

warranty as if the druggist had said, "I promise you that this packaged drug is the same as your prescription." [35]

The inclusion of affirmations of fact as a possible basis for express warranties reflects more than an understanding of the commercial realities of the bargaining process; in addition, it is a reaction against the notion that ideas of contract law ought to be separated from ideas of tort law. Without the clear statement in the Code, it could be argued that an affirmation of fact (when false) sounds in tort and should give rise to remedies of fraud and deceit rather than to form the basis of contractual remedies. This attempt to decide cases woodenly through a system of classification has already been discussed and criticized.[36] That discussion need not be repeated except to emphasize that the Code quite properly rejects any attempt to distinguish between statements which appear to create tort liability and those which appear to create contractual liability; either an affirmation of fact or a promise will satisfy the express warranty section of the Code.

§ 66. Basis of the Bargain

An express warranty is not created simply because the seller has affirmed a fact or made a promise about the goods. That affirmation or promise (as well as the description, sample, or model under the remaining subsections of section 2–313(1)) must become a "part of the basis of the bargain" before an express warranty has been created. These words are undefined—and are probably undefinable. However, the idea of the Code is that every bargain results from several factors —factors such as the buyer's desire to obtain the goods, his willingness to exchange cash or credit for those goods, the seller's desire to obtain the price, and his willingness to exchange available goods for that price.

These factors are not exclusive; many bargains have a broader base. If the seller is a merchant, the buyer may reasonably believe that the goods are merchantable even though nothing is said to this effect.[37] At other times the words and conduct of the parties may give the seller reason to know the particular purpose for which the buyer is making the purchase and may also give the seller reason to know that the buyer is relying on the seller's skill and judgment in selecting or furnishing suitable goods for the buyer's purpose.[38] These bargains rest—at least in part—on these assumptions, and warranties are implied in the resulting sale. On still other occasions a "part of the basis

---

35. *See also* Seely v. White Motor Co., 63 Cal.2d 9, 403 P.2d 145, 45 Cal.Rptr. 17 (1965); Inglis v. American Motors Corp., 3 Ohio St.2d 132, 209 N.E.2d 583 (1965).

36. § 54 *supra.*

37. UCC § 2–314.

38. UCC § 2–315.

of the bargain" may be statements made by the seller about the goods or his exhibition of samples or models. In those situations the statements, samples, or models become warranties that the goods will conform to the statements, samples, or models. The Code does not state whether the "part" which is involved must be significant or whether it may be minor; nor does the Code define what constitutes the "basis" of a bargain. These decisions are left to the court and the jury, acting under the general direction of the Code.[39]

Such decisions were quite properly left to the court and jury. The facts of sales transactions are too variable to permit the promulgation of specific rules in a statute. The seller's statements may have been made weeks or months before the sale [40] or they may have been made moments before—or even after [41]—the sale; the particular statement may have been clearly one of fact or it may have bordered on opinion; [42] the statement may have been made in national advertising to the public generally [43] or it may have been made to the buyer at the time of the sale; the buyer may have examined the goods or he may have purchased without examination; [44] and so on. As combinations of these factors vary from case to case, the base on which the resulting bargain rested will vary. The Code's direction, however, is clear: determine the basis on which the bargain rested; if a part of this basis was the seller's affirmation of fact or a promise, his exhibition of a sample or a model, or a description of the goods, there is an express warranty that the goods will conform to the statement or to that sample or model.

§ 67.   Basis of the Bargain—Statements Made After the Sale

The Uniform Sales Act required that the buyer rely on the affirmation of fact or promise before an express warranty had been created. The full text of the applicable section was as follows:

39. When the facts are disputed, the question of express warranty is for the jury. Sylvia Coal Co. v. Mercury Coal & Coke Co., 151 W.Va. 818, 156 S.E.2d 1 (1967).

40. Leavitt v. Fiberloid Co., 196 Mass. 440, 82 N.E. 682 (1907); Powers v. Briggs, 139 Mich. 664, 103 N.W. 194 (1905). Cf. Ransberger v. Ing, 55 Mo. App. 621 (1894).

41.   § 67 infra.

42. Similar words in relation to the sale of a second-hand automobile were treated differently in Adams v. Peter

Tramontin Motor Sales, Inc., 42 N.J. Super. 313, 126 A.2d 358 (App.Div. 1956); and Wat Henry Pontiac Co. v. Bradley, 202 Okl. 82, 210 P.2d 348 (1949). See § 70 infra.

43. Sylvestri v. Warner & Swasey Co., 398 F.2d 598 (2d Cir. 1968) (express warranty through pictures and words in brochure); Randy Knitwear, Inc. v. American Cyanamid Co., 11 N.Y.2d 5, 226 N.Y.S.2d 363, 181 N.E.2d 399 (1962); Rogers v. Toni Home Permanent Co., 167 Ohio St. 244, 147 N.E.2d 612 (1958). See § 68 infra.

44.   § 88 infra.

Any affirmation of fact or any promise by the seller relating to the goods is an express warranty if the natural tendency of such affirmation or promise is to induce the buyer to purchase the goods, and if the buyer purchases the goods relying thereon.[45]

The Code dropped the reliance test in the section on express warranties, substituting the "basis of the bargain" test, but retained the need for reliance in the section on the implied warranty of fitness for purpose.[46] The extent to which this change represents a change in the substance of the law of express warranties requires further analysis.

First, the easy case: if the seller's statements would have met the test of the Uniform Sales Act, the "basis of the bargain" test of the Code has been satisfied. Therefore, if the seller's affirmation of a fact or promise would naturally tend to induce the buyer to make the purchase and if the buyer does rely in making his purchase, the affirmation or promise has become a part of the basis of the resulting bargain. Thus, a petition has stated a cause of action under the Code when the petition alleges that the seller agreed to sell and to plant grass sprigs in the buyer's yard; that the buyer questioned the advisability of sprigging in the month of October; that the seller expressly warranted that October was not too late to sprig this type of grass and that the cold weather would not damage it; that the buyer relied on these warranties; and that the cold weather did kill the grass. Such a petition contains all of the elements of an express warranty—either under the Uniform Sales Act or under the Code.[47] The Sales Act would require a discussion of natural tendencies and of reliance; the Code requires a finding of the basis of the bargain.

Second, the harder case: granting that reliance will satisfy the Code's "basis of the bargain" test, is reliance an essential element of that test? This question is not easily answered, in large part because of the varying factual patterns which can present it. For example, the seller's statements may come after the sale has been made; or the seller's statements may come before the sale but the buyer may not have heard them (as with advertisements which the buyer did not read), or the buyer may have heard them but examined the goods to

---

45. Uniform Sales Act § 12. *See* Murphy v. National Iron & Metal Co., 71 Ariz. 323, 227 P.2d 219 (1951); Midland Loan Fin. Co. v. Madsen, 217 Minn. 267, 14 N.W.2d 475 (1944); Richardson v. Coffman, 87 Iowa 121, 54 N.W. 356 (1893). However, if the statement of the seller would naturally induce reliance, no further proof of reliance was needed. Steiner v. Jarrett, 130 Cal.App.2d 869, 280 P.2d 235

(1954); Bregman Screen & Lumber Co. v. Bechefsky, 16 N.J.Super. 35, 83 A. 2d 804 (App.Div.1951).

46. UCC § 2–315.

47. Bell v. Menzies, 110 Ga.App. 436, 138 S.E.2d 731 (1964). The buyer must also have given notice of the breach or he will be barred of any remedy. UCC § 2–607(3). § 143 *infra.*

ascertain if the seller's statements were true, or the buyer may have heard them but later signed a writing which disclaimed all warranties. Each of these cases presents a situation in which the Uniform Sales Act seller could have argued that there was no warranty because there was no reliance at the time of the purchase. The Code analysis of these problems is presented in this and the next two sections of this text, with this section emphasizing the effect of statements made after a sale.

Consider the following hypothetical situation:

A young lady visited a self-service drug store and selected a tube of eye-shadow from a display rack. She took the eye-shadow to the check-out counter where she paid the clerk the price of the product. As the clerk was placing the eye-shadow in a sack, she said, "This is our finest eye-shadow. It is absolutely harmless to the eyes." The young lady took the purchase home, used the eye-shadow as directed, and suffered a painful burn when some of the cosmetic fell into the corner of her eye.

Prior to the Code there was authority that this statement would not amount to an express warranty; the statement of the clerk did not induce the purchase.[48] The Code has eliminated any reference to reliance in the creation of express warranties, although it retained reliance for the implied warranty of fitness for purpose.[49] The Code test is whether the clerk's statement was a "part of the basis of the bargain." A "bargain" is not something that occurs at a particular moment in time, and is forever fixed as to its content; instead, it describes the commercial relationship between the parties in regard to this product. The word "bargain" is not encrusted with pre-Code concepts which had attached themselves to contract formation—notions that a contract came into existence at some specific point in time, some split second when offer and acceptance coincided, thereafter to be binding unless a new contract complete with the trappings of agreement and consideration superseded the old one. The Code's word is "bargain"—a process which can extend beyond the moment in time that the offeree utters the magic words, "I accept." In the eye-shadow

---

48. Beckett v. F. W. Woolworth Co., 376 Ill. 470, 34 N.E.2d 427 (1941).

49. *Compare* UCC § 2–313 *with* UCC § 2–315. From this it can be argued that the drafters intended to change the reliance test of the Uniform Sales Act when express warranties are involved. "In actual practice affirmations of fact made by the seller about the goods during a bargain are re-garded as part of the description of those goods; hence no particular reliance on such statements need be shown in order to weave them into the fabric of the agreement. Rather, any fact which is to take such affirmations, once made, out of the agreement requires clear affirmative proof. The issue normally is one of fact." UCC § 2–313, Comment 3.

purchase case, the clerk's statements are a part of the entire *bargain* even though they did not induce the *contract*.

As long as the seller would allow the buyer to exchange or return the product purchased, the buyer's forbearance from returning the goods can be the necessary consideration to support the seller's promise made after the sale.[50] Even if the seller's statement is made at a time when the buyer does not have the privilege of return, that statement may be so closely connected with the sale that it is still a *part* (note the Code word; the statements need not be the sole basis) of the basis of the *bargain*. However, even in those cases in which the court is convinced that the bargain had been completed prior to the seller's statements, those statements could be a modification of the completed agreement.[51] No consideration is needed for a Code modification, and it is reasonable to assume that a buyer would agree to an expansion of his warranty protection. Therefore, statements made in brochures and pamphlets included within the package which was closed (or even sealed) at the time of purchase can be the source of express warranties even though the buyer did not read the brochure or pamphlet prior to the moment he made his purchase. This conclusion can be based either on the expanded concept of bargain or on a modification of a bargain-already-made.

Whether statements in brochures and pamphlets included with the goods in a sealed package can limit a seller's liability is quite a different problem. As long as the seller was expanding the buyer's protection it was reasonable to assume that the buyer would consent to the statements as a part of the bargain between the parties. However, there is no reason to assume that a buyer would consent to a hidden disclaimer of warranties or limitation of liabilities.[52] The problem of disclaimers is discussed elsewhere in this text.[53]

§ 68. Basis of the Bargain—Statements Made Prior to the Sale

The great bulk of the express warranty cases rest on statements made, or samples or models exhibited, prior to the sale. As has already been pointed out, if the seller's statements would naturally tend to induce the purchase and if the buyer relied on those statements in

---

50. See discussion and pre-Code cases cited in 1 S. Williston, Sales § 211 (rev. ed. 1948).

51. UCC § 2–209. This Code section is discussed in § 43 *supra*. The affirmations of fact and promises on a label are also implied warranties under UCC § 2–314(2) (f). A distinction between the express and implied warranties is necessary when implied warranties have been effectively disclaimed. §§ 74, 76 *infra*.

52. Admiral Oasis Hotel Corp. v. Home Gas Indus., Inc., 68 Ill.App.2d 297, 216 N.E.2d 282 (1965).

53. §§ 86–88 *infra*.

making the purchase, an express Code warranty has been created.[54] Such a case caused no difficulty under the Uniform Sales Act, and will cause no difficulty under the Code. Under the Code, however, the analysis ought not be in terms of reliance. Instead, the analysis should be in terms of the "basis of the bargain." [55] When a seller has affirmed a fact, made a promise, or described his product, or when the seller has exhibited a sample or model of the goods, and the parties continue to deal at least partially on the basis of what the seller said or showed the buyer, the seller's statements (or sample or model) will be a part of the basis of the bargain reached—and will create an express warranty. This was the sequence of events in the sale of the grass sprigs, already discussed.[56] It also represents the sequence of most factual patterns involving express warranties.[57] True, it makes no difference in the easy case whether the analysis is in terms of "reliance" or "basis of the bargain"; a warranty arises under either test. A modification of the facts, however, will illustrate the need for following the Code test.

First, suppose that the buyer did not hear or read the seller's statements regarding his product. There is no question but that the seller affirmed a fact or made a promise about his goods; the difficulty is that the statements were made outside the hearing of the buyer.[58] For example, a seller may have advertised his product in magazines and brochures which were never read by the buyer. Assuming that these magazines and brochures contained affirmations as to the quality of the goods sold, the buyer did not rely upon those affirmations when he made his purchase. Nevertheless, could these affirmations become a part of the basis of the bargain between the seller and buyer?

---

54. § 67 *supra.*

55. UCC § 2–313.

56. Bell v. Menzies, 110 Ga.App. 436, 138 S.E.2d 731 (1964), discussed in § 67 *supra.*

57. *E. g.,* Sylvestri v. Warner & Swasey Co., 398 F.2d 598 (2d Cir. 1968); Rogers v. Toni Home Permanent Co., 167 Ohio St. 244, 147 N.E.2d 612 (1958); Lawner v. Englebach, 433 Pa. 311, 249 A.2d 295 (1969).

58. An example of such a case, other than the one mentioned in the text, is the sale of a product to a patient while under anesthesia in a hospital. *See* Cheshire v. Southampton Hosp. Ass'n, 53 Misc.2d 355, 278 N.Y.S.2d 531 (Sup.Ct.1967), which doubted the existence of a sale because the product involved (a surgical pin) was probably a part of an overall service under the doctrine of Perlmutter v. Beth David Hosp., 308 N.Y. 100, 123 N.E.2d 792 (1954). *But cf.* Orthopedic Equip. Co. v. Eutsler, 276 F.2d 455 (4th Cir. 1960). *See also* Jackson v. Muhlenberg Hosp., 96 N.J.Super. 314, 232 A.2d 879 (L. Div.1967), where the product was blood. The court entered summary judgment against the patient on claims based on strict liability and implied warranty but found an express warranty in a statement attached to the blood container. The case was reversed on appeal and a trial ordered, on the ground that the record was too meagre to enter a final decision. 53 N.J. 138, 249 A.2d 65 (1969).

Cases have disagreed as to the answer to this question,[59] but those which hold that the unread advertisement may constitute a warranty reach the preferable result—and the result which is more consistent with the intention of the Code. The common law lawyer, steeped in the tradition of treating warranty coverage solely as a matter of contract, may object to such a result. How can a buyer claim the *consensual* protection of an affirmation or a promise when the buyer knows nothing of the affirmation or promise? Posing the question in this way overlooks the history of warranty protection. The buyer sues "on a contract" only because the legal system has forced him to classify his cause of action as contract or tort. What is involved are a product and an injury, either to a person or to property. The court's task is to determine whether that injury was caused by a defect in the product, and any statements made by the seller designed to induce the public to buy his product are relevant in making this determination.[60] The "basis of the bargain" includes the dickered terms,[61] but is not limited to them. The "basis of the bargain" is also the item purchased, and a part of that bargain includes the statements which the seller made about what he sold.

Second, suppose that the seller's statements were made, the description given, or the sample or model exhibited, before the sale; that the buyer heard or read the statements or description, or saw the exhibits; and that the delivered goods did not conform to the statements, description, sample, or model—whichever was involved; but that the seller claimed that the buyer did not rely on anything which the seller said or did prior to the sale. Since there was no reliance, the seller would argue, there has been nothing attributable to the seller which can be considered a *part of the basis of the bargain;* therefore, there is no warranty under section 2–313.

Many factual patterns can present this question. The claimed defect may have been obvious, or would have been obvious on examination; the buyer may have examined the goods before the contract and either have found or missed the defect; or the buyer may have brought in his own expert to determine whether the goods did

---

59. Speed Fastners, Inc. v. Newsom, 382 F.2d 395 (10th Cir. 1967) (brochure not read by buyer does not constitute express warranty); Lonzrick v. Republic Steel Corp., 6 Ohio St.2d 227, 218 N.E.2d 185 (1966) (fact that advertisement was not read is not sound basis for denying recovery in tort based on warranty). See Annot., 75 A.L.R.2d 112, 128–33 (1961). The advertisements could also be used to show the scope of implied warranty under UCC § 2–314. Compare the reliance test in Restatement (Second) of Torts § 402B (1965).

60. Walcott & Steele, Inc. v. Carpenter, 246 Ark. 93, 436 S.W.2d 820 (1969).

61. UCC § 2–313, Comment 1. Further, if the advertisement is read after the sale but before the injury, a modification under UCC § 2–209 could result. § 67 *supra.*

conform to the seller's representations. As the facts change, so may the result. Thus, no single rule can provide an answer to all of these factual patterns. The Code, however, sets out certain principles which will aid in deciding these cases, even though the decision in each must necessarily turn on its own facts.

1. The affirmation of fact, the promise, or the description must be interpreted before it can be determined whether there has been a warranty covering the particular defect.[62] The words used by the seller must be read in the way in which the buyer should reasonably have understood them. Thus, if a seller asserts that a second-hand automobile is in "excellent shape," it must first be decided whether those words are an affirmation of fact or "merely the seller's opinion or commendation of the goods." [63] Even if it is determined that they amount to an affirmation of fact under the circumstances involved, they may not cover an obvious defect. If the automobile involved had a rusted fender and door panel, the words "excellent shape" made to the buyer who was examining the automobile could well have been meant to be limited to the mechanical condition of the engine, so that if something was faulty with the engine, there would be a default—but the existence of the obvious rust would not amount to a breach. Likewise, statements made by the buyer to the seller about the performance of the goods must be interpreted against the background of the prior negotiations of the parties.[64]

2. The Code requires only that the statements of the seller (or the description, sample, or model) become a *part* of the basis of the bargain; it is not necessary that they become the sole basis of the bargain. If a buyer has examined the goods prior to the purchase and did not discover the defect, the warranty is not excluded.[65] If the buyer discovered the defect—but bought anyway—such a purchase will still often rest both upon what the buyer discovered and upon what the seller said. What the buyer discovered caused doubts, but those doubts were at least partially removed by the representations made. Those representations have, therefore, become a *part* of the basis of the bargain. For example, suppose that a seller had a used boring mill for sale; that the seller represented that the mill had a

---

62. § 48 *supra.*

63. § 70 *infra.*

64. General Electric Co. v. United States Dynamics, Inc., 403 F.2d 933 (1st Cir. 1968).

65. "The warranty need not be the sole inducement. The buyer may rely both on the seller's statements and on his own judgment. Even examination by the buyer does not excuse the seller from liability for words which amount to an express warranty if the defect was not detected." Bregman Screen & Lumber Co. v. Bechefsky, 16 N.J. Super. 35, 41, 83 A.2d 804, 807 (App. Div.1951). For a Code case, see General Electric Co. v. United States Dynamics, Inc., 403 F.2d 933 (1st Cir. 1968).

spindle speed of up to 1,300 revolutions per minute; that the buyer inspected the mill and noticed that the instruction sheet indicated that its maximum speed was only 358 revolutions per minute; but that the buyer nevertheless purchased the mill. On these facts one court correctly held that the representations of the seller were a *part* of the basis of the bargain.[66] The buyer had purchased both on the basis of what he saw and what he was told by the seller. Thus, an inspection of the goods—even an inspection which discovers that the seller's statements might be false—will not necessarily bar recovery for breach of express warranty.[67]

This conclusion is strengthened by other provisions in the Code. Section 2–316 eliminates *implied* warranties for defects that should have been discovered on an examination of the goods prior to their purchase. That section is limited to implied warranties, thus making it clear that express warranties are not automatically eliminated when a buyer has inspected.[68]

3. The Code does require, however, that the seller's statements (or the sample or model) become a part of the *basis* of the bargain. If the resulting bargain does not rest at all on the representations of the seller, those representations cannot be considered as becoming any part of the "basis of the bargain" within the meaning of section 2–313. Admittedly, there will not be many cases in which the seller's representations will have spent themselves prior to the purchase (most often a buyer who discovers that the seller's representations are false will refuse to purchase), but just as parties may codify or rescind contracts already entered into,[69] so may they determine that prior statements made by the seller are no longer to be considered a part of their negotiations. This determination may come from an express understanding—as where the seller, before the bargain is struck, tells the buyer that he is withdrawing a specific statement that he made about the goods—or it may come from the conduct of the parties. An example of the latter might include a case in which the seller's statements are made so long before the contract of purchase that a reason-

---

66. City Mach. & Mfg. Co. v. A. & A. Machinery Corp., 4 UCC Rep. 461 (U.S. Dist.Ct.E.D. N.Y.1967). *See also* General Electric Co. v. United States Dynamics, Inc., 403 F.2d 933 (1st Cir. 1968), discussed in § 73 *infra*.

67. Norris v. Parker, 15 Tex.Civ.App. 117, 38 S.W. 259 (1896). *See* 1 S. Williston, Sales § 207 (rev. ed. 1948).

68. The seller need not intend to warrant in order to have an express warranty. Some early cases required such an intent (*e. g.*, M'Farland v. Newman, 9 Watts (Pa.) 55, 60 (1839)), probably as a carry-over from such decisions as Chandelor v. Lopus, 3 Cro.Jac. 4, 79 Eng.Rep. 3 (Ex.1603), discussed in 54 *supra*. As to the present law, see UCC § 2–313, Comment 3.

69. § 43 *supra*.

able person in the place of the buyer ought to have realized that the seller's past representations were no longer applicable.[70]

The buyer who examines and discovers a defect could conceivably also be purchasing without a warranty that a seller's prior affirmation would have created.[71] This result (no warranty) ought to be reached only if the trier of fact is convinced that the representation formed no part of the basis of the bargain. As was pointed out above, an examination will not eliminate an express warranty whenever the buyer relies even partially on the seller's statements made prior to the purchase.

In determining whether a seller's statement (or a description, sample, or model) has formed any part of the basis of the bargain, evidence of the negotiations between the parties is admissible. The court's task is to determine the foundations upon which the final bargain rested.[72] There is no one factor which is determinative, but perhaps the best single indicator of the basis of the bargain is the price which the buyer agreed to pay. If the price did not reflect the existence of the defect or the possibility that the article sold was not genuine—that is, if the buyer paid full price for the goods—the probabilities are that the seller's prior statements did form at least a part of the basis of the bargain. If, however, the price paid indicates that the parties were exchanging the risk that the goods might be faulty or not genuine, there is evidence that the seller's statements did not form a part of the basis of the bargain.[73] Each case must be determined on its own facts, with the scales weighted in favor of a finding that prior statements made by the seller have become an express warranty. This should not, however, obliterate the test: did the affirmations of fact or promises made by the seller, did any descriptions, or any samples or model exhibited become a part of the basis of the bargain? If so, an express warranty has been created. If not, there is no express warranty.

---

70. A doubtful example of this principle is Smith v. Denholm & McKay Co., 288 Mass. 234, 192 N.E. 631 (1934), where the court held that a seller's representations as to the first sale did not carry over to the second and third sales of the same product. *See also* Ransberger v. Ing, 55 Mo.App. 621 (1894). The better rule is stated in Leavitt v. Fiberloid Co., 196 Mass. 440, 82 N.E. 682 (1907); Powers v. Briggs, 139 Mich. 664, 103 N.W. 194 (1905).

71. Sylvia Coal Co. v. Mercury Coal & Coke Co., 151 W.Va. 818, 156 S.E.2d 1 (1967).

72. UCC § 2–313, Comment 4.

73. Sylvia Coal Co. v. Mercury Coal & Coke Co., 151 W.Va. 818, 156 S.E.2d 1 (1967). *See* UCC § 2–314, Comment 7.

§ 69.　Express Warranties and the Parol Evidence Rule

A type of case which arises with some frequency involves the Code sections on express warranty and the Code's parol evidence rule. The following example typifies these cases:

A buyer has purchased goods which he now claims to be defective, and supports his claim by attempting to introduce evidence of an express warranty made by the seller prior to the sale. The seller denies that an express warranty was made. If this were all there was to the dispute, the court would have before it a factual problem: did the seller affirm a fact or make a promise, was there a description, or was a sample of model exhibited—as the case may be—which became a part of the basis of the bargain between the buyer and seller? The buyer's evidence and the seller's evidence would be admitted, and the trier of fact would resolve the issue. However, assume that the seller urged that the buyer's evidence is not admissible because of a signed writing which contains a clause stating (a) that there were no warranties, express or implied, beyond those contained in the writing (and the warranty alleged by the buyer is not a part of this writing), and (b) that the writing is the exclusive evidence of the agreement between the parties.

Portions of this problem have been discussed in detail in other sections of this text. However, because of the frequency with which this factual pattern is repeated, the issues presented are collected at this point, with footnote references to the longer textual discussions. The principal issues involve the statute of frauds, the parol evidence rule, and the meaning of the phrase "basis of the bargain."

1. *Statute of frauds.* The seller would not be successful in a claim that the Code's statute of frauds prevents introduction of the buyer's evidence of a prior warranty. The buyer's evidence may consist of a writing in which the seller supposedly made the express warranty or it may be testimony of oral representations and promises made by the seller. The statute of frauds makes neither of these inadmissible. In the case of the writing, the answer is clear. The statute of frauds requires a writing, and one exists. The answer is just as clear when the express warranty rests on oral testimony. All that the statute of frauds requires is that there be some writing which (1) sets forth the quantity of goods sold and (2) is sufficient to indicate that a contract for sale was made between these parties. The writing introduced by the seller will satisfy these requirements.[74]

2. *Parol evidence rule.* This is the doctrine which will cause the buyer his greatest difficulties; in fact, there are some courts which would exclude the buyer's evidence simply because it "contradicts"

---

74. § 24 *supra.*

unambiguous language in a written agreement.[75] This result (that is, no warranty) may be correct in a particular case, but rigid application of an unsupportable version of the parol evidence rule will, on occasion, lead to unsupportable results.

The no-warranties portion of the written clause could be used by the seller as a base for two arguments:

a. This clause indicates that the alleged express warranty, if made, was rescinded prior to the moment of the parties' agreement. The buyer, therefore, did not rely on the prior representations, and those representations did not become any part of the basis of the bargain between the buyer and seller.[76] This argument, if accepted, would result in the no-warranties clause removing from the factual pattern one of the essential elements of the express warranty section: that the statements, descriptions, samples, or models must become a "part of the basis of the bargain" before a warranty is created.

b. The buyer's evidence of a prior warranty contradicts the written statement that no warranties were made; as such, the buyer's evidence is inadmissable under the parol evidence rule.[77] This argument, if accepted, allows the no-warranty clause to form a barrier preventing the trier of fact from considering whether the representations of the seller were a part of the basis of the resulting bargain.

The exclusive-evidence-of-agreement portion of the written clause could form the basis for a third argument for the seller:

c. The buyer's evidence of a prior warranty also contradicts the written statement that the writing is the sole evidence of the parties' agreement; however, even if the evidence of the prior warranties is somehow "consistent" with the writing, nevertheless it is not admissible to add to a writing which represents the complete and exclusive statement of the terms of the parties' agreement.[78] The result of this argument, if accepted, is similar to that of b, above: the evidence of the alleged prior representations never goes to the trier of fact.

What should be done with these arguments? One thing which could be done with them is to accept them and refuse to allow the buyer's evidence to be admitted. A court may do this when it concludes that the buyer's evidence is so unbelievable that even if the jury were to return a verdict for the buyer, the court would have to enter a judgment for the seller on this question—notwithstanding the

75. Green Chevrolet Co. v. Kemp, 241 Ark. 62, 406 S.W.2d 142 (1966); Will Laboratories, Inc. v. White Rock Pen Corp., 4 UCC Rep. 848 (N.Y.Sup.Ct. 1967). *But see* UCC § 2–202, Comment

76. UCC § 2–313(1).

77. UCC § 2–202.

78. UCC § 2–202(b).

verdict.[79] It is easier to tell the buyer that his evidence is inadmissible than to tell him that he is not to be believed.

Putting these cases to one side (those in which the judge concludes that reasonable men could not believe the buyer's version of the pre-agreement negotiations), what Code issues are presented by the seller's arguments outlined above? One problem which the court must decide is whether any part of the parol evidence rule prevents admission of the buyer's evidence.[80] While it may at first appear that the buyer's evidence does contradict the no-warranties provision of the writing, the court is not justified in keeping the buyer's evidence from the trier of fact unless it is determined that the writing was "intended by the parties as a final expression of their agreement with respect to such terms as are included therein." Did the *parties* (not just one of them) intend that the no-warranties provision was the final expression of their agreement relating to express warranties?[81] If so, but only if so, is the judge justified in keeping this evidence from the jury. Here ideas developed in the section of this text dealing with unconscionability are material.[82] If the clause providing that there are no warranties was part of a printed form which was not discussed with the buyer and if there was no justifiable expectation on the part of the seller that the buyer assented to that clause, the *parties* did not intend that clause to be the final expression of their understanding of warranties.[83] The clause, in such a case, unfairly surprises the buyer and should not limit the introduction of his evidence. If, on the other hand, the seller had justifiable reason to understand that the buyer was assenting to a purchase without warranties, the "intended by the parties" test of the parol evidence rule has been met.

This same analysis must be made for the exclusive-evidence-of-the-contract clause contained in the writing. Such a clause is an indication that the parties intended to have their rights and duties determined by the promises and conditions contained in the writing, and not by promises or representations which were exchanged at some prior time—whether those promises and representations were consistent or inconsistent with the writing. Such a clause, however, ought not be considered as conclusive evidence that the *parties* intended to merge all of their prior understandings into the written document. The clause

79. *See* Eskimo Pie Corp. v. Whitelawn Dairies, Inc., 284 F.Supp. 987 (S.D.N.Y. 1968); Whirlpool Corp. v. Regis Leasing Corp., 29 A.D.2d 395, 288 N.Y.S.2d 337 (1968); 3 A. Corbin, Contracts § 542 (1960).

80. The Code's parol evidence rule is discussed in § 53 *supra*.

81. Hull-Dobbs, Inc. v. Mallicoat, 57 Tenn.App. 100, 415 S.W.2d 344 (1966).

82. § 44 *supra*.

83. § 48 *supra*.

may have been obtained by fraud, it may have been obtained by oppression, it may have been obtained under circumstances which made it clear to the seller that the buyer did not know the clause was included in a printed form and therefore did not intend that the writing be the exclusive evidence of their agreement, or it may have been obtained under circumstances which indicate that the seller could not reasonably have expected that the buyer assented to the clause.[84]   In these instances the writing was not intended either as a final expression of their agreement with respect to the merging of prior understandings or as the complete and exclusive statement of all of the terms of their agreement.[85]   In short, under the Code the finality of a writing cannot be determined solely by looking at the writing; the background of the negotiations and of the execution of the document is relevant evidence to determine the parties' intention.

As is pointed out in another section of this text, there is no parol evidence problem when the express warranty rests on a description of the goods which has been included in the writing or in the exchanged memoranda.[86]   Nor is there a parol evidence rule problem when the seller's affirmation of fact or his promises are contained in the writing. In these cases there is no "prior agreement" or "contemporaneous oral agreement" involved.   All that is involved is a problem of construing a writing (or set of writings) which both create and destroy warranties at the same moment.[87]   How the Code solves this problem is discussed elsewhere.[88]

3. *Basis of the bargain.*   If the court determines that the buyer's evidence is admissible, the trier of fact must determine whether the seller made an affirmation of fact or a promise about the goods, whether a description was used, or whether a sample or model was shown, and whether—if one of these events occurred—that event became a "part of the basis of the bargain."   What a particular bargain was based upon cannot be determined solely by reading the writing or writings involved—even if that writing contains a statement that it represents the entire agreement of the parties.   The court must search out the factors that produced the agreement and surrounded the writing. Principles to aid in reaching this determination have been listed and briefly discussed in a prior section.[89]

---

84. §§ 34, 36–37, and 44 *supra.*

85. For a case where the court found the writing to be ambiguous, see Leveridge v. Notaras, 433 P.2d 935 (Okl.1967).   Generally, see §§ 48–49, and 53 *supra.*

86. § 71 *infra.*

87. UCC § 2–316(1).

88. §§ 71, 87 *infra.*

89. § 68 *supra.*

§ 70. Statements of Fact Distinguished from Statements of Opinion

The Uniform Sales Act provided that no "affirmation of the value of the goods, nor any statement purporting to be a statement of the seller's opinion only shall be construed as a warranty." [90] The seller was allowed to make some assertions about his goods without having those assertions become express warranties. These assertions are often called sales-talk or "puffing." Under the early warranty law almost anything said by the seller fell within this classification as long as it was not fraudulent or the seller did not use the word "warrant"—or perhaps some similar word.[91] The history of the law of warranty has been a continual restriction of the area of permissible puffing and an expansion of the number of situations in which the statements made by the seller amount to an affirmation of fact or a promise.[92] This trend continued under the Uniform Sales Act even though two types of statements were exempted from construction as a warranty: (1) affirmations of value, and (2) statements purporting to be the seller's opinion only.

The Code, after providing that neither formal words nor specific intent is needed to create an express warranty, continues: "an affirmation merely of the value of the goods or a statement purporting to be merely the seller's opinion or commendation of the goods does not create warranty." [93] The word "merely" has been inserted in the affirmation-of-value exemption—indicating an intention to restrict further the area of permissible puffing—and "only" in the opinion portion has become "merely." However, the addition of "commendation" could conceivably cause difficulty. Almost every statement made by the seller—including his affirmations of fact and promises—could be viewed as a commendation of the goods and, therefore, as not creating warranties. While this is a *conceivable* source of difficulty in statutory construction, courts ought not (and will not) use this added word to expand the situations in which affirmations of fact and promises are interpreted as permissible sales talk.[94] The tests under the two statutes are sufficiently similar so that pre-Code cases can continue as authority under the Code.[95]

90. Uniform Sales Act § 12.

91. § 54 *supra.*

92. Kabatchnick v. Hanover-Elm Bldg. Corp., 328 Mass. 341, 103 N.E.2d 692 (1952) (real estate; action for deceit).

93. UCC § 2–313(2).

94. *E. g.,* Jacobs Pharmacy Co. v. Gipson, 116 Ga.App. 760, 159 S.E.2d 171 (1967) (seller gave his "commendation" of a packaged drug; court held that a warranty existed).

95. Examples of statements which have been held to be puffing, or sales talk, include: a statement by a salesgirl that the product was "wonderful" and would "enhance" the buyer's hands, Jacquot v. Wm. Filene's Sons, 337 Mass. 312, 149 N.E.2d 635 (1958); a statement by the seller that his nine-

Court decisions on these problems do not turn on a careful analysis of statutory language, and properly so. The line between warranty and puffing is one that evades specific rules. The problem is that of determining the basis of the bargain—the justifiable expectations of the buyer—and words that are warranties in one situation can be sales talk in another, depending upon their impact on the resulting bargain. The answer is to be determined by the trier of fact from the surrounding circumstances and the manner in which the words were used.[96] For example, in one case a seller told a dealer that the goods were "readily saleable," and the court held that these words were puffing, not a warranty.[97] In another case a seller represented to a farmer that goods were saleable; the court held this to be a misrepresentation of fact and allowed rescission even though the buyer inspected the goods and had a merchant aid him in this inspection.[98] A similar difference can be found in the cases when the seller has stated that a product is "good".[99] A statement that a second-hand automobile is "perfect" and that the buyer "couldn't buy a better car" was puffing according to the facts of one case;[1] but an assurance that a second-hand car "is in A–1 shape" was held to be a warranty by another court.[2] Generally, statements as to the fitness of an animal for breeding purposes are regarded as sales talk, but one court held that the seller's statements in that case amounted to a warranty.[3]

Statements as to the value of goods are often cited as the primary example of puffing. The Code specifically excepts "an affirmation merely of the value of the goods" from the express warranty coverage.

year old yacht was "in perfect shape as she is my Pride and Joy," Keating v. DeArment, 193 So.2d 694 (Fla.Ct. App.1967), limited in Brown v. Hall, 221 So.2d 454 (Fla.Ct.App.1969); a statement that a power-activated tool was "safe to use," Hollenbeck v. Ramset Fasteners, Inc., 267 N.C. 401, 148 S.E.2d 287 (1966); a statement that roses were "very fine stock," Stumpp & Walker Co. v. Lynber, 84 N.Y.S. 912 (App.T.1903); and, under the Code, a statement that goods sold were "of good quality, that good results would be obtained," and that the buyer would "be pleased" with the product's operation, Olin Mathieson Chem. Corp. v. Moushon, 93 Ill.App.2d 280, 235 N.E. 2d 263 (1968). Many pre-Code cases are cited in 1 S. Williston, Sales § 203 (rev. ed. 1948).

96. Hagedorn v. Taggard, 114 A.2d 430 (D.C.App.1955); Jackson v. Gifford, 264 P.2d 313 (Okl.1953) ("we do not sell sick hogs"); Sylvia Coal Co. v. Mercury Coal & Coke Co., 151 W.Va. 818, 156 S.E.2d 1 (1967).

97. Regal Motor Prods., Inc. v. Bender, 102 Ohio App. 447, 139 N.E.2d 463 (1956).

98. Foote v. Wilson, 104 Kan. 191, 178 P. 430 (1919).

99. Compare Saunders v. Cowl, 201 Minn. 574, 277 N.W. 12 (1938), with Keenan v. Cherry & Webb, 47 R.I. 125, 131 A. 309 (1925).

1. Adams v. Peter Tramontin Motor Sales, 42 N.J.Super. 313, 126 A.2d 358 (App.Div.1956).

2. Wat Henry Pontiac Co. v. Bradley, 202 Okl. 82, 210 P.2d 348 (1949).

3. Adrian v. Elmer, 178 Kan. 242, 284 P.2d 599 (1955).

Nevertheless, there are times when the seller's statements of the value of what he has sold amount to more than a "mere" expression of opinion; they go further and affirm a fact about the goods. When a seller tells a buyer that he has a $1,000 bracelet for sale, he may (depending on the circumstances of the transaction) be affirming facts about that bracelet's quality. If so, the statement is not *merely* one of the value of the goods.[4]

Summarizing the thousands of opinions which have dealt with the problem of just when a statement of opinion becomes an affirmation of a fact is impossible. A part of the impossibility results from the nature of the task. In one sense, every statement made by a seller is nothing more than his opinion as to the goods or how the goods will operate; yet at some point he makes his statement in a manner and under such conditions that the buyer does not understand that *only* this seller's opinion is involved. It is at that point that the seller has left the puffing stage of his negotiations and has crossed into the area of express warranty. Perhaps the best test that can be suggested as to when this line has been crossed comes from the basis of the bargain test contained in section 2–313(1). The Comments pose the question thus: "What statements of the seller have in the circumstances and in objective judgment become a part of the basis of the bargain?"[5] Those that have are warranties; those that have not are sales talk. This does not prevent the issue from being one of fact, but it indicates that the Code is not establishing two different tests within section 2–313. The addition of the value-opinion-commendation language only restates the test that was developed in subsection (1).

---

4. Johnson v. City Co. of New York, 78 F.2d 782 (10th Cir. 1935); Foote v. Wilson, 104 Kan. 191, 178 P. 430 (1919); Lawner v. Engelbach, 433 Pa. 311, 249 A.2d 295 (1969) (decided under Code). In Pettibone Wood Mfg. Co. v. Pioneer Constr. Co., 203 Va. 152, 122 S.E.2d 885 (1961), a statement by the seller as to cost of operating goods was held not to be a warranty.

5. UCC § 2–313, Comment 8. Many of the recent cases which have held that the seller's statements did not rise to the stature of a warranty have found alternative bases on which to rest their decision, almost as if the conclusion that only "puffing" was involved was not a sufficient reason for deciding against the buyer. These cases can be explained on the basis of the statements made in the text. *E. g.*, Shay v. Joseph, 219 Md. 273, 149 A.2d 3 (1959) (no reliance); Maupin v. Nutrena Mill, Inc., 385 P.2d 504 (Okl. 1963) (no causal relation).

§ 71. Description of the Goods

There were some old English cases,[6] and even a few decisions in this country,[7] which held that a description of the goods did not create a warranty. Evidently, describing goods fell within the area of permissible puffing and sales talk. Any chance for these cases to develop into a general principle of law was blocked by the Uniform Sales Act which provided that descriptions created *implied* warranties.[8] The Code has continued the idea that warranties may be created by descriptions, but has moved them into the section on *express* warranties.

> Any description of the goods which is made part of the basis of the bargain creates an express warranty that the goods shall conform to the description.[9]

The differences between an express and an implied warranty can be over-emphasized. Once a court has decided that a warranty exists, it makes no difference whether that warranty is called express or implied; in either event the seller must comply or be liable for breach, and his liability is not diminished because the warranty involved is only implied.[10] Nevertheless, there were good reasons for changing the description warranty to one that is classified as "express."

First, the factual background which produces the description warranty is similar to that which produces the affirmation-of-fact warranty (which is an express warranty). For example, when a seller states that he has a certain brand of goods for sale, he is affirming a fact about those goods (that they are of the brand stated) and he is, at the same time, describing them. Under the Code there is no need to try to sort out descriptions from affirmations of fact; they both create express warranties.

Second, this process of sorting the express affirmation-of-fact warranty from the implied description warranty could have been important under the Uniform Sales Act when implied warranties had been effectively disclaimed, and when the words which the seller used in

---

6. In Budd v. Fairmaener, 8 Bing. 48, 131 Eng.Rep. 318 (C.P.1831), seller signed a receipt in the following words: "Received of Mr. *Budd* 10*l.* for a grey four year old colt, warranted sound in every respect." The court held that there was no warranty as to the age of the colt. Tindal, C. J., said, "I should say that, upon the face of this instrument, the intention of the parties was to confine the warranty to soundness, and that the preceding statement was matter of description only." *Id.* at 52, 131 Eng. Rep. at 320.

7. Shambaugh v. Current, 111 Iowa 121, 82 N.W. 497 (1900); Willard v. Stevens, 24 N.H. 271 (1851); Rollins v. Northern Land & Logging Co., 134 Wis. 447, 114 N.W. 819 (1908).

8. Uniform Sales Act § 14.

9. UCC § 2–313(1) (b).

10. Shreve v. Casto Trailer Sales, Inc., 150 W.Va. 669, 149 S.E.2d 238 (1966).

talking about his goods bordered on a description but conceivably could have risen to the level of an affirmation of fact. Under the Code the court need not concern itself with trying to distinguish the indistinguishable. No matter how the words are classified (whether as description or affirmation of fact), an express warranty is involved— and the disclaimer of implied warranties will have no effect on the warranty.[11]

Having classified description warranties as express, the Code solves the disclaimer problem in a sensible manner. Most agreements contain some description of the goods sold. The description may be sketchy (such as "one lawn mower," "one Spangler television set, Model No. 21–456P," or "two carloads Grade A eggs, large") or it may be detailed (as when blueprints and specifications are involved),[12] but a description is a natural part of all agreements and is usually included in any writing adopted by the buyer and seller. On some occasions that writing also attempts to disclaim all express and implied warranties, and a conflict is presented: the description created a warranty which was quickly disclaimed.

The Code resolves this conflict in a reasonable manner. The buyer can quite properly assume that any disclaimer in the writing does not mean that the buyer will not receive the goods which he ordered. It is reasonable for him to believe that he is entitled to the described goods, and that the seller cannot perform his agreement by shipping something different—even though there is a disclaimer of express warranties. The Code protects this justified expectation of the buyer.

Evidence of the warranty is admissible even though it *contradicts* the disclaimer clause. The parol evidence rule operates only on prior agreements and contemporaneous oral agreements; the description, being a part of the writing or writings, is neither of these.[13] Therefore, the description used in the agreement is admissible evidence of a warranty.

When the evidence is admitted, the court will have before it a writing which both creates an express warranty and then limits or negates all express warranties. What should be done with such a

---

11. Berk v. Gordon Johnson Co., 232 F.Supp. 682 (E.D.Mich.1964) (equipment described as "Kosher operation"; all warranties, except a warranty of repair, were stated to be waived by the buyer).

12. A number of pre-Code cases are collected in footnote 17 to 1 S. Williston, Sales § 205 (rev. ed. 1948). Other examples include Klein v. Asgrow Seed Co., 246 Cal.App.2d 87, 54 Cal. Rptr. 609 (1966) ("VF-36" tomato seeds); Santor v. A & M Karagheusian, Inc., 44 N.J. 52, 207 A.2d 305 (1965) (Grade # 1 carpet).

13. UCC § 2–202. See §§ 50–53 *supra*. For a discussion of the problems presented if the description is oral and precedes a writing, see § 69 *supra*.

writing?   Have warranties been created or have they been disclaimed?
The Code's answer is both clear and sensible: to the extent that it is
reasonable, construe these clauses as consistent; to the extent that such
construction is unreasonable (as it would be in the assumed case if the
seller is arguing that the disclaimer negates the warranty by description), the "negation or limitation is inoperative." [14]   By making the
description warranty express, rather than implied, the Code brings
the description of goods within this provision, and the seller has warranted that the goods shall conform to the description.

One of the principal differences between the affirmation-of-fact
warranty and the description warranty is that the latter need not be
"made by the seller." [15]   The buyer can describe the goods which he
wishes to purchase, and if that description becomes a part of the basis
of the bargain, an express warranty has been created.   Thus, when a
buyer sends his purchase order to the seller stating the goods he wishes
to purchase and the seller responds by shipping goods, a description
warranty has been created.   Likewise, blueprints and specifications
submitted by the buyer will create a warranty that the goods shall
conform, if those blueprints and specifications become a part of the
basis of the bargain.[16]

§ 72.   Sample or Model

The final method of creating an express warranty is through the
use of samples or models.   The basic framework of this warranty is
the same as the others:

> Any sample or model which is made part of the basis of the
> bargain creates an express warranty that the whole of the
> goods shall conform to the sample or model.[17]

Since either a sample or a model will suffice for the creation of a
warranty, the court need not distinguish between the two, but the
exhibited item must qualify as a sample or a model.   The Comments
suggest that a sample is that which is drawn from the bulk of the goods,
and a model is that which "is offered for inspection when the subject
matter is not at hand and which has not been drawn from the bulk of
the goods." [18]   Thus, a model may exist even though there is yet no bulk

14.   UCC § 2–316(1).   Walcott & Steele,
Inc. v. Carpenter, 246 Ark. 93, 436 S.
W.2d 820 (1969).   Problems of interpretation of contractual language are
discussed elsewhere in this text.   See
§§ 46–49 supra for a general treatment
and §§ 64, 70 supra for an application
of these principles to warranty cases.
See also Corbin, The Interpretations
of Words and the Parol Evidence Rule,
50 Cornell L.Q. 161 (1965).

15.   Compare UCC § 2–313(1) (a) with
(1) (b).

16.   UCC § 2–313, Comment 5.   For a
discussion of the meaning of "basis
of the bargain," see §§ 66–68 supra.

17.   UCC § 2–313(1) (c).

18.   UCC § 2–313, Comment 6.

of goods, as where the seller has exhibited an item which has yet to be produced or acquired by the seller. A model need not be the same size as the finished product; it may be a smaller scale of the goods to be delivered to the buyer.[19]

The sample or model must be made a "part of the basis of the bargain" before a warranty is created.[20] One way to express this idea is to place the emphasis on the concept of *sample* and *model*: that which is exhibited must be shown as a sample or a model of the goods to be delivered, and not just to suggest what the bulk of the goods will be like. To be a sample, the goods exhibited must be drawn from the bulk and represented in such a way as to lead the buyer reasonably to believe that the seller is claiming that all of the goods sold will be like the item shown; to be a model, the goods shown must be represented in such a way as to lead the buyer reasonably to believe that the goods when delivered will be like the item shown.[21] In these cases the sample or model has become at least a part of the basis of the bargain, and a warranty has been created.

There are other cases, however, in which an item is represented only to suggest or to illustrate to the buyer what the delivered goods will be like.[22] A reasonable buyer in such a situation would not conclude that all of the goods purchased will conform precisely to the exhibited item. For example, a buyer who purchased 10,000 bricks after examining one which had been shown him by the seller could be held to understand that the bricks which were delivered would not all conform [23] in size, shape, and color to the one which he examined. In that sense, the examined brick was not a "sample," or, if it was, its precise size, shape, and color did not become a part of the basis of the bargain between the parties.[24] Nevertheless, the exhibited brick could well have been a "sample" of the general characteristics of the bricks to be purchased—that is, of their general size, shape, color, and hardness. If it did become a sample in this more general sense, and if that sample was the basis of the bargain, an express warranty has been created that the goods would conform to the more general characteristics of the exhibited single brick—but not to its precise characteristics.

---

19. See § 73 *infra*.

20. This concept is discussed in §§ 66–68 *supra*.

21. Baltimore Mach. & Equip., Inc. v. Holtite Mfg. Co., 241 Md. 36, 215 A.2d 458 (1965). In this case the seller argued that the item exhibited was only a guide or suggestion; the court found a warranty. *See also* Graulich Caterer, Inc. v. Hans Holterbosch, Inc., 101 N.J.Super. 61, 243 A.2d 253 (App.Div. 1968) (food sample).

22. Wood v. Michaud, 63 Minn. 478, 65 N.W. 963 (1896).

23. UCC § 2–106(2).

24. Washington Fruit & Produce Co. v. Ted Mirski Co., 24 Agri.Dec. 1559, 3 UCC Rep. 175 (U.S.Dept. of Agriculture 1965).

Thus, the problem is one of interpreting the meaning of the acts of the parties. When the item was exhibited, what was its meaning to the buyer? Did he reasonably believe that the bulk of the goods would conform to the item, or did he reasonably believe that the item only illustrated the general nature of what was to be received? This is similar to any problem of interpretation [25] with the acts of the parties becoming at least as important as the words they used.

Very seldom will a sale be made solely from a sample or a model. Affirmations of fact, promises, sales talk, and descriptions will often accompany the negotiations which led up to the sale. On occasion, there will be an inconsistency between what is shown and what is said. The delivered goods may conform to the sample or model, but not to the statements which the seller made about the goods—or the delivered goods may conform to the statements but not to the sample or model. What is the scope of the warranty in these cases?

The Code suggests three tests which are to be used in answering this question. These tests are drawn from section 2–317:

1. Whenever reasonable, warranties are to be construed as consistent with each other and as cumulative. If the sample creates a warranty of strength and the affirmation of fact creates a warranty of durability, these warranties are to be accumulated. The buyer has an express warranty of strength *and* durability.

2. If "such construction is unreasonable the intention of the parties shall determine which warranty is dominant."

3. In determining intent, "the following rules apply:

    "(a) Exact or technical specifications displace an inconsistent sample or model or general language of description.

    "(b) A sample from an existing bulk displaces inconsistent general language of description . . .."

These tests can be summarized under a single Code principle: "the intention of the parties shall determine which warranty is dominant." [26] Such a test sounds reasonable. If the parties had a common intention at the time they reached their agreement and if that common intention can now be discovered, that intention should of course be enforced. The words they used and the samples and models they exhibited may have had a common meaning to them, and the court should give effect to that meaning. All too often, however, no common intention can now be discovered. The seller reasonably in-

25. §§ 46–53 *supra*.   26. UCC § 2–317.

tended one thing, and the buyer another. To try to apply the intention of the *parties* is to hide the working tools out of which an answer to this problem must be fashioned.

Courts will undoubtedly rely on their common law heritage in solving this problem of interpretation. They can talk about an objective intention, rather than a subjective intention. They can use the word "reasonable" or "justified" in characterizing the intention of one party, and the adjective "unreasonable" or "unjustified" in labelling the intention of the other party. What this talk will come down to, however, is that the intention of the *parties* cannot be applied here; instead, the intention of one of the parties must be selected. Since it was the buyer to whom the samples will most often be shown and to whom the words will have been said, it will properly be the buyer's intention (that is, his "reasonable intention") which is controlling.[27] Nevertheless, there may be cases in which the buyer exhibited the samples and detailed the descriptions. Here the seller's understanding could become controlling. The problems of interpretation are discussed elsewhere in this text.[28]

In other instances a sample or model will have been shown and that sample or model will have become the basis of a bargain, yet the writing will have included a statement that there are no warranties and that the writing is the exclusive evidence of the parties' agreement. In such a case the express warranty by sample has collided with a writing which attempts to exclude warranties. Such a collision calls into operation the usual rules of interpretation; it also raises the difficulties of the parol evidence rule. These have been discussed in prior sections and need not be repeated.[29]

---

27. "[I]n mercantile experience the mere exhibition of a 'sample' does not of itself show whether it is merely intended to 'suggest' or to 'be' the character of the subject-matter of the contract. The question is whether the seller has so acted with reference to the sample as to make him responsible that the whole shall have at least the value shown by it." UCC § 2–313, Comment 6. Earlier this Comment states that "there is no escape from the question of fact." For a case which reaches the result suggested in the text, see General Electric Co. v. United States Dynamics, Inc., 403 F.2d 933 (1st Cir. 1968). This case is discussed in § 73 *infra*.

Nordstrom Law of Sales HB—15

28. § 48 *supra.*

29. §§ 53, 69 *supra*. See Neville Chem. Co. v. Union Carbide Co., 294 F.Supp. 649 (W.D.Pa.1968), *aff'd* 422 F.2d 1205 (3d Cir. 1970), for an application of the ideas in these sections to a case involving a sample or model, but the disclaimer applied only to implied warranties. *See also* Will Laboratories, Inc. v. White Rock Pen Corp., 4 UCC Rep. 848 (N.Y.Sup.Ct.1967), where the parol evidence rule was applied to prevent admission of evidence to prove an express warranty by sample.

§ 73. Sample or Model—Scope of the Warranty

When a sample or model has become a part of the basis of the bargain, the warranty which is created is that the *whole* of the goods shall conform to the sample or model.[30] The warranty is not satisfied if a portion (or even a major portion) of the goods conforms; the whole of the goods must conform.[31] The sample or model becomes the basis for determining the subject matter of the parties' agreement, just as the affirmations of fact or promises of the seller define what was intended to be sold when this type of express warranty is involved.[32]

The use of a small-scale model may cause special problems in determining the scope of the warranty given. In one case the buyer purchased storm windows after examining a smaller model of the ones he intended to buy. In the model the windows fit their frames tightly, even when operated with a tilting device. When the full-scale windows were installed, the fit was quite different. As the size of the window expanded, the lack of an inside support became critical, and the actual windows rattled—letting in the wind, snow, and rain. In one sense the product conformed to the model: it contained the same number of pieces arranged in exactly the same way as found on the model. In another sense, however, the product did not conform: the windows did not fit snugly when closed. What does the language, "conform to the sample or model," mean? Does it mean that the larger product must operate in the same fashion as the smaller model, or is it sufficient if the larger product has the same physical features?

The court read the implied warranties of merchantability and fitness for purpose into the express warranty by sample and held that a jury question had been presented as to whether the product sold was merchantable and fit for its intended purpose.[33] While this is an acceptable method of solving the problem, a more direct answer could have been found by construing the express warranty by sample as including a warranty that the product sold would operate as efficiently as the model which became the basis of the bargain.

Another type of case which may cause difficulty in determining the scope of the sample or model warranty involves a factual pattern in which the seller has made statements or promises as to the quality of a product, but has allowed the buyer to examine a sample or model which does not measure up to the warranted quality. If the buyer

---

30. UCC § 2–313(1) (c).

31. For pre-Code law, *compare* F.A.D. Andrea v. Dodge, 15 F.2d 1003 (3d Cir. 1926) *with* 1 S. Williston, Sales § 250 (rev. ed. 1948).

32. § 65 *supra*.

33. Loomis Bros. Corp. v. Queen, 17 Pa.D. & C.2d 482 (C.P.1958).

fails to discover the discrepancy between the statements or promises and the operation of the sample or model, does the examination negate the express warranties that were made? Another way to state this question would be: is the affirmation of fact (or promise) made by the seller still a part of the basis of the bargain even though the buyer has examined the goods?

No single answer can be given to this question, but these guides are contained in the Code:

First, the examination does not automatically negate *express* warranties. The Code provides that an examination (or a refusal to examine) a sample or model prevents the creation of *implied* warranties as to any defects "which an examination ought in the circumstances to have revealed to" the buyer; [34] but nothing is said in this subsection as to the effect of examination on express warranties.

Second, the words relevant to the creation of an express warranty are to be construed as consistent with conduct (examination) tending to negate the warranty, if reasonable; but if such a construction is unreasonable, the negation is inoperative.[35]

Third, the warranty created by the words is to be construed as consistent and as cumulative with the warranty created by the sample, if reasonable; otherwise, the intention of the parties is to determine the dominant warranty.[36] This intention of the parties becomes another way of looking at the "basis of the bargain" between the buyer and the seller. Both present questions of fact which turn on the particular factors of the case involved.[37]

An example of the application of these ideas to a specific case is found in *General Electric Co. v. United States Dynamics, Inc.*[38] There the seller sold a gas purifying machine which had been designed to remove oxygen from nitrogen in a pipe line. Before the sale the buyer had tested a small-scale model for over a year and had found that the model did remove the oxygen. The advertisements of the model also stated that "No hydrogen mixes with the main gas stream." When the buyer purchased the large machine its purchase order required in part that "No other impurities should be introduced into the effluent nitrogen," and the seller's letter of acceptance guaranteed that the apparatus would "purify the quantity of gas specified to the level

---

34. UCC § 2–316(3) (b).

35. UCC § 2–316(1). See § 68 *supra*.

36. This test is discussed in § 72 *supra*.

37. For a case in which inspection was held to exclude an express warranty

by sample, see Sylvia Coal Co. v. Mercury Coal & Coke Co., 151 W.Va. 818, 156 S.E.2d 1 (1967).

38. 403 F.2d 933 (1st Cir. 1968).

required." Thus, there were affirmations of fact, a description, and a promise that the nitrogen would be pure; there was also an examination of a model which satisfied the buyer that no *oxygen* remained with the nitrogen.

When the machine began operation it was learned that *hydrogen* remained in the main stream of gas. This defect could not be cured, and a further test of the model indicated that it, too, allowed hydrogen in the main stream. The court had, therefore, a case in which there were elements of an express warranty of purity, combined with a lengthy examination of a model which did not completely purify but during which the buyer did not discover the defect. The case was made more difficult for the buyer, who was trying to rescind his purchase, because the seller had no test facilities and had relied on the buyer's reports of satisfaction.

Nevertheless, the court granted summary judgment for the buyer. The court intimated that the buyer's reports as to the successful operation of the machine were not admissible under the Code's parol evidence rule, but stated: "Wholly apart from the question whether a small-scale model can be considered a 'sample' of a much larger device, inspection could not offset express warranties."[39] As a statement of general law, this may be too broad; however, in the context of the facts of this case, the statement is unobjectionable. The buyer did rely on both his inspection (for oxygen removal) and the statements of the seller (for the removal of other gases). The statements became, therefore, a part of the basis of the bargain and created an express warranty that no hydrogen would remain in the main stream of gas.

3. IMPLIED WARRANTIES

§ 74. Overview of Implied Warranties

There are two implied warranties under the Code: that of merchantability and that of fitness for purpose. These warranties are *implied*, rather than *express*. The differences between these two types of warranties can be over-emphasized. Certainly the express warranty is not "better" than one that is implied. Once a court has found that a warranty exists, the liability of the seller is not diminished just because the breach pertains to an implied warranty.[40]

---

39. *Id.* at 935.

40. There is no need to imply a warranty once an express warranty is found. Inglis v. American Motors Corp., 3 Ohio St.2d 132, 209 N.E.2d

583 (1965). However, a finding of an express warranty is not inconsistent with the existence of implied warranties. Vandenberg v. Siter, 204 Pa. Super. 392, 204 A.2d 494 (1964).

What difference there is between the express and implied warranties is one of degree—not of kind. With the express warranty some affirmation of fact or promise has been made by the seller, or the goods have been described, or some sample or model has been shown. It is against these words or acts that the conformity of the delivered goods is measured. On the other hand, the implied warranty arises from the nature of the sale—the warranty of merchantability if the seller is a merchant with respect to goods of that kind,[41] and the warranty of fitness for a particular purpose if the seller (merchant or not) has reason to know the buyer's particular purpose and that the buyer is relying on the seller's skill or judgment in selecting or furnishing suitable goods.[42] Quite naturally, in a particular sale these warranties shade into each other, and all may exist. For example, the buyer may have told the seller the purpose for which he needs certain goods and that he is relying on the seller to furnish goods that will meet that purpose. Such a seller, in discussing the goods with the buyer, may well have made affirmations of fact about the goods to be sold and, in writing out the sales slip, will probably have described the goods which he is selling. If the seller is a merchant, this example presents a factual background for the existence of express warranties and of both of the implied warranties. It is extremely difficult, if not impossible, to determine the point at which words and conduct giving rise to an express warranty cease and words and conduct giving rise to implied warranties begin. Fortunately there is usually no reason to try to discover such a point. The words, conduct, writings, trade usages, course of performance, and course of dealing—all of these go into the parties' bargain, and it is from this bargain that warranties emerge.[43] Whether those warranties are "implied" or "express" is a matter of degree—not of kind.

There were at least two reasons, however, why the drafters of the Code may have drawn the distinction between the express and the implied warranties. The first is that of history. It is generally easier to continue a concept that has become familiar than to discard it in favor of the novel or new. Courts have long talked about "implied" terms in contracts;[44] over one hundred years ago the court, in the famous case of *Jones v. Just*,[45] found a warranty of merchantability

---

41. UCC § 2–314.

42. UCC § 2–315.

43. §§ 50–52 *supra.*

44. **One of the best known cases is** Wood v. Lucy, Lady Duff-Gordon, 222 N.Y. 88, 118 N.E. 214 (1917): "The law has outgrown its primitive stage of formalism when the precise word was the sovereign talisman, and every slip was fatal. It takes a broader view today. A promise may be lacking, and yet the whole writing may be 'instinct with an obligation,' imperfectly expressed." *Id.* at 91, 118 N.E. at 214.

45. L.R. 3 Q.B. 197 (1868).

through the process of implication: "where a manufacturer undertakes to supply goods, manufactured by himself, or in which he deals, but which the vendee has not had the opportunity of inspecting, it is an implied term in the contract that he shall supply a merchantable article."[46] The Uniform Sales Act drew the same distinction.[47] Rather than to adopt some new system of labelling warranties, the drafters simply accepted those that had been given to them by history.

Why draw any distinction between the express and the implied warranty? Why not just have "warranties" without concern over some modifying adjective? The Code's answer lies in the section on disclaimer, and this becomes the second reason which might have prompted the drafters to continue to draw a line between the warranty that is express and the one that is implied. Implied warranties do not rest on some specific affirmation of fact or promise made by a seller; they do not arise out of a description of the goods; and they do not owe their existence to a sample or model which was exhibited. Implied warranties are created against a much less specific background; they arise because the seller happens to be a merchant or has knowledge about the buyer's purpose and reliance. In short, the Code rests on the assumption that implied warranties are less apt to create specific impressions in the mind of the reasonable buyer than are express warranties where, for example, the seller has asserted a fact about the goods he is selling. Once this assumption is made, the next step comes easily. The disclaimer of the implied warranty does not call for language as specific as does the attempted disclaimer of the express warranty. The Code takes the step because it allows implied warranties to be disclaimed with comparatively little difficulty, but makes it extremely difficult to disclaim express warranties.[48]

Certainly a commercial code could be constructed around warranties, without concern over their type. The Uniform Commercial Code, however, took a different approach and retained a distinction between express and implied warranties. The following sections of this text examine the two implied warranties—that of merchantability and of fitness for purpose.

---

46. *Id.* at 203.

47. Uniform Sales Act §§ 14–15. Section 16 created an implied warranty in a sale by sample. This was changed by the Code to an express warranty. *See* § 72 *supra.*

48. UCC § 2–316; §§ 87–88 *infra.*

§ 75. Implied Warranty of Merchantability

The implied warranty of merchantability is established in one sentence: "Unless excluded or modified (Section 2–316), a warranty that the goods shall be merchantable is implied in a contract for their sale if the seller is a merchant with respect to goods of that kind." [49]

This sentence contains three limitations. First, this warranty may be excluded or modified under section 2–316.[50] Second, it is implied only if the seller is a "merchant with respect to goods of that kind." This text has already discussed the meaning of "merchant" under the Code; that discussion will not be repeated.[51] It is sufficient to note that the Code's concept of merchant is double- (or perhaps, triple-) headed.[52] It includes persons who deal in goods of the kind involved, and it also includes persons who hold themselves out as having knowledge of the practices or goods involved. The warranty of merchantability is limited to persons who have the merchant status in respect to goods of the kind involved—whether they are dealing in those goods or holding themselves out as having knowledge as to those goods.[53] Therefore, there is no implied warranty of merchantability in a contract of sale in which the seller is a non-merchant or in which the seller is a merchant with respect to some goods or practices but not with respect to the goods sold in this particular case.[54] If the seller falls within the specified class of merchants, it makes no diifference whether the buyer is a merchant or a non-merchant. Third, the warranty of merchantability is implied in a contract for the sale of goods. Because of the definition, present sales are included as well as contracts to sell goods at a future time.[55] However, leases, bailments, gifts, and other non-sales are not directly within the coverage of this section of the Code.[56] Likewise, sales of real estate, rights in action, shares of stock, and other items which do not fall within the definition of "goods" are not directly affected by this section.[57]

---

49. UCC § 2–314(1).

50. §§ 86–88 *infra.*

51. § 33 *supra.*

52. UCC § 2–104(1).

53. UCC § 2–104, Comment 2. As to the requirement of good faith applicable to non-merchants, see UCC § 1–203.

54. It is not necessary that the seller normally sell this particular type of goods if the seller customarily sells the general line of merchandise manufactured by the manufacturer of these particular goods. Mutual Services of

Highland Park, Inc. v. S.O.S. Plumbing & Sewerage Co., 93 Ill.App.2d 257, 235 N.E.2d 265 (1968) (abstract published only).

55. UCC § 2–106(1).

56. McKone v. Ralph's Wonder Market, Inc., 27 Mass.App.Dec. 159 (1963). The possibility of using the Code for transactions which are not sales is examined in § 21 *supra.*

57. UCC § 2–105(1), discussed in § 22 *supra.* Some courts are implying warranties in the sale of buildings. Carpenter v. Donohoe, 154 Colo. 78, 388 P.2d 399 (1964); Bethlahmy v. Bechtel, 91 Idaho 55, 415 P.2d 698 (1966);

If these limitations are met, and if the warranty is not excluded or modified, there is an implied warranty that the goods shall be "merchantable." The Code meaning of that word is examined in the following section of this text.

§ 76. Minimum Standards of Merchantability

It would be inaccurate to suggest that the Code defines merchantability. What the Code does in section 2–314 is to set the minimum standards of merchantability. The statutory language is that goods "to be merchantable must be *at least* such as . . ." More may be required by the parties' agreement, course of dealing, or usage of trade,[58] but the minimum standards assure the buyer that if he does not receive goods which conform at least to normal commercial expectations, he will have a course of action open by which he can secure compensation for losses suffered. Even though the seller was careful not to make one assertion of fact or promise about the goods, the ordinary buyer in the normal commercial transaction expects that the goods which he has just purchased will not turn out to be completely worthless.[59] As Lord Ellenborough colorfully said in one case: "The purchaser cannot be supposed to buy goods to lay them on a dunghill."[60] On the other hand, a buyer who has purchased goods without obtaining an express warranty as to their quality cannot reasonably expect that those goods will be the best of all possible goods of that kind. The Code's protection lies between these extremes:

Goods to be merchantable must be at least such as

(a) pass without objection in the trade under the contract description; and

(b) in the case of fungible goods, are of fair average quality within the description; and

(c) are fit for the ordinary purposes for which such goods are used; and

(d) run, within the variations permitted by the agreement, of even kind, quality and quantity within each unit and among all units involved; and

Schipper v. Levitt & Sons, 44 N.J. 70, 207 A.2d 314 (1965); Humber v. Morton, 426 S.W.2d 554 (Tex.1968). For a later opinion in *Humber v. Morton*, see 448 S.W.2d 494 (Tex.Ct.Civ.App. 1969). *But cf.* Mitchem v. Johnson, 7 Ohio St.2d 66, 218 N.E.2d 594 (1966).

58. UCC § 2–314, Comment 6.

59. *Cf.* Restatement (Second) of Torts § 402A (1965), quoted in § 54 *supra*. That section requires the product to be in a "defective condition unreasonably dangerous" to the user, consumer, or his property.

60. Gardiner v. Gray, 4 Camp. 144, 145, 171 Eng.Rep. 46, 47 (K.B.1815).

(e) are adequately contained, packaged, and labeled as the agreement may require; and

(f) conform to the promises or affirmations of fact made on the container or label if any.[61]

Each of these subsections is connected with an "and." There is, therefore, a breach of the implied warranty of merchantability if the goods fail to meet any one of these minimum standards. Even though the goods would pass without objection, the warranty of merchantability has not been fulfilled if those goods are not adequately packaged; likewise, adequate packaging is not sufficient to satisfy this warranty if the goods would not pass without objection.

a. *Pass without objection in the trade under the contract description.* Two parts of this standard are important. The first is the contract description. What is it that was purchased and sold? Until this has been determined, the expectations of the trade cannot be ascertained.[62] If the item is second-hand, less is expected in the way of quality than if the item is purchased new.[63] At this point the implied warranty of merchantability overlaps the express warranty by description.[64] The contract description gives rise to an express warranty; the contract description is also important in measuring the scope of the implied warranty of merchantability. As long as implied warranties are not disclaimed it makes no difference whether the resulting warranty is express of implied; if, however, implied warranties are disclaimed, there is no reason why the "pass without objection" test could not be used to give content to the scope of the express warranty— which was not disclaimed.

The second part of the test that is important is found in the language, "pass without objection in the trade." The standards are those set by "the trade," not by either the overly-meticulous or the overly-indulgent buyer. Difficulties will be encountered in determining both the extent of "the trade" and its geographical boundaries, but the purpose of the drafters was to seek out an average group—one that dealt with the product on a routine basis and one that would, in most instances, have standards by which the quality of the product could be measured. Again, the product need not be the best that the trade has to offer; it is only necessary that the goods "pass without objection."

---

61. UCC § 2–314(2).

62. Neville Chem. Co. v. Union Carbide Corp., 294 F.Supp. 649 (W.D.Pa.1968), *aff'd* 422 F.2d 1205 (3d Cir. 1970).

63. Chamberlain v. Bob Matick Chevrolet, Inc., 4 Conn.Cir. 685, 239 A.2d

42 (1967); Johnson v. Fore River Motors, Inc., 26 Mass.App.Dec. 184 (1963).

64. § 71 *supra*.

This subsection implies that the default is known at the time that the test is applied.[65] For example, a canned ham with a cup of ground glass imbedded in the middle of the ham will pass without objection in the trade as long as the can is sealed. Indeed, that very can has passed from producer to distributor to retailer (and even to the consumer) without a single objection as to its contents. The test, however, is not whether the sealed container passes without objection. The test is more rigid: now that the defect in the product is known, would the product pass without objection in the trade under its contract description?

b. *In the case of fungible goods, are of fair average quality within the description.* This subsection applies to fungible goods the same tests as were applied in the prior subsection. " 'Fair average' is a term directly appropriate to agricultural bulk products and means goods centering around the middle belt of quality, not the least or the worst that can be understood in the particular trade by the designation, but such as can pass 'without objection.' Of course a fair percentage of the least is permissible but the goods are not 'fair average' if they are all of the least or worst quality possible under the description." [66] The merchant-seller is not impliedly warranting that the fungibles are of the best quality within the contract description; he is, however, warranting that they would pass without objection and measure up at least to a fair and an average quality.

Both this and the prior subsection refer to the contract description against which the merchantability of the goods is to be measured. As has already been indicated, this reference causes a possible overlap with express warranties; it also brings to implied warranties ideas of "basis of the bargain" which are applied to express warranties.[67] Through the contract description the court can determine what was sold and what was purchased. For example, a contract for "Grade A eggs, large" sets the baseline from which the fair average quality is to be measured. It also indicates the test against which the eggs are to pass "without objection." Change the contract description to "Grade B eggs, large" or to "Grade A eggs, medium," and a different measure will be applied to determine the merchantability of the delivered eggs. As this point the Comments suggest that in "cases of doubt as to what

65. Sams v. Ezy-Way Foodliner Co., 157 Me. 10, 170 A.2d 160 (1961); John A. Brown Co. v. Shelton, 391 P.2d 259 (Okl.1964). Annots., 77 A.L.R.2d 7, 61–63 (food), and 77 A.L.R.2d 215, 243–44 (1961) (beverages). Pre-Code cases are collected in 1 S. Williston, Sales § 242 (rev. ed. 1948). The conclusion that the Code adopts the result of the *Sams* case is strengthened by UCC § 2–314

(2) (c)—the goods must be fit for their ordinary purposes. *See also* Jackson v. Cushing Coca-Cola Bottling Co., 445 P.2d 797 (Okl.1968).

66. UCC § 2–314, Comment 7. For a pre-Code case, see Gossler v. Eagle Sugar Ref., 103 Mass. 331 (1869).

67. §§ 66–68 *supra*.

quality is intended, the price at which a merchant closes a contract is an excellent index of the nature and scope of his obligation under the present section." [68]

c. *Are fit for the ordinary purposes for which such goods are used.* This is the key thought—the heart—of the merchantability warranty. When a merchant sells goods of the kind in which he deals, there is a warranty that the goods purchased will be fit for their ordinary purpose. Shoes must have their heels attached so that they will not break off under normal use,[69] but if those shoes are used for mountain climbing, there is no implied warranty that the heels will be fit for this extraordinary purpose—unless, of course, the elements of a warranty of fitness for purpose are present.[70] Likewise, shoes are warranted against producing dermatitis,[71] shotgun shells against premature explosion,[72] marine engines against excessive smoking,[73] machinery against defective operation,[74] rivet studs against splitting,[75] and hair lotion against scalp burns.[76]

A Common Pleas decision from Pennsylvania indicates the scope of this implied warranty. In that case the buyer purchased a log chain from the seller who was engaged in the business of selling farm equipment and hardware. At the request of the buyer, the seller welded hooks on one end of the chain. The buyer used the chain to haul a truck up a dirt road, the chain broke, and the truck was damaged. The buyer brought suit, claiming a breach of the implied warranty of merchantability; the seller demurred, arguing that the ordinary purpose of a log chain is to haul logs—not trucks. The court properly overruled the demurrer.[77] The problem is that of determining the ordinary purpose of a "log chain" with hooks welded on one end. This purpose can-

68. UCC § 2–314, Comment 7. *See* Moore v. Mathieuu, 13 F.2d 747 (9th Cir. 1926); Sylvia Coal Co. v. Mercury Coal & Coke Co., 151 W.Va. 818, 156 S.E.2d 1 (1967).

69. Chairaluce v. Stanley Warner Management Corp., 236 F.Supp. 385 (D. Conn.1964).

70. UCC § 2–315, Comment 2. See Standard Packaging Corp. v. Continental Distil. Corp., 259 F.Supp. 919 (E.D.Pa.1966), *aff'd* 378 F.2d 505 (3d Cir. 1967).

71. Nederostek v. Endicott-Johnson Shoe Co., 415 Pa. 136, 202 A.2d 72 (1964).

72. Allen v. Savage Arms Corp., 52 Luz. Leg.Reg. 159, 2 UCC Rep. 974 (Pa.C.P. 1962).

73. Hunt v. Perkins Mach. Co., 352 Mass. 535, 226 N.E.2d 228 (1967).

74. Graco v. Bucciconi Engineering Co., 407 F.2d 87 (3d Cir. 1969).

75. Speed Fastners, Inc. v. Newsom, 382 F.2d 395 (10th Cir. 1967).

76. Newmark v. Gimbel's, Inc., 54 N.J. 585, 258 A.2d 697 (1969).

77. Robert H. Carr & Sons, Inc. v. Yearsley, 31 Pa.D. & C.2d 262 (C.P. 1963).

not be determined by looking in a dictionary or by reading other cases. Evidence is needed to prove that this use of a log chain (pulling a truck) is within the ordinary purposes of such a chain, and this question of fact will not be precluded by use of a demurrer.

The warranty of merchantability is broader than that the goods will do the ordinary job for which they were made. They must also, unless the further warranty is disclaimed, do the job safely.[78] The hair lotion might do an excellent job of putting a wave in a woman's hair but, if it also causes dermatitis in a substantial number of users, the lotion is not *fit* for its ordinary purpose. An insecticide which kills insects is not *fit* for its ordinary purpose if it also causes injury to animals.[79] Cattle feed which contains sufficient nutrients to keep cattle alive (and even to fatten them) is not *fit* for its ordinary purpose if it also causes sterility in bulls.[80] Thus, fitness for ordinary purpose is a broader concept than just that of doing a single job; it contains ideas of doing that job safely. However, the law does not require that the goods sold be accident-proof. A hammer is fit for its ordinary purpose even though it is capable of mashing thumbs, and shoes may be merchantable even though they slip on wet asphalt.[81] There is no escape from the proposition that the issue is one of fact for the jury: were the goods fit for their ordinary purposes?

d. *Run, within the variations permitted by the agreement, of even kind, quality and quantity within each unit and among all units involved.* When the agreement calls for the delivery of units of goods, the warranty of merchantability applies to each unit as well as to all the units involved. "But precautionary language has been added as a reminder of the frequent usages of trade which permit substantial variations both with and without an allowance or an obligation to replace the varying units." [82]

e. *Are adequately contained, packaged, and labeled as the agreement may require.* There are difficulties in interpreting the meaning of this warranty. These difficulties center on the meaning of the word

---

78. See § 81 *infra* for an expanded discussion of this idea.

79. Holowka v. York Farm Bureau Coop. Ass'n, 78 York Legal Rec. 121, 2 UCC Rep. 445 (Pa.C.P.1963). For a later opinion, see 82 York Legal Rec. 73 (Pa.C.P.1968), relying on Miller v. Preitz, 422 Pa. 423, 221 A.2d 320 (1966). *Miller v. Preitz* was overruled in Kassab v. Central Soya, 432 Pa. 217, 246 A.2d 848 (1968).

80. Kassab v. Central Soya, 432 Pa. 271, 246 A.2d 848 (1968).

81. Fanning v. LeMay, 38 Ill.2d 209, 230 N.E.2d 182 (1967). As with express warranties (§ 63 *supra*), the creation of implied warranties does not make the seller an insurer against loss by the buyer. The buyer must prove that a breach of warranty caused the loss. McMeekin v. Gimbel Bros., Inc., 223 F. Supp. 896 (W.D.Pa.1963).

82. UCC § 2–314, Comment 9.

"require" and the extent to which the last five words ("as the agreement may require") modify "contained" and "packaged". This subsection could be read to mean that the goods must be adequately contained and packaged, and they must also be labeled as the agreement may require. Under this reading the test of the container and the package is their adequacy; the test of the labeling is both adequacy and the requirements of the agreement. The sentence structure, however, would indicate that the requirements of the agreement modify the adequacy of the container and the package, as well as the labels.

How this subsection is interpreted will make a difference in results. The word "require" could be read to mean that the parties must have thought about the containers, packages, and labels and have entered into a specific agreement about them before an implied warranty as to their merchantability will arise. Such a reading would prevent this subsection from being used when there was no specific agreement regarding the containers, packages, or labels—as, for example, when a housewife has purchased bottled goods from a local grocery store. If the bottle (container) is defective and if that defect causes injury (as when the bottle is being opened), a restrictive reading of "require" would necessitate a search for implied warranties as to the bottle in other sections of the Code.[83]

There is no good reason why the word "require" ought to be read this narrowly. It the parties have specifically dealt with the problem of containers, an express warranty has been created; the seller will have made promises or affirmations of fact regarding those containers. Therefore, the word "require" ought to be read in its context of implied warranties—the goods have been sold under an agreement which contains no specific language about the container, the package, or the labels; nevertheless, if the agreement does relate to goods which must be contained, packaged, and labeled in some manner so that they will be useful to the buyer, the agreement does impliedly "require" the containers, packages, and labels; and this requirement is measured against the kind of goods covered by the agreement. Thus, an agreement to purchase goods packaged in a bottle requires a stronger container if the lid is to be pried or twisted off than if the lid is easily lifted off. Failure to provide such a container is a breach of warranty.

83. For example, it could be argued that the container was "goods" and was sold to the buyer. This would mean that the container must also be "merchantable." Some pre-Code law was to the contrary. Torpey v. Red Owl Stores, Inc., 228 F.2d 117 (8th Cir. 1955). Other cases found the warranty. Renninger v. Formost Dairies, Inc., 171 So.2d 602 (Fla.Ct.App.), *cert.* *denied* 177 So.2d 480 (Fla.1965); Hadley v. Hillcrest Dairy Inc., 341 Mass. 624, 171 N.E.2d 293 (1961) (where bottle was loaned, not sold). *Compare* McKone v. Ralph's Wonder Market, Inc., 27 Mass.App.Dec. 159 (1963), *with* Harris v. Great Atlantic & Pacific Tea Co., 23 Mass.App.Dec. 169 (1962).

f. *Conform to the promises or affirmations of fact made on the container or label if any.* This text has already presented an argument that promises and affirmations of fact made on labels or containers create express warranties.[84] This section of the Code makes it clear that they are also implied warranties. As long as implied warranties are not disclaimed it makes no difference whether such statements are classified as express or implied warranties. If an effective disclaimer is involved, there is still the possibility that the statements on labels and containers amount to express warranties.

These are the six minimum standards of merchantability. They should be viewed as *minimum* standards; more may be required in a specific case—depending primarily on the course of prior dealings between these parties and on the requirement of the trade which is involved.[85] Nevertheless, even these minimum standards give buyers assurance that the goods which they purchase measure up to the usual purpose for which those goods are ordinarily used.

§ 77. Food Cases

The sale of food to be eaten off the premises of the seller is subject to the same Code warranties as is any other commodity. Thus, affirmations of fact or promises by the seller about the food will create express warranties that the food conforms to those affirmations or promises. The affirmations or promises could be made directly to the buyer, through advertising, on the labels placed on the containers, or in any one of countless other ways.[86] Further, an implied warranty of merchantability and, under proper facts, an implied warranty of fitness for purpose could be applicable to the sale of food to be eaten off the premises.[87]

The pre-Code cases which caused difficulties were those which involved the serving of food to be eaten on the premises—that is, food served in a restaurant, hotel, corner drug store, or similar establishment. Several cases actually held that there was no warranty that the food was merchantable; the poisoned guest had to rely on cumbersome concepts of negligence in his attempts to recover for

---

84. §§ 67–68 *supra.* Walcott & Steele, Inc. v. Carpenter, 246 Ark. 93, 436 S. W.2d 820 (1969).

85. UCC § 2–314(3).

86. §§ 65–68 *supra.*

87. The implied warranty of merchantability is specifically covered by the second sentence of UCC § 2–314(1). There is no reason why, if the seller has the requisite knowledge, a warranty under UCC § 2–315 could not also be implied. *See* Finocchiaro v. Ward Baking Co., —— R.I. ——, 241 A.2d 619 (1968), but Rhode Island has adopted an amended version of UCC § 2–315.

damages suffered.[88] How courts could reach such a result is a monument to the orderly mind of the lawyer. Every transaction had to be placed within its proper category, and from this categorization flowed the answers to all legal problems. This transaction— the serving of food to be eaten on the premises—was, said some courts, the rendition of a service or perhaps the grant of a license to eat as much of what was served as the guest desired; the transaction was, however, not a sale of the food; warranties attach to sales; and because this transaction was not a sale, there was no warranty of merchantability.[89]

There are, of course, many ways to attack such "logic." Certainly the statement that there are warranties in sales cases does not compel the conclusion that there are no warranties in non-sales cases. It is not hard to conceive of warranties attaching themselves to the quality both of goods and services, at least when the reasons for implying warranties in *service* cases are as compelling as those underlying the implication of warranties when *goods* are sold.[90] The Code could have accepted this approach, and included a section or two on the warranties which attached themselves to the rendition of services. The Code's solution was, however, much more straight-forward. After providing that "a warranty that the goods shall be merchantable is implied in a contract for their sale if the seller is a merchant with respect to goods of that kind," the Code added this sentence:

> Under this section the serving for value of food or drink to be consumed either on the premises or elsewhere is a sale.[91]

There is no question as to the intention of the drafters: pre-Code cases which refused to imply a warranty of merchantability in the case of the restaurant and hotel are changed by the Code.[92]

---

88. The leading cases are Lynch v. Hotel Bond Co., 117 Conn. 128, 167 A. 99 (1933); Nisky v. Childs Co., 103 N.J.L. 464, 135 A. 805 (Ct.Err. & App. 1927). *See also* Albrecht v. Rubinstein, 135 Conn. 243, 63 A.2d 158 (1948); Yeo v. Pig & Whistle Sandwich Shops, Inc., 83 Ga.App. 91, 62 S.E.2d 668 (1950); Kenney v. Wong Len, 81 N.H. 427, 128 A. 343 (1925).

89. Not all pre-Code cases held that there was no sale. The leading case finding a warranty was Friend v. Childs Dining Hall Co., 231 Mass. 65, 120 N.E. 407 (1918). *See also* Bark v. Dixson, 115 Minn. 172, 131 N.W. 1078 (1911); Eisenbach v. Gimbel Bros., 281

N.Y. 474, 24 N.E.2d 131 (1939); Ford v. Waldorf System, Inc., 57 R.I. 131, 188 A. 633 (1936); Annot., 7 A.L.R.2d 1027 (1949).

90. § 21 *supra.*

91. UCC § 2–314(1).

92. Georgia and New Jersey were two states which refused to find an implied warranty. Both have indicated that the Code has changed their prior holdings. Ray v. Deas, 112 Ga.App. 191, 144 S.E.2d 468 (1965); Sofman v. Denham Food Service, Inc., 37 N.J. 304, 181 A.2d 168 (1962) (dictum because the Code was not yet effective;

There are two limitations on the implied warranty of merchantability of food and drink. First, this warranty is made only by the person who is a merchant with respect to food. The non-merchant makes no such warranty. Thus, the warranty is implied in the case of the restaurant, hotel, inn, drive-in, and corner drug store which serves food for value; it is not implied when the housewife serves a dinner for friends or even for a bridge club where the members pay dues to defray the costs of the meal. There will be difficult cases between these extremes. For example, is a church which is sponsoring a church supper a "merchant" with respect to the food? Is a club which has organized and charged for a summer picnic a "merchant" with respect to the food served? Each of these in-between cases will turn on its own special facts. If the church has hired a dietician to plan and serve meals, the definition of merchant has been met. However, if the church is only the location where some group has met to sponsor an evening meal, the definition of merchant—so far as the church is concerned—has not been satisfied.[93]

Second, the food must be served "for value." This criterion will be met in most cases. The hotel, restaurant, or drug store normally charges a price for the meal and that price will satisfy the value requirement. Even the water, salt, and pepper which appear to be served gratuitously are compensated for in the price of the meal, and meet the value test.[94] There will, however, inevitably be those cases which raise doubts as to whether the merchant has served the food "for value." Like those involving the question of whether the server of the food is a "merchant," each of these cases must be handled on its own facts. One answer might lie in the Code's broad definition of value.[95] A more definitive answer arises out of the Code's policies for implying warranties. This topic has already been explored and will not be repeated here.[96]

yet court refused to apply pre-Code innkeeper rule to food served in cafeteria.).

93. The concept of merchant is expanded in § 33 *supra*.

94. Yochem v. Gloria, Inc., 134 Ohio St. 427, 17 N.E.2d 731 (1938).

95. UCC § 1–201(44). As to an employee who received board as a part of his compensation, see Bark v. Dixson, 115 Minn. 172, 131 N.W. 1078 (1911).

96. §§ 21–22 *supra*. The opening words of the second sentence of UCC § 2–314(1) ("Under this section") have also caused concern. Do they mean that *only* under UCC § 2–314 is the serving of food for value to be considered a "sale," leaving to common law the question of whether the serving of food for value is a "sale" under UCC §§ 2–313 and 2–315? Certainly, these words can be given this meaning, but it is more probable that the drafters were emphasizing the change in the laws of some states, and providing that a warranty of merchantability

Once the implied warranty is found, its scope is determined as with any warranty of merchantability.[97] There is, however, one problem which has special application to the food cases. Suppose that a restaurant serves for value a chicken salad; that the salad contains a chicken bone sliver which becomes lodged in the throat of the purchaser; and that the purchaser claims damages based upon a theory of breach of warranty.[98] Is food "defective" (that is, unmerchantable) when the claimed defect is a natural part of the food involved, or must the claimed defect be foreign to the food (like a glass sliver in the salad) before the warranty has been breached? Courts reached different conclusions prior to the Code and, since the Code contains no section specifically dealing with this question, the battle can continue to be waged along its pre-Code battle lines. One group of cases based its conclusion of no defect on the ground that the natural item was to be expected in the food. "Bones which are natural to the type of meat served cannot legitimately be called a foreign substance, and a consumer who eats meat dishes ought to anticipate and be on his guard against the presence of such bones."[99] This group of cases did not, however, require the same consumer to be on his guard against foreign objects—thus the distinction was drawn on the basis of what was foreign and what was natural to food involved.[1] Another group of cases rejected this distinction:

> The "foreign-natural" test applied as a matter of law does not recommend itself to us as being logical or desirable. It is true one can expect a T-bone in T-bone steak, chicken bones in roast chicken, pork bone in a pork chop, pork bone in spareribs, a rib bone in short ribs of beef, and fish bones in a whole baked or fried fish, but the expectation is based

does arise "under this section." Therefore, express warranties and an implied warranty of fitness for purpose (as in a nursing home where a special diet is prescribed by the owner) could arise under the Code if the facts create these warranties.

97. § 76 *supra.*

98. There is also the possibility of the purchaser's claiming damages on the basis of strict liability. *See* § 54 *supra.* This presents the problem as to whether the food is "defective" under Restatement (Second) of Torts § 402A (1965).

99. Mix v. Ingersoll Candy Co., 6 Cal.2d 674, 682, 59 P.2d 144, 148 (1936). *See*

also Allen v. Grafton, 170 Ohio St. 249, 164 N.E.2d 167 (1960). For a colorful opinion under the Code holding no breach of warranty where a fish bone in fish chowder caused injury, see Webster v. Blue Ship Tea Room, Inc., 347 Mass. 421, 198 N.E.2d 309 (1964).

1. *E. g.*, Goetten v. Owl Drug Co., 6 Cal.2d 683, 59 P.2d 142 (1936). A Code case involving a foreign substance in the goods (grease in bread) is Finocchiaro v. Ward Baking Co., —— R.I. ——, 241 A.2d 619 (1968). Cases are collected in 2 L. Frumer and M. Friedman, Products Liability 653–91 (1968).

not on the naturalness of the particular bone to the meat, fowl, or fish, but on the type of dish served containing the meat, fowl, or fish. There is a distinction between what a consumer expects to find in a fish stick and in a baked or fried fish, or in a chicken sandwich made from sliced white meat and in roast chicken. The test should be what is reasonably expected by the consumer in the food as served, not what might be natural to the ingredients of that food prior to preparation. What is to be reasonably expected by the consumer is a jury question in most cases. . . .[2]

The problem takes on aspects of assumption of risks: what risks does the customer assume when he purchases food? One group of cases states that he assumes the risk of objects which are natural to the type of food involved; the other makes the question one of fact but refers the risk to the specific food as prepared. One case took this basic idea and went so far as to hold that the customer assumed the risk that the fish which was ordered might be infected with ciguatera poison.[3] This case ought not be approved, any more than a manufacturer ought to be allowed to escape liability for a defective product on the ground that purchasers know that a small percentage of all mass-produced goods will contain defects. The Code has made this type of liability one of the costs of doing business, and courts should not revert to the doctrine of *caveat emptor* to nullify the Code.

§ 78. Implied Warranty of Fitness for Particular Purpose

The second implied warranty of quality is that of fitness for a particular purpose (as contrasted to the implied warranty under section 2–314 that the goods will be fit for their *ordinary* purpose.) The Code provides in section 2–315:

> Where the seller at the time of contracting has reason to know any particular purpose for which the goods are re-

---

2. Betehia v. Cape Cod Corp., 10 Wis. 2d 323, 331–32, 103 N.W.2d 64, 68–69 (1960). This opinion collects many cases on both sides of the foreign-natural test. For a case allowing a plaintiff to recover simply because the food was stale (hard roll; broken tooth), see Scanlon v. Food Crafts, Inc., 2 Conn.Cir. 3, 193 A.2d 610 (1963). The "foreign-natural" and "reasonable expectation" tests are discussed in Hunt v. Ferguson-Paulus Enterprises, 243 Or. 546, 415 P.2d 13 (1966). For a case allowing the guest of the purchaser to recover (privity problem), see Conklin v. Hotel Waldorf Astoria Corp., 5 Misc.2d 496, 161 N.Y. S.2d 205 (City Ct.1957). Food may be unmerchantable even though it contains no deleterious or foreign objects if it is inedible because of its taste or smell. Martel v. Duffy-Mott Corp., 15 Mich.App. 67, 166 N.W.2d 541 (1968).

3. Bronson v. Club Comanche, Inc., 286 F.Supp. 21 (D. Virgin Islands 1968). On assumption of risk, generally, *see* § 84 *infra*.

quired and that the buyer is relying on the seller's skill or judgment to select or furnish suitable goods, there is unless excluded or modified under the next section an implied warranty that the goods shall be fit for such purpose.

A number of Code cases have used this warranty section when there was no need that it be used.[4] For example, if the seller knows the purpose for which the buyer wants the goods and also knows that the buyer is relying on the seller to select suitable goods, but if the seller goes on to say, "These goods will fill your needs," the statement of the seller can easily be construed as an express warranty. Likewise, if the buyer's use of the goods is the ordinary use of those goods, the implied warranty of merchantability is sufficient without resorting to the warranty of fitness for a particular purpose. In the latter situation the buyer's particular purpose coincides with the ordinary use of the goods, and either section 2–314 or section 2–315 will give the buyer the protection he needs.

This "over-use" of the implied warranty of fitness for a particular purpose was mentioned, not to object to such over-use, but to stress the interrelation of the Code warranties.[5] The parties' bargain has produced certain understandings—either express or implied, or both. These understandings may produce Code warranties which overlap without a clear dividing line. This is as it should be. Any attempt to force a line of demarcation between types of warranties would be trying to create differences where none exists in the commercial agreement. The only possible objection to an over-use of the warranty of fitness for a particular purpose is that courts might lose sight of the specific problems which section 2–315 is intended to resolve. This section of the text will emphasize those problems— with the understanding that the fitness warranty may also be used to reach other cases even though those cases are covered by other Code warranty provisions.

The warranty of fitness for purpose rests on what the seller has reason to know[6] at the time of contracting (not on the seller's knowledge at some later time). He must have reason to know two things: first, the particular purpose for which the buyer requires the goods; *and* second, that the buyer is relying on the seller's skill or judgment to select or to furnish suitable goods.[7] These two require-

4. *E. g.,* Sawyer v. Pioneer Leasing Corp., 244 Ark. 943, 428 S.W.2d 46 (1968); Scanlon v. Food Crafts, Inc., 2 Conn.Cir. 3, 193 A.2d 610 (1963).

5. UCC § 2–317. *See* Loomis Bros. Corp. v. Queen, 17 Pa.D. & C.2d 482 (C.P.1958), discussed in § 73 *supra.*

6. Actual knowledge is not required; reason to know will suffice. UCC § 1–201(25). *See also* UCC § 1–201(27).

7. Normally, the seller will be a merchant but this warranty is not limited to merchants. Compare UCC § 2–314. Non-merchants may impliedly warrant

ments are connected by an "and"; both must exist before the warranty will be implied. It is not enough that the seller has reason to know the use to which the buyer intends to put the goods unless the seller also has reason to know that the buyer is relying on the seller's skill or judgment to select or furnish suitable goods. On the other hand, the reliance factors are in the disjunctive; the second requirement is satisfied on the basis of the seller's skill *or* judgment to select *or* furnish suitable goods.[8] The seller need not both select and furnish; either will suffice.

The scope of the fitness warranty is well illustrated in two decisions. In the first, the stucco walls of the buyer's house were chalky and powdery. The buyer took this problem to the seller—a retail paint merchant—who recommended a certain brand of paint. The buyer applied the paint, carefully following the directions which had been given by the seller. Less than five months later the paint began to peel, flake, and blister. This time the buyer had to have the surface sandblasted, evidently to remove the paint which the seller had sold the buyer. In a suit by the buyer against the seller,[9] the court found that the necessary elements of an implied warranty of fitness for purpose existed: the seller had reason to know the particular purpose for which the buyer wanted the paint and that the buyer was relying on the seller's judgment in selecting the proper paint. The paint selected may well have been "merchantable"— that is, fit for its ordinary purposes. However, this buyer had not asked for paint for its ordinary purpose, but for one particular purpose which the buyer made known to the seller. There was, therefore, a warranty of fitness for that purpose. The court further found that the warranty was breached, and affirmed a judgment for the buyer. "The implied warranty of fitness is not founded on negligence; . . . nor is it founded on fraud or lack of good faith."[10] It rests upon the requirements of the Code.

In the second decision, the buyer ordered from the seller boxes for packaging liquor bottles; he also ordered acetate bands to encircle the boxes. The seller furnished boxes and bands, both of which the court found to be merchantable. When the buyer attempted to insert the boxes in the shipping cases, the fit was so tight that

---

that goods sold are fit for a particular purpose. UCC § 2–315, Comment 4.

8. The "selection" may be the process of the seller's taking the goods off the shelf or it may be the seller's choice of goods from the wholesaler. Ring-

stad v. I. Magnin & Co., 39 Wash.2d 923, 239 P.2d 848 (1952).

9. Catania v. Brown, 4 Conn.Cir. 344, 231 A.2d 668 (1967).

10. *Id.* at 346, 231 A.2d at 670.

the bands tore off on the sides of the shipping case cells. The buyer had to insert the liquor boxes in glassine bags to reduce the contact between the band and the sides of the cells. When the seller sued the buyer for the price,[11] the buyer claimed that the warranty of fitness for purpose had been breached, and counterclaimed for his damages. The court, however, found that the "evidence was insufficient to justify a finding that the seller had reason to know that the banded goods were required for the particular purpose of facilitating their insertion into the cells of the shipping case of undisclosed dimensions, and that the buyer relied on the seller's skill or judgment to select or furnish suitable goods for that purpose." [12] A judgment for the seller for the price was affirmed.

These two cases present the operation of the fitness-for-purpose warranty.[13] In the first, the elements of knowledge and reliance were present. In the second, the seller undoubtedly knew that the liquor boxes would have to be placed in some shipping container, but the court found that he had no reason to know that the buyer was relying on the seller to submit boxes and bands that would fit in a particular container. In the first, the warranty of fitness for purpose gave the buyer a cause of action; in the second, no warranty beyond that of merchantability existed.

All warranties require a close look at the facts of the bargain; the warranty of fitness requires an especially close look at those facts. The goods, by hypothesis, are merchantable and conform to all express warranties that were made. The difficulty is that those goods do not perform some particular function that the buyer expected they would. Before the seller will be held liable in damages for this failure of the goods, it must be shown that the seller had reason to know (1) the particular purpose for which the goods were required [14] and (2) that the buyer was relying on the seller's skill or judgment to select or furnish suitable goods.[15] This reason to know is measured as of the time of the contract. If these conditions are met, but only if they are met, is there a warranty of fitness for the buyer's particular purpose.

11. Standard Packaging Corp. v. Continental Distil. Corp., 378 F.2d 505 (3d Cir. 1967).

12. *Id.* at 509.

13. See also Boeing Airplane Co. v. O'Malley, 329 F.2d 585 (8th Cir. 1964); Paullus v. Liedkie, 92 Idaho 323, 442 P.2d 733 (1968).

14. No warranty of fitness for purpose was implied when the seller of engine parts did not have reason to know buyer's engine had been modified. Mennella v. Schork, 49 Misc.2d 449, 267 N.Y.S.2d 428 (Dist.Ct.1966).

15. Where the buyer did not rely on the seller's skill or judgment, there is no warranty of fitness for purpose, Vacuum Concrete Corp. of America v. Berlanti Constr. Co., 206 Pa.Super. 548, 214 A.2d 729 (1965).

§ 79. Use of Patent or Trade Names

The Uniform Sales Act contained this subsection:

> In the case of a contract to sell or a sale of a specified article under its patent or other trade name, there is no implied warranty as to its fitness for any particular purpose.[16]

This subsection produced some amazing results. For example, in one case the buyer decided to install a new boiler in his skating rink, went to the seller for assistance, and relied entirely upon the knowledge and skill of the seller in selecting the size and type of boiler (all of which was known to the seller). The negotiations resulted in a writing for the purchase and sale of a "1–5–28–5 section Ideal Sectional Boiler." Even the seller admitted that the boiler which was installed was two sizes smaller than was needed to do the required job. Nevertheless the court refused to award the buyer damages, holding that the "trade-name" subsection set out above nullified any implied warranty of fitness.[17] Just because the final writing referred to the object purchased by its trade name, there was no warranty that the product would do the job for which the buyer made his purchase—even though the elements of this warranty otherwise existed.[18]

The Uniform Commercial Code has deleted the reference to contracts to sell goods by their patent or trade names. The result is that the warranty of fitness for purpose is not eliminated simply because the writing lists the goods sold by their patented or trade name.[19] Under the Code, "the existence of a patent or other trade name and the designation of the article by that name, or indeed in any other definite manner, is only one of the facts to be considered on the question of whether the buyer actually relied on the seller, but it is not of itself decisive of the issue. If the buyer himself is insisting on a particular brand he is not relying on the seller's skill and judg-

16. Uniform Sales Act § 15(4).

17. Matteson v. Lagace, 36 R.I. 223, 89 A. 713 (1914).

18. Not all courts construed the Uniform Sales Act so narrowly. Iron Fireman Coal Stoker Co. v. Brown, 182 Minn. 399, 234 N.W. 685 (1931). *See also* Drumar Mining Co. v. Morris Ravine Mining Co., 33 Cal.App.2d 492, 92 P.2d 424 (1939); E. Edleman & Co. v. Queen Stove Works, Inc., 205 Minn.

7, 284 N.W. 838 (1939); Sperry Flour Co. v. De Moss, 141 Or. 440, 18 P.2d 242 (1933); Green Mountain Mushroom Co. v. Brown, 117 Vt. 509, 95 A.2d 679 (1953); and discussion in 1 S. Williston, Sales § 236a (rev. ed. 1948). Cases are collected in Annots., 59 A.L.R. 1180 (1929), s. 90 A.L.R. 410 (1934).

19. Appeal of Reeves Soundcraft Corp., 2 UCC Rep. 210 (Armed Services Bd. of Contract Appeals, 1964).

ment and so no warranty [of fitness] [20] results.[21]   But the mere fact that the article purchased has a particular patent or trade name is not sufficient to indicate nonreliance if the article has been recommended by the seller as adequate for the buyer's purpose." [22]

The parol evidence rule ought not keep out evidence of prior oral conversations giving rise to the warranty of fitness unless both parties intended the later writing to be exclusive on the question of warranties.[23]   That intent is not shown solely because the writing describes the goods by their brand name.

§ 80.   Blood Cases

One of the oddities of the current law of sales is the way that courts treat cases involving the transfusion of blood which turns out to be contaminated.   The typical factual pattern which presents the problem is roughly equivalent to this: the hospital patient is advised by his doctor that a blood transfusion is needed to save life or speed recovery; the patient is seldom in a position to question this advice or to aid in the selection of the blood; the blood is procured by the doctor from the hospital, but separately billed to the patient; the hospital had purchased that blood from a blood bank which had received the blood (either by purchase or gift) from countless people who were not given a thorough examination before the blood was accepted; and the blood which this patient received was contaminated, causing further illness—usually hepatitis.   Fortunately, these cases are rare, but this is little solace to the patient who entered the hospital to be made well but who contracted a disease because of the blood which was introduced into the patient's body.

The most famous of the blood cases is Perlmutter v. Beth David Hospital.[24]   The facts were much like those set out above, and the patient brought suit against the hospital.   The hospital moved to dismiss the complaint; the lower courts denied the motion, but, on appeal and with three judges dissenting, the Court of Appeals of New York reversed and held that insofar as the patient had attempted to recover

---

20.   These words are not in the Comment; nevertheless, the warranty of merchantability would exist (if the necessary elements of that warranty are present) even if the buyer is insisting on a particular brand of goods. *See* UCC § 2–314.

21.   This may be an overstatement.   If the buyer insists on a particular brand of goods but if the seller has reason to know the buyer's purpose for the goods and that the buyer is relying on the seller's judgment in selecting a particular model or size within that brand, the facts of a warranty of fitness could exist.

22.   UCC § 2–315, Comment 5.

23.   §§ 53, 69 *supra*.   *But see* Thorman v. Polytemp, Inc., 2 UCC Rep. 772 (N.Y. County Ct.1965).

24.   308 N.Y. 100, 123 N.E.2d 792 (1954).

for breach of warranty, no cause of action had been stated. The basis of the opinion is reminiscent of the pre-Code food cases—the contract involved is one for services, is not divisible, is not within the law of sales, and there are therefore no warranties. The conclusion of the court is summarized in this paragraph from the opinion:

> The supplying of blood by the hospital was entirely subordinate to its paramount function of furnishing trained personnel and specialized facilities in an endeavor to restore plaintiff's health. It was not for blood—or iodine or bandages—for which plaintiff bargained, but the wherewithal of the hospital staff and the availability of hospital facilities to provide whatever medical treatment was considered advisable. The conclusion is evident that the furnishing of blood was only an incidental and very secondary adjunct to the services performed by the hospital and, therefore, was not within the provisions of the Sales Act.[25]

Other courts have followed the lead of *Perlmutter* and have denied warranty protection to the patient, leaving him only a possible action in tort.[26]

Some patients have tried to recover damages from the blood bank for the contaminated blood. This has been more successful, but most courts still refuse to extend the coverage of implied warranties from the blood bank to the patient.[27] Evidently, these are illnesses which the patient must bear without recompense because his contract was one for services, rather than a sale.[28]

From the standpoint of the patient it is difficult to conceive of a stronger case for implying the warranties of merchantability and fitness for purpose. The patient was relying on his doctor and on the doctor's source of supply to furnish suitable blood. Both the doctor and the hospital had reason to know of this reliance and to know the

---

25. *Id.* at 106, 123 N.E.2d at 795.

26. Sloneker v. St. Joseph's Hosp., 233 F.Supp. 105 (D.Colo.1964); Koenig v. Milwaukee Blood Center, Inc., 23 Wis. 2d 324, 127 N.W.2d 50 (1964). For cases denying recovery in suits for negligence or violation of state pure food and drug acts, see Balkowitsch v. Minneapolis War Memorial Blood Bank, Inc., 270 Minn. 151, 132 N.W. 2d 805 (1965). For a possible suit on express warranty, see Jackson v. Muhlenberg Hosp., 96 N.J.Super. 314, 232 A.2d 879 (L.Div.1967), *rev'd per curiam* 53 N.J. 138, 249 A.2d 65 (1968) (record too meagre).

27. Whitehurst v. American Nat'l Red Cross, 1 Ariz.App. 326, 402 P.2d 584 (1965) (denying recovery); Community Blood Bank, Inc. v. Russell, 196 So. 2d 115 (Fla.1967) (denying defendant's motion to dismiss); Balkowitsch v. Minneapolis War Memorial Blood Bank, Inc., 270 Minn. 151, 132 N.W. 2d 805 (1965) (denying recovery).

28. Massachusetts amended UCC § 2–316 to provide that the implied warranties do not apply to "a contract for the sale of human blood, blood plasma or other human tissue or organs from a blood bank or reservoir of such other tissues or organs." Mass.Gen.Laws Ann. ch. 106, § 2–316(5) (Supp.1968).

particular purpose for which the blood was needed. Further, the blood selected was not even merchantable—that is, neither would it pass without objection in the "trade" nor was it fit for its ordinary purpose. The reason why no warranties are to be implied, according to these courts, is that the blood was not "sold" to the patient. The transaction involves services rather than goods.

The first difficulty with this conclusion is that it is just that—a conclusion. There is nothing inherent in the transfusion of blood that makes the transaction either a "service" or a "sale." The legal system has looked at the transaction and has decided that a service is involved, but that system could just as well have emphasized the billing of the patient and concluded that a sale was involved. After all, the price of all goods contains a large percentage for services that were involved in preparing, transporting, and distributing those goods. In fact, in many items the cost of the services performed on the goods far exceeds the value of the raw material involved. Nevertheless, courts have no difficulty in concluding that the distribution of these items is a *sale* of *goods*. What is so different about the transfusion of blood— especially when it is remembered that the patient is complaining that the blood (not the service in transfusing) was unmerchantable?

The second difficulty with the conclusion reached by the courts is that it stops short of analyzing the problem involved. Granting that a service rather than a sale is involved, why should not warranties be implied in the rendition of services? It is no answer to say that warranties are implied in sales; this is not a sale; therefore, there are no implied warranties.[29] Courts are implying warranties in areas other than those falling within the Uniform Commercial Code.[30] What is so different about the transfusion of blood?

The answer to these questions cannot be determined by trying to find a sale or a service, or by quibbling about whether the entire transaction is one involving goods or non-goods. The answer probably lies in two features of the typical transfusion of contaminated blood case, features that were present in *Perlmutter*. First, the defendant is a hospital (or a blood bank). It is not in business for a profit—even though its charges for rooms, meals, and "services" are sufficient to support a number of people who are working for a profit. Second, the courts have thus far been convinced "that there is today neither a means of detecting the presence of the jaundice-producing agent in the donor's blood nor a practical method of treating the blood to be used for transfusions so that the danger may be eliminated . . ..[31]

29. See Koenig v. Milwaukee Blood Center, Inc., 23 Wis.2d 324, 127 N.W. 2d 50 (1964). See § 22 *supra*.

30. §§ 21-22 *supra*.

31. 308 N.Y. 100, 106, 123 N.E.2d 792, 795.

The problem is, therefore, a real one for the hospital. If warranties are implied, liability will exist even though there is no medical way to detect or prevent the harm. This has not prevented the implication of warranties in transactions involving other products,[32] but it may be sufficient in cases of the kind here presented. The court is making a policy choice: it is preferable to allow the hospital to experiment on life-saving processes without fear of legal liability, making the individual bear the entire loss when the experiment proves unsuccessful, than to spread the risk to all who use the hospital.[33] This may be a wise decision with the new medical processes—such as organ and tissue transplants—which are being attempted; or it may be an unwise decision because it promotes early experimentation before sufficient research has been accomplished.

This is the problem that the courts should face—not the surface one of whether a service or a sale of goods is involved. The answer turns on many factors, including the availability and cost of insurance against these losses. For example, if medical science is now at the place where it can forecast with reasonable accuracy the number of patients who will receive hepatitis from blood transfusions and if the hospital can insure against the liabilities which will flow from the use of contaminated blood, the cost of this insurance can be spread among all who require blood transfusions without bringing ruinous losses on the hospital. In any event, this approach to the problem would make it clear that the language of *Perlmutter* and its progeny does not exempt the hospital from liability for poisoned food served in its cafeteria, for poisoned food served to a patient,[34] for prescribing the wrong diet to a patient, for using contaminated medicine or bandages, or for insertion of medical devices (such as metal pins in bones) where it is possible to determine before the insertion that the device is defective [35] —even though all could be viewed as a part of the hospital's "services."

---

32. Vlases v. Montgomery Ward & Co., 377 F.2d 846 (3d Cir. 1967) (avian leukosis in chickens); Green v. American Tobacco Co., 154 So.2d 169 (Fla. 1963), *cert. denied* 377 U.S. 943, 84 S. Ct. 1349, 12 L.Ed.2d 306 (1964) (cancer from cigarette smoke). The history of the *Green* litigation is traced in § 82 n. 49 *infra.*

33. *Cf.* Restatement (Second) of Torts § 402A, Comment *k* (1965).

34. Unless, of course, hospitals are generally immune to suit. Forrest v. Red Cross Hosp., Inc., 265 S.W.2d 80 (Ky.1954).

35. Picker X-Ray Corp. v. Frerker, 405 F.2d 916 (8th Cir. 1969). *But see* Cutler v. General Electric Co., 4 UCC Rep. 300 (N.Y.Sup.Ct.1967).

§ 81. Non-conformity

Prior sections have discussed the standards which goods must meet to satisfy the seller's warranty obligations. These standards are based on the law of contracts and proceed from the idea that a sale is a consensual relation between the seller and buyer. The agreement between the parties establishes the warranties, express and implied, or the standards against which the quality of the goods is to be tested. Goods are conforming when "they are in accordance with the obligations under the contract";[36] goods which do not measure up to the contractual obligations are non-conforming.

The tort approach to substandard goods is similar to that of the Code. Under tort law the test of non-conformity is framed in terms of negligence or strict liability—which the *Restatement (Second) of Torts* codifies with the cryptic phrase: "product in a defective condition unreasonably dangerous to the user or consumer or to his property . . . ."[37] Both the Code and tort tests work reasonably well with the majority of sales problems in which a claim has been made that the seller's goods have produced an injury. When a merchant sells an automobile with no brakes or with defective brakes, when a local grocer sells contaminated meat, or when the owner of a dress shop sells a cocktail robe that bursts into flames on casual contact with a stove burner, there is little difficulty in finding that the goods involved were "non-conforming."[38] Likewise, there would be little difficulty in finding that these same goods were "defective" and "unreasonably dangerous." These goods were not safe for their intended use.

This text has already examined these core problems, and an earlier section concluded that the warranty of merchantability is broader than simply that the goods will do the job for which they were sold.[39] The goods must also, unless the further warranty is disclaimed, do the job "safely." If the facts of the cases on which this conclusion was based are now examined, certain common features emerge. In those

36. UCC § 2–106(2).

37. Restatement (Second) of Torts § 402A (1965), discussed in § 54 *supra*.

38. These holdings can be supported under UCC §§ 2–314 or 2–315, or both. The cocktail robe case, Ringstad v. I. Magnin & Co., 39 Wash.2d 923, 239 P.2d 848 (1952), suggested that the merchant seller has an obligation to *select* safe goods. *See also* Kuriss v. Conrad & Co., 312 Mass. 670, 46 N.E.2d 12 (1942). The seller of raw pork is entitled to expect that it will be cooked before eaten, Silverman v. Swift & Co., 141 Conn. 450, 107 A.2d 277 (1954), but only to the extent of ordinary cooking, Holt v. Mann, 294 Mass. 21, 200 N.E. 403 (1936). A chair not safe to stand on is defective, Phillips v. Ogle Aluminum Furniture, Inc., 106 Cal.App.2d 650, 235 P.2d 857 (1951), but shoes which injure the plaintiff's feet because improperly fitted do not create liability for the retail seller of those shoes, Dubbs v. Zak Bros., 38 Ohio App. 299, 175 N.E. 626 (1931).

39. § 76 *supra*.

cases (1) the goods would have caused harm (bodily or economically) to a substantial number of users had any one of them purchased the goods, (2) the defect was discoverable by the seller had he taken the time to examine the goods, (3) the injury which resulted was foreseeable once the defect was known, and (4) the person who was harmed had no reason to know that the goods would cause this particular harm. In this type of case the contractual obligations of the seller, unless disclaimed, require a safe product; supplying unsafe goods does not satisfy the obligations of the contract; and such goods are "non-conforming."

There are, however, other cases that are not so easily decided. These are challenging the principles on which many product liability decisions rest. As yet, these "other cases" have not produced general principles which can be presented in the usual textbook fashion. They are, nevertheless, the most difficult of the current sales problems and merit some mention in any textual treatment of the law of sales, even though no single solution can be developed.

There are many ways to group these cases. One would be by examining what is meant by the word "safely" in the conclusion that a product must not only do the job for which it was sold, but that it must do that job "safely". In a very real sense there is no such thing as a *safe* product. An otherwise wholesome candy bar can produce serious illness when eaten by a diabetic, and even a non-diabetic can become ill by eating too many of these same candy bars. Similarly, a person can drill a hole in his hand with an electric drill, leave the keys in his automobile and have it stolen and wrecked, or suffer a severe electrical shock while trying to repair his plugged-in television set. Were these goods "safe" even though their use resulted in injury? Were these goods "safe" when it is possible to manufacture an electric drill so that it will operate only when both hands are on the handle, to design an automobile so that the driver will be warned when he has left the keys in the ignition with the engine turned off, and to construct a television set so that the electrical contact is broken when the back is removed? Was the candy bar "safe" even though no way has yet been devised to place a warning in the candy to tell the consumer when he is about to eat one too many bites?

There is, in addition, another group of cases challenging the bases on which product liability rests. These cases involve situations in which the scientific knowledge was not far enough advanced at the time the goods were produced to predict that the goods might have a harmful side effect. The manufacture of cigarettes during the first half of this century may be an example of this phenomenon. If it is true that cancer was not linked to cigarette smoking during those years (that is, if medical knowledge had not advanced to the point where it could predict that cigarettes were not "safe" when smoked by some people), ought cigarettes be classed as non-conforming goods under the Code, or defective goods under the law of torts, so as to create liability now that medical science believes that it has found such a link? Other examples can also be found in the drug industry. A drug which has been carefully tested according to current test standards may show no harmful side effects until years after its first use. The manufacturer or seller of such a drug had no way to foresee its unsafe features at the time of the sale. If later medical evidence proves that the drug did produce the injury, was the drug non-conforming or defective when it was sold?

Neither the Code test (non-conformity) nor the tort test of strict liability (defective product unreasonably dangerous) specifically answers these questions. Both are ambiguous. Under the Code, when do the obligations of the contract include safety from injury? Under tort law, when is a product "defective"? Is it defective when it produces injury? Evidently not because the defective product must also be *unreasonably* dangerous—leaving the idea that reasonable danger is insufficient to satisfy the strict liability requirements.

Since neither body of law produces specific answers, courts have been required to proceed on a case-by-case basis. From these cases discernible issues have emerged. These issues often reinforce each other; at other times they cut across each other. The following sections of this text will consider the problem of safety from the basis of these questions:

1. To what extent is it necessary that the manufacturer or seller be able to foresee that the goods have the capacity of producing the injury complained of?

2. To what percent of the population must the goods be potentially harmful before they will be considered non-conforming or defective?

3. To what extent will the plaintiff's knowledge that the product is capable of producing injury prevent that product from being classified as non-conforming or defective when it does produce injury? [40]

§ 82. Non-conformity—Foreseeability of Injury

There are conflicting opinions as to the role which foreseeability ought to play in determining liability for breach of warranty. Some points, however, are relatively clear and these can be stated at the outset.

---

40. For a related basis for seeking product liability, see Noel, *Products Defective Because of Inadequate Directions or Warnings*, 23 S.W.L.J. 256 (1969).

First, to the extent that the defendant-seller expressly warrants his product as being safe, foreseeability on his part is not required as a condition to liability.[41] In such a case the seller is expressly assuming the risks that the goods may cause injury, even from unknown and unknowable defects, and the court will not disturb the agreement made by the parties. This rule operates only if the seller has expressly warranted the safety of his product; the scope of the warranty requires an interpretation of the words or acts of the seller. This problem has already been discussed.[42]

Second, problems centering on foreseeability are therefore limited to implied warranties and to liability in tort. At this point different types of foreseeability must be distinguished. The first level of foreseeability involves those cases in which the seller is arguing that he believed that the goods which he sold were safe because he used all the care he could in marketing those goods. Examples include the retailer who is selling goods in a sealed container (and arguing that he could not foresee that inside the container was some object that made the goods unsafe for human consumption) and the manufacturer who urges that it used extreme care in manufacturing the goods. While at one time the retailer might have been successful in his argument when he sold goods in a sealed container,[43] this position is fast becoming nothing more than a bit of history in the law of sales.[44] The test for these products is their merchantability; that is, whether the goods would pass without objection in the trade. In determining whether goods will pass without objection, the measuring stick is their condition as discovered by the buyer or consumer.[45] The test for these cases could, therefore, be stated not as one for the need of actual foreseeability of the defect or injury, but as one of objective foreseeability: once the true condition of the goods is known, was it foreseeable that the goods in that condition would produce injury?

The second level of foreseeability is the one that has produced the problems and is the one as to which there have been diverse results. Here the manufacturer and seller had no scientific means of

---

41. *See* Pritchard v. Liggett & Myers Tobacco Co., 350 F.2d 479 (3d Cir. 1965), *cert. denied* 382 U.S. 987, 86 S.Ct. 549, 15 L.Ed.2d 475 (1966), *modified* 370 F.2d 95 (3d Cir. 1966), *cert. denied* 386 U.S. 1009, 87 S.Ct. 1350, 18 L.Ed.2d 436 (1967); Toole v. Richardson-Merrell, Inc., 251 Cal.App. 2d 452, 60 Cal.Rptr. 398 (1967).

42. §§ 48–52, 70 *supra*.

43. *See* 1 S. Williston, Sales § 242 n. 13 (rev. ed. 1948).

44. *Id.* n. 15; Sams v. Ezy-Way Foodliner Co., 157 Me. 10, 170 A.2d 160 (1961); Newmark v. Gimbel's, Inc., 54 N.J. 585, 258 A.2d 697 (1969) (application of cosmetic by beautician); Ryan v. Progressive Grocery Stores, 255 N.Y. 388, 175 N.E. 105 (1931).

45. § 76 *supra*.

determining that the product would produce a harmful side effect. At the time that the goods were manufactured and sold they appeared to everyone to be "safe." No doctor, no engineer, no chemist, or no physicist could predict that the product involved had the inherent capability of producing the injury now complained of. The product was bought and used; the injury resulted; and now scientific knowledge has advanced to the point that a causal link between the use of the product and the resulting injury appears clear. Placing this problem in the realm of the hypothetical for the purpose of emphasizing its scope, suppose that ten years from now it is discovered that the use of what is now thought of as a safe product (say woolen sweaters) is "proved" to cause a painful body condition (say arthritis). Should the manufacturers and sellers of woolen sweaters be liable to arthritic sufferers who prove this causal relation for the bodily discomfort and immobility resulting from wearing woolen sweaters?

One way to express this problem is by asking whether foreseeability is a necessary requirement for recovery under either warranty or strict liability. Having stated the problem in this form, cases have disagreed. The blood cases, already discussed, tend to indicate that inability to foresee the non-conformity of the goods is a complete defense to liability for blood containing hepatitis virus.[46] Some drug cases have reached the same result;[47] others have disagreed.[48] The same diversity is found in the cigarette cases.[49] Assuming that

46. § 80 *supra*. The blood cases have emphasized that there is no scientific method of detecting the presence of jaundice-producing viruses in the blood. Perlmutter v. Beth David Hosp., 308 N.Y. 100, 123 N.E.2d 792 (1954). Thus, these cases have a similarity to the problem discussed in the text. However, to the extent that the number of patients acquiring hepatitis through blood transfusions is statistically predictable, the blood cases are also similar to the warranty problems of any seller whose quality control devices are inadequate to assure 100% safety in his product.

47. Cudmore v. Richardson-Merrell, Inc., 398 S.W.2d 640 (Tex.Civ.App. 1965), *cert. denied* 385 U.S. 1003, 87 S.Ct. 705, 17 L.Ed.2d 542 (1967).

48. Davis v. Wyeth Laboratories, Inc., 399 F.2d 121 (9th Cir. 1968); Gottsdanker v. Cutter Laboratories, 182 Cal. App.2d 602, 6 Cal.Rptr. 320 (1960). *See also* Vlases v. Montgomery Ward & Co., 377 F.2d 846 (3d Cir. 1967).

49. The wrongful death action by Mary Green (as administratrix of her husband's estate) against American Tobacco Co. for her husband's death from lung cancer is a good example of the divergence of opinions. A jury trial resulted in a verdict for the defendant which the Fifth Circuit Court in a 2–1 decision affirmed. Upon plaintiff's motion for a rehearing, the court certified a question of applicable state law to the Florida Supreme Court. Green v. American Tobacco Co., 304 F.2d 70, 85 (5th Cir. 1962). The only question certified to the Florida court, and the only one answered by it, was whether the law of Florida imposed upon a manufacturer an absolute liability for breach of implied warranty when the manufacturer could not by the reasonable application of human skill and foresight have known that users of the product would be endangered. The court answered the question affirmatively saying, "No reasonable distinction can, in our opinion, be made between the physical or practical impossibility of obtaining

there was no medical basis during the first half of this century for linking cancer with the smoke of cigarettes, ought cigarette manufacturers bear the liability for the harm caused by their product which was sold during those 50 years, now that there is evidence of the causal relation? Stated in terms of foreseeability: as long as the cigarette manufacturers had no scientific basis for foreseeing the harm that would come from their product, was that product nonconforming in that it did not do the job for which it was made—and do it *safely*?

The difficulty with framing this question in terms of foreseeability is that it misdirects the attention of the legal system. One of the bases for warranty liability is that it spreads the risk of non-conforming products among all users of that product. To the extent that a seller can foresee a statistical number of injuries from his product, he is able to add to the cost of each item an amount which will produce a fund large enough either to purchase insurance against the losses or to build a fund which will pay the resulting judgments. However, to the extent that the injuries are scientifically unforeseeable, a seller cannot accumulate such a fund—and risks are not being spread. They are simply being shifted from the injured consumer to the seller and manufacturer.[50] Liability becomes absolute. More than that it becomes insurance; the manufacturer is called upon to insure the safety of his product, even against unknowable losses. The overall thrust of the cases thus far would indicate that the courts are not ready to take this step.

The problem of this section of the text can be illustrated by a group of cases which involve both tort and warranty liability, and which are still in the process of determining the basis upon which that liability ought to rest. These are the automobile design cases.[51]

knowledge of a dangerous condition, and scientific inability resulting from a current lack of human knowledge or skill." 154 So.2d 169, 171 (Fla.1963).

The Circuit Court on the basis of this answer, reversed the judgment and remanded for a trial solely on the issue of whether the cigarettes were "reasonably" fit and wholesome. 325 F.2d 673 (1963).

At a second jury trial a verdict was again rendered for defendant. At a hearing of the Fifth Circuit *en banc* with 1 judge dissenting, the lower court was reversed and judgment entered for the plaintiff on the issue of liability with orders to retry the issue of damages. 391 F.2d 97 (1968).

On a petition for rehearing *en banc*, the Court in an 8–3 *per curiam* opinion adopted the reasoning of the prior dissent (391 F.2d at 106) that the scope of the implied warranty was "reasonably wholesome or fit," rather than one of absolute liability. It thus overruled its earlier determination and affirmed the judgment of the lower court. 409 F.2d 1166 (1969).

50. For at least a partial answer to this argument, see James, *The Untoward Effects of Cigarettes and Drugs: Some Reflections on Enterprise Liability*, 54 Calif.L.Rev. 1550 (1966).

51. Restatement (Second) of Torts § 398 (1965). These problems are not lim-

One lawsuit involved a plaintiff who was injured in a head-on collision. His cause of action against the manufacturer alleged that his injuries resulted from the negligent design of the steering assembly, negligent failure to warn of the inherently dangerous condition of the steering assembly placement, and breach of express and implied warranties of merchantability and intended use. There was no claim that the negligence or breach of warranty caused the collision—only that the automobile's design caused the injuries to be more severe than they otherwise would have been. Restating this contention in the terms presented in this section of the text, the plaintiff was claiming that, although the automobile performed the transportation function, it did not perform that function as safely as it ought to when exposed to a collision.

The district court granted a summary judgment for the manufacturer,[52] reasoning that the manufacturer's duty was to design an automobile which was reasonably safe when driven and which contained no latent or hidden defects. The duty to warn was limited to latent defects which rendered the product "unsafe for its intended use. . . . The intended use of an automobile does not include its participation in head-on collisions and, therefore, there was no duty on the part of the defendant to warn [that] in the event of such a collision the plaintiff might be injured."[53] On appeal, the Eighth Circuit reversed and remanded.[54] The disagreement with the district court centered on the "intended use" of an automobile coupled with ideas of foreseeability:

> We think the "intended use" construction urged by General Motors is much too narrow and unrealistic. Where the manufacturer's negligence in design causes an unreasonable risk to be imposed upon the user of its products, the manufacturer should be liable for the injury caused by its failure to exercise reasonable care in the design. These injuries are readily foreseeable as an incident to the normal and expected use of an automobile. While automobiles are not made for the purpose of colliding with each other, a frequent and inevitable contingency of normal automobile use will result in collisions and injury producing impacts. No rational basis exists for limiting recovery to situations

ited to automobiles. Bailey v. Montgomery Ward & Co., 6 Ariz.App. 213, 431 P.2d 108 (1967).

52. Larsen v. General Motors Corp., 274 F.Supp. 461 (D.Minn.1967).

53. *Id.* at 464–65.

54. Larsen v. General Motors Corp., 391 F.2d 495 (8th Cir. 1968). For a case quoting *Larsen* favorably, see Mickle v. Blackmon, 252 S.C. 202, 166 S.E.2d 173 (1969).

where the defect in design or manufacture was the causative factor of the accident, as the accident and the resulting injury, usually caused by the so-called "second collision" of the passenger with the interior part of the automobile, all are foreseeable. Where the injuries or enhanced injuries are due to the manufacturer's failure to use reasonable care to avoid subjecting the user of its products to an unreasonable risk of injury, general negligence principles should be applicable. The sole function of an automobile is not just to provide a means of transportation, it is to provide a means of safe transportation or as safe as is reasonably possible under the present state of the art.[55]

The court added that the manufacturer had no duty to make the automobile accident-proof "or even one that floats on water, but such manufacturer is under a duty to use reasonable care in the design of its vehicle to avoid subjecting the user to an unreasonable risk of injury in the event of a collision." [56]

A later decision indicates that the Eighth Circuit is not requiring the construction of an accident-proof car.[57] Other courts have agreed.[58] However, the attempt to draw a line between the duty to make the steering assembly safer in the event of a collision and the no-duty to make an automobile which will float on water presents the problem of this section of the text. It certainly would not take too much imagination on the part of automobile manufacturers to foresee that some automobiles do fall into the water and that lives are lost because the automobile does not float. Why did the court cut off the duty short of the floating automobile?

The answer to this question can probably be best found if the idea of foreseeability is ignored and attention is focused on the concept of risk-shifting, already discussed, and on the ultimate costs involved in making products safer. The immediate result of a finding of product liability may be the bankruptcy of concerns producing the product or a withdrawal of that product from the market, or both.[59] That product may never be remarketed (even though it benefited thousands of per-

---

55. Larsen v. General Motors Corp., 391 F.2d 495, 502 (8th Cir. 1968). *See also* Darryl v. Ford Motor Co., 440 S.W.2d 630 (Tex.1969) (strict liability in tort).

56. *Id.*

57. Schneider v. Chrysler Motors Corp., 401 F.2d 549 (8th Cir. 1968), and cases there cited.

58. Schemel v. General Motors Corp., 384 F.2d 802 (7th Cir. 1967), *cert. denied* 390 U.S. 945, 88 S.Ct. 1030, 19 L.Ed.2d 1134 (1968).

59. The suggestion of bankruptcy is not fanciful. See Rheingold, *The MER/29 Story—An Instance of Successful Mass Disaster Litigation*, 56 Calif.L. Rev. 116 (1968).

sons) just because the financial risks to the seller are too great; or, if it is placed on the market again, the cost will be increased or the design changed to give greater safety.[60] These changes will benefit many consumers who would otherwise have been injured in the use of the product, but this benefit is gained at a cost to the public—a cost in the design and price of the product, or even in its complete unavailability. The problem becomes one of balancing the interests of these groups. For example, the almost-completely safe automobile can be built. It would have a top speed of around 20 miles an hour and look something like the World War II tank. Should a court force this type of automobile on the public—which may well not be able to afford such a product or which may not care at all for the design—under the understandable quest for safer goods?

The answer so far has been that it should not. The product must not contain hidden or latent defects so far as its foreseeable and intended use is concerned, but it need not be accident-proof. The legal skirmishes, however, are far from over. Those who are injured through use of goods will continue to press their claims that the goods were non-conforming or defective. Sellers and manufacturers will continue to claim that the injury suffered was not foreseeable, either because scientific knowledge had not advanced that far at the time of the sale or because the plaintiff was not using the goods for their intended purpose. The court decisions have, as yet, presented no pattern from which an answer can be drawn. About the best that can be done at the present time is to suggest that the distinction between conforming and non-conforming goods, as far as this question is concerned, results from a determination of the point at which the gains to the public in obtaining safer goods outweigh the costs to the public in design and in the price charged. Somewhere around this point courts will conclude that the goods are "non-conforming." [61]

§ 83. Non-conformity—Foreseeability of Plaintiff

A second problem in determining when goods are non-conforming centers on the number of people to whom the goods must be potentially harmful: are implied warranties limited to the normal person or do they also include those people whose reactions are abnormal? This problem is usually not mentioned in cases involving such items as poisoned food, defective machines, or candy bars with pieces of glass

---

60. The availability of insurance may prevent the threat of liability from being a substantial deterrent to marketing new products or changing old products. *Cf.* Restatement (Second) of Torts § 402A, Comment *k* (1965).

61. Dickerson, *Products Liability: How Good Does a Product Have to Be?*, 42 Ind.L.J. 301 (1967); Spengler, *The Economics of Safety*, 33 Law & Contemp.Prob. 619 (1968).

imbedded in their centers. These items are potentially harmful to almost anyone who uses them. It is true that there may exist a few people who have built up an immunity to the poison, who can withstand the electrical shock when the machine shorts out, and there are even a few carnival performers who may not be injured by swallowing a sliver of glass. There may, therefore, be someone for whom nearly every product is "safe"; yet the safety of these products—that is, their merchantability—is measured against their use by the "normal" person. Since the products discussed above would be harmful to the vast majority of the population, they are classified, usually without discussion, as non-conforming goods. If the consumer proves that he was in fact injured by those goods and otherwise meets the tests for warranty (or strict liability), he will be allowed to recover from the seller of those goods.[62]

There are, on the other hand, some goods which are "safe" for use by the majority but cause harm when used by a smaller segment of the population which is allergic to the goods or to one of its ingredients. If one of those who has such an allergy uses the goods and is injured, were the goods (as to him) "non-conforming"? Does the warranty of merchantability extend not only to the person whose reactions are "normal," or does it also reach the one whose reactions are "abnormal"?

The cases which raise this problem usually involve some kind of drug, lotion, or cosmetic (some substance applied to or ingested into the body), but on occasion they involve other chattels.[63] The typical factual pattern would be:

A purchaser bought a face lotion from her local drug store and applied the lotion according to directions. A few days later she noticed that her skin was dry, flaky, and inflamed. She immediately stopped using the lotion, but the redness increased into severe facial burns which have left permanent scars. A doctor will testify that two of the lotion's ingredients caused these particular burns, but the doctor will also testify that the normal person would have had no adverse reaction to those ingredients. Do implied warranties reach only the normal person or do they also extend to those whose reactions are abnormal?

Statements in court opinions indicate that there are two rules as to the law applicable to injuries resulting from allergic reactions to goods. One group of cases states that implied warranties are limited to injuries which would have been caused to those persons whose reactions are normal, and that goods are not non-conforming simply be-

---

62. §§ 74 et seq. *supra.*

63. *E. g.,* Flynn v. Bedell Co., 242 Mass. 450, 136 N.E. 252 (1922) (fur collar on a coat).

cause the person with abnormal reactions was injured through their use.[64] If those statements are accepted at their face value, a consumer could not recover for the injuries which he received from the use of a product unless he could also show that his reactions were normal—that is, that more than one-half of the population would have suffered a similar injury from the use of that product.

Another group of cases contains a much less stringent test for the consumer. He need not show that a majority would have had the same reaction; he need only show that a significant number of people, an appreciable class, would have had the same reaction.[65] This appreciable class must be greater than one but may be considerably short of a majority. In states following this view, the scope of implied warranties is increased and the number of goods which are non-conforming is greater. The result of these cases is summarized in this sentence:

> To establish a breach of warranty, the plaintiff must show (1) that the product contains a substance or ingredient which has a tendency to affect injuriously an appreciable number of people, though fewer in number than the number of normal buyers, and (2) that he has, in fact, been injured or harmed by the use of the product.[66]

The second requirement must not be overlooked. It is not enough to show that the consumer used the product and suffered the injuries. The causal relation must also be proved. The defective product must have caused the injuries complained of.[67]

One way to summarize American law as to a seller's liability for injuries caused to persons with allergic reactions is to accept at face value the statements which courts have made about their rules. This would require a determination as to whether a particular jurisdiction accepts the "normal reaction" rule or the "appreciable class" rule,

---

64. "[I]f the article could be worn by any normal person without harm, and injury is suffered by the purchaser only because of a supersensitive skin, there is no breach of the implied warranty of reasonable fitness of the article for personal wear." Ross v. Porteous, Mitchell & Braun Co., 136 Me. 118, 122, 3 A.2d 650, 653 (1939). Bonowski v. Revlon, Inc., 251 Iowa 141, 100 N.W.2d 5 (1959) (testimony that 1 in 5 million had a similar allergy); Casagrande v. F. W. Woolworth Co., 340 Mass. 552, 165 N.E.2d 109 (1960) (also discussion of "significant number" test); Bradt v. Hollaway, 242 Mass. 446, 136 N.E.2d 254 (1922). Cases are collected in Annot., 26 A.L.R.2d 963 (1952).

65. Corneliuson v. Arthur Drug Stores, Inc., 153 Conn. 134, 214 A.2d 676 (1965); Reynolds v. Sun Ray Drug Co., 135 N.J.L. 475, 52 A.2d 666 (Ct.Err. & App.1947); Esborg v. Bailey Drug Co., 61 Wash.2d 347, 378 P.2d 298 (1963). But cf. Scanlon v. Food Crafts, Inc., 2 Conn.Cir. 3, 193 A.2d 610 (1963).

66. Crotty v. Shartenberg's-New Haven, Inc., 147 Conn. 460, 467, 162 A.2d 513, 516 (1960).

67. Landers v. Safeway Stores, 172 Or. 116, 139 P.2d 788 (1943); F. W. Woolworth v. Garza, 390 S.W.2d 90 (Tex. Civ.App.1965).

and the answer to a particular problem would then turn on which jurisdiction's law was applicable to the facts.   However, when the facts
and holdings of those cases which have said that the "normal reaction" rule is being applied are analyzed, much of the difference between
the rules disappears.   Those cases involve situations in which the plaintiff either failed to prove that the product caused the injury or failed
to show that his reaction was anything other than unique.   Thus, the
facts of these cases would produce the same result—no liability—under
the test of the second rule.   There is, therefore, considerable doubt as
to whether there are two rules and, since the more recent cases have
talked in terms of the "appreciable number" approach, this would now
appear to be the prevailing view in determining the non-conformity
of goods.[68]

Perhaps these cases can be adequately explained on the basis of
foreseeability, only this foreseeability centers on injury to this plaintiff.   That explanation could be framed along the following lines.   As
long as the number of persons who would be injured by a product is
extremely small, the manufacturer and seller cannot reasonably foresee
the existence of such a group.   When the number who might be injured
is increased to an appreciable portion of the population, that number
merits protection even at the expense of the majority—and the manufacturer and seller can be held reasonably to have foreseen its existence.[69]

The difficulty with this explanation is that it states the conclusion as to liability in terms of another conclusion (foreseeability).[70]
Even the unique consumer can be "foreseen" in the sense that medical
science can predict his existence.   There are few ingredients for which
there is not someone somewhere with an allergic reaction to them.   If
that person could recover damages (and the damages could be substantial if the allergic reaction is violent) solely on a showing that *he* suffered an injury from the product, many products would be removed
from the market even though they are beneficial to the vast majority,
or their price might be increased to an almost prohibitive level.   The
problem, therefore, is not one of foreseeability (a result is foreseeable
if a court holds it to be so), but it is a determination of what risks ought
to be shifted to the seller.   This involves a policy decision as to the
point at which the good to the public through safer products outweighs
the cost to the public through higher prices and perhaps even unavail-

68.   Howard v. Avon Products, Inc., 155
      Colo. 444, 395 P.2d 1007 (1964).

69.   *E. g.*, Vanoven v. Hardin, 233 Ark.
      301, 344 S.W.2d 340 (1961).

70.   § 82 *supra.*

ability of the goods. As long as the class which might be injured is insignificant in size, the gains to the public in having the product are paramount.

Approaching the cases in this manner explains another phenomenon of court decisions. Suppose that the manufacturer can predict that an appreciable number of persons may be injured by the use of the product. Is it necessary that the product be removed from the market to protect the seller from warranty liability? Clearly not. The seller may escape liability through a properly prepared disclaimer.[71] If the seller gives an adequate warning of the dangers that might be involved if the product is used by one with abnormal allergic reactions or if he includes directions for a satisfactory patch test, his chances of liability will be considerably lessened.[72] If the allergic consumer uses the product despite these warnings, it can be held that he has "assumed the risk" of his injuries—another way of stating that the majority can continue to enjoy the product without paying for injuries which the allergic user could have avoided. These ideas are captured in the use of the word "innocently" in the following statement:

> [I]t would appear reasonable to require of a plaintiff, seeking to establish a breach of such [implied] warranties, when confronted with the defense of allergy or hypersensitivity, that such plaintiff produce substantial evidence which, with reasonable inferences therefrom, will support findings that: (a) the product involved contains a harmful ingredient; (b) such ingredient is harmful to a reasonably foreseeable and appreciable class or number of potential users of the product; and (c) plaintiff has been innocently injured in the use of the product in the manner and for the purpose intended.[73]

Even with the rule thus restated, there are still a number of questions to be answered. These center primarily on how the size of the appreciable class is to be determined. One court has held that four to five percent of the population is an "appreciable class" for the goods

---

71. UCC § 2–316. As to the effect of disclaimers on the tort action, see Helene Curtis Indus., Inc. v. Pruitt, 385 F.2d 841 (5th Cir. 1967), cert. denied 391 U.S. 913, 88 S.Ct. 1806, 20 L. Ed.2d 652 (1968); Vandermark v. Ford Motor Co., 61 Cal.2d 256, 391 P.2d 168, 37 Cal.Rptr. 896 (1964); Restatement (Second) of Torts § 395, Comment *k* (1965).

72. Wright v. Carter Products, Inc., 244 F.2d 53 (2d Cir. 1957), Barton v. Myers, 1 Mich.App. 460, 136 N.W.2d 776 (1965); Noel, *Products Defective Because of Inadequate Directions or Warnings*, 23 S.W.L.J. 256 (1969); Dillard and Hart, *Product Liability: Directions For Use and the Duty to Warn*, 41 Va.L.Rev. 145 (1955). For tort liability, see Restatement (Second) of Torts § 401 (1965). As to the duty to warn a bystander injured by a bolt picked up and thrown by a power lawn mower, see Sills v. Massey-Ferguson, Inc., 296 F.Supp. 776 (N.D.Ind.1969).

73. Esborg v. Bailey Drug Co., 61 Wash. 2d 347, 358, 378 P.2d 298, 304 (1963).

there involved (hat bands);[74] whether it can be a smaller group remains to be determined. The effect of the patch test on determining the size of the group has not yet been explored by court opinions. There are some people who are not allergic to the small doses involved in a patch test, yet are allergic when the product is used over a larger area of the body. If the consumer is injured when the product is used over the larger body area (or in its larger quantity), is the appreciable class determined by the number who would have suffered harmful effects after having taken the patch test or by the number who would have been injured without taking the test? Logic points to the former number—which should be smaller in size and, therefore, less likely to be an "appreciable" number of the population—if this question is considered as an attempt to balance the product's good against the costs of making it safer. Finally, the lawyer will have many trial problems in proving the number who are allergic to the ingredients which harmed the plaintiff. In most cases, he will have to rely on expert medical testimony to establish his case.[75]

§ 84. Non-conformity—Assumption of Risk

Courts have long disagreed as to whether contributory negligence on the part of the consumer [76] or his assumption of certain risks [77] would amount to a defense to a suit for breach of warranty. The Code does not deal directly with this problem. Therefore, this disagreement can continue in spite of the Code's adoption and in spite of the doctrine of strict tort liability.[78]

As far as sales law is concerned, the problem centers on the risks which were shifted by the parties' agreement. To the extent

---

74. Zirpola v. Adam Hat Stores, Inc., 122 N.J.L. 21, 4 A.2d 73 (Ct.Err. & App.1939). One out of 500 was not enough in Jacquot v. Wm. Filene Sons Co., 337 Mass. 312, 149 N.E.2d 635 (1958).

75. These problems are discussed in Note, 46 Cornell L.Q. 465 (1961).

76. Denying contributory negligence as a defense: Kassouf v. Lee Bros., Inc., 209 Cal.App.2d 568, 26 Cal.Rptr. 276 (1962) (food); Simmons v. Wichita Coca-Cola Bottling Co., 181 Kan. 35, 309 P.2d 633 (1957); Jarnot v. Ford Motor Co., 191 Pa.Super. 422, 156 A. 2d 568 (1959). Allowing contributory negligence as a defense: Nelson v. Anderson, 245 Minn. 445, 72 N.W.2d 861 (1955); Schneider v. Suhrmann's South Temple Meat Co., 8 Utah 2d 35, 327 P.2d 822 (1958). For the diffi-

culties involved in distinguishing contributory negligence from proximate cause, see Dallison v. Sears, Roebuck & Co., 313 F.2d 343 (10th Cir. 1962).

77. Brown v. Chapman, 304 F.2d 149 (9th Cir. 1962); Barefield v. LaSalle Coca-Cola Bottling Co., 370 Mich. 1, 120 N.W.2d 786 (1963); Poretz v. R. H. Macy & Co., 119 N.Y.S.2d 211 (Sup. Ct.1953) (dealing with injuries from apparent hazards). See Annot., 4 A. L.R.3d 501 (1965).

78. The traditional distinction between contributory negligence (failure to discover the defect) and assumption of risk (knowledge of the defect, but use of the product anyway) is contained in countless cases. E. g., Kleppe v. Prawl, 181 Kan. 590, 313 P.2d 227 (1957).

that the buyer should reasonably understand at the time of the sale that he is buying the goods without a warranty that those goods are safe for use, he is assuming the risk of injury suffered through the use of those goods.[79] The easy case is the dynamite which explodes in the way that it was intended to explode and injures the purchaser who was standing too close at the time of detonation. One way to explain the result (no liability on the part of the seller of the dynamite) is to say that the purchaser assumed the risk of this kind of injury; another way is to hold that the goods were in fact conforming in that they did the job for which they were intended—a job which involved some hazard of injury. Likewise, a purchaser who bought an automobile knowing that it had no brakes (or that it would not float on water) cannot recover for injuries suffered when he drove the automobile into a tree because the brakes would not stop the automobile (or into a lake because he wanted to see if the automobile would float). The harder cases involve such questions as to whether the purchaser has assumed the risk of injury when he has failed to follow a recommended patch test before using a product, when he has failed to follow directions printed on a box in which the product is sold,[80] when he eats food which he has reason to know might be poisoned,[81] or when he continues to use a product after he learns of its capability of harm.[82] Each of these cases presents a question of fact which can be phrased in terms of assumption of risk or in the Code language of conforming goods.

There is another group of Code sections which applies to some of these cases. These sections are found in the part of Article 2 dealing with remedies. They make it clear that a buyer can recover only for the loss which *results* from a breach of warranty.[83] To the extent that a buyer has assumed a risk, a court can justify a holding of no seller liability by saying that the loss *resulted* not from the breach of warranty, but from the user's own carelessness. This much can be said of these Code sections: the concept of cause and effect is sufficiently broad so that a court can allocate loss depending on how it determines the risks to have been shifted by the agreement or conduct of the parties. The doctrine of assumption of risk is a convenient way to express this policy decision.

---

79. *See* UCC § 2–316.

80. Jacobs Pharmacy Co. v. Gipson, 116 Ga.App. 760, 159 S.E.2d 171 (1967).

81. Bronson v. Club Comanche, Inc., 286 F.Supp. 21 (D. Virgin Islands 1968).

82. Poretz v. R. H. Macy & Co., 119 N.Y.S.2d 211 (Sup.Ct.1953). Similar

cases are presented when food contains bones or other items natural to the food but harmful to the eater. This problem was discussed in § 77 *supra*. As to the duty to a bystander who is injured, see Sills v. Massey-Ferguson Co., 296 F.Supp. 776 (N.D. Ind.1969).

83. UCC §§ 2–714, 2–715.

§ 85.   Overlap between Express and Implied Warranties

The Code contains a section dealing with the interpretation of express and implied warranties. The basic principle is that warranties are to be construed as consistent with each other whenever reasonable; when such construction is not reasonable "the intention of the parties shall determine which warranty is dominant."[84] The intention test and the problems involved in construing seemingly inconsistent express warranties have already been discussed.[85]

There are two types of cases which have not been discussed: (1) those situations which involve both the implied warranties of merchantability and fitness for a particular purpose, and (2) those situations which involve both express and implied warranties. The Code's mandate remains the same: these warranties—whether express or implied—are to be construed as cumulative if such construction is reasonable; otherwise the intention of the parties will be controlling.[86] Normally the express and implied warranties will be consistent (and cumulative),[87] but to aid in the solution of those rarer cases in which some inconsistency makes the cumulative construction unreasonable, the Code adds:

> Express warranties displace inconsistent implied warranties other than an implied warranty of fitness for a particular purpose.[88]

The Comments indicate that this rule of construction—as well as the others set out in this section—"are not absolute but may be changed by evidence showing that the conditions which existed at the time of contracting make the construction called for by this section inconsistent or unreasonable."[89]

D.   LIMITATIONS ON AND EXCLUSION OF WARRANTIES

§ 86.   Disclaimers

The law of sales is usually viewed as a specialized branch of the more general law of contracts. This view of sales brings to the subject a number of pre-conceived ideas—ideas such as freedom of contract, unconcern over the adequacy of consideration, the need for assent, and the application of conditions. The traditional view of

---

84. UCC § 2–317.

85. § 72 *supra*.

86. L & N Sales Co. v. Stuski, 188 Pa. Super. 117, 146 A.2d 154 (1958).

87. Vandenberg v. Siter, 204 Pa.Super. 392, 204 A.2d 494 (1964).

88. UCC § 2–317(c).

89. UCC § 2–317, Comment 3.

contracts is that parties are free to work out the terms of their agreement, and courts will do the best they can to make sense out of what the parties did. Since this is the law of contracts, it automatically becomes the law of sales.[90]

Such an approach can explain the warranties in a sales agreement. Express warranties rest on the dickered terms of the parties' "deal." Implied warranties rest on the reasonable expectations of a buyer when nothing was said about the quality of the goods sold.

Disclaimer of warranty coverage springs from the same idea. Freedom of contract means what it says. Parties to an agreement ought to be free to provide that the buyer is purchasing goods without any warranties, express or implied—that he is purchasing the goods in whatever condition they now may happen to be, and without any promises (or only certain specified but limited promises) from the seller as to the quality of those goods. The Code has a section allowing warranties to be excluded or modified.[91] This section (2–316) is divided into four subsections but can be more easily understood if its ideas are grouped under three headings:

1. The disclaiming of express warranties.[92]

2. The disclaiming of implied warranties.[93]

3. The limitation of remedies for breach of warranty.[94]

These ideas are discussed in the following sections of this text, but before moving to the detailed analysis of the problems involved, a general overview of the results of recent cases may help explain the direction in which the law of sales may be moving. Under the early notions of *caveat emptor* the seller was allowed to sell his wares in almost any condition as long as he was not fraudulent or did not make what today would be called an express warranty as to their quality.[95] Modern cases take quite a different approach. Warranties are implied from the nature of the sale; express warranties are found in words and acts which before would have been condoned under the rubric of "puffing" or sales talk. Further, it is

90. UCC § 1–103. This Code section is discussed in § 32 *supra*.

91. UCC § 2–316.

92. UCC § 2–316(1), discussed in § 87 *supra*.

93. UCC § 2–316(2) and (3), discussed in § 88 *infra*.

94. UCC § 2–316(4), discussed in § 89 *infra*.

95. § 54 *supra*. That section of the text shows that warranty suits were recognized before assumpsit could be viewed as a separate cause of action. Thus, the idea that warranties *must* rest on contract law (as was assumed in the opening paragraphs of this section of the text) is open to question. *See* Lonzrick v. Republic Steel Corp., 6 Ohio St.2d 227, 218 N.E.2d 185 (1966).

becoming increasingly difficult to disclaim those warranties. Using ideas of inconspicuousness and unconscionability, courts are striking down an increasing number of disclaimer clauses. Legislatures and governmental agencies are continually adding to the list of products which must meet certain minimum standards of quality before they can be sold to the public. It may be that in the not-too-distant future ideas of warranties and disclaimers will be completely removed from the area of contract law, and sellers will make certain warranties as to minimum quality and safety just because they have sold the goods—with no opportunity to disclaim those warranties. With certain products we may already be at this point.[96]

§ 87.   Disclaimers—Express Warranties

Subsection (1) of section 2–316 provides:

> Words or conduct relevent to the creation of an express warranty and words or conduct tending to negate or limit warranty shall be construed wherever reasonable as consistent with each other; but subject to the provisions of this Article on parol or extrinsic evidence (Section 2–202) negation or limitation is inoperative to the extent that such construction is unreasonable.

This subsection serves two principal functions. First, it provides a rule of interpretation for agreements which contain words and conduct which both create and negate (or limit) express warranties. The Code's command is to interpret these words and conduct as consistent whenever reasonable. An example of the application of this portion of section 2–316(1) is found when a writing describes goods in one clause and then provides in another clause that the seller has made no express warranties. In such a case it is reasonable to assume that the disclaimer was meant to apply to qualities which were not implicit in the description.

The second function of section 2–316(1) is to state a rule of construction when all attempts to interpret the agreement as consistent have failed. When such an impasse has been reached, the express warranty is given precedence over the disclaimer—subject to the limited operation of the Code's parol evidence rule. These problems have already been discussed and are summarized here only to present a complete analysis of the Code's disclaimer clause.[97]

96. An example may be the automobile industry. Larsen v. General Motors Corp., 391 F.2d 495 (8th Cir. 1968), discussed in § 82 *supra*. For a case contrary to the "predictions" in the text, see Marshall v. Murray Oldsmo- bile Co., 207 Va. 472, 154 S.E.2d 172 (1967).

97. Problems of interpretation and construction of the parties' agreement are discussed in § 71 *supra*; the appli-

Perhaps the best way to summarize the impact of section 2–316
(1) is this: there is only one way for the seller to be certain that
there are no express warranties in a sale—and that is not to use
words or conduct which would be relevant to the creation of an express warranty.[98] Although such advice is most difficult to put into
practice, a seller ought not affirm a fact or make a promise about
the goods, accept a description of the goods, or have anything to do
with a sample or model of the goods.[99] If he has done any of these
things, a later attempt to limit or negate the express warranty which
was created is "inoperative." The seller's only hope in such a case
would be to show that the buyer understood, before the contract,
that the grounds on which an express warranty might rest were withdrawn by the seller.[1] In such a case, the words or conduct which
otherwise would create an express warranty will not become a "part
of the basis of the bargain" between the buyer and seller, and no
warranty will have been created—not because it was negated by
section 2–316 but because the requirements of the express warranty
section (2–313) were not met.[2]

§ 88. Disclaimers—Implied Warranties

The Code provides three methods by which implied warranties
may be modified or excluded. These are: (1) by the buyer's examining the goods or refusing to examine them; (2) by a course of dealing,
course of performance or usage of trade; or (3) by certain language.[3]
These are discussed below.

EXAMINATION OF THE GOODS

The Code provides that:

> [W]hen the buyer before entering into the contract has ex-
> amined the goods or the sample or model as fully as he desired
> or has refused to examine the goods there is no implied war-
> ranty with regard to defects which an examination ought in
> the circumstances to have revealed to him . . ..[4]

cation of the parol evidence rule to
express warranties is outlined in § 69
supra.

98. Berk v. Gordon Johnson Co., 232
F.Supp. 682 (E.D.Mich.1964); Walcott
& Steele, Inc. v. Carpenter, 246 Ark.
93, 436 S.W.2d 820 (1969).

99. UCC § 2–313.

1. Admiral Oasis Hotel Corp. v. Home
Gas Indus., Inc., 68 Ill.App.2d 297,

216 N.E.2d 282 (1966); Diepeveen v.
Larry Vogt, Inc., 27 N.J.Super. 254,
99 A.2d 329 (App.Div.1953).

2. §§ 66–68 *supra.*

3. UCC § 2–316.

4. UCC § 2–316(3) (b).

Several points in this subsection deserve mention. First, the subsection does not purport to provide a method by which express warranties are to be limited or excluded; it refers only to implied warranties. Nevertheless, an examination might prevent an express warranty from arising. Express warranties are created by some affirmation of fact or promise made by the seller, or by a description, sample, or model of the goods—providing that at least one of these events has become a "part of the basis of the bargain" between the parties. An examination or a refusal to examine may, in a particular case, indicate that no part of the bargain rested on any statement made by the seller, or on a description which was made, or on any sample or model which was shown. If so, but only if so, will there be no express warranty.[5] In the more usual case the examining buyer will have purchased both on the strength of his examination and on statements made by the seller (or on descriptions, samples, or models). In these cases the *"part of the basis of the bargain"* test has been met, and an express warranty accompanies the sale.[6]

Second, only those defects which an examination ought in the circumstances to have revealed to the buyer will be excluded from implied warranty coverage. A warranty against latent defects will still be implied if the remaining conditions of warranty are met.

Third, it is only an *examination* or a refusal to *examine* which limits or excludes implied warranties. The concept of examination must be distinguished from the Code's concept of inspection. Inspection occurs most frequently after the goods have been delivered to the buyer pursuant to a prior contract for their sale.[7] Its purpose is to aid the buyer in determining whether the delivered goods conform to the contract—whether the buyer must accept and pay for the goods or whether he may reject them. An examination, on the other hand, occurs (if at all) before the contract has been entered into, and determines the scope of the contractual obligations of the parties—that is, it determines just what it is that the buyer purchased.

Fourth, the "refusal to examine" portion of this subsection requires a "refusal." It is not sufficient that the buyer have had an opportunity to examine and have failed to do so. The seller must demand that the buyer examine and the buyer must "refuse" to do so.[8]

Finally, the examination need not be of the goods. It is sufficient if the buyer examines a sample of those goods. Therefore, if the buyer,

---

5. §§ 64–73 *supra.*

6. General Electric Co. v. United States Dynamics, Inc., 403 F.2d 933 (1st Cir. 1968). Additional cases are cited and discussed in § 68 *supra.*

7. Inspection is covered by UCC §§ 2–512 and 2–513; examination by UCC § 2–316(3) (b). Inspection is discussed in §§ 120–24 *infra.*

8. UCC § 2–316, Comment 8.

prior to entering into a contract, has examined a sample of the goods which he is about to purchase, there are no implied warranties as to defects which that examination ought to have revealed to him.[9]

Course of Dealing, Course of Performance, and Usage of Trade

The meaning of these concepts is discussed elsewhere in this text.[10] Their application to disclaimers rests on the notion that each of them aids in determining the meaning of the parties' agreement. The language that the parties used in expressing their agreement is apt to have been chosen in the background of any usage of the trade in which they are engaged or of any prior course of dealing between those parties. Further, a course of performance of this contract is evidence of how the parties intended the words they used. To the extent that any one of these indicates that the parties intended to limit or exclude implied warranties, that intention will be given effect.

Language of the Parties

The basic idea here is the same as in the prior paragraph: since warranties arise out of agreement, implied warranties will be limited or excluded to the extent that the parties have agreed to the limitation or exclusion.[11] The difficulty arises in determining just when the parties have *agreed* to limit or exclude the implied warranties. The Code suggests two methods by which this agreement may be shown but, before discussing these methods, the Code's approach to the concept of "agreement" must be summarized. The approach has been applied to disclaimers, and court decisions can be understood only against this background.

An agreement is the bargain of the parties in fact as found in the language they used, the circumstances surrounding the use of that language, and (when applicable) any course of dealing, course of performance, and usage of trade.[12] If a writing is involved, this is excellent evidence of their agreement. It is, however, not the sole evidence. To the extent permissible under the Code's parol evidence rule,[13] all of the circumstances surrounding the execution of that writing will

---

9. Sylvia Coal Co. v. Mercury Coal & Coke Co., 151 W.Va. 818, 156 S.E.2d 1 (1967); Appeal of Reeves Sound-craft Corp., 2 UCC Rep. 210 (Armed Services Bd. of Contract Appeal, 1964).

10. §§ 50–52 *supra.*

11. "Disclaimers and limitations of certain warranties and remedies are matters for bargaining." State *ex rel.* Western Seed Production Corp. v. Campbell, 250 Or. 262, 442 P.2d 215, 217 (1968).

12. UCC § 1–201(3), discussed in § 47 *supra.*

13. UCC § 2–202, discussed in § 53 *supra.*

also be considered to determine the parties' bargain. Finally, the requirement that the contract, or any clause of the contract, not be unconscionable [14] cuts across all of Article 2. Therefore, simply because the seller included a printed disclaimer clause in his acknowledgment or in the form signed by the buyer is not conclusive on the question of whether that clause was a part of the parties' bargain. If its inclusion unfairly surprises the buyer or amounts to oppression, the disclaimer clause will be stricken or limited to avoid any unconscionable result. These ideas apply to all clauses in the writing; it is not surprising that courts have applied them to what may be the most important clause for the disappointed buyer—the creation and exclusion of warranties.

With these ideas as a background, the Code provides that there are two types of language which may be used to exclude or modify implied warranties. The first is the common expressions of "as is," "with all faults," or similar language which—and this is the important test—"calls the buyer's attention to the exclusion of warranties and makes it plain that there is no implied warranty." [15] The idea with the use of these expressions is that there are certain statements made by sellers which most buyers would normally understand as limiting or excluding implied warranties. If the seller uses these words and has no reason to know that this particular buyer does not understand their import, the implied warranties of merchantability and fitness for purpose will have been disclaimed.[16] These words will have alerted the buyer that he is buying the goods without warranties and supposedly the parties will have taken this into account in setting the price.[17] A court ought not later increase the contractual obligations of the seller (by adding a warranty) when the goods prove defective any more than it should increase the contractual obligations of the buyer (by increasing the price) when the goods prove not to be defective. The parties have distributed the risks of defectiveness and the risk should be left where the parties placed it.

There is a second method by which the seller may limit or exclude implied warranties. This is contained in the following subsection:

Subject to subsection (3), to exclude or modify the implied warranty of merchantability or any part of it the lan-

14. UCC § 2–302, discussed in § 44 *supra.*

15. UCC § 2–316(3) (a). *Cf.* Hull-Dobbs, Inc. v. Mallicoat, 57 Tenn.App. 100, 415 S.W.2d 344 (1966), where the words "in its present condition" were used.

16. Chamberlain v. Bob Matick Chevrolet, Inc., 4 Conn.Cir. 685, 239 A.2d 42 (1967); Belvision, Inc. v. General Electric Co., 46 Misc.2d 952, 260 N.Y.S. 2d 579 (App.Term.1965).

17. Delta Air Lines, Inc. v. Douglas Aircraft Co., 238 Cal.App.2d 95, 47 Cal.Rptr. 518 (1965). Annot., 24 A.L. R.3d 465 (1969).

guage must mention merchantability and in case of a writing must be conspicuous, and to exclude or modify any implied warranty of fitness the exclusion must be by a writing and conspicuous. Language to exclude all implied warranties of fitness is sufficient if it states, for example, that "There are no warranties which extend beyond the description on the face hereof." [18]

This subsection appears to provide sellers with an easy way to rid themselves of unwanted implied warranties. All they need do is to adopt the suggested language in their forms and add a phrase that states that there is no warranty of merchantability.[19] Apparently, this language, which would not be noticed by many non-merchant buyers, would make the sale one which carried no implied warranties.

The Code has not generally had this effect. Courts have worked with two ideas to limit the force of the printed disclaimer. The first is built into the quoted subsection: the written disclaimer must be "conspicuous." This word is defined as follows:

> "Conspicuous": A term or clause is conspicuous when it is so written that a reasonable person against whom it is to operate ought to have noticed it. A printed heading in capitals (as: NON–NEGOTIABLE BILL OF LADING) is conspicuous. Language in the body of a form is "conspicuous" if it is in larger or other contrasting type or color. But in a telegram any stated term is "conspicuous." Whether a term or clause is "conspicuous" or not is for decision by the court.[20]

Accordingly it has been held that a printed disclaimer is not conspicuous when it is a part of a clause entitled "warranty," is printed in the same size and color of type as the remaining parts of the form, or is printed on the reverse side of a pad of forms.[21] In these cases there is

---

18. UCC § 2–316(2).

19. Construction Aggregates Corp. v. Hewitt-Robins, Inc., 404 F.2d 505 (7th Cir. 1968), cert. denied 395 U.S. 921, 89 S.Ct. 1774, 23 L.Ed.2d 238 (1969); Cox Motor Car Co. v. Castle, 402 S.W. 2d 429 (Ky.1966); Marshall v. Murray Oldsmobile Co., 207 Va. 972, 154 S.E. 2d 140 (1967).

20. UCC § 1–201(10).

21. E. g., Marion Power Shovel Co. v. Huntsman, 246 Ark. 149, 437 S.W.2d 784 (1969); Hunt v. Perkins Mach.

Co., 352 Mass. 535, 226 N.E.2d 228 (1967); Zabriskie Chevrolet, Inc. v. Smith, 99 N.J.Super. 441, 240 A.2d 195 (L.Div.1968). The Zabriskie case also raises the problem of the disclaimer received as a part of a printed "warranty" long after the contract of sale was entered into. As to this, see also Tiger Motor Co. v. McMurtry, 284 Ala. 283, 224 So.2d 638 (1969); Mack Trucks of Arkansas, Inc. v. Jet Asphalt & Rock Co., 246 Ark. 99, 437 S.W.2d 459 (1969); Admiral Oasis Hotel Corp. v. Home Gas Indus., Inc., 68 Ill.App.2d 297, 216 N.E.2d 282 (1965) Diepeveen v. Larry Vogt, Inc.,

no reason to believe that the reasonable buyer would have noticed the disclaimer; there is no basis for saying that the clause is a part of the parties' *agreement,* or bargain; and to apply it after the goods have proved to be defective would be unfairly to surprise the buyer.

The second idea which has limited the impact of the printed disclaimer is that of unconscionability. Even if the buyer knows of the seller's attempted disclaimer (so that the test of conspicuousness is met), it is still possible that an enforcement of the attempted disclaimer would produce an unconscionable result. This is particularly true in industries in which the form contract between the buyer and seller is as standard as the product which is sold, where the buyer has no opportunity to bargain about the terms of the agreement, and where a purchase of the same article from another seller will involve the same disclaimer. In these cases the entire industry—or a large portion of it—has attempted to seize upon the Code's permissive use of disclaimers to free the industry from troublesome and expensive warranty claims. As could be expected, courts have refused to allow such an attempt.[22] Although it has been argued that the Code section on unconscionability should have no application to disclaimers where the Code spells out specifically how to disclaim the implied warranties,[23] the cases quite properly are using the section on unconscionability to strike the oppressive disclaimer just as it would any other clause. This subject is discussed in greater detail elsewhere in this text.[24]

§ 89. Limitation of Remedies

When a warranty has been successfully disclaimed the buyer has no cause of action for a supposed breach of that warranty. The disclaimer has removed the warranty and the seller is not in de-

27 N.J.Super. 254, 99 A.2d 329 (App. Div.1953). See discussion in § 66 *supra.*

22. The leading case is Henningsen v. Bloomfield Motors, Inc., 32 N.J. 358, 161 A.2d 69 (1960), discussed in § 92 *infra.* Others include Zabriskie Chevrolet, Inc. v. Smith, 99 N.J.Super. 441, 240 A.2d 195 (L.Div.1968); Wilson Trading Corp. v. David Ferguson, Ltd., 23 N.Y.2d 398, 297 N.Y.S.2d 108, 244 N.E.2d 685 (1968).

23. UCC § 2–316(2) does not state that if the mandate of that section is followed, implied warranties are automatically excluded. It states minimum requirements only. Even the last sentence only indicates what *language* is sufficient, leaving open the question

of whether that language is to be a part of the parties' contract. UCC § 1–201(11). Comment 3 to UCC § 2–719 is troublesome when it states that the "seller in all cases is free to disclaim warranties in the manner provided in Section 2–316"—apparently indicating that if the *formalities* of that section are followed, disclaimers will result. Marshall v. Murray Oldsmobile Co., 207 Va. 972, 154 S.E.2d 172 (1967), supports this conclusion. Compare, however, UCC § 2–719(3) which allows limitation of consequential damages if not unconscionable. Certainly, the drafters did not intend that different results could be obtained by drafting under UCC § 2–316 rather than UCC § 2–719.

24. § 44 *supra.*

fault. In this sense, the successful disclaimer has removed all remedies which the buyer would have had without the disclaimer.

There are some instances in which the seller is willing to make warranties but would like to limit the remedies which the buyer would normally have following a default. For example, the seller may not want to leave the determination of damages to later litigation and may prefer, instead, to negotiate a liquidated damage clause.[25] More frequently the seller will attempt to limit the buyer's remedies for a breach of warranty to a repair or replacement of the defective part—and then only if the buyer has brought the defect to the attention of the seller within a certain period of time following the sale. If this clause is effective, the buyer's remedies will be constricted from those which would otherwise have been available following the seller's default.

There is a considerable body of non-Code law on the validity and impact of these clauses.[26] Code cases, however, are controlled by section 2–719. This section provides in part:

> [T]he agreement may provide for remedies in addition to or in substitution for those provided in this Article and may limit or alter the measure of damages recoverable under this Article, as by limiting the buyer's remedies to return of the goods and repayment of the price or to repair and replacement of non-conforming goods or parts. . . .

Notice that this section has application beyond the repair-or-replacement agreement already discussed. It allows both the buyer and the seller to add or substitute remedies and to limit or alter the measure of damages. One use of this section might be to provide the "other proper circumstances" in which the buyer is entitled to specific performance [27] despite the pre-Code reluctance of courts to grant equitable remedies solely because the parties had agreed that such remedies were proper.

Because section 2–719 states rules which apply to both sellers and buyers, a discussion of its impact could have been included in the chapter on remedies. However, its principal application will be with agreements by which the seller has attempted to limit the buyer's remedies following a breach of warranty. In this respect

25. UCC § 2–718(1); Denkin v. Sterner, 10 Pa.D. & C.2d 203 (C.P.1956). The seller's liquidated damages are discussed in § 181 *infra*; the buyer's in § 154 *infra*.

26. Annot., 84 A.L.R.2d 318 (1962). For a Code case applying UCC § 2–719 to limit a buyer's damages, see Wyatt Industries, Inc. v. Publicker Industries, Inc., 420 F.2d 454 (5th Cir. 1969).

27. § 158 *infra*.

the primary use of 2–719 agreements will be similar to that of disclaimer clauses—except that, under section 2–719, *all* remedies are not taken from the buyer. Thus, the operation of section 2–719 was included at this point in the text.

Section 2–719 allows parties to increase or decrease available remedies providing three conditions are met. These are: (1) the variation in remedies must be contained in the parties' agreement; (2) an exclusive or limited remedy must not have failed "of its essential purpose"; and (3) an attempt to limit or exclude consequential damages must not be unconscionable.

The requirement that the agreement contain the alteration of basic Code remedies brings into play those ideas discussed in the prior section of this text. The limitation must be a part of the parties' bargain in fact. If it is contained in a printed clause which was not conspicuous or brought to the buyer's attention, the seller had no reasonable expectation that the buyer understood that his remedies were being restricted to repair and replacement. As such, the clause cannot be said to be a part of the bargain (or agreement) of the parties.[28]

The reference to the essential purpose of a remedy is troublesome. The entire subsection reads as follows:

> Where circumstances cause an exclusive or limited remedy to fail of its essential purpose, remedy may be had as provided in this Act.[29]

Remedies do not have "purposes"—let alone an essential purpose. People have purposes in entering into agreements, but these purposes may differ depending upon whether the buyer or the seller is being considered. If the seller prepared the form which severely limits any remedy which the buyer has in the event of default, it is not unreasonable to believe that the seller's "purpose" was exactly that which is spelled out in the clause. His purpose was that of selling goods and limiting liability for defects later discovered. The buyer's "purpose" may well have been different; he may have wanted the goods and full remedies in the event of a breach. To talk about a purpose—as the Code does—confuses the test which the court should apply in determining whether to enforce the limitation-of-remedies clause. The Comments indicate what the drafters had in mind: "where an apparently fair and reasonable clause because of circumstances fails in its purpose or operates to deprive either

28. Klien v. Asgrow Seed Co., 246 Cal. App.2d 87, 54 Cal.Rptr. 609 (1966) (Code not in effect but court discussed application of Code to facts).

29. UCC § 2–719(2).

party of the substantial value of the bargain, it must give way to the general remedy provisions of this Article.[30]

The clause must have an apparent fairness and reasonableness —that is, appear to be fair and reasonable at the time it was agreed upon by the parties. If it cannot meet this test, the clause is unenforceable. If it does meet this test, the limitation of remedies still will not be effective if later circumstances indicate that the limitation "operates to deprive either party of the substantial value of his bargain." This last phrase is not found in the Code, and a court could conceivably hold that here the Code and the Comments conflict—thus, the Code must prevail.[31] However, courts have not— and undoubtedly will not—reach such a conclusion.[32] The "value of the bargain" test is sound, and it carries into section 2–719 the same ideas which were applied to disclaimers. For example, suppose that a buyer has purchased an automobile and has signed a standard form contract which contained a clause limiting his remedies to a repair or replacement of a defective part. Such a clause will operate fairly and reasonably if the brakes fail at a time when the driver could bring the automobile to a stop without a collision.[33] New brakes can be installed (or the old brakes repaired) and the buyer will have the benefit of his bargain. However, if the brakes fail causing the automobile to be damaged and the buyer injured, repairing the old brakes or installing new brakes deprives the buyer of the value of his bargain. The circumstances of the collision have made what appeared to be a fair and reasonable remedy wholly unfair and unreasonable. In Code terms this clause has failed of its essential purpose, and Code remedies ought to be given this buyer—despite the limitation-of-remedies clause. On the other hand, if the buyer had understood that his warranties were to be limited even if the goods were destroyed or damaged due to a defect in the goods, the limitation of remedies undoubtedly affected the price paid and should be enforced by the court.[34] Even though the results vary in these cases, the test remains the same: what was the parties' bargain and does the limitation of remedies deprive the buyer of that bargain?

---

30. UCC § 2–719, Comment 1.

31. § 6 *supra*.

32. Wilson Trading Corp. v. David Ferguson, Ltd., 23 N.Y.2d 398, 297 N.Y.S. 2d 108, 244 N.E.2d 685 (1968); Vandenberg v. Siter, 204 Pa.Super. 392, 204 A. 2d 494 (1964). For a case involving a failure to replace or repair a defective part, see Cox Motor Car Co. v. Castle, 402 S.W.2d 429 (Ky.1966).

33. *Compare* Wilson v. Scampoli, 228 A.2d 848 (D.C.App.1967) (a case citing UCC § 2–508 but probably resting on UCC § 2–719; see § 105 *infra*), *with* Zabriskie Chevrolet, Inc. v. Smith, 99 N.J.Super. 441, 240 A.2d 195 (L.Div. 1968).

34. Delta Air Lines, Inc. v. Douglas Aircraft Co., 238 Cal.App.2d 95, 47 Cal.Rptr. 518 (1965).

The final Code requirement is that a clause which limits or excludes consequential damages must not be unconscionable. The entire subsection states:

> Consequential damages may be limited or excluded unless the limitation or exclusion is unconscionable. Limitation of consequential damages for injury to the person in the case of consumer goods is prima facie unconscionable but limitation of damages where the loss is commercial is not.[35]

Ideas of unconscionability already developed in this text would apply to this section of the Code.[36]

E. PERSONS PROTECTED

§ 90. Privity of Contract—Users and Consumers

This chapter began with an assertion that many of the problems involved in product liability cases have been clouded by the lawyer's attempt to solve these problems by classifying the factual pattern as either tort or contract.[37] The lawyer is comforted by reasoning that this particular plaintiff ought to win or lose because what *really* is involved is a tort—or a contract. Of course, neither of these is *really* involved. What the legal system faces is a dispute between two parties arising out of a series of events which the Code calls "a transaction in goods." The task of the legal system is to solve that dispute as fairly as it can. When the claim is that the seller caused the plaintiff's injuries through the sale of defective goods, this means determining where the risks of loss from those goods ought to be placed. This question should not be solved by some automatic classification of the factual pattern into a concept invented by lawyers. Instead, the answer to this question in a products liability case ought to turn on the answer to at least these three questions:

> 1. Which parties in the chain of distribution ought to be liable?

---

35. UCC § 2–719(3).

36. Ford Motor Co. v. Tritt, 244 Ark. 883, 890A, 430 S.W.2d 778 (1968); *In re* Granite Mills (Cowen), 29 A.D.2d 303, 287 N.Y.S.2d 765 (1968); §§ 44, 88 *supra* and §§ 103, 153 *infra*.

An agreement limiting the buyer to a return of the purchase price was upheld as one basis for the decision in Dow Corning Corp. v. Capitol Aviation Corp., 411 F.2d 622 (7th Cir. 1969).

37. See the discussion and citations in § 54 *supra*.

2. For what kinds of defects ought those parties be liable?

3. To whom ought this liability extend?

Most of the issues surrounding these questions have now been examined in some detail, but one problem remains: to whom ought this liability extend?

The historical answer to this question has turned, in large measure, on how the factual pattern has been classified. If the sale is viewed as a contract, is it not "logical" that parties to the contract are the only ones who can recover for a default (that is, for defective goods)? A non-party certainly should have no contractual rights against the seller who sold defective goods.[38] If the injury from the sale is classified as a tort, the need for a plaintiff who is a contractual party is not present, but tort concepts of fault, proximate cause, and foreseeability intrude upon the solution. The recent growth of strict liability in tort has been prompted in large part by a desire to combine the contractual notions of liability without fault with the tort notions that the injured party need not be a party to the sales contract.[39]

The 1962 Official Text of the Code took a partial step in the direction of expanding the group of persons who could recover for breach of the seller's warranty and provided in section 2–318:

> A seller's warranty whether express or implied extends to any natural person who is in the family or household of his buyer or who is a guest in his home if it is reasonable to expect that such person may use, consume or be affected by the goods and who is injured in person by breach of the warranty. A seller may not exclude or limit the operation of this section.

---

38. Ballard & Ballard Co. v. Jones, 246 Ala. 478, 21 So.2d 327 (1945); Pelletier v. Dupont, 124 Me. 269, 128 A. 186 (1925); Long v. Flanigan Warehouse Co., 79 Nev. 241, 382 P.2d 399 (1963); Odom v. Ford Motor Co., 230 S.C. 320, 95 S.E.2d 601 (1956).

A mother purchased a new dress as a gift for her daughter; the daughter wore the dress and was burned when it caught fire; and the daughter sued the seller, with one count in warranty, evidently alleging that the goods were highly inflammable. The seller's demurrer was sustained. "The implied warranty imposed by law does not run with the article sold, and only the purchaser may recover for a breach of warranty." R. H. Macy & Co. v. Vest, 111 Ga.App. 85, 86, 140 S.E.2d 491, 492 (1965).

The author is not serious about the "certainly" in the text. The textual statement was made to emphasize the fallacy of the contract-tort distinction.

39. Lack of privity is not a defense to strict liability cases. Schipper v. Levitt & Sons, 44 N.J. 70, 207 A.2d 314 (1965); Santor v. A & M Karagheusian, Inc., 44 N.J. 52, 207 A.2d 305 (1965); Darryl v. Ford Motor Co., 440 S.W.2d 630 (Tex.1969); Dippel v. Sciano, 37 Wis.2d 443, 155 N.W.2d 55 (1967). Nor need notice be given the seller. McCormack v. Hankscraft Co., 278 Minn. 322, 154 N.W.2d 488 (1967), 281 Minn. 571, 161 N.W.2d 523 (1968).

The step was meant to be only partial. There was no thought that this section (2–318) was to set the maximum boundaries for the group of third parties who could recover when injured by defective goods. The Code had set the minimum coverage, and further development even as late as 1964, was to come through case law.[40]

Nevertheless, many courts have read section 2–318 as if it attempted to state for once and for all the entire group of non-parties who would be allowed to recover for breach of express and implied warranties.[41] A nephew living next door was held to be in the "family" of the buyer, but the court intimated that a nephew that lived across the country might not be.[42] Whether an employee is in the business "family" of the employer is a question on which courts have divided,[43] sometimes with surprising results. For example, an employee who personally purchased champagne for his employer (a hotel) was allowed to recover from the seller when the champagne bottle exploded,[44] but an employee who did not make the purchase was denied recovery from the seller for injuries sustained from an exploding bottle of soda water.[45] Although a guest in the buyer's home is specifically covered by section 2–318, a guest in the buyer's automobile is not.[46] Bystanders have had a difficult time showing the requisite privity, but have been successful in a few cases.[47] Further, some courts have drawn a distinction between economic losses and personal injuries.[48] All in all,

40. In Report No. 2 of the Permanent Editorial Board for the Uniform Commercial Code 39–40 (1965) the Board rejected an amendment to UCC § 2–318 which would have abolished privity (as had been done at that time in the Virginia and Wyoming versions of the Code). As pointed out later in this text, the proposed amendment (as alternatives to UCC § 2–318) was made two years later.

41. E. g., Myers v. Council Mfg. Co., 276 F.Supp. 541 (W.D.Ark.1967); Galanek v. Howard Johnson, Inc., 24 Mass.App.Dec. 134 (1962); State ex rel. Western Seed Corp. v. Campbell, 250 Or. 262, 442 P.2d 215 (1968), cert. denied 393 U.S. 1093, 89 S.Ct. 862, 21 L.Ed.2d 784 (1969).

42. Miller v. Preitz, 422 Pa. 383, 221 A. 2d 320 (1966), overruled on another point Kassab v. Central Soya, 432 Pa. 217, 246 A.2d 848 (1968).

43. Speed Fastners, Inc. v. Newsom, 382 F.2d 395 (10th Cir. 1967); Delta Oxygen Co. v. Scott, 238 Ark. 534, 383 S.W.2d 885 (1964); Haley v. Allied

Chem. Corp., 353 Mass. 325, 231 N.E. 2d 549 (1967); Nederostek v. Endicott-Johnson Shoe Co., 415 Pa. 136, 202 A.2d 72 (1964).

44. Yentzer v. Taylor Wine Co., 414 Pa. 272, 199 A.2d 463 (1964).

45. Hochgertel v. Canada Dry Corp., 409 Pa. 610, 187 A.2d 575 (1963).

46. Marcus v. Spada Bros. Auto Service, 41 Pa.D. & C.2d 794 (C.P.1967).

47. Mitchell v. Miller, 26 Conn.Supp. 142, 214 A.2d 694 (Super.Ct.1965); Kuschy v. Norris, 25 Conn.Supp. 383, 206 A.2d 275 (Super.Ct.1964); Piercefield v. Remington Arms Co., 375 Mich. 85, 133 N.W.2d 129 (1965).

48. Seely v. White Motor Co., 63 Cal.2d 9, 403 P.2d 145, 45 Cal.Rptr. 17 (1965); Price v. Gatlin, 241 Or. 315, 405 P.2d 502 (1965). Contra Santor v. A & M Karagheusian, Inc., 44 N.J. 52, 207 A. 2d 305 (1965); Inglis v. American Motors Corp., 3 Ohio St.2d 132, 209 N.E. 2d 583 (1965).

an amazing body of case law has been built around section 2–318.[49] It is not surprising that some courts have turned to strict liability in tort to reach what those courts believe to be sensible results.

There was no need to leave the Code and its comprehensive scheme of solving product liability problems. The courts could have accepted the invitation of the drafters and have used section 2–318 only as a minimum coverage, protecting others when they merited protection.[50] Some state legislatures have deviated from the 1962 Official Text by specifically expanding the group protected by Code warranties.[51]

In 1966 the Permanent Editorial Board for the Uniform Commercial Code recognized the growing case law and the lead taken by several legislatures. The Board recommended two optional amendments to the 1962 version of 2–318 set out above. Those amendments are:

Second alternative:

A seller's warranty whether express or implied extends to any natural person who may reasonably be expected to use, consume or be affected by the goods and who is injured in person by breach of the warranty. A seller may not exclude or limit the operation of this section.

Third alternative:

A seller's warranty whether express or implied extends to any person who may reasonably be expected to use, consume or be affected by the goods and who is injured by breach of the warranty. A seller may not exclude or limit the operation of this section with respect to injury to the person of an individual to whom the warranty extends.

Amendments to the Comments state that the "second alternative is designed for states where the case law has already developed further [than the present version of section 2–318] and for those that desire to expand the class of beneficiaries. The third alternative goes further, following the trend of modern decisions as indicated by Restate-

---

49. Guest of a purchaser in a restaurant, Bronson v. Club Commanche, Inc., 286 F.Supp. 21 (D. Virgin Islands 1968); Galanek v. Howard Johnson, Inc., 24 Mass.App.Dec. 134 (1962) (guest is not within coverage of UCC § 2–318). Subpurchasers have had a difficult time recovering. Myers v. Council Mfg. Corp., 276 F.Supp. 541 (W.D.Ark.1967); see § 91 infra.

50. E. g., Speed Fastners, Inc. v. Newsom, 382 F.2d 395 (10th Cir.1967);

Dealers Transp. Co. v. Battery Distrib. Co., 402 S.W.2d 441 (Ky.1965); Dippel v. Sciano, 37 Wis.2d 443, 155 N.W.2d 55 (1967). As to the Code's notice requirements, see §§ 139–45 infra.

51. E. g., Finocchiaro v. Ward Baking Co., — R.I. —, 241 A.2d 619 (1968). UCC § 2–318 was omitted from the Code as enacted in California and Utah.

ment of Torts (Second) § 402A . . . in extending the rule beyond injuries to the person." [52]

The drafters of the Code have indicated their intention to abolish the older notions of privity of contract and to substitute, in its place, a test of whether the person who was injured by the breach of warranty "may reasonably be expected to use, consume or be affected by the goods." This does not mean that this particular person (Ben Buyer, Sam Smith, or whoever was injured) must have been foreseen by the seller. It is sufficient that the injured person is a member of a class of persons who could reasonably be expected to be affected by the goods. For example, a hair lotion may be made for use by professional beauticians only, and be clearly marked to this effect. If a bottle of this lotion is used by someone who is not a professional beautician and that person is injured by the lotion, either of the above alternatives might prevent that person from recovering warranty damages from the seller of the lotion. The problem would be whether the seller could reasonably expect non-professionals to acquire and use the lotion.[53]

Legislatures can and should compel the abolition of privity doctrines in warranty cases by adoption of one of the two alternatives to section 2–318—preferably the third alternative. However, even the 1962 Official Text can be read to reach this result and, fortunately, most courts are reading the Code in this manner.

§ 91. Privity of Contract—Manufacturers

The prior section considered what some courts call "horizontal privity." There is another type of privity problem which has been discussed in several cases and which is called "vertical privity." The difference between these two types of problems can be described in this way: a manufacturer sells his goods to a wholesaler who sells them to a retailer; the retailer sells those goods to a consumer who uses them or gives them to some third party who uses them. As goods are moving "down" the distributive chain from manufacturer to consumer, the contractual relationships (or sales) are "vertical." When they are placed in the hands of the ultimate purchaser, they have left the commercial distributive chain and the connection between the ultimate purchaser and the person who was injured by their use can be described as "horizontal." [54] For horizontal privity

---

52. Report No. 3, Permanent Editorial Board for the Uniform Commercial Code 14 (1967).

53. *See* Helene Curtis Indus., Inc. v. Pruitt, 385 F.2d 841 (5th Cir. 1967), *cert. denied* 391 U.S. 913, 88 S.Ct. 1806, 20 L.Ed.2d 652 (1968).

54. See the concurring and dissenting opinion of Mr. Justice Jones in Miller v. Preitz, 422 Pa. 383, 398–413, 221 A.2d 320, 328–35 (1966).

the injured party is trying to place himself in the position of the buyer and take advantage of warranties made to the buyer; for vertical privity the buyer (or the one in his place) is attempting to take advantage of warranties made by those who did not "sell" to the buyer.

A moment's thought will convince even the skeptic that the goods have moved neither vertically nor horizontally, and that this method of describing privity problems is only a graphic way of indicating the different function which goods have in commerce. With vertical privity, goods are the subject of several sales to become available for their ultimate use; with horizontal privity, those goods are being used by the public usually for the purpose for which they were manufactured.

The problem of vertical privity under the Code arises in this way: all of the sections dealing with warranties of quality relate to "sellers"; [55] the Code defines a seller as one who sells or contracts to sell goods; [56] and a sale consists in the "passing of title from the seller to the buyer for a price." [57] Thus, the manufacturer sells to the wholesaler, the wholesaler to the retailer, and the retailer to the buyer. Each of these is a separate sale and, arguably, creates warranties only to the purchaser at that sale and to those included within section 2–318. The manufacturer's warranties would, under this argument, be made to the wholesaler (note the reference to "his" buyer in section 2–318) and to those who are guests in "his"—the wholesaler's—home. Since the person ultimately injured by the goods fits none of these categories, the injured party would have no cause of action against the manufacturer or, by like reasoning, against the wholesaler. The injured party would be limited to an action against the retailer who would have to proceed up the distributive chain for reimbursement.[58] Not only might the need for "vertical privity" produce multiple lawsuits, but it could also cause difficulties if one of the sellers in the vertical chain of privity turned out to be insolvent.

55. UCC §§ 2–313, 2–314, and 2–315.

56. UCC § 2–103(1) (d).

57. UCC § 2–106(1).

58. These could be separate suits with problems of conflicting findings of fact in the separate suits, or (where permitted by state law) a third-party action could be used by the defendant to bring the manufacturer into the litigation. See Rule 14, Fed.R. Civ.P. The third-party action would require that the manufacturer be subject to the jurisdiction of the state in which the defendant is being sued. The defendant-seller could, in the alternative, use the vouching-in procedures of UCC § 2–607(5). For possible constitutional limitations on UCC § 2–607(5), see Comment, *Constitutional Limitations on Vouching*, 118 U.Pa. L.Rev. 237 (1969).

Some courts have read the Code to have this limited meaning in granting warranty protection.[59] Such a reading is not required nor was it intended by the drafters. One of the Comments states that section 2–318 "is neutral and is not intended to enlarge or restrict the developing case law on whether the seller's warranties, given to his buyer who resells, extend to other persons in the distributive chain." [60] The drafters indicated in this sentence that they did not intend to take a position on the need for vertical privity, but were leaving this problem to case law. Therefore, the Code ought not be quoted to require a need for privity of contract between the manufacturer and the person who is injured by a defect in the goods.

Most of the recent cases have discarded any need for vertical privity. They rest on the premises that it is the manufacturer who, through mass advertising campaigns, has created a market for the goods; that it is in the interest of the manufacturer that the consumer buy and use the goods; and that it is the manufacturer of non-conforming goods who will ultimately bear the loss if multiple lawsuits are required instead of a direct action.[61] In short, there is no good reason to substitute three lawsuits to do what can be done in one.

An example of the recent cases is *Kassab v. Central Soya*,[62] a decision of the Supreme Court of Pennsylvania which overruled an earlier case requiring vertical privity as a condition to maintaining an action against the manufacturer.[63] The court rejected any notion that there should be a dichotomy between tort and contract in product liability cases, found that the Code does not attempt to treat the problem of vertical privity, and added:

> We now believe that the time has come to recognize that the same policy reasons underlying the food cases also underlie cases involving defective non-edibles which cause injury. When it is considered that continued adherence to the requirements of vertical privity results merely in perpetuating a needless chain of actions whereby each buyer must seek redress for breach of warranty from his own immediate seller until the

59. Price v. Gatlin, 241 Or. 315, 405 P.2d 502 (1965) (economic loss); Henry v. John W. Eshelman & Sons, 99 R. I. 518, 209 A.2d 46 (1965) (*but see* Finocchiaro v. Ward Baking Co., —— R.I. ——, 241 A.2d 619 (1968)); Leach v. Wiles, 58 Tenn.App. 286, 429 S.W.2d 823 (1968); Annots., 17 A.L.R.3d 1010, 1130–34 (1968); 16 A.L.R.3d 683 (1967).

60. UCC § 2–318, Comment 3.

61. *E. g.*, Randy Knitwear, Inc. v. American Cyanamid Co., 11 N.Y.2d 5,

226 N.Y.S.2d 363, 181 N.E.2d 399 (1962); Rogers v. Toni Home Permanent Co., 167 Ohio St. 244, 147 N.E.2d 612 (1958). *But see* Brendle v. General Tire and Rubber Co., 304 F.Supp. 1262 (M.D.N.C.1969) (applying North Carolina law).

62. 432 Pa. 217, 246 A.2d 848 (1968).

63. Miller v. Preitz, 422 Pa. 383, 221 A.2d 320 (1966).

actual manufacturer is eventually reached, and in memorializing the unwarranted notion that a change in the caption of a complaint can completely alter the result of a lawsuit, our course becomes well marked. Vertical privity can no longer commend itself to this Court.[64]

§ 92.   Henningsen v. Bloomfield Motors, Inc.[65]

Claus Henningsen decided to purchase a Mother's Day gift for his wife—not the usual flowers or candy, but a new automobile. He visited Bloomfield Motors (a Plymouth dealer), told the dealer of the intended gift, and signed a purchase order for a Plymouth Plaza "6" Club Sedan. This commonplace transaction began a series of events which forms the basis for a review of many of the ideas presented in this chapter and indicates how sales law can be used to shift losses which occur when goods do not measure up to their warranted quality.

Ten days after the new Plymouth was delivered to Mrs. Henningsen she was driving on Route 36 in Highlands, New Jersey, at around 20 miles an hour when something cracked under the hood, the steering wheel spun in her hands, and the automobile veered to the right and crashed into a brick wall. At that time the odometer registered only 468 miles. Mrs. Henningsen sued Bloomfield Motors and Chrysler Corporation (the manufacturer of the Plymouth) for the injuries she received, and Claus Henningsen joined in the action. The complaint was based upon negligence and upon breach of express and implied warranties, but the negligence count was dismissed by the court. The jury returned a verdict against both defendants, who appealed. The Supreme Court of New Jersey unanimously affirmed[66] and discussed the following problems:

PRIVITY

The suits against Chrysler raised questions which this text has separated into problems of vertical and horizontal privity.[67] As to vertical privity the arguments of Chrysler were that implied warranties accompany sales, Chrysler's only sale was to Bloomfield Motors, and there was no sale between Chrysler and either of the Henningsens to which these warranties could attach. The court's answer was that such privity between manufacturer and buyer was not needed.

The limitations of privity in contracts for the sale of goods developed their place in the law when marketing conditions

64. Kassab v. Central Soya, 432 Pa. 217, 246 A.2d 848, 856 (1968).

65. 32 N.J. 358, 161 A.2d 69 (1960).

66. *Id.*

67. § 91 *supra.*

were simple, when maker and buyer frequently met face to face on an equal bargaining plane and when many of the products were relatively uncomplicated and conducive to inspection by a buyer competent to evaluate their quality. . . . With the advent of mass marketing, the manufacturer became remote from the purchaser, sales were accomplished through intermediaries, and the demand for the product was created by advertising media. In such an economy it became obvious that the consumer was the person being cultivated. Manifestly, the connotation of "consumer" was broader than that of "buyer." He signified such a person who, in the reasonable contemplation of the parties to the sale, might be expected to use the product. Thus, where the commodities sold are such that if defectively manufactured they will be dangerous to life or limb, then society's interests can only be protected by eliminating the requirement of privity between the maker and his dealers and the reasonably expected ultimate consumer. In that way the burden of losses consequent upon use of defective articles is borne by those who are in a position to either control the danger or make an equitable distribution of the losses when they do occur.[68]

As to horizontal privity Chrysler was joined by Bloomfield Motors in arguing that, even if an implied warranty of merchantability was made to Claus Henningsen, that warranty did not extend to Mrs. Henningsen. The court dismissed this argument, relying primarily on an earlier New Jersey tort action in which the wife of a tenant was allowed to recover damages from the landlord for injuries received when the landlord defaulted in his covenant to deliver the premises in good repair.[69] Noting the growth of the contract theory of warranty law from the original tort action of deceit, the court continued:

> An awareness of this evolution makes for ready acceptance of the relaxation of rigid concepts of privity when third persons, who in the reasonable contemplation of the parties to a warranty might be expected to use or consume the product sold, are injured by its unwholesome or defective state.[70]

---

68. Henningsen v. Bloomfield Motors, Inc., 32 N.J. 358, 379, 161 A.2d 69, 80–81. The court also noted that some jurisdictions hold that express warranties through advertising run directly to the buyer who purchases in reliance thereon. *Id.* at 385, 161 A.2d at 84.

69. Faber v. Creswick, 31 N.J. 234, 156 A.2d 252 (1959). There would be no

difficulty in dismissing this argument under the Code. *See* UCC § 2–318 and § 90 *supra.*

70. Henningsen v. Bloomfield Motors, Inc., 32 N.J. 358, 414, 161 A.2d 69, 100.

The 1962 version of UCC § 2–318 would reach the same result since Mrs. Henningsen was in the "family" of the purchaser. § 90 *supra.*

Neither horizontal nor vertical privity was a defense to the actions brought by the Henningsens. Further, the court was willing to use precedents from tort law to help shape its conclusions under the law of sales.[71]

IMPLIED WARRANTIES

Mr. Henningsen signed a standard form order blank which contained printing on both sides of a single sheet of paper. Six-point type on the front indicated that the front and back of the order comprised the entire agreement between the parties and that Mr. Henningsen agreed to all of the printed matter contained on the form. On the back was the warranty provision which, first, expressly warranted certain parts to be free from defects and, second, declared that this express warranty was in lieu of all other warranties. The express warranty was limited to a replacement of the defective part (within time and mileage limitations) if the part was sent to the factory, transportation charges prepaid, and if examination disclosed to the satisfaction of Chrysler that the part was defective.[72] The defendants argued that these clauses prevented the creation of any implied warranty of merchantability, or at least limited the remedies available for breach.

The court, however, held otherwise. Characterizing the terms of the warranty as a "sad commentary upon the automobile manufacturers' marketing practices," [73] the court pointed out that the standard form contract had "metamorphosed the warranty into a device to limit the maker's liability." [74] The attempt to limit liability when a part was defective made any security given by the warranty illusory. Further, "the express warranty against defective parts and workmanship is not inconsistent with an implied warranty of merchantability." [75] Therefore, unless the disclaimer was effective, an implied warranty that the automobile was merchantable ran from Chrysler to Mr. and Mrs. Henningsen.

An implied warranty on the part of Bloomfield Motors was found with less judicial effort. The purchase contract was between the dealer and Claus Henningsen, and an implied warranty was annexed to that agreement by force of statute. The attempt to limit liability was ineffective for the same reasons that it failed as to Chrysler Corporation. Thus, unless the disclaimer was effective, an implied warranty that the automobile was merchantable also ran from the dealer to Mr. and Mrs. Henningsen.

---

71. § 54 *supra*.

72. § 89 *supra* discusses limitation of remedies available for breach of warranty.

73. Henningsen v. Bloomfield Motors, Inc., 32 N.J. 358, 375, 161 A.2d 69, 78.

74. *Id.* at 375, 161 A.2d at 78.

75. *Id.*

DISCLAIMER

As was pointed out in the prior paragraphs, the standard form agreement attempted to disclaim all warranties except that the manufacturer would replace defective parts—and then only under very limited circumstances. The court held that this disclaimer and the attempt to limit liability to replacement were both void as contrary to public policy; today, the result could be reached by holding these clauses to be unconscionable.[76] Unfair surprise and oppression were found by the court. Unfair surprise existed because the jury could find that the fine print on the back of the order did not direct Mr. Henningsen's attention to the clauses or, even if he saw the clause, an ordinary reasonable person would not understand that he was relinquishing claims for personal injuries that might flow from the use of the defective automobile. Oppression existed because the writing was a standard form presented by the great majority of manufacturers on a take-it-or-leave-it basis.[77] There was no opportunity to bargain as to the warranties.

> From the standpoint of the purchaser, there can be no arms length negotiating on the subject. Because his capacity for bargaining is so grossly unequal, the inexorable conclusion which follows is that he is not permitted to bargain at all. He must take or leave the automobile on the warranty terms dictated by the maker. He cannot turn to a competitor for better security.

> . . . The lawmakers did not authorize the automobile manufacturer to use its grossly disproportionate bargaining power to relieve itself from liability and to impose on the ordinary buyer, who in effect has no real freedom of choice, the grave danger of injury to himself and others that attends the sale of such a dangerous instrumentality as a defectively made automobile. In the framework of this case, illuminated as it is by the facts and the many decisions noted, we are of the opinion that Chrysler's attempted disclaimer of an implied warranty of merchantability and of the obligations arising therefrom is so inimical to the public good as to compel an adjudication of its invalidity.[78]

---

76. § 44 *supra.* That section suggests that unconscionability is a product either of unfair surprise or of oppression.

77. § 88 *supra.* For a contrary conclusion, see Marshall v. Murray Oldsmo-

bile, Inc., 207 Va. 972, 154 S.E.2d 140 (1967).

78. Henningsen v. Bloomfield Motors, Inc., 32 N.J. 358, 403–04, 161 A.2d 69, 94–95.

BREACH OF THE IMPLIED WARRANTY

Only one additional step was needed to hold the defendants liable for the injuries that followed. The court had found that an implied warranty of merchantability had been made by Chrysler Corporation and by Bloomfield Motors, that the attempt to disclaim this warranty and to limit its impact to replacement of the defective parts had failed, and that privity of contract was not needed between either of the Henningsens and the defendants. This, however, was not enough to support liability on the part of the defendants who are not insurers of the safety of their product. The Henningsens had to go further and show that a defect in the product caused the injuries of which they complained.[79] The court held that the expert evidence which they introduced at the trial was sufficient to support the verdict of the jury. The result was an affirmance of the judgments in favor of both of the plaintiffs.

SUMMARY

Henningsen arose prior to the adoption of the Code in New Jersey. It cannot, however, be disregarded as a Code precedent. The language of the court and its analysis of the legal problems presented are equally applicable to Article 2 of the Uniform Commercial Code. Product liability cases can be solved by sales law or by the doctrine of strict liability. A change in the classification of the cause of action ought not affect the rights and obligations of the parties.

79. § 81 *supra.*

CHAPTER V

PERFORMANCE OF THE SALES CONTRACT

Analysis

A. INTRODUCTION

2. Right of Inspection

A. INTRODUCTION

§ 93. General Performance Obligations of Seller and Buyer

Section 2–301 sets out the general performance obligations of the parties to a contract for the sale of goods:

> The obligation of the seller is to transfer and deliver and that of the buyer is to accept and pay in accordance with the contract.

The Code, therefore, affirms the principal purpose of the law of sales: to facilitate both the distribution of goods to buyer and the payment of the purchase price to the seller.

The obligations of both parties is to be determined "in accordance with the contract." The parties may determine the time, place, and method of delivery as well as when the buyer must accept the goods and pay the price. For example, the agreement may require that the seller deliver the goods "F.O.B. seller's tank car, Pacific Coast." Tendering a bill of lading which indicates that the goods were shipped from Dallas, Texas, does not fulfill the seller's delivery obligation.[1] Likewise, the parties may agree that the buyer must pay cash on delivery of the goods—or the buyer may be given a period of time after delivery (such as 30, 60, or 90 days) to pay the price.[2] In either event the terms of the agreement determine the scope of the parties' obligations.

This text has already considered problems of interpreting the agreement of the parties. The principles developed at that point are equally applicable to any decision as to obligations of performance.[3]

There will be instances in which the parties will have said nothing about certain portions of their delivery or payment obligations. It may be that the seller has agreed to deliver 10,000 pairs of shoes at a

---

1. Mitsubishi Goshi Kaisha v. J. Aron & Co., 16 F.2d 185 (2d Cir. 1926).

2. If the parties have not agreed that the buyer is to be extended credit, payment is due at the time and place at which the buyer is to receive the goods. UCC § 2–310(a).

3. §§ 46–53 supra.

stated price, but that nothing was said as to when the delivery was to be made, whether the shoes were to be delivered in lots or all at one time, or whether the delivery was to be made at the seller's or buyer's place of business. Also, the parties may have said nothing about whether the buyer was to pay in cash or by check, or whether he was to have a period of time after receiving the shoes to pay the price. The absence of these terms from the agreement does not mean that there are no obligations of the contract regarding them. General contract law and the Code fill in many of these "open" terms. This problem is discussed in detail in other sections of this text.[4] The result, however, is that the contract of the parties determines their performance obligations.

§ 94.   Doctrine of Concurrent Conditions

Unless the parties have otherwise agreed, tender of payment by the buyer and tender of delivery by the seller are concurrent conditions. This result is accomplished primarily through two Code sections:

> Tender of delivery is a condition to the buyer's duty to accept the goods and, unless otherwise agreed, to his duty to pay for them. Tender entitles the seller to acceptance of the goods and to payment according to the contract.[5]

> Unless otherwise agreed tender of payment is a condition to the seller's duty to tender and complete any delivery.[6]

Therefore, unless the parties have set up some other order of performance, the seller must tender the goods to trigger the buyer's obligation to pay for them, and the buyer must tender the price to trigger the seller's obligation to deliver the goods. The practical implication of this rule is that the seller is not in default, even though the date set for delivery has gone by, unless the buyer has tendered the price; and the buyer is not in default, even though the date set for the payment of the price has gone by, unless the seller has tendered the goods.[7]

---

4. §§ 38–39 *supra.*

5. UCC § 2–507(1).

6. UCC § 2–511.(1)

7. This was not always the rule in the sale of goods. At one time a seller could recover the purchase price even though he did not allege a tender of the goods. Nichols v. Raynbred, Hobart 89, 80 Eng.Rep. 238 (K.B.1615). But Lord Mansfield established an order of performance in Kingston v. Preston, 2 Doug. 689, 99 Eng.Rep. 437 (K.B.1773), and this is continued in the Code as well as the general law of contracts. Cameras for Industry, Inc. v. L. D. Precision Components Corp., 49 Misc.2d 1044, 268 N.Y.S.2d 860 (App.T.1966) *modified* 30 A.D.2d 526, 290 N.Y.S.2d 525 (1968) (decided under the Uniform Sales Act). *See* Kelly Constr. Co. v. Hackensack Brick Co., 91 N.J.L. 585, 103 A. 417 (Ct.Err. & App.1918), a decision which would be partially changed by UCC § 2–307.

The parties can, of course, change this order of performance. For example, the seller can agree to extend credit to the buyer; in this event the buyer need not tender during the period of credit in order to put the seller in default. Likewise, the buyer can agree to pay a portion or all of the purchase price in advance of the delivery date set for the goods; in this event the seller need not tender delivery prior to the date set for delivery in order to put the buyer in default.

Nevertheless, the rule from which the Code begins in determining the order in which the parties must perform their obligations is that of concurrent conditions. In these cases the lawyer ought not overlook the need for tender to trigger the obligation of the other party to perform because, unless that obligation is triggered, the failure to deliver or to pay is not a default.

B. PERFORMANCE OBLIGATIONS OF THE SELLER

1. WARRANTY AND TENDER OBLIGATIONS

§ 95. Warranty Obligations

The seller's basic performance obligation is contained in section 2–301 of the Code:

> The obligation of the seller is to transfer and deliver and that of the buyer is to accept and pay in accordance with the contract.

There are minor syntactic difficulties with this section. The principal one is that of determining just what is modified by the words "in accordance with the contract." Are these words a limitation solely on the buyer's obligations (or perhaps only on his obligation to pay), or do they also modify the seller's obligation to transfer and deliver?

It may well be that the drafters were concerned primarily with making certain that the buyer would not be required to pay for the goods at the time of their delivery if the contract had extended a period of credit to him; thus they added the modification after the buyer's payment obligation.[8] Nevertheless, the idea that the contract is to control all of the parties' obligations is central to Article 2 and especially to section 2–301. The seller is to transfer and deliver what? The only answer that makes sense is that he is to transfer and deliver

---

8. In UCC § 2–507(1), quoted in § 94 *supra*, there are two references to the parties' agreement, the first of which is clearly limited to the buyer's obligation to pay.

the goods which he promised to the buyer[9] and he is to deliver those goods at the time and place agreed upon. In short, the seller is obligated to transfer and deliver *conforming* goods at the time and place which *conform* to the contract between the parties.[10]

The primary implication of this conclusion is that the tendered goods must conform to the warranties of title and of quality which accompanied the contract for their sale.[11] This brings into the seller's obligations those warranties which were discussed in the prior chapter of this text. If the goods do not conform to the warranties of quality or title, the seller has failed to perform his general obligation and—if the buyer has made a proper tender or if tender has been excused— the seller will be liable under an appropriate remedy for breach of contract. If the goods do conform to the contract and if the tender was proper, the seller has performed his contractual obligations, the tender has triggered the buyer's obligation to accept the goods,[12] and the seller will be awarded an appropriate remedy if the buyer fails to make a payment when due. Therefore, the prior chapter presents the principal discussion of a seller's obligations under a contract for sale or a sale of goods.

§ 96. Tender Obligations

The seller performs by tendering delivery. The Code definition of tender relaxes the requirement of those common law cases which held that the seller had to attempt physically to hand the goods to the buyer:

> Tender of delivery requires that the seller put and hold conforming goods at the buyer's disposition and give the buyer any notification reasonably necessary to enable him to take delivery . . . .[13]

Thus, tender is performed by two acts: (1) putting and holding conforming goods at the buyer's disposition—and in an appropriate case this may be done at the seller's place of business; and (2) giving the buyer a notification which will enable him to take delivery. Two ex-

---

9. In UCC § 2–511(1) the seller's tender is described as a duty; in § 2–503(1) "tender" is defined in terms of conforming goods. More in point is UCC § 2–601 which gives the buyer the privilege of rejection "if either the goods or the tender of delivery fail in any respect to conform to the contract."

10. UCC § 2–503(1). In installment contracts the tender obligations are less rigorous to obligate the buyer to accept the goods. Any deviation from the terms of the contract would, how-

ever, be a default and give the buyer an action for damages. § 104 *infra*.

11. Zabriskie Chevrolet, Inc. v. Smith, 99 N.J.Super. 441, 240 A.2d 195 (L. Div.1968) (quality); Campbell v. Pollack, 101 R.I. 223, 221 A.2d 615 (1966) (title).

12. UCC § 2–507.

13. UCC § 2–503(1); Aetna Ins. Co. v. Maryland Cast Stone Co., 254 Md. 109, 252 A.2d 872 (1969).

amples will indicate how this concept works and, at the same time, will introduce the operation of the Code on the performance obligations of the seller.

Case # 1. Ben Buyer and Dealer entered into a contract for the purchase and sale of a new automobile. As soon as both parties signed the writing, Dealer had his employees get the automobile ready for delivery to Buyer. The extra equipment was added, the motor tuned, bolts tightened, and the entire automobile was cleaned. In Code terms the seller was in the process of making the goods *conform* to the contract. Once the goods did conform, the seller was ready to tender. Since delivery to Buyer was not required by their contract, Dealer could tender by placing this automobile in the showroom (or on the lot), holding it for Buyer's disposition, and giving Buyer notification that he could come by and pick it up.[14] The seller has performed; the purchaser's obligations to accept and to pay have been triggered.

In some instances the seller cannot tender by holding the goods at his place of business. If the purchaser had selected a new refrigerator, a large television set, or a bulky machine, the agreement between the parties may (and probably would) require the seller to deliver the goods to the buyer's address. The Code makes this clear by providing in section 2–503(1):

> The manner, time and place for tender are determined by the agreement and this Article, and in particular
>
> (a) tender must be at a reasonable hour, and if it is of goods they must be kept available for the period reasonably necessary to enable the buyer to take possession; but
>
> (b) unless otherwise agreed the buyer must furnish facilities reasonably suited to the receipt of the goods.

The reference to the need for a tender "at a reasonable hour" is especially important in those few cases in which the seller would like to have the buyer default (as in a rising price market). The seller cannot put the buyer in default by tendering at an unreasonable hour. This requirement is a specific example of the general obligation of good faith imposed on all parties in the performance of a contract.[15]

Case #1 presented a situation in which the seller tendered the goods without intervention of an intermediary. When the buyer and seller are separated by a considerable distance so that the goods must be shipped by an independent transporter (railroad, steamship, trucker, or airline), the seller's tender becomes more complicated.

14. UCC § 2–308(a) discussed in § 39   15. UCC § 1–203.
supra.

Case # 2. In addition to automobiles, Dealer (located in Cincinnati, Ohio) also sold new tires. Dealer sent a purchase order for 500 tires to Seller, located in Akron, Ohio. Seller would like to sell the tires but does not have a delivery service which includes Cincinnati and does not want to release possession of the tires until Dealer has paid the price. On the other hand, Dealer does not have a pick-up service that includes Akron and does not want to pay the price until he is assured that he will receive the tires.

Seller's tender in Case #2 will be accomplished through some intermediary—in this case probably by train or truck, although in other cases the goods could be shipped by boat or airplane. Assume that Seller sent Dealer an acknowledgment of the Dealer's order and took 500 conforming tires to the local freight depot of Crosscountry Railroad.[16] The tires would be put into the possession of the railroad in one of two ways: (1) if Seller has a sufficiently large load so that it will fill a freight car, Seller may have his employees load the car; or (2) if the load is smaller than a full freight car, the goods will be turned over to the local freight agent and the railroad employees will do the loading. In either event, some provision is made for paying the freight charges from Akron to Cincinnati (seller's point to buyer's point), and the freight agent will sign a receipt for the goods. This receipt is called a "bill of lading."[17]

A bill of lading is, however, more than a receipt for the goods. A bill of lading is also a document of title,[18] and a negotiable bill of lading evidences that the holder of the bill is entitled to the goods which it covers.[19] The bill of lading also represents a contract between the carrier and the shipper of the goods. Printed on the back of the form, sometimes in incredibly small type, are the terms and conditions of the transportation agreement. Liability for loss, obligation to pay freight charges, right of the carrier to sell unclaimed goods, conditions on claims, and so on are covered.

A bill of lading is negotiable in only two instances: (1) if by its terms the goods are to be delivered to bearer or to the order of a named

---

16. For a discussion of the Code problems involved if the acknowledgment contains terms which are different from or additional to those found in the order form, see § 37 *supra.*

17. UCC § 1–201(6). *See* Gastwirth v. P. Mashbitz & Sons, 414 Pa. 445, 200 A. 2d 766 (1964), where one of the documents involved was held not to be a bill of lading.

18. UCC § 1–201(15).

19. The definition of "holder" is contained in UCC § 1–201(20). Documents of title are covered in Article 7 of the Code. Rights acquired by due negotiation of a negotiable document of title include title to the goods. UCC § 7–502. *Cf.* UCC § 7–503. Rights acquired in absence of due negotiation are listed in UCC § 7–504. Warranties on negotiation or transfer are covered by UCC § 7–507.

person; or (2) where recognized in overseas trade, if the bill runs to a named person or assigns. In all other instances the bill is non-negotiable.[20] Thus, the typical uniform order bill of lading (printed on yellow paper) contains the clause "consigned to the order of." The typical uniform straight bill of lading (printed on white paper) states simply "consigned to." The first is negotiable; the second is non-negotiable.

Returning to the second example, assume that Seller had taken a negotiable bill of lading from Crosscountry Railroad. Crosscountry is obligated to deliver the tires to any holder—either the original consignee, or someone to whom the bill has been duly negotiated.[21] Seller can have Dealer's name entered on the bill as the consignee, or Seller could enter its own name as consignee and endorse the bill to Dealer. In either event Dealer will be entitled to the goods when they arrive in Cincinnati, and can secure possession by delivering the bill of lading to the Cincinnati agent of Crosscountry Railroad.

How Seller tenders in Case #2 depends upon the terms of the agreement between Dealer and Seller. It is now necessary to go back and focus on the buyer's order and the seller's acknowledgment which were mentioned briefly in stating the hypothetical facts. These will undoubtedly have said something about the delivery of the goods, and will have created either a shipment or a destination contract. The seller's method of performance under each of these is considered in the next three sections of this text.[22]

§ 97. Performance Obligations in Shipment and Destination Contracts

All contracts for the sale of goods impose on the seller the obligation to tender delivery of the goods.[23] In most contracts the parties have agreed as to the place where this tender is to be made. Such an agreement may be expressed in words or may be implied from trade customs or prior dealings of these parties.[24] There are, however, some contracts in which no place of delivery has been agreed upon by the parties. As to these the place of delivery is determined by the following rules: *Rule #1*, if the contract is for the sale of identified goods and if the parties know the location of those goods, that location is the place of delivery;[25] and *Rule #2*, if Rule #1 is not applicable, the seller's place of business (or, if he has no place of business, his residence) is the place of delivery.[26]

---

20. UCC § 7–104.

21. UCC §§ 7–301(1), 7–403. Consolidated Packing Co. v. Capitol Packing Co., 389 F.2d 505 (1st Cir. 1968).

22. See also § 100 *infra* for a discussion of the use of a sight draft.

23. UCC § 2–301.

24. §§ 51–52 *supra.*

25. UCC § 2–308(b).

26. UCC § 2–308(a). See the discussion in § 39 *supra.*

The rules set out above will have little impact on the great bulk of commercial transactions because in most instances the parties will have agreed on the place of delivery.[27]   Their agreement may, of course, provide for delivery at any place and under any conditions to which they have consented, but the more common agreements are of two kinds: (1) those in which the buyer agrees to pick up the goods at a designated place (usually the seller's place of business) without the seller's having any responsibility for moving the goods, and (2) those in which the seller assumes responsibility for transporting the goods to the buyer.

The second kind of case (that in which the seller is authorized or required to transport the goods) is also divided by the Code into two groups: shipment contracts and destination contracts.[28]   In a *shipment* contract the seller tenders delivery at the point of shipment, and risk of loss passes to the buyer "when the goods are duly delivered to the carrier." [29]   In a *destination* contract the seller tenders delivery at the stated destination, and risk of loss passes to the buyer "when the goods are there duly so tendered as to enable the buyer to take delivery." [30]   It therefore becomes important in all delivery contracts to determine whether the seller is required to deliver the goods at a particular destination or whether the contract is satisfied by the seller's shipping the goods to the buyer.

Whether a shipment or a destination contract is involved depends upon the agreement of the parties.   If the parties have stated their intention, that intention will control.   If the intention is not stated, the court will be called upon to determine whether an agreement to deliver can be implied from what the parties did and said.[31]   This calls into play the usual rules of contract interpretation already discussed in this text.[32]   In addition, two sections of the Code are particularly helpful:

1.   The Code provides that unless "otherwise agreed   .   .   .   if the seller is authorized to send goods he may ship them under reservation, and may tender the documents of title, but the buyer may inspect the goods after their arrival before payment is due unless such inspection is inconsistent with the terms of the contract.   .   .   . " [33]   The

---

27.   UCC § 2–308, Comment 1.

28.   Risk of loss is discussed in §§ 130–36 *infra.*

29.   UCC § 2–509(1) (a).

30.   UCC § 2–509(1) (b).

31.   According to the Comments, shipment contracts are normal and desti-nation contracts are variant.   Specific agreement or commercial understand-ing is necessary to create a destina-tion contract.   UCC § 2–503, Comment 5.

32.   §§ 46–53 *supra.*

33.   UCC § 2–310(b).

authorization to ship may be found in trade usage, course of performance, course of dealing, or the terms of the agreement involved.[34] In this respect, the fact that the parties are located in distant cities will often be sufficient to authorize shipment by the seller.[35] Thus, in Case #2 in the prior section of this text, the seller of the tires would undoubtedly be authorized to ship those tires to the buyer on a carrier, and to use a bill of lading in connection with that shipment.[36]

2.   Another section of the Code which is of aid in determining whether a shipment or a destination contract is involved is section 2–319 which defines the F.O.B. and F.A.S. terms. That section provides in part:

> (1) Unless otherwise agreed the term F.O.B. (which means "free on board") at a named place, even though used only in connection with the stated price, is a delivery term under which
>
> (a) when the term is F.O.B. the place of shipment, the seller must at that place ship the goods in the manner provided in this Article (Section 2–504) and bear the expense and risk of putting them into the possession of the carrier; or
>
> (b) when the term is F.O.B. the place of destination, the seller must at his own expense and risk transport the goods to that place and there tender delivery of them in the manner provided in this Article (Section 2–503);
>
> (c) when under either (a) or (b) the term is also F.O.B. vessel, car or other vehicle, the seller must in addition at his own expense and risk load the goods on board. If the term is F.O.B. vessel the buyer must name the vessel and in an appropriate case the seller must comply with the provisions of this Article on the form of bill of lading (Section 2–323).[37]

---

34. §§ 50–52 *supra.*

35. The contract will usually authorize the seller to send the goods to the buyer. UCC § 2–310(b) allows such a seller to ship under reservation.

36. The buyer's right of inspection is discussed in §§ 120–24 *infra.* See also UCC § 2–310, Comment 4.

37. The F.A.S. seller's port or dock contract is also a shipment contract. UCC § 2–319(2); Tex-O-Kan Flour Mills Co. v. Nord, 18 So.2d 50 (La.Ct.App.1944); The W. Ferdinand Armstrong (Eastern Gas & Fuels Ass'n v. Howard), 69 F.Supp. 824 (S.D.N.Y.1946) (involving an F.A.S. buyer's dock contract). The C.I.F. and C. & F. contracts are also shipment contracts. UCC § 2–320. AMCO Transworld, Inc. v. The M/V Bambi, 257 F.Supp. 215 (S.D. Tex.1966).

An important part of this definition is the phrase "delivery term": "F.O.B. . . . is a delivery term." These initials (F.O.B.) tell where the seller is to make his tender of delivery. In an F.O.B. seller's point contract the seller tenders at the point of shipment; in an F.O.B. buyer's point contract the seller tenders at the point of destination.[38] Therefore, the F.O.B. (or the F.A.S. vessel—which the Code defines as meaning "free alongside") term aids in determining whether a shipment or destination contract is involved, and indicates how the seller is to perform his obligations under the agreement.[39]

§ 98. Tender in a Shipment Contract

In a shipment contract the seller tenders at the point of shipment and, if the tender was proper, the risk of loss passed to the buyer when the goods were delivered to the carrier.[40] The problem is that of determining the elements of a *proper* tender. The seller is tendering at a point distant from the buyer; typically, the buyer has no one present to assure that the goods will be given proper care during shipment or that the bill of lading will be forwarded promptly so that the buyer can obtain the goods from the carrier when they arrive in buyer's city. Thus the seller in a shipment contract ought to be required to take reasonable precautions to protect the buyer's interest in the goods while they are in transit.[41]

The Code contains such a requirement, accomplishing the result through the concept of tender. The general Code section on the manner of the seller's tender of delivery (2–503) provides that the seller must comply with section 2–504 in all shipment contracts. That section (2–504) provides:

> Where the seller is required or authorized to send the goods to the buyer and the contract does not require him to deliver them at a particular destination, then unless otherwise agreed he must
>
> > (a) put the goods in the possession of such a carrier and make such a contract for their transportation as

---

38. As to risk of loss, see § 132 *infra*.

39. Electric Regulator Corp. v. Sterling Extruder Corp., 280 F.Supp. 550 (D. Conn.1968). The seller has tendered goods under an "F.O.B. trucks, job site" contract when it has manufactured goods and asked for delivery instructions which were not forthcoming. Aetna Ins. Co. v. Maryland Cast Stone Co., 254 Md. 109, 253 A.2d 872 (1969).

If the contract calls for delivery "ex ship," delivery is required from a ship which has reached the named port of destination and the place where goods of the kind involved are usually discharged. UCC § 2–322.

40. § 97 *supra*.

41. The Uniform Sales Act gave this protection in section 46.

may be reasonable having regard to the nature of the goods and other circumstances of the case; and

(b) obtain and promptly deliver or tender in due form any document necessary to enable the buyer to obtain possession of the goods or otherwise required by the agreement or by usage of trade; and

(c) promptly notify the buyer of the shipment.

Failure to notify the buyer under paragraph (c) or to make a proper contract under paragraph (a) is a ground for rejection only if material delay or loss ensues.[42]

The result of this section is that the seller's performance obligations under a shipment contract extend beyond that of delivering conforming goods to the carrier.[43] The choice of the type of carrier (and even the carrier itself) must be reasonable.[44] If the type of goods involved requires prompt delivery, sending by railroad or by truck rather than by airplane would be an improper tender if a material loss or delay occurs. The same result would follow if the contract with the carrier turns out to be unreasonable. Failure to require a refrigerator car for frozen goods or failure to declare the full value of the goods would not obligate the buyer to accept and pay for those goods if they are destroyed during shipment.[45]

Prompt notification of the shipment must be given in all cases, whether called for by the contract or not. This notification in credit shipments comes most often through the invoice; in documentary sales it comes through the documents. "It is also usual to send on a straight bill of lading but this is not necessary to the required notification. However, should such a document prove necessary or convenient to the buyer, as in the case of loss and claim against the carrier, good faith would require the seller to send it on request." [46] Once again, the failure to notify is a ground for rejection only if material loss or delay ensues. The Code does not expressly consider whether the loss or delay must result from the failure to notify, but such a requirement will probably be read in by the courts. The Comments do indicate, however, that the parties may make prompt notification—such as by

42. The buyer's right of rejection is discussed in § 141 *infra*.

43. The Code requires the seller to "put the goods in the possession of" the carrier. UCC § 2–504(a). Placing a portion of the goods in the carrier's possession is not a proper tender if the contract of sale is entire. *See* Lewis v. Farmers Grain & Milling Co., 52 Cal.App. 211, 198 P. 426 (1921); § 102 *infra*.

44. *See* Cargill, Inc. v. Thibault Milling Co., 230 Ark. 890, 328 S.W.2d 362 (1959).

45. UCC § 2–504, Comment 3; Miller v. Harvey, 221 N.Y. 54, 116 N.E. 781 (1917). Cases are cited in 2 S. Williston, Sales §§ 278a, 278b (rev. ed. 1948).

46. UCC § 2–504, Comment 5.

wire or cable—an express ground for rejection even though the buyer does not suffer any loss.[47]

The final requirement in a shipment contract is that the seller tender the documents necessary for the buyer to obtain possession of the goods.[48] This completes the buyer's protection because, with the documents, he can obtain the goods from the carrier or, in the event of loss, proceed against the carrier under the contract of shipment.[49] The seller who has complied with these provisions of section 2–504 has a cause of action against the buyer if the buyer refuses to accept the goods and pay their price as agreed upon.[50] The remedies of a seller are discussed in other portions of this text.[51]

§ 99. Tender in a Destination Contract

The second type of delivery contract is a destination contract in which the seller is obligated to tender conforming goods at the point of destination.[52] Since the goods must conform to the contract at the time they are tendered,[53] it usually makes no difference to the buyer how the goods were transported from the place of shipment or whether a reasonable contract was made with any carrier which might be involved.[54] If the goods in fact conform when they reach their destination, the buyer has received what he contracted for; if they do not conform, the buyer may reject the goods.[55] In either event the buyer is protected against losses or delays which occur during shipment. Therefore, the Code need not (and does not) contain provisions for the destination contract—as it does for shipment contracts—which protect the buyer as to the kind of carrier selected or the nature of the contract made with that carrier. The normal tender requirements already set out in this text protect the buyer in the destination contract.[56]

There are some destination contracts which involve documents. The Code makes it clear that the necessary documents must be tender-

---

47. *Id.*

48. UCC § 2–504(b).

49. UCC § 7–301(1).

50. Permalum Window & Awning Mfg. Co. v. Permalum Window Mfg. Corp., 412 S.W.2d 863 (Ky.1967).

51. §§ 161 et seq. *infra.*

52. § 97 *supra.*

53. § 96 *supra.*

54. These matters are important when the tender is at the seller's point—that is, in a shipment contract. § 98 *supra.*

55. UCC § 2–601.

56. Specifically, these requirements include (1) the need for conforming goods being put and held at the buyer's disposition, (2) proper notice to the buyer, (3) tender at a reasonable hour kept open for a reasonable time, and (4) any further requirements contained in the parties' agreement. § 96 *supra.*

ed to the buyer as a part of the seller's obligations. Two examples are described in the Code: the first is the documentary sale in which the contract expressly requires the seller to deliver documents; [57] the second is the situation in which the goods are in possession of a bailee and are to be delivered without being moved.[58] In the latter case the seller performs by tendering either a negotiable document of title covering the goods or an acknowledgment by the bailee of the buyer's right to possession of the goods.[59]

§ 100.   Use of a Sight Draft

A hypothetical problem was included in a prior section of this text for the purpose of introducing the methods by which a seller may perform his contractual obligations whenever goods are to be sent by carrier.[60]   That hypothetical involved a seller located in Akron, Ohio, and a buyer in Cincinnati, Ohio. The buyer sent a purchase order to the seller for 500 tires, and the seller responded with an acknowledgment of the order. This exchange of forms probably resulted in a legally enforceable agreement—that is, a contract—between the parties.[61] The prior discussion has pointed out that all of the seller's performance obligations cannot be determined until the delivery terms of that contract are known.[62] Did the parties agree on a shipment or a destination contract? Were documents required or only authorized?

The assumption will now be made that this contract is like the typical delivery transaction: the tires were to be shipped F.O.B. seller's point (Akron) with documents authorized but not required. This arrangement would be classified as a shipment contract [63] with the seller's performance obligations being measured by the seller's tender at the point of shipment. Therefore, the seller would be required to put 500 conforming tires into the possession of a carrier, make a reasonable contract for their delivery to the buyer, obtain a bill of lading from the carrier, deliver this bill of lading to the buyer, and promptly notify the Cincinnati buyer that the tires have been shipped.[64] When the

---

57.   UCC § 2–503(5). Documentary sales are those in which documents are required, not just authorized.   § 123 *infra*.

58.   UCC § 2–503(4).

59.   *Id.;* Whately v. Tetrault, 29 Mass. App.Dec. 112 (1964).

60.   § 96 *supra*.

61.   § 37 *supra*.

62.   §§ 97–99 *supra*.

63.   Permalum Window & Awning Mfg. Co. v. Permalum Window Mfg. Corp., 412 S.W.2d 863 (Ky.1967); UCC § 2–308, Comment 1.

64.   UCC § 2–504. The bill of lading is prima facie evidence of its authenticity, genuineness, and facts stated in the document by the carrier. UCC § 1–202.

seller has performed these acts he has tendered the goods, obligating the buyer to accept and to pay in accordance with the contract.[65]

If the seller had agreed to extend credit to the buyer, the endorsed bill of lading could be sent directly to the buyer so that he could go to the Cincinnati freight depot and pick up the tires by surrendering the bill of lading. The seller would then invoice the goods to the buyer and collect the price when the time for credit had expired. However, in the hypothetical presented it was stated that the seller did not want to release possession of the tires until the price had been paid and that the buyer did not want to pay the price until the tires had been received. This creates momentary difficulties because the Akron seller will not want to put the bill of lading into the possession of the Cincinnati buyer until the buyer has paid the price, and the buyer will not want to pay the price until he has received the bill of lading. It appears that a stalemate will result unless the buyer and seller get together at some point between these two cities and exchange the bill of lading for the price.

Businessmen have, however, worked out a method of solving this problem without leaving their respective cities. The seller will take the bill of lading to an Akron bank and draw a draft on the buyer. A draft is similar to a check, except this draft will be drawn on the buyer instead of on a bank in which funds have already been deposited.[66] The draft will order the buyer to pay the purchase price for the tires (assume that this price is $12,000) to the order of the seller's bank. The main portions of the draft will look like this:

$12,000   Akron, Ohio, March 15, 1970
....

                                     Akron First Bank
AT SIGHT pay to the order of ....

Twelve thousand and no/100
.... Dollars

Bill of lading attached.

To: Buyer Company
Through: Cincinnati Third Bank

                    Alexander C. Carpentera
                    _____
                    for Seller Corporation

---

65. UCC § 2–507(1); §§ 98–99 *supra*.

66. Negotiable drafts and checks are covered in Articles 3 and 4 of the Code. Both are defined in UCC § 3–104.

The words "at sight" tell the buyer that payment is to be made when the draft is presented (hence the name "sight draft"), although in other instances the draft could be made payable at some future definite date.[67]

The seller is now ready to complete the transaction for the sale of the tires. Carpentera—for the seller—will endorse the order bill of lading to the buyer, or he could endorse it to bearer. He will attach the endorsed bill to the draft and leave both with Akron First Bank. Seller Corporation is willing to trust Akron First Bank as its collecting agent even though it would not trust the credit of the buyer. Akron First Bank will endorse the draft (not the bill of lading) under a sentence reading substantially as follows:

> Pay to the order of any
> bank or trust company.

Often the stamped endorsement will add "Prior endorsements guaranteed", but this is not required by the Code.[68]

Akron First Bank will send both the draft and the bill of lading to Cincinnati Third Bank (as noted on the draft). When these documents arrive in Cincinnati the buyer will be notified. An employee of the buyer can go to a local office of Cincinnati Third Bank, pay the draft—or arrange a loan with Cincinnati Third Bank—and pick up the endorsed bill of lading. Since the banking transaction usually occurs more quickly than the time needed for shipment, the buyer will have the bill of lading before the goods arrive at buyer's point. The carrier will call the buyer when the goods arrive (the buyer's name and address were included in the bill of lading as the person to be notified when the goods arrive at their destination). The buyer will deliver the endorsed bill to the carrier and receive the goods. The $12,000, through various transfers of bank credits, will be credited to the account of the seller in his Akron bank. The goals of both the buyer and seller have been accomplished: the seller was able to retain control of the goods through the bill of lading until the price was paid, and the buyer did not have to pay the price until he was assured that the goods were on the carrier.

---

67. The use of a time draft (or "trade acceptance," as it is sometimes called) is a method of extending credit to the buyer. Some sellers prefer the trade acceptance to open credit because the trade acceptance can be discounted by the seller during the credit period. The buyer must "accept" the trade acceptance before receiving the goods if payable more than three days after presentment. UCC §§ 2-514, 4-503. "Acceptance" is the drawee's—here, the buyer's—signed engagement to honor the draft as presented. UCC § 3-410.

68. UCC § 4-207.

§ 101. Use of a Letter of Credit

A seller is afforded considerable financial protection by using a sight draft in a sale involving documents. The buyer will not be able to obtain the documents until the draft has been paid and, without possession of negotiable documents, the buyer cannot obtain the goods from the carrier.[69] Therefore, if the draft (that is, the price) is not paid, the seller can retain possession of the goods and is not left to his remedy for full price against a distant defendant who might turn out to be insolvent.

The sight draft, however, has its limitations. For example, the draft does not assure the seller that the buyer will want the goods when they arrive. If the buyer has changed his mind and no longer wants the goods, he can refuse to pay or to accept the draft and leave the goods in the possession of the carrier. A distant seller facing this problem must make arrangements for the goods to be returned or sold and, if those goods are subject to rapid deterioration, those arrangements must be made quickly or the entire shipment will be lost. It is true that such a seller will have a cause of action against the buyer, but any litigation will have to be commenced in a state with judicial jurisdiction over the buyer and this may be several hundred miles from the seller's place of business. Perhaps more important, though, is that sellers do not sell goods to obtain lawsuits; they sell goods to secure payment in ordinary course. The draft gives substantial assurance that payment will be made, but the draft does not afford the seller protection in those situations in which the buyer has changed his mind about wanting the goods.

A seller who wants more assurance of payment than is given by a sight draft can demand a letter of credit before shipping the goods. The function of a letter of credit is readily understood if the basic problem is recalled. With the sight draft the distant seller did not want to release possession of the goods to the buyer until the buyer had paid the price; the seller considered in this section of the text does not even want to ship the goods until the buyer has paid the price. The buyer could send the cash in advance of shipment, but he is not interested in sending several thousand dollars to a seller until the goods have been shipped. Such a buyer and seller could work out some way to put the money in escrow with a trusted third party (like a bank), the money to be held until the third party receives the documents indicating that the goods have been shipped and then to be released to the seller. Such an arrangement could be worked out, but this has not been the usual course of business for these transactions.

---

69. Discussed in § 100 *supra*.

Instead, this trusted third party—that is, the bank—issues a letter of credit to the seller. Letters of credit are used most often in international sales but are sometimes a part of inland sales. The nature of a letter of credit can be inferred from its name. First, it is a letter. The letter is written by the bank to the seller. Second, it is a credit. The letter contains a promise by the bank either to pay or to accept drafts presented by the seller on the buyer when those drafts are accompanied by documents of title under the conditions specified in the letter.[70] This letter of credit originates in a bank selected by the buyer and is forwarded, or cabled, to a bank in the seller's city which advises the seller of the issuance of the credit. The originating bank is the "issuer"; the buyer is the "customer"; the advising bank is called the "advising bank" which may or may not confirm the credit;[71] and the seller is the "beneficiary." A letter of credit may be revocable or irrevocable, but the latter type is the only one which is thoroughly protective because, unless otherwise agreed, "once an irrevocable credit is established as regards the customer it can be modified or revoked only with the consent of the customer and once it is established as regards the beneficiary it can be modified or revoked only with his consent."[72]

Neither the issuer of a credit nor the advising bank is concerned with the underlying sale. The issuer is superimposing its credit on the contract for sale and, although the issuer will receive the documents, it does not intend to take possession of the goods. Instead the issuer will deliver the documents to the buyer under whatever financial arrangements were made with the buyer at the time the credit was obtained, and the buyer will use those documents to claim the goods from the carrier.

The seller receives greater protection with the letter of credit than he received with only the sight draft because, on compliance with the conditions in the letter, the issuer becomes liable to the seller for the amount of the draft—up to the amount of the remaining credit.[73]

70. UCC § 5–103.

71. *Id.*

72. UCC § 5–106(2). A revocable credit may be "modified or revoked by the issuer without notice to or consent from the customer or beneficiary." UCC § 5–106(3). *Cf.* UCC § 5–106(4).

73. Custom is to be read into the statement of condition to determine whether the seller has complied with those conditions. Thus, a credit conditioned upon submission of *full set* of bills of lading was satisfied when but one of the set of two bills of lading was presented together with bank indemnity against loss from absence of other bill of lading. Dixon, Irmaos & CIA. Ltda. v. Chase Nat'l Bank, 144 F.2d 759 (2d Cir. 1944), *cert. denied* 324 U.S. 850, 65 S.Ct. 687, 89 L.Ed. 1410 (1945). For opposing comments on this case read Backus and Harfield, *Custom and Letters of Credit: the Dixon, Irmaos Case,* 52 Colum. L.Rev. 589 (1952); Honnold, *A Footnote to the Controversy Over the Dixon Case, Custom and Letters of Credit: the Position of the Uniform Commercial Code,* 53 Colum.L.Rev. 973 (1953). *See* UCC § 5–113, Comment 4, and UCC § 2–323(2).

Thus, the seller has obtained the credit not only of the buyer, but also of the bank issuing the letter of credit.[74]

§ 102. The Perfect Tender Rule

In many kinds of contracts the performance obligations of one party are triggered by the substantial performance of the promise of the other contracting party.[75] Full performance is not required; substantial performance will suffice.[76] The Code, however, adopts the general rule applicable to commercial contracts: "if the goods or their tender of delivery fail in any respect to conform to the contract," [77] the buyer may, among other courses of action, reject all of the goods. Both the goods and the tender must conform to the contract. A nonconforming tender is a sufficient ground for rejection even though the goods do conform. Further a failure *in any respect* to conform is the basis for rejecting the tender. The Code, therefore, adopts as its basic rule the requirement of a perfect tender by the seller. "There is no room in commercial contracts for the doctrine of substantial performance." [78]

There are several exceptions to the perfect tender rule. These exceptions are considered in the following sections of this text and should be consulted to determine the complete scope of the seller's performance obligations. Nevertheless, whenever the basic rule is applicable, only full performance—unless the defect falls within the idea of *de minimis*—will obligate the buyer to accept the goods and to pay their price. The buyer may, of course, elect to accept the defective performance, but he is not required to do so.[79]

A good illustration of the common law perfect tender rule arises out of facts which occurred during World War I.[80] A buyer ordered 300 crates of Australian onions to be shipped in March under a C.I.F. San Francisco contract from Australia to the United States. At this time there was only one ship sailing each month between the Australian port of shipment and San Francisco; thus, unless the onions could be loaded on the March ship, the seller could not deliver the onions during the time required by the contract.

74. The buyer's obligation to pay is suspended by a proper letter of credit but, upon dishonor of the credit, is reinstated. UCC § 2–325(2).

75. 3A A. Corbin, Contracts §§ 700–12 (1960).

76. Jacob & Youngs, Inc. v. Kent, 230 N.Y. 239, 129 N.E. 889 (1921).

77. UCC § 2–601.

78. Mitsubishi Goshi Kaisha v. J. Aron & Co., 16 F.2d 185, 186 (2d Cir. 1926).

79. §§ 142, 150 *infra*.

80. Prescott & Co. v. J. B. Powles & Co., 113 Wash. 177, 193 P. 680 (1920).

The seller had 300 crates of the ordered onions ready for shipment (we can assume that he had them sitting on the dock) when the United States took space in the ship to carry wheat to the United States (and we can assume that the wheat was necessary for the "war effort"). As a result the seller was permitted to load only 240 crates. A draft and the attached bill of lading were tendered to the buyer who refused to pay the draft or accept the onions—because in the meantime the buyer had decided that he did not want any onions and had attempted to cancel the entire order, not knowing that only 240 crates had been shipped. The onions were sold at a loss, and the seller sued to recover his damages. The lower court granted full recovery to the seller. The buyer appealed and the Supreme Court of Washington reversed.

The court was willing to assume that the action of the United States in commandeering the space on the ship would have provided a defense to the seller if he had been sued for failure to ship the entire 300 crates, but when the seller sues on the contract "it is essential to a recovery that a full performance be shown, and no excuse not provided for in the contract will justify a recovery where the performance is partial only, save only an act of the buyer in rendering performance impossible or a waiver by it." [81] Likewise, if the goods are not up to their warranted quality,[82] or are delivered after the date specified in the agreement,[83] or if the documents are not in their agreed-upon form,[84] the buyer may reject the tender and successfully defend an action for breach on his part.

This rule has even been applied to transactions in which the seller has tendered more goods than were called for by the contract between the parties. Thus, a tender of 53 tons of metal scrap is not a proper

---

81. *Id.* at 181, 193 P. at 682.

82. *In re* A. W. Cowen & Bros., Inc., 11 F.2d 692 (2d Cir. 1926). *Cf.* Ingle v. Marked Tree Equip. Co., 244 Ark. 1166, 428 S.W.2d 286 (1968). If the buyer accepts non-conforming goods, he may nevertheless revoke his acceptance under the conditions stated in UCC § 2–608. Revocation of acceptance differs from rejection in that the non-conformity must "substantially impair its value" to the buyer. Thus, once goods have been accepted, insubstantial non-conformity is not sufficient to allow the buyer to return the goods. Lanners v. Whitney, 247 Or. 223, 428 P.2d 398 (1967); Rozmus v. Thompson's Lincoln-Mercury Co., 209 Pa.Super. 120, 224 A.2d 782 (1966). Another difference between rejection and revocation of acceptance lies in the party having the burden of proof. If the buyer is seeking to reject, the seller bears the risk of persuading the trier of fact that the performance conformed; if the buyer is seeking to revoke acceptance, the buyer bears the risk of persuading the trier of fact that the performance was non-conforming. Miron v. Yonkers Raceway, Inc., 400 F.2d 112 (2d Cir. 1968). See § 143 *infra*.

83. Graves v. Flynn, 63 So.2d 619 (La.Ct.App.1953); Philip Carey Mfg. Co. v. General Prods., Co., 89 R.I. 136, 151 A.2d 487 (1959). *Cf.* Cartozian & Sons v. Ostruske-Murphy, Inc., 64 Wash.2d 1, 390 P.2d 548 (1964).

84. Mitsubishi Goshi Kaisha v. J. Aron & Co., 16 F.2d 185 (2d Cir. 1926).

tender of the seller's performance obligations under an agreement calling for the sale and purchase of 30 to 40 tons of metal scrap.[85] Such a tender fails to conform to the contract, and the Code allows the buyer to reject the tender. In some instances application of this rule can be justified. The buyer ought not to be compelled to accept a substantial burden which was not imposed upon him by his agreement, and having to sort the correct amount or quality from the mass tendered, or having to pay an additional sum for taking the whole mass, can be such a burden that courts should hold that the seller has not performed his contractual promise. There are, however, some situations in which application of the rule cannot be justified and in these cases pre-Code courts held that a tender of more goods than were ordered was a sufficient performance. These are cases in which the burden of selection from the mass was not great and the buyer was not required to take care of shipping the excess goods back to the seller.[86] The same result should follow if the seller tenders an extra item or two of the kind ordered to be certain that there is a sufficient quantity of conforming goods—if the seller is willing to let the buyer keep the entire amount at no increase in the total price.[87] The Code should continue these pre-Code results despite the adoption of the perfect tender rule.

2. LIMITATIONS ON THE PERFECT TENDER RULE

§ 103. Agreement Limiting Buyer's Remedies

The full text of section 2–601 is as follows:

> Subject to the provisions of this Article on breach in installment contracts (Section 2–612) and unless otherwise agreed under the sections on contractual limitations of remedy (Sections 2–718 and 2–719), if the goods or the tender of delivery fail in any respect to conform to the contract, the buyer may
>
> (a) reject the whole; or
>
> (b) accept the whole; or
>
> (c) accept any commercial unit or units and reject the rest.

---

85. Perry v. Mount Hope Iron Co., 16 R.I. 318, 15 A. 87 (1888).

86. UCC § 2–612, Comment 5; Davis v. Adams, 18 Ala. 264 (1850).

87. Alfred Shrimpton & Sons v. Warmack, 72 Miss. 208, 16 So. 494 (1894).

Even if the seller is not willing to let the buyer keep the increased tender at the gross contract price, the buyer may accept the tender. List & Son v. Chase, 80 Ohio St. 42, 88 N.E. 120 (1909); Pressure Cast Prods. Corp. v. Page, 261 Wis. 197, 51 N.W.2d 898 (1952). See UCC § 2–605.

This section establishes the perfect tender rule already discussed: [88] if the goods or the tender fail *in any respect* to conform to the contract, the buyer may reject the entire shipment. Such a rule defines the seller's performance obligation. Both the goods and their tender must conform to the contract.[89] This rule is subject, however, to several limitations or exceptions, two of which are indicated in section 2–601. Installment contracts and situations in which the parties have agreed to limit their remedies are specifically exempted from the requirement of a perfect tender. This section discusses the "unless otherwise agreed" exception; the following section of this text deals with the seller's performance obligations in an installment contract.

The parties may agree to limit their remedies in instances in which there is a default. That limitation on remedies may be in the form of a liquidated damage clause [90] or any agreement which provides for remedies in addition to or in substitution for those provided by Article 2.[91] The typical clause affecting the seller's obligation to perform is one which substitutes the right to have defective parts repaired or replaced in place of the right to reject or revoke acceptance on discovery that the goods do not conform to the contract. If this clause is effective, the buyer will not be able to reject non-conforming goods which can be made conforming through repair or replacement of a defective part.[92] An example of the operation of such a clause can be shown through the following hypothetical example: a buyer purchased a new refrigerator from a seller, and when the refrigerator was delivered by the seller to the buyer one of the doors was damaged and the motor was defective. If the agreement between the buyer and seller contained no limitation on the buyer's remedies, the buyer could reject the tender and recover damages based upon his rightful rejection. If the agreement contained an effective limitation of the buyer's remedies, the buyer could not reject the refrigerator but the seller would be obligated to repair the defective parts.[93]

The general guidelines for determining the effectiveness of a provision in an agreement limiting the buyer's remedies have already

88. § 102 *supra.*

89. §§ 95–96 *supra.*

90. UCC § 2–718; § 154 *infra.*

91. UCC § 2–719. This section is quoted in part in § 89 *supra.*

92. Where the seller refuses to give consideration to a well-founded complaint, there has been a breach of warranty although the warranty given limited remedies to repair or replacement. The normal measure of recovery would be the cost of repair, but when the buyer did not know the cause of the difficulty, the measure was the market value of the goods. Cox Motor Car Co. v. Castle, 402 S.W. 2d 429 (Ky.1966).

93. Evans Mfg. Corp. v. Wolosin, 47 Luz.Leg.Reg. 238 (Pa.C.P.1957).

been presented.[94] Those guidelines apply to the specific repair-or-replacement limitation. They include:

1. The requirement that the *agreement* provide for the limitation on the buyer's privilege to reject non-conforming goods. "Agreement" means the bargain of the parties in fact as found in the language they used or as implied from the circumstances surrounding their negotiations.[95] Thus, if the buyer understood (subjectively) that he was purchasing goods which could not be rejected or returned if they failed to conform to the contract, that understanding will be given effect by the court. Likewise, the agreement may rest on principles of objective mutual assent—that is, it may be found in circumstances which justify the seller in reasonably assuming that the buyer was agreeing to a repair-or-replacement limitation. However, if the trier of fact believes that the buyer did not subjectively understand that such a provision was a part of the agreement and that the seller had no reasonable basis for assuming that the buyer did so understand (as where the printed provision in a form contract was neither conspicuous nor brought to the buyer's attention and where the form was signed by the buyer without the buyer's having had an opportunity to comprehend the printed clauses), there is no *agreement* limiting the buyer's remedies, and the printed clause is no bar to rejection of non-conforming goods.[96]

2. The repair-or-replacement limitation must not fail of its essential purpose.[97] If it does fail, Code remedies (including rejection) would be available to the buyer.

3. Even if the repair-or-replacement provision is otherwise effective, it will become unenforceable in limiting consequential damages in those instances in which the provision is unconscionable. A common illustration of how such a provision may become unconscionable can be found with the hypothetical buyer who decided to purchase a new refrigerator. Suppose that the seller carefully explained that the refrigerator could not be rejected if non-conforming but that the defective parts would be repaired or replaced; that repair or replacement would be the buyer's sole remedy against the seller; and that the form which the buyer was about to sign contained a provision covering this understanding. Suppose further that the seller pointed out the printed provision and gave the buyer ample opportunity to read the entire form. If the delivered refrigerator had a defective motor, the seller would have the opportunity to replace the motor, and the buyer could not rightfully reject the goods on the grounds that they were non-conform-

---

94. § 89 *supra*.

95. UCC § 1–201(3).

96. Klein v. Asgrow Seed Co., 246 Cal. App.2d 87, 54 Cal.Rptr. 609 (1966).

97. This requirement is analyzed in § 89 *supra*.

ing. However, if the defective motor caused a fire in the buyer's house and damaged the kitchen and injured the buyer, limitation of the buyer's remedies to a new motor (or even to a repaired refrigerator) could well be an unconscionable application of that limitation. The buyer who is buying goods for his personal, family, or household use would probably understand the typical repair-or-replacement limitation to apply to the goods but not to damages sustained through the use of defective goods. Applying the provision outside its reasonably understood scope would be unconscionable.[98] Accordingly, the Code provides that limitation "of consequential damages for injury to the person in the case of consumer goods is prima facie unconscionable but limitation of damages where the loss is commercial is not." [99]

The result of an effective provision limiting buyer's remedies to repair or replacement ameliorates some of the harshness of the perfect tender rule to the extent that the buyer cannot reject a non-conforming tender which can be made conforming. Whether the clause will also limit the buyer's damages in the event of injury through use of the defective goods depends upon the factors discussed above.

§ 104. Installment Contracts

The installment contract forms another exception to the perfect tender rule—the Code rule which allows the buyer to reject any tender which does not conform in every respect to the contract.[1] With the installment contract the seller may trigger the buyer's obligation to accept and pay for the goods even though the seller has tendered less than complete performance. The failure to perform completely is, of course, a breach for which the seller is liable in damages; in that sense a "perfect tender" is still required by the Code. Nevertheless, something short of a perfect tender will obligate the installment contract buyer to accept the goods and pay their price (less damages suffered); in that sense the "perfect tender" rule is relaxed by the Code.[2]

98. Henry v. W. S. Reichenbach & Son, 45 Pa.D. & C.2d 171 (C.P.1968). Another type of clause which attempts to limit buyer's remedies is the one in which the buyer is required to give notice of defects within a specific number of days from the date the goods have been delivered or be barred of any remedy. When the defects would not become apparent within the specified time period, these clauses have been held unconscionable. Neville Chem. Co. v. Union Carbide Corp., 294 F.Supp. 649 (W.D.Pa.1968), aff'd 422 F.2d 1205 (3d Cir. 1970). The unconscionability is a question of law for the court. Wilson Trading Corp. v. David Ferguson, Ltd., 23 N.Y.2d 398, 297 N.Y.S.2d 108, 244 N.E.2d 685 (1968); § 44 supra.

99. UCC § 2–719(3). "Consumer goods" are defined in UCC § 9–109(1), and this definition is applicable to Article 2. UCC § 2–103(3).

1. § 102 supra.

2. UCC § 2–612.

This is not a distinction without a difference. The privilege of rejection can be a powerful weapon. In a shipment contract the goods will most often be at the buyer's place of business when they are rejected. The seller—who may be hundreds of miles away—will be called upon to determine whether goods which are now in a railroad yard in the buyer's city are in fact non-conforming and, if they are, how best to dispose of them.[3] Further, if the perfect tender rule applies, the seller knows that in any lawsuit he will be called upon to prove that the goods and their tender were in complete conformity with the contract even though this particular tender was only one of several called for by the contract. The time and expense involved for the seller may cause a buyer to reject in the hopes of forcing a compromise price. The Code recognizes the interests of the seller by obligating the buyer to take goods even though they do not conform in every respect to the contract; the Code also recognizes the interests of the buyer by requiring the seller to pay damages for his default, no matter how trivial.

The Code rules with respect to installment contracts can be summarized as follows:

1. The parties may agree that accurate conformity in the quality of the goods is a condition to the duty of the buyer to accept an installment delivery.[4] They must, however, *agree* to such a provision. A clause to this effect inserted in the buyer's form does not necessarily show agreement—even if the seller signed the form. Before such a clause will be enforced, that clause "must, however, have some basis in reason, must avoid imposing hardship by surprise and is subject to waiver or displacement by practical construction."[5]

2. When there is no such effective agreement, the Code divides a seller's defective performances under installment contracts into two kinds: first, those which involve a defect in the *required* documents and, second, those which involve other defects. The first kind of defect is considered below. The second requires a further division: those which do not substantially impair the value of that installment, and those which do substantially impair the value of that installment. The insubstantial impairment tenders cannot be rightfully rejected by the buyer. In these cases the seller is not obligated to make a perfect tender to trigger the buyer's obligation to pay for the goods, although

---

3. The merchant buyer's duties following a rightful rejection give some protection to such a seller. UCC § 2–603. The buyer's options as to salvage of goods rightfully rejected are detailed in UCC § 2–604.

4. UCC § 2–612 does not contain the usual "unless otherwise agreed" language, but UCC §§ 1–102(3) and (4) read with UCC § 2–612 provide a statutory basis for the statement in the text.

5. UCC § 2–612, Comment 4.

the seller will be required to respond in damages for any harm suffered by the buyer because of the defective tender.

These divisions leave a group of cases in which (1) the seller's tender was defective, (2) there was no agreement between the parties requiring a perfect tender by the seller, (3) the defect was not in the required documents, and (4) the defect caused a substantial impairment in the value of the tendered installment.[6] The result is a group of cases in each of which the seller has not even substantially performed his contractual promise. Still the buyer cannot rightfully reject the seller's tender if the tender can be "cured" and if the seller gives adequate assurance of its cure.[7] At this point the Code is attempting to keep the goods moving in commerce even though the initial tender by the seller was substantially defective. The group of cases referred to above would, therefore, be decided as follows: if the substantial defect cannot be cured, the buyer may reject;[8] if it can be cured but the seller fails to give the necessary assurance, the buyer may reject; if the defect can be cured and the seller gives the necessary assurance, the buyer may accept but, if the seller later fails to cure, the buyer may at that time revoke his acceptance and return the goods to the seller.[9] The result is a statutory scheme by which the seller is protected against rejection when he can "cure," and by which the buyer is assured of getting the goods he ordered.

There is some difficulty in determining the meaning of "cure" as applied to the installment contract. The Code's section on "cure" covers more cases than just the installment contract. It allows a seller

---

6. The statutory language provides that the "buyer may reject any installment which is non-conforming if the non-conformity substantially impairs the value of that installment and cannot be cured or if the non-conformity is a defect in the required documents; but if the non-conformity does not fall within subsection (3) and the seller gives adequate assurance of its cure the buyer must accept that installment." UCC § 2–612(2).

One problem presented by this subsection is how to measure the value of an installment so that it can be determined whether the defective tender substantially impaired that value. Is that value to be measured against the requirements of the contract, the needs of the buyer, the willfulness of the seller's default, or some external standard of value? In this respect the reference in UCC § 2–608 ("substantially impairs its value *to him*") is more explicit and probably represents

what the drafters had in mind under UCC § 2–612(2). This test also applies to situations involving anticipatory repudiation. UCC § 2–610. A good general discussion of substantial performance is contained in 3A A. Corbin, Contracts §§ 709–10 (1960).

7. UCC § 2–612(2), quoted in the prior footnote, causes some difficulty in reaching the conclusion in the text, but the textual statement appears to represent the intention of the drafters.

8. Graulich Caterer Inc. v. Hans Holterbosch, Inc., 101 N.J.Super. 61, 243 A.2d 253 (App.Div.1968).

9. UCC § 2–608(1) (a); § 153 *infra*. If the buyer fails to allow the seller to cure, damages sustained through use of the defective goods are not recoverable from the seller. Robertson Mfg. Co. v. Jefferson Tile Co., 5 UCC Rep. 119 (N.Y.Sup.Ct.1968).

to cure a defective tender which has been rejected when the time for performance has not expired or when the seller had reasonable grounds to believe that his non-conforming tender would be accepted—providing in either case that proper notice has been given.[10] Therefore, if an installment seller has tendered an installment prior to the delivery date, the buyer could not rightfully reject that tender even if it varied substantially from the requirements of the contract—providing that the defect could be cured within the time set for delivery and providing that the seller gave adequate notice of his intention to cure.

The general section on cure presents two problems when applied to defective installment tenders. The first is relatively minor: the cure section is conditioned on a prior rejection by the buyer while the installment section prevents rejection if cure is possible. Courts should have no trouble in following the installment section. The second is more troublesome. Cure requires a "conforming" tender or delivery. Does this mean that the installment seller must make a perfect tender when correcting a substantial default or is it sufficient if he corrects the delivery so that it substantially conforms to the contract? Neither the Code nor the Comments suggest an answer. Nevertheless, the policy of the installment section should prevail and a cure which removes any substantial impairment of value ought to suffice to trigger the buyer's obligation to accept and pay.

3.   Where there is no effective agreement and the defect is in the *required* documents (*e. g.*, the absence of an insurance document in a C.I.F. contract), the doctrine of substantial performance has no application. Any defect is a sufficient basis for rejection. "Even in such cases, however, the provisions on cure of tender apply if appropriate documents are readily procurable." [11]

4.   The Code rules discussed thus far apply only to rejection or acceptance of the defective installment. When may the buyer treat the delivery of a defective installment as a breach of the entire contract? The Code provides this answer:

> Whenever non-conformity or default with respect to one or more installments substantially impairs the value of the whole contract there is a breach of the whole. But the aggrieved party reinstates the contract if he accepts a nonconforming installment without seasonably notifying of cancellation or if he brings an action with respect only to past installments or demands performance as to future installments.[12]

---

10.   UCC § 2–508; § 105 *infra*.

11.   UCC § 2–612, Comment 4.

12.   UCC § 2–612(3). When this section is applicable the buyer may also reject the defective installment even though the seller offers to cure the defective tender. UCC § 2–612(2).

The buyer may not use this subsection to declare a breach of the whole contract solely because the seller's failure to deliver one or more installments made it unlikely that further deliveries would be forthcoming. If the probability of obtaining future deliveries concerns the buyer, he must use the section on the right to demand adequate assurance that those deliveries will be made, and only if he fails to get the assurance may he cancel future performances under an installment contract.[13] The Code's test for an immediate cancellation is whether the default as to the installments substantially impairs the value of the whole contract.[14] This is a question of fact for each case. Further, the sentence on reinstatement of the contract indicates a Code policy to continue the installment contract if the aggrieved party gives an indication that he wants it continued.

The subsection quoted above applies also to defaults by installment buyers. Nonpayment of an apportionable part of the entire price gives the seller the privilege of treating the entire contract as breached only if that nonpayment substantially impaired the value of the entire contract. If the nonpayment causes the seller concern that future deliveries will be met by similar failures to pay, the seller must rely on the section on adequate assurances. However, "a seller may withhold a delivery pending payment for prior ones, at the same time delaying his decision as to cancellation." [15]

5. These rules as to installment contracts substantially vary the perfect tender rule. The extent to which they will apply to commercial transactions depends on how broadly an "installment contract" is defined. If defined narrowly, there will be few cases to which the doctrine of substantial performance will be applicable; if defined broadly, the number of cases will be increased. The Code commands the broad interpretation:

> An "installment contract" is one which requires or authorizes the delivery of goods in separate lots to be separately accepted, even though the contract contains a clause "each delivery is a separate contract" or its equivalent.[16]

§ 105. Cure

Another limitation on the seller's need to make a perfect tender as a condition to the buyer's obligation to accept and pay for the goods arises out of the seller's right to cure a defective tender. Cure is allowed by section 2–508 in two situations:

---

13. UCC § 2–609.

14. Myers v. Anderson, 98 Colo. 394, 56 P.2d 37 (1936); Graulich Caterer Inc. v. Hans Holtersbosch, Inc., 101 N.J. Super. 61, 243 A.2d 253 (App.Div.1968).

15. UCC § 2–612, Comment 7; Rau Fastener Co. v. Trailmark Outdoor Prods., Inc., 4 UCC Rep. 1171 (N.Y.Sup. Ct.1968).

16. UCC § 2–612(1).

(1) Where any tender or delivery by the seller is rejected because non-conforming and the time for performance has not yet expired, the seller may seasonably notify the buyer of his intention to cure and may then within the contract time make a conforming delivery.

(2) Where the buyer rejects a non-conforming tender which the seller had reasonable grounds to believe would be acceptable with or without money allowance the seller may if he seasonably notifies the buyer have a further reasonable time to substitute a conforming tender.

In one sense section 2–508 does not limit the seller's obligation to deliver or tender conforming goods. Even when he cures, the seller must eventually either "make a conforming delivery" or "substitute a conforming tender." [17] However, section 2–508 allows sellers in some situations to make a second delivery or tender when they learn that the first was non-conforming. In these situations the perfect tender need not be made the first time but may be made at some later date. In this sense section 2–508 does act as a limitation on the seller's obligation to deliver conforming goods.

The first type of cure covered by section 2–508 is not novel to the Code; pre-Code law recognized the right of a seller to correct a tender if he did so prior to the contract time for delivery.[18] Such a rule is based on fairness to the seller without causing harm to the buyer. When a seller has made an early delivery, that fact alone ought not prevent him from withdrawing that delivery if it turns out to be non-conforming and tendering conforming goods on or before the date set for delivery. A typical example can arise with a contract to deliver a certain model refrigerator, "aqua green in color," on or before March 1. Assume that on February 20 the seller delivered a refrigerator, but when he uncrated it in the buyer's home he noticed that the one he had put on the truck was beige in color. If the seller immediately told the buyer that he would take the beige refrigerator back to the store and have the aqua green model installed before March 1, the cure requirements of section 2–508 have been met. The seasonable notice pro-

---

17. "Cure" in an installment contract may require only a delivery of goods which substantially conform to the contract. § 104 *supra*. In single delivery contracts "conforming" under UCC § 2–508(2) must mean conforming except as to the date of delivery.

18. Lowinson v. Newman, 201 App.Div. 266, 194 N.Y.S. 253 (1922); Portfolio

v. Rubin, 196 App.Div. 316, 187 N.Y.S. 302 (1921), *aff'd.* 233 N.Y. 439, 135 N.E. 843 (1922). Other cases are cited in 2 S. Williston, Sales § 459 (rev. ed. 1948); Hawkland, *Curing an Improper Tender of Title to Chattels: Past, Present and Commercial Code,* 46 Minn.L. Rev. 697 (1962).

tected the buyer, and the early mistake ought not prevent the seller from performing within the time specified by the contract.[19]

This subsection cannot be applied mechanically by holding that in every instance a delivery on or before the contract date can correct an improper tender or delivery. The goods may be of a kind which the buyer needs on the date specified—not a few hours later—and the early non-conforming tender could cause the buyer reasonably to believe that conforming goods would not be forthcoming from the seller. Such a buyer may have made immediate alternative contracts to fill his needs, and a later attempt to cure within the contract time would be ineffective because a seasonable notice had not been given the buyer.[20]

This problem can be illustrated by assuming that a canner had a contract with a tomato grower by which the grower had agreed to deliver a specified kind and quality of tomatoes, "to be delivered on March 1." If the seller delivered the wrong kind of tomatoes during the morning of March 1, which delivery the canner-buyer rejected, the seller would have to give almost immediate notice that conforming tomatoes would be delivered later that same day—or else his attempted delivery in the afternoon of March 1 could be an ineffective attempt to cure. The canner may have arranged his plant and labor force so that he would begin canning operations on March 2. Such a buyer need not speculate as to whether he will receive the tomatoes from the seller, and if he has made a substitute contract with another grower before receiving notice from the first seller, the later notice from the seller would not be "seasonable." [21]

The second type of cure presents ideas not found in pre-Code law. It allows sellers in some instances to cure even after the date set for performance. The problem is to determine those instances in which a late cure is permissible. The primary difficulty is to determine the subject of the "which" clause: "Where the buyer rejects a non-conforming tender which [what?] the seller had reasonable grounds to believe would be acceptable. . . ." Two readings are possible: "which [tender] the seller had reasonable grounds to believe would be acceptable," or "which [non-conforming tender] the seller had reasonable grounds to believe would be acceptable." The change in the subject of this clause affects the number of cases covered by this subsection.

---

19. Robertson Mfg. Co. v. Jefferson Tile Co., 5 UCC Rep. 119 (N.Y.Sup.Ct. 1968). The Comments state that cure within UCC § 2–508(1) can occur even though the buyer has returned the goods and received a refund of the purchase price. UCC § 2–508, Comment 1. A mutual assent rescission would prevent the operation of such cure, but the buyer's unilateral rejection would not. Lowinson v. Newman, 201 App. Div. 266, 194 N.Y.S. 253 (1922).

20. Seixas v. Ockershausen, 7 N.Y.St. Rep. 256, 43 Hun 559 (Sup.Ct.1887).

21. UCC § 2–508, Comment 1.

Consider the following hypothetical factual patterns:

Case # 1: A seller and buyer entered into a contract for the sale and purchase of a new color television set of a specified make and model. Between the time of the making of the contract and the date set for delivery the manufacturer introduced a new model of the set ordered. The seller, knowing that the new model was not the one ordered by the buyer but reasonably believing that the buyer would prefer the improved model, delivered the new model to the buyer for the original price. The buyer may reject the tender because it did not conform to the contract. If the buyer does reject, can the seller cure by having a reasonable time beyond the contract date to correct his non-conforming tender?

The answer ought to be that he can. This answer can be reached by using either "tender" or "non-conforming tender" as the subject of the "which" clause in section 2–508(2). This seller knew that his tender did not conform to the agreement of the parties but reasonably believed that this non-conforming tender would be acceptable to this particular buyer. Such a seller should be given additional time to make his tender conforming when he is faced with a surprise rejection.[22]

Case # 2. Assume the same contract for the sale and purchase of a specified make and model color television set. Instead of delivering the new and improved model of the ordered set the seller delivered the old model which was packed in a sealed box in the condition which it was received from the manufacturer. Although the seller believed that the delivered set was conforming, it was in fact defective: all pictures were bright red and no amount of adjustment in the home would correct the defect. Can this seller cure by having a reasonable time beyond the contract date to correct the non-conforming tender?

If it is assumed that there was a contract date for the delivery (which has now passed) and that the buyer did not agree to allow cure as his remedy against this seller, the answer ought to be that such a seller does not have additional time to correct the defect. Such a seller did not know that his tender was non-conforming. Therefore, the only way which section 2–508(2) would protect him would be by using "tender" as the subject of the "which" clause, and by arguing that what section 2–508(2) means is that whenever a seller believes that his tender is a conforming tender he has reasonable grounds for believing that the tender would be acceptable to the buyer. One court

22. Bartus v. Riccardi, 55 Misc.2d 3, 284 N.Y.S.2d 222 (City Ct.1967).

has so read this Code section, but the case could rest equally well on the limitation of remedies agreement which undoubtedly accompanied that sale.[23]

Such a reading of section 2–508(2) should be rejected. It would make the reference to money allowance redundant; a seller who believes that his tender is conforming has no reason to consider a reduction in the price of the goods. It would extend the time for performance in nearly every contract by some undetermined reasonable time, contrary to the general obligations of the seller to deliver according to the terms of the contract. Finally, the seller in Case #2 is in the same position as the great bulk of sellers who find they are mistaken as to the quality of their goods. Such sellers do not merit additional time to do what they agreed to do by a date which has now passed. Thus, this subsection (2–508(2)) should be limited to sellers who knew their tender was non-conforming but who reasonably believed that their buyers would accept the non-conforming tender—only to meet a surprise rejection.[24]

The parties may agree that the seller is not to be allowed to cure a non-conforming tender, and such an agreement will be given effect by courts.[25] As with other agreement problems the appearance of such a clause in a buyer's form is not conclusive even though the seller signed the form. The court must determine whether the clause was a part of the parties' bargain in fact. "If the clause appears in a 'form' contract evidence that it is out of line with trade usage or the prior course of dealing and was not called to the seller's attention may be sufficient to show that the seller had reasonable grounds to believe that the tender would be acceptable." [26]

The parties may also agree to expand the seller's right to cure a defective tender—even to the point of making repair or replacement by the seller the exclusive remedy of the buyer. This type of agreement and its problems are discussed elsewhere in this text.[27]

---

23. Wilson v. Scampoli, 228 A.2d 848 (D.C.App.1967). *Cf.* Zabriskie Chevrolet, Inc. v. Smith, 99 N.J.Super. 441, 240 A.2d 195 (L.Div.1968).

24. The Comments are not helpful in determining how UCC § 2–508(2) is to be read. They state that the reasonable grounds to believe "can lie in prior course of dealing, course of performance or usage of trade as well as in the particular circumstances surrounding the making of the contract." UCC § 2–508, Comment 2. To the extent that these factors influence the meaning of the words used by the parties in reaching agreement, they make the tender conforming. §§ 46–52 *supra*. To the extent that these factors do not give meaning to the agreement, the reference to them by the drafters supports the position of the text. The seller, knowing of the prior course of dealing, etc., thought that his tender would be acceptable.

25. UCC §§ 1–102(3) and (4).

26. UCC § 2–508, Comment 2.

27. §§ 89, 103 *supra*.

Section 2–508 does not give the buyer the right to demand that the seller cure a defect in his tendered product; the section deals only with the seller's right to cure. This, however, should cause no difficulty. If the parties want to give the buyer a right to demand cure, they may put it in their agreement. Even if such a provision is not a part of the contract, the buyer's general remedies give the buyer the needed protection. The buyer may be able to reject, revoke acceptance, or (at the least) keep the goods and collect damages caused by any non-conformity in the tender.[28]

§ 106. Loss of the Buyer's Privilege of Rejection

The Code's perfect tender rule rests primarily on two portions of section 2–601. The first, which has already been discussed, defines the quality of the tender required by the seller: "if the goods or the tender of delivery fail in any respect to conform to the contract . . .." Notice that the test of performance is not one of substantial non-conformity or of substantial impairment of value. When section 2–601 is applicable, *any* non-conformity in the goods or their tender will suffice.

Will suffice for what? This is the critical question in determining the effect of a non-conformity, and its Code answer is the second portion of section 2–601 which is needed to establish the perfect tender rule as defined in a prior section of this text. To illustrate the importance of the Code answer, suppose that section 2–601 began exactly as it does now (that is, defined the quality of the seller's necessary tender in terms of *any* non-conformity in the goods or their tender) but went on to provide that the effect of such a non-conformity would be that the seller would be liable for any damages caused the buyer and stated that only a *substantial* non-conformity would allow the buyer to refuse the goods. Such a provision would have been a restatement of general contract law.[29] Any party who does not perform according to his contractual promises must compensate the other party for resulting injuries, but substantial performance usually obligates the other party to accept what has been tendered.[30]

This, however, is not the answer given by section 2–601. That section grants the buyer three options when any non-conformity is

---

28. § 139 *infra.*

29. 3A A. Corbin, Contracts §§ 700–12 (1960). Cases supporting the statement in the text are cited and discussed by Professor Corbin. The Code's test is presented in § 102 *supra.*

30. *E. g.,* Kauffman v. Raeder, 108 F. 171 (8th Cir. 1901); Harvey v. White, 213 Cal.App.2d 275, 28 Cal.Rptr. 601 (1963); Meador v. Robinson, 263 S.W. 2d 118 (Ky.1953); Antonoff v. Basso, 347 Mich. 18, 78 N.W.2d 604 (1956); Plante v. Jacobs, 10 Wis.2d 567, 103 N.W.2d 296 (1960). *But see* Glazer v. Schwartz, 276 Mass. 54, 176 N.E. 613 (1931).

involved: (1) he may reject all of the goods; (2) he may accept all of the goods; or (3) he may accept any commercial unit or units and reject the rest. The privilege of rejection completes the impact of the perfect tender rule. Not only does any non-conformity in the seller's tender open the seller to a possible damage claim but it also allows the buyer to refuse the goods. Having rightfully refused the goods, the buyer is not obligated to pay the price or respond in damages.

This text has already discussed three instances in which a perfect tender is not required to trigger the buyer's obligation to accept the goods. These involve situations in which the parties have agreed to limit the buyer's remedies, in which an installment contract is involved, or in which the seller has a right to cure a defective tender.[31] A fourth instance can now be added: those cases in which the Code takes from the buyer his privilege of rejecting the goods or any part of them. If the buyer has lost his privilege of rightful rejection, he is obligated to accept the goods even if they do not conform to the contract.[32]

Once goods have been accepted the only way that a buyer can obligate the seller to retake those goods is by revoking his acceptance. If the Code allowed revocation of acceptance for any non-conformity, the perfect tender rule would have been continued even though the buyer had accepted. However, revocation of acceptance is allowed only in limited instances and one of the requirements is that the non-conformity must substantially impair the value of the goods to the buyer.[33] Therefore, once the privilege of rejection is lost, the fact that the tender by the seller was not "perfect" is not crucial in determining whether the buyer must accept and pay for the goods. Of course, any non-conformity must be compensated in damages which can be deducted from the price if it has not been paid.[34]

A complete discussion of when and how a buyer loses his privilege of rejection is included elsewhere in this text.[35] That discussion should be consulted to complete the Code's exceptions to the perfect tender rule.

31. §§ 103–05 *supra*.

32. UCC § 2–606(1) (b).

33. UCC § 2–608(1).

34. UCC § 2–717.

35. §§ 141–44 *infra*.

3. EXCUSE FROM PERFORMANCE

§ 107. Statement of the Problem

The Code contains three sections which state general principles relieving the seller from full performance of his contractual obligations. They can be rationalized within the law of contracts in several ways. They can be explained under language of excuse, impossibility, impracticability, or even implied promise or condition. The most accurate way, however, to explain these sections is to consider the risks which the parties shifted by their agreement.

Agreements are expressed most often in terms of words, and words can be an imprecise method of stating what the parties intended. For example, if A agreed to work for B for five years in exchange for B's promise to pay a salary at stated intervals, the form of the agreement would probably be in terms of an unconditional promise by A to work for those five years. Nevertheless, if B fails to pay a required installment of the salary, A will in most cases be excused from performing further—at least until the salary is paid. The law explains this privilege of A by constructing an order of performance and making B's payment an implied condition of A's obligation to continue to perform.[36] Further, if A were to die during the five year period, A and his estate would in most cases be "excused" from performance.[37] The law explains this result by holding that A's death made his promise impossible to perform, but A's death did not make it impossible for his estate to pay damages. Nevertheless, courts quite properly hold that A's estate would not be liable in damages for B's loss during the portion of the contract period which A did not perform. The words chosen by the parties in expressing their agreement were absolute and unconditional ("A promises to work for B for five years"); yet in the bulk of cases the parties did not intend to shift to A the risks that B would not pay on time or that A might die during the contract period. When the court is convinced that unconditional words were not intended to shift the risk of the events which in fact occurred, the party is relieved from performance—and from paying damages for his nonperformance. The most accurate way to explain this result is to recognize that contracts are devices by which parties are allowed to shift risks involved in the occurrence or nonoccurrence of future events but that the words they chose to accomplish this result are not necessarily conclusive in deter-

---

36. 3A A. Corbin, Contracts §§ 675–76 (1960).

37. Clifton v. Clark, 83 Miss. 446, 36 So. 251 (1904). *Cf.* Mendenhall v. Davis, 52 Wash. 169, 100 P. 336 (1909). An early explanation of the rule is contained in Yerrington v. Greene, 7 R.I. 589 (1863), a case where the employer died. Other cases are cited in 6 A. Corbin, Contracts § 1335 (1962).

mining whether a particular risk was or was not shifted. Obligations may be stated in unconditional form only because the parties failed to consider the event which did occur.

The task of deciding what risks were shifted by the agreement (in Code terms, determining just what the "contract" was) is one of the more difficult problems facing a court in contract actions. If the court believes that the parties intended to place the responsibility for the occurrence or nonoccurrence of the event on either of the parties, that intention ought to prevail. Often, however, the court is confronted with a complete lack of intention—the parties did not even consider the problem. In such a situation the court has no alternative but to decide where the loss ought to fall. It cannot escape a decision on this question because even a dismissal of the action results in placing a portion of the risk on one of the parties. For example, if B sued A's estate for damages arising out of A's failure to perform the balance of his five year contract when A died, a dismissal of that suit has placed the risk of A's death on B to this limited extent: B cannot shift to A's assets the loss which occurred when A did not perform the work which the words of his unconditional promise indicated he would perform. B must bear the resulting losses because the contract (that is, the legally enforceable obligations arising out of the agreement) did not place on A the risk of A's continuing survival. B does not, however, bear the "risk" of A's death in the sense that B now becomes liable for any damages to A's estate, and normally B is not required to continue paying A's salary. There is no escape from the fact that the court's decision on the problem of which party ought to bear certain risks is a policy determination. The result can be masked in language of implied intent, which one is the "expert," or impossibility of performance, but these expressions are shorthand methods of stating that one party or the other ought to assume responsibility for the events which occurred—or did not occur.[38]

Three sections of the Code apply these ideas to contracts for the sale of goods. They deal with situations which occur most frequently in commercial contracts and state the policies to be applied when the parties did not turn their attention to the problem now facing the court. The first section deals with casualty to identified goods,[39] the second with substitute performance,[40] and the third with excuse because of a failure of presupposed conditions.[41] Each of these is discussed in the following sections of this text.

---

38. See Transatlantic Fin. Corp. v. United States, 124 U.S.App.D.C. 183, 363 F.2d 312 (1966); 6 A. Corbin, Contracts §§ 1328, 1331, 1337 (1962).

39. UCC § 2–613; § 108 *infra*.

40. UCC § 2–614; § 109 *infra*.

41. UCC § 2–615; § 110 *infra*.

§ 108. Casualty to Identified Goods

Section 2–613 brings into the law of sales a doctrine applicable to the law of contracts [42] but attempts to make the result of cases arising under this doctrine more predictable than they were at common law. That section provides:

> Where the contract requires for its performance goods identified when the contract is made, and the goods suffer casualty without fault of either party before the risk of loss passes to the buyer, or in a proper case under a "no arrival, no sale" term (Section 2–324) then
>
> (a) if the loss is total the contract is avoided; and
>
> (b) if the loss is partial or the goods have so deteriorated as no longer to conform to the contract the buyer may nevertheless demand inspection and at his option either treat the contract as avoided or accept the goods with due allowance from the contract price for the deterioration or the deficiency in quantity but without further right against the seller.

This section contains several conditions which must be satisfied before the relief given in subsection (a) and (b) is available to the parties. Those conditions vary depending on whether the contract is or is not a "no arrival, no sale" contract.

The "no arrival, no sale" term in an agreement is sometimes used in overseas destination contracts, often when the seller is reselling goods which have been shipped by another. The purpose of such a term is to make clear to the buyer that the seller is not taking the risk that the goods are conforming or that they will arrive at their destination.[43] The term may also be used when the seller is willing to take the risk that the goods may be lost during shipment but is not willing to take the added responsibility of liability for damages to the buyer if the goods do not arrive. Whenever the term is used the seller, unless the parties have otherwise agreed, "must properly ship conforming goods and if they arrive by any means he must tender them on arrival but he assumes no obligation that the goods will arrive unless

---

42. An early case is Taylor v. Caldwell, 3 Best & S. 826, 122 Eng.Rep. 309 (1863), where a hired hall was destroyed after the execution of the contract but before the date set for performance. The Uniform Sales Act §§ 7–8 adopted the basic principle of impossibility. Pre-Code law is discussed in 1 S. Williston, Sales §§ 160–165 (rev. ed. 1948). The distinction between the divisible and entire contract has been abandoned "in favor of adjustment in business terms." UCC § 2–613, Comment Changes.

43. See J. A. Kirsch & Co. v. Benyunes, 105 Misc. 648, 174 N.Y.S. 794 (Sup.Ct. 1919), aff'd 191 App.Div. 904, 180 N.Y.S. 940 (1920).

he has caused the non-arrival."[44] Therefore, the seller is in default if he either ships non-conforming goods or causes the non-arrival. Further, if the goods do arrive, he must tender them to the buyer; the seller does not retain the option of tendering or of not tendering such goods. On arrival there is a sale to the buyer.

If goods under such a contract are partially lost, if they have deteriorated so that they no longer conform, or if they arrive late, the buyer is entitled to the relief provided for by subsection (b) of section 2–613, set out above.[45] In theory, he would also be entitled to the relief in subsection (a) but since total avoidance of the contract is a part of the meaning of a "no arrival, no sale" contract, there is no special reason to rely on this part of section 2–613.

Section 2–613 provides for avoidance or partial avoidance of some contracts which do not contain the "no arrival, no sale" term. The conditions on the operation of this section to these contracts are:

1. The goods must be "identified" when the contract is made. Section 2–501 defines when identification occurs, and applies both to existing and to future goods.[46] The requirement in section 2–613 that the goods be identified "when the contract is made" could be read to limit section 2–613 to goods which are existing at the time of the execution of the contract. Such a reading would eliminate from the protection of section 2–613 those goods which were destroyed before the contract was made as well as any goods which were identified after the contract was made but lost before delivery. This limited reading of section 2–613 should be rejected. The drafters meant to include goods already destroyed [47] and, in proper circumstances, even future goods which had been identified before their destruction should fall within the policies of section 2–613. Perhaps the closest synonym for "identified" in this section is "specified." If the purchased goods are specified by the contract (as that one refrigerator and no other, or that machine to be built and no other), the first condition of section 2–613 has been met.

2. The contract must "require" that the identified goods be delivered in performance of the contract. The section has no application to the usual contract for the sale of goods in which the seller is not required to deliver a particular item of goods but may deliver any goods fitting the contract description. The first two conditions should be read together to understand the impact of section 2–613; the con-

---

44.   UCC § 2–324(a).

45.   UCC § 2–324(b).

46.   § 126 *infra*.

47.   UCC § 2–613, Comment 2.

tract must obligate the seller to deliver a specific item, and no other item (not even one that looks just like the one ordered) will satisfy the contract.[48]

3. The goods must suffer casualty.

4. The casualty must be suffered without the fault of either party. The inference from this requirement is that if the buyer is at fault, he will remain obligated to purchase, but if the seller is at fault, he will remain obligated to deliver.

5. The risk of loss must not have passed to the buyer. If the risk has passed to the buyer, the section has no application and the contract is not partially or wholly avoided by any casualty to the goods.[49]

When these five conditions are met, the resulting factual pattern is one which falls within the discussion of the prior section of this text. A loss has occurred which it is reasonable to assume the parties did not contemplate at the time of their agreement. Who ought to bear that loss? The Code's answer is to divide the kinds of losses into two groups: total and partial. As a matter of draftsmanship this division was unnecessary because the chances of a buyer's accepting goods that were totally destroyed are too remote to be of concern to any drafter of a statute. Nevertheless, the drafters chose to make the division and no serious quarrel can be made with that choice.

If the loss is total, the contract is "avoided." The seller is not obligated to deliver; the buyer is not obligated to pay. Neither party is in default for the failure to perform; both are excused from their obligations. This avoidance is different from the limitations on the perfect tender rule.[50] In the latter cases the seller was allowed to tender something less than full performance and still obligate the buyer to purchase, but the seller remained liable for the defect in his tender. With the excuse from performance the buyer is not obligated to take what is tendered and the seller is not liable in damages for the defect in his tender. Section 2–613 is an example of an excuse from performing a contractual promise.[51]

---

48. Section 2–613 of the 1952 Official Text of the Code stated the first two requirements in these words: "Where the contract relates to identified goods which are irreplaceable or are treated by the parties as unique for purposes of the contract . . .."

49. §§ 130–36 *infra*. It is, of course, possible for the agreement to allocate the risk of loss. That agreement is binding on the parties. Generally, see 6 S. Williston, Contracts § 1972A (rev. ed. 1938); UCC §§ 1–102(3) and (4).

50. §§ 103–06 *supra*.

51. The buyer would be entitled to a return of any payments made on the contract price. "So, if the contract becomes impossible of performance, the relation ends, and the money advanced can be recovered back." William F. Mosser Co. v. Cherry River Boom & Lumber Co., 290 Pa. 67, 72, 138 A. 85, 87 (1927). This rule is recognized in Kelly v. Bliss, 54 Wis. 187, 11 N.W. 488 (1882); Restatement of Contracts § 468 (1932).

If the loss is partial, the contract is wholly avoided only if the buyer so chooses. The seller, therefore, cannot use casualty to a portion of the goods as a basis for escaping from a portion of a contract which turned out to be unprofitable for the seller. The buyer is given the right to inspect the goods to decide whether to accept the goods or to avoid the entire contract. If the buyer decides to accept, "due allowance" is to be made from the contract price. On some occasions the computation of this allowance will be mechanical—as where a specific portion of the goods has been destroyed but the remaining portion has not been harmed. On other occasions a determination of the amount will be extremely difficult. Suppose, for example, that the seller has agreed to sell goods worth $12,000 for a contract price of $10,000; that the goods are partially destroyed under the conditions set out in the first paragraph of section 2–613; that the casualty reduced the value of the goods to $9,000; but that the buyer elected to accept the goods "with due allowance from the contract price." Thus, the buyer's liability begins with the $10,000 contract price but is to be reduced by a "due allowance." How should this allowance be computed? If it is $1,000 (the contract price less the value of the goods after partial loss—that is, $10,000 less $9,000), the seller will have been paid in full for the goods delivered even though he would have lost $2,000 had the goods not been partially destroyed. If the allowance is $3,000 (the value of the goods before less their value after the partial loss—that is $12,000 less $9,000), the buyer will receive his entire $2,000 gain on the sale even though the seller has performed only a part of the agreement and is excused from performing the remainder. Perhaps the best method of solving this type of case is to reduce the contract price by an amount determined by multiplying the contract price by the percentage of deterioration. In the supposed case the goods deteriorated 25 per cent in value, and the contract price should be reduced $2,500. This will leave the seller with a recovery of $7,500 for $9,000 worth of goods. In this way the buyer retains the profitableness of his contract for the goods delivered, and the seller is not required to stand the loss for the portion of the contract excused. That the drafters intended this method of computing recovery can be supported by the Code statement that the buyer can accept the partially destroyed goods with due allowance "but without further right against the seller." [52]

---

52.   UCC § 2–613(b).

§ 109. Substitute Performance

Some contracts for the sale of goods contain an agreement as to the berthing,[53] loading, or unloading facilities which are to be used in the performance of the seller's promise to deliver. Others may contain a provision as to the type of carrier or manner of delivery to be used by the seller. These provisions become a part of the seller's contractual obligations, and the perfect tender rule would require that the seller comply before the buyer becomes obligated to accept and pay for the goods.[54] The perfect tender rule is, however, relaxed in section 2–614(1):

> Where without fault of either party the agreed berthing, loading, or unloading facilities fail or an agreed type of carrier becomes unavailable or the agreed manner of delivery otherwise becomes commercially impracticable but a commercially reasonable substitute is available, such substitute performance must be tendered and accepted.

This subsection has no application if all that is involved is a seller who has found that the agreed facilities, carrier, or manner of delivery has become financially burdensome. The facility must "fail"; the carrier must become "unavailable"; the manner of delivery must become "commercially impracticable." When any of these tests is met and a commercially reasonable substitute is available, that substitute performance must be "tendered and accepted."[55] This subsection is similar to sections 2–613 and 2–615 in that the occurrence of any one of the conditions in section 2–614(1) excuses the seller from performing the contract according to its express terms. It is unlike sections 2–613 and 2–615 in that when any one of the conditions of section 2–614(1) occurs *and* when a commercially reasonable substitute is available, the seller must tender the substitute and the buyer must accept it.[56] The buyer may not refuse to accept the substitute tender (as he may, for example, when a section 2–613 casualty has partially destroyed the goods),[57] and the buyer may treat the seller as being in default if the substitute performance is not made.

---

53. "[B]erth . . . the place where a ship lies when at anchor or at a wharf." Webster's Third New International Dictionary 207 (1966).

54. § 102 *supra.*

55. If a commercially reasonable substitute is not available, the seller would be excused from performing if the facts brought the case within UCC § 2–615. See § 110 *infra. Cf.* § 102 *supra.*

56. If the seller accepted the risks that the usual manner of delivery might not be available, UCC § 2–614(1) does not allow the seller to recover in quantum meruit for the increased costs of a substitute performance. *See* Transatlantic Fin. Corp. v. United States, 124 U.S.App.D.C. 183, 363 F.2d 312 (1966).

57. § 108 *supra.*

The operation of section 2–614(1) is illustrated by this quotation from the Comments: "The differing lines of solution are contrasted in a comparison of International Paper Co. v. Rockefeller, 161 App.Div. 180, 146 N.Y.S. 371 (1914) and Meyer v. Sullivan, 40 Cal.App. 723, 181 P. 847 (1919). In the former case a contract for the sale of spruce to be cut from a particular tract of land was involved. When a fire destroyed the trees growing on that tract the seller was held excused since performance was impossible. In the latter case the contract called for delivery of wheat 'f. o. b. Kosmos Steamer at Seattle.' The War led to cancellation of that line's sailing schedule after space had been duly engaged and the buyer was held entitled to demand substituted delivery at the warehouse on the line's loading dock. Under this Article, of course, the seller would also be entitled, had the market gone the other way, to make a substituted tender in that manner." [58]

§ 110.   Excuse by Failure of Presupposed Conditions

Section 2–615 has no counterpart in prior uniform legislation but is based upon common law principles developed by courts over the last several decades.[59] The ideas which it seeks to capture are difficult to state in terms of a general rule; therefore, the drafters might have been better advised had they omitted any statutory reference to the problem of excuse through mistake and allowed courts to continue

---

58.   UCC § 2–614, Comment 1.

59.   Mistake of one or both parties can enter the contractual arrangement at four different times: (1) prior to the mutual assent stage; (2) at the time of agreement; (3) after the agreement but during the process of reducing the terms of the agreement to writing; and (4) in the performance of the contract. UCC § 2–615 deals primarily with (1): the assumptions which the parties took with them to the process of agreement. Examples of pre-Code cases include Dansby v. Buck, 92 Ariz. 1, 373 P.2d 1 (1962); Farhat v. Rassey, 295 Mich. 349, 294 N.W. 707 (1940); Costello v. Sykes, 143 Minn. 109, 172 N.W. 907 (1919); Ward v. Reisdorf, 55 S.D. 322, 226 N.W. 339 (1929). This idea overlaps the problems of warranty where a seller is "mistaken" as to the quality of goods delivered. See § 54 *supra.* Mistake which enters at the time of agreement is illustrated by the famous case of the two ships named "Peerless." Raffles v. Wichelhaus, 2 H. & C. 906, 159 Eng.Rep. 375 (Ex.1864). Other typical cases are

Bell v. Carroll, 212 Ky. 231, 278 S.W. 541 (1925); Vickery v. Ritchie, 202 Mass. 247, 88 N.E. 835 (1909). It might be possible to fit some of the goods cases involving this type of mistake problem within UCC § 2–615. The third type of mistake is often called mistake in integration and, when the necessary elements are present, reformation is the proper remedy. Mills v. Schulba, 95 Cal.App.2d 559, 213 P.2d 408 (1950); Crabb v. Chisum, 183 Okl. 138, 80 P.2d 653 (1938); Travelers Ins. Co. v. Bailey, 124 Vt. 114, 197 A.2d 813 (1964); Edmiston v. Wilson, 146 W. Va. 511, 120 S.E.2d 491 (1961). For a case involving warranty of goods, see Whipple v. Brown Bros. Co., 225 N.Y. 237, 121 N.E. 748 (1919). As to the effect of the parol evidence rule, see § 53 *supra.* The fourth type of mistake is illustrated by the person who overpays a debt. The usual remedy to recover the overpayment is quasi-contract. Simms v. Vick, 151 N.C. 78, 65 S.E. 621 (1909). The Code contains no specific sections on the latter two types of mistake.

their case law development of this problem.[60]   Such was not their decision, and this section is now a part of the Code:

> Except so far as a seller may have assumed a greater obligation and subject to the preceding section on substituted performance:
>
> (a) Delay in delivery or non-delivery in whole or in part by a seller who complies with paragraphs (b) and (c) is not a breach of his duty under a contract for sale if performance as agreed has been made impracticable by the occurrence of a contingency the non-occurrence of which was a basic assumption on which the contract was made or by compliance in good faith with any applicable foreign or domestic governmental regulation or order whether or not it later proves to be invalid.
>
> (b) Where the causes mentioned in paragraph (a) affect only a part of the seller's capacity to perform, he must allocate production and deliveries among his customers but may at his option include regular customers not then under contract as well as his own requirements for further manufacture. He may so allocate in any manner which is fair and reasonable.
>
> (c) The seller must notify the buyer seasonably that there will be delay or non-delivery and, when allocation is required under paragraph (b), of the estimated quota thus made available for the buyer.

The central thrust of section 2–615 is found in subsection (a).[61]   A failure to deliver or a delay in delivery is excused if the performance has become impracticable (the Code did not use the word "impossible") because of either of two events: (1) the occurrence of a contingency the non-occurrence of which was a basic assumption on which the contract was made, or (2) the compliance in good faith with some governmental order.[62]

As has already been pointed out, these are not new ideas to the law of contracts.[63]   They stem from the realization that the words

---

60. Case law development could occur through UCC § 1–103.

61. To the extent that parties allocate the risk, there can be no excuse. Friedman v. Grevnin, 360 Mich. 193, 103 N.W.2d 336 (1960). See the opening clause of UCC § 2–615.

62. If one party has assumed the risk of governmental interference, that party is not excused by a governmental or-

der. Security Sewage Equip. Co. v. McFerren, 14 Ohio St.2d 251, 237 N.E. 2d 898 (1968). The risk of closing the Suez Canal by the Egyptian government was held to have been assumed by the shipping company. Transatlantic Fin. Corp. v. United States, 124 U.S.App.D.C. 183, 363 F.2d 312 (1966).

63. § 107 *supra*.

which parties use to express their agreement only inartfully state some of the risks which those parties intended to shift. For example, a buyer who needs goods in the future may be willing to enter into a contract to purchase those goods to assure himself of a source of supply at a fixed price. He is willing to give up the chance that the goods could be bought later from another source for a lesser price. In short, the buyer is willing to assume the risk that the goods will decline in price before the delivery date. On the other hand, the seller may be willing to promise to supply those goods in exchange for an assured market and price. Such a seller is willing to assume the risk that he could later be able to sell those same goods at an increased price. If such a buyer and seller can agree on the other terms, the words which they use to state their agreement as to the delivery of the goods may be extremely general, with few contingencies or exceptions. Nevertheless, their "deal" rested on several basic assumptions which were never expressed—assumptions such as that the seller had correctly multiplied the unit price of the goods by the number to be delivered,[64] that war would not intervene to make delivery impossible or the source of supply extremely limited, or that the quality of the goods sold was not wholly different from the understanding of the parties at the time of agreement.[65] If their basic assumptions turn out to be incorrect and events occur which they assumed would not occur, enforcing the words which they used is to make for the parties a contract to which they never agreed. If the law did not recognize that words must be understood in the background of their use, even simple contracts would have to be expressed in writings the size of a large volume.

The law is not that foolish. It has recognized that certain events fall outside the risks assumed by the parties and it has excused performance if one of those events occurs and upsets the *basic* assumptions of the parties. The Code adopts that rule for the sale of goods. The assumptions must, however, be *basic*. Although the seller assumed that the price of goods would remain constant or might even decline, an increase in price will not call for the application of section 2–615. This was a risk which the seller took when he received an assured market for the goods.[66] "But a severe shortage of raw materials or of supplies due to a contingency such as war, embargo, local crop

64. Mathematical errors are considered in Geremia v. Boyarsky, 107 Conn. 387, 140 A. 749 (1928). Omissions were involved in M. F. Kemper Constr. Co. v. City of Los Angeles, 37 Cal.2d 696, 235 P.2d 7 (1951). *See generally* 3 A. Corbin, Contracts §§ 606–12 (1960).

65. Sherwood v. Walker, 66 Mich. 568, 33 N.W. 919 (1887).

66. United States v. Wegematic Corp., 360 F.2d 674 (2d Cir. 1966) (seller assumed risk through warranties); Comment, 59 Mich.L.Rev. 98, 103–05 (1960).

failure, unforeseen shutdown of major sources of supply or the like, which either causes a marked increase in cost or altogether prevents the seller from securing supplies necessary to his performance, is within the contemplation of this section." [67]

Subsection (b) continues the general trend of pre-Code law.[68] Some sellers will have a number of contracts similar to the one with this particular buyer. If the impracticability of making full delivery affects only a portion of the goods, such a seller must allocate among his customers the goods which he has, but may include regular customers even though they are not then under contract.[69] The seller, however, is not allowed to make a profit out of the intervening impracticability by contracting to sell at the higher rates which may result following a casualty, thus reducing the share which must be allocated to the lower-priced contracts. Thus, the Code requirement of apportionment becomes a specific example of the application of the general doctrine of good faith in the performance of contracts.[70] Although the Code does not say so specifically, the seller would have to deliver his production to one buyer if this is the only buyer or customer that he has at the time of the intervening impracticability.

Subsection (c) requires that the seller notify the buyer seasonably that there will be a delay in delivery or a non-delivery and of any estimated quota which will be made available to the buyer. Section 2–616(2) gives the buyer a reasonable time, not to exceed 30 days, to give the seller written notice as to whether the buyer will terminate the contract or modify the contract by agreeing to take his available quota in substitution for the promised performance. If the buyer does not give this notice, the contract lapses with respect to the deliveries affected. This procedure provides considerable certainty for the parties who face a disruption resulting from the failure of a presupposed condition.

The drafters of the Code were satisfied in codifying, in sections 2–613 and 2–615, principles of impossibility and of mistake which had already received general acceptance in this country. Unfortunately they did not go further and consider how losses ought to be apportioned following a casualty or impracticability which excused the seller's further performance. Suppose, for example, that the buyer had made

---

67. UCC § 2–615, Comment 4.

68. Haley v. Van Lierop, 64 F.Supp. 114 (W.D.Mich.), *aff'd* 153 F.2d 212 (6th Cir. 1945); County of Yuba v. Mattoon, 160 Cal.App.2d 456, 325 P.2d 162 (1958); 6 S. Williston, Contracts § 1962 (rev. ed. 1938).

69. UCC § 2–615. Notice must be given by the seller under UCC § 2–615(c). Failure to give notice would bar the seller from claiming excuse. UCC § 2–615(a).

70. UCC § 1–203.

a down payment and that none of the goods had been delivered at the time of the intervening casualty or impracticability. Under section 2–613 the buyer may treat the contract as avoided; under section 2–615 the failure to deliver is not a breach of the seller's duty to deliver. It is, therefore, clear that the drafters did not intend to allow such a buyer to recover from the seller any damages which the buyer suffered by the failure to deliver. However, is the buyer entitled to a recovery of the down payment which he made? The non-Code American rule allows this recovery, and nothing in the Code prevents the continued application of this rule to the sale of goods.[71] If these were the only damage problems arising from the operation of these two sections, the drafters ought not be criticized for failing to state existing law (even though they believed it necessary to state the general rule of impossibility).

Unfortunately, other damage problems occur when the seller has incurred expenses prior to the intervening impossibility and those expenses (1) did not benefit the buyer and (2) are not recoverable from some other source. For example, a seller—in reliance on the contract with the buyer—may have begun construction of goods before the issuance of a governmental order making further performance impracticable. Are those expenses involved in commencing the construction recoverable, in whole or in part, from the buyer? Are they to be deducted from any down payment which the buyer has paid before that down payment is to be returned? If so, what should be the result when the expenses exceed the down payment?[72] Had the drafters turned their attention to the difficult question of how to apportion losses following intervening casualty or impracticability, confused areas of case law could have been eliminated, and the Code might have served as a model for the solution of similar problems in non-goods cases.

The seller who has partially performed prior to excuse from further performance does not present as difficult a Code problem. He is entitled to the contract price of goods accepted[73] (this may cause interpretation problems if the price was set for the complete delivery

71. *E. g.*, Cochrane v. Forbes, 257 Mass. 135, 153 N.E. 566 (1926); Panto v. Kentucky Distilleries & Warehouse Co., 215 App.Div. 511, 214 N.Y.S. 19 (1926). Other cases are collected in Annot., 144 A.L.R. 1317 (1943).

72. The leading English case concerned with these problems is Fibrosa Spolka Akcyjna v. Fairbairn Lawson Combe Barbour, Ltd., [1943] A.C. 32, [1942] 2 All E.R. 122. This decision was followed with the adoption by Parliament of the Law Reform (Frustrated Contracts) Act of 1943, 6 & 7 Geo. 6, c. 40 (1943). The American and English cases are discussed in several comments on this case. *E. g.*, 6 A. Corbin, Contracts §§ 1367–72 (1962); Comment, 69 Yale L.J. 1054 (1960); Comment, 46 Mich.L.Rev. 401 (1948).

73. UCC § 2–607(1).

and not on a per unit basis) and is discharged from liability for further performance. Therefore, damages for failure to complete the delivery ought not be deducted from the contract price.

C. PERFORMANCE OBLIGATIONS OF THE BUYER

1. ACCEPTANCE AND PAYMENT

§ 111. Comparison of Seller's and Buyer's Obligations

The buyer's method of tender and his performance obligations are not as complicated as those of the seller. The reason for the distinction arises out of the nature of the commercial undertaking by the parties. The seller has promised to deliver a given quantity of goods of a certain quality. Deciding whether he has performed opens questions of warranties of quality and title as well as how the goods must be tendered to the buyer. Disclaimers, limitations of remedies, installment contracts, the right to cure, the distinction between shipment and destination contracts, and excuse from performance become important in measuring whether the seller has tendered and whether he has performed his obligations under a contract for sale.[74]

The buyer, on the other hand, normally has agreed to but one thing—to pay the price at a specified time and place. There are, on occasion, problems of interpreting that agreement—problems of deciding just how much the buyer did promise to pay for the goods or when he agreed to make the payment [75]—but these problems do not arise as frequently and are often not as complicated as those that can be involved in determining whether goods measure up to their warranted quality and whether their tender conformed to the contract between the parties.

In discussing the performance obligations of the buyer two questions must be distinguished:

(1) What acts must the buyer perform to obligate the seller to perform his part of the sales agreement?

(2) What obligations does the buyer have once the seller has properly tendered conforming goods?

---

74. These problems are discussed in §§ 86–89, 97–99, and 103–10 *supra*.

75. *E. g.*, Col-Tex Ref. Co. v. Coffield & Gutherie, Inc., 196 F.2d 788 (5th Cir. 1952); Martin v. A. W. Moeller & Son, 241 Iowa 1033, 44 N.W.2d 345 (1950); Giguere v. Bisbee Buick Co., 152 Me. 177, 126 A.2d 283 (1956). Code problems of price are created by UCC § 2–305 discussed in § 38 *supra*. Problems are also created by UCC § 2–304 when the price may be payable in money "or otherwise." Mortimer B. Burnside & Co. v. Havener Sec. Corp., 25 A.D.2d 373, 269 N.Y.S.2d 724 (1966). A disagreement as to price caused the litigation in Associated Hardware Supply Co. v. Big Wheel Distributing Co., 355 F.2d 114 (3d Cir. 1966).

These are the same questions which have already been considered, except in reverse, in connection with the seller. The first is directed toward a determination of the necessary conditions precedent to the buyer's obtaining a cause of action against the seller. If the seller's obligations are conditioned on the prior or concurrent performance of some act by the buyer, failure of the condition to occur prevents the seller's obligation from arising. The seller will not be in default and no cause of action will lie against him. The second question assumes that the seller has performed his necessary conditions (in most cases, has properly tendered conforming goods) and that the buyer is called upon to perform his obligations to prevent a default on his part.

Only the answer to the second question involves a discussion of any "obligation" on the part of the buyer. Neither the buyer nor the seller is *obliged* to tender—that is, a failure to tender does not give rise to a cause of action against the party who failed to make the tender. The only result of a failure to tender is that no cause of action has arisen against the other party; thus, if both seller and buyer fail to tender, neither is in default.[76] In this sense the sub-headings of this chapter are partially inaccurate ("Performance Obligations of the Seller" and "Performance Obligations of the Buyer"), but a completely accurate title becomes so long as to be unwieldy or so cryptic as to be meaningless. The following sections of this text consider both the buyer's necessary tender and his obligations once the seller has performed any necessary conditions precedent.

§ 112. Mechanics of Tender of the Price

The buyer's tender obligations can be introduced through the following hypothetical factual pattern:

A seller and buyer agreed to the sale and purchase of a television set for a total price (including taxes) of $425. The agreement was reached and a writing was signed on July 1. The seller agreed to deliver the set to buyer's home on July 5. Nothing was said about the terms of payment and no custom, course of performance, or course of dealing indicated that the buyer was to be extended credit in paying the price. Assume that as of July 6 the seller had not delivered the set and the buyer had made no effort to hand $425 in cash to the seller. Is the seller in default of his obligation to deliver the television set?

The Code's beginning point in answering this question is found in section 2–511:

> Unless otherwise agreed tender of payment is a condition to the seller's duty to tender and complete any delivery.

76. § 94 *supra.*

Before the seller has a *duty* to deliver (1) the buyer must have tendered payment or (2) there must have been an agreement that the buyer need not tender payment. If neither (1) nor (2) has occurred, the seller had no duty to deliver and his failure to deliver—even though July 5 has come and gone—was not a default of any duty on his part.

In the hypothetical set out above there are no facts on which to base a conclusion that the seller agreed to extend credit to the buyer. There was no express agreement that the buyer was to have 30, 60, or any other number of days to pay the price, and there is no basis for implying such an agreement. Absent such an agreement payment is due at the time the buyer is to receive the goods.[77] A change of the facts to insert a credit term (either open or secured credit) will change this result. The seller's duty to deliver in those cases will be measured by the agreement; if the goods are to be delivered solely on the basis of the buyer's credit (as with a typical charge account), the seller is obligated to deliver even though the buyer has made no payment; if the goods are to be delivered partly on the buyer's credit and partly on the basis of the buyer's down payment, a tender of the down payment will be a condition to the seller's duty to deliver.[78] However, on the facts set out above there is nothing to indicate that the parties have "otherwise agreed" and, unless the buyer has tendered payment, the seller had no duty to deliver on July 5.

Has the buyer tendered payment? The temptation may be strong to conclude that the buyer has not tendered because he made no attempt to hand $425 in cash to the seller. However, that conclusion should not be reached until the applicable tender sections are analyzed.

1. *How much must be tendered?* The Code's language is that "payment"[79] must be tendered. A tender of 10%, 50%, or even 99%

---

77. UCC § 2–310(a). It is recognized that this section states when and where "payment" is due; it does not expressly indicate when or where a "tender of payment" should be made. *Cf.* UCC § 2–511. Therefore, an argument is available that UCC § 2–310 should be limited to a determination of when and where a buyer is obligated to pay following a conforming tender by the seller. §§ 39, 111 *supra.* The text has rejected this limited reading of UCC § 2–310 and has accepted the principle that the buyer must tender at the time and place he would be obligated to pay had the seller delivered conforming goods. This is the position taken in 2 S. Williston, Sales § 450 (rev. ed. 1948).

It is possible to waive a condition and, if it is waived, the non-occurrence of the condition is not a defense to a suit for breach. § 42 *supra* and 1 S. Williston, Sales § 190 (rev. ed. 1948). Thus, a seller could waive tender as a condition of delivery, thereby extending credit to the buyer.

78. For the date on which credit begins to run, see UCC § 2–310(d). A seller who has agreed to sell on credit and who, before the goods are delivered, discovers the buyer to be insolvent may refuse delivery except for cash. UCC § 2–702(1) discussed in § 163 *infra.* Even if the buyer is not insolvent, a seller who has not performed may demand adequate assurances if reasonable grounds for insecurity have arisen. UCC § 2–609.

79. UCC § 2–511(1).

of the price is not sufficient. Unless credit has been extended, the buyer obligates the seller to deliver the goods only by tendering the entire price.

2. *What must be tendered?* The drafters could have defined the buyer's tender obligations in terms of cash. Paraphrasing the seller's obligations,[80] they could have provided that "tender of payment requires that the buyer put and hold legal tender at the seller's disposition and give the seller any notification reasonably necessary to enable him to receive the legal tender." They could have so provided, but they did not. Instead, they stated:

> Tender of payment is sufficient when made by any means or in any manner current in the ordinary course of business unless the seller demands payment in legal tender and gives any extension of time reasonably necessary to procure it.[81]

The buyer need not have cash; a check will suffice. The seller need not, however, take the check but may demand the cash if he gives the buyer an extension of time reasonably needed to procure the cash. Therefore, if the buyer tenders the check late in the afternoon of the date set for delivery and payment, the seller has a choice. He may accept the check and thereby suspend the buyer's underlying obligation until the check is presented and paid or dishonored,[82] or he may refuse the check and demand cash. If this demand creates commercial surprise, the buyer must also be given a reasonable extension of time (perhaps until the morning of the next banking day). Failure to grant the extension means that the original tender by check is sufficient and the seller is obligated to deliver the goods.[83]

3. *When and where must the tender be made?* Payment is due at the time and place that the buyer is to *receive* the goods—not at the time and place of shipment or delivery.[84] The only exception to this rule is for documentary sales—that is, sales in which the buyer has agreed to pay against documents of title—and for these cases payment is due at the time and place at which the buyer is to receive the documents of title.[85]

It becomes necessary, therefore, to determine in each case just where the goods (or, in the exceptional documentary sales cases, where

---

80. § 96 *supra*

81. UCC § 2–511(2).

82. UCC §§ 2–511(3), 3–802. The interrelation of these sections is discussed in Mansion Carpets, Inc. v. Marinoff, 24 A.D.2d 947, 265 N.Y.S.2d 298 (1965). If the goods have been delivered and the check later dishonored, the seller's right to retake the goods is covered by

UCC §§ 2–403 and 2–507(2) and discussed in §§ 166, 168–71 *infra*.

83. Silver v. The Sloop Silver Cloud, 259 F.Supp. 187 (S.D.N.Y.1966).

84. UCC § 2–310(a). The buyer's right to inspect before payment is preserved in UCC § 2–310(b).

85. UCC § 2–310(c).

the documents) are to be received. If the buyer is to receive the goods at the seller's place of business, that is the place at which the buyer must tender his payment. Thus, if the television set involved in the hypothetical were a portable which the buyer had agreed to pick up on July 5, tender of payment would require the buyer to go to the seller's place of business during working hours on the 5th of July and there tender a check for the full amount of the price. On the other hand, if the seller is to ship the goods under either a shipment or destination contract, the buyer may tender at the point that the goods were to have been received. The facts of the hypothetical problem indicate that this latter type of contract is involved; the seller was to deliver the goods to the buyer's home and it is at the buyer's home that the tender must be made.

4. *How may a tender be made if the seller is not present at the time and place for tender?* The last problem is a practical one. How can a buyer tender either a check or cash to a person who is not present at the place the goods or documents were to have been received? With documents there is usually a bank involved and tender can be made at that place, but with goods which never arrive it is difficult for the buyer to make a formal tender to an absent seller. The Code does not contain any specific provisions describing what a buyer is to do in this type of situation. Pre-Code law would indicate, however, that all such a buyer must do is to prove that at the time and place that the goods were supposed to have been received the buyer had sufficient funds (either in cash or in his checking account) and that someone was present with authority to tender the payment had the goods arrived.[86] Therefore, it may well be that the buyer in the hypothetical problem with which this section began did make the necessary tender to obligate the seller to deliver the television set. Whether he did will require a further look into the facts of the buyer's financial position on July 5, but if the tender was proper, the failure of the seller to deliver is a default for which he may be held liable in damages.

§ 113. Obligations and Rights Generally

The prior section of this text dealt with the problem of the buyer's tender. In essence, the question there considered was: what must a buyer do to obligate the seller to perform his promises under a contract for the sale of goods? This section of the text begins the discussion of a problem which has many points of similarity to the question of tender but which has an entirely different legal impact: once the seller has properly tendered conforming goods, what are the buyer's rights and

---

86. Catlin v. Jones, 52 Or. 337, 97 P.
546 (1908).

obligations under a contract for the sale of goods? The difference in the legal impact of these problems has already been mentioned. If a buyer fails to tender, the only consequence is that the seller's obligation to perform has not been triggered; but if a buyer fails to perform an obligation under the contract, the buyer will be liable to the seller in some remedy based upon a default of the buyer's promise.[87]

Notice the assumption on which this portion of the text rests: the seller must have made a proper tender of conforming goods. Until there has been a proper tender of conforming goods, the buyer has no obligation to perform. What is a "proper tender" and what are "conforming goods" has been considered under the seller's performance obligations.[88]

The buyer's basic obligations are introduced in section 2–507(1):

> Tender of delivery is a condition to the buyer's duty to accept the goods and, unless otherwise agreed, to his duty to pay for them. Tender entitles the seller to acceptance of the goods and to payment according to the contract.

The buyer's obligations under a contract for sale are, therefore, two. He must accept the goods *and* he must pay for them in accordance with the contract. What the seller wants in most cases is that the buyer pay the price at the time or times specified in the agreement. Whether the buyer does something called "acceptance" is usually of little or no moment to the seller. However, the Code uses the concept of acceptance to control the various remedies available to the seller. When the buyer wrongfully fails to accept goods (that is, when the seller's tender was proper), the buyer has defaulted in one of his obligations under the Code and the seller may recover damages even though the price is not yet due.[89] Likewise, if the buyer accepts and retains the goods but fails to pay the price due, he is in default and liable for the price.[90]

The buyer's basic right under the Code is the right to inspect the goods, always before acceptance and often before paying the price.[91] Exercise of the right to inspect assures the buyer that the seller's tender was conforming.

These obligations and this right are discussed in the following sections.

---

87. §§ 93–94, 112 *supra.*

38. §§ 95–110 *supra.*

89. UCC § 2–703. If the failure to accept was rightful, the buyer has remedies under UCC § 2–711. See Chapter VII *infra.*

90. UCC § 2–709.

91. UCC § 2–513. The right to inspect before payment is lost in documentary sales. UCC §§ 2–512, 2–513(3). This problem is discussed in § 123 *infra.* In theory the right to inspect before acceptance may also be lost because UCC § 2–513 begins with the familiar "unless otherwise agreed" language.

§ 114.   Obligation to Accept the Goods

When the seller performs his obligations under a contract for sale by properly tendering conforming goods, the buyer is under a duty to accept those goods. The Code defines when acceptance occurs, but this definition was included primarily for situations in which the seller has tendered non-conforming goods which the buyer has not seasonably rejected.[92] However, one part of the definition is applicable here: acceptance occurs when the buyer "after reasonable opportunity to inspect the goods signifies to the seller that the goods are conforming. . . ."[93] Reading this back into section 2–507, the buyer is obliged, following a proper tender of conforming goods, to signify to the seller that the goods do conform to the contract.

Obtaining such a signification can be important to the seller. Once he has it—that is, once the goods have been accepted—the seller may proceed to recover the price stated in the contract.[94] Such a seller is not limited to a damage remedy. Further, the seller is not obligated to retake the goods if the buyer later changes his mind and wants to return the conforming goods. Following an acceptance the goods are the buyer's and the seller is entitled to the price of those goods.

The prior paragraph should not be read to mean that the seller cannot, if he desires, retake conforming goods if the buyer signifies that he no longer wants them and tenders them back to the seller. While the seller is not obligated to take them back, he may treat the buyer's request as an offer for an accord and satisfaction and accept that offer by retaking the goods.[95] The seller's rights following such an accord depend upon its terms.[96] He may or may not be able to hold the buyer for damages suffered, depending upon his reasonable understanding of the buyer's offer of return. Such a seller may have difficulties under the Bankruptcy Act if the buyer files a petition in bankruptcy, or one is filed against him, within four months of the transfer. The transfer of the goods in most cases would be in satisfaction (or partial satisfaction) of an antecedent debt (the price) and, if the tests for a preference are met, the buyer's trustee in bankruptcy could avoid the preference.[97]

---

92. UCC § 2–606. This section is discussed in § 142 *infra*.

93. UCC § 2–606(1) (a).

94. UCC § 2–709; § 178 *infra*. Other consequences of acceptance are discussed in §§ 142–43 *infra*.

95. General Air Conditioning Corp. v. Fullerton, 227 Ark. 278, 298 S.W.2d 61 (1957).

96. Citizens & Southern Bank v. Union Warehouse & Compress Co., 157 Ga. 434, 122 S.E. 327 (1924).

97. A full discussion of the Bankruptcy Act is beyond the scope of this text. However, the preference sections of the Act (30 Stat. 562 § 60 (1898), hereinafter cited Bankruptcy Act; 11 U. S.C.A. § 96 (1964)) could be applied to avoid the transfer if the elements

The obligation to accept has another consequence. If the buyer fails to accept a proper tender of conforming goods, the buyer has "wrongfully rejected" the goods under section 2–703. The seller may refuse to transfer the goods to the buyer and proceed to recover damages. Thus the buyer's acceptance obligation is important in opening remedies to the seller.

§ 115. Obligation to Pay the Price

The buyer's obligation to pay for the goods is determined by the agreement between the parties. In some instances the buyer has agreed to submit a letter of credit or to pay the price in advance of the seller's tender. The "unless otherwise agreed" language of section 2–507 and the general contract law of conditions obligate the buyer to pay or to deliver the letter of credit even though the seller has not yet tendered.[98]

Putting these cases to one side, the buyer is obligated to pay the price only when the seller has tendered the goods, and even then payment is due "according to the contract." [99] This language is sufficiently broad so that any arrangements between the parties—whether arising out of express language or trade customs, course of performance, or course of dealing—will be effective. For example, the agreement may give the buyer a period of credit, allow him to receive the goods after accepting a time draft, require him to pay with legal tender or a check at the time of delivery, provide for payments against a sight draft, or contain some combination of these methods of payment. If it does, such an agreement controls the buyer's obligation to pay the price.

Absent an agreement, the Code fills out the payment term in much the same manner as has already been discussed in the section dealing with the buyer's tender:[1]

1. The seller's proper tender of conforming goods obligates the buyer to pay the entire price.[2] The Code does not recognize any stat-

---

of a preference are present. 3 Collier, Bankruptcy ¶60.07[1] (14th ed 1969). The fraudulent transfer section might also be applicable (Bankruptcy Act § 67; 11 U.S.C.A. § 107 (1964)). *See* 4 Collier, Bankruptcy ¶¶67.29 et seq. (14th ed. 1969). A seller selling on credit should, of course, seek protection at the time of the contract of sale by use of Article 9 of the Code. This Article is the subject of the excellent treatise, G. Gilmore, Security Interests in Personal Property (1965).

98. UCC § 2–507, Comment 2.

99. UCC § 2–507(1).

1. § 112 *supra*. The question discussed there is: what acts must the buyer perform to obligate the seller to deliver? The problem in this section is: assuming that the seller has performed any necessary conditions precedent, what are the buyer's performance obligations?

2. UCC § 2–507.

utory credit term; the buyer has a length of time to pay only if credit is a part of the agreement.

2. Payment by check (or by "any means or in any manner current in the ordinary course of business") is sufficient "unless the seller demands payment in legal tender and gives any extension of time reasonably necessary to procure it." [3] If the sales contract had expressly provided for legal tender, the buyer would not be given added time to procure cash. It is only the surprise demand for legal tender that is protected against;[4] the Code does not allow the buyer, by use of a check, to extend the time for his performance when it should have been clear that a check would not be accepted.

3. Payment is due, not at the time and place of the seller's tender (even though it is the "tender" which triggers the buyer's obligation to pay), but at the time and place the buyer is to receive the goods.[5] This rule has its greatest impact in shipment contracts. For instance, suppose that a seller has agreed to sell goods, F.O.B. seller's city, to be shipped to the buyer. The seller tenders at his city,[6] but the payment is due where the goods are to be received—that is, the buyer's point. Further, payment is not due until the time the goods are to arrive *and* the buyer has had an opportunity to inspect them.[7] The normal method of handling this type of payment would be through the use of a sight draft with documents of title. When the goods arrive in the buyer's city, the carrier will allow inspection (unless the seller had instructed the carrier not to allow the inspection) and, if the goods are conforming, the buyer will be obligated to pay the draft. Having received payment for the draft, the bank will release the bill of lading and the buyer may pick up his goods from the carrier.

This type of case could create a problem in interpreting the Code. Suppose that the seller's tender to the carrier was proper so that the risk of loss passed to the buyer;[8] however, the goods were lost in transit. The Code is explicit that the risk of loss is on the buyer, but could the buyer successfully argue that payment was not due until the goods were *received*? The answer should be that he cannot. Under section

---

3. UCC § 2–511. This section is discussed in § 112 *supra*.

4. UCC § 2–511, Comment 3.

5. UCC § 2–310(a).

6. UCC § 2–319.

7. UCC § 2–310(b). Even in a shipment contract F. O. B. buyer's plant, the buyer has a right to inspect the goods before payment. *See* Marmond Spring Co. v. Triangle Instrument Co., 4 UCC Rep. 302 (N.Y.Sup.Ct.1967). The agreement may provide for payment before inspection. If it does, such an agreement is controlling. UCC § 2–310(b); § 123 *infra*.

8. Electric Regulator Corp. v. Sterling Extruder Corp., 280 F.Supp. 550 (D. Conn.1968).

2–507 payment is due at the time and place the buyer "is to receive" the goods. This language eliminates any argument that the buyer owed the price at the point of seller's tender; it was not designed to keep the effective risk of loss on the buyer.[9] Nevertheless, confusion results when the Code goes on to say that in shipment non-documentary sales "the buyer may inspect the goods after their arrival before payment is due." If the goods have never arrived, the buyer cannot inspect and (so the argument would go) has no obligation to pay. This argument should be rejected. The right of inspection assumes that the goods have in fact arrived, and its purpose is to assure the buyer that the seller did tender conforming goods. If the goods did not arrive, the buyer has no possibility of inspecting; but if the seller can prove that he did make a conforming tender, the buyer is obligated to pay the price if the goods were lost or damaged "within a commercially reasonable time after risk of their loss has passed to the buyer."[10]

4. With documentary sales the buyer is obligated to pay the price at the time and place the documents are to be received regardless of where the goods are to be received.[11]

Failure to pay the price when it is due opens to the seller the remedies provided in Part 7 of Article 2. These remedies are discussed elsewhere in this text.[12]

§ 116.   Use of a Negotiable Instrument

If a buyer has signed a negotiable instrument (draft, check, or note) in connection with the purchase of goods, some of the payment obligations already discussed will be changed. For example, suppose that a buyer purchased goods on credit and signed only a contract document in which he promised to pay for the goods within 90 days from delivery. If that buyer should discover that the goods did not conform to the contract, he may deduct from the price those damages which he suffered by reason of the default, or, if he acts promptly, return the goods and resist an action for their price. This result will follow even though the seller had assigned his right to payment and the assignee was the one pressing for payment.[13]

---

9. Compare the problems under Uniform Sales Act § 42. 2 S. Williston, Sales §§ 447–48b (rev. ed. 1948).

10. UCC § 2–709; Sadler Mach. Co. v. Ohio Nat'l Inc., 202 F.2d 887 (6th Cir. 1953); § 178 *infra*.

11. UCC § 2–310(c).

12. §§ 163 et seq. *infra*.

13. Sponge Divers' Ass'n v. Smith Kline & French Co., 263 F. 70 (3d Cir. 1920); Parker v. Funk, 185 Cal. 347, 197 P. 83 (1921); Rice v. Friend Bros., 179 Iowa 355, 161 N.W. 310 (1917). The rights against the seller under the Code are set out in UCC §§ 2–711, 2–717. Assignment is covered in UCC § 2–210. While the problem of this section of the text is not specifically treated, the pre-Code law should be continued since only the "rights" of

Insert a negotiable instrument into this factual pattern and the result may well be changed.[14] Suppose that the same buyer had also signed a negotiable note by which he promised to pay the price 90 days from the date of the note. As long as the seller held the note the seller (holder) would be subject to any defense that the goods were not conforming,[15] but if the buyer sought to assert this defense against an assignee (holder) of the note who had the status of a "holder in due course," he would discover that the holder in due course could recover the full amount of the note without deduction for the non-conformity in the goods.[16] True, the seller would remain liable for his default, but the buyer's damages could not be offset against any recovery by the holder in due course. This difference in the buyer's liability has obvious practical implications when the seller is located at some distant point or is of doubtful solvency.

The reasons for affording the holder in due course of a negotiable instrument a more favored treatment than is given to the assignee of a simple contract right rests on the policy that the use of certain types of instruments ought to be promoted in commercial transactions. To the extent that a person knows that he will be given this favored treatment if he buys for value, in good faith, and without certain types of notice, he is more willing to purchase negotiable instruments (or so the argument goes) and they will find ready acceptance in commerce. This policy favoring negotiability of certain types of instruments cuts across the sales policy of allowing the buyer to withhold his damages from the purchase price or, in some cases, of forcing the goods back on the seller and having no liability for the price—and the policy favoring negotiability has been given the greater weight.[17]

the assignor may be assigned. UCC § 2–210(2).

14. A negotiable instrument is defined in UCC § 3–104.

15. Although a payee may be a holder in due course (UCC § 3–302, Comment 2), he would not take free of defenses of any party to the instrument with whom he has dealt. UCC § 3–305(2). Normally the maker or drawer would be such a party. On this basis Saale v. Interstate Steel Co., 27 A.D.2d 1, 275 N.Y.S.2d 532 (1966), aff'd 19 N.Y. 2d 933, 281 N.Y.S.2d 340, 228 N.E.2d 397 (1967), can be criticized.

16. Federal Factors, Inc. v. Wellbanke, 241 Ark. 44, 406 S.W.2d 712 (1966). The requirements of a holder in due course are set out in UCC § 3–302; his rights are listed in UCC § 3–305.

17. There are instances in pre-Code law in which the assignee was so closely connected with the transaction between seller and buyer that the assignee was denied any protection of the holder in due course status. Commercial Credit Corp. v. Orange County Mach.Works, 34 Cal.2d 766, 214 P.2d 819 (1950); Mutual Fin. Co. v. Martin, 63 So.2d 649 (Fla.1953); Unico v. Owen, 50 N.J. 101, 232 A.2d 405 (1967). The extent to which this doctrine will survive the Code is in doubt, Root v. John Deere Co. of Indianapolis, Inc., 413 S.W.2d 901 (Ky.1967), yet it seems a safe prediction that courts will continue the pre-Code doctrine. Notes given in connection with sales of consumer goods are becoming a favorite subject of legislation, with the holder in due course defense being taken from assignees in various ways. One is to provide that a *negotiable* note

Negotiable instruments are the subject of Articles 3 and 4 of the Code. A full treatment of the impact of these two Articles on the buyer's payment obligations digresses substantially from a consideration of Article 2 and is, therefore, outside the scope of this text.

§ 117. Use of a Credit Card

The buyer's use of a credit card in making his purchases may also change some of the payment obligations which have been discussed in prior sections of this text. Unfortunately, all that can be done at this time is to suggest legal problems which may arise out of credit card purchases; case law and legislation are as yet too scanty to form the basis of general conclusions.

The consumer credit card came into widespread use during the late 1940's but is not referred to in the Uniform Commercial Code. There is no reason why credit cards should have been included in Article 2, but a good argument can be made that a separate Article should have been drafted to cover the legal problems arising out of their use and misuse. Credit cards have a sufficient resemblance to negotiable instruments and to letters of credit (all are devices indicating promises of future payment) so that some separate statutory treatment would have been warranted. They were, however, omitted from the Code; therefore, common law principles supported by statutes where applicable will undoubtedly control the answers to legal problems created by their use.

There are two types of credit cards: the two-party, or "bipartite" card, and the three-party, or "tripartite" card.[18] If the seller issues the credit card, as is common with department store cards, the arrangement is bipartite—only the seller and buyer are parties to transaction. In issuing the card the seller has agreed to deliver goods to the buyer on the strength of the buyer's credit; in exchange the buyer has agreed to pay for the goods within the credit period. Normally this is 30 days or, if a revolving credit account is involved, some longer period of time depending on the balance owed by the buyer. The ac-

---

cannot be a part of the installment sale and that the buyer cannot agree to give up his defenses if sued by any assignee of the contract right. *E. g.*, McKinney's N.Y.Pers.Prop. Law § 403 (1962). Another is to require the words "consumer note" to be printed on the face of the note, which is then not a *negotiable* instrument. *E. g.*, Mass.Gen. Laws Ann. ch. 255, § 12C (1968). Compare Uniform Consumer Credit Code §§ 2.403, 2.404. The consumer is also receiving judicial relief from the full impact of the holder in due course defense. *E. g.*, Jones v. Approved Bancredit Corp., —— Del. ——, 256 A.2d 739 (1969); Unico v. Owen, 50 N.J. 101, 232 A.2d 405 (1967).

18. For a general discussion of credit cards, see South, *Credit Cards: A Primer*, 23 Bus.Law 327 (1968); Comment, *The Tripartite Credit Card Transaction: A Legal Infant*, 48 Calif. L.Rev. 459 (1960); Note, 35 U.Cin.L. Rev. 424 (1966).

tual sale resembles the normal extension of credit, with the credit card identifying the buyer as one who is entitled to purchase on credit. The buyer is, of course, not obligated to pay at the time the goods are delivered by the seller since the parties have agreed to exchange the goods for the buyer's promise to pay on the future date.[19] The arrangement fits neatly within section 2–507(1) with the seller's tender entitling him to the buyer's acceptance of the goods and "to payment according to the contract."

A tripartite arrangement exists when the card is issued by someone who is neither the seller nor the buyer. Typical of this type of card are those issued by banks, major oil companies, local associations of merchants, Diners' Club, and American Express. The tripartite card involves three separate contracts: (1) the contract between the issuer of the card and the holder; (2) the contract between the issuer of the card and the seller by which the issuer agrees to purchase certain accounts at some percentage of face value (sometimes 100% but often less) under stated conditions; and (3) the contract of sale between the seller and the cardholder.[20] The normal transaction with a tripartite card would unfold like this: the buyer selects an item of merchandise displayed by the seller; instead of paying cash or asking for direct credit from the seller, the buyer presents his tripartite credit card; the seller completes the sales slip, imprints the card's embossed lettering onto the upper portion of the slip, and asks the buyer to sign on the appropriate line; the seller sells the account (that is, assigns the contract right to payment) to the issuer of the card; the issuer collects and sorts the accounts and, at stated periods, submits a bill to the holder of the card; and the holder pays the issuer for the purchases made and reported during the last month. The issuer of the card finds this arrangement to be profitable either through the discount received when it purchased the accounts from the merchant or through charges assessed against holders who do not pay their bills in full by a stated date, or both. The seller finds the arrangement profitable—even if he must sell the accounts at a discount—because he is able to secure immediate cash and not be put to the expense of maintaining a credit department. The buyer finds this arrangement tolerable because he can buy on credit without the necessity of carrying several plastic credit cards in his pocket, as he must with the bipartite cards.

Sometimes, however, things do not go as planned. A thief or an imposter may use someone else's card and accumulate hundreds of

19. § 115 *supra*.

20. Davenport, *Bank Credit Cards and the Uniform Commercial Code*, 1 Valparaiso L.Rev. 218 (1967).

dollars in charges—only to disappear, leaving the issuer with the loss unless it can be shifted to one of the other parties to the transaction. On other occasions the buyer may purchase goods on the strength of his tripartite card, discover that the goods do not measure up to their warranted quality, and attempt to deduct from the price the damages which he suffered (as the Code allows him to do),[21] only to be met by a claim from the issuer that the buyer must pay it the full price and argue with the seller about damages. In both of these instances the payment obligations discussed above [22] are sought to be varied. In the first the defendant is being asked to pay for goods which he neither received nor agreed to buy; in the second a buyer is being asked to pay in full for defective goods. The following sections of this text consider these two problems: the holder's obligation to pay for credit card purchases made (1) by an unauthorized user after the card has been lost or stolen or (2) by an authorized user when the goods do not measure up to their warranted quality.

§ 118.   Credit Cards—Unauthorized Purchases

Both the bipartite and tripartite cards create legal problems when the card has been lost or stolen and an unauthorized person has used the card to make purchases before the holder notified the issuer in writing that the card had disappeared. Remove the credit card from this problem and the answer is simple. Had the seller sold on unsecured credit to a person who fraudulently represented himself to be the defendant, the defendant would not be responsible for the purchases. The seller's only contract was with the defrauder and, unless the defrauder could be found and turned out to be financially responsible, the seller would bear the loss. Further, any assignee from the seller would have no greater rights against the defendant than the seller-assignor would have had.[23] Even the use of a negotiable instrument would not change this result. The defrauder's forgery of the defendant's name as maker of a note (or as drawer of a check) would not bind the defendant—even if the instrument had been negotiated to a holder in due course.[24]

The introduction of the credit card into this basic factual pattern may, however, change this result—whether the credit arrangement is bipartite or tripartite. Credit cards are issued in one of two ways. Some are issued after an application has been completed and signed by the holder. Usually these application forms contain a statement to the effect that the person signing the form

21. UCC § 2–717.

22. § 115 *supra*.

23. Cases in support are cited in § 116 *supra*.

24. UCC § 3–404.

will be responsible for all purchases made with the card from its date of issue to the time that the card is returned or the issuer notified in writing that the card has been lost. Traditional contract doctrines can be employed to determine whether this statement is a part of the contract between the parties and, if so, whether it can be interpreted to include responsibility for unauthorized purchases.[25]

Other credit cards are mailed to a list of prospective users without waiting for applications. This is most often done with the tripartite card where the issuer is interested in capturing as much as it can of the lucrative consumer finance charges (usually 18%, but sometimes ranging much higher) involved in long-term credit sales. To make the plan attractive to merchants it is necessary to have widespread use of the card, and the direct mailing plan has been adopted by some issuers. Such a plan rules out the use of the application form, but issuers have inserted the liability-until-written-notice provision either on the front or back of the card.[26] Some have also included the provision in the literature enclosed with the mailing. The hope of the issuer is that these printed clauses will make the holder liable for unauthorized purchases once he has used the card—that is, that a contract arose when the card was used, and the printed clause is a part of that contract. Thus, the first theory on which holder of a card may be liable for unauthorized purchases is that of contract: the holder promised to pay for goods sold to anyone who had possession of the card providing the sale was made before the issuer had written notice of the card's disappearance.

Another theory on which the holder may be liable for unauthorized purchases is that of tort: the issuer's loss was caused by the negligence of the holder in the manner in which he guarded the card (which according to most credit card terms "remains the property of the issuer") and in his failure to notify the issuer in writing of the card's loss. The response of the legal system to these claims for payment presents a mixture of these two theories.

Some state legislatures have enacted credit card statutes.[27] The statutes enacted thus far have been of little aid to the holder. They approve the validity of the liability-until-written-notice provisions if the holder has used the card or if he had requested in

---

25. §§ 46–53 *supra*.

26. *E. g.*, one oil company has printed the following on the back of its card: "By acceptance of this card, customer named hereon agrees to the terms of issue, and assumes responsibility for purchases made through its use prior to its surrender to . . ., or prior to the receipt by . . . of written notice of its loss or theft."

27. Ill.Rev.Stat. ch. 121½, § 381 (Supp. 1969); N.Y.Gen.Bus.Law § 512 (McKinney 1968); Wisc.Stat.Ann. § 895.45 (Supp.1968).

writing that the card be issued. The holder of the unsolicited card is given some protection in that the liability-until-written-notice statement on the card must be "conspicuously" printed in a certain size type. There is also statutory authority for limiting the amount of the holder's liability for unauthorized purchases, with a variation in the amount depending on whether the card has a signature panel.[28] One result of these statutes is that presumably a holder would have no contractual liability for unauthorized purchases made on a card sent, unsolicited, in the mail and lost before it was used—however, even here the statutes do not foreclose a common law action of negligence against the holder arising out of the loss of the card. The result of these statutes appears, on the whole, to provide the issuer with the protection it demands but to give little or no attention to the plight of the cardholder.

The conclusion drawn in the prior sentence is necessarily equivocal (it states only what "appears" to be the impact of the credit card statutes) because as yet there has not been sufficient litigation to indicate how the courts will interpret these statutes. One court has held that its local statute (New York) did not make the holder liable for unauthorized purchases when the holder did not know that the card was lost.[29] That court also found a duty owing by the seller-issuer "to the customer that it will not permit this credit status of the customer to be abused." [30] Abuse was found when the thief was allowed to make 237 purchases within 30 days. A question which the case leaves unanswered is what the court would have decided if the first few of the 237 purchases would have been large enough to make it financially attractive for the issuer to separate those few purchases for separate recovery. As to those purchases (if within the holder's credit limit) it would have been difficult for the court to have found credit card "abuse" which was so easily found when all 237 purchases were the subject of the suit.

Court response to the liability-until-written-notice provision on the card has varied. For example, two New York cases have enforced the provision, one of them holding that the holder's liability did not end when she notified the issuer by telephone.[31] A third

---

28. Ill.Rev.Stat. ch. 121½, § 382 (Supp. 1969). For a criticism of this type of inducement to use signed cards, see Comment, *Credit Cards: Distributing Fraud Loss*, 77 Yale L.J. 1418, 1426 n. 51 (1968).

29. Allied Stores v. Funderburke, 52 Misc.2d 872, 277 N.Y.S.2d 8 (Civ.Ct. 1967).

30. *Id.* at 878, 277 N.Y.S.2d at 15.

31. Uni Serv Corp. v. Vitiello, 53 Misc. 2d 396, 278 N.Y.S.2d 969 (Civ.Ct.1967); Texaco, Inc. v. Goldstein, 34 Misc.2d 751, 229 N.Y.S.2d 51 (N.Y.Mun.Ct.1962), *aff'd mem.* 39 Misc.2d 552, 241 N.Y.S. 2d 495 (Sup.Ct.1963).

New York case, discussed in the prior paragraph, denied liability on the part of the holder when he did not know that the card was missing and the seller-issuer failed to exercise due care by allowing the unusual activity in the holder's account.

Courts in two other jurisdictions have also found for the holder. The leading case is *Union Oil Co. v. Lull*,[32] where the Oregon Supreme Court first interpreted the arrangement between the issuer and holder as "imposing a risk of loss upon the defendant [holder] for sales made through the use of the card prior to receipt of notice by plaintiff [issuer] that the card was lost or stolen." [33] It then likened the holder to a gratuitous indemnitor or surety and stated that the creditor (issuer) was obligated to do nothing which would be injurious to the surety (holder). The burden of proving reasonable care was placed on the issuer.[34] Under the facts of this case this meant that the issuer would have to show that due diligence was exercised at the time of each sale—whether made by an employee of the issuer or by an independent dealer who made the sale. A judgment for the issuer was reversed and a new trial ordered. Since the goods involved were sold at several gasoline stations across the country, the decision on burden of proof may have effectively disposed of the case favorably to the holder.

A California court, which followed *Lull* on the issuer's burden of proof, dismissed the issuer's case against the holder—instead of remanding for a new trial—because of the provisions contained in the agreement between the seller and the issuer.[35] Under this agreement the issuer was to buy all "valid" charges represented by a charge slip containing the signature of the holder which was "the same" as that on the card. Since these conditions had not been met, the court concluded that the issuer's purchase of the forged charge slips constituted an attempt to retain the seller's goodwill—rather than damages—and that an advertising account should be charged with the amount involved rather than the account of the holder.

32. 220 Or. 412, 349 P.2d 243 (1960).

33. *Id.* at 425, 349 P.2d at 249. The credit card in *Lull* stated that the holder "guaranteed" payment for all sales made with the card. Since credit cards no longer normally carry the "guarantee" language, the value of *Lull* as precedent may be limited.

34. *Contra* Duke v. Sears, Roebuck & Co., 441 S.W.2d 524 (Tex.1969). For a later history of this case, see 446 S.W. 2d 886 (Tex.Ct.Civ.App.1969).

35. Diners' Club, Inc. v. Whited, Civ. No. A10872 (L.A.Super.Ct.App.Div. Aug. 6, 1964), discussed in Bergsten, *Credit Cards—A Prelude to the Cashless Society*, 8 B.C.Ind. & Com.L.Rev. 485, 494–5 (1967) and in Note, 43 N.C.L. Rev. 416 (1965). For other cases involving the cardholder's liability (but not a liability-until-written-notice clause) see Comment, *Credit Cards: Distributing Fraud Loss*, 77 Yale L.J. 1418, 1421 n. 20 (1968).

Although several cases have refused to impose liability on the holder of a card for unauthorized sales, no court has as yet questioned the validity of the liability-until-written-notice clause. To the extent that the seller exercises due care when making sales to the thief, these clauses appear to be an effective method of shifting losses to the cardholder—that is, to someone who has not received the purchased goods. However, the validity of these clauses merits further analysis. If a card is sent unsolicited, contains no signature panel, and the liability provision is found only in microscopic print buried on the reverse side of the card, distorted by advertising and embossing, a serious question can be raised as to whether the legal system ought to hold that the provision has been "consented" to by the holder.[36] Was the issuer reasonable in believing that the holder understood the liability clause?

The validity of the clause should be tested against ideas of unconscionability. Clearly the holder has no opportunity to bargain over the terms of the credit card, and liability-until-written-notice provisions are contained on almost all major cards. The holder's only choice is to take the card or to refuse it, and this may not be a "choice" in view of the advertising which issuers employ to promote the use of their cards. However, endorsement of the liability provisions by some state legislatures and the fact that the holder is in the best position to discover the card's loss suggest that it is unlikely that courts will invalidate the liability clause as unconscionable. Instead, until legislation is adopted which requires a different approach, courts will continue to decide cases under a blend of contract and tort law—using language in their opinions which will give credit card issuers hope that they can draft some provision which will irrevocably bind cardholders to pay for all purchases made on the strength of the card, but reaching decisions which in the main will relieve cardholders from this onerous burden.

§ 119. Credit Cards—Holder's Defenses

The use of credit cards may create a second type of problem. Suppose that a cardholder used his card to make a purchase on credit, that between the time of the delivery of the goods and the date for payment of the charge the holder discovered that the goods did not measure up to their warranted quality, and that the holder would like to deduct from the price the damages suffered by reason of the non-conformity—or return the goods and resist any attempt

---

36. See Macaulay, *Private Legislation and the Duty to Read—Business Run by IBM Machine, the Law of Con-* *tracts and Credit Cards*, 19 Vand.L. Rev. 1051 (1966).

to recover the price.[37]   This is the type of defense which traditionally would be cut off by the use of a negotiable instrument which had been negotiated to a holder in due course who had not dealt with the buyer.[38]   Will this defense also be unavailable in a credit card transaction?

There should be no difficulty when a bipartite card is used. Here the seller of the goods and issuer of the card are the same person. The card is used as a means of identifying the purchaser as the one entitled to credit, and the sale is the normal extension of credit by a seller to a buyer. The buyer would retain his right to offset his damages against the price or, if he acted within the provisions of the Code, to return the goods and resist all attempts at price recovery. The seller is, by definition, in default of his promise to deliver conforming goods and all of the Code remedies are available to the buyer.[39]   Any provision in the credit application which attempted to take these remedies from the buyer would be subject to attack on the ground that the provision was unconscionable.[40]

Difficulties can arise when a tripartite card is used. Here the one extending the credit is a "stranger" to the sale and has not defaulted on any of its obligations to the cardholder. Nevertheless, the general rule of contract law is that the assignee of a claim takes that claim subject to all defenses which the obligor had against the assignor.[41]   Unless the credit card issuer can place itself in a better position than that occupied by the seller of the goods, the buyer will be able to use his breach of warranty claim to diminish the issuer's recovery. This "better position" is usually sought through an agreement with the cardholder that the issuer takes the claim free of any defenses which the cardholder may have against the seller. The validity of these clauses, while once questioned in some jurisdictions,[42] appears to be upheld by section 9–206(1):

> Subject to any statute or decision which establishes a different rule for buyers or lessees of consumer goods, an agreement by a buyer or lessee that he will not assert against an assignee any claim or defense which he may

---

37. The buyer's right to deduct damages is given by UCC § 2–717. See § 156 *infra*. The buyer's courses of action on discovery of the seller's default is discussed in §§ 141–45 *infra*.

38. UCC § 3–305.

39. UCC § 2–711.

40. UCC § 2–302 discussed in § 44 *supra*. If the provision afforded the buyer a limited remedy, the provision could also be attacked through UCC § 2–719, discussed in § 89 *supra*.

41. Schenuit v. International Fin. Corp., 148 Md. 403, 130 A. 331 (1925). Other cases are cited in 4 A. Corbin, Contracts §§ 892 et seq. (1951). Compare UCC § 9–318.

42. Quality Fin. Co. v. Hurley, 337 Mass. 150, 148 N.E.2d 385 (1958).

have against the seller or lessor is enforceable by an assignee who takes his assignment for value, in good faith and without notice of a claim or defense, except as to defenses of a type which may be asserted against a holder in due course of a negotiable instrument under the Article on Commercial Paper (Article 3) . . . .

Four points about this section should be underscored. First, it is conceivable that courts will hold that section 9–206 has no application to credit card transactions. The credit card is typically used with unsecured credit while section 9–206 appears in Article 9—the Article dealing with secured transactions—and creates a type of limited negotiability for documents which do not qualify as negotiable under Article 3.[43] However, the purpose of Article 9 expressed through section 9–206 closely parallels the purpose of the tripartite credit card. Both involve methods of financing the seller of goods through the assignment of accounts by giving protection to the assignee. Thus, the policy of section 9–206 is applicable to credit card transactions.

Second, if section 9–206 is applicable to the credit card transaction, the cardholder will not be aided by the statutory exception for defenses which may be asserted against a holder in due course. The maker of a negotiable note cannot successfully assert a breach of warranty claim against an assignee of that note who qualifies as a section 3–305 holder in due course.[44] Thus, if the cardholder-issuer relationship is analogized to that of the maker-assignee, the cardholder will not be able to use the section 9–206 exception to assert a breach of warranty claim against the issuer.

Third, the section allows legislatures and courts to develop rules protecting buyers of consumer goods. Since consumer goods are usually involved with credit card purchases, a court is free to ignore the waiver-of-defense clause in most tripartite credit card transactions. Indeed, the developing case law and legislation which prevents the transferee of what would otherwise be a negotiable note from acquiring the rights of a holder in due course when consumer goods have been sold should be applicable to a credit card transaction presenting essentially the same facts.[45]

---

43. UCC § 3–104. See the discussion in United States v. First Nat'l Bank, 263 F.Supp. 298 (D.Mass.1967).

44. § 116 *supra.*

45. Unico v. Owen, 50 N.J. 101, 232 A.2d 405 (1967). Other authority is discussed in § 116 *supra.* For an application of these ideas to UCC § 9–206, see James Talcott, Inc. v. Gee, 266 Cal.App.2d 384, 72 Cal.Rptr. 168 (1968); Star Credit Corp. v. Molina, 6 UCC Rep. 70 (N.Y.Civ.Ct.1969), State statutes include Mass.Gen. Laws Ann. ch. 255, § 12(c) & ch. 255D, § 10(6) (1968); Wash.Rev. Code Ann. § 63.14.-020 (Supp.1968).

Fourth, even if a jurisdiction does not have special rules for sales of consumer goods, section 9–206 cuts off buyer's defenses only if there is an agreement to that effect. Thus, it is important to search the issuer-cardholder and the seller-cardholder agreements to determine whether such a provision is included therein. The unsecured credit card sale is typically represented only by a sales slip, and the waiver-of-defenses provision is not usually included in that transaction. Instead, tripartite credit card arrangements which contain this provision do so by a statement either in the application for credit or on the card issued to the holder. If this statement is enforced as written, the holder will be required to pay the issuer for defective goods and present his damage claim to the seller. In some instances this will be a perfectly satisfactory remedy for the buyer. If he dealt with a reputable merchant who is convinced that the goods were defective, those goods will be replaced or repaired to the buyer's satisfaction. In other instances, however, the seller may be insolvent or have gone out of business; the seller may be located in a distant city—a common problem with nationwide credit systems; or there may be tactical advantages in asserting a breach of warranty claim as a defense to rather than as the basis for a separate suit.

There are, therefore, situations in which the holder would like to attack the validity of the waiver-of-defenses clause and to assert against the issuer his breach of warranty claims. Three methods of attack have been suggested. These are:

1. An argument that the clause is not a part of the issuer-holder "contract." If the waiver is found on the reverse side of the card, buried in small print, a court ought to hold that the waiver is not the bargain of the parties in fact.[46] Likewise, if the clause is found in a brochure which accompanied an unsolicited card and the brochure is devoted in the main to extolling the virtues of the card, it may not be reasonable for the issuer to expect that the cardholder understood that he was to make payments to the issuer even if he had a dispute with the seller. In this event, the brochure is not the bargain of the parties in fact and not a part of their contract.

2. An argument that even if the clause is a part of the contract, a proper interpretation of the language indicates that the language chosen does not apply to a breach of warranty claim. This requires a study of the particular provision involved, read as it would be read by the mythical reasonable person signing the application or reading the card or brochure.[47]

---

46. UCC § 1–201(3); § 47 *supra*.

47. *E. g.*, General Elec. Corp. v. Beyerlein, 30 A.D.2d 762, 292 N.Y.S.2d 32 (1968). Documents are set out in Davenport, *Bank Credit Cards and the Uniform Commercial Code*, 1 Valparaiso L.Rev. 218, 246–54 (1967).

3. An argument that even if the clause is a part of the contract and applicable to this case, it ought not be enforced against the buyer of consumer goods (and, by analogy, consumer services). Waiver-of-defenses clauses might make commercial sense when the buyer and seller are both merchants, but the consumer merits full protection of warranties given him. To the extent that an issuer of a credit card is allowed to recover without regard to the conformity of the goods, express and implied warranties may effectively be taken from the buyer.[48] At this point the current developments in respect to holders in due course of negotiable notes given in connection with the sale of consumer goods are directly applicable.[49]

It may be that the decision on the validity of these clauses in the sale of consumer goods will turn on the language of the agreements involved. If the agreement between the issuer and holder makes no mention of the assignment of claims but is drafted like a letter of cred-

---

One issuer of a tripartite credit card has attempted to protect itself against the holder's defenses. In the material which was included with the card mailed to prospective cardholders appeared this statement: "Any dispute between a Member [the seller] and a Holder will be settled by them, and indebtedness shall be paid to the [Issuer] even though such dispute exists." Whether this enclosure (a) is a part of the contract between the parties and (b) if so, whether it sufficiently informs the cardholder that his defenses have been cut off by the assignment remain to be seen. Is there any *indebtedness* as long as the holder has a valid defense against the seller? Is the issuer agreeing that the holder and seller *will* settle their dispute? Finally, there is the question discussed in this text: will these clauses be upheld when the card is used to purchase consumer goods or services?

48. UCC § 9–206(2); L & N Sales Co. v. Stuski, 188 Pa.Super. 117, 146 A.2d 154 (1958).

49. § 116 *supra*. A frontal attack on the waiver-of-defenses clause as unconscionable under UCC § 2–302 would be hard to sustain. UCC § 9–206(1) is general legislative approval of such agreements in secured transactions. The similarities between the purposes of financing through assignment of secured claims and the transfer of accounts under a tripartite credit card arrangement are sufficiently similar so that the policy of UCC § 9–206 ought to sustain the credit card waiver-of-defense clause against any sweeping claim of unconscionability. Beam v. John Deere Co., 240 Ark. 107, 398 S.W.2d 218 (1966); First Nat'l Bank v. Husted, 57 Ill.App.2d 227, 205 N.E.2d 780 (1965). However, such a frontal attack is not necessary when the transaction involves consumer goods since these transactions may be excluded from the operation of UCC § 9–206.

There will be difficulties in some jurisdictions with non-Code statutes which provide that the assignee of a non-negotiable right takes subject to the same defenses as are available against the assignor. Massachusetts has such a statute, Mass.Gen. Laws Ann. ch. 231, § 5 (1956) and has held that a waiver-of-defenses clause is contrary to the public policy of the state. Quality Fin. Co. v. Hurley, 337 Mass. 150, 148 N.E.2d 385 (1958). The effect of the Code on such statutes and cases is in doubt. General Elec. Credit Corp. v. Noblett, 268 F.Supp. 984 (W. D.Okl.1967), *rev'd* 400 F.2d 442 (10th Cir.), *cert. denied* 393 U.S. 935, 89 S. Ct. 295, 21 L.Ed.2d 271 (1968); General Elec. Corp. v. Beyerlein, 30 A. D.2d 762, 292 N.Y.S.2d 32 (1968). *Beyerlein*, limiting *Hurley* to consumer goods cases, is consistent with the consumer goods exception of UCC § 9–206(1).

it,[50] the issuer may convince a court that its transaction is separate from the seller-holder contract and that the issuer is not subject to any infirmities in that transaction. On the other hand, if the agreements involved are drafted on the basis of contractual principles of assignment, the courts may apply the usual rules regarding assignment and hold that the issuer-assignee has no greater rights than its seller-assignor.[51]

This position has a surface appeal but only because it is the kind of argument familiar to lawyers. What is involved is a problem of which of two parties (issuer or holder) *ought* to bear the risks involved with a seller who disputes the breach of warranty claim or who is financially unable to respond in damages. The answer should not turn on how carefully the issuer's attorney drafted documents which are not readily comprehensible to the cardholder who succumbed to the cashless society advertising of the issuer. This is a policy question to be answered by a consideration of competing policies.

On one side is the issuer of the card who is supplying credit to aid both the cardholder and the seller. Rules of law which make this business too expensive will result either in the withdrawal of financial institutions from the business or in the increase in the price of goods and credit to be passed on to all cardholders.

On the other side is the consumer who has no understanding of the difference between bipartite and tripartite credit cards. He has, however, used his card to buy goods on credit, and those goods have turned out to be defective. When the issuer demands payment the tripartite cardholder will have difficuties in even forcing the seller into any issuer-holder litigation. Attempts to implead the seller must satisfy jurisdictional and venue requirements,[52] but even if these can be satisfied, a motion to dismiss will probably be granted because of the lack of common issues and facts between the two suits.[53] Further, the Code's vouching-in procedures would be of no aid to such a holder-buyer. The only sanction against a seller who does not respond to the vouching-in notice is that the seller will be bound by any determination of fact common to the two controversies.[54] If the waiver-of-defenses clause eliminates the holder's breach of warranty claim from

---

50. UCC Article 5; Bergsten, *Credit Cards—A Prelude to the Cashless Society*, 8 B.C.Ind. & Com.L.Rev. 485, 512–13 (1967); Davenport, *Bank Credit Cards and the Uniform Commercial Code*, 1 Valparaiso L.Rev. 218, 234–40 (1967).

51. Comment, *The Tripartite Credit Card Transaction: A Legal Infant*, 48 Calif.L.Rev. 459, 468–69 (1960).

52. 3 J. Moore, Federal Practice ¶¶ 14.-27–.28 (1968).

53. F. James, Civil Procedure § 10.20 (1965).

54. UCC § 2–607(5) (a).

the issuer-holder suit, there is no common determination of fact involved, and the seller has no reason to enter that litigation.

The result is that if the waiver-of-defenses clause is upheld, the holder-buyer must pay the issuer and institute a separate suit against his reluctant seller. If the waiver clause is not upheld, the holder-buyer will be able to set off his damages, and the issuer must take action against the reluctant seller. This returns to the question posed earlier: should the holder or the issuer bear the risks involved when a seller disputes the breach of warranty claim or becomes insolvent?

One reason to conclude that these risks should be placed on the issuer is that he, more than the buyer, trusted the financial credit of the seller. In the usual tripartite credit card arrangement, the buyer entered into a purchase transaction. Only in a very limited sense did he rely on the seller's credit and, as long as the buyer had not paid for the goods, it was the seller who was trusting the buyer's credit. The issuer, on the other hand, is a business engaged in the purchase (in some form) of the seller's accounts. It is in a much better position to determine the credit standing of the seller because it is dealing with credit arrangements. Often the issuer in fact relies on the credit of the merchant-seller by inserting a clause in the issuer-seller agreement that the seller will repurchase any accounts disputed by the holder. It is, therefore, not difficult to conclude that it is the issuer (not the holder) who trusted the credit of the seller and who should take the accounts subject to any defenses which the holder may have that affect the seller's financial standing—no matter how clearly the waiver-of-defenses clause was drafted.

There is an additional reason to place these risks on the card issuer. Both the holder and the issuer trusted the honesty and standards of dealing of the seller—the buyer in purchasing goods and the issuer in purchasing accounts receivable. However, the issuer is in a much stronger position to police the seller who habitually passes off poor quality merchandise on the public. The issuer can bring the strength of its future financial backing to bear on sellers who refuse to recognize valid claims from their buyers. This strength will be much more effective than the complaints of individual buyers and should aid in bringing these sellers up to the Code's standard of merchantability and fair dealing.

The problems arising out of the use (and misuse) of credit cards merit comprehensive study by state legislatures, not sporadic statutes which do little more than to affirm the desires of issuers to be able to choose between holders and sellers when a dispute arises. In the meantime courts will be forced to reach hard decisions without legislative guidance. When the problem involves a determination of whether the issuer ought to be allowed to proceed against a cardholder free from any defenses which the holder may have against the seller, the answer ought not turn on the niceties of the language used by the issuer's attorneys in the documents they drafted. Instead the answer should respond (1) to the policies underlying the Uniform Commercial Code and other statutes regulating consumer sales and loans, (2) to the differences between the risks which a financer and a purchaser should assume, and (3) to the realization that the issuer is often in the stronger bargaining position to assure honest dealing between seller and buyer. On balance, these policies favor allowing the holder to assert his defenses when sued by the issuer of a tripartite credit card.

2. RIGHT OF INSPECTION

§ 120. Nature of the Right of Inspection

The buyer's "right" of inspection serves a needed function in the performance of contracts for the sale of goods. Unfortunately, the nature of this "right" is not clear from the statutory language; however, an understanding of the function which inspection plays in the performance process aids in interpreting the Code. This function can be illustrated by assuming that buyers had no right of inspection and considering the following factual pattern:

A seller and buyer entered into a contract for the sale of goods, the seller to deliver the goods to the buyer. Nothing was said about credit; thus the buyer was obligated to pay on delivery.[55] The seller showed up at the buyer's place of business on the appointed day with a truck filled with boxes in which the seller claimed were the specified quantity of conforming goods. The buyer requested the privilege of looking inside the boxes to assure himself that the goods were those ordered. The seller refused, repeated his claim that the goods were conforming, and demanded payment of the purchase price.

If we assume that the buyer has no right to inspect, a buyer in a case like the one set out above faces troublesome alternatives. If he pays the price and the goods turn out to be non-conforming, the buyer could reject (or revoke acceptance) and sue for a refund of the amount paid plus compensation for damages suffered.[56] In theory this may be an adequate remedy, but in practice it may be extremely inadequate. The buyer has had to advance money for a truckload of boxes, hoping that the seller will not be insolvent if it later turns out that the goods inside those boxes were non-conforming—but knowing that the only way he can be assured of getting his money back, even against a solvent seller, is by taking the initiative as the plaintiff in a lawsuit.

---

55. UCC § 2–310(a).   56. UCC § 2–711.

On the other hand, if the buyer refuses to pay the price, he faces the unhappy prospect of being sued and having the seller prove that the goods were in fact conforming.[57] Of course, the buyer could successfully defend this suit with evidence that the goods were not conforming—and that his rejection was rightful—but this evidence is difficult to obtain when the information of conformity is in the possession of the seller. Therefore, without a right of inspection a buyer is placed in a most awkward position: he either invests the purchase price in the hope that the goods conform or he refuses the investment with the risk that he will be held in default of his contract promise to pay the price.

One answer to such a buyer could have been that if he wants the protection of an inspection, he can make it a part of the agreement to purchase the goods. The Code, however, has taken the opposite position.[58] The right to inspect is a part of every contract unless the parties have agreed otherwise. The contrary agreement may be express (as where the parties have stated that the buyer "shall have no right to inspect before payment") or it may arise out of the nature of transaction (as where the buyer has agreed to pay against documents of title).

The principal Code section is 2–513. Subsection (1) establishes the right with this language:

> Unless otherwise agreed and subject to subsection (3), where goods are tendered or delivered or identified to the contract for sale, the buyer has a right before payment or acceptance to inspect them at any reasonable place and time and in any reasonable manner. When the seller is required or authorized to send the goods to the buyer, the inspection may be after their arrival.

This subsection will cause difficulties in deciding whether the buyer's demands are "reasonable," but these will be problems of fact turning on the nature of the goods and the agreement between the parties.[59] A more difficult threshold problem is that of determining the nature of the buyer's "right." At least two possibilities could be asserted. First, the right may be promissory only—that is, the buyer's right of inspection arises out of an implied promise made by the seller, which promise is not also a condition on the buyer's obligation to pay. Un-

---

57. UCC § 2–703.

58. UCC § 2–513. For the distinction between the Code's concept of examination and its concept of inspection, see § 88 *supra*.

59. The parties may agree on what is a reasonable time. UCC § 1–204 (1). It may also be established by custom. Valley Nat'l Bank v. Babylon Chrysler-Plymouth, Inc., 53 Misc. 2d 1029, 280 N.Y.S.2d 786 (Sup.Ct.) *aff'd mem.* 28 A.D.2d 1092, 284 N.Y.S. 2d 849 (1967).

der this construction of section 2–513(1) the seller's failure to allow the buyer to inspect would be a default for which the buyer could recover damages but which would not prevent the buyer's obligation to pay the price from arising provided that the seller could prove that the goods were in fact conforming. The second possible construction of section 2–513(1) is that the right to inspect is a condition on the buyer's obligation to pay—that is, unless the seller allows the buyer to inspect the goods, the tender is defective and the buyer has no obligation to pay the price or accept the goods.[60]

A substantial argument can be made that the language of the Code compels the promissory interpretation. Tender of delivery is a condition to the buyer's duty to accept and pay, and a tender entitles the seller to acceptance and payment.[61] Tender is defined as requiring that the seller "put and hold conforming goods at the buyer's disposition and give the buyer any notification reasonably necessary to enable him to take delivery." [62] Nothing is said about the tender's having to include time for inspection by the buyer. Therefore (goes this argument) if conforming goods were properly put at the buyer's disposition and the appropriate notice given, the buyer is obligated to pay even though the seller refused to allow an inspection. The most that the buyer would have would be an action for the damages which arose out of the seller's failure to allow the *promised* inspection. Normally these damages would be only nominal because the tendered goods either conformed to the contract (in which event the breach of the inspection promise caused no harm) or they did not conform to the contract (in which event the harm arising out of the breach of the inspection promise is the same as that arising out of the promise to deliver conforming goods).

This argument should be rejected. To interpret section 2–513(1) as creating only a promissory right of inspection ignores the function which an inspection serves in the performance of a contract for the sale of goods. Its purpose is to give the buyer some assurance that what has been delivered to him conforms to that which he purchased. The buyer is entitled to this assurance before he accepts and pays the price, or he is left with the same troublesome choices that he had with-

---

60. "A condition creates no right or duty of and in itself, but is merely a limiting or modifying factor. If it is breached or does not occur, the promisee acquires no right to enforce the promise. A promise raises a duty to perform and its breach subjects the promisor to liability and damages, but does not necessarily excuse performance by the other party. . . ." United States v. Schaeffer, 319 F.2d 907, 911 (9th Cir. 1963), *cert. denied* 376 U.S. 943, 84 S.Ct. 798, 11 L.Ed.2d 767 (1964). A general discussion of the distinction between promise and condition is contained in 3A A. Corbin, Contracts § 633 (1960).

61. § 94 *supra*.

62. UCC § 2–503(1).

out the right of inspection. Unless the buyer has agreed to pay without inspecting, there is no good reason to leave him with this dilemma. The drafters did not mean to create a "right" under section 2–513(1) only to have that "right" dissipated by construing it solely as a promise. The only way to protect the buyer is to construe the 2–513(1) right as a *condition* to the buyer's performance obligations—that is, to make allowance of inspection a necessary part of the seller's tender.[63] That the drafters intended this conclusion is clear from the following Comment:

> [W]here the seller is demanding payment on delivery he must first allow the buyer to inspect the goods in order to avoid impairing his tender unless the contract for sale is on C.I.F., C.O.D., cash against documents or similar terms negating the privilege of inspection before payment.[64]

Under this reading of section 2–513(1) the failure to allow inspection impairs the seller's tender. If the tender is improper, the buyer may reject the goods [65] and refuse to pay the price.[66] Further, since the rejection was rightful, the buyer could (if he had made the proper tender) hold the seller liable for any damages suffered.[67] This text will proceed on the basis that this is the nature of the buyer's "right" of inspection.

The buyer may, of course, waive the condition by not exercising his right of inspection.[68] The Code does not require him to inspect but says that he has a "right" to do so if he desires. Further, the buyer may waive this right as to payment but retain it as to acceptance,[69] so that if, after payment, he discovers that goods are non-conforming, he may still reject or revoke acceptance if he can meet the other requirements of these courses of action.[70]

§ 121. Time, Place and Manner of Inspection

The Code does not attempt to detail the time, place, or manner of inspection. Instead, it properly leaves these matters to a case-by-case

63. Imperial Prods. Co. v. Capitol Chem. Co., 187 App.Div. 599, 176 N.Y. S. 49 (1919), *aff'd* 228 N.Y. 528, 126 N.E. 911 (1920). The buyer's right to inspection under the Uniform Sales Act was covered by § 47. The courts held that the right of inspection was a condition, disagreeing as to whether the condition was precedent or subsequent. 3 S. Williston, Sales §§ 472–74 (rev. ed. 1948).

64. UCC § 2–503, Comment 2. Leading to the same conclusion are UCC §§ 2–310, 2–606(2) (b).

65. UCC § 2–601.

66. UCC § 2–711(1).

67. *Id.*

68. Tennessee-Virginia Constr. Co. v. Willingham, 117 Ga.App. 290, 160 S.E. 2d 444 (1968).

69. UCC § 2–513, Comment 2.

70. §§ 141–43 *infra.*

determination under the general mandate that the buyer has a right to inspect "at any reasonable place and time and in any reasonable manner." [71] Because of the variety of goods that can be the subject of sale, this was as specific as the drafters could be. Some goods can be inspected on the loading dock by a casual observation; others may require a test run in the factory or a chemical analysis in the research laboratory. As long as the buyer selects a place, time, and manner of inspection that is "reasonable", he may withhold acceptance and payment until the inspection is completed.[72]

There is one type of problem, however, for which the Code is specific as to the place of the inspection. Many sales contracts require or authorize the seller to deliver the goods to the buyer's residence, city, or place of business.[73] Examples include the consumer who has purchased a new refrigerator from a local retailer and the businessman who has bought several hundred machines from a manufacturer thousands of miles away. The retailer will select a refrigerator from his stock and deliver it to the consumer's residence; the manufacturer will select and package the machines and ship them by carrier to the buyer's city, most probably using a sight draft (or a time draft if credit is extended) and documents of title. Where are buyers allowed to inspect when the goods are delivered to them? The Code does not leave this question to the test of reasonableness but provides: "When the seller is required or authorized to send the goods to the buyer, the inspection may be after their arrival." [74] The consumer may inspect the refrigerator in his house; the businessman may inspect the machines while they are still in the possession of the car-

---

71. UCC § 2–513(1).

72. For a case in which the court found that the time of inspection was too late, see Michael M. Berlin & Co. v. T. Whiting Mfg., Inc., 5 UCC Rep. 357 (N.Y.Sup.Ct. 1968).

73. §§ 97–99 *supra*.

74. UCC § 2–513(1). This follows the general pre-Code law. Olsen v. Mc-Maken & Pentzien, 139 Neb. 506, 297 N.W. 830 (1941); Inland Seed Co. v. Washington-Idaho Seed Co., 160 Wash. 244, 294 P. 991 (1931); 3 S. Williston, Sales § 480 (rev. ed. 1948).

The parties could select some point other than the place of arrival for inspection. This was allowed under pre-Code law (3 S. Williston, Sales § 480 (rev. ed. 1948)) and the "unless otherwise agreed" language of UCC § 2–513 (1) should carry over to the last sen-

tence of that section. If not, UCC § 1–102(4) should provide the needed statutory authority.

The Code language is that inspection *may* be after arrival. Could the buyer change the place of inspection by demanding the exercise of the right at the place of shipment? Since the point of arrival was selected for the benefit of the buyer, there would normally be no good reason why the buyer could not select a point more beneficial to the seller, at least if the buyer gave prompt notice of his desire to inspect at the place of shipment. Code authority can be found in the "may" already referred to and in the general requirements of reasonableness which occur in the prior sentence of UCC § 2–513(1). Pre-Code law is scarce, but agrees with the suggested solution contained in this note. *E. g.*, Phoenix Iron & Steel Co. v. Wilkoff Co., 253 F. 165 (6th Cir. 1918).

rier. If the manufacturer had agreed to deliver the machines to the buyer's place of business, then this would be the "arrival" point and the buyer could inspect at his place of business.

This result is not changed simply because the risk of loss may have been on the buyer during shipment. The machines may have been ordered under an F.O.B. seller's point contract, and the seller may have made a proper tender at the place of shipment so that the risk that those goods might be lost in transit shifted to the buyer. Nevertheless, the Code accepts the sensible position that the buyer need not have someone inspect those goods at the time they were delivered to the carrier but may wait until their arrival. A contrary decision would effectively deny the right of inspection to many buyers because they do not have agents at the point of shipment. Therefore, even though the seller may have made a proper tender of conforming goods so that the risk of loss shifted to the buyer, the buyer retains the right of inspection which he may exercise after the goods arrive to assure himself that conforming goods were in fact sent by the seller.[75] If his inspection reveals (or should have revealed) that the goods were conforming at their point of tender, the buyer is obligated to accept them and to pay for them according to the contract.[76] If his inspection reveals that the goods were not conforming at their point of tender, the buyer may reject the goods and resist any efforts by the seller to recover their price.[77]

The allowance of inspection after arrival creates momentary difficulties when combined with the conclusion drawn in the prior section of this text. There it was argued that the right to inspect is a condition on the buyer's duty to accept and pay for the goods and that, if the seller refused to allow the inspection, the tender was improper— allowing the buyer to reject the goods and refuse to pay their price. As long as the goods arrive, the two ideas reinforce each other and operate without legal difficulties. However, if the goods are lost in transit after the risk of loss has passed to the buyer,[78] the buyer cannot inspect "after their arrival." Does this mean that the tender is improper—since the buyer has lost his right to inspect—and that such a buyer could successfully resist a suit for the price of the goods?

Even though the conclusion drawn in the prior section might lead to this result, the answer is that the buyer in such a case could not use the right of inspection to defeat a suit for the price. The Code's policy in placing the risk of loss on a buyer following proper tender in a shipment contract is based upon the commercial decision that from

75. UCC § 2–310, Comment 1.

76. UCC §§ 2–507, 2–607(1).

77. UCC §§ 2–601, 2–711.

78. UCC § 2–509; §§ 130–36 infra.

that point of time on (or at least for a commercially reasonable time thereafter) the buyer ought to bear the "risk" that the goods might be lost. "Risk" means that if those goods are lost, the buyer is nevertheless obligated to perform his contractual promise—that is, to pay the price.[79] The right of inspection cannot be used to upset the more specific treatment of risk of loss. Therefore, an exception must be made to the conclusion drawn in the prior section of this text: the right of inspection on arrival is a condition on the buyer's obligations to accept and pay unless the risk of loss has shifted to the buyer *and* the goods are destroyed before they arrive. If these two events have occurred, the buyer will be liable for the price even though he cannot inspect.

The parties may agree on the length of time within which the buyer is to be allowed to inspect.[80] Such an agreement is binding unless the time selected is "manifestly unreasonable." [81]

§ 122. Expenses of Inspection

The Code deals expressly with the problem of which party bears the expenses of inspection:

> Expenses of inspection must be borne by the buyer but may be recovered from the seller if the goods do not conform and are rejected.[82]

The buyer may not shift the cost of inspection to the seller if the buyer decides to accept non-conforming goods; the goods must be non-conforming *and* rejected before the section is applicable.

The rule of this Code section may be changed by the agreement of the parties.[83] If it is not changed, the buyer's expenses of inspecting goods which turn out to be non-conforming (and are rejected) are incidental damages and recoverable under the express language of section 2–715(1).

§ 123. Exceptions to the Right of Inspection

The statutory rule that the buyer has a right to inspect goods before payment or acceptance is subject to this introductory phrase: "Unless otherwise agreed and subject to subsection (3) . . .."

---

79. UCC § 2–709(1) (a). *See also* UCC § 2–321 and the Comment.

80. UCC § 2–513(1) is expressly subject to other agreements of the parties.

81. UCC § 1–204(1). UCC § 2–302 could also be applicable. For Code cases in which the parties' agreement as to time for inspection was not enforced,

see Wilson Trading Corp. v. David Ferguson, Ltd., 23 N.Y.2d 398, 297 N.Y.S.2d 108, 244 N.E.2d 685 (1968); Vandenberg v. Siter, 204 Pa.Super. 392, 204 A.2d 494 (1964).

82. UCC § 2–513(2).

83. UCC § 2–513, Comment 4.

Subsection (3)—which is quoted and discussed below—lists types of contracts in which the buyer is obligated to pay without inspection. Each of these types of contracts is one in which the parties normally understand that payment of the price must precede inspection; therefore, subsection (3) can be considered as a specific example of the more general proposition that parties may, by agreement, vary their Code created rights and duties.[84]

ACCEPTANCE WITHOUT INSPECTION

It would be an extremely odd case in which the parties had agreed that the buyer must accept the goods without having the right to inspect them first. In by far the great majority of commercial contracts the buyer has purchased some described kind of goods, and he is entitled to what he bought. The seller cannot force some different kind of goods on the buyer, and the buyer retains the right to inspect that which is delivered to determine whether it conforms to the contract. Even when the buyer buys goods "as is," he is entitled to inspect to see if the delivered goods are a different type of merchandise and to reject the tender if the goods are not those purchased. The Comments suggest that the only time the buyer must accept before inspection is when the sale is of "this thing";[85] however, even here the buyer is entitled to the "thing" bought, and if the seller delivers a different "thing," the buyer can reject. Therefore, a fairly safe conclusion is that a buyer may always inspect before *acceptance*. The problems center on whether a buyer may always inspect before he must *pay* for the goods.

PAYMENT WITHOUT INSPECTION

There are situations in which a seller is willing to sell his goods only if the buyer agrees to pay for them without an inspection. Consider, for example, the seller who has an order from an overseas buyer but who fears that the buyer will misuse the right of inspection before payment to make false claims as to the goods' non-conformity and thereby be able to force a price reduction. The distance between the seller and the delivered goods may be so great that it becomes so inconvenient and expensive to determine the validity of the buyer's claims that it is necessary to settle quickly at a reduced price for the goods. Such a seller may say to his buyer that he is willing to sell the goods only if the buyer will pay in advance or on arrival of the necessary documents and, if the goods turn out to be non-conforming, seek a recovery of the purchase price. If the buyer is willing to make the pur-

84. UCC § 1–102(3).　　　　　85. UCC § 2–513, Comment 1.

chase on this basis, the seller's possession of the price gives added protection against the necessity of making quick decisions about claims which may turn out to be false.

A common way of expressing this type of overseas agreement is through the C.I.F. or C. & F. contract. The use of these terms means, in the first case, that the quoted price includes the cost of the goods, insurance, and freight;[86] in the second case it means that the quoted price includes the cost of the goods and their freight.[87] Thus the buyer knows the total price he is obligated to pay for the goods without any increase due the cost of freight. Important to these two types of contracts is this section of the Code:

> Under the term C.I.F. or C. & F. unless otherwise agreed the buyer must make payment against tender of the required documents and the seller may not tender nor the buyer demand delivery of the goods in substitution for the documents.[88]

The C.I.F. and C. & F. contracts are examples of contracts in which the buyer has agreed to pay against documents and has lost his right of inspection before payment[89]—but not before acceptance. The only Code exception to this rule (other than the common "unless otherwise agreed" language) is:

> Unless otherwise agreed where the contract provides for payment on or after arrival of the goods the seller must before payment allow such preliminary inspection as is feas-

86. UCC § 2–320(1). Pre-Code law allowed the seller to prepay the freight or deduct it from the invoice. Dixon, Irmaos & CIA, Ltda. v. Chase Nat'l Bank, 144 F.2d 759 (2d Cir. 1944), *cert. denied* 324 U.S. 850, 65 S.Ct. 687, 89 L.Ed. 1410 (1945), and cases cited therein. The Code requires that the seller "obtain a receipt from the carrier . . . showing that the freight has been paid or provided for." UCC § 2–320(2) (b). Thus, unless the agreement so provides, the seller cannot ship the goods, freight collect, even if the freight costs are deducted from the invoice. UCC § 2–320, Comment 5.

87. UCC § 2–320(1); AMCO Transworld, Inc. v. M/V Bambi, 257 F.Supp. 215 (S.D.Tex.1966).

88. UCC § 2–320(4).

89. Madeirense Do Brasil v. Stulman-Emrick Lumber Co., 147 F.2d 399 (2d Cir.), *cert. denied* 325 U.S. 861, 65 S.Ct. 1201, 89 L.Ed. 1982 (1945) (C. & F. contract); Obrecht v. Crawford, 175 Md. 385, 2 A.2d 1 (1938) (C.I.F. contract). The C.I.F. buyer must pay on arrival of documents even if the contract does not provide for payment against documents. E. Clemens Horst Co. v. Biddell, [1912] A.C. 18. For a construction of C.I.F. contracts with inconsistent terms, see 2 S. Williston, Sales § 280f (rev. ed. 1948).

ible; but if the goods are lost delivery of the documents and
payment are due when the goods should have been delivered.[90]
Notice that the *contract* must provide for payment on or after arrival. Inspection is not allowed before payment simply because the goods
happen to arrive before the documents.

Because the Code accepts the mercantile practice of allowing the
C.I.F. and C. & F. contracts to eliminate the buyer's right of inspection
before payment, there is a need to assure the buyer that the goods sent
will be properly loaded, that the freight will be paid, that the necessary
invoices and documents will be obtained and forwarded promptly to
the buyer, and (in the C.I.F. contract) that insurance will cover the
normal risks of loss. The Code contains these assurances.[91]

There are other sales in which the seller wants to require payment before inspection. He may accomplish this with a C.O.D. contract or by a contract which provides for payments *against* documents. This latter agreement is often called a documentary sale and
is not to be confused with the agreement in which the seller is simply
authorized or required to ship with documents. Unless the contract
between the parties provides that the buyer is to pay *against* those documents, the buyer may inspect before he pays even though the seller
uses documents of title to complete the sale.

The principles developed above are made a part of the Code by
section 2–513(3). Section 2–513(1) establishes the buyer's general
right of inspection before payment or acceptance subject to the introductory phrase: "Unless otherwise agreed and subject to subsection
(3) . . .." That subsection (3) provides in full:

> Unless otherwise agreed and subject to the provisions of
> this Article on C.I.F. contracts (subsection (3) of section
> 2–321), the buyer is not entitled to inspect the goods before
> payment of the price when the contract provides
>
> (a) for delivery "C.O.D." or other like terms; or
>
> (b) for payment against documents of title, except
>   where such payment is due only after the goods
>   are to become available for inspection.

These points deserve emphasis: (1) the reference to C.I.F. contracts is to the subsection quoted above on preliminary inspection
where feasible;[92] (2) the buyer's right to inspect is removed only as a

---

90. UCC § 2–321(3). The first two subsections of UCC § 2–321 "provide for
a shift to the seller of the risk of
quality and weight deterioration during shipment . . .." UCC § 2–
321, Comment.

91. UCC § 2–320(2).

92. UCC § 2–321(3).

condition to payment, not to acceptance; (3) the important document in determining whether the buyer has waived his right to inspect before payment is the contract between the parties, not the method by which the seller chooses to ship the goods; and (4) even when the contract provides for payment against documents, the buyer may inspect before payment if "payment is due only after the goods are to become available for inspection." The fact that the goods happened to arrive before the documents does not satisfy this last condition.[93] It is only when the contract between the parties delays payment until the goods arrive that the goods have become "available for inspection."

SUMMARY

The result of this statutory pattern can be summarized thus: the buyer always has a right to inspect goods before accepting them or before paying for them unless he has given up that right in his contract with the seller; the seller's refusal to allow inspection when the right has not been contracted away is a defective tender (unless the goods were lost or destroyed after their risk of loss passed to the buyer) allowing the buyer to reject and resist payment, and such refusal is also a breach if the buyer has performed any necessary conditions on his part;[94] in very few contracts (none?) will the buyer have waived inspection before acceptance; but in some contracts the buyer will have agreed to pay before inspecting. In this last situation the buyer is obligated to pay even though the goods are non-conforming and the seller refuses inspection—if the seller's tender is otherwise proper. This summary is subject to one final Code exception:

(1) Where the contract requires payment before inspection non-conformity of the goods does not excuse the buyer from so making payment unless

(a) the non-conformity appears without inspection; or

(b) despite tender of the required documents the circumstances would justify injunction against honor under the provisions of this Act (Section 5–114).

(2) Payment pursuant to subsection (1) does not constitute an acceptance of goods or impair the buyer's right to inspect or any of his remedies.[95]

Subsection (2) makes express that which otherwise would have had to have been implied from the section establishing the buyer's right to inspect. Subsection (1) carves out two instances in which the buyer may refuse to pay even though the contract requires payment without inspection. The reference to section 5–114 deals with a defect in

93. UCC § 2–513, Comment 5.   95. UCC § 2–512.

94. § 120–21 *supra*.

the documents. The other instance is when the non-conformity "appears without inspection." Evidently this refers to such situations as the C.O.D. record album which, when delivered, rattles in such a manner as to indicate that the contents have been shattered. In these cases the buyer is not obligated to pay for goods even though he agreed to do so without inspection.[96]

§ 124. Exceptions to the Requirement That the Details of Inspection Must be "Reasonable"

In absence of an agreement section 2–513(1) provides that the place, time, and manner of inspection must be "reasonable." Because what is or is not "reasonable" may be both obscure and subject to hindsight determination by the trier of fact, the parties may wish to agree on the details of inspection. Section 2–513(1) gives them this privilege. The "unless otherwise agreed" language modifies not only the buyer's right to inspect but also the statement that the inspection is to be "at any reasonable place and time and in any reasonable manner." Therefore, the parties may agree on the details of the buyer's inspection, and this agreement will be controlling in the event a controversy arises.[97]

Agreeing as to a place and method of inspection may cause other problems not anticipated by the parties. Suppose, for example, that the contract of sale required the seller to manufacture or produce certain goods within extremely close tolerances and gave the buyer one week to inspect all deliveries—with the inspection to take place in the buyer's laboratory. The terms of the contract were "F.O.B. seller's city" with nothing said about time of payment.

Prior sections of this text have indicated that the buyer has a right to inspect before payment or acceptance of these goods.[98] This section supports the conclusion that the buyer will have one week to perform this inspection, that the place of the inspection is not the carrier's yard but the buyer's laboratory, and that the method of inspection will involve measurements for exact size or content. However, has the agreement as to inspection changed the point where the risk of loss is to shift? Has it postponed the time that the goods are to be identified to the contract so that the buyer will not have an insurable

---

96. Shaking the package enough to hear the rattles is a kind of "inspection." Even looking at a crushed box could qualify as an "inspection." Nevertheless, the drafters meant to excuse the buyer from his payment obligation in situations in which the apparent non-conformity "is one which is evident in the mere process of taking delivery." UCC § 2–512, Comment 3.

97. UCC § 1–204(1) also allows the parties to agree as to what is a reasonable time. See discussion and cases cited in § 121 *supra*.

98. §§ 120–22 *supra*.

interest in the goods until after the inspection? What happens if the buyer's laboratory is destroyed by fire after the goods are shipped by the seller and before they arrive at the buyer's city? Is the contract avoided or may either of the parties insist that the buyer inspect in some other reasonable manner? In answer to these questions the Code provides:

> A place or method of inspection fixed by the parties is presumed to be exclusive but unless otherwise expressly agreed it does not postpone identification or shift the place for delivery or for passing the risk of loss. If compliance becomes impossible, inspection shall be as provided in this section unless the place or method fixed was clearly intended as an indispensable condition failure of which avoids the contract.[99]

99. UCC § 2–513(4).

CHAPTER VI

TITLE, INSURABLE INTEREST, AND RISK OF LOSS

Analysis

A. TITLE TO GOODS

A. TITLE TO GOODS

§ 125. Importance of Title Under the Code

One of the hallmarks of the pre-Code law of sales was its emphasis on the concept of title. Writing in the late-1930's Professor Karl Llewellyn (who became the Chief Reporter for the Code) put it this way: "The approach of prevailing Sales doctrine, before or apart from the [Uniform Sales] Act and in it, is this: Unless cogent reason be shown to the contrary, the location of Title will govern every point which it can be made to govern. It will govern, between the parties, risk, action for the price, the applicable law in an interstate transaction, the place and time for measuring damages, the power to defeat the other party's interest, or to replevy, or to reject; it will govern, as against outsiders, leviability, rights against tort-feasors, infraction of criminal statutes about sales, incidence of taxation, power to insure." [1]

---

1. Llewellyn, *Through Title to Contract and a Bit Beyond*, 3 Law: A Century of Progress 80, 87 (1937).

There were many difficulties with a legal system which attempted to solve sales problems through a search for an all-pervading title. People do not care one whit where title, as such, is located. They want to know if the law will protect their possession of goods and whether an insurance company can be compelled to pay if those goods are destroyed. Buyers are interested in remedies against defaulting sellers, and sellers are interested in remedies against defaulting buyers. Both want to know who bears the risk of loss if goods are destroyed in transit, and manufacturers have a financial concern as to whether they must pay a property tax on goods still in their possession on the tax date but subject to a contract for sale. These are the problems that worry people, and the only time they become concerned about "title" is when their lawyer tells them that the answer to their problems turns on who has the title to the goods involved.

Nevertheless, title might have been a satisfactory method of solving legal problems if there had been some objective method of determining its location, but a title to goods has neither form nor substance. It is a concept created by lawyers and its location is wherever lawyers place it.[2] Some judges were astute enough to realize that different policy considerations were involved when they were faced with a question of who ought to pay a tax from those involved in a risk of loss problem. These judges manipulated the title concept to produce sensible results in the cases before them. Others, however, slavishly followed title precedents from cases presenting problems strikingly different from the ones under consideration and reached indefensible results. Thus, the single-title concept of sales produced uneven results and obstructed any careful analysis of the problems lying at the root of the factual patterns involved.[3]

There was, however, an even greater difficulty. The idea that there was a single title whose transfer could be pinpointed in every sale made sense only in those simple cases reminiscent of a medieval economy—those in which the buyer picked up the goods purchased and paid cash at the moment of delivery. These are the cash-on-the-barrelhead sales, and a title passing from the seller to the buyer can be hypothesized without much difficulty. As soon as the transaction

---

2. Under the Uniform Sales Act the location of title was a matter of intent. Uniform Sales Act §§ 18–19. The same rule existed at common law. The difficulty was that parties often had no intent at all about the location of title because they did not think in these terms. *See* Cadillac Mach. Co. v. Mitchell-Diggins Iron Co., 205 Mich. 107, 171 N.W. 479 (1919); George Boiko & Co. v. Atlantic Woolen Mills,

Inc., 195 App.Div. 207, 186 N.Y.S. 624 (1921), *aff'd mem.* 234 N.Y. 583, 138 N.E. 455 (1922). Another difficulty arose out of the courts' willingness to ignore express statements of intent. *See* Low v. Pew, 108 Mass. 347 (1871).

3. Note, *The Effect of Prepayment Upon the Buyer's Right to Goods*, 37 Colum.L.Rev. 630, 634 (1937).

became more complicated the single-title fiction would no longer work. The introduction of deferred payments, security agreements, financing from the third parties, or delivery by carrier from a warehouse located at a point distant from both the seller's and buyer's place of business required a fluid concept of title with its bits and pieces held by all parties to the transaction. The single-title concept did not reflect commercial practices.

At the urging of Professor Llewellyn and other scholars the drafters of the Code discarded the notion that the principal method of solving sales problems should turn on the search for a single (or as Llewellyn called it, a "lump") title. The Code's approach can be summarized thus: specific problems are identified and solutions to those problems are established without concern as to who has title or the time a title might have passed from seller to buyer. "The purpose is to avoid making practical issues between practical men turn upon the location of an intangible something, the passing of which no man can prove by evidence and to substitute for such abstractions proof of words and actions of a tangible character." [4] It was, however, impossible for the drafters to foresee all of the problems that might arise in a sales transaction. Some method of solution had to be supplied for these problems, and a section on title was inserted to provide an answer for these unforeseeable cases. Also, a considerable body of non-sales law existed which was geared to the title determination (examples include taxation of personalty, attachment, larceny, and insurability). [5] The Code section on title allows this law to continue until such time as it, too, searches out the policies involved in these questions and rids itself of the lump-title approach. [6]

The Code's title section states its purpose in the opening two sentences of section 2–401:

> Each provision of this Article with regard to the rights, obligations and the remedies of the seller, the buyer, purchasers or other third parties applies irrespective of title to the goods except where the provision refers to such title. Insofar as situations are not covered by the other provisions of this Article and matters concerning title

---

4. UCC § 2–101, Comment.

5. *E. g.*, Indiana Ins. Co. v. Fidelity General Ins. Co., 393 F.2d 204 (7th Cir. 1968) (insurance); Southern First & Casualty Co. v. Teal, 287 F.Supp. 617 (D. S.C.1968) (insurance); O'Brien v. Isaacs, 32 Ill.2d 105, 203 N.E.2d 890 (1965) (taxation); Underwood v.

Commonwealth, 390 S.W.2d 635 (Ky. 1965) (criminal law); Wickham v. Levine, 47 Misc.2d 1, 261 N.Y.S.2d 702 (Sup.Ct.1965) (regulation of sale).

6. As the court did in *In re* Yale Express Sys., Inc., 370 F.2d 433 (2d Cir. 1966), 384 F.2d 990 (2d Cir. 1967).

become material the following rules apply: [then follows a series of rules which are summarized in the next section of this text].

The result is to reverse pre-Code law. No longer is title the primary tool for solving a sales problem.[7] The Code provides solutions through a series of "if . . . then . . ." sections: if such-and-such facts occur, then the solution is so-and-so. Title continues to be of importance for residuary problems and for those cases in which the Code makes specific reference to title.

This latter group of cases is not large. Several Code sections refer to documents of *title,* but these have no application to the introductory rule of section 2–401. Beyond these, title is referred to in sections 2–106 (definition of a sale), 2–312 (warranty of title), 2–326 (goods are deemed to be on sale or return even though the person delivering the goods has reserved title), 2–327 (title does not pass in a sale on approval), 2–403 (a person with voidable title has power to transfer title to a good faith purchaser for value, and an entrustee has power to transfer the rights—title?—of the entruster to a buyer in ordinary course of business), 2–501 (the seller retains an insurable interest as long as he retains title to the goods), and 2–722 (a person with title can sue third persons for injury to the goods). The problems raised by these sections are solved through discovery of title.

Risk of loss was one of the problems which pre-Code law solved by determining who had the title to the goods.[8] Goods were at the seller's risk until the property (the Uniform Sales Act's word for "title") was transferred to the buyer. After the transfer the goods were at the buyer's risk. The Uniform Sales Act recognized that it was not always proper for the risk to follow title and provided two exceptions: (1) a seller's retention of title as security for the buyer's obligation to pay the price did not prevent the risk from passing to a buyer in possession, and (2) a delay in the delivery of goods caused by the fault of the buyer or seller placed on the

---

7. William F. Wilke, Inc. v. Cummins Diesel Engines, Inc., 252 Md. 611, 250 A.2d 886 (1969); Evans Prods. Co. v. Jorgensen, 245 Or. 362, 421 P.2d 978 (1966). *See* UCC § 9–202.

8. Tarling v. Baxter, 6 Barn. & C. 360, 108 Eng.Rep. 484 (1827), is an early nineteenth century example of the application of this rule. This rule was codified into the Uniform Sales Act § 22. Examples of American cases applying the rule include Wing v. Mid-Continent Seeds, Inc., 170 Kan. 242, 225 P.2d 78 (1950); Gilligham v. Phelps, 5 Wash.2d 410, 105 P.2d 825 (1940). Textual statements are contained in Williston, *Delivery as a Requisite in the Sale of Chattel Property,* 35 Harv.L.Rev. 797 (1922); Williston, *The Risk of Loss After an Executory Contract of Sale in the Common Law,* 9 Harv.L.Rev. 106 (1895).

party who was at fault the risk of any loss which might not have occurred except for the fault.[9]

The Code divorces the question of risk from a determination of title; thus there is no longer any reason to search for title in order to decide who bears the risk that the goods might be destroyed or lost. Title has become an immaterial consideration for the risk problem. Instead, the Code contains two sections on risk of loss. Both are written in the typical format; if the facts are these, then this party bears the risk of loss. The first of these two sections deals with risk of loss in absence of breach [10] and the second deals with the effect of breach on risk of loss.[11] The rules contained in these Code sections are discussed in later portions of this Chapter.[12]

§ 126.   Rules as to Passage of Title

It is fortunate, for a reason other than those listed in the prior section, that the passage of title plays only a minor role in the solution of commercial law problems. The Code section on when title passes [13] and its companion section on when goods are identified to the contract [14] present construction difficulties which would require extensive litigation if the drafters had continued the pre-Code emphasis on title as the basis for solving commercial problems. Since this emphasis was not continued, most of these difficulties will arise only with non-Code cases which continue to be solved through the single-title concept.

The Code's title rules are contained in section 2–401 and can be summarized thus:

Rule # 1. Title to goods cannot pass under a contract for sale prior to the time those goods are identified to the contract.[15] Until identification no agreement and no acts by the parties can affect title. Therefore, it becomes important to determine just when identification can occur.

Identification of existing goods turns, in the first instance, on the agreement of the parties. "Such identification can be made at any

---

9. Uniform Sales Act § 22. Rules as to passage of title were contained in Uniform Sales Act §§ 18–19. For application of these sections, see Sadler Mach. Co. v. Ohio Nat'l, Inc., 202 F.2d 887 (6th Cir. 1953); Radloff v. Bragmus, 214 Minn. 130, 7 N.W.2d 491 (1943).

10. UCC § 2–509.

11. UCC § 2–510.

12. §§ 130–36 *infra.* Even though title is no longer relevant to the risk of loss problem, some courts continue to talk as if it were. *E. g.,* Whately v. Tetrault, 29 Mass.App.Dec. 112 (1964).

13. UCC § 2–401.

14. UCC § 2–501.

15. UCC § 2–401(1).

time and in any manner explicitly agreed to by the parties." [16]   The emphasis in this rule should be placed on the word "explicitly." Implied agreements will not suffice, but (the Comments add) an agreement may be explicit even though not found in the terms used in the particular transaction.   "Thus, where a usage of the trade has previously been made explicit by reduction to a standard set of 'rules and regulations' currently incorporated by reference into the contracts of the parties, a relevant provision of those 'rules and regulations' is 'explicit' within the meaning" of the section on identification.[17]   Here is one place where a court could have difficulty in applying the Code to specific factual patterns: when does an agreement stop being implied and become explicit?   The answer of the drafters appears to turn on whether some writing somewhere can be referred to as containing the identification provision.

Absent explicit agreement identification occurs (according to section 2–501):

(a) when the contract is made if it is for the sale of goods already existing and identified;

(b) if the contract is for the sale of future goods [18] other than those described in paragraph (c), when goods are shipped, marked or otherwise designated by the seller as goods to which the contract refers;

(c) when the crops are planted or otherwise become growing crops or the young are conceived if the contract is for the sale of unborn young to be born within twelve months after contracting or for the sale of crops to be harvested within twelve months or the next normal harvest season after contracting whichever is longer.

These rules apply whenever the parties have not explicitly agreed on some other time of identification.[19]   Thus, it can be concluded that title to goods cannot pass (no matter what the parties say about

16. UCC § 2–501(1).

17. UCC § 2–501, Comment 3.

18. "Future goods" are goods which are not both existing and identified. UCC § 2–105(2).   Thus, title to existing goods which are not "identified" when the contract is made cannot pass to the buyer until the goods are "designated" by the seller.   Whether title passes at the moment of designation depends upon the application of the other title-rules discussed in this sec-tion of the text. If the sales contract allows the buyer to designate the goods, identification would occur on the buyer's designation (*see* UCC § 2–501, Comment 1), and title would pass at that time and place. This last conclusion is more difficult to obtain from Code language, but would prob-ably be reached under the "explicitly agreed" language of UCC § 2–401(1).

19. Draper v. Minneapolis-Moline, Inc., 100 Ill.App.2d 324, 241 N.E.2d 342 (1968).

title) as to existing goods which are not identified, as to future goods before designation, or as to unplanted crops or unborn young which are not conceived.

These situations will cover most of the cases facing a court for decision, but there are troubles with factual patterns falling between the sections. For example, what is the difference between "identified" existing goods and "designated" future goods? What help is it to define the time of identification in terms of whether the goods are identified? When are crops "growing"? Are apples growing when the tree is planted, when the leaves come out in the spring, when the blossoms begin to form, or not until the apple itself is discernible? As far as title is concerned many of these problems will remain of academic interest only, but since identification is also tied to insurable interest, some of these questions may call for answers in the context of which party is covered by insurance. The guide suggested by the drafters is found in this Comment sentence: "In view of the limited effect given to identification by this Article, the general policy is to resolve all doubts in favor of identification."[20] Whether this policy can be found in the statute is another question.

The first title-rule thus becomes: title cannot pass from the seller to the buyer until the goods are identified to the contract. Section 2–401 states this rule in absolute terms, surrounding it with other title-rules which are subject to modification by explicit agreement of the parties. Therefore, it appears that the drafters of the Code meant to prohibit buyers and sellers from passing title prior to the time that the goods are identified to the contract.[21] This makes sense—or at least it makes no sense to allow parties to pass title to future goods which cannot be designated as belonging to the buyer.

Notice that this first title-rule does not state that title does pass to the buyer the moment that the goods are identified; it only prevents passage of title prior to identification. Once the goods are identified, the other title-rules control when and where title passes.

Rule # 2. When goods have been identified to the contract the buyer obtains a "special property" in those goods. This term is not defined, but it is used in section 2–401 as an interest different from "title." The only other place "special property" is mentioned in

---

20. UCC § 2–501, Comment 2.

21. UCC § 2–401, Comment 2. This construction of UCC § 2–401 has not overlooked the impact of UCC § 1–102 (3); it concludes that the title section has "otherwise provided" that the parties may not agree to pass title prior to identification. UCC § 2–105(2). This is consistent with pre-Code law. Uniform Sales Act § 17.

Article 2 is in section 2–502 which gives the buyer a right to goods on the seller's insolvency. Thus, once goods are identified the buyer can recover those goods from an insolvent seller providing that the buyer meets the other tests of section 2–502 and providing that those tests survive attack under the Bankruptcy Act.[22]

Rule # 3. Any reservation of title by the seller as to goods which have been shipped or delivered to the buyer is limited to a reservation of a security interest.[23] The purpose of this rule is to make Article 2 consistent with Article 9, the Article which establishes a comprehensive scheme for the regulation of security interests in personal property and fixtures. One type of problem dealt with in Article 9 is seller-credit extended in part on the security of goods. A common example involves a seller who has transferred possession of goods to a buyer who does not pay the entire purchase price on delivery of the goods. Such a seller may retain a security interest in those goods so that if the buyer refuses or is unable to pay the price as it becomes due, the seller can foreclose and apply the proceeds of the foreclosure sale against the price.[24] The seller prefers this procedure, rather than an unsecured action for the price, in those situations in which other creditors are competing for a share of the buyer's estate. To the extent that the security has value the seller is given a priority over other creditors of the buyer.

Article 9 contains many safeguards to protect third parties who have dealt with the goods as belonging to the buyer from loss of those goods to overreaching secured creditors. The seller-buyer security agreement must describe the collateral and be signed by the buyer,[25] the debtor must have rights in the goods which are the collateral for the credit extended, the seller must give value,[26] and the seller's security interest must be perfected. In many instances perfection means that the seller must file some public notice of his security interest so that potential creditors can decide whether to lend additional funds to the buyer.[27]

---

22. Note, *Bankruptcy and Article Two of the Uniform Commercial Code: The Right to Recover the Goods Upon Insolvency*, 79 Harv.L.Rev. 598 (1966); Note, *The Uniform Commercial Code and an Insolvent Seller's Possession of Goods Sold*, 104 U.Pa.L.Rev. 91 (1955). See § 160 *infra*.

23. Wooden v. Michigan Nat'l Bank, 117 Ga.App. 852, 162 S.E.2d 222 (1968); Recchio v. Manufacturers & Traders Trust Co., 55 Misc.2d 788, 286 N.Y.S. 2d 390 (1968).

24. UCC § 9–504.

25. UCC § 9–203(1). The textual paragraph is not intended as a comprehensive statement of the law of secured transactions. For example, the writing may be dispensed with if the collateral is pledged to the secured party. *Id.* The paragraph indicates the general safeguards afforded creditors of and purchasers from the buyer-debtor.

26. UCC § 9–204.

27. UCC § 9–302.

This third title-rule harmonizes Article 2 with Article 9. A seller cannot escape the proscriptions of Article 9 by having the buyer agree that title is to remain in the seller until the purchase price is paid. The Code provides that such a reservation (no matter what words are chosen) is no more than a reservation of a "security interest," the type of interest to which Article 9 applies.

Rule # 4. Subject to the three rules set out above and subject to Article 9, section 2–401 provides that title to goods passes from the seller to the buyer in any manner and on any conditions explicitly agreed on by the parites.[28] The agreement must be explicit and will not be implied from the intention of the parties.[29] It need not, however, be found in the same document as the other terms of the sale; if the title agreement is written in some other document to which reference is made by the sales contract, this reference is sufficient to satisfy the requirements of the fourth title-rule.

Rule # 5. When there is no explicit agreement as to the time and place title is to pass from seller to buyer, section 2–401 establishes fixed rules as to passage of title depending on whether delivery is to be made by moving the goods. When delivery is to be made without moving the goods:

(a) if the seller is to deliver a document of title, title passes at the time when and the place where he delivers such documents; or

(b) if the goods are at the time of contracting already identified and no documents are to be delivered, title passes at the time and place of contracting.[30]

When delivery is to be made by moving the goods, title passes to the buyer "at the time and place at which the seller completes his performance with reference to the physical delivery of the goods."[31] Notice that title may pass before the goods are delivered. The test is the time and place at which the seller *completes his performance.*

---

28. Silver v. The Sloop Silver Cloud, 259 F.Supp. 187 (S.D.N.Y.1966).

29. *Cf.* Uniform Sales Act § 18; Mitchell v. Gilmour, 256 App.Div. 893, 9 N.Y.S.2d 45 (1939). Several cases have suggested that the question of title is for the jury. *E. g.,* Metropolitan Auto Sales Corp. v. Koneski, 252 Md. 145, 249 A.2d 141 (1968); Knotts v. Safeco Ins. Co. of Am., 78 N.M. 395, 432 P.2d 106 (1967). *Cf.* Park County Implement Co. v. Craig, 397 P.2d 800 (Wyo. 1964).

30. UCC § 2–401(3). Cases are collected in Annot., 17 A.L.R.3d 1010, 1081 (1968).

31. UCC § 2–401(2); Motor Ins. Corp. v. Safeco Ins. Co. of Am., 412 S.W. 2d 584 (Ky.1967); Newhall v. Second Church & Soc., 349 Mass. 493, 209 N.E.2d 296 (1965); Jordan v. Butler, 182 Nev. 626, 156 N.W.2d 778 (1968); Gantman v. Paul, 203 Pa.Super. 158, 199 A.2d 519 (1964). The same rule was applied to the time an interest passed under a lease. First Nat'l Bank & Trust Co. v. Smithloff, 119 Ga.App. 284, 167 S.E.2d 190 (1969).

In a shipment contract this would be at the point of shipment although the buyer will not receive the delivery until the goods reach their destination.[32] Nevertheless, title has passed to the buyer at the point of shipment. In a destination contract this would be at the destination.[33] These rules are not changed by the seller's reservation of a security interest or by the use of a document of title which is to be delivered at a different time or place.

The Comments focus the fifth title-rule into one idea which is helpful in understanding the intention of the drafters. The test in both branches of this rule is that of determining when and where the seller committed himself in regard to specific goods.[34] In shipment contracts it is the point of shipment; in destination contracts it is the point of delivery; in contracts under which the goods are not to be moved it is the delivery of documents, if any, or the making of the contract if there are no documents.

These are the five basic title-rules. There are gaps and inconsistencies. Fortunately, not many commercial law problems will turn on a determination of title, and most of the inconsistencies will remain of academic interest only. However, the job that the drafters did is probably better than could be expected with such a nebulous concept as title to goods. The single idea that emerges from section 2–401 is that title will not pass from seller to buyer until goods are "existing" (whatever this may mean in hard cases) but, once goods do exist, title is to pass at the earliest moment that the seller commits those goods to the contract. This principle may aid in reaching solutions in those cases which fall between sections of the Code and in those cases covered by two inconsistent sections.[35]

Rule # 6. There is one additional title-rule. What happens to title when goods are rejected by the buyer?

A rejection or other refusal by the buyer to receive or retain the goods, whether or not justified, or a justified revocation of acceptance revests title to the goods in the

---

32. *In re* Eastern Supply Co., 1 UCC Rep. 151 (U.S.Dist.Ct.W.D.Pa.1963) (decided under 1952 Code).

33. §§ 98–99 *supra.*

34. UCC § 2–401, Comment 4.

35. Most courts have held that the title rules of the Code apply to determine, as between seller and buyer, who has title to an automobile. *See, e. g.,* Semple v. State Farm Mut. Auto. Ins. Co., 215 F.Supp. 645 (E.D.Pa.1963); Park County Implement Co. v. Craig, 397 P.2d 800 (Wyo.1964). As to title to airplanes subject to federal registration, see American Aviation, Inc. v. Aviation Ins. Managers, Inc., 244 Ark. 829, 427 S.W.2d 544 (1968). As to title to cattle subject to state regulation, see Pugh v. Stratton, 22 Utah 2d 190, 450 P.2d 463 (1969).

seller. Such revesting occurs by operation of law and is not a "sale." [36]

The rejection may be rightful or wrongful, but the revocation of acceptance must be justified. Thus, a buyer who has accepted the goods delivered cannot by unilateral action revest title in the seller unless his revocation of acceptance meets the Code tests for such a revocation.[37]

B. INSURABLE INTEREST

§ 127. The Basic Rules

Section 2–501 contains separate rules to be used in determining when the buyer and seller have an insurable interest in goods. According to this section the seller retains an insurable interest as long as he retains title to or a security interest in the goods; [38] the buyer obtains an insurable interest upon identification of those goods.[39] Since goods can be identified to a contract for sale even though the seller has reserved a security interest in those goods, it is possible for both the seller and the buyer to have insurable interests in the same goods. In such a situation both parties have an economic interest in the goods and both should be able to insure their interests.

There may be times, however, in which a party with a substantial economic interest in the continued existence of the goods does not have an insurable interest under the first two subsections of section 2–501. For example, a seller may have identified goods to the contract and by explicit agreement have given up title to the buyer. Nevertheless, if those goods remain in the possession of the seller, the seller may wish to insure his interest against loss through negligence. With neither title nor a reserved security interest remaining in the seller, the first two subsections of section 2–501 would deny the seller any insurable interest. Likewise, a buyer under a requirements contract may have an economic interest in not having his operations disrupted through casualty to the seller's plant, but since the goods could be destroyed before designation, the first two subsections of section 2–501 would deny the buyer any insurable interest.[40]

36. UCC § 2–401(4).

37. Tennessee-Virginia Constr. Co. v. Willingham, 117 Ga.App. 290, 160 S.E. 2d 444 (1968). Title does not revest in the seller on buyer's failure to pay the price. Jordan v. Butler, 182 Neb. 626, 156 N.W.2d 778 (1968).

38. UCC § 2–501(2).

39. UCC § 2–501(1).

40. These examples are suggested in 1955 N.Y.Law Rev.Comm'n Rep. (vol. 1) 463–65.

The drafters recognized that there were instances in which the buyer and seller might have legitimate economic interests which were not protected by the Code rules on insurable interest, and they added the following subsection (3) to 2–501: "Nothing in this section impairs any insurable interest recognized under any other statute or rule of law." [41] States are thus free to adopt legislation or refer to case law broadening the insurable interest rules found in the Code. Thus, the Code accepts non-Code rules as supplementing the specific Code provisions on insurable interest.

The following sections of this text discuss the Code rules as to the insurable interests of the buyer and seller under a contract for the sale of goods. These rules probably do not merit the textual space devoted to them. In the first place, section 2–501 is not that hard to read. It states fairly clearly the mechanics of determining when the seller and buyer have insurable interests in goods. Textual treatment can do little more than to explain the context of the Code words, suggest how the section can be used in the typical cases, and point out a few places where section 2–501 has left obvious gaps in possible insurance coverage—gaps that will be quickly filled by courts. In the second place, section 2–501 does little more than to adopt non-Code law. The "heart" of that section is subsection (3), quoted above: all non-Code rules about insurable interest are made a part of the Code, whether those rules come from statutes or case law. This subsection will take care of the hard cases and to write about those would require a separate text on insurance law. To write about the Code rules which have been added to each state's general rules on insurable interest (as this text does) can be accomplished relatively quickly since, in general, these rules pertain to the easy—and typical—cases.

A much more difficult problem would be to attempt to determine why the drafters of the Code decided to include a section on insurable interest when their ultimate decision was to rely so heavily on non-Code law. Given this decision, would it not have been better to say nothing about insurable interest? Perhaps the drafters wanted to be certain that they had freed the buyer's insurable interest from vestiges of title concepts. If so, would it not have been preferable to work out a uniform concept of insurable interest rather than to rely on state law which could vary from state to state? This approach would have required an examination of the policies underlying the older requirements that a person have an *insurable interest* before he is allowed to recover under a policy of insurance, a decision

---

41. This subsection did not appear in the 1952 Official Text of the Code but was added in 1955.

as to which (if any) of these policies were worthy of perpetuation, and consideration of new policies growing out of the commercial needs of businessmen. This is exactly the type of decision which went into other Code sections when the drafters freed commercial law from the lump title concept. It is strange that they believed that some type of lump insurable interest concept ought to be retained.

Were this problem approached in the same manner as other Code problems at least this much should have found its way into Code language: anyone who bears the risk of loss should have an insurable interest in the goods. This leads to a broader concept— one that challenges the existence of a need for an "insurable interest" in property: ought not the test of whether an insured should be allowed to recover under a policy of property insurance depend solely upon whether the destruction of the goods caused that person a "loss"? Why not free property insurance from any notion that the person insured must have something that can be called an "insurable interest" and simply inquire into whether the destruction of the goods caused that person some type of financial detriment?[42] If it did and if the insurance policy purported to cover that detriment, the insurance company should indemnify the insured for his loss. In short, property insurance should be viewed as a contract of indemnification with no concern as to whether an "insurable interest" apart from loss suffered can be found to exist.

Such an approach to insurance on goods is probably contained through subsection (3),[43] but it is not found in the identification-title rules of the first two subsections of section 2–501. About the best that can be said for what was done by the Code is that it took a middle ground—neither breaking with the past nor embracing the concept of straight indemnification. However, some of the language used by the Code is sufficiently ambiguous so that a court can take this step if it so desires.

§ 128. Buyer's Insurable Interest

A buyer obtains an insurable interest in goods "by identification of existing goods as goods to which the contract refers even though the goods so identified are non-conforming and he has an

---

42. "Property insurance is essentially and entirely a contract of indemnity. Hence an interest for the loss of which the contract provides indemnity is an absolute essential to the valid existence of the contract." W. Vance, Handbook on the Law of Insurance § 28 (3d ed. 1951).

43. *Id.* § 29. A possible justification for the Code's rules on insurable interest is that it removes, in the typical cases, any argument that the insurable interest must exist at the time the contract is made. *Id.* § 30.

option to return or reject them."[44]   The buyer has no Code insurable interest in future goods; the goods must be both existing and identified before the buyer obtains an insurable interest.[45]

The Code does not define when goods become "existing." In most cases there will be no problem in making this determination. When the buyer has ordered such goods as an automobile, one hundred television sets, or a thousand cans of beans, common understanding will be relied upon to indicate whether the automobile, television sets, or cans of beans "exist." However, common understanding can on occasion be deceptive. Goods begin as raw materials and pass through several processes before they reach the ultimate consumer. In one sense the automobile "exists" when its separate component parts have been collected and are ready for assembly. At least this much is true: the automobile "exists" for Code purposes even though the process of assembling the parts was incomplete so that the buyer had the privilege of rejecting the tendered object.[46] Thus, a partially or improperly assembled item satisfies the Code's existence requirement, leaving the problem of how complete an assembly is necessary before the component parts have an existence as the goods referred to by the contract.

This problem is answered in large part by the second requirement for an insurable interest: there must be an "identification" of the existing goods. Normally the identification will require some overt act by at least one of the parties. It may come through an explicit agreement, through the making of the contract if the existing goods are identified at the time of the contract, by designating goods if the contract called for future goods, or through one of the special rules for crops and unborn young of animals.[47] The act of designating goods as the ones to which the contract refers will usually not take place until those goods are so far assembled that they would be considered as "existing" in the common understanding of businessmen. Therefore, many of the conceptual problems involved in when goods are both existing and identified will disappear when this test is applied to specific sets of facts.

Thus, a buyer who purchases specific goods which are designated by the parties at the time of contract ("this automobile" or "those particular television sets") acquires an insurable interest in those

---

44. UCC § 2–501(1).

45. First Nat'l Bank & Trust Co. v. Smithloff, 119 Ga.App. 284, 167 S.E.2d 190 (1969). Pre-Code law is discussed in 4 J. Appleman and J. Appleman, Insurance Law and Practice § 2291 (rev. vol. 1969).

46. UCC § 2–501(1).

47. Identification is discussed in § 126 *supra*.

goods at the moment the contract is made.[48] The buyer has this insurable interest even though the risk of loss of those goods may still be with the seller, even though the seller may still retain the title to those goods, and even though the seller also has an insurable interest in those same goods. The Code has separated such problems as risk of loss and insurable interest from the question of who has the title to the goods.[49]

If the buyer has purchased future goods other than crops or un-born young of animals, he acquires an insurable interest in those goods the moment they are shipped, marked, or otherwise designated by the seller as goods to which the contract refers.[50] Thus, when the seller selects from goods on hand those which he intends to deliver to the buyer and marks them in such a way as to designate them as those going to the buyer, the buyer acquires at that moment an insurable interest in those goods. Again the seller may have retained title, may still bear the risk that the goods might be lost, and may also have an insurable interest in the same goods. These conclusions are immaterial in determining that the buyer also has an insurable interest in the goods.

Therefore, for the great bulk of cases the problem of knowing just when goods become "existing" is of no particular importance. Identification will solve most of the close questions. However, there remain cases clustering on the edges of those discussed which are not so easily solved. If a buyer has agreed to purchase the entire output of the seller, at what moment of time does the buyer acquire an insurable interest in goods still in the possession of the seller? The buyer certainly has such an interest by the time the goods are shipped to him; it is also clear that he has an insurable interest at an earlier time if the seller has marked the goods as belonging to the buyer. However, since this hypothetical buyer is purchasing all of the seller's output, are not the goods "designated" as the buyer's the moment that they come from the seller's production line?

There are business reasons for giving such a buyer an insurable interest in these goods even though they have not been tagged or specially marked as belonging to the buyer. The buyer's business could be as seriously disrupted by destruction of these goods as it would have been had the goods been marked or shipped before the

---

48. UCC § 2–501(1) (a); National Compressor Corp. v. Carrow, 417 F.2d 97 (8th Cir. 1969) (party with insurable interest allowed to sue third party for injury to goods). *See* Draper v. Minneapolis-Moline, Inc., 100 Ill.App. 2d 324, 241 N.E.2d 342 (1968).

49. § 125 *supra*.

50. UCC § 2–501(1) (b). An insurable interest in growing crops and unborn animals arises automatically under the tests of UCC § 2-501(1) (c).

casualty.[51] Nevertheless, the Code concept of "identification" appears to require a separate act whenever future goods are involved, preventing the buyer from acquiring an insurable interest prior to the time that the seller has marked the output as belonging to the buyer.[52] The case would be even more difficult for the buyer (1) when his contract is for a portion of the seller's output (has the seller *designated* certain goods for this buyer through the production process when other purchasers of the same output are also involved?), or (2) when his contract is for the entire output of the seller but the goods had not been completely assembled or produced at the time of their destruction (are goods *existing* and *identified* when partially assembled or when their component parts have been acquired by the seller but not assembled at all?).

A solution to problems in which identification does not rest on some overt and unambiguous act can be found in two places. The first is the Code Comment which provides: "In view of the limited effect given identification by this Article, the general policy is to resolve all doubts in favor of identification."[53] Although no specific statutory language can be found which supports this conclusion, the Comment deserves judicial approval in the construction of section 2–501. The problem is to determine whether a buyer has a sufficient interest in goods so that he can insure against loss by casualty. Allowing early identification by resolving doubts in favor of insurability does not provide the buyer with a windfall because he will be allowed to recover from the insurance company only the loss suffered.

There is a second approach to the Code which can extend the buyer's insurable interest beyond the instances listed in section 2–501 (1). That approach was suggested in the prior section of this text and can be summarized thus: the Code's enumeration of situations in which the buyer has an insurable interest in *goods* is not exclusive. Under local law the buyer who does not have an insurable interest in goods may have an insurable interest in the seller-buyer *contract* or in the *profits* which would have arisen out of that

51. The buyer will have a cause of action against a seller who fails to deliver goods called for by the contract, UCC § 2–711, unless such doctrines as those described in UCC §§ 2–613 and 2–615 are applicable. §§ 107–10 *supra*. Even though the buyer may have a damage suit, there are reasons why he might prefer to recover on an insurance policy, leaving the insurance company to whatever subrogation claims it may have.

52. Identification of growing crops and unborn animals is automatic; identification of other future goods requires designation. UCC §§ 2–501(1) (b) and (c).

53. UCC § 2–501, Comment 2.

contract.[54] Conceivably such a buyer might also have an insurable interest, under some local statute or decision, in goods which have not yet been identified to the contract. This local law is made a part of the Code by virtue of the following subsection: "Nothing in this section [2–501] impairs any insurable interest recognized under any other statute or rule of law." [55] Therefore, a buyer has whatever insurable interest is given him by local non-Code law plus an insurable interest in the goods upon their identification to the contract.

§ 129. Seller's Insurable Interest

The buyer normally acquires his insurable interest when the seller does some act which designates certain goods as those referred to by the seller-buyer contract.[56] This designation will usually occur prior to the time of—or no later than the same time as—the risk of loss has passed to the buyer. Therefore, except for perhaps a peculiar factual pattern or two, a buyer will have an insurable interest in goods during all the time during which he bears the risk of their loss.

On the other hand, the seller does not lose his insurable interest through the act of identification. Section 2–501(2) provides a different time-line for the termination of the seller's insurable interest: "The seller retains an insurable interest in goods so long as title to or any security in the goods remains in him . . .." The Code tests are two: (1) Does the seller have title to the goods? (2) Does the seller have a security interest in the goods? If either of these questions is answered in the affirmative, the seller has retained his insurable interest. The result can be that both the buyer and seller have an insurable interest in the same goods at the same time—as where the seller has tagged or marked goods to be shipped to the buyer but has not yet passed title to the buyer.

In the normal case the Code rules as to the seller's insurable interest will operate as follows:

1. *Prior to delivery*. Title usually passes from the seller to the buyer at the time that the seller has completed his performance with reference to the physical delivery of the goods.[57] In a destination contract this performance is completed when tender is made at the destination; in a shipment contract title passes at the time and place of "shipment." [58] Section 2–401 does not define the precise moment of

---

54. The subject of insurable interest is discussed in 4 J. Appleman and J. Appleman, Insurance Law and Practice §§ 2121 et seq. (rev. vol. 1969); E. Patterson, Essentials of Insurance Law §§ 22–33 (2d ed. 1957); W. Vance, Handbook on the Law of Insurance §§ 28–30 (3d ed. 1951).

55. UCC § 2–501(3).

56. § 128 *supra*.

57. § 126 *supra*.

58. UCC § 2–401(2).

"shipment" and precision may be necessary when a court must decide whether the seller still retained his insurable interest. Since the basic rule of section 2–501(2) centers on the time that the seller has finally committed himself to the delivery,[59] section 2–504 can be used to give meaning to "shipment"—and title would pass at the time the goods are placed in the possession of the carrier. Therefore, for the normal case the seller will have an insurable interest in all goods in his possession prior to their delivery to the buyer. The basis of such an interest is the seller's title to the goods.

As with pre-Code cases the lump-title concept will cause difficulties in the not-so-normal situation. There will be situations in which the seller ought to have an insurable interest even though title has passed from the seller to the buyer, and no security interest has been reserved. For example, a seller in possession of goods sold to a buyer may (for some reason) have agreed that title was to pass at the time of the contract. Such a seller has no title, no security interest, and according to the Code no insurable interest. Also a seller on an open credit sale in which the buyer is to pick up the goods at some future date may find a court deciding that title passed at the time of contracting.[60] Destruction of the goods in cases like these is a legitimate concern of such a seller, especially if the risk of loss has not yet passed to the buyer. In these situations other local rules on insurable interest may protect the seller.[61] If so, the insurance policy can be written to cover the seller's interest in the goods or in the contract;[62] if not, the transaction should be planned so that the seller retains a security interest or title until the risk of loss has passed to the buyer and the purchase price has been paid.

---

59. UCC § 2–401, Comment 4.

60. UCC § 2–401(3)(b) can be read to produce this result. The problem is to determine the scope of the phrase "where delivery is to be made without moving the goods." Included are cases in which the goods are in a warehouse and the sale is made by documents of title, UCC § 2–401(3)(a), but does the phrase also include the over-the-counter cash sales by retail merchants? If so, problems of insurable interest will arise when the moment of contracting (passage of title) precedes by a substantial length of time the moment the buyer receives the goods (passage of risk loss; UCC § 2–509(3)). As to how the phrase should be read, compare UCC § 2–503 (4) where the same idea is combined with the requirement that the goods are in the possession of a bailee.

61. *E. g.*, McKinney's N.Y. Ins. Law § 148 (1966) which defines insurable interest as including "any lawful and substantial economic interest in the safety or preservation of property from loss, destruction or pecuniary damage." These rules are made applicable to the Code by virtue of UCC § 2–501(3).

62. E. Patterson, Essentials of Insurance Law §§ 24–26 (2d ed. 1957). The possibility of credit insurance and its ramifications are discussed in W. Vance, Handbook on the Law of Insurance § 201 (3d ed. 1951). *See generally* 9 J. Appleman and J. Appleman, Insurance Law and Practice §§ 5241–52 (1943).

2. *After delivery.* If the goods have been delivered to the buyer who has paid the entire purchase price, the seller will usually have no concern about insuring those goods. They now belong to the buyer and he will bear the risk of their loss from casualty. One time such a seller would have a concern about those goods would be when the buyer rejects or rightfully revokes his acceptance. In these instances the Code provides that title revests in the seller, and an insurable interest could rest on the title concept.[63]

If the goods have been delivered to the buyer on credit, the seller has a claim for the purchase price. Usually the risk of loss of those goods will be on the buyer and their loss through casualty will be no defense to a suit for their price. However, if the buyer is insolvent, the seller's suit will result in a judgment worth only a fraction of the full claim. Such a seller might like to insure the goods to protect his interest if the goods are destroyed. The Code provides that such a seller has an insurable interest to the extent that he reserved a security interest in the goods.[64] If the seller was willing to rely on the open credit of the buyer, he gave up all interest in the goods—including his insurable interest.[65] On the other hand, if he reserved a security interest in the goods, he relied both on the credit of the seller and on the value of the goods in the event of nonpayment of the price—and he is given an insurable interest in those goods.

There usually will be no difficulty in determining when a seller has reserved a security interest or in valuing that interest. The typical sale will involve a buyer who has signed the appropriate documents giving the seller a security interest in the goods sold. Often the seller will also have filed a financing statement with the proper local officers. In Code terms this security interest has become enforceable because of the writing, it has attached to specific collateral, and it has been perfected by filing.[66] The seller has obtained maximum protection under Article 9 of the Code. Not only can he foreclose or redeem but he will also be given the priority protection af-

---

63. UCC § 2–401(4).

64. UCC § 2–501(2). A reservation of title is a reservation of a security interest. UCC § 2–401(1).

65. UCC § 2–702(2) could be the basis of an exception to this statement. As long as the seller can reclaim the goods he arguably has a sufficient interest in those goods to support an insurance claim. The difficulty is that UCC § 2–702(2) is not drafted in terms of "title." The definition of "security interest" may be broad enough to include the seller's interest in goods on the buyer's insolvency. UCC § 1–201(37). This interpretation may cause problems under Article 9, but a court which desires to give the UCC § 2–702 seller an insurable interest on the basis of a reserved security interest can except the transaction from Article 9 by virtue of the "created by contract" language of UCC § 9–102(2). See UCC § 9–113.

66. UCC §§ 9–203 (enforceability); 9–204 (attachment); 9–302 (perfection). Some interests may be perfected without filing. An index of these interests is contained in UCC § 9–302(1).

forded by Article 9. Such a seller has made his security interest as valuable as Article 9 allows. That interest is insurable under section 2–501, and any insurance recovery should reflect the value of that interest to the seller—unless the policy places a contractual limitation on the amount of recovery.[67]

Troublesome insurance questions can arise when a seller (who has attempted to retain a security interest in goods which have suffered casualty) has failed to qualify his security interest for maximum Article 9 protection. Suppose such a seller did not perfect his security interest or did not obtain a written security agreement signed by the debtor. Does that seller nevertheless have a "security interest in the goods" for the purpose of section 2–501(2)?

Section 2–501(2) does not require that the seller's security interest be either perfected or enforceable. It states that the seller has an insurable interest "so long as title to or any security interest in the goods remains in him . . . ." The Code's definition of "security interest" requires neither perfection nor enforceability;[68] these are added by Article 9 to determine the amount of protection that the security interest is to be given. Therefore, an unperfected or even an unenforceable security interest should qualify for an insurable interest under section 2–501(2). The harder problem is to value such an interest in the event of loss. Failure to perfect does not affect the seller's right to redeem but would cause him to lose a priority race.[69] An unenforceable security interest will not allow the seller to redeem or to obtain Code priority, but such an interest is not valueless because a later writing or change of possession apparently meets the Code test of enforceability. Answers to these valuation questions will turn on the language of the policy and the facts of each case.[70]

A security interest which has not attached presents a different problem—and, fortunately, one which will occur very infrequently under an Article 2 transaction. Attachment contains the notion of the security interest seizing upon the goods—the security interest "attaches" itself to the goods. Until the moment of attachment the seller would have no security interest *in the goods*, as required by section 2–501(2), and no Code insurable interest.

---

67. *E. g.*, Motors Sec. Co. v. Aetna Life Ins. Co., 17 So.2d 316 (La.Ct.App.1944).

68. UCC § 1–201(37). See UCC § 2–401 (1) which defines "security interest" for a seller who has reserved title.

69. *E. g.*, UCC § 9–312.

70. "If the insured has suffered no loss with respect to the property covered by the policy, there is, of course, no liability on the policy for there is nothing for the insurer to indemnify." Flint Frozen Foods, Inc. v. Firemen's Ins. Co., 8 N.J. 606, 610, 86 A.2d 673, 674–75 (1952) (the holder of a security interest had been paid by the debtor; the debtor was not allowed to recover under the policy insuring the secured party's interest).

C. RISK OF LOSS

§ 130. Relation of Title to Risk of Loss

It is sometimes necessary to determine whether the buyer or seller is to bear the risk of loss to goods. For example, a local retailer may have entered into a contract to sell a fur coat to a buyer who had paid the price but left the coat with the retailer to be monogrammed or tailored. Before the buyer picked up the coat, it was stolen or destroyed by a fire. Is the loss of the coat at the risk of the retailer or of the buyer? That same retailer may have ordered 50 fur coats from a furrier in a distant city, the coats to be shipped F.O.B. seller's city. During shipment the coats were destroyed by a collision and ensuing fire. Is the loss of these 50 coats at the risk of the furrier or the retailer? Would the result be changed if the coats shipped had not conformed to the contract between the parties or if the contract had called for shipment F.O.B. buyer's city? These are but examples of the many situations in which parties to a sale can become concerned about which one of them bears the risk of loss.

The Code contains two sections directly applicable to this general problem. The first deals with the risk of loss in absence of breach;[71] the second considers the effect of breach on risk of loss.[72] Each contains separate rules as to when the risk has been shifted to the buyer. There is, however, one principle which applies to all risk of loss problems. This principle is summarized in one sentence from the Comments:

> The underlying theory of these sections on risk of loss is the adoption of the contractual approach rather than an arbitrary shifting of the risk with the "property" in the goods.[73]

No longer is the question of title of any importance in determining whether a buyer or a seller bears the risk of loss. It is true that the person with title will also (and incidentally) often bear the risk that the goods may be destroyed or lost; but the seller may have title and the buyer the risk, or the seller may have the risk and the buyer the title. In short, title is not a relevant consideration in deciding whether the risk has shifted to the buyer.[74]

---

71. UCC § 2–509.

72. UCC § 2–510.

73. UCC § 2–509, Comment 1.

74. § 125 *supra*. Even a court that seems to understand this Code rule cannot avoid writing a paragraph on when title passes. *E. g.*, William F. Wilke, Inc. v. Cummins Diesel Engines, Inc., 252 Md. 611, 250 A.2d 886 (1969). For a case in which the court let the risk of loss turn on the title question, see Diefenbach v. Gorney, 93 Ill.App.2d 51, 234 N.E.2d 813 (1968).

This is a negative principle, indicating only what should *not* be considered in determining who bears the risk. The positive rules are examined in later sections of the text.[75]

§ 131. Code's Approach to Risk of Loss

The Code sections on risk of loss seek to solve two problems. Both presuppose a seller-buyer contract for the sale of goods. At some point in the process of manufacturing and distributing goods the risk that those goods may be lost or destroyed is on the seller. If the seller is a retailer or wholesaler, he bears the risk while the goods are on his shelves and before he has agreed to sell them to the buyer; if the seller is a manufacturer, he bears the risk as the goods come off the production line; if the seller is a producer, he bears the risk while the crops are growing or the raw materials are in the ground. After the contract and after conforming goods have been placed in the possession of the buyer, the buyer bears the risk. There is, therefore, a shift in the risk of loss at some point in time during the making and performance of a contract for sale. Determining the exact moment when this risk has shifted is important to the parties so that they will know which of them ought to insure against loss and so that disputes between them following casualty to the goods can be speedily solved. *Problem #1*: At what precise point in time does the risk of loss as to conforming goods shift from the seller to the buyer?

On some occasions the buyer may have defaulted on his contractual promise to pay before the goods are delivered to him, or the seller may have delivered non-conforming goods to the buyer. Both of these events disrupt the normal commercial transaction. In the first the seller retained conforming goods which, following their destruction, have a reduced value. Sometimes they are worthless; sometimes they can be sold for scrap. In the second the buyer had goods in his possession, but not the goods ordered. If the buyer bears the risk as to these non-conforming goods, their destruction forces the buyer to pay for something which he did not order; if the seller bears the risk, he may recover from the buyer nothing for goods which were lost at a time when the seller had no control over their safety. The risk of loss rules applicable when there has been no default do not work satisfactorily in the event of breach. *Problem #2*: What effect does a breach by either the buyer or seller have on shifting the risk of loss for goods subsequently destroyed?

These two problems are considered in separate Code sections. The first is the subject of section 2–509; the second, of section 2–510.

75. §§ 131–36 *infra*.

Section 2–509. The Code begins with the assumption that the risk of loss is on the seller until some event occurs to pass that risk to the buyer. Rather than stating some all-inclusive single rule applicable to every situation, the Code (in section 2–509) lists three types of cases and establishes for each the point in time when the risk of loss passes to the buyer: [76]

1. Those in which the contract requires or authorizes the seller to ship the goods by carrier. These contracts may be either shipment or destination contracts. [77]

2. Those in which the goods are held by a bailee and are to be delivered without being moved. Typically, this type of case involves goods held by a warehouseman which are being sold to the buyer without removal from the warehouse. Often a negotiable warehouse receipt is transferred by the seller to the buyer, but the receipt may be non-negotiable or the arrangement may be less formal with no receipt having been issued by the bailee.

3. Those not falling within 1 or 2 above. This is the residuary rule and includes such situations as those in which the buyer is to pick up the goods at the seller's place of business or residence as well as those in which the seller is to deliver the goods to the buyer by some means other than by "carrier."

Each of these three situations involves separate policy considerations as to when risk of loss ought to pass; thus, separate rules are stated for each. These rules are outlined in the following sections of this text, but two exceptions should be noted. First, the parties may agree as to which one is to bear the risk of loss. [78] This agreement may be completely different from or only a slight modification of the Code rules. The parties must, however, "agree" before this exception is applicable. A printed clause hidden in a maze of fine print raises the same problems as to "agreement" as it did with other attempts to displace Code rules by printed documents. [79] Second, in a sale on approval the seller bears the risk of loss until the goods are accepted by the buyer. [80]

---

76. If goods are destroyed or lost before the risk of loss has passed to the buyer, the seller will normally be required to supply further conforming goods or be in default. There are, however, instances in which casualty to identified goods will relieve the seller from further contractual obligations. UCC § 2–613. This problem is discussed in § 108 *supra.*

77. § 97 *supra.*

78. UCC § 2–509(4). For a pre-Code case, see Industron Corp. v. Waltham Door & Window Co., 346 Mass. 18, 190 N.E.2d 211 (1963).

79. §§ 44, 47–52 *supra.*

80. UCC § 2–509(4). Sales on approval are discussed in § 41 *supra.*

Section 2–510. The general subject of section 2–510 is the effect which a breach has on risk of loss. Three types of cases are included. The first is that in which the tender by the seller so fails to conform to the contract as to give the buyer a right to rejection. The second type of case is that in which the buyer has accepted the goods but has later rightfully revoked his acceptance. Both of these are situations in which the seller is in default. The third type of case dealt with by section 2–510 is the buyer's breach—those in which the seller has identified goods as belonging to the buyer but, before the risk has passed to the buyer, the buyer has repudiated or is otherwise in breach. Once again different commercial policies are involved in each of these situations and different rules are stated by the Code.[81]

§ 132. Goods Shipped by a Carrier

The first Code rule on risk of loss involves those situations in which the goods are to be shipped by carrier. "Carrier" is not defined in Article 2, but the reference is to some organization independent from either the seller or buyer—the railroad, airline, and trucking company are examples.[82] The rule is contained in section 2–509 and is as follows:

> (1) Where the contract requires or authorizes the seller to ship the goods by carrier
>
> > (a) if it does not require him to deliver them at a particular destination, the risk of loss passes to the buyer when the goods are duly delivered to the carrier even though the shipment is under reservation (Section 2–505); but
> >
> > (b) if it does require him to deliver them at a particular destination and the goods are there duly tendered while in the possession of the carrier, the risk of loss passes to the buyer when the goods are there duly so tendered as to enable the buyer to take delivery.

This section applies whether the contract "requires" or "authorizes" the seller to ship the goods by carrier. Another Code section gives the seller this authority whenever he is to send the goods to the buyer.[83] Thus, the authorization to ship is a part of most sales contracts when the seller and buyer are located at any distance from each

---

81. §§ 135–36 *infra.*

82. 1956 Recommendations of the Editorial Board for the Uniform Commercial Code 59.

83. UCC § 2–310(b). The "required or authorized" language parallels UCC § 2–504 which deals with the seller's obligations under a shipment contract.

other, and is a part of all sales contracts containing an F.O.B., C.I.F., or like term.[84]

Section 2–509(1)(a) states the risk of loss rule in shipment contracts: if the seller duly delivers goods to the carrier, the risk of loss passes to the buyer on delivery to the carrier. Later loss or damage to those goods leaves the buyer liable for the price if the loss or damage occurred "within a commercially reasonable time after risk of their loss has passed to the buyer."[85] This latter requirement is found in section 2–709, the section dealing with the seller's action for the price, and its relation to risk of loss is puzzling. If the risk has passed to the buyer, why must the loss occur within a "commercially reasonable time" in order to make the buyer liable for the agreed price of the goods? Suppose, for example, that the buyer and seller entered into a shipment contract, that the seller duly delivered conforming goods to the carrier, but that the carrier wrongfully held the goods for a commercially unreasonable time before the goods were lost in transit. The risk passed to the buyer on delivery to the carrier, but does the buyer escape price liability because the loss did not occur within a commercially reasonable time after the delivery? If so, the risk of loss has effectively been shifted back to the seller by section 2–709 in spite of section 2–509—except for those cases in which the buyer paid in advance of the shipment.

Other sections of the Code indicate that the price section (2–709) ought not be read to change the risk of loss in the supposed situation. Section 2–507 provides that tender of delivery "is a condition to the buyer's duty to accept the goods and, unless otherwise agreed, to his duty to pay for them. Tender entitles the seller to acceptance of the goods and to payment according to the contract." Section 2–709 was not meant to take this right to payment from the seller when a third party (the carrier) has defaulted in its obligations. The carrier's default extends the "reasonable time" requirement of section 2–709, and the buyer continues to bear both the risk of loss and the liability for price. His action is against the carrier; the buyer does not have a defense against the seller's price action.

That this was the purpose of the "commercially reasonable time" language of section 2–709 is clear from the history of this section. The 1952 version of section 2–709 provided that the seller could recover the price when, among other things, the goods had been lost or damaged after risk of their loss had passed to the buyer. There was

---

84. UCC §§ 2–319, 2–320. The references of these sections to "risk" reinforce the rules of UCC § 2–509(1). In an "ex ship" contract the risk of loss does not pass to the buyer "until the goods leave the ship's tackle or are otherwise properly unloaded." UCC § 2–322.

85. UCC § 2–709(1)(a); § 178 *infra*.

no limitation as to when this loss must occur. The New York Law Revision Commission objected to this text because "the Code provides no limit on the time during which seller may hold goods at buyer's risk." [86] The type of case that troubled the Commissioners was one in which the risk of loss had passed to the buyer but in which the seller was still *holding* the goods at the time of the casualty. Examples can be drawn from either the destination or shipment contract. In a destination contract involving a delivery by carrier, the risk of loss passes on a proper tender by the carrier; in a shipment contract involving delivery by a carrier, the risk of loss passes on a proper delivery to the carrier. In either event the buyer's wrongful refusal to accept the goods leaves the goods with the carrier, subject to the seller's orders. The Commissioners did not believe that the buyer ought to bear the risk of loss of those goods forever. Only if casualty occurred to the goods within a commercially reasonable time after the wrongful refusal to accept should the buyer be liable for their price; otherwise, the loss ought to fall on the seller—the one with control over the goods.

In response to the Commission's criticism the drafters inserted the "commercially reasonable time" language in sections 2–709 and 2–510(3). There was no objection as to how the 1952 rule operated when the goods had been lost while in the control of a carrier; the concern was about those situations in which the seller retained control after the risk had shifted to the buyer.[87] However, the addition of the time limitation to section 2–709 (rather than dealing with the problem exclusively in the risk of loss sections) could produce cases like the one set out above: that is, one in which the seller in a shipment contract had duly delivered goods to a carrier, the carrier had held the goods for a commercially unreasonable time without shipping them to the buyer, and the goods were then destroyed by some casualty. In such a case the risk of loss would have passed to the buyer on delivery to the carrier but the seller would not be able to recover the price under a literal application of the language of section 2–709. Fortunately such cases will be rare; however, when they do arise, the court should take account of how the 2–709 time limitation became a

---

86. 1955 N.Y. Law Rev. Comm'n (vol. 1) 489.

87. One type of case which the drafters undoubtedly had in mind was Reliance v. James Walker Co., 129 Md. 475, 99 A. 597 (1916). The "commercially reasonable time" language was added in 1956 to meet "the point made by the New York Commission that the seller should not be able to hold the goods at the buyer's risk indefinitely." 1956 Recommendations of the Editorial Board for the Uniform Commercial Code 78.

The distinction between the shipment and destination contract is discussed in § 97 *supra*. See Storz Brewing Co. v. Brown, 154 Neb. 204, 47 N.W.2d 407 (1951).

part of the Code and apply that limitation only when the seller had control of the goods following passage of the risk of loss to the buyer.

The principal problem under section 2–509(1)(a) is that of determining the meaning of the words "duly delivered." This much is clear: until delivery to the carrier the risk of loss in a shipment contract remains with the seller; and, even on delivery to the carrier, the risk does not pass to the buyer unless the goods have been *duly* delivered. The difficulty comes in detailing the requirements which change a plain delivery into a due delivery. These words are not defined, but appear to carry with them some notion that the seller's delivery to the carrier must conform to the contract with the buyer. If the contract called for a refrigerator, the delivery to the carrier of a water softener ought not place on the buyer the risk that the softener would be lost in transit. Likewise, if the contract required air shipment, delivery to a trucking company ought not transfer the risk of loss.

The Comments support this construction by suggesting that this word ("duly") was used to incorporate into section 2–509 the tender requirements of a shipment contract.[88] Under those requirements the seller must: (1) put the goods in the possession of such a carrier as is reasonable; (2) make a reasonable contract for their transportation; (3) obtain and promptly deliver or tender the necessary documents; and (4) promptly notify the buyer of the shipment.[89] Certainly if the seller does these four things and, in addition, makes certain that the goods involved conform to the contract,[90] there has been a due delivery and the risk has shifted to the buyer. The problem centers on how much short of this ideal performance will satisfy section 2–509 (1)(a).

The initial temptation is to state flatly that any default by the seller removes the case from section 2–509 (after all, the section is entitled: "Risk of Loss in the Absence of Breach") and prevents the risk from passing on delivery to the carrier. This may, however, be reading too much into the single word "duly." It may be that the scheme of the Code allows something short of perfect performance by the seller to satisfy the delivery to a carrier requirements of section 2–509. For example, section 2–510(1) provides:

> Where a tender or delivery of goods so fails to conform to the contract as to give a right of rejection the risk of their loss remains on the seller until cure or acceptance.

88. UCC § 2–509, Comment 2.

89. UCC § 2–504. Failure to make a proper contract for the value of goods lost in transit prevented the seller from recovering the price in Miller v. Harvey, 221 N.Y. 54, 116 N.E. 781 (1917). Tender in a shipment contract is discussed in § 98 *supra*.

90. § 95 *supra*.

The implication from this section is that some non-conformities do not prevent the risk of loss from shifting to the buyer. It is only a non-conformity which gives the buyer a right of rejection that keeps the risk of loss on the seller.[91] The delivery of the water softener in place of the refrigerator or the selection of truck transportation in place of an agreed-upon air shipment would give the buyer the right to reject. However, if the buyer-seller contract had been an installment contract and the non-conforming goods delivered to the carrier did not *substantially* impair the value of that installment to the buyer, the buyer could not reject—and the risk of loss would shift to the buyer in spite of the seller's breach.[92] Thus, the word "duly" does not always carry with it a requirement of a perfect tender, but only a tender which is sufficient to prevent the buyer from rejecting the goods on their arrival.[93]

The second type of contract covered by section 2–509(1) is the destination contract. When the seller is required to deliver goods at

---

91. This implication is strengthened by a look at the history of UCC § 2–510 (1). The 1952 Official Text provided: "Where a tender or delivery of goods fails to conform to the contract the risk of their loss remains on the seller until cure or acceptance." The New York Law Revision Commission pointed out that this language would leave the risk with the seller in an installment contract even if the default were minor—contrary to UCC § 2–612. 1955 N.Y. Law Rev. Comm'n (vol. 1) 494–95. The Code was amended to its present form. 1956 Recommendations of the Editorial Board for the Uniform Commercial Code 60.

92. Other problems with UCC § 2–509 (1) (a) include:

1. How is this section to be read with the last sentence of UCC § 2–504? Failure to notify the buyer or failure to make a proper contract is a ground for rejection only if material delay or loss "ensues." Suppose a seller fails to notify the buyer of the shipment; the goods arrive in buyer's city; but because he did not hear from the seller, the buyer did not pick up the goods. While they were in the possession of the carrier the goods suffered casualty. This would be a ground for rejection and the risk would not be on the buyer. If, however, the casualty occurred in transit, the failure to notify did not contribute to the buyer's loss. Should the risk of loss nevertheless be on the seller? The word "ensues" in UCC § 2–504 is ambiguous. A loss did *follow* the failure to notify but the loss was in no way *caused* by the failure to notify. Should "ensues" be read to require some causal effect? The purpose of UCC § 2–504 would seem to require an affirmative answer.

2. How is the concept of cure to be read into UCC § 2–509(1) (a)? See UCC § 2–510, Comment 2. The difficulty is that "cure" does not operate until the buyer has rejected. UCC § 2–508. Thus, if non-conforming goods have been delivered to the carrier so as to give the buyer "a right of rejection" the risk does not pass to buyer until rejection and cure. See § 105 *supra*.

3. How is a defect in documents to be treated? This defect gives the buyer the privilege of rejection and will prevent the risk of loss from being shifted until he accepts. UCC §§ 2–504(b), 2–510(1).

93. Thus, the broad language of the opinion in William F. Wilke, Inc. v. Cummins Diesel Engines, Inc., 252 Md. 611, 250 A.2d 886 (1969), should be limited to the facts of that case— a contract calling for the delivery of a single item. For a discussion of when the buyer may reject, see §§ 102–06 *supra*.

their destination, their risk does not shift on delivery to a carrier but only when the goods are duly tendered at the point of destination so "as to enable the buyer to take delivery." [94] Once again the Code uses the word "duly." The meaning here is the same as that discussed above: the tender must be such as requires the buyer to accept the goods. This necessitates looking (1) at the agreement between the parties to determine the quality of the goods ordered and any contractual limitations on the privilege of rejection, (2) at the goods delivered to determine whether they conform to the contract (or, in the case of deliveries under an installment contract, whether they substantially conform), and (3) at the mechanics of the tender. This last requirement would make section 2–503 applicable in determining whether the risk of loss had been shifted to the buyer. The carrier's tender in a destination contract must be at a reasonable hour and be kept open for a period of time reasonably necessary for the buyer to take possession. In addition, any necessary documents must have been delivered by the seller.

The resulting patterns under both of these contracts (shipment and destination) are similar. The seller begins with the risk of loss. He shifts it to the buyer when he has taken such action as is needed to place on the buyer the duty of accepting the goods. At that moment the buyer bears the risk of loss of those goods. If the buyer wrongfully refuses those goods and returns them to the control of the seller, the seller effectively regains the risk after a commercially reasonable time.

§ 133. Goods in Possession of a Bailee

There are some sales in which the goods bought and sold are in the possession of a bailee and the sale is to be completed without moving the goods. As an example, grain stored in a warehouse may be sold to a buyer who has no intention of ever removing that grain from the warehouse. His only intention may be that of reselling the grain to a purchaser who also plans to leave the grain with the warehouseman for a substantial period of time before obtaining possession to grind the grain into flour or to distill it into liquor. Each of these sales will be completed without moving the grain, and to keep the risk of loss on the original owner until he has "delivered" the goods to the buyer or until the buyer has "received" the goods would be commercially unrealistic. Some point in time short of actual receipt of the goods must be chosen to shift the risk—or the original owner would continue to bear that

---

94. A contract calling for delivery F.O.B. buyer's point shifts the risk of loss to buyer at the destination. Electric Regulator Corp. v. Sterling Extruder Corp., 280 F.Supp. 550 (D. Conn. 1968).

risk although the price had been paid and control of the goods turned over to the buyer weeks or months before the loss.

The Code's key to risk of loss in these cases lies in the concept of control of the goods.[95] The warehouseman of grain would most probably have issued some receipt to show that he had stored the grain for the owner and would deliver it according to certain terms. This receipt is a document of title under the Code.[96] If negotiable, the holder has control over the grain in the sense that the bailee is obligated to deliver on presentation of the document; [97] if non-negotiable, the holder has less assurance that presentation will entitle him to the grain but notice to the bailee will give him that assurance or inform him that some prior party has a right to the grain.[98] Therefore, control of the document of title (plus a reasonable time to check with the bailee if the document is non-negotiable) is a sufficient control of the goods to shift the risk to the buyer.

There are cases, however, in which the bailee has not issued a document of title. A racing car may be stored at a garage; a yacht

---

95. Pre-Code law placed the risk on the person who held the title, and title could pass to the buyer although the goods were in the possession of the seller. Radloff v. Bragmus, 214 Minn. 130, 7 N.W.2d 491 (1943); § 125 *supra*. The Code rejected this union between the holder of title and the bearer of the risk, and substituted several tests which this text has summarized under the "control" concept. Risk of loss passes to the buyer on *receipt* of the goods if the seller is a merchant, on *receipt* of documents (receipt plus reasonable time to present a non-negotiable document) when goods are held by a bailee, and on *delivery* to a carrier in a shipment contract. The point where the drafters may not have followed the "control" concept is in destination contracts and in sales by non-merchants. In these cases risk passes on tender, but with the destination contract the buyer does not obtain the risk until he has an opportunity to take delivery. § 132 *supra*. The drafters equated their rules on risk with their conclusion as to who would be most likely to insure. UCC § 2–509, Comment 3. *Cf.* UCC § 2–510. A check of several insurance policies (although admittedly not a comprehensive study) indicated that it was difficult to state which party was more likely to have general insurance coverage. The policy language was ambiguous and did not harmonize with Code concepts. Therefore, the "control" concept was suggested as an alternative method of summarizing the bulk of the Code's risk of loss rules. Certainly, the idea of control is not contrary to the notion of probability of insurance; the person in control of goods is the one who probably will think about insuring them against loss, as the above-cited Comment suggests. Nor is the idea of placing the risk on the one in control a novel idea. In the middle of the thirteenth century Bracton stated that when "a purchase and sale have been contracted for, as aforesaid, before delivery and after, the risk of the thing bought and sold regards him generally who holds it, unless it has been otherwise agreed upon from the beginning, because in truth, he who has not delivered a thing to the purchaser, is still himself the lord of it . . .." 1 H. Bracton, De Legibus et Consuetudinibus Angliae 493 (Twiss ed. 1878).

96. UCC § 1–201(15). See also the definitions in UCC § 7–102.

97. UCC §§ 7–403, 7–502.

98. UCC § 7–504(2). *See generally*, Proctor & Gamble Distributing Co. v. Lawrence Am. Field Warehousing Corp,. 16 N.Y.2d 344, 266 N.Y.S.2d 785, 213 N.E.2d 873 (1965).

may be docked for the winter at a marina; or a horse may be stabled on a farm in Kentucky. The arrangement between the owners of these goods and their bailees may have been very informal with no document of any kind having been issued by the bailees. Nevertheless, the owner of the car, yacht, or horse ought to be able to sell without requiring the buyer to take immediate possession. The new owner may want to leave the car in the garage, the yacht in the marina, or the horse on the farm—being satisfied to have the bailee become his (rather than the former owner's) bailee. Control is again the key factor. When the buyer has converted the seller's bailee into the buyer's bailee he has a sufficient control over the goods that the risk of their loss ought to shift.

This text purposely withheld any discussion of how a seller performs a contract for the sale of goods held by a bailee (and to be delivered without being moved) because this discussion, while not difficult, underscores the Code's time of shifting the risk of loss. The performance problem centers on what the seller must do to trigger the buyer's obligation to accept the goods and to pay for them according to the terms of the contract.[99] This is a unilateral act on the part of the seller—usually a tender of the goods or documents, or both. If the buyer refuses the seller's conforming tender, the buyer is in default and is liable to the seller for that default, but whether the buyer should bear the risk of loss of those goods following a wrongful rejection is a different problem. Since risk is generally the result of some type of control over the goods, the unilateral tender by the seller is not sufficient to shift the risk. Thus, although a buyer may be liable in damages for a wrongful rejection, later destruction of those goods could be at the seller's risk.

These general ideas are applied to sales in which the goods are held by a bailee and are sold without being moved. Specifically, the rules on performance and passage of risk for these cases are:

1. *Negotiable documents.* If a negotiable document of title covering the goods is involved, the seller tenders performance by *tendering* the negotiable document;[1] however, the risk of loss shifts to the buyer only on his *receipt* of the document.[2] "Receipt" carries with it the idea that the buyer has taken physical possession of the document;[3] thus, if the buyer refuses the seller's tender, the goods in the possession of the bailee remain at the seller's risk. Tender begins the delivery which is not complete until receipt.[4]

---

99. §§ 95–102 *supra.*

1. UCC § 2–503(4) (a).

2. UCC § 2–509(2) (a).

3. *Cf.* UCC § 2–103(1) (c).

4. UCC § 2–509, Comment 4.

2. *Non-negotiable documents.* Tender of a non-negotiable document is a sufficient tender of performance "unless the buyer seasonably objects." [5] If the buyer does object, the seller must find some other way to perform—perhaps by obtaining and tendering a negotiable document or by procuring the bailee's acknowledgment of the buyer's right to the goods. When the bailee receives notice of the buyer's rights to the goods, those rights are fixed as against the bailee and all third parties.

Receipt of non-negotiable documents does not shift the risk to the buyer. The reason for this rule undoubtedly arises out of the fact that the buyer, although he holds the non-negotiable document, can lose his rights to creditors of the seller, to certain purchasers from the seller, or to the bailee himself.[6] The buyer is protected against such third parties only from the time he gives notice to the bailee. Risk of loss, therefore, remains on the seller until the buyer has had a reasonable time to present the non-negotiable document to the bailee, and a refusal to honor the document defeats the tender.[7]

3. *No documents involved.* When the bailee holds goods for which no documents have been issued and the seller wants to sell those goods without moving them, the seller can perform in one of two ways. He can either (1) deliver to the buyer a writing which directs the bailee to deliver the goods to the buyer, or (2) procure from the bailee an acknowledgment that the buyer is entitled to the goods. If the seller chooses the first method of performance, tender and risk of loss are determined by the same rules as if a non-negotiable document had been involved.[8] If the seller chooses the second method of performance, tender is accomplished by procuring the acknowledgment,[9] and risk of loss passes "on acknowledgment by the bailee of the buyer's right to possession of the goods." [10]

In the usual case these rules will work with no difficulty. If the buyer is given a writing which directs the bailee to hold or deliver the goods on the buyer's order, the buyer has a reasonable time to present that writing—and the risk of loss will not shift until that time has expired. If the seller procures the bailee's acknowledgment that the goods are being held for the buyer, the buyer has immediate control over the goods and risk passes at that time.[11] One case which might cause difficulty is that in which the seller procured the bailee's acknowledgment without notifying the buyer that he had taken such action. For this kind of case the court ought to read into this section

---

5. UCC § 2–503(4) (b).

6. UCC § 7–504(2).

7. UCC §§ 2–503(4) (b), 2–509(2) (c).

8. *Id.*

9. UCC § 2–503(4) (a).

10. UCC § 2–509(2) (b).

11. Whately v. Tetrault, 29 Mass.App. Dec. 112 (1964).

of the Code the general requirements of notice as a part of a necessary tender and should keep the risk of loss on the seller until the buyer has notice that the acknowledgment has been obtained.[12]

§ 134. Residuary Rules

Section 2–509(3) contains the residuary risk of loss rules—rules for those cases in which there was no agreement by the parties as to which was to bear the risk, in which the seller was neither authorized nor required to ship the goods by carrier, and in which the goods were not held by a bailee to be delivered without being moved. These residuary rules are stated in these words:

> In any case not within subsection (1) or (2), the risk of loss passes to the buyer on his receipt of the goods if the seller is a merchant; otherwise the risk passes to the buyer on tender of delivery.[13]

The merchant rule conforms to the general Code policy of placing the risk on the party who has control of the goods at the time of their loss. Risk does not pass until the buyer has *received* the goods; however, the non-merchant seller can shift the risk even though he retains control of the goods—risk passes when the non-merchant seller *tenders* delivery.

The difference in these two rules can be easily illustrated. Suppose that a buyer agreed to purchase a used automobile and to pay the price and to take delivery as soon as the seller had the brakes relined. The seller had the work done, telephoned the buyer, and told him that he could pick up the automobile at his convenience. Before the buyer took possession the automobile was destroyed by a fire in the seller's garage. If the seller was a merchant, the risk of loss problem would turn on whether the buyer had received the goods; since the buyer had not taken physical possession, the risk would remain on the seller. However, if the seller was not a merchant, the risk problem would center on whether the seller had tendered delivery. Had he put and held conforming goods at the buyer's disposition and given the appropriate notice? If so, the risk would be on the buyer.

Whether a seller had tendered delivery requires a showing (1) that the goods were conforming, (2) that they were put and held "at the buyer's disposition," and (3) that the notice reasonably enabled the buyer to take delivery.[14] There are difficulties in reading these

---

12. See the definition of tender in UCC § 2–503(1) discussed in § 96 *supra*.

13. UCC § 2–509(3).

14. UCC § 2–503(1). This section has been discussed so far as it relates to the acts which a seller must perform to place a buyer in default. §§ 93–102 *supra*.

requirements into the Code section on risk of loss. The contents of the notice (or the contents of the notice plus the prior understandings of the parties) must let the buyer know where the goods are held so that he can go there and take delivery; otherwise the notice would not reasonably "enable him to take delivery." That much is clear, but when the goods are destroyed before the buyer does take delivery, does the notice requirement also include a time factor? Must the notice be given long enough before the casualty so that the buyer had a reasonable time to take delivery of the conforming goods prior to their destruction? Further, what is the meaning of the phrase, "at the buyer's disposition"? Are goods held at the buyer's disposition if the contract requires the buyer to perform some act (like paying the price) as a condition precedent to his obtaining delivery, or must the tender be unconditional? Certainly the tender need not be unconditional when the problem is whether the acts of the seller were sufficient to place the buyer in default—and the Comments recognize this [15]—but this conclusion does not necessarily control the answer to the risk of loss problem. Ought the risk of loss shift even though the buyer must perform some act before he can obtain delivery? The answers to these questions cannot be found in specific Code language; they will turn on how courts feel about placing the risk on a party who does not have control of goods which suffer destruction.[16]

Returning to the Code's residuary risk of loss rules: risk passes to the buyer on his receipt of the goods if the seller is a merchant, otherwise the risk passes to the buyer on tender of delivery. In the usual sale by the merchant application of these rules will cause few complications. Suppose that a buyer had entered into a contract with a retail seller of sewing machines to purchase a specific floor model sewing machine. This buyer would have an insurable interest in that sewing machine at the moment the contract was made but the risk of its loss would remain with the seller until the buyer's receipt of the machine—and "receipt" requires that the buyer take physical possession of the goods.[17] If the sewing machine was destroyed while still in the seller's store or while on the seller's truck en route to the buyer's home, the risk remains on the seller.[18] Likewise, if a buyer had agreed to purchase a diamond ring from a jeweler but had left the ring to be engraved, the risk would not pass to the buyer even though the price had been paid, the engraving had been completed, and the buyer had

---

15. UCC § 2–503, Comment 2.

16. One court which found that tender was not complete mentioned lack of buyer's control. Deitch v. Shamash, 56 Misc.2d 875, 290 N.Y.S.2d 137 (Civ. Ct.1968).

17. UCC § 2–103(1) (c).

18. Delivery on the seller's truck is not a shipment by "carrier." § 132 *supra*.

been notified that he could pick up the ring.[19] Neither the buyer of the sewing machine nor the buyer of the ring had as yet taken physical possession of the goods. Holding the ring for the purpose of deciding whether to purchase or of admiring a purchase already made (but with the intention of returning the goods to the retail seller for further modification) does not amount to a "receipt" for the Code's risk of loss rules. The Code shifts the risk of loss when a merchant-seller loses control of the goods—at that moment of time when the buyer has physical possession of the goods *as a buyer*.

These rules apply even though the buyer is also a merchant. Thus, if a merchant is selling to a merchant, the Code's residuary rule shifts the risk to the buyer on receipt of the goods.[20] However, this rule will be of only limited application in such a case because in many sales by a merchant to another merchant, the contract will authorize or require the seller to ship the goods by carrier.

Two problems with this section remain. First, receipt of goods is defined to mean "taking physical possession of them."[21] Ordinarily the moment that the buyer takes possession will be readily determined. He will place the item in his hand and walk out of the store, he will get into his new automobile and drive away, or he will have the seller deliver and place the item in his home or place of business. In these cases the buyer's "possession" is clear. Unfortunately, however, "possession" is a concept which has caused much common law litigation and a diversity of definitions. Inevitably there will be Code problems on whether the purchaser from a merchant-seller took possession of the goods before they were destroyed. The seller's delivery man, not finding the buyer at home, may leave the goods (for example, the sewing machine) on the buyer's front porch or with a neighbor. Has the buyer taken physical possession of such goods? Does it make a difference if the porch is enclosed or open, whether the buyer lives in an apartment or a single residence, whether the delivery man was following a common practice of the seller in leaving the goods with someone other than the buyer, or whether the buyer was informed of the location of the goods? Answers to these questions are not easy, and common law decisions on the meaning of possession in cases involving larceny, title, or conversion afford little aid in reaching these answers.[22] Here the problem is whether risk of loss should shift to the buyer; perhaps the Code's

---

19. UCC § 2–509, Comment 3.

20. Conte v. Styli, 26 Mass. App. Dec. 73 (1963). The court incorrectly relied on passage of title to determine that the risk had shifted to the buyer. § 130 *supra*. The result appears correct, however, in that the facts state that the buyer had taken possession of the goods.

21. UCC § 2–103(1) (c).

22. Shartel, *Meanings of Possession*, 16 Minn.L.Rev. 611 (1932).

concept of control of the goods is the best guide that can be given in solving deviant cases.

Second, the residuary risk of loss rules distinguish between the merchant and the non-merchant. Usually this distinction will not be hard to make. The manufacturer who sells goods which it has manufactured is a merchant in that sale; the wholesaler and retailer selling goods of the kind which they normally sell are merchants for those sales.[23] There will, however, be those troublesome cases in which it is difficult to determine whether a particular seller falls within the Code's definition of merchant. For example, a manufacturer selling an old machine which was used in the factory is not selling goods of the kind in which the manufacturer "deals." To make such a seller a merchant (and to keep the risk of loss from shifting until the buyer has received the machine) a court would have to conclude that, by its occupation, the manufacturer or some agent is holding itself out "as having knowledge or skill peculiar to the practices or goods involved." [24] Concluding that every seller of used goods is a merchant because of his knowledge of those *goods* would cause difficulty with other Code sections which depend on a finding that the seller is a merchant,[25] but an emphasis on the *practice* of insuring goods could be employed to expand the number of sellers falling within the merchant definition for risk of loss. Most sellers do have a knowledge about the practices of caring for and insuring goods and, for the purpose of section 2–509(3), can be considered "merchants" even though the goods sold are not of the kind in which they usually deal.

The residuary risk of loss rules will not be difficult to apply in the great majority of cases. For these cases the Code has established principles through which it can be determined, with considerable certainty, whether the risk has passed to the buyer of goods. Parties to a commercial transaction deserve this certainty so they can plan their insurance coverage. There will, however, be a few cases in which this certainty is lost. Summarizing, these include:

---

23. § 33 *supra.*

24. UCC § 2–104(1).

25. The Code did not intend to make every seller of used goods a "merchant" simply because the seller had knowledge concerning those goods. Too many other Code sections would become meaningless. For example, the "good faith" requirement requires objective good faith for a merchant, UCC § 2–103(1)(b), but only subjective honesty for the non-merchant, UCC § 1–201(19). Thus, Mattek v. Malofsky, 42 Wis.2d 16, 165 N.W.2d 406 (1969), would not be applicable to the casual buyer. *See also* UCC §§ 2–205, 2–603, and 2–605. The Code accomplishes this distinction by limiting the goods and practices portion of the definition of merchant to a person who *by his occupation* holds himself out as having the requisite knowledge or skill. UCC § 2–104(1).

1. Those instances in which it is difficult to determine whether this seller was a merchant. This problem will be important when the seller has tendered the goods but the buyer has not yet received them. In view of the Code's general concept of placing the risk on the party in control of the goods, close questions should be resolved in favor of finding the seller to be a merchant. This result can be reached by emphasizing the "practices" portion of the definition of merchant and recognizing that the practices involved when the risk of loss question is presented are those of caring for the goods and insuring them.

2. Those instances in which the seller is a merchant and the problem is whether the buyer has possession of the goods. Once again, an emphasis on control will aid in the solution of these cases: has the parties' relationship to the goods so changed that the buyer now has control of the goods? Notice that it is not enough that the seller have lost control; the Code requires that the buyer have received the goods.

3. Those instances in which the seller is not a merchant and the problem is whether the seller has tendered delivery. With this question control is no longer important. The seller clearly has control because, by hypothesis, the buyer has not yet received the goods. The definition of tender and the Comments' stress on which party is more apt to have insured [26] will allow the courts to reach sensible results in specific cases. However, even if it is concluded that the risk has passed to the buyer on tender, the buyer will not be liable for the price unless the goods are lost or damaged within a commercially reasonable time after risk of their loss has passed to the buyer.[27] This rule will protect those buyers who have not paid the price at the time of the loss and the goods have remained in the control of their sellers for a commercially unreasonable length of time after risk has passed and before their loss.

§ 135. Effect of Seller's Breach

Prior sections of this text have discussed the time when risk of loss passes from the seller to the buyer in absence of breach by either party.[28] Two subsections of section 2–510 indicate the effect which a breach by the seller has on the risk of loss rules:

> (1) Where a tender or delivery of goods so fails to conform to the contract as to give a right of rejection the risk of their loss remains on the seller until cure or acceptance.

> (2) Where the buyer rightfully revokes acceptance he may to the extent of any deficiency in his effective insurance

---

26. UCC § 2–509, Comment 3.

27. UCC § 2–709(1) (a); § 132 *supra.*

28. §§ 132–34 *supra.*

coverage treat the risk of loss as having rested on the seller from the beginning.

When the Buyer has a Right of Rejection

When non-conforming goods are tendered or delivered by the seller, the buyer may in some instances reject the goods. Later portions of this text develop the instances in which rejection is allowed.[29] For example, if the contract calls for a single delivery of goods and if no other limitation on rejection is applicable, the buyer can reject for any non-conformity in the goods or tender of delivery.[30] On the other hand, if the contract calls for delivery of the goods in installments, the buyer may reject an installment if the non-conformity substantially impairs the value of that installment and cannot be cured.[31] It is only when the non-conformity is sufficient to give the buyer the privilege of rejection that the risk of loss remains on the seller.

Where the contract requires or authorizes the seller to ship the goods by carrier, section 2–510(1) only restates the risk of loss rule obtained from section 2–509(1). In a shipment contract the risk passes when the goods are *duly* delivered to the carrier; in a destination contract the risk passes when the goods are *duly* tendered to the buyer. This adverb ("duly") carries into section 2–509 the requirement that the delivery or tender must sufficiently comply with the contract so as to prevent the buyer from rejecting the goods.[32]

Section 2–510(1) does, however, limit the operation of the merchant-seller rule when the goods are not to be shipped by carrier. Under section 2–509(3) the risk passes when the buyer receives the goods. A buyer may receive goods (that is, take physical possession of them)[33] and still have the privilege of a later rejection.[34] An inspection by a buyer of goods in his possession may prove that the goods were non-conforming—or substantially non-conforming, in the case of an installment contract. As long as the buyer has the privilege of rejection the risk of loss remains on the seller.[35] Even though the buyer has control of the goods, he does not have their risk if they were so non-conforming as to give him the privilege of rejecting them. Only cure or acceptance of such goods shifts the risk to the buyer.

---

29. § 141 *infra*.

30. UCC § 2–601.

31. UCC § 2–612.

32. § 132 *supra*.

33. UCC § 2–103(1) (c).

34. Zabriskie Chevrolet, Inc. v. Smith, 99 N.J.Super. 441, 240 A.2d 195 (L.Div. 1968). *Cf.* UCC § 2–602(2) (b).

35. William F. Wilke, Inc. v. Cummins Diesel Engines, Inc., 252 Md. 611, 250 A.2d 886 (1969).

When the Buyer has Rightfully Revoked Acceptance

Acceptance of goods precludes their rejection.[36] Thus, as soon as goods are accepted the buyer can no longer use section 2–510(1) to keep the risk of loss on the seller. It may, however, turn out that the accepted goods were non-conforming. In limited instances the buyer's acceptance may be revoked—similar in effect to the pre-Code notion of rescission.[37] These instances are discussed in detail in another portion of this text and will not be repeated here.[38] It is sufficient at this time to notice that the effect of a successful revocation of acceptance is similar to that of a rightful rejection: the non-conforming goods are thrown back on the seller, and the buyer has the same rights and duties with regard to the goods involved as if he had rejected them.[39]

Risk of loss following a rightful revocation of acceptance is handled differently from a rightful rejection of the goods. The risk remains on the seller from the beginning of the transaction—but only to the extent of any deficiency in the buyer's effective insurance coverage. The operation of this rule is illustrated by the following hypothetical case:

Suppose a buyer had paid the full price—$10,000—for goods which he had accepted without discovering their non-conformity and under circumstances which made it difficult to discover the non-conformity. Thereafter the defect was discovered and the buyer revoked his acceptance, giving timely notice to the seller. Before the seller could remove the goods from the buyer's possession the goods were destroyed by a fire. The buyer's insurance coverage on these goods was $6,000. The buyer may treat the risk of loss to the extent of $4,000 as having rested on the seller from the beginning of this transaction. Further, if the buyer had not paid the price (presumably he would not have recovered the $6,000 from the insurance company), the seller would not be able to recover the price from the buyer following the loss.[40] Since this section of the Code treats the risk of loss as having rested on the seller, the seller's insurance carrier would have no subrogation rights against the buyer on the contract of sale for any amounts paid by the seller's insurance carrier on account of this loss.[41]

---

36. UCC § 2–607(2).

37. Lawner v. Engelbach, 433 Pa. 311, 249 A.2d 295 (1969).

38. § 143 *infra*.

39. UCC § 2–608.

40. UCC § 2–709. Since the risk of loss did not pass, that portion of UCC § 2–709 would not aid the seller. The seller, however, might argue that he is entitled to the price because the goods were "accepted." This argument should be rejected if the buyer has rightfully revoked his acceptance. § 143 *infra*.

41. UCC § 2–509, Comment 3.

§ 136. Effect of Buyer's Breach

The effect of a default by the buyer is outlined in section 2–510(3):

> Where the buyer as to conforming goods already identified to the contract for sale repudiates or is otherwise in breach before the risk of their loss has passed to him, the seller may to the extent of any deficiency in his effective insurance coverage treat the risk of loss as resting on the buyer for a commercially reasonable time.

Several conditions must be met before this section is applicable. First, the goods must be *conforming*—that is, they must be "in accordance with the obligations under the contract." [42] Any non-conformity, whether minor or substantial, prevents the seller from using section 2–510(3). The impact of this requirement can be exemplified through the installment contract where a buyer can reject a defective tender only if the non-conformity substantially impairs the value of that installment and cannot be cured.[43] In situations in which the non-conformity is not great enough to allow the installment-contract buyer to reject, the non-conformity would nevertheless operate to keep the entire risk on the seller even though the buyer had repudiated or was otherwise in breach.

Second, the goods must be *identified* to the contract. The seller cannot transfer any of the loss to the buyer simply by showing that a warehouse full of goods was destroyed and, had it not been for this casualty, some of those goods would have been used to fill the buyer's order. The goods must have been existing and identified at the time of the contract or they must have been marked or otherwise designated by the seller as the goods to which the contract with the buyer refers.[44]

Third, the goods must have been *already* identified to the contract. This is a time reference: at the moment some event occurs the goods must have been "already" identified. The difficulty arises in determining the precise event referred to by the word "already." Several constructions are possible,[45] but only two are probable: the goods must have been "already" identified (1) when the buyer defaulted or (2) when the loss occurred. The choice between these two constructions assumes importance depending on the sequence in which the

---

42. UCC § 2–106(2).

43. UCC § 2–612; § 104 *supra*.

44. UCC § 2–501; § 126 *supra*.

45. For example, one construction of UCC § 2–510(3) might be that the goods must be identified before their risk of loss passes to the buyer. This construction has been rejected because identification in some form is always required before risk of loss passes. §§ 132–34 *supra*. The reference in UCC § 2–510(3) to the time risk of loss passes is connected with the buyer's breach—not identification.

three events (breach, identification, and loss) occurred. Those three factors can be combined in six sequences:

Case 1.　Identification .... Breach .... Loss
Case 2:　Identification .... Loss .... Breach
Case 3:　Breach .... Identification .... Loss
Case 4:　Breach .... Loss .... Identification
Case 5:　Loss .... Breach ...... Identification
Case 6:　Loss .... Identification ...... Breach

Since Cases 4 through 6 assume that identification occurred after the loss, they will be disregarded. Section 2–510(3) requires conforming goods to be identified, and goods which have suffered casualty are in no sense "conforming."

Case 1 causes no difficulty with the "already identified" portion of section 2–510(3). Under that Case the identification occurred before both the breach and the loss; thus the goods were already identified at both critical times. In this respect Case 2 is like Case 1, but the result of shifting some of the loss to the Case 2 buyer is strange and probably not anticipated by the drafters. Adding dates to Case 2 produces this situation: assume a contract which called for delivery by the seller on June 15; on June 10 seller identified goods to the contract by marking them with the buyer's name; two days later the seller's warehouse and the identified goods were destroyed by fire; on June 14 the buyer, not knowing of the fire, called the seller and repudiated his order. One reading of section 2–510(3) would place the risk of loss on buyer to the extent of any deficiency in the seller's insurance coverage. The goods were conforming when identified, they were "already" identified at the time of loss and breach, and the risk had not passed to the buyer. This reading should be rejected because the loss occurred before the buyer did anything to justify shifting any portion of the loss to him.[46] Perhaps the best statutory

---

46. The policy underlying UCC § 2–510 (3) is difficult to discover. Consider the type of case covered by this section: the seller has identified conforming goods to the contract but has not gone far enough in performance to shift the risk of loss to the buyer; the seller has not effectively insured those goods for their full value; and the goods are destroyed or lost without the fault of either party. The buyer's breach makes him liable in damages, but usually not for the full price of the goods. UCC § 2–709 (the reference in UCC § 2–709(1)(b) is to goods which, when not destroyed, are not reasonably capable of being re-sold). Why should the buyer's breach shift any portion of the risk, beyond those damages, to the buyer? If the buyer had not been in default, the seller would bear the full risk. What is there in the default that ought to make the buyer bear any portion of the risk?

The Uniform Sales Act § 22(b) provided: "Where delivery has been delayed through the fault of either the buyer or seller the goods are at the risk of the party in fault as regards any loss which might not have occurred but for such fault." The last part of this rule required a showing that the fault caused the loss. Tweedle Bros. Inc.

method of reaching this conclusion is to emphasize that section 2–510 (3) allows the seller to treat the risk as on the buyer "for a commercially reasonable time," and to hold that this time begins to run with the buyer's breach. Since, in Case 2, the goods were already destroyed at the time of breach, their risk is determined without reference to section 2–510(3).[47]

Case 3 is the one which causes difficulties of construction. Here the buyer defaulted and the seller followed by identifying goods to the contract. Those goods were later lost through some casualty. Were these goods "already" identified so that this requirement of section 2–510(3) is satisfied? Restating a question already asked: must the identification precede the breach or is it sufficient if it precedes the loss?

There are good commercial reasons for identification following breach. The seller may be interested in taking advantage of his resale remedy or in pursuing his suit for full price.[48] If the word "already" refers to the time of breach, the Case 3 seller will not be able to treat any of the risk as having rested on the buyer even though that seller was following Code procedures to obtain a remedy. Some authorities have assumed that the Case 3 seller is protected by section 2–510(3),[49] and their position is strengthened by the fact that the risk rests on the buyer only for a "commercially reasonable time."[50] The

---

v. Berliner, 226 Or. 509, 360 P.2d 557 (1961). This need to show cause and effect conforms to the general contract principle that an aggrieved party is to be compensated for losses which were *caused* by the defaulter.

However, UCC § 2–510(3) moves in a different direction. No requirement of causation can be found in the express language of that subsection and it is difficult to read it into its sweeping command. True, some losses suffered by the seller will be the result of the buyer's breach—as where goods are destroyed after the date scheduled for delivery but which remained in the seller's possession only because the buyer defaulted. However, the section also applies when the destruction occurs after the breach but before the date scheduled for delivery. In such a case the buyer's breach is a fortuitous event which the seller can seize upon to recoup uninsured losses (e. g., the "layaway" in which the buyer had missed a payment at the time of loss; 1955 New York Law Rev. Comm'n Rep. (vol. 1) 498–99 (Case No. 6)). The text has already suggested that a par-

tial requirement of causation can be read into UCC § 2–510(3) when the breach occurs after the casualty, but to read it into the many variations of Case 1 would require judicial revision of UCC § 2–510(3). The Comments are of no help. The reference to "contract breaker" in Comment 3 is ambiguous. About the best that can be said about the policy underlying this subsection is that the risk remains on the seller unless the buyer has defaulted after conforming goods have been identified, and a default at this time "justifies" shifting losses to such a buyer even though those losses were in no way caused by the default.

47. *Cf.* UCC § 2–613 discussed in § 108 *supra.*

48. UCC §§ 2–706, 2–709.

49. 1955 New York Law Rev. Comm'n Rep. 498 (Case No. 4). This argument is supported by UCC § 2–704.

50. This language was not a part of the 1952 Code and the Report of the New York Law Revision Commission cited

seller could not identify after breach and keep the risk on the buyer for an unduly long period of time, but (goes this argument) he can identify after breach and place a part of the risk on the buyer for a commercially reasonable time.

Nevertheless, the syntax of section 2–510(3) favors the reading that the goods must have been "already" identified at the time of breach. Loss is not referred to in section 2–510(3); breach is specifically mentioned. The connection between identification and breach is clearly made by the statutory language. Further, if the reference is to identification at the time of loss, there was no reason to include the word "already." Conforming goods cannot be identified following casualty and, on the assumption that something was meant by the inclusion of that word, the only probable meaning is that the goods must have been identified at the time of breach.

As a fourth condition to the application of section 2–510(3), the breach must occur *before the risk of loss has passed to the buyer.* If the risk has passed under any of the branches of section 2–509, the buyer's later breach does not operate to return some of that risk to the seller's insurance carrier.

When these four conditions are met, the seller may to the extent of any deficiency in his effective insurance coverage treat the risk as resting on the buyer for a commercially reasonable time. The addition of the time period is understandable. The seller will have control of the goods (if they have been received by the buyer, the risk will have passed) and ought not be able to keep a portion of the risk on the buyer for an unduly long period of time.

A puzzling part of this section is the reference to the deficiency in the effective insurance coverage. A return to Case 1, with some added facts, illustrates the difficulties. Suppose that a contract calls for delivery of goods on June 15. On June 1 the buyer paid $5,000 on a total contract price of $12,000, with the balance to be paid on delivery. On June 10 the seller identified the goods to the contract; on June 12 the buyer repudiated; and on June 14 the goods were destroyed. The Code places the risk on the buyer "to the extent of any deficiency in his [the seller's] effective insurance coverage." If the seller had no insurance, the buyer would bear $7,000 of the risk.[51] If the seller had $12,000 of effective insurance, the buyer would bear

---

in the prior footnote was written prior to its addition to the Code.

51. This figure assumes that the property is "worth" $12,000. If the seller is a merchant and can replace the goods for a wholesale cost of (say) $9,000, the buyer's liability ought to be reduced accordingly. The buyer is not liable on the contract for the contract price, but bears the risk of loss of the goods. The buyer has no contractual liability because the seller cannot meet the conditions of UCC § 2–703 once the goods are destroyed.

none of the risk—and ought, under principles of restitution, to be able to recover most of the $5,000 down payment.[52] The difficulties arise when the insurance coverage is between these extremes. If the policy specifically limits the seller's recovery to $7,000, none of the risk would rest on the buyer, and the buyer would have to look to his insurance carrier for recovery of the $5,000 down payment. What, however, is the result if the seller's insurance policy allows the seller to recover the value of his "interest" in the goods? Could not the insurance company successfully argue that the "effective" insurance here is only the amount that the seller was unable to recover from the buyer because of the buyer's insolvency? If the buyer is able to pay $7,000, there is no effective seller's insurance on these goods, and the entire risk of loss is therefore on the buyer.[53] In short, is not this language circuitous?

There is little doubt but that the drafters meant to answer the questions raised in the prior paragraph in the negative, and their position can be supported by reading sections 2–509 and 2–510(3) together. The risk of loss is on the seller because none of the events listed in section 2–509 has occurred. Thus, the seller's insurance carrier is liable for the value of the seller's interest in those goods, or $7,000.[54] This determination is to be made without reference to section 2–510(3). After (but only after) this determination is made, buyer's breach becomes important to a recovery of any deficiency. To accept the arguments posed in the prior paragraphs is to give the seller's insurance company a kind of subrogation—a result specifically proscribed by the Comments.[55]

Section 2–510(3) combines with the two subsections dealing with a breach by the seller to place a portion of the risk of loss on the "contract breaker." As long as the interests of the buyer and seller are fully insured, this becomes a device by which the losses can be dis-

---

52. Under some policies the insured is allowed to recover the full value of the goods undiminished by contractual rights against third parties. *E. g.*, Alexandra Restaurant, Inc. v. New Hampshire Ins. Co., 272 App.Div. 346, 71 N.Y.S.2d 515, *appeal granted but rearg. denied* 272 App.Div. 996, 73 N.Y.S.2d 637 (1947), *aff'd* 297 N.Y. 858, 79 N.E.2d 268 (1948). Under other policies the insured is entitled only to indemnity. *E. g.*, Flint Frozen Foods, Inc. v. Firemen's Ins. Co., 8 N.J. 606, 86 A.2d 763 (1952). The variation in insurance policy language is one factor that makes generalizations about UCC § 2–510(3) unreliable.

53. This is not the meaning given the word "effective" by the Comments. UCC § 2–510, Comment 3.

54. Some support for this position can be obtained from two non-Code cases. Springfield Fire & Marine Ins. Co. v. Boswell, 167 So.2d 780 (Fla.Ct.App. 1964) (real estate); Southern Produce Co. v. American Ins. Co., 166 So.2d 59 (La.Ct.App.), *writ of review refused* 246 La. 863, 167 So.2d 675 (1964) (valued policy).

55. UCC § 2–510, Comment 3.

tributed between the insurance carriers. However, when the defaulting party is not insured these subsections applied indiscriminately can
result in the shifting of losses which are in no way connected with the
default. Judicious use of section 2–510 is needed so that cases which
unintentionally fall within its terse language (like Case 2, above) are
excluded by court decision.

CHAPTER VII

REMEDIES

Analysis

A. INTRODUCTION

418

A. INTRODUCTION

§ 137. Overview of the Code's Treatment of Remedies

Part 7 of Article 2 of the Code contains several sections detailing the remedies available to parties to a sales transaction. Two sections within this Part are essential to an understanding of Code remedies. The first is section 2–703 which indexes the seller's remedies; the second is section 2–711 which indexes the buyer's remedies. Each of these sections lists four events which must occur ("triggering events" to the applicability of the section) before the remedies listed therein are available. In addition, other sections create remedies independently from sections 2–703 and 2–711; that is, those remedies can be obtained even though none of the triggering events of sections 2–703 and 2–711 has occurred. Examples include the seller's action for price (2–709), the buyer's action for damages for breach when the goods have been accepted (2–714), and the right of one party to some remedy on the insolvency of the other party (2–502 and 2–702). In addition, other portions of the Code have a direct bearing on remedies available. For example, section 2–403 limits the power of a seller (or owner) to pursue goods which have fallen into the hands of a third-party purchaser. However, section 2–701 makes it clear that Article 2 does not impair the remedies for breach of an obligation collateral to the contract for sale.

This Chapter of the text deals with these various remedies. The general scheme of this Chapter involves, first, an analysis of the buyer's remedies on default of the seller and, second, an analysis of the seller's remedies on default of the buyer. Although not all of the problems fit neatly within this pattern, such an approach was chosen because it mirrors the Code's presentation of remedies.

§ 138.　Code Protected Interests on Breach of Contract [1]

On breach of a contract for the sale of goods three interests of the parties contend for judicial protection. These are the expectation, reliance, and restitution interests,[2] discussed below:

1. *The expectation interest.* When the parties enter into an agreement, certain hopes—or expectations—are created by the respective promises. When the agreement concerns the purchase and sale of goods, the buyer expects to receive those goods and the seller expects to receive the price. If the agreement is also a contract, the Anglo-American legal system has traditionally protected this expectation interest upon the default of one of the parties.[3] Protection may come through remedies which award the nondefaulting promisee the property which was promised—remedies such as specific performance

---

1. Substantial portions of this section and parts of other sections dealing with restitution recoveries appeared in Nordstrom, *Restitution on Default and Article Two of the Uniform Commercial Code*, 19 Vand.L.Rev. 1143 (1966). Reprinting is with permission of the Vanderbilt Law Review. As to waiver of breach, see UCC § 1–107 and § 43 *supra*.

2. These interests are developed fully in Fuller and Perdue, *The Reliance Interest in Contract Damages*, 46 Yale L.J. 52 (1936), 46 Yale L.J. 373 (1937). An excellent discussion of Code reme-dies appears in Peters, *Remedies for Breach of Contracts Relating to the Sale of Goods Under the Uniform Commercial Code: A Roadmap for Article Two*, 73 Yale L.J. 199 (1963).

3. Miller v. Robertson, 266 U.S. 243, 45 S.Ct. 73, 69 L.Ed. 265 (1924); Bachman v. Fortuna, 145 Conn. 191, 141 A. 2d 477 (1958); Ficara v. Belleau, 331 Mass. 80, 117 N.E.2d 287 (1954); Spitz v. Lesser, 302 N.Y. 490, 99 N.E.2d 540 (1951); Norwood v. Carter, 242 N.C. 152, 87 S.E.2d 2 (1955); Donald W. Lyle, Inc. v. Heidner & Co., 45 Wash. 2d 806, 278 P.2d 650 (1954).

and replevin.[4] Protection may also come through an award of the full contract price [5] or through damages measured by the difference between the contract price and the market value of the promised performance.[6] Other "formulas" have been worked out by courts for varying factual patterns, but each has this common theme: each seeks to award the non-defaulting party the gain which he expected to make had the defaulting party performed.

2. *The reliance interest.* In reliance on contractual promises, some promisees may have lost more than a hoped-for performance; they may have incurred obligations, spent money, or transferred or consumed property. The reliance losses may have been valuable only in relation to the performance, and when the performance was not forthcoming, may be valueless to the promisee. The promisee is now in a worse position than he would have been had only his expectations been thwarted. Not only has he lost his hoped-for gains but he has also suffered a decrease of assets. Thus, reliance losses present a more compelling case for legal intervention than the failure to obtain an expected gain. Nevertheless, courts have had difficulty defining the limits of separate protection of the reliance interest.[7] The trend,

---

4. As to specific performance: "When land is the subject matter of the agreement, the inadequacy of the legal remedy is well settled and specific performance will be decreed unless there are circumstances which make it inequitable or impossible to do so." Gulf Oil Corp. v. Rybicki, 102 N.H. 51, 52, 149 A.2d 877, 879 (1959). *See also* Kjeldgaard v. Carlberg, 168 Neb. 662, 97 N.W.2d 233 (1959); Gartrell v. Stafford, 12 Neb. 545, 11 N.W. 732 (1882); Springs v. Sanders, 62 N.C. 71 (1866). When goods are the subject matter of the agreement, specific performance is allowed whenever "the goods are unique or in other proper circumstances." UCC § 2–716(1). As to a specific performance of a contract to sell stock, see Waddle v. Cabana, 220 N.Y. 18, 114 N.E. 1054 (1917); Comment, 51 Mich.L.Rev. 408 (1953).

As to replevin: under the Uniform Sales Act the buyer's right to replevy goods turned on whether title had passed to the buyer. 3 S. Williston, Sales § 594 (rev. ed. 1948). The circumstances under which a buyer may obtain replevin in a Code state are detailed in UCC § 2–716(3).

5. UCC § 2–709; John I. Haas, Inc. v. Wellman, 186 F.2d 862 (9th Cir. 1951).

6. UCC § 2–714(2); Sauer v. McClintic-Marshall Constr. Co., 179 Mich. 618, 146 N.W. 422 (1914). As to the meaning of "value," see 5 A. Corbin, Contracts §§ 1004–05 (1964).

7. A part of the difficulty in developing rules for reliance losses may be caused by a failure to distinguish various kinds of reliance losses. Expenses may be incurred:

(1) Prior to the time the agreement was entered into. These expenses are not recoverable; they were not made in reliance on any contract promise and are not attributable to breach. The party was willing to make these expenses to obtain the agreement of the other party. Protection of these expenses comes in obtaining the contracted-for performance or its equivalent. Manning v. Pounds, 2 Conn.Cir. 344, 199 A.2d 188 (1963); Chicago Coliseum Club v. Dempsey, 265 Ill.App. 542 (1932); Norton & Lamphere Constr. Co. v. Blow & Cote, Inc., 123 Vt. 130, 183 A.2d 230 (1962). *See* 5 A. Corbin, Contracts § 1034 (1964); Annot., 17 A.L.R.2d 1300, 1314 (1951).

(2) After the agreement and prior to its breach. These expenses are generally the basis of a recovery to the extent that they are reasonable, foreseeable, and are of no value to the promisee.

however, suggests that a nondefaulting promisee will be awarded compensation for his reliance losses upon the promisor's default, such compensation being decreased by any provable loss which the promisee would have suffered had there been no breach.[8]

3. *The restitution interest.* In reliance on contractual promises, some promisees may have conferred a benefit upon the promisor. For example, in a contract for the sale of goods the buyer may have made a prepayment on the price or the seller may have made a partial delivery. The position of the promisee is similar to his position when reliance losses are involved: the promisee has suffered a loss by the transfer of assets. There is, however, an apparent and important distinction between the reliance and the restitution interests. When what is described as the restitution interest is involved, the promisee's loss has been coupled with a benefit to the promisor.[9] Therefore, there is a double reason for protecting the restitution interest. Despite this, the restitution remedies have grown haphazardly and it was not

---

Columbia Motors Co. v. Williams, 209 Ala. 640, 96 So. 900 (1923); Abrams v. Reynolds Metals Co., 340 Mass. 704, 166 N.E.2d 204 (1960); Security Store & Mfg. Co. v. American Rys. Express Co., 227 Mo.App. 175, 51 S.W.2d 572 (1932). Annot., 17 A.L.R.2d 1300 (1951). Recovery for these expenditures cannot exceed the contract price. Restatement of Contracts § 333 (1932).

(3) After the breach, often in an attempt to lessen damages. There is authority that such expenses cannot be recovered when they are the cost of litigation against the defaulting party. Chicago Coliseum Club v. Dempsey, 265 Ill.App. 542 (1932). However, if the expenses are incurred by the nondefaulting party in a reasonable effort to decrease his damages, many cases allow a recovery of those expenses. Casey v. Nampa & Meridian Irrigation Dist., 85 Idaho 299, 379 P.2d 409 (1963); Rench v. Hayes Equip. Mfg. Co., 134 Kan. 865, 8 P.2d 346 (1932); Atholwood Dev. Co. v. Houston, 179 Md. 441, 19 A.2d 706 (1941); Eastern Advertising Co. v. Shapiro, 263 Mass. 228, 161 N.E. 240 (1928); Restatement of Contracts § 336 (1932). Annot., 84 A.L.R. 171 (1933).

8. In addition to the cases cited note 7 *supra*, see L. Albert & Son v. Armstrong Rubber Co., 178 F.2d 182 (2d Cir. 1949); DePaolo v. DeRomo, 346 Pa. 654, 31 A.2d 158 (1943); Allen v. Elliott Reynolds Motor Co., 33 Tenn.

App. 179, 230 S.W.2d 418 (1950). Some courts have stated that the defaulter is estopped to claim that the nondefaulting party would have suffered a loss on the agreement if performed. United States v. Behan, 110 U.S. 338, 48 S.Ct. 81, 28 L.Ed. 168 (1884); American Can Co. v. Garnett, 279 F. 722 (9th Cir. 1922); Lloyd v. American Can Co., 128 Wash. 298, 222 P. 876 (1924). Other courts place the burden of proof on the defaulting party to show that the nondefaulter would have suffered a loss. L. Albert & Son v. Armstrong Rubber Co., *supra* this note; Holt v. United Security Life Ins. & Trust Co., 76 N.J.L. 585, 72 A. 301 (Ct.Err. & App.1909). Under either approach, however, when profits are not recoverable because they cannot be proved with "certainty," reliance expenses provide an alternative measure of recovery. Restatement of Contracts § 333, comment c (1932).

9. This is the "plus-minus" analysis in W. Keener, Quasi-Contracts 163 (1926) and F. Woodward, Quasi-Contracts § 274 (1913). Not always is an economic loss to the promisee necessary to have a benefit to the promisor. In Acme Mills & Elevator Co. v. Johnson, 141 Ky. 718, 133 S.W. 784 (1911), the defaulting party gained by the breach but the promisee suffered no economic loss. The court refused to transfer the gain to the promisee.

until this century—and probably not until the *Restatement of Restitution* had its impact upon lawyers and judges—that anything resembling an organized approach was taken toward protection of the restitution interest.[10]

The Code, accepting most of the pre-Code law of remedies, seeks to protect these interests in varying degrees. The remainder of this Chapter will use these words (expectation, reliance, and restitution interests) as discussed above and will indicate the extent of their Code acceptance.

B. SELLER IN DEFAULT

1. THE BUYER'S COURSES OF ACTION

§ 139. The Code's Approach to Buyer's Remedies

The Code contains several sections devoted to a presentation of the remedies of an aggrieved buyer.[11] In summary, these sections allow an aggrieved buyer to select an appropriate remedy from the following:

1. Recover as much of the price as he has paid.

2. Recover damages under formulas which are not strikingly different from pre-Code rules on damages.

3. "Cover" and recover the added costs incurred in procuring substitute goods—without being limited by a later finding of "market value."

4. In a proper case, obtain the goods through specific performance or replevin.

5. In some situations in which the seller becomes insolvent, recover the goods by tendering performance.[12]

In addition, remedies not specifically mentioned in the Code may be available to an aggrieved buyer through the Code's adoption of general principles of law and equity.[13]

---

10. Dawson, *Restitution or Damages?*, 20 Ohio St.L.J. 175 (1959). "Unless the contrary clearly appears, expressions of 'cancellation' or 'rescission' of the contract or the like shall not be construed as a renunciation or discharge of any claim for an antecedent breach." UCC § 2–720.

11. The buyer's remedies are indexed in UCC § 2–711. Damages are covered in UCC §§ 2–713, 2–714, and 2–715. Money recoveries based on "cover" are granted by UCC § 2–712. Specific performance and replevin are the subject of UCC § 2–716.

12. UCC § 2–502.

13. UCC § 1–103.

Each Code remedy has its specific conditions which are discussed in later sections of this text. Before beginning this detailed discussion, however, two observations should make the Code's approach to a buyer's remedies more understandable

First, the basic pattern of a buyer's remedies is similar to that found in non-Code law. In some instances the buyer can obtain the goods themselves either through specific performance, replevin, or on the seller's insolvency. These, however, are limited instances. In the great number of cases the aggrieved buyer must be satisfied with a money substitute for the goods which the seller failed to deliver.[14] The cover remedy makes the measure of damages more in accord with commercial practices, but this does not change the fact that the Code continues the general pre-Code law of substituting damages for the goods which the seller promised to deliver.

There is much to be said both for and against such an approach. Policy arguments can be framed in favor of making specific performance the buyer's basic remedy. After all, the seller did promise to deliver goods and, if the seller has those goods, why should he be allowed to retain them in default of his contractual promise? Should not contract law seek to promote commercial stability by making people perform their contractual promises? At the least, regular award of specific performance decrees would serve as a warning to sellers who are about to default and might be the necessary impetus to make those sellers perform.

On the other hand, contract law generally (except for contracts for the sale of land)[15] and the Code specifically have rejected the idea that specific performance ought to be the basic remedy for an aggrieved purchaser. Goods are usually available from many sources and, except for spite, it generally makes little difference to the buyer whether he obtains those goods from the seller or from some third party—as long as the buyer is not required to pay more for those goods than the price set in his contract. Also, the legal system relies on influences other than its remedies to cause reluctant parties to perform their contractual promises. When these outside influences break down it is probably better to let one party refuse to perform, and to

---

14. The Comments state that Article 2 "seeks to further a more liberal attitude than some courts have shown in connection with the specific performance of contracts of sale." UCC § 2–716, Comment 1. Whether courts will accept this invitation remains to be seen. *See* Hilmor Sales Co. v. Helen Neushaefer Div. of Supronics Corp., 6 UCC Rep. 325 (N.Y.Sup.Ct. 1969).

15. Purchaser's right to specific performance: McCullough v. Newton, 348 S.W.2d 138 (Mo.1961); Gartrell v. Stafford, 12 Neb. 545, 11 N.W. 732 (1882); Epstein v. Gluckin, 233 N.Y. 490, 135 N.E. 861 (1922). Vendor's right to specific performance: Freeman v. Paulson, 107 Minn. 64, 119 N. W. 651 (1909); Spring v. Sanders, 62 N.C. 71 (1866).

maintain a semblance of order and confidence in the commercial world by substituting money for the promised performance—except in those few cases where the goods themselves are needed to right a wrong which cannot be approximately corrected through an award of money. On balance, the drafters must have been influenced by the latter arguments because they retained the basic pre-Code law and used damages as the usual recovery, leaving specific recovery for the exceptional case.

The second observation is less theoretical. Code remedies presuppose that the buyer has followed a course of action which leads to the remedy he desires—and deserves. The courses of action available to the buyer must be understood to appreciate the remedial sections of the Code. They involve:

1. An analysis of the particular default involved.

2. A choice between rejection and acceptance of non-conforming goods.

3. An understanding of the meaning and impact of "acceptance."

4. A knowledge of when and how an acceptance can be revoked.

5. An understanding of the effect of retaining non-conforming goods.

These are discussed in the following sections of this text.

§ 140. Types of Defaults by Sellers

Three types of defaults by sellers are envisioned by the Code: the first occurs when a seller repudiates his promise before the date set for performance; the second occurs when there has been no repudiation but the seller fails to make any delivery; and the third occurs when the seller does deliver goods but the goods or their tender fails to conform to the contract.[16] When the seller has repudiated or failed to make a delivery, the buyer may proceed directly to a remedy. No rejection or notice is needed, most probably because the seller in these cases reasonably should know that he has not performed.

The non-conforming tender is the type of default which requires the buyer to follow carefully one of the courses of action open to him by the Code. Here the seller may not know that his tender did not conform to the contract and he should be alerted to the buyer's claims. Perhaps the non-conformity can be cured [17] or perhaps the seller may be able to take some action to minimize the damages which the buyer

---

16. UCC §§ 2–711, 2–714.   17. § 105 *supra*.

will suffer. In any event, the Code requires that the buyer take certain action if he intends to claim a remedy for a non-conforming tender. The action which he must take is neither burdensome nor difficult, but it does give the seller some protection in a transaction which the buyer claims has gone awry.

§ 141. Rejection of the Goods

When non-conforming goods are tendered the buyer has a choice: he may accept the goods or he may reject them. With a single delivery contract the goods may be rejected "if the goods or the tender of delivery fail in any respect to conform to the contract." [18] With installment contracts the buyer may reject an installment only if the non-conformity "substantially impairs the value of that installment and cannot be cured or if the non-conformity is a defect in the required documents" or if the default with respect to one installment impairs the value of the whole contract.[19] It is true that the Code gives the buyer a third choice when the contract involves the delivery of more than one commercial unit. In these cases the buyer may accept one or more of the commercial units and reject the rest.[20] This allows a type of partial acceptance—which the Comments caution must be exercised in good faith—but it is, like the principal choice, an option either to accept or reject, with the option limited to commercial units rather than to the whole of the goods.

If the buyer decides to reject the goods, he must do so "within a reasonable time after their delivery or tender" and a rejection "is ineffective unless the buyer seasonably notifies the seller." [21] The first two requirements for an effective rejection are, therefore, to make the decision reasonably quickly after the goods have been tendered or delivered and to give seasonable notice to the seller. Requiring that this action be taken *reasonably* and *seasonably* takes some certainty out of the Code, but an approach which inserted a specific number of days (or hours) would create more hardship than it alleviated.[22] A

---

18. UCC § 2–601 and § 102 *supra*. The privilege of rejection is severely limited in sales within The Perishable Agricultural Commodities Act, 46 Stat. 531 (1931), 7 U.S.C.A. § 499a et seq. (1964). L. Gillarde Co. v. Joseph Martinelli & Co., 168 F.2d 276, *opinion amended on rehearing* 169 F.2d 60 (1st Cir.), *cert. denied* 335 U.S. 885, 69 S.Ct. 237, 93 L.Ed. 424 (1948).

19. UCC § 2–612 and § 104 *supra*.

20. UCC § 2–601(c). For a discussion of partial rejection, see § 146 *infra*.

21. UCC § 2–602(1). The buyer's duties as to rejected goods are detailed in UCC § 2–602(2).

22. "Reasonable time" and "seasonably" are defined in UCC § 1–204. These definitions are about as helpful as could be expected. The question is one of fact for the jury, Trailmobile Div. of Pullman, Inc. v. Jones, 118 Ga. App. 472, 164 S.E.2d 346 (1968); Schneider v. Person, 34 Pa.D. & C.2d 10 (C.P.1964), but trade usage is admissible. Valley Nat'l Bank v. Baby-

noticeable defect in a piece of machinery or an easily seen fracture in a horse's leg requires more prompt action by the buyer than does a latent defect in yarn sold to be knitted into sweaters or in flower bulbs sold to be grown during the next growing season.[23] The seller is entitled to prompt notice so that he can investigate the facts, but the notice provision should not be construed to create a trap for the buyer. About the best that can be said is that the words "reasonable" and "seasonable" were inserted in the Code so that the trier of fact could reach a just result under the facts of the individual case.

The next requirement for an effective rejection is that the buyer not have waived his objection to the goods. "Waiver" is a word that has been given many meanings by courts and it is used in two other sections in Article 2 without definition.[24] In connection with rejection, however, the drafters used the word only in the title to the section (2–605) and then defined fairly carefully what they meant by a waiver —without using that word in the text of the section. A waiver which will prevent a rejection can occur in only two instances. The first involves payment by the buyer against documents when the buyer has not reserved his rights. In this instance the buyer is precluded from recovering the payment "for defects apparent on the face of the documents." [25] The second involves a defect in the tender which the buyer did not mention when he gave his seasonable notice of rejection to the seller. Before such a defect is waived the defect must have been (1) unstated in the notice, *and* (2) ascertainable by a reasonable inspection, *and* (3) one which "the seller could have cured if stated seasonably," *or*, between merchants, one not mentioned in a further writing "when the seller has after rejection made a request in writing for a full and final written statement of all defects on which the buyer proposes to rely." [26] Unless these conditions are met, the buyer has not waived his basis for rejection simply because he failed to state that basis in his notice of rejection. The result is the Code's attempt to balance the harm that would be done to a buyer if he is precluded from relying on unstated defects against the harm that would be done

lon Chrysler-Plymouth, Inc., 53 Misc. 2d 1029, 280 N.Y.S.2d 786 (Sup.Ct.), *aff'd mem.* 28 A.D.2d 1092, 284 N.Y.S. 2d 849 (1967).

23. Miron v. Yonkers Raceway, Inc., 400 F.2d 112 (2d Cir. 1968); Ingle v. Marked Tree Equip. Co., 244 Ark. 1166, 428 S.W.2d 286 (1968); Zabriskie Chevrolet, Inc. v. Smith, 99 N.J.Super. 441, 240 A.2d 195 (L.Div.1968); Vandenberg v. Siter, 204 Pa.Super. 392, 204 A.2d 494 (1964); Wilson Trading Corp. v. David Ferguson, Ltd., 23

N.Y.2d 398, 244 N.E.2d 685, 297 N.Y. S.2d 108 (1968). Attempted rejection of steel thirteen weeks after delivery because steel was undersize was not timely. Michael M. Berlin & Co. v. T. Whiting Mfg., Inc., 5 UCC Rep. 357 (N.Y.Sup.Ct.1968).

24. UCC §§ 2–208 and 2–209. The problem is discussed in § 43 *supra*.

25. UCC § 2–605(2).

26. UCC § 2–605(1).

to a seller if the buyer is allowed to state one (or no) reason for rejection and later to substitute a different reason. This idea is also applicable to situations in which the buyer has accepted goods but later attempts to recover damages for the seller's breach. If the waiver section (2–605) is applicable, the buyer is precluded "from relying on the unstated defect to justify rejection *or to establish breach.*" [27]

The final requirement for an effective rejection is that it occur prior to an acceptance. "Acceptance of the goods by the buyer precludes rejection of the goods . . . ." [28] Acceptance and the effect thereof are discussed in the following sections of this text.

After a rightful rejection a merchant buyer has certain duties as to the goods in his possession or control. These duties are spelled out in section 2–603 and are designed to protect the seller's interest in goods which are being held by the merchant buyer without placing onerous burdens on the merchant buyer. The basic statutory duty of such a buyer is to follow "reasonable instructions" from the seller, but even in absence of such instructions the merchant buyer must make reasonable efforts to resell goods which are perishable or threaten to decline in value speedily. That same section (2–603) places two limitations on the buyer's duties: first, the merchant buyer need not take any action if the seller has an agent or place of business at the market where the goods were rejected—in these cases the seller can protect himself; and second, instructions are not "reasonable" if, following a demand for indemnity, the seller fails to furnish indemnity for the buyer's expenses. There is at least one other instance in which the instructions ought not be held to be "reasonable," and that is when a buyer with a security interest in the goods (under the conditions of section 2–711(3)) is requested to return those goods to the seller.

Section 2–603 also gives the buyer who has rightfully rejected goods but resold them pursuant to section 2–603 a right to reimbursement out of the proceeds of the sale. That reimbursement is to include expenses in caring for and selling the goods—including a commission for the sale. If that buyer has a security interest in the goods under section 2–711(3), he may also be reimbursed for the expenses listed in that subsection.

If the seller fails to give instructions and if the goods are not perishable (or threaten to decline in value speedily), section 2–604 gives the buyer the option of (1) storing the goods, (2) reshipping them, or (3) reselling them with reimbursement as above discussed.

---

27. *Id.* (Emphasis supplied.)

28. UCC § 2–607(2). As to the seller's right to cure, see § 105 *supra.*

That section provides that the exercise of any of these options is not an acceptance or a conversion of the goods.

These duties and options are also available to a buyer who has revoked acceptance. Section 2–608(3) provides: "A buyer who so revokes has the same rights and duties with regard to the goods involved as if he had rejected them."

§ 142. Acceptance of the Goods

The alternative to rejecting the goods is accepting them. The buyer must either reject or accept the tendered goods and, if he attempts to do neither, the Code provides that he has accepted. The only way that a buyer could both reject and accept the same goods would be first to reject and later to change his course of action and decide to accept.[29]

"Acceptance" is a defined Code term. It occurs when the buyer says he will take the goods, when he fails to make an effective rejection,[30] or when he does some act inconsistent with the seller's ownership. The second method is the catch-all provision. When a rejection is not effective it is an acceptance. The section on acceptance (2–606) is set out below:

(1) Acceptance of goods occurs when the buyer

    (a) after a reasonable opportunity to inspect the goods signifies to the seller that the goods are conforming or that he will take or retain them in spite of their non-conformity; or

    (b) fails to make an effective rejection (subsection (1) of Section 2–602), but such acceptance does not occur until the buyer has had a reasonable opportunity to inspect them; or

    (c) does any act inconsistent with the seller's ownership; but if such act is wrongful as against the seller it is an acceptance only if ratified by him.

(2) Acceptance of a part of any commercial unit is acceptance of that entire unit.

Accepting goods has several effects beyond that of precluding a later rejection of the same goods. These are:

1. Acceptance requires the buyer to pay for the goods at the contract rate.[31] If the accepted goods and their tender conform to the

---

29. UCC § 2–606, Comment 4.

30. Hudspeth Motors, Inc. v. Wilkinson, 238 Ark. 410, 382 S.W.2d 191 (1964).

31. UCC § 2–606(1).

contract, the seller is entitled to the full contract price without deduction. However, if the buyer has accepted non-conforming goods, he may deduct from the contract price the damages suffered—providing the buyer has given proper notice of the non-conformity.[32]

2. Acceptance of non-conforming goods can change the Code requirement of the contents of the notice which must be given to the seller to preserve an action in damages. When a buyer rejects goods his notice must alert the seller of the rejection so that the seller can make some disposition of those goods. The notice given in relation to accepted goods may, however, be much more informal as long as the buyer seeks only damages (rather than to revoke his acceptance).[33] The Code language is that after a tender has been accepted "the buyer must within a reasonable time after he discovers or should have discovered any breach notify the seller of breach or be barred from any remedy." [34] Here the notice given is not that the buyer is rejecting or revoking acceptance—only that there has been a breach. The purpose of this notice is to inform the seller that the "transaction is troublesome" so that, hopefully, the parties will begin negotiations which will lead to a settlement of their dispute short of litigation.[35] As long as the contents of the notice (which is not required by the Code to be in writing) meet this test, the notice should be sufficient to preserve the rights of the buyer who has accepted the goods.

3. Acceptance of non-conforming goods probably extends the time in which notice of a defect can be given. Both the buyer who rejects non-conforming goods and the buyer who accepts non-conforming goods but wishes to recover damages must give the seller notice within a reasonable time, but the statutory language as to the date on which the reasonable time begins to run differs in these two situations. The rejection notice must be given within a reasonable time after their "delivery or tender". With accepted goods the notice must be given within a reasonable time after the buyer "discovers or should have discovered any breach." Undoubtedly this latter test was meant to extend the time within which the buyer could act to preserve his rights, and courts have indicated that this is how these sections should be

---

32. UCC § 2–714; § 150 *infra*. If damages are allowed, they may be subtracted from the contract price. UCC § 2–717; § 156 *infra*.

33. Manfredi v. James C. Fettes, Inc., 352 Mass. 775, 226 N.E.2d 365 (1967); Babcock Poultry Farm v. Shook, 204 Pa.Super. 141, 203 A.2d 399 (1964); UCC § 2–607, Comment 4.

34. UCC § 2–607(3) (a).

35. UCC § 2–607, Comment 4; L. A. Green Seed Co. of Arkansas v. Williams, 246 Ark. 454, 438 S.W.2d 717 (1969) (must allege notice in complaint); Babcock Poultry Farms, Inc. v. Shook, 204 Pa.Super. 141, 203 A.2d 399 (1964).

read.[36] These decisions reach a proper result; rejection requires quicker decisions from both parties, and the notice provisions ought to reflect this. However, there are language difficulties in separating the time for the rejection notice from the time for giving notice after nonconforming goods have been accepted when the defect is of the kind which should have been (but was not) discovered at the time the goods were delivered. In such a situation the time of delivery is the same as the time that the buyer should have discovered the defect. The Code could be read to make the "reasonable time" periods the same so that when the buyer has lost the privilege of rejection he has also lost the right to damages following an acceptance. However, the Code ought not be read in this manner. The need for a quick decision is usually not present when the buyer has accepted and more time should be given a buyer who has retained the goods and seeks only damages for their defects.[37]

4. Acceptance of goods has another consequence. It shifts the burden of proof from the seller to the buyer. When an attempted rejection is timely and the problem facing the court is whether that attempted rejection was wrongful, the seller bears the burden of proving that the goods and their tender were conforming (or, in the case of installment contracts, did not substantially impair the value of the installment or could have been cured). However, when a buyer claims that his seller has defaulted on a contract to sell goods which have now been accepted, the buyer bears the burden of establishing the seller's breach.[38] The reason for changing the party who bears the burden of proof once the goods are accepted arises out of an understanding of the Code's scheme as to the courses of action open to the buyer. Rejection will normally come, if at all, fairly soon after the goods have been tendered or delivered, but claimed breaches in connection with accepted goods may not be made until a longer period of time after delivery of the goods. The claimed defect may have arisen out of something that the buyer did to the goods while they were in his possession rather than from a defect at the time of their delivery and, since the seller will have little or no knowledge of the buyer's treatment of the goods, the Code wisely placed on the buyer the burden of establishing breach once goods have been accepted.[39]

---

36. Miron v. Yonkers Raceway, Inc., 400 F.2d 112 (2d Cir. 1968); Lanners v. Whitney, 247 Or. 223, 428 P.2d 398 (1967).

37. UCC § 2–607, Comment 4; § 145 *infra*. Greater liberality in computing the time period is important under UCC § 2–607 because the failure to give proper notice bars all remedies. General Foods Corp. v. Bittinger Co., 31 Pa.D. & C.2d 282 (C.P.1963); Sig Hoffman, Inc. v. Victory Spud Serv., Inc., 25 Agri.Dec. 1175, 3 UCC Rep. 977 (U.S. Dept. of Agriculture 1966).

38. Miron v. Yonkers Raceway, Inc., 400 F.2d 112 (2d Cir. 1968); Tennessee-Virginia Constr. Co. v. Willingham, 117 Ga.App. 290, 160 S.E.2d 444 (1968); Burge Ice Machine Co. v. Dickerson, 60 Ill.App.2d 266, 210 N.E.2d 243 (1965).

39. UCC § 2–607(4).

5. Another consequence of acceptance lies in the increased difficulty of requiring the seller to retake possession of the goods on the grounds that they were non-conforming at the time of their tender. This problem is considered in the following section.

§ 143. Revoking Acceptance of the Goods

Even though the buyer has accepted the goods it may still be possible for him to require the seller to retake those goods if they do not conform to the contract. The Code's term for this course of action is "revocation of acceptance"— not "rescission," a word with many non-Code meanings.[40]

Revocation of acceptance is like rejection in that, if it is effective, the goods will be treated as if they were the seller's.[41] Revocation of acceptance, however, is available in a more limited number of instances of non-conformity than would have been rejection. Rejection is available in single delivery contracts for *any* non-conformity in the goods or their tender. Revocation of acceptance, however, is an available course of action to a buyer only if the non-conformity in the goods or a commercial unit "substantially impairs its value to him" and if the buyer accepted

(a) on the reasonable assumption that its non-conformity would be cured and it has not been seasonably cured; or

(b) without discovery of such non-conformity if his acceptance was reasonably induced either by the difficulty of discovery before acceptance or by the seller's assurances.[42]

Thus, when a buyer knows or should have known of a defect before he accepted the goods and did not assume that the defect would be cured by the seller, there can be no revocation of that acceptance even though the defect substantially impaired the value of the goods to the buyer. An insubstantial impairment never allows revocation of acceptance;[43]

---

40. UCC § 2–608; § 146 *infra*.

41. UCC § 2–608(3). If the goods are in the possession of the buyer and are rejected or the acceptance revoked, merchant buyers are obligated to follow reasonable instructions from the seller. UCC § 2–603. The buyer has a security interest in those goods for payments made and for certain expenses. UCC § 2–711(3). The goods may be sold to enforce the security interest as if the buyer were an aggrieved seller. UCC § 2–706.

42. UCC § 2–608(1). For a discussion of partial revocation of acceptance, see § 146 *infra*.

43. Rozmus v. Thompson's Lincoln Mercury Co., 209 Pa.Super. 120, 224 A.2d 782 (1966). For a discussion of the meaning of substantial impairment, see Campbell v. Pollack, 101 R.I. 223, 221 A.2d 615 (1966).

a substantial impairment allows revocation of acceptance only in the limited number of cases covered by the above quoted Code section.

The privilege of revoking acceptance can be lost unless it occurs within a reasonable time after the buyer "discovers or should have discovered the ground for it and before any substantial change in condition of the goods which is not caused by their own defects." [44] The relation of this length of time to the promptness with which a buyer must reject has already been discussed. Unless the buyer acts within this time limit he will not be allowed to revoke his acceptance of the goods [45] and, even though he acts within the reasonable time limit, the revocation of acceptance will not be effective if the condition of the goods has been substantially changed for reasons other than those arising out of the defect.[46] Further, revocation is "not effective until the buyer notifies the seller of it." [47] The notice must be of "it"—that is, of the revocation of acceptance. Thus, the buyer must do more than simply tell the seller that the goods are defective; he must inform the seller that the goods are being returned.

The Code is not clear on the effect of the buyer's use of the goods following an attempted revocation of acceptance. Use following a rejection amounts to an acceptance, but no similar section is found in regard to a buyer's further use after he has properly revoked an acceptance. Nevertheless, courts have held that such a use bars the revocation and requires the buyer to retain the goods.[48] This result can be justified either on the basis of the policy underlying the Code's courses of action open to a buyer or on the statutory language stating that the use—with knowledge of the defects—amounts to a second acceptance which cannot be revoked under the applicable section on revocation of acceptance.

---

44. UCC § 2–608(2).

45. Green Chevrolet Co. v. Kemp, 241 Ark. 62, 406 S.W.2d 142 (1966); Hudspeth Motors v. Wilkinson, 238 Ark. 410, 382 S.W.2d 191 (1964); Shreve v. Casto Trailer Sales, Inc., 150 W.Va. 669, 149 S.E.2d 238 (1966).

46. This requirement will cause difficulties in instances in which the buyer has changed the goods not knowing of the defect. *But cf.* Grandi v. Lesage, 74 N.M. 799, 399 P.2d 285 (1965).

47. UCC § 2–608(2). For a discussion of the time periods involved in the notices given to revoke acceptance, see Lanners v. Whitney, 247 Or. 223, 428 P.2d 398 (1967).

48. Ingle v. Marked Tree Equip. Co., 244 Ark. 1166, 428 S.W.2d 286 (1968); F. W. Lang Co. v. Fleet, 193 Pa.Super. 365, 165 A.2d 258 (1960). Not all use prevents rejection or revocation of acceptance. Where the seller gives continued assurance that defects will be remedied, use does not prevent return of the goods for breach of warranty. Trailmobile Div. of Pullman, Inc. v. Jones, 118 Ga.App. 472, 164 S.E.2d 346 (1968). Another situation in which use of the goods following revocation may not bar later revocation is that in which the use is necessary to mitigate damages. Code support for such a result can be found in UCC § 2–715. Also, the buyer may inspect, test, and sample the goods under the conditions detailed in UCC § 2–515.

§ 144. Retention of the Goods

The buyer may elect to retain non-conforming goods in spite of their non-conformity or he may be required to keep them because his rejection or revocation of acceptance was ineffective. Such a buyer is required to pay for the goods at their contract rate, but may be able to deduct from the contract price the damages which he suffered.[49] Before the buyer can deduct damages from the price or recover damages from the seller, the buyer must have given the appropriate notice.[50] This problem has already been discussed.[51]

§ 145. Summary of the Buyer's Courses of Action

The prior sections have presented the buyer's courses of action when he receives non-conforming goods or a non-conforming tender. He first may choose between rejection and acceptance. If he rejects properly, the goods are treated as belonging to the seller. If he accepts, the buyer may have a further choice between keeping the goods and revoking his acceptance. If the revocation is proper, the goods are treated as belonging to the seller—just as with a rejection. However, even if the buyer is required to retain the goods, he has not lost his remedy for damages caused by the non-conformity. An understanding of a buyer's remedies rests on a understanding of these courses of action.

Throughout this process runs the requirement of notice. The buyer must notify the seller of the rejection or of the revocation of acceptance. Even if the buyer has accepted the goods and intends to retain them, he must notify the seller of the defect or be barred from any remedy. This notice requirement has caused some courts to solve product liability cases on the basis of strict liability in tort where notice is supposedly not needed.[52] Certainly this is one way to reach a sensible result in cases in which the courts believe that the giving of early notice was not essential to a just result in the particular case, but the Code is not so inflexible that it is necessary to throw the Code aside when notice to the seller did not follow within a few days of the discovery of the defect.[53] The purpose of notice is to allow the parties to

---

49. UCC §§ 2–607(1), 2–717; §§ 146–57 *infra.*

50. UCC §§ 2–607(3) (a), 2–717.

51. § 142 *supra. See* UCC § 2–607, Comment 4.

52. *E. g.,* Greenman v. Yuba Power Prods., Inc., 59 Cal.2d 57, 377 P.2d 897, 27 Cal.Rptr. 697 (1962) (Uniform Sales Act); Santor v. A & M Kara-

gheusian, Inc., 44 N.J. 52, 207 A.2d 305 (1965); Wights v. Staff Jennings, Inc., 241 Or. 301, 405 P.2d 624 (1965); Dippel v. Sciano, 37 Wis.2d 443, 155 N.W. 2d 55 (1967) (general inapplicability of Code).

53. UCC § 2–607, Comment 4; Nugent v. Popular Markets, Inc., 353 Mass. 45, 228 N.E.2d 91 (1967). *See also* Piercefield v. Remington Arms Co., 375 Mich. 85, 133 N.W.2d 129 (1965).

negotiate a settlement of their dispute. The construction of "reasonable time" under the Code can take account of the facts of the case involved and can support the Comment statement:

> The time of notification is to be determined by applying commercial standards to a merchant buyer. "A reasonable time" for notification from a retail consumer is to be judged by different standards so that in his case it will be extended, for the rule of requiring notification is designed to defeat commercial bad faith, not to deprive a good faith consumer of his remedy.[54]

2. THE BUYER'S MONETARY RECOVERIES

§ 146. Recovery of the Purchase Price Paid

When one of the four triggering events of section 2–711 has occurred, the buyer may recover any portion of the purchase price which he has paid. As an illustration of this principle assume that the buyer and the seller have entered into a contract for the sale of goods, that the contract price was $10,000, that the buyer had paid $3,000 down, and that the seller delivered non-conforming goods which the buyer rightfully rejected. Such a buyer is entitled to a return of the $3,000 which he paid. Recovery can be justified either on the basis that the buyer *lost* that amount or on the basis that the seller *gained* that amount from the transaction in which the seller defaulted.

This principle is not new to the law. It is reflected in the usual measure of recovery for breach of contract in which the *unpaid* contract price is subtracted from the value of the goods.[55] If the goods in the supposed case were worth the contract price ($10,000) on the date set for performance, application of the damage formula produces an award of $3,000—the buyer's restitution interest.[56] If the goods were worth more than $10,000, $3,000 of the total recovery represents the down payment and the remainder is the buyer's expected gain which would have accrued through performance. If the goods were worth less than $10,000 on the date set for performance, the buyer can never-

---

54. UCC § 2–607, Comment 4.

55. Pettaway v. Commercial Automotive Service, Inc., 49 Wash.2d 650, 306 P.2d 219 (1957); 3 S. Williston, Sales § 599 n. 13 (rev.ed. 1948). When the buyer has paid nothing on the purchase price, the court often ignores stating the "unpaid" portion of the formula. Philippi v. Pacific Grains, Inc., 225 Or. 57, 356 P.2d 438 (1960). The Code reaches this result by using contract price as the base for figuring damages under UCC §§ 2–712 and 2–713 but returning to the buyer the portion of the price paid. UCC § 2–711 (1).

56. § 138 *supra.*

theless recover the entire $3,000 on his rejection of the goods.[57] The pre-Code explanation of this result (which puts the buyer in a better financial position than he would have enjoyed had the seller performed) was in terms of rescission: the defaulter's breach allowed the aggrieved party to rescind the contract and seek restitution of the amounts paid under the contract.[58]

The Code's approach to a recovery of the down payment is more straight-forward. No longer is the buyer forced to elect between rescission and affirmance of the contract, approaches which created difficult (and needless) problems of election of remedies.[59] "Rescission" is a term not found in the Code to describe the buyer's courses of action following a default by his seller.[60] In its place section 2–711 states that where one of the four triggering events occurs, "the buyer may cancel and whether or not he has done so may in addition to recovering so much of the price as has been paid" either (1) cover and have damages based on his cover contract or (2) recover damages for non-delivery. Important here are two concepts. First, cancellation is not necessary for a recovery of the down payment; the buyer may have this amount even though he has not cancelled. Second, even if the buyer has cancelled and recovered his down payment, he may also have damages.[61] Code damages are not inconsistent with an award of the price paid by the buyer.

The buyer is entitled to a return of his down payment (plus cover damages or the more usual measure of damages) only if one of the four triggering events of section 2–711 has occurred. Each of these events

---

57. Bush v. Canfield, 2 Conn. 485 (1818); Palmer, *The Contract Price as a Limit on Restitution for Defendant's Breach*, 20 Ohio St.L.J. 264 (1959).

Leveridge v. Notaras, 433 P.2d 935 (Okl. 1967), decided under the Code, allowed the buyer to recover the purchase price paid although the buyer alleged that the goods were worth less than the price paid. The buyer sought this recovery on a theory of rescission, but the Code basis should have been rejection or revocation of acceptance.

58. Boomer v. Muir, 24 P.2d 570 (Cal. App. 1933). The notion that the rescission of the contract somehow destroys the contractual relationship between the parties is, however, fallacious. The Code's emphasis on cancellation is preferable. UCC § 2–106 (4).

59. Uniform Sales Act § 69; 3 S. Williston, Sales §§ 611–612a (rev. ed. 1948).

60. Lawner v. Englebach, 433 Pa. 311, 249 A.2d 295 (1969). The remedy under the Code is adequate and the buyer has no equity action for rescission based on breach, Casey v. Philadelphia Auto Sales Co., 428 Pa. 155, 236 A.2d 800 (1968). *But cf.* Lanners v. Whitney, 247 Or. 223, 428 P.2d 398 (1967). "Rescission" is used in UCC § 2–721 and finds its way (inaccurately) into some Code cases. *E g.*, Tiger Motor Co. v. McMurty, 284 Ala. 283, 224 So.2d 638 (1969).

61. The buyer has a right to his down payment less use value. Byrd v. Moore Ford Co., 116 Ga.App. 292, 157 S.E.2d 41 (1967). He may also recover damages. Lanners v. Whitney, 247 Or. 223, 428 P.2d 398 (1967). For cancellation of an installment contract, see Graulich Caterer Inc. v. Hans Holterbosch, Inc., 101 N.J.Super. 61, 243 A.2d 253 (App.Div.1968).

is one in which the buyer ends up without the goods: (1) the seller failed to make the required delivery; (2) the seller repudiated; or the tendered goods so failed to conform to the contract that the buyer (3) rightfully rejected or (4) justifiably revoked his acceptance. If any one of these events has occurred, the seller either still has the goods or has a right to their return. In addition, he holds the down payment made by the buyer. Since the seller is not entitled to both, the amount paid on the price must be returned.[62] If, however, the default consisted of tendering non-conforming goods which the buyer decided to retain, neither section 2–711 nor any other Code section allows the buyer to recover his down payment. In such a case the buyer is limited to his damage remedy.[63]

The pre-Code doctrine of election of remedies caused difficulties for the buyer when the contract required the delivery of several items and some (but not all) of the goods delivered were non-conforming. Such a buyer was faced with a choice. He could rescind and recover the price paid, but if he did, he was required to rescind entirely and return all of the goods; alternatively, the buyer could pursue a damage remedy.[64] This requirement was relaxed in installment sales and when the contract was divisible, but these exceptions provided the courts with crude tools with which to fashion appropriate solutions to specific cases.

The Code extends the possibility of the buyer's price recovery when the seller delivers non-conforming goods and the buyer desires to keep some but not all of the tendered goods. The Code reaches this result by allowing the buyer to reject or revoke acceptance of commercial units, not requiring the buyer to choose between keeping all or none of the goods.[65] Once the buyer has rightfully rejected or justifiably revoked his acceptance, section 2–711 operates to allow the buyer to recover both the price and damages—whether or not the buyer has cancelled. The principal problem is that of determining when partial rejection or revocation of acceptance is available to the buyer, and this requires an understanding of the Code's distinction between the single delivery and the installment contract.

With the single delivery contract—and subject to the limitations already discussed—if the goods or their tender of delivery fail *in any respect* to conform to the contract, the buyer may "accept any com-

---

62. Zabriskie Chevrolet, Inc. v. Smith, 99 N.J.Super. 441, 240 A.2d 195 (L.Div. 1968).

63. UCC § 2–714; § 150 *infra*.

64. Reno Sales Co. v. Pritchard Indus. Inc., 178 F.2d 279 (7th Cir. 1949); cases cited in 3 S. Williston, Sales § 608b (rev. ed. 1948).

65. UCC § 2–601(c).

mercial unit or units and reject the rest." [66] There is no requirement that the unit or units accepted be conforming. The buyer could, if he desired, accept the non-conforming units and reject those that conform to the contract; or he could accept some non-conforming and some conforming units and reject the remainder.[67] With the installment contract (that is, one which requires or authorizes the delivery of goods in separate lots to be separately accepted) the "buyer may reject any installment which is non-conforming if the non-conformity substantially impairs the value of that installment and cannot be cured or if the non-conformity is a defect in the required documents . . . ." [68] This language changes the rejection test from one of *any* non-conformity to a requirement of *substantial* impairment of value, and it prevents rejection of any installment if the defect can be cured. More important to the present discussion, however, is that this Code section (2–612) gives the buyer the privilege of rejecting the installment—not the commercial units within the installment. This may have been an oversight by the drafters (because they did give the buyer the privilege of revoking acceptance of commercial units without regard to the type of contract involved) but the language of the Code would require the buyer either to accept or to reject the entire installment and would not allow him to select commercial units within that installment for acceptance or rejection.[69]

Revocation of acceptance is allowed by section 2–608. This section has already been discussed,[70] that discussion emphasizing the limited number of situations in which a buyer can revoke acceptance of goods. Those limitations are applicable to attempts to recover the price because before any 2–711 remedy is available to the buyer, he must have *justifiably* revoked acceptance (or one of the other three events must have occurred). If the buyer can meet the limitations of section 2–608, he may revoke his acceptance either of the entire lot or of any commercial unit "whose non-conformity substantially impairs its value to him . . . ." The words "to him" are added to the test which appeared in the installment contract section of the Code (2–612), but they will undoubtedly be implied in section 2–612. Important to price recovery and to damages is that the revocation of acceptance of a commercial unit is limited to the unit which is non-conforming. The buyer cannot (as he could with rejection under the single delivery contract) select the units he wishes to return to the seller, keeping some non-conforming units and returning some units that do conform.

---

66. *Id.*

67. UCC § 2–601, Comment 1.

68. UCC § 2–612(2); § 104 *supra.*

69. When the buyer may treat the entire installment contract as breached is discussed in § 104 *supra.*

70. § 143 *supra.*

Having rightfully rejected or justifiably revoked acceptance, the buyer can recover the price which he paid for the "goods involved." There are problems facing the buyer who desires to keep only a portion of the delivered or tendered goods, among them the selection of a rational basis for apportioning the price when the goods were sold for a lump price rather than for a unit price. Nevertheless, the Code does expand the protection of the buyer's price recovery following a default by the seller.

§ 147. "Cover" Damages

The Uniform Sales Act contained five sections specifically dealing with remedies of the buyer.[71] Section 67 applied to situations in which the seller had failed to deliver the goods and title had not passed to the buyer. Subsection (3) provided this measure of damages:

> Where there is an available market for the goods is question, the measure of damages, in the absence of special circumstances showing proximate damages of a greater amount, is the difference between the contract price and the market or current price of the goods at the time or times when they ought to have been delivered, or, if no time was fixed, then at the time of the refusal to deliver.

The theory underlying this measure of recovery is not complicated. The basic purpose of contractual recoveries is to place the aggrieved party in the financial position he would have occupied had there been no default.[72] In a contract for the sale of goods the buyer is entitled to the goods on the promised date and at the agreed-upon price. If the seller fails to deliver those goods, the buyer will normally be able to purchase similar goods within a few days of the date set for delivery. Since most goods have a fairly well defined market price, damages computed by subtracting contract price from market value will put the buyer in the position that he would have occupied had the seller performed. The buyer's only outlay will be the contract price; any additional amount will have been paid by the defaulting seller.[73] To this recovery must be added consequential damages suffered and any payments which the buyer made on the price, but the basic formula of the Uniform Sales Act worked reasonably well in the great number of cases.

---

71. Uniform Sales Act §§ 66–70.

72. This purpose is adopted as a part of the Code in UCC § 1–106(1).

73. The textual statement follows the course of American decisions by over-looking such noncompensable costs as attorney fees. Any discussion of a major overhaul of our legal system to include attorney fees as a part of damages is outside this text. § 1 *supra*.

There were, however, some troublesome cases which did not lend themselves to the market-value-minus-contract-price formula.[74] Consider, for example, the buyer who had agreed to purchase a specially manufactured item for which there was no defined market value. When his seller refused to deliver the item purchased, the buyer faced a dilemma. He needed the goods (and had a contractual "right" to them), but to be certain that he would be fully compensated the buyer had to make his substitute purchase at an amount which the trier of fact would later determine to be the "market value." At this point the hindsight of the trier of fact second-guessing the acts of the buyer —who could use only foresight—produced doubtful results.[75] The market-value formula allowed the defaulting seller to introduce evidence that the second purchase was not made at the market price even though it was made in complete commercial good faith and, if the trier of fact found the market value to be less than the contract price for the substitute goods, this measure of damages required a judgment for the lesser amount.

The Code retains the market-value formula [76] (but changes it to "market price"); however, the Code also contains a new measure of recovery to aid in the solution of some cases which were not adequately handled through prior law. This new measure centers on the concept of "cover"—the privilege of the buyer to make a substitute purchase in place of the goods which were not delivered by the seller. Section 2–712 provides:

> (1) After a breach within the preceding section the buyer may "cover" by making in good faith and without unreasonable delay any reasonable purchase of or contract to purchase goods in substitution for those due from the seller.

> (2) The buyer may recover from the seller as damages the difference between the cost of cover and the contract price together with any incidental or consequential damages as hereinafter defined (Section 2–715), but less expenses saved in consequence of the seller's breach.

> (3) Failure of the buyer to effect cover within this section does not bar him from any other remedy.

The buyer of the specially manufactured item which the seller failed to deliver is no longer required to second-guess the trier of fact on the

---

74. Orester v. Dayton Rubber Mfg. Co., 228 N.Y. 134, 126 N.E. 510 (1920), discusses some of these cases.

75. *E. g.*, Missouri Furnace Co. v. Cochran, 8 F. 463 (W.D.Pa.1881) (installment contract for coal to be delivered in future); Sauer v. McClintic-Marshall Constr. Co., 179 Mich. 618, 146 N.W. 422 (1914) (contract for structural steel needed by buyer to complete building).

76. UCC § 2–713.

question of market value when the buyer decides to purchase substitute goods. If the buyer makes a reasonable substitute purchase in good faith and without unreasonable delay, the damages will be measured by the difference between the cost of cover and the contract price. This approach to monetary recoveries comes much closer to meeting the needs of commerce than did the market-value formula of prior law. Of course, this section is not limited to "specially manufactured" goods—that example was chosen only because it was an easy example of goods for which there was no ready market value. Any buyer can take advantage of the cover damages providing he can meet the requirements of section 2–712. These are:

1. There must be a breach within the meaning of section 2–711. The seller must have repudiated or failed to make a required delivery, or the buyer must have rightfully rejected or justifiably revoked his acceptance.[77] These are all situations in which the buyer does not have the goods; he has thrown them back on the seller or never received them. Cover is not available if the buyer has accepted and retained the goods (even though they are non-conforming) or if he is obligated to accept them under conditions in which he cannot justifiably revoke that acceptance.

2. The substitute purchase must be made in good faith.[78] For the non-merchant this means that the buyer must have exercised honesty in fact in making the purchase; the merchant must meet this test and also observe reasonable commercial standards of fair dealing in the trade.[79] It is difficult to fit the idea of factual honesty into the repurchase transaction. Are some purchases made "honestly" and others "dishonestly"? Evidently the drafters intended that the buyer ought not be allowed to make his substitute purchase at what he realized was an inflated price so that he could pass the increased cost to the seller under section 2–712. Policing these infrequent cases can be handled either under this concept of honesty in fact or through the further requirement that the purchase be "reasonable."

The observation of commercial standards by merchants is important, however. If good commercial practices require checking prices with a number of sellers before making the substitute purchase, those practices must be followed if the buyer is to be allowed to take advantage of the measure of recovery contained in section 2–712. On the other hand, if the buyer has immediate need for the goods and commercial standards of fair dealing are satisfied by his ordering the

---

77. §§ 141, 143, 146 *supra.*

78. The buyer must have made a purchase before UCC § 2–712 is applicable.

Draper v. Minneapolis-Moline, Inc., 100 Ill.App.2d 324, 241 N.E.2d 342 (1968).

79. UCC §§ 1–201(19), 2–103(1) (b).

substitute goods after checking with only one supplier, the good faith requirement of section 2–712 has been met.

3. The substitute purchase must be reasonable and made without any unreasonable delay. These requirements, when combined with the good faith test, form the basis for judicial policing of cover contracts. The buyer ought to recover damages which will place him in the same financial position he would have occupied had the seller performed, and the buyer will no longer be required to second-guess the trier of fact on a later determination of market value. Nevertheless, the buyer is not free to set his damages by making just any second contract. Concepts of reasonableness and of good faith assure that the buyer acted fairly and honestly in making his substitute purchase—whether that buyer is a merchant or a non-merchant—and that a merchant-buyer also followed the commercial standards of his trade. Whether the substitute contract was made at "market price" is relevant evidence in reaching a decision on the reasonableness of the purchase and the good faith of the buyer, but just because the court might later find that this particular substitute contract was made in excess of the market price does not require a determination that the 2–712 measure of damages is inapplicable.[80] The test is not one of whether the purchase was at market; the test is the good faith of the buyer in making a reasonable purchase without unreasonable delay.

4. The goods purchased must be "in substitution" for those due from the seller. Most often the second purchase will be of the same type of goods as those promised by the seller, but identity is not required by section 2–712. It is sufficient if they are "commercially usable as reasonable substitutes under the circumstances of the particular case."[81] Further, credit may be substituted for cash, and different delivery terms may be involved. Each of these deviations presents factual problems for the trier of fact (including, in some cases, the possibility of an adjustment of the damages awarded) and an accumulation of deviations makes the case more difficult for the buyer to fit within the reasonable purchase test of section 2–712, but this section does not require identity between the two contracts—only that the goods purchased be "in substitution" for those due from the seller.[82]

When these four tests are met the buyer's basic recovery is the cost of cover less the contract price (adjusted under section 2–711 for

---

80. UCC § 2–712, Comment 2. *Cf.* Jefferson Credit Corp. v. Marcano, 60 Misc.2d 138, 302 N.Y.S.2d 390 (Civ.Ct. 1969).

81. UCC § 2–712, Comment 2.

82. Borochoff v. Breman, 85 Ga.App. 256, 68 S.E.2d 915 (1952); Benj. Harris & Co. v. Western Smelting & Ref. Co., 381 Ill. 443, 45 N.E.2d 639 (1943).

any amounts paid down by the buyer). Thus, if a contract called for the sale of certain goods at a contract price of $7,000, the seller defaulted, and the buyer covered by following the requirements of section 2–712(1) at a cost of $8,200, the buyer's basic recovery would be $1,-200—even though the "market" is later determined to be $7,500 for these goods. If that buyer had paid $500 on the purchase price, his recovery would be increased to $1,700. In addition, the buyer will recover his incidental and consequential damages less expenses saved because of the seller's breach (as, for example, when the substitute goods allowed the buyer to dispense with some cost in processing which would have been incurred with seller's goods).[83]

The final subsection of section 2–712 can cause some difficulty. That subsection provides: "Failure of the buyer to effect cover within this section does not bar him from any other remedy." This much is clear: the buyer may decide not to make a second purchase in substitution for the goods which seller promised but did not deliver. Such a buyer is not barred from pursuing some other remedy. Likewise, a buyer who attempted to cover but who waited an unreasonably long time, or who made an unreasonable purchase, or who bought in bad faith has not lost any other remedy which he may have for the seller's default.[84] These buyers have failed to "effect cover" within the meaning of section 2–712(3).

Difficulties will arise in determining exactly when a buyer *effects* cover. First the easier case: suppose that a non-merchant buyer made a substitute contract which met the tests of section 2–712(1). Is such a buyer obligated to use the damage formula of section 2–712 (2), or may he (by emphasizing the word "may" in that subsection) disregard that formula and recover damages based on the market price of the goods? If this question is raised by a buyer who made his substitute contract with the intention of using the section 2–712 (2) formula but who later discovered that he had made the second purchase at below market price, the answer should be foreshadowed by pre-Code law: this buyer ought to be limited to his section 2–712 (2) recovery.[85] This was the loss he suffered, and giving him dam-

---

83. The punctuation of UCC § 2–712(2) indicates that the saved expenses should be subtracted from the total damages—not from only the incidental and consequential damages. Thus, if the increased cost through cover is $1,200, the incidental damages are $100, and the expenses saved are $200, buyer should recover $1,100 under UCC § 2–712.

The expenses must be saved "in consequence of the seller's breach." UCC § 2–712(2). *See* 5 A. Corbin, Contracts § 1038 (1964).

84. The failure to cover may, however, affect other remedies. *E. g.*, UCC §§ 2–715(2)(a), 2–716.

85. May Hosiery Mills v. Munford Cotton Mills, 205 Ala. 27, 87 So. 674 (1920); Iron Trade Prods. Co. v. Wilkoff Co., 272 Pa. 172, 116 A. 150 (1922). *Compare* UCC § 2–712, Comment 3, *with*

ages based on cost of cover puts him in the position he would have been had the contract been performed.

Few cases are, however, this clear. Consider, second, the more likely situation in which this question will be raised. A merchant has a number of orders with several suppliers and he places orders from time to time to keep his stock sufficient to meet his demands. For example, a shoe manufacturer may have contracts with several tanneries to purchase leather; a lawn mower manufacturer may be purchasing its carburetors from four or five sources on a regular basis; or a retail grocer may be constantly looking for a less expensive source of sacks and bags. When a seller to one of these merchants defaults, how can a trier of fact determine whether the buyer *effected* cover through one of his normal purchases? If the defaulting seller can find that his buyer made a later purchase at below market, that seller would like to claim that this purchase limited the buyer's damages— and the preceding paragraph concluded that this claim had merit when made against the casual buyer. However, could not the merchant have made the below-market purchase even if the seller had not defaulted and have reaped the gain represented by the goodness of his purchase? Further, is it not likely that he would have done so irrespective of the buyer's breach? If so, there is little reason to pass that gain, as a windfall, to the defaulting seller.[86]

§ 148. Damages for Non-delivery

Section 2–713 provides for the traditional market-value-minus-contract-price measure of damages [87] and presents several problems of statutory construction:

> (1) Subject to the provisions of this Article with respect to proof of market price (Section 2–723), the measure of damages for non-delivery or repudiation by the seller is the difference between the market price at the time when the buyer learned of the breach and the contract price together with any incidental and consequential damages provided in this Article (Section 2–715), but less expenses saved in consequence of the seller's breach.

UCC § 2–713, Comment 5. These can be harmonized only if "cover" has the meaning given to it by UCC § 2–712(1) —the repurchase under the conditions of that subsection. Once he makes the repurchase (i. e., "covers"), he no longer has the choice of damage recoveries.

86. The difficulties of determining when a buyer was effecting cover could have been solved by inserting a notice requirement similar to the one a seller must give to take advantage of the resale remedy. UCC § 2–706.

87. 5A A. Corbin, Contracts § 1101 (1964); 3 S. Williston, Sales § 599 (rev. ed. 1948).

(2) Market price is to be determined as of the place for tender or, in cases of rejection after arrival or revocation of acceptance, as of the place of arrival.

The operation of this section can be illustrated through a series of hypothetical factual patterns.

Case # 1. Seller agreed to sell and Buyer to buy a new machine— "new" in the sense that it had not been used prior to the sale. The usual price of these machines was $10,000 but Seller agreed to give Buyer a 10% discount, setting the price at $9,000. Delivery was scheduled for July 1, Seller to deliver the machine to Buyer. Seller did not deliver the machine and has no legal excuse for his failure to deliver.

Such a buyer could cover by following the requirements of section 2–712. If he followed this procedure, his measure of damages would be that which was discussed in the prior section of this text.[88] Suppose, however, that this particular buyer did not cover—he may have changed his mind about needing such a machine, or the substitute purchase which he made may not have been "reasonable," or any one of a number of events might have occurred which made the 2–712 approach unattractive. Nevertheless, this buyer has lost the $1,000 gain which he would have had if the seller had performed, and this expectation interest is protected by the general law of contracts and by the Code.[89] Specifically, section 2–713 would apply. Case #1 is a factual pattern in which there has been no delivery, and the measure of recovery begins with subtracting the contract price ($9,000) from the market price ($10,000). To this would be added incidental and consequential damages, and expenses saved would be subtracted from the total. Since the facts of Case #1 show no such damages or expenses, the buyer's section 2–713 recovery would be $1,000—the same amount which he would have received if he had covered at market price.[90]

The suggested solution to Case #1 assumed that the market price of this machine was $10,000. This is probably a safe assumption under the facts of that Case. However, it should not be concluded that the Code's "market price" is necessarily the same as the price at which the goods are "listed" for sale. Section 2–713(2) gives guidance as to the place and time at which market price is to be determined, but it offers no functional definition of the term. For example, it does not tell what

88. § 147 *supra*. Some have argued, however, that the expectation interest should be protected only through cover and that cover should be made mandatory unless the aggrieved party is willing to cancel without liability. Revised Uniform Sales Act, Comment on Section 58–A (1941), at pages 247–48.

The Uniform Commercial Code rejected compulsory cover.

89. § 138 *supra*.

90. Any payments on the price are also recoverable. § 146 *supra*.

market should be examined to ascertain the prevailing price. Is it the wholesale or retail market that is important? [91] Once this is determined, should the market be limited to franchised dealers of the product who sell only at list price or should the market be expanded to include discount stores which sell at below list prices?

Although "market price" is not defined by the Code, that term will continue to carry the pre-Code concept of the price that would have been paid in a theoretical market—generally defined as the price which a willing buyer would have paid and for which a willing seller would have sold the goods in a perfect market.[92] There are few

91. For a discussion, see Illinois Cent. R. R. v. Crail, 281 U.S. 57, 50 S.Ct. 180, 74 L.Ed. 699 (1930). Wholesale price was allowed in Marshall v. Clark, 78 Conn. 9, 60 A. 741 (1905) (reported as Righter v. Clark in the Atlantic Reporter), but a retailer was given profits in suit against a wholesaler by the court's use of retail, rather than wholesale, price in Sun Co. v. Burrus, 139 Va. 279, 123 S.E. 347 (1924).

92. Determining "market price" by the selection of the price of comparable goods will serve well the majority of cases involving the sale of goods. E. g., Southern Pac. Milling Co. v. Billiwhack Stock Farm, 50 Cal.App.2d 79, 122 P.2d 650 (1942); Charles Street Garage v. Kaplan, 312 Mass. 624, 45 N.E.2d 928 (1942). No specific number of comparable sales is needed to establish market price, Parmenter v. Fitzpatrick, 135 N.Y. 190, 31 N.E. 1032 (1892), but a price fixed by a combination among sellers will not set market price, Lovejoy v. Michels, 88 Mich. 15, 49 N.W. 901 (1891). There are, however, instances in which a more refined definition of market price will be needed; these require an analysis of the structure of the market involved. For example, Treas. Reg. §§ 1.613(3) and (4) (1968) list the factors which are to be applied in determining the representative market or field price to be used in computing the percentage depletion deduction. Among these factors are: the geographic extent of the relevant market, identification of like kind and grade of the product, frequency and volume of sales, the existence of a substantial number of unrelated buyers and sellers no one of whom controls a substantial portion of the sales or purchases, and the existence of accommodation or tie-in sales.

Economic analysis identifies three market structures in which market price is determined. The first is the ideal market discussed in the text. Such a market is identified by the existence of many buyers and sellers, by complete information of existing supply conditions and of all prices of units sold, by the absence of control over price by any party, and by the freedom of any party to enter and depart from the market. P. Samuelson, Economics 466–67 (7th ed. 1967).

The second market structure is the imperfectly competitive market. Such a market is identified by relatively few sellers who sell either (1) an identical product or (2) a product which is technologically the same but differentiated by its trade-name. In this market the seller cannot sell all of his output without depressing the price which buyers will be willing to pay. Thus, there is an incentive for the relatively few sellers to exercise discretion over the price of their product—predicting the response of their competitors to their changes in price. E. Chamberlin, The Theory of Monopolistic Competition, Ch. 4 (8th ed. 1962).

The complete monopoly is the third structure used by economists to explain the determination of market price. Here there is a single seller of a single product for which there is no close substitute. The expected pricing conduct of the seller in these circumstances, absent public regulation, is that its price will be set higher than it would be in a competitive market and that an incremental monopoly profit will be enjoyed by the seller. P. Samuelson, Economics 481 (7th ed. 1967).

perfect markets, and the willing buyer and seller are nothing more than constructs which reflect a judicial quest for a baseline from which damages can be computed. Despite this drawback, the concept of market price has utility in resolving the dispute before the court. There are many goods for which a representative price has been determined in a market context. Enough lawn mowers, television sets, pencils, men's suits, desks, and typewriters are sold each month so that a representative price for these items is established by the market; the Code accepts such price for the purpose of section 2–713 damages. There are, however, other goods for which no objective price exists. A painting by an old master, steel which has been shaped to form a special product, and a computer constructed to perform a unique task have no selling price set in a market of competing buyers and sellers; nevertheless, even for these items the Code allows the parties to introduce evidence as to the price for which these items would sell under theoretical conditions in a market situation comparable to the one in which the parties were actually dealing. Between these extremes of mass-produced goods and the one-of-a-kind item several gradations are possible. The goods may be in short supply in the geographical area where the seller promised to deliver them, but they may be available a few hundred miles away. There may be only a few (or even none) of the contracted-for goods in existence on the date set for performance, but production schedules indicate that within a month or two an ample supply will be available to the buyer. These are but examples of the gradations of varying market conditions which create difficulties in price determination. In an attempt to introduce some certainty into this process of valuation, the Code contains specific answers to these questions:

1. As of what time is market price to be determined? Goods may fluctuate in price between date of the contract and the time the dispute is tried in court. For example, the machine discussed in Case #1 may have been selling for $10,000 on the date the contract was entered into, for $12,000 on the date of the scheduled delivery, and for $8,000 on the date the dispute is being litigated. The Code provides that the market price "at the time when the buyer learned of the

---

Determination of "market price" must take account not only of the market structure involved, but also of the practice of discriminatory pricing—a practice of a seller of charging two prices for the same product sold in two distinct markets. For example, a manufacturer of spark plugs may charge $1.00 per plug under its own name and sell the same plug for $.49 under the label of a discount house.

F. Rowe, Price Discrimination under the Robinson-Patman Act, Chs. 4 and 5 (1962). The tying arrangement is another trade practice which may generate an "artificial" price for a product. See United States v. Loew's, Inc., 371 U.S. 38, 83 S.Ct. 97, 9 L.Ed.2d 11 (1962); Turner, *Validity of Tying Arrangements Under the Antitrust Laws*, 72 Harv.L.Rev. 50 (1958).

breach" is the critical time.[93]   In Case #1 the buyer learned of the breach when the machine was not delivered; thus, July 1 would be the time of valuation.   This gives the buyer that sum of money which, when added to the unpaid contract price, equals the market price of the machine on the day the buyer learned of the breach.   A theoretical difficulty with the Code's time line is that a buyer cannot often make his second purchase the moment he learns of the breach.   If the price is fluctuating, the amount awarded will not reflect the cost of the goods at a time that the buyer can reasonably be expected to make the purchase.   However, when a buyer does in fact make a substitute purchase, he can seek recovery under section 2–712 which requires only that there be no unreasonable delay.

2.   As of what place is market price to be determined?   The machine may sell for $10,000 at the buyer's city but for only $9,200 at the seller's city.   The Code's answer is set forth above: "Market price is to be determined as of the place for tender or, in cases of rejection after arrival or revocation of acceptance, as of the place of arrival." [94] The Comments state that the Code has again followed the baseline which would have been used had the buyer covered, but has converted the recovery into a damage formula based upon market price.[95]   This, however, may not be a proper reading of the Code.   The buyer who has rejected but who decides to cover may find that the "reasonable" cover contract must be made at the place of tender rather than the place of rejection.   Nevertheless, section 2–713 damages would be measured at the point of rejection for the buyer who did not cover.

3.   If there is no evidence of a market price available at the time and place mentioned above, how is market price to be determined? Here the Code presents only a partial answer:

> If evidence of a price prevailing at the times or places described in this Article is not readily available the price prevailing within any reasonable time before or after the time described or at any other place which in commercial judgment or under usage of trade would serve as a reasonable substitute for the one described may be used, making any proper allowance for the cost of transporting the goods to or from such other place.[96]

---

93. UCC § 2–713(1). Compare the time line for the seller's damages on breach by a buyer. UCC § 2–708; § 175 *infra*.

94. UCC § 2–713(2).

95. UCC § 2–713, Comment 1.

96. UCC § 2–723(2). For a pre-Code case using price at nearest market plus cost of transportation, see Sundt v. Tobin Quarries, Inc., 50 N.M. 254, 175 P.2d 684 (1946). "Evidence of a relevant price prevailing at a time or place other than the one described in this Article offered by one party is not admissible unless and until he has given the other party such notice as the court finds sufficient to prevent unfair surprise." UCC § 2–723(3).

This answer is "partial" because there will remain instances in which there is insufficient commerce in a given product to discover a "market" for it—as where the contract is for the sale of unique goods (and, for such a contract, specific performance may be the best remedy for the buyer). These cases will be solved as they were prior to the enactment of the Code with appraisals and expert testimony providing the trier of fact with guides from which to base its judgment of a "market price." [97]

Case # 2. Return to the basic facts of Case #1: a contract between Seller and Buyer for a machine worth $10,000, a price set by the parties at $9,000, and a breach by Seller. In Case # 1 it was assumed that the breach arose out of the failure of Seller to deliver the machine to Buyer. For Case #2 assume that Seller did deliver a machine which Buyer discovered to be defective and that Buyer either rightfully rejected or justifiably revoked his acceptance. Does section 2–713 provide a remedy for this Buyer?

The answer ought to be that section 2–713 does provide a remedy the parties at $9,000, and a breach by Seller. In Case #1 it was as- ceptance of a defective tender. The Comments suggest that this should be the answer when they state that the section 2–713 remedy is "completely alternative to cover under the preceding section and applies only when and to the extent that the buyer has not covered." [98] This would indicate that the drafters meant at least this much: any time that a buyer could cover and recover damages under section 2–712, that buyer is free to elect not to cover and can recover damages under section 2–713.

The difficulty in reaching this interpretation is that section 2–713 provides that its measure of recovery applies in cases of "non-delivery or repudiation." The Case #2 Seller has not repudiated; has he done something which qualifies as a "non-delivery"? If this question is answered negatively, section 2–713 has no application once goods have been delivered even though the goods are non-conforming and are later thrown back on the seller. Such an answer would require the buyer to search elsewhere for a measure of damages.[99]

---

97. UCC § 2–723, Comment. As to admissibility of price quotations contained in journals, newspapers, and periodicals, see UCC § 2–724. As to the competency of testimony as to price quoted by a relative of the buyer, see **Draper v. Minneapolis-Moline Co.,** 100 Ill.App.2d 324, 241 N.E.2d 342 (1968).

98. UCC § 2–713, Comment 5.

99. UCC § 2–714 could be used to produce a result similar to that of UCC § 2–713. There are, however, differences. For example, the time and place baseline of UCC § 2–714(2) is the point of acceptance rather than the time the buyer learned of the breach

Some support can be marshalled for such an argument. For example, the word "non-delivery" is also used in section 2–615 where its apparent meaning is limited to situations in which the seller failed to make any delivery—but not to include cases involving delivery of non-conforming goods. Despite this, the use of the word "non-delivery" in section 2–713 compels the broader meaning. This conclusion is based on two other Code provisions:

The first is section 2–711(1) which lists the four triggering events (two of which are rightful rejection and justifiable revocation of acceptance) and provides that when one of these occurs the buyer may, among other things, cover *or* "recover damages for non-delivery as provided in this Article (Section 2–713)." The second is section 2–713(2) which provides a place for measuring market price "in cases of rejection after arrival or revocation of acceptance." Thus, both of the sections involved use the word "non-delivery" to include two kinds of cases: those in which the seller has not delivered and those in which the seller has delivered but the buyer has exercised the privilege of returning the goods to the seller. The result is that "non-delivery" in section 2–713 ought to be read to mean those situations in which the delivery by the seller was not effective to obligate the buyer to retain the goods. If the transaction results in the buyer's not having this obligation because of a default by the seller, there has been no effective delivery and damages can be based upon this "non-delivery."

§ 149. Damages on Repudiation

The measure of recovery following a repudiation by the seller presents a perplexing problem in statutory construction—so perplexing that Code amendments are needed to produce uniform results. All this text can do is to state the problems created by the Code and to suggest a solution which can be justified on notions of what the law ought to be. This solution will be framed in terms of Code policies but it is readily admitted that other policies can be found by those who believe that other results are preferable.

The problems begin with section 2–713 which was quoted in full in the prior section of this text.[1] Two hypothetical factual patterns were presented, around which a discussion of the buyer's recovery in "non-delivery" cases was developed. That method of presentation will be continued with the emphasis being shifted to the "repudiation" language of 2–713.

and the place of tender found in UCC § 2–713. Nevertheless, UCC § 2–714 (1) is sufficiently flexible to provide a necessary measure of damages. This text takes the position that Case #2 should be solved by UCC § 2–713 and that UCC § 2–714 is applicable to situations in which the buyer has accepted *and retained* the goods. *See* UCC § 2–714, Comment 1.

1. § 148 *supra.*

Case # 3. On January 10 Seller agreed to sell and Buyer to buy a new machine—"new" in the sense that it had not been used prior to the sale. The usual price of these machines was $10,000 but Seller agreed to give Buyer a 10% discount, setting the price at $9,000. Seller promised to deliver the machine to Buyer on July 1. During February the price of these machines rose sharply and Seller became unhappy with the contract. On March 2 Seller wrote to Buyer complaining about the deal and demanding that an additional $1,500 be added to the contract price. The letter was received on March 4 and Buyer is interested in learning what rights he has against Seller. As of March 4 it is impossible to know whether the increase in the price of these machines is temporary or whether they will cost even more on the delivery date, July 1.

One problem facing the Case #3 buyer is that of proving that the seller had "repudiated" the contract.[2] It is tempting to conclude that this is not a substantial problem when the seller has *demanded* a higher price for a machine which he was contractually obligated to sell for $9,000. Is this not a statement by the seller that he is renouncing his promise to deliver on July 1 and will reinstate that promise only if the buyer consents to the higher price? If so, the seller has "repudiated" and the section 2–713 damages are available to the buyer.[3] However, the more reasonable interpretation of seller's letter may fall short of a renunciation. It may be only a firm request for a substitute contract, made with the understanding that if the request is refused, the seller will reluctantly deliver the machine on July 1 for the $9,000. If this is the proper interpretation, there has been no repudiation and both parties remain contractually obligated to perform their promises.[4]

The ambiguous statement—that is, the one which is neither a clear-cut renunciation nor a simple appeal to the buyer's conscience for added money—is common in these cases. The seller often does not want to default but, in a rising market, is faced with a loss which he believes ought to be shared by the buyer. Perhaps a firm request will

2. "Repudiation" is not defined by the Code. Nevertheless, it is clear that the word was used in the sense of an anticipatory breach. For example: (1) UCC § 2–610 uses "repudiation" in connection with a performance not yet due, and (2) UCC §§ 2–703 and 2–711 use "repudiation" as one of several kinds of breaches distinguished from a failure to pay or make delivery. Thus, a statement made after payment or delivery was due cannot amount to a "repudiation." Holden & Martin v. Gilfeather, 78 Vt. 405, 409, 63 A. 144, 146 (1906); Restatement of Contracts § 318 (1932).

3. The leading case is Hochster v. De La Tour, 2 Ell. & Bl. 678, 118 Eng. Rep. 922 (Q.B. 1853). The repudiation may be by acts as well as statements. Restatement of Contracts § 318 (1932).

4. *E. g.,* Dingley v. Oler, 117 U.S. 490, 6 S.Ct. 850, 29 L.Ed. 984 (1886); McCloskey & Co. v. Minweld Steel Co., 220 F.2d 101 (3d Cir. 1955); 4 A. Corbin, Contracts §§ 973–74 (1951).

produce the desired response. The problem is that of determining whether that "firm request" crossed the line and became an anticipatory breach.[5] The answer requires a careful look at the facts of each case and often leaves the buyer in an awkward position. If he comes to the incorrect conclusion, he may discover either that he will have no goods delivered to him on July 1 or that he will be obligated to take those goods from two sources.

The Code has given partial relief to a party faced by an ambiguous statement from the other contracting party. Section 2–609 states the general rule that a "contract for sale imposes an obligation on each party that the other's expectation of receiving due performance will not be impaired." The buyer, faced with a possible repudiation, has had his expectation of receiving delivery "impaired." Likewise, a seller who finds that his buyer's financial position makes it doubtful that payment will be made as promised has had his expectation of receiving payment "impaired."[6] Thus, section 2–609 applies to both parties—not just to buyers or sellers. This section continues:

> . . . When reasonable grounds for insecurity arise with respect to the performance of either party the other may in writing demand adequate assurance of due performance and until he receives such assurance may if commercially reasonable suspend any performance for which he has not already received the agreed return.[7]

A party may invoke section 2–609 only when *reasonable* grounds for insecurity arise; he may not demand assurances on a whim. Thus, the Case #3 buyer still faces a factual question—and he may predict incorrectly what a court will do when it reviews those facts. However, the test is less demanding than it was with the common law anticipatory breach problem. There the buyer had to decide whether the seller's letter was a *breach;* under section 2–609 he must decide only whether that letter gave him reasonable grounds for *insecurity* as to the seller's future performance.[8]

Once section 2–609 is invoked the party using that section may do two things: (1) he may demand an adequate assurance of performance[9] and (2) until he receives that assurance may "if commercially reasonable" suspend any performance for which he has not already received the agreed return. This section does not allow the insecure

---

5. This difficulty is illustrated by the correspondence and discussions in Reliance Cooperage Corp. v. Treat, 195 F.2d 977 (8th Cir. 1952).

6. UCC § 2–609, Comment 1.

7. UCC § 2–609(1).

8. Lockwood-Conditionaire Corp. v. Educational Audio Visual, Inc., 3 UCC Rep. 354 (N.Y.Sup.Ct.1966).

9. For a discussion of the meaning of "adequate assurance," see UCC § 2–609, Comment 4.

party to recall deliveries or payments already made, but only to suspend a performance not yet accomplished.[10] The seller may refuse to make a delivery or the buyer may withhold a prepayment even though the time stated in the contract for the delivery or payment has arrived. This right to suspend performance is not unlimited; it exists only until the assurances are received.

Case #3 buyer, if in doubt as to whether the seller's letter amounted to a repudiation, could use section 2–609 and demand adequate assurance that the seller will deliver the machine on July 1. If that assurance is received, there would be no repudiation and no remedy available to the buyer. If the assurance is not received within a reasonable time—not exceeding 30 days—the Code provides that there has been a "repudiation" of the contract. This would remove the ambiguity of the seller's position and allow the buyer to proceed under section 2–713 for damages.

The perplexing Code problem facing a buyer following a repudiation by his seller is that of determining *when* the market price of the goods will be measured. The answer most often given by common law courts was that the damages should be measured as of the time set for performance, and the repudiation did not accelerate this date.[11] This rule was applied by some courts even though the buyer had covered prior to performance date and had bought substitute goods at a lesser price than their market price on the performance date.[12] The performance-date rule for measuring market price was not unanimous, however, with some courts selecting alternative dates depending on the facts of the case.[13]

The answer given by the Code appears deceptively easy if only section 2–713 is studied: "the measure of damages for non-delivery or repudiation by the seller is the difference between the market price at the time when the buyer learned of the breach and the contract price.

10. Thus, a seller who has delivered goods on credit to a buyer who becomes insolvent cannot use UCC § 2–609 to promote a "repudiation." Such a seller's remedy lies with UCC § 2–702. *See* § 160 *infra*.

11. McJunkin Corp. v. North Carolina Natural Gas Corp., 300 F.2d 794 (4th Cir. 1961), *cert. denied* 371 U.S. 830, 83 S.Ct. 43, 9 L.Ed.2d 68 (1962); Compania Engraw Commercial & Indus. S.A. v. Schenley Distillers Corp., 181 F.2d 876 (9th Cir. 1950); Continental Grain Co. v. Simpson Feed Co., 102 F. Supp. 354 (E.D.Ark.1951), *modified on appeal*, 199 F.2d 284 (8th Cir. 1952).

Pre-Code cases are collected in Comment, *A Suggested Revision of the Contract Doctrine of Anticipatory Repudiation*, 64 Yale L.J. 85, 91–99 (1954); Annot., 34 A.L.R. 114 (1925).

12. Segall v. Finlay, 245 N.Y. 61, 156 N.E. 97 (1927).

13. Renner Co. v. McNeff Bros., 102 F. 2d 664 (6th Cir.), *cert. denied* 308 U.S. 576, 60 S.Ct. 92, 84 L.Ed. 483 (1939); Goldsmith v. Stiglitz, 228 Mich. 255, 200 N.W. 252 (1924); Cron & Dehn, Inc. v. Chelan Packing Co., 158 Wash. 167, 290 P. 999 (1930).

. . . ." [14] Apparently, the buyer "learned of the breach" at the time he received the repudiation, and damages are set as of that moment. This solution would leave the court with the task of determining just when the repudiation occurred, but once that date was known the damages could be determined.

Trouble arises when this measure is read in light of other Code sections. Section 2–610 provides an option for the non-repudiating party:

> When either party repudiates the contract with respect to a performance not yet due the loss of which will substantially impair the value of the contract to the other, the aggrieved party may
>
> (a) for a commercially reasonable time await performance by the repudiating party; or
>
> (b) resort to any remedy for breach (Section 2–703 or Section 2–711), even though he has notified the repudiating party that he would await the latter's performance and has urged retraction; and
>
> (c) in either case suspend his own performance or proceed in accordance with the provisions of this Article on the seller's right to identify goods to the contract notwithstanding breach or to salvage unfinished goods (Section 2–704).

The aggrieved party may treat the repudiation as final, but he is not required to do so. He may wait for a commercially reasonable time to ascertain whether the repudiating party will change his mind and, during that time, may urge retraction without concern over a doctrine of election of remedies.[15] This privilege of waiting for a commercially reasonable time creates the conflict with the "learned of the breach" date set by section 2–713. If prices are rising (as they may well be when the seller has defaulted), it makes no sense to tell a buyer that he may await a seller's performance in spite of a repudiation but that, if he does and if the performance is not forthcoming, the buyer's damages will be measured at the time he learned of the repudiation. Such a rule would effectively destroy the Code-created privilege under section 2–610.

One way to solve this problem involves a play on words, but is one that finds respectable support in pre-Code law. Section 2–713 uses the language "learned of the *breach.*" Section 2–610 speaks of *repudiation.* Since "repudiation" is not defined by the Code, it can

---

14. UCC § 2–713(1). The buyer is also entitled to incidental and consequential damages less expenses saved. *Id.*

15. Aura Orchards v. A. Peltz & Sons, Inc., 27 Agri.Dec. 1546, 6 UCC Rep. 149 (U.S. Dept. of Agriculture 1968).

be treated as meaning the unilateral act of the seller which is not a breach until accepted by the buyer. Thus, the buyer learns of the breach (2–713) when he decides to accept it or when the commercially reasonable time (2–610) has expired.[16] This gives an odd twist to the word "learned," but since it reaches a sensible result, this interpretation could be accepted without too many difficulties.

The problem, however, is not that easily solved. Section 2–713 opens by referring to section 2–723. That section (2–723) begins with this subsection:

> If an action based on anticipatory repudiation comes to trial before the time for performance with respect to some or all of the goods, any damages based on market price (Section 2–708 or Section 2–713) shall be determined according to the price of such goods prevailing at the time when the aggrieved party learned of the repudiation.

"Learned of the breach" has become "learned of the repudiation." Therefore, the argument made to harmonize section 2–610 with section 2–713 becomes even more difficult to make. The drafters were not consciously differentiating a "repudiation" from a type of "breach."

The difficulties, however, are deeper than a distinction between words. Section 2–723 provides a time for determining market price when the case is tried before the date set for performance, and the date picked is the time the aggrieved party learned of the repudiation. Implied in this rule is the negative proposition: if the case is tried after the date set for performance, some other time is to be picked in measuring market price. Theoretically all kinds of dates are possible, but the only one which makes sense in the context of section 2–723 is that time set for performance.

Thus, it appears that the Code presents several answers to the question of when market price should be determined following repudiation by a seller.[17] Section 2–713 selects the date the buyer learned of the breach which may be changed by section 2–610 to mean the date the buyer accepted the repudiation, but which section 2–723 moves to the time of performance (except for the situation in which the trial arises prior to that date and, for sake of trial convenience, the time the buyer learned of the repudiation is used). In short, it looks as if the problem of measuring damages following a repudiation

16. Pre-Code law is discussed in 4 A. Corbin, Contracts § 981 (1951).

17. Whether the seller's "offer" to complete the contract at a higher price sets a limit on recovery is not considered by the Code. The problem is discussed in Lawrence v. Porter, 63 F. 62 (6th Cir. 1894), and generally in 5 A. Corbin, Contracts § 1043 (1964).

was either not considered by the drafters or was considered on different occasions and resolved differently each time it was considered.

Statutory history lends support to the first conclusion. Article 2 of the Code was based in large part upon an earlier draft of a Uniform Revised Sales Act. The 1944 version of that Act contained a section strikingly similar to the present version of the Code's section 2–713(1)—except no reference was made to repudiation.[18] The 1952 Code repeated the basic idea of the Uniform Revised Sales Act by providing: "The measure of damages for non-delivery is the difference between the price current at the time the buyer learned of the breach and the contract price. . . ." Again, no mention was made of a measure of recovery for repudiation. Selecting the time the buyer learned of the breach (rather than the date set for delivery) can be justified in a non-delivery case because in some shipment contracts the buyer does not *learn* of the failure to ship until after the goods fail to arrive. This may be several days after the date on which the seller was obligated to perform, and a recovery based on market price on the date the buyer learned of the breach allows these buyers additional time to measure their recovery.

In 1956 section 2–713 was amended in several respects. The cross-reference to 2–723 was added, "current" prices became "market" prices, and a later reference to saved expenses was clarified. Additionally, and without explanation, the words "or repudiation by the seller" were added to section 2–713.[19] There is no indication in the stated reasons for this addition that the drafters considered how section 2–713 would fit within the other Code sections on repudiation.

The result, therefore, is that time for measuring damages on repudiation by the seller is a problem which was not adequately dealt with by the drafters of the Code. Amendments are needed to correct this situation. Until the amendments are proposed and adopted, the best course of action for a buyer like the one in Case #3 is to cover and proceed under section 2–712 for his damages. Such a buyer must act without "unreasonable delay," but he need not make his cover contract the very moment he learned of the breach. His attempts to get the seller to retract and the time necessary to go into the market to purchase substitute goods will affect the reasonableness of the buyer's delay in covering. For those cases in which the buyer cannot or

---

18. "The measure of damages for non-delivery is the difference between the contract price and the price current at the time the buyer learned of the breach and at the place for tender together with any incidental and consequential damages under Section 117 but less any expense saved in conse-

quence of the seller's breach." Uniform Revised Sales Act § 115 (1944 draft).

19. 1956 Recommendations of the Editorial Board for the Uniform Commercial Code 79–80.

does not cover, some solution must be provided by courts when the buyer seeks damages in a constantly rising market. That solution cannot rest on precise Code language; it must be sought in Code policies. The policies which seem controlling here are:

1. The privilege afforded by section 2–610 to an aggrieved party to wait a commercially reasonable time to learn whether the repudiating party will retract his repudiation.

2. The privilege given a buyer to cover and to have his section 2–712 damages computed as of the date of cover. This cover contract need not be made immediately upon the buyer's learning of the breach; it is sufficient if it is made without an unreasonable delay.

3. The stated purpose of the drafters to make the section 2–713 recovery a complete alternative to cover.

4. The general policy of making results under the Code turn on commercial practices and of not forcing surprising results on the parties to a contract for the sale of goods.

The result of these policies would measure the buyer's damages against a repudiating seller not at the moment that the buyer learned of the breach or the repudiation, but at such reasonable time thereafter as the buyer could in good faith have entered into a reasonable contract to purchase substitute goods. Such a measure would provide a section 2–713 remedy which was "completely alternative to cover"—as suggested by the Comments.[20]

§ 150.　Damages When Goods are Retained

According to its title, section 2–714 provides the buyer's measure of recovery for his seller's breach in regard to goods which have been accepted by the buyer. The evident scheme of the Code's damage remedies for a buyer is this: sections 2–711, 2–712, and 2–713 provide the measure of damages when the seller has defaulted and the buyer either did not receive the goods or, having received them, rightfully returned them to the seller; section 2–714 provides the measure of recovery when the seller has defaulted but the buyer has retained the goods. The primary reason for distinguishing between these two types of cases is that when the buyer returns the goods (or never receives them) he is entitled to a return of all of the purchase price which he paid and, in addition, compensation for the loss of his expectation interest.[21] On the other hand, when the buyer has retained

---

20. UCC § 2–713, Comment 5. For a suggestion as to a different time-line for measuring damages through a tort theory, see Peters, *Remedies for Breach of Contracts Relating to the Sale of Goods Under the Uniform Com-* *mercial Code: A Roadmap for Article Two*, 73 Yale L.J. 199, 261–63 (1963). *See also* UCC § 2–721.

21. The interests of a party to a sales contract are discussed in § 138 *supra*.

defective goods, any monetary recovery must reflect the fact that the buyer's assets have been increased—and the seller's decreased—by the value of the retained goods.

An understanding of the Code's scheme as to damages is important because the scope language of the two branches of section 2–714 does not state, with precision, the application of section 2–714. Subsection (1) deals with the measure of recovery for a non-conformity in tender and triggers its application with this introductory phrase: "Where the buyer has accepted goods and given notification . . . ." This subsection applies when the goods have been accepted *and retained* (even though the words, "and retained," are not contained in section 2–714(1)), with section 2–711 providing the measure of recovery when the goods have been accepted but when that acceptance has been justifiably revoked.[22] Subsection (2) has no scope language but begins by stating that the "measure of damages for breach of warranty is . . . ." The subsection (2) formula—value difference—was not meant to be applied when conforming goods were never delivered, nor was it meant to be applied when non-conforming goods were delivered but rightfully returned to the seller. The intended scope of section 2–714 is more accurately stated in a Comment than it is in the text of the Code: "This section deals with the remedies available to the buyer after the goods have been accepted and the time for revocation of acceptance has gone by."[23]

There are two damage formulas set out in section 2–714:

1. When there is any non-conformity of tender, the buyer may recover "the loss resulting in the ordinary course of events from the seller's breach as determined in any manner which is reasonable."[24]

2. When there has been a breach of warranty the measure of damages is "the difference at the time and place of acceptance between the value of the goods accepted and the value they would have had if they had been as warranted, unless special circumstances show proximate damages of a different amount."[25]

In addition and in "a proper case any incidental and consequential damages under the next section may also be recovered."[26] Thus, a

---

22. Concern over the precise application of UCC § 2–714(1) may be academic only because the damage formula of that subsection is so broad that it can reflect whether the buyer has the goods or whether they have been returned to the seller.

23. UCC § 2–714, Comment 1.

24. UCC § 2–714(1).

25. UCC § 2–714(2).

26. UCC § 2–714(3). This reference to UCC § 2–715 can be used in product liability cases (where the non-conforming goods cause personal injuries) to recover damages beyond the value decrease in the goods. § 153 *infra*.

buyer "in a proper case" may recover both incidental and consequential damages as well as damages under section 2–714(1) or under section 2–714(2).

There is some difficulty in determining what types of defaults are covered by 2–714(1). The Code language is "any non-conformity of tender." This could be read to mean any non-conformity in the mechanics of tender but not in the quality of goods delivered. For example, if conforming goods are delivered a day late, there has been a non-conformity in the tender.[27] Likewise, in a shipment contract the failure to obtain and promptly to deliver necessary documents is a non-conforming tender even if the conforming goods arrive on the contract date.[28] Subsection (1) covers these cases but is it limited to these types of defaults? The Comments indicate that it is not so limited but also includes deliveries of non-conforming goods.[29] This is the preferable reading of section 2–714(1). Two bases can be suggested to support an expanded reading of section 2–714(1)—a reading which brings breach of warranty cases within its scope. First, the definition of "tender" includes the requirement that the goods be conforming;[30] thus, a tender is non-conforming when either the quality of the goods or the mechanics of their delivery fails to conform to the contract. Second, and more important, the formula of section 2–714(1) is the broad catch-all measure of recovery which is needed to make any code work; it can be used to resolve the odd cases which do not fit within the usual damage patterns.

Subsection (2) of section 2–714, on the other hand, states the usual measure of damages following a breach of warranty where the buyer has retained the delivered goods: value of the goods if they would have been as warranted less the value of the goods which were accepted. To the extent that the delivered goods are worth less than conforming goods would have been worth, the buyer is allowed damages to compensate him for this loss in value.[31] The following examples illustrate the application of this formula:

Case # 1. Seller sold Buyer an automobile warranting that it was "in all respects as good as new." The purchase price of $2,650

---

27. UCC § 2–503(1); §§ 96, 102 *supra.*

28. UCC § 2–504(b); § 98 *supra.*

29. UCC § 2–714, Comment 2.

30. UCC § 2–503(1).

31. City Mach. & Mfg. Co. v. A. & A. Machinery Corp., 4 UCC Rep. 461 (U. S.Dist.Ct. E.D.N.Y.1967); Klein v. Asgrow Seed Co., 246 Cal.App.2d 87, 54 Cal.Rptr. 609 (1966) (goods involved were seeds and value difference was measured by product of seeds; UCC § 2–715 could have been used to reach same result); Cox Motor Car Co. v. Castle, 402 S.W.2d 429 (Ky.1966); Santor v. A & M Karagheusian, Inc., 44 N.J. 52, 207 A.2d 305 (1965); Babcock Poultry Farm, Inc. v. Shook, 204 Pa.Super. 141, 203 A.2d 399 (1964) (goods were chickens; warranty related to egg production; value difference included decreased egg production).

was paid in full. Buyer discovered that the automobile had been in a wreck before it was sold to him and, even though repaired, was not "as good as new." Had the automobile been in the conditioned warranted, it would have had a value of $2,650, but in its delivered condition it had a value of $2,000.[32] The section 2–714(2) formula produces a damage recovery in the amount of $650 [33]—the same result reached in pre-Code cases.[34] Had Buyer discovered the breach of warranty after he had accepted the goods but before he paid the price, Buyer would be liable for the entire price [35] but could deduct damages from the amount due.[36]

Case # 2. Assume the facts of Case #1 except that the automobile would have been worth $3,000 if it had been in the condition warranted but was worth only $2,350 as delivered. In Case #2 Buyer had a profitable contract. Had Seller delivered conforming goods, Buyer's assets would have been increased $350 since he would have acquired goods worth that much more than the price he was obligated to pay. The section 2–714(2) measure of recovery remains at $650 (value of conforming goods, $3,000, minus the value of the goods accepted, $2,350), and Buyer has paid a net amount of $2,000 for goods which are worth $2,350. His $350 expectation interest has properly been protected by section 2–714(2).[37]

Case # 3. Assume the facts of Case #1 except that the automobile would have been worth only $2,300 if it had been in the condition warranted but was worth $1,650 as delivered. In Case #3 Seller had a profitable contract. Had Seller delivered conforming goods, Seller's assets would have been increased $350 since he would have acquired that much more in cash than he was obligated to transfer in goods. The section 2–714(2) measure of recovery remains at $650 ($2,300 minus $1,650), and Seller has received $2,000 for goods which

---

32. Market price and market value are discussed in § 148 *supra* footnote 92. Value need not be proved with mathematical certainty. L. A. Green Seed Co. v. Williams, 246 Ark. 454, 438 S.W. 2d 717 (1969) (consequential damages). Published price quotations are evidence of value. Jerome Kantro Co. v. Summers Bros., Inc., 27 Agri.Dec. 129, 5 UCC Rep. 135 (U.S.Dept. of Agriculture, 1968). Cost of repair is evidence of decrease in value. Willred Co. v. Westmoreland Metal Mfg. Co., 200 F.Supp. 59 (E.D.Pa.1961) (for an earlier opinion, see 200 F.Supp. 55 (E. D.Pa.1959)).

33. Union Motors, Inc. v. Phillips, 241 Ark. 857, 410 S.W.2d 747 (1967).

34. Bracker v. American Nat'l Food, Inc., 133 Cal.App.2d 338, 284 P.2d 163 (1955); Sanchotena v. Tower Co., 74 Idaho 541, 264 P.2d 1021 (1953); Truesdale v. Friedman, 270 Minn. 109, 132 N.W.2d 854 (1965). Cases are collected in 3 S. Williston Sales § 613 (rev. ed. 1948).

The giving of appropriate notice is a condition to any of the buyer's remedies. UCC § 2–607(3) (a); §§ 142, 145 *supra*.

35. UCC § 2–607(1).

36. UCC § 2–717.

37. § 138 *supra*.

are worth $1,650. Now the expectation interest of Seller has been protected by section 2–714(2).

Protection of a seller's expectation interest in a situation like that presented in Case #3 was probably an oversight by the drafters. A seller who is in substantial default of his promise to deliver conforming goods ought not be allowed compensation for any "goodness" of the bargain which he made; at the most he merits protection only to the extent of the value which his defective performance has benefited the buyer.[38] In Case #3 the seller's recovery should be limited to $1,650 —the value of the goods accepted and retained by the non-defaulting buyer. Whether courts will reach this result by use of other portions of the Code [39] or by judicial legislation remains to be seen—but such a result ought to be reached by some method. Restitution remedies were generally overlooked by the drafters of the Code and a recognition of this fact should prevent courts from concluding that they are bound by the statutory damage formulas when those formulas produce inequitable results.

In addition to his section 2–714 damages the buyer is also entitled to lost profits and to damages for injuries to person or property caused by the defective goods, providing the conditions of section 2–715 are met.[40] Damages for breach of the warranty of title are considered elsewhere in this text.[41]

§ 151.　Additional Recovery—Justification

One of the goals of contractual remedies is that of compensation— putting the aggrieved party in the same financial position he would have occupied had the contract been performed.[42] This goal is reflect-

---

38. 5A A. Corbin, Contracts § 1124 (1964) (stating principle when defaulter is plaintiff, but results ought not turn on whether the defaulter was able to hide the breach long enough to be paid —thus making him a defendant in the action).

39. Perhaps the "special circumstances" language of UCC § 2–714(2) can be used. Other sections which may aid the buyer are UCC §§ 1–106 and 2–714(1). The difficulty is that the Code begins by giving the seller *contract price* for goods accepted, UCC § 2–607 (1), and deducts damages from the contract price, UCC § 2–717. This works well in the normal seller-default cases (Cases #1 and #2 in the text), but not for the odd case, Case #3). Until judicial opinions interpret the Code, Case #3 buyers should con-

sider cancelling and asking for a return of the entire purchase price, enforcing their security interest in he goods if the price is not returned. UCC § 2–711; § 146 *supra*; § 157 *infra*.

40. §§ 151–53 *infra*. Some courts have used the "special circumstances" language of UCC § 2–714(2) to support the same result as would be reached under UCC § 2–715. Keystone Diesel Engine Co. v. Irwin, 411 Pa. 222, 191 A. 2d 376 (1963). Other courts have used the language of UCC § 2–714(1) to support a recovery of lost profits. Seely v. White Motor Co., 63 Cal.2d 9, 45 Cal.Rptr. 17, 403 P.2d 145 (1965).

41. § 61 *supra*.

42. UCC § 1–106.

ed in many of the damage formulas already discussed. In a market in which a buyer can readily make a substitute purchase, a recovery of the cost of cover less any unpaid portion of the purchase price will place the buyer in the same financial position as if the contract had been performed by the seller—that is, the buyer will have obtained the needed goods at a net price equal to the price he agreed to pay the seller.[43] In those instances in which the buyer does not cover, compensation will normally be obtained by awarding damages measured by the market price of the promised goods less the unpaid contract price [44] (when the buyer does not have the goods) or the difference between the value of the goods as warranted and the value of the goods as accepted [45] (when the buyer retains the defective goods).

There are, however, situations in which these formulas will not compensate the aggrieved buyer for his losses. An example is the product liability case.[46] When the non-conformity in the goods has caused personal injury or property damage, each of the above formulas falls short of making the buyer "whole." The buyer's measure of damages ought to take account not only of the decreased value of the defective goods delivered but also of the injuries proximately caused by the seller's default. Another example can be found in those cases in which the buyer's contract with the seller is but one fact in a chain of events which the buyer believed would lead him to an expected profit. When the seller fails to deliver the contracted-for goods and the buyer is unable to obtain substitute goods from another source, the buyer will have lost his anticipated profits from collateral transactions which he would have entered into had the goods been delivered. The buyer's measure of damages ought to take account of these collateral losses if he is to be compensated. Finally, there are those situations in which the seller has delivered non-conforming goods which do not cause personal injury or property damage and which, although returned to the seller, can be replaced by the buyer so that the buyer does not suffer any collateral losses. Even so, the buyer may have incurred expenses in caring for those goods during the time they were in his possession, and the buyer's measure of damages ought to take account of these expenses.

The Code contains two sections which give flexibility to monetary recoveries. The first is section 2–714(1) which expresses an extremely broad damage formula ("the loss resulting in the ordinary course of events from the seller's breach as determined in any manner which

---

43. § 147 *supra.*

44. §§ 148–49 *supra*

45. § 150 *supra.*

46. The warranty problems in product liability cases are discussed in §§ 54–55, 63–92 *supra.*

is reasonable") and is triggered by an equally ambiguous event ("any non-conformity of tender"). Almost any default can be brought within this event and any of the traditional damage recoveries can be justified under the stated formula. There are, however, two difficulties with using this section to shape monetary recoveries. First, its breadth gives no direction as to how Code damages should be measured. Second, this section is applicable only when goods have been accepted and retained; thus it is of no aid to the buyer where there has been a repudiation, a failure to deliver, a rightful rejection, or justifiable revocation of acceptance.[47]

The section more directly applicable is section 2–715. That section is incorporated by reference into cover damages, damages for non-delivery or repudiation, damages for breach in regard to accepted goods, and should be considered as impliedly incorporated into recoveries of the purchase price.[48] Section 2–715 provides for recovery, in a proper case, of the buyer's incidental and consequential damages. It is the "safety valve" for buyer's recoveries—the section which brings sufficient flexibility into the Code so that a court can tailor the measure of damages to fit the facts of individual cases. The following two sections of this text consider the application of section 2–715 to buyer's monetary recoveries.

§ 152.   Additional Recovery—Incidental Damages

Section 2–715(1) provides:

> Incidental damages resulting from the seller's breach include expenses reasonably incurred in inspection, receipt, transportation and care and custody of goods rightfully rejected, any commercially reasonable charges, expenses or commissions in connection with effecting cover and any other reasonable expense incident to the delay or other breach.

The damages allowed by this subsection can be grouped roughly under the heading of reliance losses.[49] In reliance on the contract the buyer may have incurred certain expenses in relation to the goods; in reliance on the seller's default the buyer may have incurred other

---

47. § 150 *supra*.

48. UCC §§ 2–712, 2–713, and 2–714 refer to UCC § 2–715 in substantially similar language. However, none of these Code sections allows the buyer to recover the purchase price paid. This is covered in UCC § 2–711(1)— which contains no reference to UCC § 2–715. This, however, was an oversight and has not prevented courts from granting such recovery. Grandi v. LeSage, 74 N.M. 799, 399 P.2d 285 (1965). This result can be justified on the grounds of common sense or by holding that one of the damage sections was used to refer to UCC § 2–715, but that the measure of recovery under that section was zero.

49. § 138 *supra*.

expenses in an attempt to lessen the losses which might otherwise have accrued. These expenses may be recovered from the seller—in addition to the buyer's other damages—in those situations in which such a recovery is necessary to compensate the buyer for his losses.[50] Thus, a buyer of an airplane who revoked his acceptance because of a breach of warranty may recover all payments which he made on the purchase price and, in addition, funds spent to repair and preserve the airplane.[51] Likewise, a buyer of a racehorse who revoked acceptance because the horse did not conform to the seller's warranties may recover the purchase price paid and, in addition, the cost of caring for and feeding the horse from the date the horse was delivered to the buyer until the date the horse was returned to the seller.[52] Reimbursement for these expenses was necessary to compensate the buyer for his losses; otherwise the buyer would have been required to bear the costs of maintaining and caring for the goods even though the seller's default prevented him from obtaining the promised performance from the seller.

In awarding incidental damages care must be taken not to overcompensate the buyer. A buyer is often willing to incur certain expenses to obtain the seller's performance. To the extent that the buyer receives the performance or its equivalent in money, he is not also entitled to an additional award for the expenses which he incurred. Awarding this additional sum would place the buyer in a better financial position than he would have enjoyed had the contract been performed by the seller.[53] This principle can be illustrated by the following cases:

Case # 1. A Kentucky buyer ordered ten tank cars of oil from a Texas seller at a specified price per gallon, F.O.B. seller's Texas refinery, the buyer to send its tank cars to pick up the oil. The buyer sent its tank cars to the Texas refinery at a cost of $900, only to be told that the seller would not deliver the oil. The price of oil had increased so that its market price at the time and place of delivery

---

50. The language of UCC § 2–715(1) may create some difficulties. The first portion appears to be limited to rightful rejection, eliminating coverage of incidental damages for cases of non-delivery, repudiation, justifiable revocation of acceptance, and acceptance and retention of non-conforming goods. See, however, UCC §§ 2–712, 2–713, and 2–714(3), UCC § 2–715, Comment 1. The Comment can be supported by the "other reasonable expense incident to delay or breach" language of UCC § 2–715(1). There is no reason why, in a proper case, at-

torney fees should not be recoverable. Gaito v. Hoffman, 5 UCC Rep. 1056 (N.Y.Sup.Ct.1968) (title warranty).

51. Lanners v. Whitney, 247 Or. 223, 428 P.2d 398 (1967) (the court talked in terms of rescission, a term not used by the Code in describing the buyer's courses of action following a default by his seller).

52. Grandi v. LeSage, 74 N.M. 799, 399 P.2d 285 (1965).

53. *See* UCC § 1–106.

exceeded the contract price by $2,500 for the quantity involved in the contract. The buyer can recover the $2,500 under principles already discussed in this text. Is the buyer also entitled to the $900 spent in reliance on the contract?

The specific Code language on which the buyer would rely comes from section 2–715(1): the $900 expense either resulted from the seller's breach or was a "reasonable expense incident to the . . . breach." Even if it is conceded that the $900 was a reasonable amount for the expense involved, the buyer's attempt to collect this sum in addition to the $2,500 should fail. The expense did not *result* from nor was it *incident* to the *breach*. The buyer was willing to spend the $900 to get the oil and would have had to deduct the $900 from any gains which might have been received under the contract. Since the damage formula has given the buyer the equivalent of performance (damages based upon the assumption that other oil could have been obtained at the time and place of delivery), the buyer is not entitled to be placed in a better financial position than performance would have put him.[54] Indeed, had the seller repudiated before the tank cars were sent to Texas, the buyer might have been able to purchase substitute oil at a closer location and have saved a portion of the $900. If so, the expenses saved should be deducted from the buyer's recovery.[55] It is only when the expenses are incident to the *breach* that they are recoverable. Thus, if oil had not been available near the point of delivery and if the buyer had been compelled to pay an added $250 to acquire the oil, this $250 would be recoverable either under section 2–715(1) or as a part of the market price of oil at the time and place the buyer learned of the breach (see section 2–723(2)).

There are situations in which the buyer is willing to forgo damages based upon protection of his expectation interest and recover damages based only upon his reliance interest. In terms of Case #1 the buyer would be arguing that he wants only the $900 spent for transportation of the tank cars and is giving up any claim for the $2,-500 lost profits. There is no reason why such a buyer should not be allowed to recover less than the total which the law would allow him. The $2,500 was a combination of $900 for reliance expenses and $1,-600 for net profits lost. If the buyer is willing to take only the lesser sum, he should be able to do so despite the emphasis of section 2–715 (1) on "breach." When the reliance expense is separated for recovery,

---

54. *See* Globe Ref. Co. v. Landa Cotton Oil Co., 190 U.S. 540, 23 S.Ct. 754, 47 L.Ed. 1171 (1903). *Accord:* Smith v. Onyx Oil & Chemical Co., 218 F.2d 104 (3d Cir. 1955). Where the charges are in excess of those which the buyer would have had to pay except for the default, those charges are recoverable. Stamford Extract Mfg. Co. v. Oakes Mfg. Co., 9 F.2d 301 (2d Cir. 1925).

55. UCC §§ 2–712, 2–713; 5 A. Corbin, Contracts § 1038 (1964).

its loss becomes as much an incident of the breach as when it was a part of the larger lost profits. All situations are not so clear, however. Consider:

Case # 2. During World War II a buyer agreed to purchase four rubber refining machines. Delivery of two of these machines was scheduled for a date which turned out to be near the end of that war. In reliance on the contract the buyer remodelled its factory at a cost of $3,000. When the seller defaulted the buyer sought to recover from the seller the cost of the remodelling, which was now worthless to the buyer.[56] The buyer was probably willing to forgo any claim for lost profits because the end of the war made it difficult to prove with certainty that any profits would have been made from rubber refiners.

The $3,000 expenditure in Case #2 is different in its nature from the sums spent to repair the airplane or to care for the racehorse. In the latter instances, when the goods were returned, the seller obtained some benefit from the buyer's prior expenditures; however, the seller of the refiners received no benefit from the remodelling of the buyer's factory. Thus, the buyer's recovery in Case #2 must rest solely on compensation for the buyer's losses with no element of restitution for the seller's gains.[57]

Did the buyer suffer a loss when the refiners were not delivered as promised? It did only if its overall gains from the use of the refiners would have produced a net profit; it did not if the use of the refiners would have produced a net loss to the business. The $3,000 spent to remodel the factory is but one item which would have gone into a determination of whether the contract would have been a profitable one. The court concluded that the buyer could recover the $3,000 "subject to the Seller's privilege to deduct from that amount any sum which upon a further hearing it can prove would have been the Buyer's loss upon the contract, had the 'refiners' been delivered on or before May 1st, 1945." [58] Such a limit is not placed on a recovery of the restitution interest.[59]

Therefore, the type of incidental damages involved in a particular case must be carefully analyzed before the extent of its protection can be safely predicted. The Code is clear that the incidental damage must *result* from or be an *incident to* the seller's default. This language should bring into the Code decisions those pre-Code cases which have dealt with recoveries now grouped under section 2–715(1).

---

56. L. Albert & Son v. Armstrong Rubber Co., **178** F.2d 182 (2d Cir. 1949).

57. Fuller and Perdue, *The Reliance Interest in Contract Damages*, 46 Yale L.J. 52, 53–55 (1936). The article is concluded in 46 Yale L.J. 373 (1937).

58. L. Albert & Son v. Armstrong Rubber Co., **178** F.2d 182, 191 (2d Cir. 1948).

59. § 146 *supra*.

§ 153.   Additional Recovery—Consequential Damages

Section 2–715(2) provides:

> Consequential damages resulting from the seller's breach include

> (a) any loss resulting from general or particular requirements and needs of which the seller at the time of contracting had reason to know and which could not reasonably be prevented by cover or otherwise; and

> (b) injury to person or property proximately resulting from any breach of warranty.

The damages allowed by subsection (a) are normally considered as being contractual in their nature; those allowed by subsection (b), as tortious in nature.

CONTRACT DAMAGES

The ideas underlying the damages allowed by section 2–715(2)(a) had their Anglo-American origins in the famous case of *Hadley v. Baxendale*.[60] In granting a new trial to the defendant on the ground that the trial judge had misdirected the jury on the question of damages, Baron Alderson stated:

> Now we think the proper rule in such a case as the present is this:—Where two parties have made a contract which one of them has broken, the damages which the other party ought to receive in respect of such breach of contract should be such as may fairly and reasonably be considered either arising naturally, i.e., according to the usual course of things, from such breach of contract itself, or such as may reasonably be supposed to have been in the contemplation of both parties, at the time they made the contract, as the probable result of the breach of it.[61]

Writers have disagreed as to whether Baron Alderson stated one rule of damages or whether he stated two (or even three) rules; however, the appraisal of the above statement which is probably the most accurate is that it states no rule at all. In one sense, all damages are "natural" once all the facts are known. A logical chain of causation can be linked between the breach and the loss if a court wants to hold the defaulting party liable for the losses suffered, or the chain can be broken if the court wants to limit recovery. In another sense, no damages are "natural" because whether the damages *arose* from a breach of contract is not an event which can be tested by the laws of nature,

---

60. 9 Ex. 341, 156 Eng.Rep. 145 (1854).   61. *Id.* at 354, 156 Eng.Rep. at 151.

the physical order of the universe, or demonstrable rules of cause and effect. Many events combined into a factual pattern—one of these events was the loss which the aggrieved party suffered and another was the default in the promised performance. How can it be determined whether the damages arose out of the *breach* as contrasted with any of the other events involved?[62] Further, as to the second part of Baron Alderson's test, most parties probably contemplate performance, not breach, when they enter into contracts and, when they do contemplate breach and say something about the measure of recovery of default, they raise difficult questions of distinguishing liquidated damages clauses from penalties. Thus, the search for contemplated damages can usually produce only fiction for an answer.[63]

The primary concern of the court in *Hadley v. Baxendale* was not that of stating an immutable rule of damages, but of obtaining control over juries in their determination of damages. Only seven years earlier that same court had approved an award against the same carrier as was involved in *Hadley* on the basis that it was up to the jury, not the judges, to decide which expenses were "reasonable."[64] *Hadley* changed this approach: no longer were jurors to be "chancellors"[65] in regard to damages arising out of breach of contract. Their awards were to be measured against what the judges thought was a fair recovery under the facts presented in court. The "normal" measure of recovery (for example, market price minus unpaid contract price) was always considered fair and was described by Baron Alderson as damages which arose "naturally." Recovery beyond the amounts which courts believe to be normal was fair only if the defaulter should have been alerted, at the time of contracting, to the particular needs of the aggrieved party. Supposedly, the defaulter could have protected himself by a special term in the agreement; not having done so, he receives what he deserves when required to pay the special and "contemplated" damages.

Notice, however, that Baron Alderson did not require the parties to bargain about the damages. Indeed, *Hadley v. Baxendale* does not even require that the damages, to be recoverable, must either (1) have

---

62. Cohen, *Field Theory and Judicial Logic*, 59 Yale L.J. 238, 251–52 (1950). Other excellent discussions include B. Cardozo, Paradoxes of Legal Science 83–85 (1928); J. Wigmore, The Science of Judicial Proof 236–39 (3d ed. 1937).

63. Kerr Steamship Co. v. Radio Corp. of Am., 245 N.Y. 284, 157 N.E. 140 (1927).

64. Black v. Baxendale, 1 Ex. 410, 154 Eng.Rep. 174 (1847). The court in Hadley v. Baxendale was so interested in gaining control over jury verdicts that it may have ignored the facts of the case in order to state its conclusion. Victoria Laundry (Windsor) Ltd. v. Newman Indus. Ltd., [1949] 2 K.B. 528, 537 (C.A.).

65. Hixt v. Goats, 1 Rolle 257, 81 Eng. Rep. 472 (K.B.1615).

in fact arisen naturally or (2) have in fact been in the contemplation of the parties. It is sufficient if the damages were either (1) such "as may fairly and reasonably be considered" as arising naturally or (2) such "as may reasonably be supposed" to have been in the contemplation of the parties. Special damages (consequential damages under the Code) need not be bargained about and agreed upon before they are recoverable.

Nevertheless, some courts have misread *Hadley v. Baxendale* as requiring an agreement, express or implied, concerning special damages as a condition upon the right of the aggrieved party to collect those damages.[66] The Code rejects this reading of *Hadley*. The statutory language requires only that the seller have reason to know at the time of contracting of the general or particular requirements and needs of the buyer. Two ideas here are important. First, the fact that the seller did not have actual knowledge of these requirements is not controlling. The test is one of reason to know—which returns to the above analysis of *Hadley*. Second, the Code does not require that the seller have reason to know the items of damage claimed by the buyer or that the total loss would be as large as is now proved. The test is less exacting. Recovery of consequential damages turns on the seller's reason to know the facts of the buyer's general or particular requirements and needs.[67] If the seller has reason to know of these facts at the time of contracting (not the time of breach), the buyer may recover consequential damages without concern over proving an implied agreement by the seller to pay these damages in the event of his default.[68]

The result of these Code sections is this: a buyer can recover his damages under sections 2–711 through 2–714 without worrying about the seller's reason to know about why the buyer needed the goods; he

---

66. Pre-Code cases include Globe Ref. Co. v. Landa Cotton Oil Co., 190 U.S. 540, 23 S.Ct. 754, 47 L.Ed. 1171 (1903); Lamkins v. International Harvester Co., 207 Ark. 637, 182 S.W.2d 203 (1944); California Press Mfg. Co. v. Stafford Packing Co., 192 Cal. 479, 221 P. 345 (1923); Sward v. Nash, 230 Minn. 100, 40 N.W.2d 828 (1950). One Code case misreads UCC § 2–715(2) (a) by requiring contemplation of the claim for lost profits. Keystone Diesel Engine Co. v. Irwin, 411 Pa. 222, 191 A. 2d 376 (1963).

67. Neville Chem. Co. v. Union Carbide Corp., 294 F.Supp. 649 (W.D.Pa.1968), *aff'd* 422 F.2d 1205 (3d Cir. 1970); Marion Power Shovel Co. v. Huntsman, 246 Ark. 149, 437 S.W.2d

784 (1969) (court found evidence did not support conclusion that seller had reason to know buyer's needs). When the damages suffered far exceeded the consideration received by the defaulting party, pre-Code courts tended to refuse an award of special damages even though the defaulter had knowledge of some facts which might have put a reasonable person on notice. Winslow Elevator & Mach. Co. v. Hoffman, 107 Md. 621, 69 A. 394 (1908); Rochester Lantern Co. v. Stiles & Parker Press Co., 135 N.Y. 209, 31 N.E. 1018 (1892). This may explain Keystone Diesel Engine Co. v. Irwin, 411 Pa. 222, 191 A.2d 376 (1963), referred to in note 66 *supra*.

68. UCC § 2–715, Comment 2.

may recover additional damages by showing that the seller defaulted, that further loss did occur from the default, that the seller had reason to know the buyer's need for the goods, and that the loss could not have been prevented by cover or otherwise. This last requirement protects the seller from the buyer's shifting losses which arose out of avoidable consequences. For example, suppose a buyer is claiming consequential damages in the form of lost profits—that is, had the seller delivered conforming goods, the buyer would have resold them at a substantial gain but, since the delivered goods were non-conforming, the buyer lost the profits he would have made on the resale. Those profits are not recoverable (even though the seller had the requisite reason to know) if the buyer could have made a substitute contract with another source of supply and thus have obtained the necessary goods to comply with his resale contract. The "or otherwise" language of section 2–715(2)(a) suggests that there may be other ways by which the buyer could have avoided his consequential losses.[69] If so, the consequential damages are not recoverable even though suffered.

Courts are properly reading into section 2–715 other pre-Code damage requirements. Consequential damages cannot be left to speculation but must be shown with the same certainty as any other element in the buyer's cause of action.[70] However, the more certain that the court is that the seller's breach caused some consequential loss the less certain must be the proof of the extent of the loss.[71] The amount which the buyer paid his subpurchaser in damages for failure to deliver (following the seller's default) is evidence of the buyer's loss —but not conclusive evidence.[72]

---

69. An offer by the seller to cure the defect could be such a case. The buyer's refusal of the offer may prevent his recovery of consequential damages. Robertson Mfg. Co. v. Jefferson Tile Co., 5 UCC Rep. 119 (N.Y. Sup.Ct.1968).

70. Harry Rubin & Sons, Inc. v. Consolidated Pipe Co., 396 Pa. 506, 153 A.2d 472 (1959). Mathematical accuracy is not required. UCC § 1–106, Comment 1. Pre-Code cases include Story Parchment Co. v. Paterson, 282 U.S. 555, 51 S.Ct. 248, 75 L.Ed. 544 (1931); Jonesboro Coca-Cola Bottling Co. v. Young, 198 Ark. 1032, 132 S.W. 2d 382 (1939); Maslow Cooperage Corp. v. Weeks Pickle Co., 270 Wis. 179, 70 N.W.2d 577 (1955).

71. Neville Chem. Co. v. Union Carbide Corp., 294 F.Supp. 649 (W.D.Pa.1968),

aff'd 422 F.2d 1205 (3d Cir. 1970); Friedman v. Parkway Baking Co., 147 Pa.Super. 552, 24 A.2d 157 (1942). Pre-Code cases relaxed the standard of proof of damages where uncertainty resulted from the defendant's wrong. Zinn v. Ex-Cell-O Corp., 24 Cal.2d 290, 149 P.2d 177 (1944) (lost profit affecting value of stock). Air Technology Corp. v. General Elec. Co., 347 Mass. 613, 199 N.E.2d 538 (1964) (loss of business opportunity). This idea should be applicable to Code cases. See generally 5 A. Corbin, Contracts §§ 1020–26 (1964).

72. Butane Products Corp. v. Empire Advertising Service, Inc., 5 UCC Rep. 361 (Mass.App.Div.1967). For the possibility of recovering interest on money withheld by subpurchasers because of seller's default, see Willred Co. v. Westmoreland Metal Mfg. Co.,

Tort Damages

Consequential damages also include injury to the person or property resulting from any breach of warranty. The primary use of this subsection will be in connection with cases involving the emerging doctrines of product liability. Those cases have already been discussed in detail and that discussion will not be repeated at this point in the text.[73]

The only damage requirement is that the injury *proximately* result from the default. Like the statement of foreseeability in *Hadley v. Baxendale,* this requirement falls short of stating a rule of mechanical application. The task of distinguishing the proximate from the remote effects of a breach can be decided only on a case-by-case basis. Definitions of proximateness have been attempted, the most common being that a proximate cause is that cause which, in the natural and continuous sequence, unbroken by any efficient intervening cause, produced the injury, and without which the injury would not have occurred.[74] Through such policy-filled words as "natural," "unbroken," "efficient," and "produces" this statement becomes nothing more than a guide by which courts can limit or expand damages depending on the facts of the case under consideration. Perhaps a more honest way of talking about a proximate cause is to rename it as a "legal" cause which must be combined with cause in fact before recovery is allowed for ensuing injuries. The idea of "legal" cause eliminates any notion that a mechanical test is involved and emphasizes that the problem is one of policy.[75] Ought the seller who defaulted in his warranty be held liable to the buyer (or some third person) for the injuries suffered?

Parties are free to bargain about and agree to the damages recoverable in event of a breach of their contract, and courts will at-

200 F.Supp. 59 (E.D.Pa.1961) (for an earlier opinion, see 200 F.Supp. 55 (E.D.Pa.1955)).

73. §§ 54–55, 63–92 *supra.* For a case applying UCC § 2–715(2) (b) to breach of warranty damage problems, see Kassab v. Central Soya, 432 Pa. 217, 246 A.2d 848 (1968) (animal food). *See also* Martel v. Duffy-Mott Corp., 15 Mich.App. 67, 166 N.W.2d 541 (1968) (food); Gardiner v. Philadelphia Gas Works, 413 Pa. 415, 197 A.2d 612 (1964) (personal injury from sale of gas).

74. *E. g.,* Roller v. Independent Silo Co., 242 Iowa 1277, 49 N.W.2d 838 (1951); Michalka v. Great Northern Paper Co., 151 Me. 98, 116 A.2d 139 (1955); Burr v. Clark, 30 Wash.2d 149, 190 P.2d 769 (1948). The test differs from the "contemplation of the parties" test under UCC § 2–715(2) (a) in that a defendant can be liable for unforeseen consequences which result in injury to person or property. Mahoney v. Beatman, 110 Conn. 184, 147 A. 762 (1929).

75. "The purpose of the definition of the term [proximate cause] is to keep jurors within correct legal bounds." Danielsen v. Eickhoff, 159 Neb. 374, 377, 66 N.W.2d 913, 915 (1954). "Liability for damages caused by wrong ceases at a point dictated by public policy or common sense." Milks v. McIver, 264 N.Y. 267, 269, 190 N.E. 487, 488 (1934).

tempt to make sense out of this agreement—as with any other clause of their bargain. However, a presumption is created for consequential damages:

> Consequential damages may be limited or excluded unless the limitation or exclusion is unconscionable. Limitation of consequential damages for injury to the person in the case of consumer goods is prima facie unconscionable but limitation of damages where the loss is commercial is not.[76]

§ 154. Liquidated Damages

Parties to a contract for the sale of goods are free, within certain limits, to agree as to the amount of damages due in the event of default. As an original proposition a strong argument could be framed to support the validity of all agreements as to damages, especially those which are designed to make breach more costly than performance. Such clauses, if enforced by courts, would cause the parties to a contract to be more secure in their assumptions that the other party's performance will be forthcoming.[77]

The law, however, has moved in a different direction. Courts believe that compensation is the fairest guideline for measuring monetary recoveries and have used this guideline to test the validity of agreements as to the amount of damages due on breach. If the agreement meets this guideline, it is enforced as a liquidated damage clause; if it fails to measure up to the rigors of court scrutiny, the clause is labelled as a penalty and its enforcement is refused.

The Code's test for these clauses is set out in the first sentence of section 2–718(1):

> Damages for breach by either party may be liquidated in the agreement but only at an amount which is reasonable in the light of anticipated or actual harm caused by the breach, the difficulties of proof of loss, and the inconvenience or non-feasibility of otherwise obtaining an adequate remedy.

With a burst of enthusiasm for the task before them, the drafters then added this sentence: "A term fixing unreasonably large liquidated

---

76. UCC § 2–719(3); § 89 *supra*.

The buyer who is seeking consequential damages should consider the income tax consequences of the theory on which he bases his cause of action. A recovery for lost profits would be income; a recovery for injury to goodwill is a return of capital. See the discussion in Raytheon Prod. Corp. v. Commissioner of Internal Revenue, 144 F.2d 110 (1st Cir.), *cert. denied* 323 U.S. 779, 65 S.Ct. 192, 89 L.Ed. 622 (1944); Farmers' & Merchants' Bank v. Commissioner of Internal Revenue, 59 F.2d 912 (6th Cir. 1932).

77. *Cf.* § 139 *supra*.

damages is void as a penalty." [78]   Such a sentence leaves the obvious question: what is to happen to a term which fixes an unreasonably small amount of damages? [79]   The Comments attempt to salvage the situation by suggesting that the section on unconscionable contracts might be used to strike the underliquidated damage clause.[80]   Certainly that section could be used for such a purpose, but there appears to be a much easier way to attack both the too-large and the too-small damage clause. The first sentence of section 2–718(1) states the *only* situations in which damages may be "liquidated." Since reference is made to the anticipated or actual harm as a part of the test of the validity of these clauses, both the too-large and too-small damage clauses are unenforceable under the tests of the first sentence of 2–718(1).

The Code, in an attempt to bring more certainty into the process of deciding which of these clauses are to be enforced, lists the elements to be considered in determining the reasonableness of an agreement stipulating the damages due on breach.[81]   These elements will be applied by courts and should, of course, be considered by the draftsman of all stipulated damage clauses. The elements are these:

1.   The amount of damage which is anticipated *or* actually ensues from the breach; and

2.   The difficulties involved in proving the loss; and

3.   The inconvenience or non-feasibility of obtaining some adequate remedy other than the stipulated damages.[82]

To be enforceable, the dollar amount selected in the agreement must be reasonable in the light of these elements.[83]   The amount selected need not equal the anticipated or actual loss, but it must bear a reasonable relation to either of these losses. Thus, if the contract involves the sale of goods with a standard market price and a readily available market, an attempt by the buyer or seller to liquidate dam-

---

78.   UCC § 2–718(1).

79.   *E. g.*, Brown-Crummer Co. v. W. M. Rice Constr. Co., 285 F. 673 (5th Cir.), *cert. denied* 262 U.S. 742, 43 S.Ct. 520, 67 L.Ed. 1210 (1923); Better Foods Markets, Inc. v. American Dist. Tel. Co., 40 Cal.2d 179, 253 P.2d 10 (1953). The limitation of remedies discussed in § 89 *supra* can be analyzed as a type of liquidated damages. When personal injuries follow a defect in the product, can UCC § 2–718(1) be used to fortify an argument that the limitation clause is unenforceable? The subject of the too-small stipulated damage clause is considered in Fritz,

"Underliquidated" Damages as Limitation of Liability, 33 Texas L.Rev. 196 (1954).

80.   UCC § 2–718, Comment 1.

81.   Pre-Code and non-Code law on liquidated damages is discussed in 5 A. Corbin, Contracts §§ 1054–75 (1964).

82.   These elements were used in pre-Code cases. Secord v. Portland Shopping News, 126 Or. 218, 269 P. 228 (1928).

83.   Denkin v. Sterner, 10 Pa.D. & C.2d 203 (C.P.1956).

ages in advance of breach will probably fail unless the amount selected is equal to (or nearly equal to) the loss which occurred. However, if consequential damages are involved, thereby making proof of loss difficult, the chances that a stipulated damage clause will be upheld are markedly increased. Even with these cases the agreed-upon damages must be a reasonable forecast of the anticipated loss; if the amount is inserted to force the seller to perform, the resulting clause will be held to be a penalty.[84] If the clause is considered a penalty, the contract is not void nor is the aggrieved party barred from his usual remedies. Instead, the clause is stricken and the defaulter is liable for the damages provided by the Code—or, in a proper case, the defaulter will be compelled specifically to perform his promise.[85]

The fact that a stipulated damage clause appears in the writing which evidences the contract between the parties is not conclusive that there has been an "agreement" as to that clause. This problem has been discussed in other contexts and that discussion is applicable here.[86] There must have been subjective mutual assent to the clause or, at the least, the party relying on the clause must have had reasonable and justified grounds for believing that the defaulter agreed to the terms of the stipulated damage clause. The Code's emphasis is on the bargain of the parties in fact, minimizing the impact which printed forms have on shaping the rights and obligations of the parties.

§ 155. Penal Damages

The Code provides that penal damages may not be recovered "except as specifically provided in this Act or by other rule of law." [87] Although the Code does not define penal damages,[88] the drafters' intention is clear when this proscription is read in context. Section 1–106 states the general remedial policy of the Code—to place the aggrieved party in as good a position as he would have been had the other party fully performed his promises. It then adds the language quoted above, indicating that a court is not to award monetary recoveries which are designed to do something more than compensate the injured party—that is, to punish the defaulter or to serve as a warning to others—unless such recoveries are specifically allowed by the Code or by some other rule of law.

---

84. The problem of whether a clause is a penalty or a liquidated damage provision is one of law for the court. Medak v. Hekimian, 241 Or. 38, 404 P.2d 203 (1965).

85. The presence of a liquidated damage clause does not bar specific performance. Manchester Dairy System, Inc. v. Hayward, 82 N.H. 193, 132 A. 12 (1926).

86. § 88 supra.

87. UCC § 1–106(1).

88. For a discussion of various meanings of "penal" laws, see Huntington v. Attrill, 146 U.S. 657, 13 S.Ct. 224; 36 L.Ed. 1123 (1892).

Article 2 (Sales) contains no provision which specifically authorizes the buyer or seller to recover penal damages on the default of the other party to the contract. The closest this Article comes to permitting such a recovery is under a portion of section 2–718 which allows a seller to retain up to $500 of the purchase price when the buyer has made a payment on the price and defaulted so that the seller justifiably withheld delivery of the goods. In this case the seller has both the goods and a portion of the purchase price. The Code allows the seller to retain the sum allowed by section 2–718 without any showing of damages; indeed, the Code apparently provides that the seller may have both his damages *and* the 2–718 award subtracted from any restitution recovery given the buyer. The buyer's recovery under section 2–718 is discussed elsewhere in this text.[89] It is there suggested that the amount which the seller can retain without showing damages may be justified within the compensation principle through a recognition that some sellers have losses which cannot be proved within the usual damage formulas, and that allowing a seller up to $500 is a recognition of these losses. If this justification is correct, section 2–718 ought not be considered as allowing a recovery of penal damages.

The Code also allows penal damages to be awarded when authorized "by other rule of law." Thus, a court can look to its common law and other statutes to determine whether one of the parties to a controversy is entitled to a recovery designed to punish the defaulter. Although a state-by-state survey of the law of penal damages is outside the scope of this text, two general observations can be made. First, the usual rule is that penal damages will not be awarded for breach of a contract for the sale and purchase of goods.[90] The failure of one party to perform a promise is not viewed as such an outrage to the business community that the defaulter should be punished. There exists a market standard for compensation, and making the plaintiff whole is a sufficient remedy to maintain order within the commercial world.

Second, there are some cases, however, in which there is a sufficient sense of indignation and outrage connected with the default so that penal damages will be allowed by some states. Generally, these are situations in which the failure to perform a promise (such as a warranty of quality) is combined with tortious conduct (such as wanton failure to determine whether the goods measured up to their

---

89. § 184 *infra*.

90. Maco Supply Corp. v. Masciarelli, 213 So.2d 265 (Fla.Ct.App.1968), *modified* 224 So.2d 329 (Fla.1969); Swinny v. Cities Serv. Oil Co., 197 So.2d 795 (Miss.1967); White v. Benkowski, 37 Wis.2d 285, 155 N.W.2d 74 (1967). Other cases involving punitive damages for breach of contracts generally are discussed in 5 A. Corbin, Contracts § 1077 (1964) and digested in Annot., 84 A.L.R. 1345 (1933).

warranted quality). There is authority to support the award of penal damages in these situations, and the Code allows the courts to continue these awards if they so desire.[91]

§ 156. Deduction of Damages From Price

When a buyer accepts goods he becomes liable for their price.[92] If those goods are non-conforming, the buyer will in some instances be able to revoke his acceptance and terminate his price liability.[93] There are, however, situations in which a buyer who has accepted non-conforming goods will be unable or unwilling to revoke his acceptance, and he will retain the goods despite their defects. Such a buyer remains liable for the price but, providing he gave the proper notice, has a claim against the seller for damages suffered.[94] The Code (in section 2–717) gives this buyer the privilege of deducting his claim from any balance owing on the price:

> The buyer on notifying the seller of his intention to do so may deduct all or any part of the damages resulting from any breach of the contract from any part of the price still due under the same contract.

The Uniform Sales Act gave the buyer the privilege of recoupment following a breach of warranty.[95] The Code allows the deduction from price for *any* breach. That breach may be in the quality of the goods, their title, their tender, or in any other provision of the contract between the seller and buyer. However, the default must be on the *same* contract as the one under which the buyer is liable for the price, and the buyer must notify the seller of his intention to deduct the damages from the price.[96]

When these conditions are satisfied the seller has a right only to the difference, if any, between the price and the damages. When these conditions are not satisfied (as, for example, where the buyer's damage claim arose out of a different contract from the one under which the seller is claiming the price) the seller has a right to the price, but

91. Toole v. Richardson-Merrell, Inc., 251 Cal.App.2d 689, 60 Cal.Rptr. 398 (1967); Grandi v. LeSage, 74 N.M. 799, 399 P.2d 285 (1965). *But see* Roginsky v. Richardson-Merrell, Inc., 378 F.2d 832 (2d Cir. 1967). For a discussion of punitive damages: (1) under Article 9, see Skeels v. Universal C.I.T. Credit Corp., 335 F.2d 846 (3d Cir. 1964); (2) under Articles 3 and 4, see Loucks v. Albuquerque Nat'l Bank, 76 N.M. 735, 418 P.2d 191 (1966).

92. UCC § 2–607(1).

93. §§ 143, 146–48 *supra*.

94. §§ 150–53 *supra*.

95. Uniform Sales Act § 69(1)(a).

96. UCC § 2–717, Comment 2. The failure to give notice would give the seller, who had not received the price, reasonable grounds for insecurity and would allow him to use UCC § 2–609. More important, failure to notify might also prevent a buyer from using UCC § 2–717.

other rules of contract law may be combined with permissive counter-claim statutes in a particular jurisdiction to reach approximately the same result as prescribed by section 2–717 of the Code. That is, these statutes generally allow the defendant to counterclaim any claim—or certainly any contract claim—which he has against the plaintiff's contract action irrespective of whether the counterclaim arose out of the same transaction.[97] Although the theory of these permissive counterclaim statutes differs from that of section 2–717 (under the counterclaim both claims are due in full with one being set off against the other; under section 2–717 the buyer is obligated to pay only the difference), a buyer can often rely on his counterclaim privilege to assert a reduction in price even though the breach arose out of a separate contract.[98] Whether this assertion should be made depends on negotiation tactics and not some provision in the law of sales.

§ 157. Security Interest in the Goods

For many types of seller's defaults the buyer has only an in personam unsecured claim against his seller. This is usually the situation in the typical product liability case. The buyer paid the price to the seller and received in return goods which the buyer asserted were non-conforming. The buyer further claims that those goods caused injury and that the seller is liable in damages for those injuries. The Code provides guides by which the conformity of the goods can be tested [99] and the damages, if recoverable, can be measured.[1] The buyer, however, has no "security" for this claim and the collectability of any money judgment depends upon the solvency of the defendant. Likewise, when a seller has failed to deliver any goods under the contract, the buyer has a cause of action to recover any portion of the purchase price paid together with damages suffered because of the default; but this buyer's claim is completely unsecured.

The principal reason that the buyer does not have security for the seller's performance arises out of the nature of the sale transaction. Buyers do not often demand a bond, a mortgage, an escrow payment, or anything else by way of security for the seller's promises. Buyers rely on the reputation of the seller or the brand name of the product, often giving little thought to their recovery in the event of a default. Once a default does occur, however, the solvency of the de-

---

97. 3 J. Moore, Federal Practice ¶ 13.18 (1968) discussing FED.R.CIV.P. 13(b).

98. Recoverable interest and service charges may make the permissive counterclaim less attractive to the buyer than use of UCC § 2–717. Further, a court *may* require separate trials, FED.R.CIV.P. 42(b), and render separate judgments, FED.R.CIV.P. 54 (b).

99. §§ 63–92 *supra.*

1. §§ 146–55 *supra.*

fendant can be of prime importance and becomes one of the reasons for the injured buyer's selection of certain parties in the chain of distribution as defendants in his cause of action.

The Code gives the buyer security for his claims in two instances. The first has already been discussed: the unpaid portion of the purchase price becomes security for any damages arising out of a breach of the same contract.[2] This type of security assumes that the buyer has retained the goods and is, therefore, liable to pay the price to the seller. To the extent that the buyer has not paid the price, he has that much security for any claim based upon a default of the same contract; when the price has been paid in full, that security is lost. The buyer satisfies his claim by deducting from the unpaid price *all or any part of the resulting damages*.[3] He is not limited to the price paid or to expenses incurred in caring for the non-conforming goods. All of his damages can be deducted.

The second section which gives the buyer security for his claims is found in the general index of the buyer's remedies—section 2–711 (3):

> On rightful rejection or justifiable revocation of acceptance a buyer has a security interest in goods in his possession or control for any payments made on their price and any expenses reasonably incurred in their inspection, receipt, transportation, care and custody and may hold such goods and resell them in like manner as an aggrieved seller (Section 2–706).

The type of case which would be covered by this section is that in which the buyer has made a down payment (as, for example, by honoring a sight draft), the seller has delivered non-conforming goods which the buyer discovers to be non-conforming only after incurring expenses in inspecting them, and the buyer has decided to reject the goods—or, if the goods have been accepted, to revoke his acceptance. The buyer is not required to return the goods and then sue the seller for his payment of the price and his expenses. He may do two things: (1) hold the goods as security for the down payment and expenses incurred;[4] and (2) sell the goods at public or private sale under the conditions detailed in section 2–706. From the proceeds of the resale the buyer may deduct the amount of payment which he made and those expenses listed in section 2–711(3). If any surplus remains after these deductions, the surplus must be turned over to the seller.[5]

---

2. § 156 *supra*.

3. UCC § 2–717.

4. Pomeroy's Inc. v. Snyder, 52 Luz. Leg.Reg. 44 (Pa.C.P.1961).

5. UCC § 2–711, Comment 2. The security interest created by UCC § 2–711 need not be represented by a security agreement and no filing is necessary for its perfection. UCC § 9–113. Un-

The extent of the security interest under section 2–711(3) is not as broad as that given under section 2–717. Under section 2–717 *any* of the buyer's damages may be deducted from the unpaid price. Under section 2–711(3) only two kinds of buyer's damages may be deducted from the resale price. Expenses in connection with the resale are not covered by section 2–711(3) but would be incidental damages protected (in an appropriate case) under section 2–717.[6] More important, market value differences and consequential damages are excluded by section 2–711(3) but fall within the "any damages" language of section 2–717. It is, therefore, important for the buyer to understand the scope of his security interests under each of these sections. This understanding may affect his decision whether to reject the goods (or revoke his acceptance) and to rely on the goods as security or to retain the goods and rely on the unpaid portion of the purchase price as his security.

3. THE BUYER'S RIGHT TO THE GOODS

§ 158. Specific Performance

The Code's test as to when specific performance is available to a buyer on default of his seller is contained in one short sentence: "Specific performance may be decreed where the goods are unique or in other proper circumstances." [7] The Code also contains a sentence on what the decree for specific performance may contain (terms and conditions as to price, damages "or other relief as the court may deem just"),[8] but this is all that is said about when the buyer may use this equity decree to obtain the goods.

The Comments suggest that Article 2 attempts "to further a more liberal attitude than some courts have shown in connection with the specific performance of contracts of sale." [9] If this was the drafters' intention, they used strange statutory language to promote that attempt. Specific performance may be decreed where the goods are "unique." Goods are unique when there are no others like them—when they are without equal.[10] Perhaps also this word has been misused enough so that a second meaning can be ascribed to the quality of uniqueness:

---

der this section the seller is the debtor; thus neither a security agreement nor filing is needed. UCC § 9–113, Comment 3.

6. A security interest for expenses spent in repair of goods was given the buyer in Lanners v. Whitney, 247 Or. 223, 428 P.2d 398 (1967).

7. UCC § 2–716(1).

8. UCC § 2–716(2).

9. UCC § 2–716, Comment 1.

10. Goods are not unique just because they were purchased at an exceptionally low price. Hilmor Sales Co. v. Helen Neushaefer Div. of Supronics Corp., 6 UCC Rep. 325 (N.Y.Sup.Ct. 1969). A horse was held to have a peculiar and unique value in Morris v. Sparrow, 225 Ark. 1019, 287 S.W.2d 583 (1956).

when the goods are very unusual or rare. Even so, a court which looks at specific performance as an uncommon remedy for contracts involving the sale of goods will have no difficulty in severely limiting the number of cases in which the remedy will be granted. On the other hand, other courts desiring to expand the number of cases for equitable relief can find uniqueness in situations short of the one-of-a-kind goods. The Comments assert that the requirements and output contracts are the "typical commercial specific performance situation" when those contracts involve a "particular or peculiarly available source or market." [11] The court which is so inclined can reach this result by calling the goods unique or by relying on the "other proper circumstances" language.[12]

The second test is less precise. Specific performance will also be decreed "in other proper circumstances." The only hint as to what the drafters meant to include in this vague test is found in a Comment indicating that inability to cover is strong evidence of "other proper circumstances." [13] If they meant this to be the courts' guide, it is disappointing that they did not at least create a statutory presumption in favor of specific performance whenever a buyer could not cover. This would have had the merit of assuring a buyer that he would get the contracted-for goods at the contract price, either from an outside source or from the seller.[14]

However, the tests chosen by the drafters were much less forceful. They probably left the buyer where he was before the Code [15] (despite the hopeful Comment) but may have made specific performance harder to obtain than it was under the Uniform Sales Act.[16] Reasons for adopting this policy as to a buyer's remedy have already been discussed, and they are not without merit.[17] Perhaps the best way to summarize the Code's position as to specific performance has already been hinted at in this section: courts are free to go on doing what they did before the Code [18]—and the best prediction of the shape of the future law is that they probably will do just that.

11. UCC § 2–716, Comment 2.

12. Eastern Rolling Mill Co. v. Michlovitz, 157 Md. 51, 145 A. 378 (1929); Curtice Bros. v. Catts, 72 N.J.Eq. 831, 66 A. 935 (Ch.1907). See the suggestions in § 89 *supra* and § 159 *infra*.

13. UCC § 2–716, Comment 2.

14. Although the drafters did not use this test for specific performance, they approximated it in the test for replevin. § 159 *infra*. This may meet any substantial criticism against the vague specific performance language.

15. Annot., 152 A.L.R. 4 (1944).

16. Uniform Sales Act § 68. Cases are discussed in 3 S. Williston, Sales § 602 (rev. ed. 1948).

17. § 139 *supra*. See also Grossfeld, *Money Sanctions for Breach of Contract in a Communist Economy*, 72 Yale L.J. 1326 (1963).

18. A good example of the diversity of court opinions is the group of World War II cases in which the buyer sought specific performance of contracts for the sale of automobiles.

§ 159. Replevin

Another remedy by which the buyer may seek to obtain possession of the contracted-for goods is replevin. Under section 2–716(3) a buyer may replevy goods which have been identified to the contract *and* where:

1. The buyer is unable to cover after making reasonable efforts to do so,[19] *or*

2. The circumstances reasonably indicate that attempts at cover would be unavailing, *or*

3. The goods have been shipped under reservation and the buyer has satisfied or tendered satisfaction of the security interest in the goods.

As with all of the buyer's remedies, the buyer must also have taken whatever action is necessary to place the seller in default before replevin is available. This problem has been discussed elsewhere in this text.[20]

The first requirement for replevin is that the goods must have been identified to the contract. Unidentified goods cannot be obtained by replevin; if the buyer hopes to obtain unidentified goods, he must do so through specific performance. The time when identification occurs has already been discussed [21] but a summary of the Code rules indicates the scope of the replevin action. First, goods can be identified at any time provided by explicit agreement of the parties. Second, where there is no explicit agreement, identification occurs (a) as to goods which are existing and identified, at the time the contract is made, or (b) as to future goods, at the time the goods are shipped, marked, or otherwise designated by the seller as referring to the seller-buyer contract.[22] There are special rules for growing crops and for the unborn young of animals, but these are of limited application.

The fact that identification is a prerequisite for replevin removes the probability that this remedy will have any widespread use against defaulting sellers. The seller controls the time of identification of future goods and, if he has decided not to deliver the goods to the buyer, the probabilities are slim that the seller will ship, mark, or designate those goods for the buyer. Further, the buyer will often

---

McCallister v. Patton, 214 Ark. 293, 215 S.W.2d 701 (1948) (denying specific performance); Heidner v. Hewitt Chevrolet Co., 166 Kan. 11, 199 P.2d 481 (1948) (granting specific performance); Fortner v. Wilson, 202 Okl. 563, 216 P.2d 299 (1950) (denying specific performance).

19. William F. Wilke, Inc. v. Cummins Diesel Engines, Inc., 252 Md. 611, 250 A.2d 886 (1969) (footnote 5).

20. §§ 94, 111–15 *supra*.

21. § 126 *supra*.

22. UCC § 2–501.

have difficulty in gathering evidence of identification when the facts are known only to the seller. Without proof of identification, replevin is not available to the buyer even though substitute goods are unobtainable. Code replevin requires the court to be able to direct the sheriff to the particular goods, and identification serves this purpose.

There will be some situations in which the buyer can prove the fact of identification. For example, where the contract is for the sale of existing and identified goods or where the contract is for the sale of future goods which have been boxed and shipped to the buyer prior to the seller's default, the buyer will have the necessary evidence of identification. Replevin will be available to such a buyer if he can also show any one of the three additional facts listed above. The one most apt to occur is a failure to obtain cover. The fact that cover is not available following reasonable efforts of the buyer indicates the commercial unavailability of the goods. In such a situation the sheriff will be instructed to obtain the identified goods from the seller and deliver them to the buyer.[23]

Section 2–716(3) allows the buyer to replevy goods when the seller has shipped under reservation and the buyer has tendered satisfaction of any reserved security interest (as by paying a sight draft). Such use of replevin appears fair to the two parties to the contract. The seller has shipped the goods prior to his default and the buyer has paid the contract price. Replevin is an appropriate remedy for the buyer. Replevin may, however, not be fair to third parties. For example, it will affect creditors of a bankrupt seller when the buyer had made a substantial prepayment for the goods and attempts to obtain them through replevin by paying only the balance of the price. If replevin is refused, the buyer will have an unsecured claim against the seller's estate but all of the creditors (including the seller) will have a portion of their claims satisfied by the goods involved in the sale. On the other hand, if replevin is granted, the buyer's claim will be satisfied completely (to the extent of the value of the goods) and the other creditors will receive only the balance of the price—an amount which could be substantially less than the value of the goods. This situation will require a determination of whether the Code is consistent with the policies underlying the Bankruptcy Act—a problem which is discussed elsewhere.[24]

---

23. If the test of commercial unavailability is considered as an "other proper circumstance" for the action of specific performance, the probabilities that the buyer will obtain the goods will be increased. Prior identification is not a prerequisite for specifc per-

formance (UCC § 2–716(1)), and an equity decree can compel the seller—not the sheriff—to turn over the goods. § 158 *supra*.

24. § 160 *infra*. UCC § 2–716 does not attempt to solve the priority problems

An appraisal of the remedies of specific performance and replevin indicates that the Code's basic remedy is not that of allowing the buyer to obtain the contracted-for goods following a default by the seller. The buyer's basic remedy is that of cover and cover damages. Failure properly to cover does not bar market value damages but does prevent the buyer from recovering avoidable consequential damages. Only in limited instances will the seller be required to deliver the goods which were the subject of the contract for sale. The concept of uniqueness and the requirement of identification limit the scope of specific performance and replevin. Nevertheless, in appropriate cases these remedies are available and, when available, require delivery of the goods to the buyer.[25]

§ 160. Insolvency of the Seller

There is one situation in which the buyer is extremely interested in receiving the goods from the seller: that in which the buyer has made substantial prepayments on the purchase price only to discover that the seller is insolvent and has not delivered the goods. There is no question but that the buyer can obtain a judgment against the seller for the amount he has paid plus his damages in not receiving the goods as promised. However, that judgment may be nothing more than a claim to be asserted in bankruptcy (and on which the buyer will receive only a percentage of its face value) or a claim which will probably be uncollectable under state procedures (if the seller is not placed in bankruptcy). Since such a buyer stands little chance of getting his money back, he would like to finish paying the price and to receive the promised goods.

Section 2–502 provides:

> (1) Subject to subsection (2) and even though the goods have not been shipped a buyer who has paid a part or all of the price of goods in which he has a special property under the provisions of the immediately preceding section may on mak-

---

which can arise when a third party contests the buyer's right to the goods. Possibly UCC § 2–403 (discussed in § 170 *infra*) can be used if the seller has sold the goods to a third party, but problems of title and the meaning of "entrusting" are involved. Intervening creditors present even more troublesome questions. The subject is considered in Peters, *Remedies for Breach of Contracts Relating to the Sale of Goods Under the Uniform Commercial Code: A Roadmap for Article Two*, 73 Yale L.J. 199, 235–39 (1963).

25. "If a negotiable document of title is outstanding, the buyer's right of replevin relates of course to the document not directly to the goods." UCC § 2–716, Comment 5.

The buyer's right to retain goods purchased from one who had no title or who had a voidable title is covered in UCC § 2–403. The problem is discussed in § 170 *infra*.

ing and keeping good a tender of any unpaid portion of their price recover them from the seller if the seller becomes insolvent within ten days after receipt of the first installment on their price.

(2) If the identification creating his special property has been made by the buyer he acquires the right to recover the goods only if they conform to the contract for sale.[26]

On the surface this section appears to give the buyer a valuable right to the goods to protect against any loss as a result of insolvency. There are, however, three difficulties which make this section of questionable value to the buyer.

First, section 2–502 applies only when the buyer has a "special property" in the goods—which he acquires on identification of the goods. The concept of identification has been discussed in detail,[27] but in summary identification occurs (absent an explicit agreement) (a) when the contract is made if the goods are existing and identified at that time, or (b) when goods are shipped, marked, or otherwise designated by the seller if the contract is for the sale of future goods.[28] Until identification the buyer has no "special property" in any goods, and section 2–502 is of no help to him. Unfortunately, 2–502 does not state *when* the buyer must have this special property in the goods. The Code language is: ". . . a buyer who has paid a part or all of the price of goods in which he has a special property . . . may . . . recover them from the seller. . . ." Must the buyer have a special property at the time he paid a part or all of the price (if so, few contracts for the sale of future goods will be within the scope of section 2–502), at the time the seller became insolvent, within the ten-day period after insolvency, at the time the buyer tendered the remainder of the purchase price, or at the time of trial? In view of the reference to identification—which includes future goods—the drafters most probably intended that the buyer must have the special property at the time he tendered the balance of the price, but this is far from clear. Nevertheless, if identification never occurs or occurs after the relevant time, the buyer will not have the requisite "special property" and cannot claim the goods under section 2–502.

Second, even if the buyer has a special property in the goods at the relevant time, he can recover those goods only if the "seller becomes insolvent within ten days after receipt of the first installment

---

26. "Subsection (2) is included to preclude the possibility of unjust enrichment which exists if the buyer were permitted to recover goods even though they were greatly superior in quality or quantity to that called for by the contract for sale." UCC § 2–502, Comment 3.

27. § 126 *supra*.

28. UCC § 2–501.

on their price." [29] A showing that the seller was insolvent when the installment was paid will not suffice. In fact, proof that the seller was insolvent prior to or at the time the buyer made his prepayment will defeat the buyer's use of section 2–502 because it prevents this second condition from being met. The buyer must show that at the time the first installment on the price was received the seller was solvent and that within ten days *thereafter* the seller became insolvent. Attempting to prove the precise moment that a business became insolvent is a venture into foolhardiness. Except for the situation in which a financial catastrophe occurs, the change from solvency to insolvency is a gradual process which is not separated by a clear-cut moment of time subject to proof in court. The ten-day provision of section 2–502 is enough, by itself, to make this section unavailable to most buyers who find they have paid a part (or all) of the purchase price to a seller who is now insolvent.

Third, even if the buyer can meet the first two requirements of section 2–502, he faces the possibility that this Code section cannot withstand attack by a trustee in bankruptcy. If the seller's insolvency has reached the point where voluntary or involuntary bankruptcy has intervened, the seller's trustee will enter the controversy armed with the Federal Bankruptcy Act. One of the primary objectives of this Act is equality of distribution of the bankrupt's assets among his unsecured creditors.[30] Section 2–502 runs counter to this objective: the buyer, through his down payment, has extended "credit" to the seller and now seeks an advantage over the seller's other creditors by receiving 100% of the seller's performance in exchange for the balance of the purchase price. This is sufficient to signal the trustee to resist the buyer's attempts at recovering the goods. If the buyer had received the goods within four months prior to the time that the petition in bankruptcy was filed, the trustee can claim that the transfer of the goods was in part for an antecedent debt (the prepayment on the price) and seek to avoid the transfer as a preference.[31] If the transfer had not been completed at the time the petition was filed but the buyer still owed a part of the purchase price, the trustee could consider rejecting the contract and allowing the buyer to prove his claim as an unsecured creditor.[32] If the transfer had not been completed at the time the petition was filed but the buyer had paid all of the purchase price, the contract would no longer be "executory" and the trustee

---

29. The buyer must also tender the unpaid portion of the purchase price. Tender of price is discussed in § 112 *supra.*

30. 3 Collier, Bankruptcy ¶ 60.01 (14th ed. 1969).

31. Bankruptcy Act § 60 (11 U.S.C.A. § 96 (1964)).

32. Bankruptcy Act § 70b (11 U.S.C.A. § 110b (1964)).

would not have the power of rejection [33] (which extends only to executory contracts); however, the trustee would have other clauses of the Bankruptcy Act to resist the buyer's claim to the goods. Chief among these would be (1) the "strong-arm clause" by which the trustee is given the rights of a lien creditor, whether or not such a creditor exists,[34] and (2) the fraudulent transfer section [35] by which the trustee could claim that the retention of possession by the seller following identification was fraudulent as to a creditor. If successful, the trustee will retain the goods as a part of the bankrupt's estate, and the buyer will be left with an unsecured claim against the estate.

The buyer has several arguments by which he can attempt to sustain the validity of section 2–502. For example, he may claim that the transfer from the seller to the buyer was complete at the time the down payment was made (when conditions of section 2–502 are met), and that there is no preference because there is no *antecedent* debt.[36] The buyer can also use section 2–402 to urge that there was no fraudulent retention of possession by the seller during the period he held the goods for the buyer. Further, the buyer could urge that the ten-day provision of section 2–502 limits that section to "quick insolvency" situations where the chances are good that the seller still had the buyer's down payment at the time of insolvency, and that the seller was fraudulent in taking the money knowing of the impending insolvency.

Answers to these problems must await court interpretation of the Code and the Bankruptcy Act.[37] Until definite answers can be given, buyers who extend credit to their sellers would be unwise to rely upon section 2–502 to give them rights in goods retained by their sellers. Buyers who desire to finance their sellers through prepayments on the purchase price should follow the procedures of Article 9, and should use section 2–502 only as an afterthought for situations in which proper planning was not possible.

33. *In re* Forney, 299 F.2d 503 (7th Cir. 1962); *In re* San Francisco Bay Exposition, 50 F.Supp. 344 (N.D.Cal. 1943). Where only a down payment had been made, the trustee's power of rejection defeated an action for specific performance. *In re* New York Investors Mutual Group, 143 F.Supp. 51 (S.D.N.Y.1956).

34. Bankruptcy Act § 70c (11 U.S.C.A. § 110c (1964)).

35. Bankruptcy Act § 70e (11 U.S.C.A. § 110e (1964)).

36. Support for this position can be gathered from pre-Code law which allowed the buyer to obtain the goods from a bankrupt seller if the buyer had title to the goods. 4A Collier, Bankruptcy ¶ 70.19[1] (14th ed. 1969).

37. These problems have been discussed by several writers. 4A Collier, Bankruptcy ¶ 70.62A[7.2] (14th ed. 1969); Kennedy, *The Trustee in Bankruptcy Under the Uniform Commercial Code: Some Problems Suggested by Articles 2 and 9*, 14 Rutgers L.Rev. 518, 556–59 (1960); Note, *Bankruptcy and Article Two of the Uniform Commercial Code: The Right to Recover the Goods Upon Insolvency*, 79 Harv.L.Rev. 598 (1966); Note, *The Uniform Commercial Code and an Insolvent Seller's Possession of the Goods Sold*, 104 U. Pa.L.Rev. 91 (1955).

C. BUYER IN DEFAULT

1. THE SELLER'S COURSES OF ACTION

§ 161. Remedial Interests of the Seller

When a buyer defaults in his contractual obligations, a seller will be interested in different types of remedies—depending on the facts of the case. For example, if he has not delivered the goods to the buyer, he may wish to withhold delivery without incurring damages for a failure to deliver. In addition, he may want damages measured by the losses resulting from the buyer's default. If the seller has delivered the goods, he may prefer an action for the full price—or he may want to cancel and recover the goods. All of these remedies have one common feature: they are directed against the buyer.

There are some instances in which the seller has lost interest in pursuing any remedy against his buyer. These occur most frequently when the seller is convinced that the buyer is insolvent and unable to pay any judgment obtained against him. In these instances the seller would like to obtain a different type of remedy—one which is enforceable against third parties. Examples include situations in which the buyer has transferred the goods to a third party, and the seller would like to recover the goods from that third party. They also include those cases in which the buyer has been placed in bankruptcy and unsecured creditors are contending for the buyer's assets. If the seller had delivered goods to the buyer on credit, the seller is most often interested in reclaiming those goods from the trustee in bankruptcy, thereby cutting down as much of the loss as possible.

Article 2 of the Code responds to these three interests of a seller: his claims against his buyer, purchasers from his buyer, and creditors of his buyer. The remedies given to such a seller are discussed in the following sections of this text. They must, however, be kept in perspective. Another Article of the Code (Article 9) provides the framework through which persons who sell on credit can obtain the maximum protection from claims of third parties. Generally this protection comes from written security agreements and filed financing statements—that is, from public notice that the seller is claiming a security interest in certain goods held by the buyer.[38] Since this is the basic

---

38. The need for a signed security agreement is covered by UCC § 9–203. General Elec. Credit Corp. v. Bankers Commercial Corp., 244 Ark. 984, 429 S.W.2d 60 (1968); *In re* Motrak Corp., 5 UCC Rep. 659 (U.S.Dist.Ct.D.Minn. 1967) (oral security agreement is not enforceable). Filing is necessary to perfect a security interest except for the situations listed in UCC § 9–302. The exceptions most apt to apply to sellers are the purchase money security interest in farm equipment having a purchase price of no more than $2,500 and in consumer goods. Lonoke Prod. Credit Ass'n v. Bohannon, 238

procedure for protecting sellers from claims of third parties and since this procedure affords a place where those third parties can learn of the sellers' interests, it should not be surprising that Article 2, which contains no requirement of public notice, affords a seller only a minimum of protection against third party claims.[39]

§ 162.   Index of the Seller's Remedies

Section 2–703 is an index of several of the seller's remedies.   In the main, these are remedies against the buyer although some (such as the right to withhold delivery or even stop delivery of goods in transit) will be applicable to prevent creditors of the buyer from requiring delivery and thereby obtaining a priority over the seller. Section 2–703 is the parallel section to the Code's index of the buyer's remedies [40] and provides the statutory answers to three questions: '(1) For what types of defaults will the seller have a 2–703 remedy?   (2) To what goods do these remedies extend?   (3) What Code remedies does a seller have on occurrence of at least one of the listed defaults?

Types of defaults.   The remedies listed in section 2–703 are open to a seller when the buyer has done at least one of four acts: wrongfully rejected the goods; wrongfully revoked his acceptance of the goods; failed to make a payment which was due on or before delivery; or repudiated with respect to a part or the whole of the contract involved.   There may be statutory difficulty with the concept of a "wrongful" rejection.   The Code gives the buyer the privilege of rejection only if the goods or their tender is non-conforming,[41] and obligates the buyer to accept conforming goods.[42]   From this it can be argued that any attempt to reject a conforming tender is not "effective" within the meaning of section 2–606(1)(b) since the buyer had no privilege of rejection, and that such an attempt results in an acceptance rather than a "wrongful" rejection.[43]   However, the intent of the drafters is clear.   The "effectiveness" of a rejection under section 2–606(1)(b) is expressly limited to the time within which the rejection must be attempted and the notice which must be given; it does not include a determination as to whether the buyer had good cause for his attempted rejection.   Therefore, a wrongful rejection is a

---

Ark. 206, 379 S.W.2d 17 (1964) (farm equipment); Recchio v. Manufacturers & Traders Trust Co., 55 Misc.2d 788, 286 N.Y.S.2d 390 (Sup.Ct.1968) (consumer goods).   However, failure to file gives the holders of a purchase money security interest in farm equipment and consumer goods only limited protection.   UCC § 9–307.   The place of filing is detailed in UCC § 9–401 and priorities in UCC § 9–312.

39.   Stumbo v. Paul B. Hult Lumber Co., —— Or. ——, 444 P.2d 564 (1968).

40.   UCC § 2–711.

41.   UCC § 2–601.

42.   UCC §§ 2–301, 2–507.   § 114 *supra.*

43.   UCC § 2–606, quoted in full in § 142 *supra.*

refusal by the buyer to accept conforming goods properly tendered.[44] A wrongful revocation of acceptance is a refusal by the buyer to retain conforming goods after their acceptance, but only if the seller has retaken possession of those goods. If the buyer retains possession of accepted goods following an attempt wrongfully to reject them, the seller would have a Code remedy for their price.[45]

The Code does not define "repudiation," but the word is used in the sense of an anticipatory breach—a breach occurring prior to the time that buyer is obligated to accept and to pay the price.[46] Thus, the section 2–703 index of remedies is available to a seller whenever the buyer failed to make a payment which was due on or before delivery or when the buyer defaulted by indicating that he would not perform his obligations when they become due. Whether statements by a buyer amount to a "repudiation" can be difficult to determine, but in doubtful cases the seller can use the section on adequate assurance to resolve disputed facts.[47]

Goods involved. As long as the seller and buyer have only one contract for a single delivery, there is no difficulty in application of section 2–703 remedies. In such cases the seller may seek his remedy with respect to the goods covered by that contract. However, if several contracts or an installment contract is involved the problem is more difficult. The Code language is that the seller may act "with respect to any goods directly affected and, if the breach is of the whole contract (Section 2–612), then also with respect to the whole undelivered balance."[48] This language will tend to limit remedies to the contract or the installment which is involved in the default; however, the seller can often use the default on one contract or installment as grounds for insecurity and demand adequate assurance from the buyer as to his future performance. If such assurance is forthcoming, the further contractual relationship between the parties will properly not be affected by an isolated default. If that assurance is not forthcoming, the buyer will be considered to have "repudiated"—and one of the four triggering events of section 2–703 has occurred.[49]

Remedies. Section 2–703 indexes several remedies which the seller may pursue against his buyer. These are:

44. UCC § 2–602, Comment 3. The rejection must meet the tests of UCC § 2–602 or it will amount to an acceptance under UCC § 2–606.

45. UCC § 2–709. §§ 143–44 *supra* and § 178 *infra*.

46. § 149 *supra* note 2.

47. UCC § 2–609. The use of this Code section by a party who faces a doubtful repudiation is discussed in § 149 *supra*.

48. UCC § 2–703.

49. UCC § 2–609(4).

1. If the goods have not been delivered, the seller may withhold the goods.[50]

2. If the goods have been put in the possession of a bailee (such as a carrier), the seller may stop delivery of those goods.[51]

3. If the seller meets the conditions of section 2–706, he may resell the goods and recover damages measured by the difference between the contract price and the amount received on resale.[52]

4. If the seller does not comply with the resale requirements, he may nevertheless recover damages measured by the difference between the unpaid contract price and the market price of the goods at the time and place for tender or, if this amount is insufficient to place the seller in as good a financial position as performance, the seller may recover damages measured by his lost profits.[53]

5. In situations within section 2–709 (which include instances in which the buyer fails to make a payment due *after* delivery) the seller may recover the contract price.[54]

6. If the goods were unidentified at the time of the buyer's default, the seller has several options: (a) he may, under certain circumstances, complete the manufacture of unfinished goods and identify them to the contract; (b) he may resell unfinished goods for their scrap or salvage value, or "proceed in any other reasonable manner"; (c) he may resell goods which have been demonstrably intended for the buyer-seller contract even though those goods are unfinished; or (d) he may identify conforming goods to the contract.[55] Having identified the goods to the contract, the seller could proceed to an appropriate remedy, such as resale or conceivably a suit for full price.

7. If the seller so desires, he may cancel the contract.

Under several of the damage recoveries the seller may also recover his incidental expenses but must deduct any expenses saved in consequence of the buyer's default.

The Code rejects any doctrine of election of remedies.[56] Therefore, the remedies listed above are cumulative and the selection of one does not, in and of itself, bar relief under some other remedy. For example, a seller may cancel the contract and still have damages for its breach. There are instances, however, in which the action taken by the seller precludes his obtaining certain of the section 2–703

---

50. § 163 *infra.*

51. § 164 *infra.*

52. §§ 173–74 *infra.*

53. §§ 175, 177 *infra.*

54. § 178 *infra.*

55. § 179 *infra.*

56. UCC § 2–703, Comment 1.

remedies. As an illustration, a seller who has withheld delivery and resold under section 2–706 cannot recover the full price of those goods from the defaulting buyer. This result rests on notions of compensation (and no more than compensation) as well as on the defined scope of the full price remedy; it does not find its basis in any election doctrine.

The following sections of this text discuss the seller's remedies from a functional basis—that is, as the seller would be most apt to seek their enforcement. In some instances he may desire control of the goods, in others he may seek damages, and in still others he may desire to recover the full price. These are the principal headings of the following portions of this Chapter.

2. THE SELLER'S CONTROL OF THE GOODS

§ 163. Withholding Delivery

If the buyer commits one of the triggering events of section 2–703, the seller may withhold delivery of the goods without his refusal to deliver being considered a default.[57] This can be illustrated with the following factual patterns:

Case # 1. Suppose that on August 1 Seller agreed in writing to sell to Buyer a color television set for $895. The terms of the writing required Buyer to pay cash on or before August 15 at which time Seller would deliver the set to Buyer. On August 16 Buyer demanded the set although he had paid no part of the price. Is Seller in default for his failure to deliver the set on or before August 15?

The problem of Case #1 is easily solved. The buyer has failed to make a payment which was due either on or just before delivery; the goods involved are the single item promised by the seller; and section 2–703 allows the seller in this type of situation to "withhold delivery of such goods." It may be that at one time the law treated the promises in a bilateral contract as independent and allowed an action by one party even though he had not performed or tendered performance,[58] but most vestiges of this approach to the order of performance were overruled in a 1773 decision by Lord Mansfield.[59] Since common sense favored the notion that the parties to most contracts had in mind an order to their performance—even though they had not expressed that order in words—the ideas of Lord Mansfield have been accepted by the general law of contracts and by the Code.

---

57. Rau Fastener Co. v. Trailmark Outdoor Prods., Inc., 4 UCC Rep. 1171 (N.Y.App.T.1968).

58. § 94 *supra.*

59. Kingston v. Preston, cited in 2 Doug. 689, 99 Eng.Rep. 437 (K.B.1773).

Thus, the inclusion in section 2–703 of the privilege of withholding delivery was not necessary to solve Case #1. Payment of the price was a condition precedent to the seller's duty to deliver [60] and, since the buyer had not tendered the entire price, the seller was not obligated to deliver—and his failure to deliver on or before the date specified in the contract was not a default. Case #1 can be solved either by ideas of concurrent conditions or by section 2–703. Both produce the same answer: the seller is not in default for his failure to deliver the goods.

Section 2–703 allows the seller to withhold delivery for the buyer's failure to make a payment due "on or before delivery." If the payment had been due after delivery (as in a credit sale), neither section 2–703 nor the doctrine of concurrent conditions would be of aid to the seller who would like to withhold delivery. Consider:

Case # 2. Assume the same facts as involved in Case #1 except that the contract required delivery by Seller on or before August 15 and allowed Buyer 30 days after delivery to pay the price. Is Seller in default for his failure to deliver the set on or before August 15?

Section 2–703 does not allow the seller to withhold delivery because none of its triggering events has occurred. Further, the general section on the duty of the seller to perform (which makes tender of payment a condition precedent to that duty) begins with the familiar "unless otherwise agreed" language—and in Case #2 the parties have otherwise agreed. Therefore, on the facts of Case #2 the seller is in default for failing to make a required delivery.

There is, however, usually a reason why the seller has refused to deliver as promised. If that reason is spite or that he misjudged the market and set too low a contract price, the failure to deliver would be a default giving the buyer remedies against the seller.[61] On the other hand, the seller may have refused to deliver because the goods were destroyed before the risk of loss had passed to the buyer or because of a transportation strike which prevented any goods from being moved. This text has already discussed the extent to which occurrences such as these excuse a seller's performance [62] and that discussion need not be repeated except to indicate that if the seller is excused, his failure to deliver is not a "default."

Another reason why the seller might wish to withhold delivery is because he has discovered the buyer to be insolvent. Consider:

Case # 3. On August 1 Seller and Buyer entered into a written agreement for the sale and purchase of a color television set for $895,

---

60.   UCC § 2–511(1).

61.   § 148 *supra.*

62.   §§ 107–10 *supra.*

delivery to be made on August 15 with payment due 30 days after delivery. On August 10 Seller discovered that Buyer was insolvent. Is Seller obligated to deliver the set on August 15?

The discovery of insolvency has altered the risks which the seller was willing to assume when he entered into the credit sale. It now appears that the seller may have only a claim against a bankrupt estate or an uncollectable judgment in exchange for the goods. Viewed thus, the seller ought to be able to withhold delivery. However, the contract may have been an especially good one for the buyer and to allow the seller to refuse delivery may force an insolvent buyer into further insolvency—passing the windfall back to his seller. The Code follows pre-Code law by providing a middle ground:

> Where the seller discovers the buyer to be insolvent he may refuse delivery except for cash including payment for all goods theretofore delivered under the contract, and stop delivery under this Article (Section 2–705).[63]

The seller in Case #3 may not simply refuse to make delivery; he may refuse to deliver unless the buyer pays cash.[64] If the buyer pays cash, he is entitled to the goods; if he does not pay cash, he is in default under section 2–703 and the seller may select an appropriate remedy against the buyer. In effect, the discovery of insolvency has converted the credit sale into a cash sale. Not only may the seller demand cash for the goods to be delivered but he may also demand cash for goods which have been "theretofore delivered under the contract." Thus, if an installment contract is involved and the seller had already delivered several items on credit before discovering the insolvency, he may refuse further deliveries unless the buyer pays cash for the items already received. This right is limited to goods delivered under *the contract*; a refusal to deliver goods unless the buyer also pays for goods delivered under other contracts between the parties is wrongful.[65]

63. UCC § 2–702(1). For the pre-Code common law, see Rock-Ola Mfg. Corp. v. Leopold, 98 F.2d 196 (5th Cir. 1938); Koppelon v. Ritter Flooring Corp., 97 N.J.L. 200, 116 A. 491 (Ct.Err. & App. 1922) (insolvency does not terminate the contract). The Uniform Sales Act § 54 reached this result through a seller's lien. Urbansky v. Kutinsky, 86 Conn. 22, 84 A. 317 (1912); 3 S. Williston, Sales §§ 506–07b (rev. ed. 1948).

64. The Code seller ought also to be able to withhold delivery where the credit term has expired. Payment would then be a condition precedent to the seller's duty to perform. UCC § 2–511.

65. *In re* Layton Fabrics, Ltd., 6 UCC Rep. 142 (N.Y.Sup.Ct.1969). This rule requires a determination of what "the contract" is. Pre-Code law drew a distinction between divisible and entire contracts, Tipton v. Feitner, 20 N.Y. 423 (1859), a distinction that will be harder to make under the Code. UCC § 2–612(1). Even though separate contracts are involved, the seller may be able to use any prior defaults as creating reasonable grounds for insecurity as to the present performance

There are two time problems with this section of the Code. First, it does not state *when* the seller must have discovered the insolvency. Certainly he must discover it before he refuses the delivery [66] and there is no difficulty if he discovers it between the date of the contract and the time set for that delivery. However, suppose the seller discovered the insolvency prior to the contract date but nevertheless agreed to sell on credit. Can such a seller change his mind and refuse delivery except for cash? The answer ought to be that he cannot except in the most unusual of circumstances. The seller accepted the risk of an uncollectable judgment when he agreed to the credit sale, and ought not later be able to change the transaction to a cash sale.

A second time-difficulty lies in determining *when* the buyer is obligated to pay the price in cash. May a seller who has discovered that his buyer is insolvent demand that the buyer pay the price on the date which the parties had scheduled for delivery and, if payment is not forthcoming, foreclose the buyer's rights under the contract? The Code is silent on the answer to this question except through such general sections as the requirement of good faith.[67] While this requirement will provide the necessary variation for the situations in which the goods or their value will deteriorate rapidly, the more general answer to the question posed ought to be that the seller may not demand cash on the date set for delivery. The buyer had until the end of the credit term to acquire the cash and an early delivery is usually for his benefit. The seller's discovery of the buyer's insolvency ought not accelerate the date the price is due; thus, in those instances in which there is not something in the nature of the goods or the transaction which requires the early delivery, the seller should not be able to foreclose the buyer's right to those goods except by demanding cash as of the date set for payment. This will require the seller to hold the goods for the buyer during the credit term if the buyer does not tender the cash at an earlier date.

The seller who has sold on credit may withhold delivery except for cash only when he discovers that the buyer is *insolvent*. Even though "insolvency" is broadly defined,[68] a seller will in some situations be required to make hard decisions as to his buyer's solvency. Consider:

Case # 4. On August 1 Seller and Buyer entered into a written agreement for the sale and purchase of a color television set for $895,

---

and withhold delivery under UCC § 2–609.

have an opportunity to secure the goods on payment of cash.

66. If insolvency is discovered after refusal to deliver, the insolvency is insufficient because the buyer did not

67. UCC § 1–203.

68. UCC § 1–201(23).

delivery to be made on August 15 with payment due 30 days after delivery. On August 10 Seller heard rumors that Buyer was not paying his debts as they matured. Is Seller obligated to deliver the set on August 15?

Rumors of insolvency are not the equivalent of insolvency. If the rumors accurately reflect the buyer's financial status, the seller may refuse delivery except for cash; if the rumors are inaccurate, a refusal to deliver according to the credit terms of the agreement would be a default.[69] A seller who is not certain as to the facts of solvency may use section 2–609, claiming that the rumors gave him "reasonable grounds for insecurity." Whether his grounds were "reasonable" is also a question of fact—but one that is less difficult to substantiate. Such a seller may in writing demand adequate assurance of performance and suspend performance ("if commercially reasonable") until he receives that assurance. Failure to give assurance would be a repudiation of the contract, allowing the seller to withhold delivery under section 2–703.[70] Therefore, a seller who is not certain that his buyer is insolvent need not make that factual decision at his peril. He may use the Code section on adequate assurances and allow the buyer to retain his bargain if he can furnish those assurances.

§ 164. Stopping Delivery

On some occasions a seller will not learn of his buyer's insolvency or default until after the goods have been placed in possession of a carrier or bailee. Such a seller may want to withhold delivery of those goods from the buyer—that is, to stop the carrier or bailee from turning the goods over to the buyer. This problem is considered in section 2–705. The three subsections of this section deal with: (1) the scope of the seller's right to stop delivery; (2) the termination of this right; and (3) the rights and duties of the carrier or bailee upon receiving the stop order.

Scope of seller's right. The seller may stop any delivery when he discovers the buyer to be insolvent. The seller may stop delivery of carload, truckload, planeload, or larger shipments of express or freight "when the buyer repudiates or fails to make a payment due before delivery or if for any other reason the seller has a right to withhold or reclaim the goods." [71] The Code does not detail these "other" reasons, but a wrongful rejection before the goods have arrived [72] or

---

69. UCC § 2–711.

70. UCC § 2–609(4).

71. UCC § 2–705(1). As to the right of a financing agency to stop delivery, see UCC § 2–506.

72. UCC § 2–703.

the giving of a check written on insufficient funds [73] would appear to be two instances in which the seller could use section 2–705 to stop delivery.

The grant of the right to stop delivery for reasons other than insolvency is an extension over the seller's rights under the Uniform Sales Act.[74] The reason for limiting stoppage in these cases to large shipments is to reduce the burden that would otherwise be placed on the carrier if the seller had the right to recall small shipments for reasons other than the buyer's insolvency.[75]

Termination of seller's right. The seller's right to stop delivery continues until: (a) the buyer receives the goods; (b) a bailee other than a carrier acknowledges to the buyer that the bailee is holding the goods for the buyer; (c) a carrier makes such acknowledgment to the buyer by reshipment or as a warehouseman; or (d) a negotiable document of title covering the goods has been negotiated to the buyer.[76] The reason the last three events terminate the seller's right to stop delivery rests in large part on a protection of the bailee or carrier. If the seller could regain possession of the goods after the bailee or carrier had indicated to the buyer that it was holding those goods for the buyer, the bailee or carrier might also be liable to the buyer on the basis of its acknowledgment or on the document of title.[77] Thus, the Comments state that the acknowledgment by the carrier that it is acting as a "warehouseman" must be by "a contract of a truly different character from the original shipment, a contract not in extension of transit but as a warehouseman." [78]

The reason that receipt of the goods by the buyer terminates the seller's right to stop delivery is that, upon receipt, delivery has been made and there is nothing left to "stop." [79] The Code defines receipt of goods as meaning "taking physical possession of them." [80] The precise moment that this event has occurred will be difficult to determine in some situations—especially with bulky goods. When these situations arise the courts will have to do the best they can to determine

---

73. UCC § 2–507(2). The seller could also stop delivery on the basis of "reasonable grounds for insecurity." UCC § 2–609. If assurance is forthcoming, the seller would have to make delivery. UCC § 2–705, Comment 1.

74. Uniform Sales Act § 57.

75. UCC § 2–705, Comment 1. "After an effective stoppage under this section the seller's rights in the goods are the same as if he had never made a delivery." UCC § 2–705, Comment 6.

76. UCC § 2–705(2).

77. *See* UCC §§ 7–301, 7–403, 7–502, and 7–504.

78. UCC § 2–705, Comment 3.

79. Stumbo v. Paul B. Hult Lumber Co., —— Or. ——, 444 P.2d 564 (1968).

80. UCC § 2–103(1) (c). Problems of "possession" are discussed in § 134 *supra*.

whether "possession" has been transferred to the buyer; they will be helped in their attempts to resolve these disputes by the Code's emphasis on *physical* possession. Telephone calls or written statements notifying the buyer that the goods are available at the freight yard or airport will not suffice as a receipt by the buyer.

Rights and duties of carrier or bailee. The basic rights and duties of the bailee (which includes a carrier because of the manner in which section 2–705(1) is written: "carrier or *other* bailee") are set out in the first two subsections of section 2–705(3):

> (a) To stop delivery the seller must so notify as to enable the bailee by reasonable diligence to prevent delivery of the goods.

> (b) After such notification the bailee must hold and deliver the goods according to the directions of the seller but the seller is liable to the bailee for any ensuing charges or damages.

The last two subsections consider the rights and duties of a bailee when a document of title has been issued for the goods. If the document is negotiable, the bailee (or carrier) is not required to obey the notification to stop delivery until the document has been surrendered.[81] If the document is non-negotiable, the carrier (notice that this rule does not include bailees other than carriers) is not required to obey a notification to stop delivery given by a person other than the consignor.[82] This latter provision is designed to prevent strangers to the contract of carriage from having a right to stop delivery. A "person in the position of a seller"—as defined by section 2–707 of the Code —is, however, given the right to stop delivery. If that person is not the consignor of a non-negotiable bill of lading, an ambiguity is created between sections 2–705 and 2–707. Since the apparent purpose of section 2–707 is to extend the rights of a "seller" to persons who, because of their relation to the transaction, are in the position of the seller, the grant of those rights by section 2–707 ought not give a person in the position of a seller greater rights than those which the seller would have had. Therefore, anyone claiming a right to stop delivery pursuant to section 2–707 must comply with the requirements of section 2–705.

Subsection (3) of section 2–705 deals only with the rights and duties between the seller and the carrier or bailee. As between the seller and the buyer, the seller has a right to stop delivery until the goods have been received by the buyer. Thus, even though a carrier

81. UCC § 2–705(3) (c).   82. UCC § 2–705(3) (d).

or bailee is not obligated to stop delivery, the buyer cannot complain if the carrier or bailee does obey the stop-delivery order.[83]

§ 165. Reclamation From the Buyer—Credit Sales

Millions of dollars worth of goods are sold each year on the strength of the buyer's credit. Goods are delivered to a buyer who promises to pay the price—sometimes plus finance charges—at a future date. That credit may be secured or unsecured. The buyer's promise to pay is "secured" when the buyer has granted the seller an enforceable security interest in collateral—most often in the goods which have been purchased. The secured transaction is governed by Article 9 of the Code, and a seller who has complied with the requirements of that Article may retake the collateral on default by the buyer.[84] The buyer's promise is "unsecured" when the seller does not have a security interest in any collateral; all the seller has is the buyer's promise to pay the price of the goods. The rights of the seller under an unsecured sale are governed by Article 2. Whether such a seller may retake the collateral following a default by the buyer is the subject of this section of the text.

Except for situations in which the buyer is insolvent,[85] the Code contains no section which specifically gives the unsecured credit seller a right to reclaim delivered goods. The closest that Article 2 comes to a grant of this right is in section 2–703 which allows an aggrieved seller to "cancel." Cancellation puts an end to the contract; arguably, this terminates any rights which the buyer has to retain the goods. The buyer's right to the goods arose out of the contract of sale which—according to this argument—has been cancelled. The seller could then urge that since the buyer no longer has any right to the goods, they should be returned to the seller.

There are many difficulties with this argument. Pre-Code law refused restitution to the credit seller in the form of specific relief.[86]

---

83. UCC § 2–705, Comment 2. As to the seller's rights if bankruptcy of the buyer intervenes, see 4A Collier, Bankruptcy ¶ 70.40 (14th ed. 1969).

84. If the security agreement is enforceable under UCC § 9–203, the secured seller may take possession after default. UCC § 9–503. His disposition of the collateral is controlled by UCC §§ 9–504 through 9–506 as well as by the security agreement. UCC § 9–201. Priorities as to third parties are covered in UCC § 9–312.

85. The seller may reclaim goods from an insolvent buyer under the conditions set forth in UCC § 2–702(2). However, because these cases involve competing claims by other creditors or purchasers, this right of the seller is discussed in the textual sections applicable to third parties. §§ 167, 169 *infra*.

86. Brand v. State, 26 Ala.App. 286, 158 So. 769 (1935); Pyrene Mfg. Co. v. Burnell, 127 Me. 503, 144 A. 649 (1929); Hayden v. Collins, 90 Utah 238, 63 P.2d 223 (1936). But see the suggestion in General Util. Corp. v. Goldman & Gorin, 108 Pa.Super. 212, 164 A. 72 (1933).

Also, allowing the seller to reclaim the goods under Article 2 would undercut many of the policies sought to be promoted through Article 9. However, the biggest difficulty lies with section 2–703—the section which the seller must use to fashion his argument for specific relief through cancellation.

Section 2–703 remedies (including the right to "cancel") are available to a seller only if at least one of four triggering events has occurred.[87] When the seller is attempting to reclaim goods which were sold on unsecured credit, the buyer has not (1) wrongfully rejected, (2) wrongfully revoked acceptance, or (3) failed to make a payment due *on* or *before* delivery. His failure was to make a payment due *after* delivery. The problem is whether the failure to make that payment was a "repudiation"—the fourth triggering event of section 2–703.

As has been pointed out elsewhere in this text, "repudiation" is not defined by the Code, but is used in the sense of an anticipatory repudiation—not as the equivalent of breach.[88] The Code uses the word "repudiation" to mean some action (or inaction) taken by one of the parties to a contract before that party has received performance and signifying that he will not perform at the scheduled time.[89] In a situation in which the buyer already has the goods, he has received "performance" and cannot "repudiate" as to the performance received. The triggering events of section 2–703 are four types of breaches, and no one is intended to include all possible breaches. Thus, the seller who has sold an unsecured credit cannot reclaim the goods on the buy-

---

It has been suggested that unique goods could be obtained by specific relief. 3 S. **Williston**, Sales § 593 n. 20 (rev. ed. 1948). Unless the general language of UCC § 1–103 is applicable, this argument will be difficult to accept under UCC § 2–703.

87. § 162 *supra*.

88. § 149 *supra* note 2. The seller has a course of action on which he can base an argument that the buyer has repudiated: first, demand assurances under UCC § 2–609; second, when those assurances are not forthcoming, claim that the buyer has repudiated under UCC § 2–609(4); and third, following a repudiation, "cancel" the contract. UCC § 2–703. This argument ought to be rejected for policy reasons discussed in the text. It can also be rejected on the basis of the language of UCC § 2–609(1). That section assumes a situation in which the non-defaulter may *suspend* per-

formance—action which cannot be taken by a seller who has delivered goods on open credit. The drafters did not intend that UCC § 2–609 would be available to allow an unsecured credit seller to reclaim goods.

89. UCC §§ 2–609, 2–610, 2–611 and 2–708. In addition to the material cited in § 149 *supra* note 2, see Gold Mining & Water Co. v. Swinerton, 23 Cal.2d 19, 142 P.2d 22 (1943); Rehart v. Klossner, 48 Cal.App.2d 46, 119 P. 2d 148 (1941); Daley v. People's Bldg., Loan & Sav. Ass'n, 178 Mass. 13, 59 N.E. 452 (1901); Scott v. Miller, 114 App.Div. 6, 99 N.Y.S. 609 (1906); Brooks v. Scoville, 81 Utah 163, 17 P.2d 218 (1932); Rottman v. Endejan, 6 Wis.2d 221, 94 N.W.2d 596 (1959); and the discussion in New York Life Ins. Co. v. Viglas, 297 U.S. 672, 56 S.Ct. 615, 80 L.Ed. 971 (1936). *But see* Crowley v. McCullough, 254 Mich. 362, 237 N.W. 50 (1931). See also Uniform Sales Act § 65.

er's failure to make a payment due after delivery of the goods. He is limited to an action for the price of the goods.

Policy arguments to support this conclusion are hard to discover when the controversy is solely between the seller and buyer. The buyer has failed to pay the price; the buyer still has the goods; the seller would like to reclaim the goods; and there are no creditors of, or purchasers from, the buyer involved in the transaction. Are there sound reasons for denying such a seller specific relief? Historically, the failure to be able to show a wrongful taking barred the remedy of replevin [90]—but most states changed this rule long ago.[91] Under the Uniform Sales Act there was a concern over the passage of title, but title is a legal concept which can be manipulated to reach desired results.[92] Also, the seller can be told that the way to reserve a right to reclaim is to put that right in some security agreement, but this only is restating the conclusion in another form. Perhaps the justification for the Code's position rests on two beliefs: (1) that recovery of full price is an adequate remedy for the seller, and (2) that in any dispute it is difficult to be certain that the controversy is really between the seller and buyer.

These beliefs are reasonable. When the seller and buyer are the only parties to the controversy a recovery of full price can be accompanied by an attachment of or levy on the goods. However, the typical case in which full price is not satisfactory to the seller is the one in which a third party is competing with the seller for the buyer's assets. That third party may be a creditor of the buyer, a representative of the buyer's creditors, or a subsequent purchaser of the goods. In these cases the controversy is not between the seller and the buyer but is between the seller and the third party. If the seller could cancel the contract with the buyer and reclaim the goods, the seller would receive a preference over the third party. It is for this kind of case that the Code (especially in Article 9) attempts to protect the interests of both the seller and the third party.[93] The seller, however, cannot use the buyer's failure to make a payment due after delivery as a basis for reclaiming the goods.

90. Goldstein v. Miami Wrecking & Salvage Co., 103 Fla. 149, 137 So. 283 (1931); Woodward v. Grand Trunk Ry., 46 N.H. 524 (1866). J. Cobbey, Replevin § 51 (1900).

91. A & A Credit Co. v. Berquist, 230 Minn. 303, 41 N.W.2d 582 (1950); Ray v. Hill, 194 Wash. 321, 77 P.2d 1009 (1938).

92. § 125 *supra.*

93. The right to reclaim goods: on the buyer's insolvency is discussed in § 169 *infra;* as against purchasers, in §§ 170–71 *infra.*

§ 166.　Reclamation From the Buyer—Cash Sales

One reason why the unsecured seller is not allowed to reclaim goods in a credit sale is that his legal position is not distinguishable from that of the buyer's other creditors.[94]　The buyer is indebted to many creditors, including this seller, and this seller ought not obtain a greater share of the buyer's assets simply because he can trace the goods which he sold to the buyer.　If, however, the seller did not rely on the buyer's unsecured credit, that seller is distinguishable from the buyer's other unsecured creditors and may be entitled to reclaim the goods.

There are several situations in which the unpaid seller's legal position is different from that of the buyer's other unsecured creditors.　A common example occurs when the seller has demanded and received a perfected security interest in the goods.　Another arises when the buyer has defrauded the seller into selling him goods on credit by misrepresenting his identity or solvency.[95]　A third situation involves the seller who has transferred goods on the strength of what he believes to be a cash payment—only to discover that the required payment was not in fact made.　A buyer may acquire the seller's goods by an exchange of counterfeit money or by delivering other goods to which he had no title.　More commonly, however, the cash-sale-gone-sour occurs when the seller accepts a check which was not honored on presentation.　These sellers have trusted the buyer's credit in only a limited sense; they believed that the buyer would deliver genuine money, goods to which he had title, or a check that would be honored.　This trust in the buyer's integrity, although a kind of "credit," is different from the type of credit extended by other unsecured creditors who trusted the buyer's promise to pay in the future.[96]

The Code recognizes the difference between cash and credit sales by providing in section 2–507(2):

> Where payment is due and demanded on the delivery to the buyer of goods or documents of title, his right as against the seller to retain or dispose of them is conditional upon his making the payment due.

Therefore, if the buyer received goods and at the same time delivered to the seller a check in payment of the amount which was then due and if that check was not honored on presentation, the seller has a

---

94.　§ 165 *supra*.

95.　§§ 167–70 *infra*.

96.　Pre-Code cases allowed specific restitution to the cash-sale seller on default of the buyer. Sprague Can-ning Mach. Co. v. Fuller, 158 F. 588 (5th Cir. 1908); Harbert v. Fort Smith Canning Co., 134 Kan. 240, 5 P.2d 849 (1931); McAllister v. Michigamme Oil Co., 230 Mich. 531, 203 N.W. 78 (1925); 2 S. Williston, Sales §§ 341–43 (rev. ed. 1948).

choice of remedies. He may sue for the price,[97] bring suit on the check,[98] or replevy the goods from the buyer. The buyer's right to *retain* the goods is conditional upon his making the payment due.

Section 2–507(2) contains two limitations on its operation. First, the buyer's right to dispose of the goods runs "against the seller." Even though the cash-sale buyer has no right to dispose of the goods until the payment due has been made, a subsequent sale of those goods to a good faith purchaser for value terminates the seller's title to the goods.[99] The subsequent purchaser acquires a good title and the original seller would lose his right to replevy the goods; on the other hand, a creditor of the buyer who had obtained an involuntary lien on the goods while they were in the buyer's possession would not acquire a good title and his lien would be subject to the seller's right to reclaim the goods if the buyer refused to make the required payment.[1]

The second limitation is found in the introductory phrase: "Where payment is due and demanded on delivery . . . ." Payment must be both due and demanded. If it is demanded when not due, the seller's tender would be non-conforming as not complying with the contract.[2] If payment is due but not demanded, the cash aspects of the transaction would have been waived and a credit sale substituted.[3] Whether a seller has *demanded* payment on delivery often raises a disputed question of fact. Sellers, eager to dispose of their goods to someone who has in the past been a good customer, may accept a post-dated check [4] or leave the goods with the buyer on the strength of his assertions that payment will be forthcoming in a matter of hours. While the transfer of payment need not be precisely simultaneous with the delivery of the goods,[5] the payment and delivery must be sufficiently close to be a part of the same transaction. The longer the seller procrastinates in reclaiming the goods once the demanded payment is not forthcoming, the greater are the chances that the trier of fact will conclude that the payment—though due—was not *demanded* on delivery. Stated another way, leaving the goods with the buyer after the seller realizes

97. UCC § 2–709.

98. UCC § 3–413. Acceptance of a check in which someone other than a bank is the drawer, maker, or acceptor suspends pro tanto the obligation until the check is dishonored; following a dishonor, suit may be brought on either the check or the obligation. UCC §§ 3–802, 2–511(2).

99. UCC § 2–403. § 170 *infra*.

1. As to the lien creditor, see § 168 *infra*. As to the good faith purchaser, see § 170 *infra*.

2. UCC §§ 2–301, 2–503, 2–711. §§ 93–94 *supra*.

3. Pre-Code cases include Neal, Morse & Co. v. Boggan, 97 Ala. 611, 11 So. 809 (1892); Frech v. Lewis, 218 Pa. 141, 67 A. 45 (1907). Cases are collected in 2 S. Williston, Sales § 346 (rev. ed. 1948).

4. UCC § 2–511, Comment 6.

5. Engstrom v. Wiley, 191 F.2d 684 (9th Cir. 1951); *In re* Helms Veneer Corp., 287 F.Supp. 840 (W.D.Va.1968).

that the payment has not been made is evidence indicating that the seller has waived the cash sale requirement.

The Comments contain an unexplained assertion: "The provision of this Article for a ten day limit within which the seller may reclaim goods delivered on credit to an insolvent buyer is also applicable here." [6] The reference is to section 2–702; the ten-day limit in section 2–702 requires that the seller demand a return of the goods within ten days after they have been received by an insolvent buyer to whom the goods were delivered on credit. There is no statutory basis for carrying this requirement into section 2–507(2)—except through notions of waiver—and a ten-day period for reclaiming under section 2–507(2) may be unduly short in situations in which a check has been returned for insufficient funds. Such a check may have passed through several indorsers and banks, not being returned to the seller until after the buyer has had the goods for more than ten days. A seller who has negotiated or transferred a check in the ordinary course of his business ought not be held to have waived his demanded payment solely because the banking process requires more than ten days to inform the seller that the check was dishonored.[7] Thus, the Comment should not be read into the Code as an absolute time limitation on the seller's right to reclaim the goods in a cash sale transaction. The Code test is whether the seller *demanded* the payment which was due on delivery. A statement by the seller to the buyer that the buyer must pay for the goods if he is to get them is sufficient unless the seller, knowing that he did not receive the payment, allows the goods to remain with the buyer without reasonable efforts to recapture them. A failure to make these "reasonable efforts" indicates that the original demand has been withdrawn and some type of credit term has been inserted into their modified agreement. The seller does not automatically have ten days in which to make up his mind, nor does he automatically lose his reclamation rights because ten days have expired.

§ 167.　Reclamation From a Lien Creditor—Credit Sales

The type of factual pattern which raises the problem of this section of the text would be as follows: On January 10 Seller sold goods to Buyer on open credit, not reserving a security interest. On January 15, Charles Creditor, an unsecured creditor of Buyer, obtained a lien on the goods by following local attachment procedures. Seller believes

---

6. UCC § 2–507, Comment 3.

7. Holding the ten-day provision applicable to UCC § 2–507 is *In re* Helms Veneer Corp., 287 F.Supp. 840 (W.D. Va.1968). Ignoring the ten-day provi-

sion are Greater Louisville Auto Auction, Inc. v. Ogle Buick, Inc., 387 S.W. 2d 17 (Ky.1965); *In re* Lindenbaum's, Inc., 2 UCC Rep. 495 (U.S.Dist.Ct. E.D.Pa.1964).

that Buyer may not be able to pay the price at the time it becomes due and would like to reclaim the goods from the lien creditor.

If the seller's belief is based on facts other than the buyer's insolvency, the seller would have no basis for recapturing the goods. He could not retake them from the buyer and the Code gives him no greater rights against a lien creditor.[8]

If, however, the seller's belief is based upon the buyer's insolvency, the Code does provide a basis on which goods can be reclaimed. Section 2–702(2) provides:

> Where the seller discovers that the buyer has received goods on credit while insolvent he may reclaim the goods upon demand made within ten days after the receipt, but if misrepresentation of solvency has been made to the particular seller in writing within three months before delivery the ten day limitation does not apply. Except as provided in this subsection the seller may not base a right to reclaim the goods on the buyer's fraudulent or innocent misrepresentation of solvency or of intent to pay.

This subsection is the counterpart of the buyer's right to obtain the goods on discovery of the seller's insolvency, but it is a much more workable section.[9] The seller may base his claim either on (1) a written misrepresentation of solvency made to the seller within three months before delivery, or (2) a demand for the goods within ten days after their receipt. The Comments require that the written misrepresentation be *addressed to* the particular seller and *dated* within three months of the delivery.[10] This would clearly include letters written to the seller [11] as well as provisions contained in the agreement of sale. Whether it also includes reports made to the seller through credit reporting agencies is more doubtful. The Comment language apparently rules out these representations when they are not addressed to the particular seller. However, the Comment language goes beyond the Code which contains no dating or addressing requirements. Written representations made through third parties should satisfy the Code (although they may not comply with the Comments) when the

---

8. § 165 *supra.*

9. § 160 *supra.* The seller need only prove that the buyer was insolvent when the goods were received; he need not prove when the buyer became insolvent. Failure to prove insolvency, however, prevents reclamation. *In re* Helms Veneer Corp., 287 F.Supp. 840 (W.D.Va.1968).

10. UCC § 2–702, Comment 2.

11. But the letters must misrepresent solvency. *In re* Units, Inc., 3 UCC Rep. 46 (U.S.Dist.Ct.D.Conn.1965). A check does not satisfy the written misrepresentation requirement unless the seller relies on the check. Theo. Hamm Brewing Co. v. First Trust & Sav. Bank, 103 Ill.App.2d 190, 242 N.E.2d 911 (1968).

buyer has supplied the information to the third party with the understanding that the third party would make the credit information available to sellers generally, and when this seller did obtain the information.[12] Whether the three-month provision has also been satisfied will depend upon any dates which are included with the information. For example, if the credit report shows that it is based upon financial data supplied more than three months before the receipt of the goods, the Code requirement would not be met even though the report was read by the seller well within that three-month period.

The seller may also reclaim goods from the insolvent buyer—even though there is no written representation of solvency—"upon demand made within ten days after the receipt" of the goods.[13] The demand that is involved in this section is a demand that the goods be returned, not that the price be paid.[14] There will be problems in determining whether ten days (as opposed to eleven days) have elapsed, but the construction of section 2–702(2) should produce these two conclusions:

1. The time period does not begin to run on shipment of the goods. Receipt is the important date.

2. The time period begins to run the day after the goods have been received. As long as the demand is made within a period ending on the tenth day "after the receipt," the statute has been satisfied.[15] Unless some other statute in the particular state excludes holidays or Sundays from this count, the time for making the demand would expire at the conclusion of the tenth calendar day after the goods have been received by the buyer.

The result of this analysis is that the unsecured seller can reclaim from the insolvent buyer goods which were sold on credit, providing

---

12. See Manly v. Ohio Shoe Co., 25 F.2d 384 (4th Cir. 1928).

13. The basis of this rule is a "tacit business misrepresentation of solvency" when purchasing goods on credit. UCC § 2–702, Comment 2. *See In re* Meislman, 105 F.2d 995, 998 (2d Cir. 1939). Pre-Code law was not as beneficial to the seller. Comment, 34 Mich. L.Rev. 850 (1936). The Code's requirement of "quick" action by the seller removes much of the impact of any change in the common law, and the exclusivity sentence makes pre-Code case law inapplicable to Code cases. UCC § 2–702(2).

14. *In re* Helms Veneer Corp., 287 F. Supp. 840 (W.D.Va.1968); Evans

Products Co. v. Jorgensen, 245 Or. 362, 421 P.2d 978 (1966). For a case which did not require the ten-day demand, see Greater Louisville Auto Auction, Inc. v. Ogle Buick, Inc., 387 S.W.2d 17 (Ky.1965). Other courts have held that the failure to make the demand bars reclamation. *In re* Childress, 6 UCC Rep. 505 (U.S.Dist.Ct.E.D.Tenn. 1969).

15. *In re* Behring & Behring, 5 UCC Rep. 600 (U.S.Dist.Ct.N.D.Texas 1968). This case also suggests that the demand may be waived if not followed promptly by some type of legal action or self-help. § 166 *supra*.

the conditions of section 2–702(2) have been satisfied.[16] The difficulty is that these goods are seldom, if ever, reclaimed *from the buyer*. Inevitably, some third party has intervened and is competing with the seller. On some occasions it is a subsequent purchaser;[17] on others it is a trustee in bankruptcy.[18] In the situation discussed in this section of the text the third party is a lien creditor who attached the goods for a claim against the buyer. Section 2–702(3) adds:

> The seller's right to reclaim under subsection (2) is subject to the rights of a buyer in ordinary course or other good faith purchaser or lien creditor under this Article (Section 2–403). Successful reclamation of goods excludes all other remedies with respect to them.

Thus, the seller's reclamation rights under 2–702(2) are subject to the rights of "a lien creditor under this Article."

The relevant inquiry thus becomes: what rights does a lien creditor have under Article 2? The Code reference is to section 2–403 which, in its first three subsections, gives rights to a good faith purchaser for value and to a buyer in ordinary course of business.[19] The only reference to lien creditors is in section 2–403(4) where the Code states that the rights of other purchasers and of lien creditors are governed by Articles 6, 7, and 9. Articles 6 (Bulk Transfers) and 7 (Documents of Title) do not deal with the problems of this section of the text; thus, the only relevant reference is to Article 9 (Secured Transactions).

Article 9 establishes a priority between security interests on the one side and several different types of interests (including competing security interests) on the other. Security interests are of two types— perfected and unperfected. Section 9–301 establishes priorities for the unperfected security interest by providing, among other things, that such an interest is subordinate to the rights of "a person who becomes a lien creditor without knowledge of the security interest and before it is perfected . . . ." Therefore, if the unsecured seller of goods on credit has a "security interest" which can be considered as unperfected, he is subordinate to the attaching creditor. Courts could conceivably conclude that this is the legal position of such a seller and that the lien creditor should prevail.[20]

---

16. In some instances the buyer may have sold the goods but the proceeds of the sale are identifiable. UCC § 2–702 would not reach these proceeds, but a constructive trust based on the misrepresentation is available in a proper case. UCC § 1–103; Greater Louisville Auto Auction, Inc. v. Ogle Buick, Inc., 387 S.W.2d 17 (Ky.1965).

17. § 170 *infra.*

18. § 169 *infra.*

19. A lien creditor is not a "purchaser." § 168 *infra.*

20. 4A Collier, Bankruptcy ¶ 70.62A [7.1] (14th ed. 1969). There are a

This has, however, not been the position reached by courts—and properly so. The notion that an *unsecured* seller has a *security* interest of any kind requires an active imagination. More important, the definition of "security interest" does not cover the reclamation rights of a seller under section 2–702(2).[21] Thus, neither Article 2 nor Article 9 gives the lien creditor any rights over the section 2–702(2) seller. Since the seller's section 2–702(2) right to reclaim is subject to the rights of lien creditors "under this Article," the justifiable conclusion is that the drafters intended the section 2–702(2) seller to prevail when competing with the lien creditor. This conclusion is supported by a proposed amendment to section 2–702(3) which eliminates the "or lien creditor" language.[22]

Judicial decisions have thus far supported this analysis of the Code—except for the last step. Rather than concluding that the Code's silence indicates that the section 2–702(2) seller should prevail, these decisions have referred to pre-Code law to determine priorities.[23] Since nearly all states granted priority to the reclaiming seller, the result is the same as that suggested above.[24] However, in those few states which prior to the Code preferred the lien creditor the result will be different—at least until the proposed amendment has been adopted in those states.

§ 168. Reclamation From a Lien Creditor—Cash Sales

This section assumes that a seller has sold goods to a buyer under a contract which required payment on delivery, that the goods were delivered and the payment demanded, but that the payment was not made. The usual situation which presents this factual pattern is one in which the buyer paid by check which was dishonored on present-

number of law review articles analyzing this problem in the context of the trustee in bankruptcy. See Braucher, *Reclamation of Goods from a Fraudulent Buyer*, 65 Mich.L.Rev. 1281 (1967). For opposing positions, see Hawkland, *The Relative Rights of Lien Creditors and Defrauded Sellers—Amending the Uniform Commercial Code to Conform to the Kravitz Case*, 67 Com.L.J. 86 (1962) and Shanker, *A Reply to the Proposed Amendment of UCC Section 2–702(3): Another View of Lien Creditor's Rights vs. Rights of a Seller to an Insolvent*, 14 W.Res.L.Rev. 93 (1962).

21. UCC § 1–201(37).

22. Report No. 3 of the Permanent Editorial Board for the Uniform Commercial Code 3 (1966). Several states have already adopted the proposed amendment.

23. *In re* Mel Golde Shoes, Inc., 403 F.2d 658 (6th Cir. 1968) (seller had preference over judgment creditor in Kentucky pre-Code law); *In re* Kravitz, 278 F.2d 820 (3d Cir. 1960) (lien creditor had preference over seller in Pennsylvania pre-Code law).

24. O'Rieley v. Endicott-Johnson Corp., 297 F.2d 1 (8th Cir. 1961); 3 S. Williston, Sales §§ 620, 637 (rev. ed. 1948); Annot., 59 A.L.R. 418 (1929). The lien creditor may, in some instances, prevail over the seller by use of the doctrine of estoppel. *In re* Rhine, 241 F.Supp. 86 (D.Colo.1965), *original opinion adhered to* 242 F.Supp. 127 (D. Colo.1965).

ment. This text has concluded that the seller had a right to reclaim the goods from the buyer.[25] However, this section of the text adds a further fact: during the time that the goods were in the possession of the buyer a creditor of the buyer levied on or attached those goods for a debt owing to the creditor by the buyer. The priority problem would then be between a cash-sale seller and a lien creditor.

In this situation the Code favors the seller and grants him priority over the lien creditor to the same extent that he would have priority over the buyer. The only difficulty in reaching this conclusion comes from section 2–507(2)—the section which conditions the buyer's right to retain or dispose of the goods when payment is due and demanded on delivery, but not made. That section states that the *buyer's* rights are so conditioned; it does not state that the *third party's* rights are also conditioned on payment. From this the lien creditor could argue that his right to the goods is unconditional and that he has priority over the seller even if the price is not paid.

The Comments, however, indicate that section 2–507(2) was written in its present form to protect good faith purchasers [26] (not lien creditors), and other Code sections support this reading. Section 2–403—the section which deals with the rights of good faith purchasers and lien creditors—affords the lien creditor protection against unperfected security interests (situations in which an Article 9 seller has sold on credit without taking the necessary steps to perfect his reserved security interest in the goods), but does not give the lien creditor priority over the seller who can reclaim under Article 2.[27] This is not simply a difference between the wording of Articles 2 and 9; it represents a judgment as to commercial policies. As long as the seller has trusted the buyer's credit to pay the price, as he does when he sells on open credit or when he fails to take the necessary action to perfect a security interest, the unpaid seller and other unsecured creditors stand on the same footing. They both trusted the credit of the buyer. Since the lien creditor first took action to acquire security, he prevails. However, when the seller transferred goods because of the buyer's misrepresentations (as when the buyer buys while insolvent) or when he sells for what he believed was the same as cash, that seller merits protection over creditors who relied only on the buyer's promise to pay.[28] Those other creditors took a business risk and cannot shift that risk to sellers who sold for cash or were defrauded.

---

25. § 166 *supra.*

26. UCC § 2–507, Comment 3.

27. Code provisions supporting this conclusion are discussed in § 167 *supra.*

28. § 166 *supra* note 96. Protection of the seller in cash sales can often rest additionally on the Code's policy of promoting the use of checks in the buyer's payment of the price. UCC § 2–511.

Further, the lien creditor cannot qualify as a "purchaser" under section 2–403 and thereby acquire the rights of a "good faith purchaser for value." A purchaser is one who takes by purchase [29]—which is defined to include only a *voluntary* transaction creating an interest in property.[30] The attachment of a lien is not a voluntary transaction; thus it is not a purchase.

ᴵ The result is that the Article 2 rights of a lien creditor are no greater than the rights which the buyer had against his seller. If the seller could not reclaim goods from his buyer, he cannot reclaim them when one of the buyer's creditors attaches those goods. On the other hand, if the seller could reclaim the goods from his buyer, he is given priority over an intervening lien creditor.[31]

§ 169. Reclamation From the Buyer's Trustee in Bankruptcy

When the buyer's insolvency has led to an adjudication in bankruptcy, the reclaiming seller will be competing against the buyer's trustee in bankruptcy for priority to the goods.

Under the Bankruptcy Act the trustee is vested with the title to all of the bankrupt's property.[32] However, in a situation in which the seller could reclaim goods, the bankrupt's title is subject to avoidance and may be avoided against the trustee unless some other provision of the Act gives the trustee greater rights than the bankrupt had. There are several sections of the Bankruptcy Act which conceivably could be applicable in a particular case,[33] but in the typical situation in which an unsecured seller is seeking reclamation the trustee would have to rely on the section which gives the trustee the rights and powers of a lien creditor—whether or not such a creditor exists.[34] The rights which a lien creditor has are measured by state law,[35] and when goods are involved this means that those rights will (except in

---

29. UCC § 1–201(33).

30. UCC § 1–201(32).

31. *See In re* Lindenbaum's, Inc., 2 UCC Rep. 495 (U.S.Dist.Ct.E.D.Pa.1964); *In re* Mort Co., 208 F.Supp. 309 (E.D. Pa.1962). Pre-Code cases holding that the lien creditor has no greater rights than the buyer include Oswego Starch Factory v. Lendrum, 57 Iowa 573, 10 N.W. 900 (1891); McAuliffe & Burke Co. v. Gallagher, 258 Mass. 215, 154 N.E. 755 (1927); Fitzsimmons v. Joslin, 21 Vt. 129 (1849).

32. Bankruptcy Act § 70a(5), 11 U.S. C.A. § 110a(5) (1964).

33. For example, atypical facts might produce a fraudulent transfer (Bankruptcy Act §§ 67d, 70e, 11 U.S.C.A. §§ 107d, 110e (1964)) or a situation in which an actual creditor—and, through him, the trustee in bankruptcy—could employ the doctrine of estoppel to resist reclamation (Bankruptcy Act § 70e, 11 U.S.C.A. § 110e (1964)). 4A Collier, Bankruptcy ¶ 70.90[2] (14th ed. 1969). Also, a consignment sale would be subject to the buyer's creditors under UCC § 2–326. § 41 *supra*.

34. Bankruptcy Act § 70c, 11 U.S.C.A. § 110c (1964).

35. Adelman v. Centaur Corp., 145 F. 2d 573 (6th Cir. 1944).

Louisiana) be measured by the Code. Thus, those portions of this text which discussed the priority problems between the reclaiming seller and the lien creditor [36] are applicable to the claims of the trustee in bankruptcy.

The conclusions drawn in those sections were:

1. *As to credit sales.* First, the seller must establish his right to reclaim under section 2–702(2). This requires a showing of insolvency of the buyer at the time the goods were received, delivery of the goods on credit, and either (a) a misrepresentation of solvency made to this particular seller in writing within three months of the delivery of goods or (b) a demand for the goods within ten days after their receipt. Second, once these facts are established the seller may reclaim the goods in all states which have removed the "or lien creditor" language from section 2–702(3) and ought to be able to reclaim them in the other states. However, in some of those other states there is judicial authority that the priorities will be determined by pre-Code law which generally—but not unanimously—favors the reclaiming seller.[37]

2. *As to cash sales.* First, the seller must establish his right to reclaim under sections 2–507 and 2–511. This requires a showing that payment was due and demanded on delivery (with section 2–310(a) aiding in determining when payment was due) and that the payment was not made. Second, once those facts are established the seller may reclaim the goods.[38]

One possible difficulty in interrelating the Code with the Bankruptcy Act to reach the results suggested above is the fact that state law can no longer be used to give certain debts a "priority," [39] and it is arguable that by allowing certain unsecured sellers to reclaim goods the Code has attempted to create a state priority. If it has, the reclamation rights under sections 2–507 and 2–702 will fail in bankruptcy proceedings.

These sections of the Code ought not be held inconsistent with the Bankruptcy Act. When a misrepresentation of solvency is involved, there is ample pre-Code authority that the seller can rescind and recapture the goods.[40] This authority supports the Code's "written misrepresentation" portion of section 2–702. However, the ten-

---

36. §§ 167–68 *supra.*

37. 4A Collier, Bankruptcy ¶ 70.62A [7.1] (14th ed. 1969).

38. *In re* Smithdale Indus., Inc., 219 F.Supp. 862 (E.D.Tenn.1963).

39. Priorities are determined by Bankruptcy Act § 64, 11 U.S.C.A. § 104 (1964).

40. 4A Collier, Bankruptcy ¶ 70.41 (14th ed. 1969).

day demand without an express showing of misrepresentation is new and could conceivably be held to create a priority rather than to follow the established notion of rescission based upon fraud. Such a position should be rejected. The Comments justify the "ten-day demand" portion of section 2–702 on the basis that receipt of goods by an insolvent buyer is a tacit business misrepresentation of solvency, thus bringing the provision within established doctrine.[41] A more forthright justification would be that the nearly unanimous decision by state legislatures to afford reclamation to an unsecured seller who acts quickly to protect his interests ought to be given effect in bankruptcy where the trustee takes on the rights and powers of a state lien creditor. The cases have quite properly assumed the validity of section 2–702 in bankruptcy proceedings.[42]

If the seller was able to recapture the goods during the four month period prior to the filing of the petition in bankruptcy by or against the buyer, that recapture ought not be considered a preference under the Bankruptcy Act if the trustee could not have resisted reclamation in the bankruptcy proceedings under those same facts.[43] The Code does, however, recognize that the seller who reacquires goods which have been delivered on credit has obtained a financial advantage over other unsecured creditors, and provides: "Successful reclamation of goods excludes all other remedies with respect to them." [44] This statement is not a model of clarity (once goods are reclaimed, what other remedy is possible with respect to the *goods?*) but undoubtedly means that once a seller is successful in reclaiming goods he has no other remedy with respect to that portion of the contract relating to the reclaimed goods. He would, however, retain all of his remedies with respect to other goods—even though covered by the same contract.

§ 170.   Reclamation From Sub-purchasers—Protection of Good Faith Purchasers

An unpaid seller who delivered goods to his buyer without reserving a security interest has only a limited right to reclaim those goods.[45] The Code further restricts that right by the protection which it affords the good faith purchaser. As a result, a seller who would otherwise be able to reclaim goods from a buyer (or even from the buyer's lien creditor or trustee in bankruptcy) may find that his

41.   UCC § 2–702, Comment 2.

42.   *In re* Mel Golde Shoes, Inc., 403 F.2d 658 (6th Cir. 1968); *In re* Kravitz, 278 F.2d 820 (3d Cir. 1960).

43.   3 Collier, Bankruptcy ¶ 60.18 (14th ed. 1969).

44.   UCC § 2–702(3).

45.   §§ 165–69 *supra*.

reclamation rights have been terminated by a transfer to a subsequent purchaser.

Article 2's protection of the good faith purchaser is contained in section 2–403—a section which deals generally with the question of what title is transferred to purchasers. Section 2–403 is, therefore, broader in scope than simply that of determining the seller's reclamation rights, and could have been considered at various other places in this text. A discussion of section 2–403 was delayed until this point, however, so that it could be presented in full against a background of the rights of a seller, owner, and buyer.

Section 2–403 states three transfer-of-title rules. These are:

Rule # 1. A purchaser acquires all of the title which his transferor had or had power to transfer. This rule is phrased in terms of purchaser-transferor rather than buyer-seller because it applies to all voluntary transactions which create an interest in goods.[46] Not only does a buyer acquire the title which his seller had, but so does a donee since—according to the Code—a donee also takes by "purchase."

The result of this first rule of section 2–403 as applied to the sales transaction can be summarized as follows. If the transferor had what the Code calls a "good title," his purchaser receives that good title. If the transferor owned a fractional interest or a life estate (or any other limited interest) in the goods, the purchaser acquires that fractional interest or life estate. On the other hand, if the transferor had no title (as, for example, if he had stolen the goods), the purchaser receives no title. The application of this rule is not changed by the good faith of any one of these purchasers. Thus, the person who purchases goods from a thief for value and in complete good faith acquires no title because his seller had none to give.[47] This was the pre-Code rule [48] and has been carried into the Code through section 2–403. In such a case the owner could reclaim his goods or maintain an action based upon a theory of conversion.

Rule # 2. The parties may agree that the purchaser will receive less title than was held by his transferor; if so, only the lesser interest will pass. There is no Code requirement that a donor give away or a seller convey all of his title. He may transfer a limited interest if that is his expressed intention, but if nothing was said by

---

46. UCC § 1–201(32). A donee takes by purchase, Berkley, Inc. v. Brettler, 354 Mass. 24, 234 N.E.2d 742 (1968), as does a pledgee, B. Ungar, Inc. v. Hammerman Bros., Inc., 5 UCC Rep. 111 (N.Y.App.T.1968).

47. P. R. Autos, Inc. v. Truelson Motors, Inc., 6 UCC Rep. 672 (N.Y.

Sup.Ct.1969); Linwood Harvestore, Inc. v. Cannon, 427 Pa. 434, 235 A.2d 377 (1967) (recognizing rule).

48. Allstate Ins. Co. v. Enzolera, 164 Neb. 38, 81 N.W.2d 588 (1957); Cotton States Mut. Ins. Co. v. Bibbee, 147 W.Va. 786, 131 S.E.2d 745 (1963); 2 S.Williston, Sales § 311 (rev. ed. 1948).

way of a limited interest, all of the transferor's title passed to his purchaser.   These first two rules are summarized in this section 2–403(1) sentence: "A purchaser of goods acquires all title which his transferor had or had power to transfer except that a purchaser of a limited interest acquires rights only to the extent of the interest purchased."

Rule # 3.   When a person has a voidable title he can pass a good title to a good faith purchaser for value; when goods have been entrusted to a merchant who deals in goods of that kind, the merchant (although he had no title) can transfer the rights of the entruster to a buyer in the ordinary course of business.   In both situations covered by the third rule of section 2–403 a seller (and he must be a "seller" because of the value requirement) has the power to transfer more title than he had.   The application of Rule #3 is expanded below.

VOIDABLE TITLE

The type of factual pattern which presents the problem solved by this portion of the third section 2–403 rule is this: A seller has sold goods but has a right to reclaim the goods from the buyer. This right to reclaim could rest either on section 2–702 (goods sold on unsecured credit to an insolvent buyer with the necessary ten-day demand or written representation of solvency)[49] or on section 2–507 (payment due and demanded on delivery, but not made).[50]   Before the seller could reclaim the goods, the buyer transferred those goods to a good faith purchaser who paid value.   The seller is now competing for priority to the goods with the subsequent purchaser.

In either of these cases the good faith purchaser for value will be given priority.   The seller, although he could have avoided his buyer's title, put his buyer in the position of an owner and is estopped to contest that ownership when it has been relied upon by a good faith purchaser for value.   The section 2–702 case is covered by this sentence from section 2–403(1): "A person with voidable title has power to transfer a good title to a good faith purchaser for value."   When the insolvent buyer purchased goods on unsecured credit, he received a title that was subject to being avoided by his seller under the conditions of section 2–702.[51]   This power to void the title is lost once the

49.   § 167 *supra.*

50.   § 166 *supra.*

51.   The seller must demand return of goods within ten days of their receipt to satisfy UCC § 2–702(2); he need not get possession within the ten days. Metropolitan Distribs. v. Eastern Supply Co., 21 Pa.D. & C.2d 128 (C.P.1959). This suggests the possibility of a sale

by the buyer after the demand but before the reclamation. Is the title of the buyer still "voidable" at the time of the sale or is it "void" so that the buyer has no power to pass a good title?   The Uniform Sales Act protected the good faith purchaser for value if the voidable title "has not been avoided at the time of the sale." Uniform Sales Act § 24. Dictum in a Code case (involving Article 8) sup-

goods are transferred to a good faith purchaser for value. Further, section 2–403 is not limited to the section 2–702 voidable title—any voidable title can ripen into good title under section 2–403. Since the Code does not define "voidable title," pre-Code notions as to this concept can be read into the Code.

This same concept could have been used to determine priorities arising out of section 2–507 cases—those in which payment was due and demanded on delivery, but not made. Once again the buyer's title is subject to being avoided, this time if the seller can meet the requirements of section 2–507. The drafters, however, did not leave this problem to judicial inquiry into whether the buyer's title was "voidable" (rather than "void") and, in section 2–403(1), listed four situations which had troubled pre-Code courts, resolving them in favor of the good faith purchaser for value. These situations are those in which:

1. The transferor was deceived as to the identity of the purchaser. These are cases in which the seller delivered goods to his buyer after being deceived into believing that the buyer was some third person, usually a man of property. If that buyer had transferred the goods to a good faith purchaser for value, pre-Code courts often looked into the intention of the seller at the time of the sale to the deceiving buyer, distinguishing situations where the misrepresentation of identity was made in a face-to-face transaction from those in which it was made by written communications.[52] No longer is this inquiry important. In either event the good faith purchaser for value is given priority.

2. The delivery was in exchange for a check which was later dishonored.[53] This is one type of case in which section 2–507 would be applicable. The delivery of the goods was "in exchange" for the check which was later dishonored. Had the seller acted quickly, he could have reclaimed the goods from the buyer, but the buyer's transfer to the good faith purchaser for value gave that purchaser a good title against the seller. If, instead of delivering the goods in exchange for the check, the seller had transferred the goods to the buyer on unsecured credit, the seller would have no right to reclaim [54] (payment

---

ports the notion that the good faith purchaser for value would be protected if he took before notice of avoidance was given. Hartford Accident & Indem. Co. v. Walston & Co., 21 N.Y. 2d 219, 234 N.E.2d 230, 287 N.Y.S.2d 58 (1967).

52. Phelps v. McQuade, 220 N.Y. 232, 115 N.E. 441 (1917).

53. Hudiburg Chevrolet, Inc. v. Ponce, 17 Wis.2d 281, 116 N.W.2d 252 (1962). As to pre-Code law *compare* Clark v. Hamilton Diamond Co., 209 Cal. 1, 284 P. 915 (1930), *with* Sullivan Co. v. Larson, 149 Neb. 97, 30 N.W.2d 460 (1948).

54. § 165 *supra*.

was not due and demanded on delivery of the goods) from the buyer or any transferee, whether or not he purchased in good faith and for value.

3. The parties agreed that the transaction was to be a "cash sale." This is another section 2–507 case. The seller could reclaim from the buyer but not from a later good faith purchaser for value. This Code provision removes any possibility of a successful argument by the seller that section 2–703 allowed him to cancel the buyer's title in a cash sale that went awry (thereby making the title "void"—not just "voidable"—and to reclaim the goods from a good faith purchaser for value).

4. The delivery was procured through fraud punishable as larcenous under the criminal law. Some pre-Code courts had been troubled by their criminal law larceny decisions which had held that no title passed on the criminal acts of the buyer, and this appeared to prevent a title from ripening in the subsequent purchaser for value.[55] This will no longer be a problem under Code. Once again, the good faith purchaser for value is given priority; the fraudulent buyer has power to transfer a good title even though he could be punished for larceny.

These four factual patterns between the seller and buyer are called transactions of purchase; in each the buyer has the power to transfer a good title. This does not mean that every subsequent purchaser terminates the seller's reclamation rights, any more than when the original buyer's title was voidable. To prevail the subsequent purchaser must prove (1) that he was a purchaser, (2) that he purchased in good faith, and (3) that he gave value. Each of these concepts is defined by the Code. A *purchaser* is a person who takes by "sale, discount, negotiation, pledge, lien, issue or re-issue, gift or any other voluntary transaction creating an interest in property." [56] *Good faith* means "honesty in fact" [57] in the transaction involved; in addition, a merchant must observe "reasonable commercial standards of fair dealing in the trade." [58] *Value* is defined to include satisfaction of a pre-existing claim or contract as well as "any consideration sufficient to support a simple contract." [59] There is, therefore, no requirement that the purchaser pay full market value for the goods, but to the extent

55. Hewitt v. Malone, 105 Ga.App. 281, 124 S.E.2d 501 (1962); Stanton Motor Corp. v. Rosetti, 11 A.D.2d 296, 203 N.Y.S.2d 273 (1960).

56. UCC §§ 1–201(32) and 1–201(33).

57. UCC § 1–201(19).

58. UCC § 2–103(1) (b). Atlas Auto Rental Corp. v. Weisberg, 54 Misc.2d 168, 281 N.Y.S.2d 400 (Civ.Ct.1967).

59. UCC § 1–201(44). Stratton Sale Barn, Inc. v. Reed, 28 Agri.Dec. 677, 6 UCC Rep. 922 (U.S. Dept. of Agriculture 1969).

that this purchaser is able to buy for less than market value, this fact is evidence that he was not acting with honesty in fact.[60]

These portions of section 2–403 provide a further limit on a seller's right to reclaim goods which have left his possession. They will be joined by rules as to agency and estoppel (through section 1–103) to protect those who act in good faith in reliance on apparent agency and ownership.[61]

ENTRUSTING

Section 2–403 has codified one type of estoppel through a doctrine which the Code has labelled as "entrusting":

> Any entrusting of possession of goods to a merchant who deals in goods of that kind gives him power to transfer all rights of the entruster to a buyer in ordinary course of business.[62]

This subsection contemplates a bailment—not a sale—to the merchant with a subsequent sale by the merchant. It sets out those instances in which the entruster loses his rights to the goods. To prevail under this subsection, the buyer must show:

1. There was an entrusting of possession. Normally, this will not be difficult to prove because "entrusting" is broadly defined as including "any delivery and any acquiescence in retention of possession regardless of any condition expressed between the parties to the delivery or acquiescence and regardless of whether the procurement of the entrusting or the possessor's disposition of the goods have been such as to be larcenous under the criminal law." [63]

2. The entrusting was to a merchant who deals in goods of that kind. The concept of merchant has already been discussed [64] and need not be repeated; however, entrusting goods to a neighbor or even to someone who is a merchant but does not deal in goods of the kind involved will not meet the requirement of section 2–403 (although such

---

60. Hollis v. Chamberlin, 243 Ark. 201, 419 S.W.2d 116 (1967).

61. An owner may be estopped to claim title against one who acted in reliance on ostensible ownership of a third party. UCC § 2–403, Comment 1. Examples of the type of case where estoppel could be used include Jackson v. Moultrie Prod. Credit Ass'n, 76 Ga. App. 768, 47 S.E.2d 127 (1948) (owner failed to deny bailee's ownership when third party made inquiry within hearing distance of owner); Lakes v. Orley, 148 Mont. 325, 420 P.2d 151 (1966)

(owner, knowing of sale by conditional purchaser to third person, did not challenge sale for several months); Arsen v. Director of Div. of Motor Vehicles, 61 N.J.Super. 131, 160 A.2d 192 (Super.Ct.1960) (owner gave bailee ownership certificate, keys, and possession of automobile but third party was not a bona fide purchaser).

62. UCC § 2–403(2).

63. UCC § 2–403(3).

64. § 33 *supra*.

a delivery might satisfy common law notions of estoppel). The type of case the Code attempts to cover is exemplified by the delivery of a watch to a jeweler for repairs or an automobile to a used car lot for sale. When an entruster delivers goods to a merchant who deals in goods of the kind involved—or allows such a merchant to remain in possession—that entruster should realize that he has placed the merchant in a position to act as owner.[65]

3. The buyer qualifies as a "buyer in ordinary course."[66] This concept is similar to that of good faith purchaser for value in that buyer must buy (that is, purchase) in good faith and without knowledge that the sale violates property rights of a third party. However, it is unlike the concept of good faith purchase for value in that the buyer must buy in *ordinary course* from a person in the business of selling goods of that kind,[67] and a purchase as a transfer in bulk or as security for or in total satisfaction of a money debt (past consideration) will not qualify the buyer for this protection. This idea combines with the entrusting requirement. Not only must the entruster place the merchant in a position to look like an owner (a "minus" for the entruster); the buyer must make his purchase in the ordinary way that purchases are made from a merchant (a "plus" for the buyer) before the entruster's rights are terminated.[68]

Finally, even if the buyer can meet the requirements of the entrusting sections of the Code, he acquires only the rights of the entruster.[69] If the entruster was a thief, having no title, the buyer in ordinary course acquires no priority over the owner. Indeed, the way these subsections of the Code are written, the buyer in ordinary course could not use the entrusting sections to ripen a voidable title held by the entruster into a good title. This may have been an oversight by the drafters (because the policies seem the same as those discussed

---

65. The entruster must know he transferred the goods to a merchant who deals in goods of that kind and the purchaser must also realize that he was buying from such a merchant. Atlas Auto Rental Corp. v. Weisberg, 54 Misc.2d 168, 281 N.Y.S.2d 400 (Civ. Ct.1967).

66. "Buyer in ordinary course" is defined in UCC § 1-201(9).

67. Makransky v. Long Island Reo Truck Co., 58 Misc.2d 338, 295 N.Y.S. 2d 240 (Sup.Ct.1968). The buyer in ordinary course obtains the title of the entruster even if sale was contrary to entruster's directions. Humphrey

Cadillac & Oldsmobile Co. v. Sinard, 85 Ill.App.2d 64, 229 N.E.2d 365 (1967).

68. When the buyer knows the merchant had no authority to sell, the buyer does not get good title unless he has purchased from an intervening purchaser with good title. Linwood Harvestore, Inc. v. Cannon, 427 Pa. 434, 235 A.2d 377 (1967). A purchaser of an automobile can be a buyer in ordinary course even though the buyer received no certificate of title. Medico Leasing Co. v. Smith, 457 P.2d 548 (Okl.1969). *Contra*, Mattek v. Malofsky, 42 Wis.2d 16, 165 N.W.2d 406 (1969).

69. The owner prevails over the secured party of the person to whom the goods

above under voidable title), and a liberal interpretation of the voidable title rules of section 2–403(1) should produce the desired consistency.[70]

§ 171. Reclamation From Secured Party of Buyer

The unpaid seller who has delivered goods to his buyer without reserving a security interest may reclaim those goods from the buyer, the buyer's lien creditor, or the buyer's trustee in bankruptcy—but only under the very limited instances already discussed.[71] However, any hopes of reclamation are lost when those goods are transferred by the buyer to a good faith purchaser for value,[72] and the buyer's secured party is a "purchaser" for the purpose of this rule. The secured party acquires his interest in the property by contract,[73] and a contract is a "voluntary transaction" within the Code's definition of "purchase." [74] Therefore, if the secured party acted in good faith and gave value, he would be protected from reclamation claims of the seller even in situations in which the security interest attached by virtue of an after-acquired property clause.[75] The discussion in the prior section of this text is applicable to this priority problem [76]—except, of course, the secured party does not receive a "good title." He receives only a security interest in the goods irrespective of any agreement between the parties as to which one has title.[77]

§ 172. Use of Constructive Trust to Claim Substitute Goods

An unpaid (and unsecured) seller has a limited right to reclaim goods from his buyer. Nevertheless, when available, the right to reclaim can be an important remedy. If the buyer is insolvent, a judgment for the price could net the seller only a small portion of his claim, but a reclamation of the goods will net the seller a full recovery for his loss—to the extent of the value of those goods. However, the

were entrusted, Cosgriff v. Liberty Nat'l Bank & Trust Co., 58 Misc.2d 884, 296 N.Y.S.2d 517 (Sup.Ct.1968), but a secured party of the buyer has priority over the secured party of the entruster. Commercial Credit Corp. v. Associates Discount Corp., 246 Ark. 116, 436 S.W.2d 809 (1969).

70. The policy of protecting buyers of goods is also expressed in Article 9. See UCC § 9–307. The relation of UCC § 2–403 to Article 9 security interests is considered in Charles S. Martin Distrib. Co. v. Banks, 111 Ga. App. 538, 142 S.E.2d 309 (1965); National Shawmut Bank v. Jones, 108 N.H. 386, 236 A.2d 484 (1967).

71. §§ 165–69 *supra.*

72. UCC § 2–403(1).

73. UCC § 9–102(2).

74. UCC § 1–201(32).

75. *In re* Hayward Woolen Co., 3 UCC Rep. 1107 (U.S.Dist.Ct.D.Mass.1967); Jordan v. Butler, 182 Neb. 626, 156 N.W.2d 778 (1968); Stumbo v. Paul B. Hult Lumber Co., —— Or. ——, 444 P.2d 564 (1968) (rule recognized in footnote 10 by court).

76. § 170 *supra.*

77. UCC § 9–202.

seller's limited Article 2 right to reclaim is lost if the goods are transferred to a good faith purchaser for value.

An owner of goods who has entrusted them to a merchant may recover those goods from the merchant under the terms of the agreement between the parties. If the merchant is insolvent, the owner is not compelled to file an unsecured claim and accept a portion of the value of the goods but may reclaim the goods in specie—thereby obtaining a larger percentage of his claim than if he were treated as a general unsecured creditor.[78] However, the owner's right of reclamation is lost if the merchant transfers the goods to a buyer in ordinary course.

The sale of the goods to the good faith purchaser for value leaves the seller with his personal cause of action against the buyer for the balance of the purchase price. Likewise, the sale by the merchant to a buyer in ordinary course gives the prior owner a personal cause of action against the merchant for the value of the goods converted. In some instances the seller (or owner) may be satisfied with such an action. If the defendant has sufficient assets to satisfy any judgment received, money will be substituted for the goods—and new goods can be obtained. Nevertheless, there are situations in which the personal cause of action is not a satisfactory remedy. If the defendant is insolvent, the unsecured personal claim will share ratably with the claims of the other creditors.

The seller (or owner) in this latter situation should consider the possibility of impressing either a constructive trust or an equitable lien on the proceeds from the sale to the third party.[79] The basis of the constructive trust is as follows: the seller (or owner) had a right to reclaim the goods as long as they were held by the buyer; the price paid by the third person is substituted for the goods; and the court will impress a trust on that price (the res of the trust) as long as the price can be traced as a part of the defendant's assets. In theory, the plaintiff is entitled to the traceable proceeds from the sale even though those proceeds have increased in value beyond the plaintiff's loss. In this sense the plaintiff is treated as the *owner* of the proceeds, and he

---

78. 4A Collier, Bankruptcy ¶ 70.39 (14th ed. 1969).

79. Restatement of Restitution §§ 202–03 (1937). As long as the buyer has the goods, the seller's remedy to obtain them is "at law." Henderson v. Gibbs, 39 Kan. 679, 18 P. 926 (1888); Glenn, *Rescission for Fraud in Sale or Purchase of Goods—Quasi Contractual Remedies as Related to Trover* *and Replevin*, 22 Va.L.Rev. 859 (1936). Once the goods are not available from the defrauding buyer, constructive trust can be maintained against traceable proceeds. Janigan v. Taylor, 344 F.2d 781 (1st Cir.), *cert. denied* 382 U.S. 879, 86 S.Ct. 163, 15 L.Ed.2d 120 (1965); Falk v. Hoffman, 233 N.Y. 199, 135 N.E. 243 (1922); Restatement of Restitution § 166 (1937).

receives any benefit from an increase in the assets which he "owns." [80] The basis of the equitable lien is similar to that of a constructive trust except that the plaintiff is limited to the amount of his loss. In this sense the plaintiff is treated as holding a *lien* on the proceeds, and the value of his loss is the amount of his lien. Because there is the possibility that these two remedies will produce different amounts of recovery, the constructive trust is limited to situations in which the defendant knowingly converted the property; the equitable lien, on the other hand, is available against either knowing or innocent converters.

These distinctions may conceivably make a difference with some Code problems, but for most cases they will remain only a difference in theory. When a seller is reclaiming goods he must act promptly, and the only asset which can be used for the trust or lien is the price which was paid to the defaulting buyer. Normally this will not have increased in value during the time involved so that the problems of distinguishing between the constructive trust and equitable lien will not often arise.

The extent to which the restitution remedies of constructive trust and equitable lien are applicable to Code cases has not been litigated. They are not specifically listed as two of the remedies (a) available to a seller who has received a check which was not honored or who has sold goods to an insolvent buyer or (b) available to an owner following sale of goods entrusted to a merchant. Nevertheless, whenever the elements of a constructive trust or equitable lien are present, section 1–103 will justify the use of these remedies in Code cases. One Code court impressed a constructive trust on the proceeds of a sale in a situation in which a buyer gave his seller a check which was later dishonored—even though the buyer had reason to believe the check would be honored on presentment.[81] Therefore, these two restitution remedies are available even though not specifically mentioned in the Code, but they should be granted only when a seller (or owner) could have reclaimed the goods in the hands of the buyer (or merchant), and the

---

80. Corn Belt Prods. Co. v. Mullins, 172 Neb. 561, 110 N.W.2d 845 (1961) (conversion); Note, 39 Mich.L.Rev. 340 (1940). The principle is set out in Restatement of Restitution § 202 (1937).

Rules to aid in tracing proceeds are contained in Restatement of Restitution §§ 210–14 (1937). For a more complete discussion of the constructive trust and equitable lien remedies, see J. Dawson, Unjust Enrichment 10–40 (1951); Dawson, *Restitution or Damages?*, 20 Ohio St.L.J. 175 (1959).

81. Greater Louisville Auto Auction, Inc. v. Ogle Buick, Inc., 387 S.W.2d 17 (Ky.1965). This case ignored the ten-day demand period and recovery was allowed against a person other than the buyer. As to the last point, see Restatement of Restitution § 208 (1937). For a discussion of the impact of the Bankruptcy Act on the constructive trust and equitable lien, see 4A Collier, Bankruptcy ¶¶ 70.25, 70.62 (14th ed. 1969).

right of reclamation was lost solely because those goods were transferred to a good faith purchaser for value (or a buyer in ordinary course). They are not available generally for every situation in which the defaulting buyer has sold goods to a third party.

3. THE SELLER'S MONETARY RECOVERIES

§ 173. Resale Damages—Introduction

When at least one of the four triggering events of section 2–703 occurs (wrongful rejection, wrongful revocation of acceptance, failure to make a payment due on or before delivery, or repudiation), the seller may resell the goods without liability for failing to deliver to the buyer.[82] In addition the seller may, if he follows the requirements of section 2–706, recover from the buyer damages measured by the contract price less the resale price, together with incidental damages but less expenses saved in consequence of the buyer's breach.[83] This measure of recovery allows the seller to establish his damages without the necessity of proving the market price of the goods.

The theory of this measure of recovery rests upon protection of the seller's expectation interest.[84] The basic purpose of contractual recoveries is to place the aggrieved party in the financial position he would have occupied had there been no default.[85] When the buyer wrongfully refused to retain the goods or indicated that he would not accept them (by failing to make a payment or by repudiating), the seller has "lost" the contract price but "gained" the goods. If the goods cannot be resold for at least the price the buyer agreed to pay, the seller's loss is the difference between these two amounts—that is, the amount he would have received had there been no default (the contract price) less the amount obtained on resale.[86] If the buyer's default caused the seller to incur additional expenses, those must be added to any recovery; if the buyer's default saved the seller expenses which would otherwise have been incurred, those must be subtracted from the recovery. The result of this process leaves the seller with a net recovery equal to the contract price and has placed him in the same financial position he would have occupied had the buyer performed. Indeed, if resale damages do not accomplish this result—as where the seller is a merchant with a sufficient supply of goods so that

82. § 162 *supra*.

83. This formula is discussed in § 174 *infra*.

84. § 138 *supra*.

85. UCC § 1–106.

86. Bruce Church, Inc. v. Tested Best Foods Div. of Kane-Miller Corp., 28 Agri.Dec. 377, 6 UCC Rep. 326 (U.S. Dept. of Agriculture (1969)).

subsequent sales could have been made irrespective of the buyer's default [87]—the seller ought not use section 2–706 as a measure of his recovery.

If the right to use resale as a basis for determining damages were not carefully limited, a seller would be able to fix his own recovery without regard to any interests of the buyer. A defaulting buyer ought to pay for the loss he caused, but he should not also be required to pay for those losses which the seller brought on himself through a careless resale (or even a friendly resale to a relative or acquaintance designed to set damages as high as possible). Thus, the Code provides certain limitations on the seller's use of resale to determine his buyer's damages. Those limitations are designed to allow the seller who follows reasonable commercial practices to have his damages determined without being subjected to a hindsight decision as to market price; at the same time they are designed to protect the defaulting buyer from capricious action by an overreaching seller.

In most resales statutory protection of the buyer is unnecessary because sellers generally are concerned about getting as much as possible out of any resale of goods—not in setting damages at as large an amount as they can. When they receive the money on the resale, they have resources which are immediately spendable; when recovery is postponed until an award of damages is made, the funds will not be available for months or years, and those sellers also face the possibility that their judgments may be uncollectable. It usually makes no commercial sense to postpone recovery of the contract price. Nevertheless, to assure fair commercial treatment of the defaulting buyer in all controversies where the seller desires to use the resale price in computing his damages, the Code has provided several limitations on the application of section 2–706.

Section 2–706 contains one overriding requirement. The resale must be made "in good faith and in a commercially reasonable manner." [88] A similar standard of fair dealing is required by Article 9 of the Code in connection with disposition of collateral following a default by the debtor and repossession by the secured party.[89] Further,

---

87. In these situations the seller has lost one sale (and one profit) if he could have made the subsequent sale even though this buyer had performed this contract. That lost profit can be compensated under the UCC § 2–708(2) formula; conceivably it could also be considered as "incidental damages" under UCC § 2–706—however, the language of UCC § 2–710 makes this reading difficult. The problem is discussed in § 177 *infra*.

88. UCC § 2–706(1). "Good faith" is defined in UCC §§ 1–201(19) and 2–103 (1) (b). The fact that the goods were resold at substantially below their retail value is evidence of commercial unreasonableness. California Airmotive Corp. v. Jones, 415 F.2d 554 (6th Cir. 1969). *Cf.* UCC § 9–507(2).

89. UCC § 9–504. There is an excellent discussion of "commercial reasonableness" in II G. Gilmore, Security In-

this is the foundation upon which the entire Code is drafted: parties to a commercial transaction must meet the reasonable standards of their trade and act in good faith. Such a standard is nebulous and subject to manipulation from case to case, but it is a feature which is needed in any code to make it work in practice. What is "fair" varies with the product, the industry, and the time the controversy occurs. The Code test allows a court to determine whether the standards of the trade were met and also to review whether those standards were "reasonable" and whether the aggrieved party acted honestly. It is true that these words can be read so often that they become close to meaningless; however, applied to the facts of particular cases they afford courts the needed basis for determining whether the defaulter has been dealt with "fairly." If he has, the seller's expectation interest has been determined and the buyer must pay the resulting damages; if he has not, the court will compute the seller's damages by section 2–708.

Unless the parties have otherwise agreed, the resale may be by either public or private sale.[90] Although the Code does not define a "public sale," the Comments indicate that the drafters intended this term to mean a sale by auction.[91] Thus, the seller has an apparent choice between a second sale by auction or by some other type of sale. However, the overriding requirement of commercial reasonableness may be used to control this choice in a particular factual pattern, especially in view of this sentence from section 2–706(2): "Sale may be as a unit or in parcels and at any time and place and on any terms but every aspect of the sale including the method, manner, time, place and terms must be commercially reasonable." Further, the resale may be by one or more contracts, or the seller may even identify the goods to an existing contract.[92] Once again, the good faith and commercial reasonableness tests would apply to these choices.

The Code establishes certain minimum requirements which must be met by the seller in making the resale. Satisfying these does not assure that the resale was made "in good faith and in a commercially reasonable manner," but the failure to comply with them prevents the seller from measuring his damages by section 2–706. These requirements are:

terests in Personal Property § 44.5 (1965).

90. UCC § 2–706(2). The "unless otherwise agreed" language is troublesome. Must this agreement be made after breach? Compare UCC § 9–506. Certainly some of the resale terms may be agreed upon pursuant to UCC § 1–102(3). UCC § 2–706(2) contains a meaningless reference to subsection

(3). Perhaps the drafters meant to refer to subsection (5) to protect good faith purchasers. This was the reference in the parallel section of the Uniform Revised Sales Act § 108 (Proposed Final Draft No. 1, 1944).

91. UCC § 2–706, Comment 4.

92. UCC § 2–706(2).

1.   Whether the resale is public or private, it must be "reasonably identified as referring to the broken contract."   A merchant cannot wait until he has made several sales of the same type of goods as involved in the seller-buyer contract and then select one of those sales as complying with section 2–706.[93]

2.   If a private sale is selected, "the seller must give the buyer reasonable notification of his intention to sell." [94]   There is no express requirement that the notice state the time and place of the resale; in fact, in many situations it would be impossible for the seller to predict the exact time of the resale.   When the goods will be resold depends in large part on the moment that an interested customer can be located. There may, however, be situations in which the commercial reasonableness of a resale requires a more complete notice than a statement that the seller intends to resell the goods.   In these situations the expanded notice ought to be given.

3.   If a public sale is selected, the Code is more explicit on the nature of the sale.   Section 2–706(4) provides that in connection with a public sale:

> (a)   only identified goods can be sold except where there is a recognized market for a public sale of futures in goods of the kind; and
>
> (b)   it must be made at a usual place or market for public sale if one is reasonably available and except in the case of goods which are perishable or threaten to decline in value speedily the seller must give the buyer reasonable notice of the time and place of the resale; and
>
> (c)   if the goods are not to be within the view of those attending the sale the notification of sale must state the place where the goods are located and provide for their reasonable inspection by prospective bidders; and
>
> (d)   the seller may buy.

The notice must state both the time and place of the public resale since, with an auction, these facts will be known to the seller.   The statement that the seller may buy at a public sale indicates that the drafters intended that a purchase by the seller at a private sale was not "commercially reasonable."

In the usual situation the resale will not bring as much as was owing by the buyer for the reason that, if the goods are worth more than

---

93.   The   identification   requirement ought to eliminate a problem which can arise under the buyer's analogous remedy of cover.   See the text accompanying footnotes 85 and 86 in § 147 *supra*.

94.   UCC § 2–706(3).   Failure to give notice bars recovery under UCC § 2–706 (1).   Foster v. Colorado Radio Corp., 381 F.2d 222 (10th Cir. 1967); Bacon Estate, 45 Pa.D. & C.2d 733 (Orphan's Ct. 1968).

the unpaid balance of the contract price, the buyer would normally be able to secure outside financing to complete the purchase. If, however, the resale does produce a sum of money greater than the unpaid contract price, the seller "is not accountable to the buyer for any profit made on the resale." [95] The seller is not selling as an agent for the buyer; he is selling the goods under a privilege granted him by the Code.[96]

Section 2–706 protects the good faith purchaser at the resale even though the seller fails to comply with requirements of that section. Subsection (5) provides that such a purchaser takes the goods "free of any rights of the original buyer." [97] Whether he acquires a good title depends on the state of the seller's title, but the good faith purchaser does cut off any claims of the defaulting buyer.

§ 174. Resale Damages—Measure of Recovery

The section 2–706 formula for computing damages consists of two parts. The first is found in all measures of recovery and can be generalized as follows: from the value of the defendant's promise subtract the value of the plaintiff's promise. Since the seller will be the plaintiff under a section 2–706 recovery, the general measure can be made specific in these terms: from the contract price subtract the resale price. The Code language states the first part of the seller's section 2–706 damages as "the difference between the resale price and the contract price." [98]

The second portion of the section 2–706 formula takes account of incidental damages caused by the breach (these must be added to the result obtained above) and the expenses saved in consequence of the breach (these must be subtracted from the result obtained above). These elements must be considered to assure that the seller's expectation interest will be fully protected—that the seller will be compensated for the default, but not overcompensated. Application of this formula can be illustrated with the following hypotheticals:

Case # 1. Seller agreed to sell and Buyer to buy goods for a contract price of $5,000. Buyer paid nothing on the purchase price but committed one of the triggering events listed in section 2–703.

95. UCC § 2–706(6). The meaning of "profit" is discussed in § 174 *infra*. A "person in the position of a seller" must account for a profit, UCC §§ 2–706(6), 2–707, as must an aggrieved buyer who is selling under UCC § 2–711.

96. Compare 3 S. Williston, Sales § 553 (rev. ed. 1948).

97. UCC § 2–706(5) does not expressly require that the good faith purchaser give value as does UCC § 2–403(1). See § 170 *supra*. However, this requirement is implicit in the requirement that the purchaser must *buy* at the resale.

98. UCC § 2–706(1).

Seller elected to resell the goods, complying with the requirements of section 2–706. Seller obtained only $4,000 on the resale, had $300 in incidental damages, and saved $75 in consequence of the default.[99] Seller is requesting that his damages be measured by section 2–706(1).

The seller's damages in Case #1 are computed under section 2–706 without difficulty. He is entitled to the contract price ($5,000) less the amount received on resale ($4,000), or $1,000. To this must be added his incidental damages of $300, and from this amount must be subtracted his savings of $75. The result is 2–706 damages of $1,225. The seller is left with a net recovery of $5,000, and he has received the contract price for the goods.[1] Not all cases are so quickly solved.

Case # 2. Assume the same facts as in Case #1 except add that Buyer had prepaid $500 on the purchase price.

The 2–706 formula for damages is the difference between the resale price and the *contract* price. Thus, a literal application of this formula will produce exactly the same damages in Case #2 as were obtained in Case #1: $1,225. However, in Case #2 the seller has an additional $500 from the buyer so that his total net receipts on this transaction would be $5,500. This recovery overcompensates the seller and produces a result contrary to the common law and to the stated policy of the Code.[2]

The recovery in Case #2 can be brought into line with the compensation principle by a judicial insertion of the word "unpaid" immediately preceding the word "contract" in section 2–706(1). This would recast the seller's recovery in Case #2 as follows: from the unpaid contract price ($4,500) subtract the resale price ($4,000), add the incidental damages ($300), and subtract the expenses saved ($75). This produces a recovery of $725 and nets the seller $5,000 on his $5,000 contract. Since nothing was paid on the Case #1 contract, the recovery there would remain the same in spite of the insertion of "unpaid" in the section 2–706 formula.

---

99. 5 A. Corbin, Contracts §§ 1038–39, 1044 (1964) discusses the general law on these elements of the formula. Incidental damages are discussed in § 180 *infra.*

1. The formula was applied and the need for proving incidental damages was discussed in Quattlebaum v. Schutt, 27 Agri.Dec. 242, 5 UCC Rep. 370 (U.S. Dept. of Agriculture 1968). A pre-Code case is Wickman v. Opper, 188 Cal.App.2d 129, 10 Cal.Rptr. 291 (1961). If Case #1 seller can supply all reasonable demand for the product involved and would probably have made the second sale even though the buyer had not defaulted, the seller is not placed in the same financial position by the UCC § 2–706 formula as he would have been had the buyer performed. Such a seller has lost one profit. Perhaps the profit can be recovered as an incidental damage, but the better approach is through UCC § 2–708(2). § 177 *infra.*

2. UCC § 1–106(1).

Insertion of the word "unpaid" can be justified on the basis of the stated compensation policy of the Code.[3] It can also be justified by comparing section 2–706 with the buyer's cover damages [4] (which takes specific account of any prepayments on the contract price) and with section 2–708. Section 2–708 states the measure of recovery for the seller who has not elected to pursue the resale remedy. That formula parallels the one found in section 2–706 except that market price is substituted for resale price and the word "unpaid" is inserted before "contract price." The drafters did not intend that a seller who had resold goods for their market price should obtain different damages depending upon which section of the Code he used to measure those damages. The reason for including the right of resale—as well as the buyer's right to cover—was to give the aggrieved party a remedy more consistent with commercial practices and to simplify recoveries by not requiring detailed proof of market prices. Thus, the word "unpaid" should be read into section 2–706 in solving Case #2 so that the seller's recovery is limited to compensation for his losses.[5]

The section 2–706 formula could also cause difficulties when the goods can be sold for more than the unpaid contract price. Such situations are rare but they occasionally occur.

Case # 3. Seller agreed to sell and Buyer to buy goods for a contract price of $5,000. Buyer paid nothing on the price but committed one of the triggering events of section 2–703. Seller elected to resell the goods, complying with the requirements of section 2–706. Seller obtained $6,000 on the resale but incurred $300 in incidental damages, saving no expenses in consequence of the default. Seller is requesting that his damages be measured by section 2–706(1).

The seller's argument that he is entitled to damages would center on two portions of section 2–706. The first is subsection (6) which states that the seller is not accountable to the buyer for any *profit* made on the resale. Thus, the seller would argue, the entire $1,000 profit is to be retained. The second is the subsection (1) formula which provides that the seller is entitled to his loss on resale (which in Case #3 would be zero) "together with" his incidental damages (which were $300). The seller would argue, therefore, that he is entitled to $300 in section 2–706 damages.[6]

---

3. *Id.*

4. UCC § 2–712 which refers only to "contract price" but which is based upon UCC § 2–711. UCC § 2–711 allows the buyer to recover "so much of the price as has been paid." Perhaps the drafters patterned the UCC § 2–706 formula after UCC § 2–712, forgetting the earlier reference to the prepayments.

5. Professor Williston read Uniform Sales Act § 64 in the same way as is suggested in the text. 3 S. Williston, Sales § 582 (rev. ed. 1948).

6. As to the right of the buyer to recover any prepayment made, see § 184 *infra.*

Such an award would put the Case #3 seller in a better financial position (by $1,300) than he would have occupied had the buyer performed. It is true that section 2–706(6) prevents the buyer from claiming any part of the "profit" made by the seller but there is no need to construe the Code to allow the seller an added $300 when that expenditure contributed, at least in part, to the receipt of that "profit." The Code policy of compensation and no more than compensation supports a denial of recovery to such a seller, and the word "profit" in section 2–706(6) can be read to mean *net* rather than *gross* profit. This interpretation is supported by pre-Code law which reached this result when the defaulting buyer was suing for restitution.[7] Hence the seller in Case #3 should be awarded no recovery against the buyer.

§ 175. Damages for Non-acceptance

Section 2–708(1) provides for the seller's traditional contract-price-minus-market-price measure of damages:

> Subject to subsection (2) and to the provisions of this Article with respect to proof of market price (Section 2–723), the measure of damages for non-acceptance or repudiation by the buyer is the difference between the market price at the time and place for tender and the unpaid contract price together with any incidental damages provided in this Article (Section 2–710), but less expenses saved in consequence of the buyer's breach.

The operation of this section can be illustrated through the following hypothetical factual patterns:

Case # 1. Seller agreed to sell and Buyer to buy a new machine— "new" in the sense that it had not been used prior to the sale. The price was set by the parties at $11,000. Delivery was scheduled for July 1, Seller to deliver the machine to Buyer. Buyer made no prepayments on the price. When the conforming machine was delivered, Buyer wrongfully rejected Seller's tender although he had no legal excuse for his failure to accept.

The seller could resell the machine and, if he followed the requirements of section 2–706, his measure of recovery would be that which has been discussed in prior sections of this text.[8] An aggrieved seller is not required, however, to resell and use section 2–706 to measure his damages.[9] He may wish to retain the goods, he may want to give them away, he may have resold but (purposely or accidentally)

---

7. Amtorg Trading Corp. v. Miehle Printing Press & Mfg. Co., 206 F.2d 103, 108 (2d Cir. 1953).

8. §§ 173–74 *supra.*

9. UCC § 2–703, Comment 1.

not followed the requirements of section 2–706, or he may have any one of a number of reasons why he would prefer to proceed on the basis of market price. The Code allows the aggrieved seller to forgo his resale remedy and to show his losses through proof of market price.

The basis of section 2–708 is that of compensation: an aggrieved seller is to be placed in the same financial position he would have occupied had the buyer performed.[10] Performance would have given the seller the price in exchange for the goods. When the buyer refused to accept and pay, the seller lost the contract price but was able to retain the goods. Thus, the value of the goods represents at least a partial compensation for the lost contract price.[11] If the goods are "worth" the unpaid contract price, the seller has not been injured and his recovery would be limited to nominal damages.[12] If the goods are "worth" less than the unpaid contract price, the seller has lost his expected gain. Section 2–708(1) recognizes these policies by providing a measure of recovery equal to the unpaid contract price less the market price of the retained goods. To this must be added incidental damages, and from this must be subtracted expenses saved in consequence of the breach.[13] Thus, if the seller in Case #1 could prove that the market price of the machine at the time and place for tender was (say) $10,000, his basic damage recovery would be $1,000. If the seller also incurred incidental damages of $300 and saved $75 in consequence of the breach, his total recovery would be $1,225.

This text has discussed several problems inherent in the concept of market price;[14] that discussion will not be repeated. Some certainty is introduced into the determination of seller's damages by the following:

1. The Code states rules applicable to the sale of goods. For many kinds of goods there is a "standard price"—not in the sense of stock market quotations, but "standard" because enough similar items are bought and sold each month so that a representative price is established by the market. The Code accepts this price for the purpose of section 2–708(1) damages. The Code also attempts to simplify

---

10. UCC § 1–106; § 138 *supra*. As to the meaning of a "wrongful rejection," see § 162 *supra*. For a pre-Code statement of the Code rule, see Rector v. De Arana, 398 S.W.2d 911 (Tex.1966).

11. Lore v All-Weather Storm Window Co., 107 A.2d 660 (D.C.App.1954).

12. Wheeler v. Cleveland, 170 Ala. 426, 54 So. 277 (1911); Nasner v. Burton, 2 Utah 2d 236, 272 P.2d 163 (1954).

13. Procter & Gamble Distrib. Co. v. Lawrence Am. Field Warehousing Corp., 16 N.Y.2d 344, 266 N.Y.S.2d 785, 213 N.E.2d 873 (1965).

14. § 148 *supra*.

some of the evidentiary problems inherent in all value determinations by making market quotations admissible.[15] Further, for those instances in which evidence of a prevailing price is not readily available, "the price prevailing within any reasonable time before or after the time described or at any other place which in commercial judgment or under usage of trade would serve as a reasonable substitute for the one described may be used, making any proper allowance for the cost of transporting the goods to or from such other place."[16] Therefore, if the seller-buyer contract called for delivery at the seller's city and there was no readily available evidence of a prevailing price at the seller's city, evidence of the price at the nearest market would be admissible. Since the seller would normally be required to transport the goods to that market to obtain that price, the transportation charges to that market should be added to his recovery.

2.   The Code establishes the time for market price determination: the time for tender.[17] This is the date on which the buyer defaulted through his non-acceptance of the goods, and this is the date that the seller could retain the goods freed from the obligation to perform. There is, therefore, a theoretical justification for the time-for-tender rule. However, in a fluctuating price market the seller may not be able to dispose of the goods until the price has either risen or fallen, and the section 2–708(1) damages may either overcompensate or undercompensate the seller. Likewise, if the buyer's breach is some time after the tender (as with a wrongful rejection or wrongful revocation of acceptance), the market price at the time for tender may not compensate the seller for his losses. A seller with legal advice can avoid the undercompensation by reselling under section 2–706 and recovering the difference between the seller-buyer contract price and the price obtained on resale. Indeed, the right of resale for the seller and cover for the buyer may be justification for the adoption of fairly rigid damage formulas which may or may not compensate for losses. A seller or buyer who is interested in "compensation" can obtain it either by reselling or covering, and damage remedies are commercially sufficient if they produce recoveries which approximate exact compensation.[18]

3.   The Code establishes the place for market price determination: the place for tender. A decision as to the point at which the seller is obligated to tender turns on the terms of the seller-buyer con-

---

15.   UCC § 2–723(1).

16.   UCC § 2–723(2); Jagger Bros., Inc. v. Technical Textile Co., 202 Pa.Super. 639, 198 A.2d 888 (1964).

17.   Compare the time for measuring the buyer's damages for non-delivery. § 148 *supra*.

18.   See the discussion in § 139 *supra*.

tract.[19] If the buyer is obligated to pick up the goods, the place for tender is where the buyer was to pick up the goods. If the seller was required to send the goods to the buyer, the place for tender may be either the point of shipment or of the destination of the goods, depending upon whether a shipment or a destination contract is involved. Thus, if the market price of the Case #1 machine had been $10,000 at the seller's city and $10,500 at the buyer's city, the subtrahend in the 2–708(1) formula would vary depending on where the seller was obligated to deliver the machine. This variance can produce results which are difficult to defend on a theory of compensation. For example, if Case #1 had involved a shipment contract and if the buyer had wrongfully rejected the goods after their arrival, the seller's section 2–708(1) recovery will be measured by the market price of the goods in the seller's city ($10,000) rather than in the buyer's city ($10,500), even though the goods were located in the buyer's city and this is the place where the seller would most likely resell them. This formula produces a basic damage recovery of $1,000 ("basic" because the seller is also entitled to incidental damages less expenses saved) against an apparent loss of only $500. The selection of the place for tender to measure the market price can be rationalized (a) by urging the value of a single damage rule that is easily applied, (b) by emphasizing that the buyer is the one in default and doubts should be resolved against a defaulter, (c) by asserting that situations involving shipping contracts and geographical price variations caused by factors other than transportation costs are rare and thus not worth a separate rule, (d) by pointing out that the seller, if he is a volume seller, may well have been able to make the second sale in the buyer's city even though the buyer had performed his contractual obligations, and (e) by referring to the common law notion that what the aggrieved party does with goods after the default is of no consequence to the defaulter.[20] Nevertheless, the Code's selection of a single geographical location for measuring damages (just as its selection of a single point in time) could, in some instances, either overcompensate or undercompensate the seller. In those instances courts can use expanded ideas of "incidental damages," "expenses saved," or the amorphous concept of "market price" to produce defensible results.

Case # 2. Assume the facts of Case #1: a contract to purchase a machine for $11,000 with delivery scheduled for July 1, and a wrongful rejection by Buyer. Assume, however, that Buyer had paid $500

---

19. §§ 96–99 *supra.*

20. Pre-Code cases are discussed in 3 S. Williston, Sales § 582 (rev. ed. 1948).

on the purchase price prior to his default and that Seller had no incidental damages or expenses saved by the default.

Section 2–708(1), unlike the section which provides the measure of recovery for resale damages,[21] uses the *unpaid* contract price as the base from which to figure the seller's damages. Therefore, while it is necessary to add the notion of unpaid contract price to the resale damages section, this concept is expressly made a part of the section 2–708(1) computation. The basic recovery under section 2–708(1) is *unpaid* contract price less the market price of the goods. In Case #2 the seller would have to prove that the market price of the goods at the time and place for tender was less than $10,500 ($11,000 contract price less the $500 prepayment) before he could have damages under section 2–708(1).[22]

Case # 3. Seller agreed to sell and Buyer to buy a new machine for $11,000. Buyer paid $500 on the purchase price. At the time and place for tender the machine had a market price of $10,800. Buyer wrongfully rejected Seller's proper tender. Seller incurred $300 in incidental damages and saved $75 in consequence of the breach.

The seller's argument that he is entitled to any damages in a situation like Case #2 would center on the "together with" language of section 2–708(1). The first portion of the damage formula produces no recovery because the market price exceeded the unpaid contract price, but the remaining portion results in damages of $225. Is the seller entitled to take these two figures and add them together (the Code states that the seller may have the first "together with" the second) to produce a recovery? This problem was discussed in connection with the seller's resale damages, and the conclusion reached there is applicable here.[23] The policy of compensation[24] supports a denial of any recovery to the seller so long as the excess of the market price over the unpaid contract price exceeds the excess of the incidental damage over the saved expenses.

Case # 4. Seller and Buyer entered into a contract for the sale and purchase of a new machine for $11,000, F.O.B. Seller's city. A conforming machine was properly tendered and accepted. Buyer, however, wrongfully revoked his acceptance and Seller accepted a return of the goods without waiving any rights he had against Buyer.

21. UCC § 2–706; § 174 *supra*.

22. Failure to prove market price prevents a recovery of substantial damages. Weiss v. Sheet Metal Fabricators, 206 Md. 195, 110 A.2d 671 (1955) (pre-Code); Ord v. Benson, 163 Neb. 367, 79 N.W.2d 713 (1956) (pre-Code);

Bacon Estate, 45 Pa.C.&D.2d 733 (Orphan's Ct. 1968).

23. § 174 *supra*.

24. UCC § 1–106. For a discussion of the buyer's recovery of any prepayments when the buyer is in default, see § 184 *infra*.

Situations like Case #4 present problems under section 2–708(1). First, damages will be measured at the time and place for tender even though the revocation may have occurred at a different place and a later time. The resulting recovery could bear little resemblance to the seller's loss. Unless the goods have appreciated in value, this alone should cause most sellers to seek their remedy under the section on resale—or to refuse to accept the wrongful return of the goods and to hold the buyer liable for the contract price.

Second, even in those cases in which the seller desires a section 2–708(1) recovery, there is a question as to whether that section is applicable. Damages are available under section 2–708(1) when there has been a "non-acceptance or repudiation." A revocation of acceptance is not a repudiation. Does it qualify as a "non-acceptance"?

An answer to this question turns on an understanding of the Code's scheme as to a seller's damages. Section 2–703 indexes all remedies, and recovery requires the occurrence of at least one of four triggering events—one of which is wrongful revocation of acceptance. Section 2–709 provides the measure of a seller's recovery when the buyer has defaulted but retained the goods—or placed the seller in a position where, although he has possession of the goods, he cannot reasonably resell them. On the other hand, sections 2–706 and 2–708 assume that the seller has the goods at the conclusion of the transaction because they reduce any recovery by the market price of the retained goods. Thus, the "non-acceptance" of 2–708(1) should not be read as limiting the applicability of that section to situations in which buyer has never accepted the goods. It should be interpreted to allow a seller to use section 2–708(1) whenever the buyer has committed at least one of the triggering events of section 2–703 and the goods have been retained by or returned to the seller.[25] Such a seller should be cautioned, however, against the use of this section except in those situations where it produces adequate compensation for his losses.

---

25. Beco, Inc. v. Minnechaug Golf Course, Inc., 5 Conn.Cir. 444, 256 A.2d 522 (1968) (goods retained; UCC § 2–708 not applicable); Tennessee-Virginia Constr. Co. v. Willingham, 117 Ga.App. 290, 160 S.E.2d 444 (1968) (accepted goods were returned to seller but seller treated them as buyer's, levying on them in his suit for the price). In Smith v. Hawkins, 323 P.2d 373 (Okl.1958), the seller took possession from the buyer after the buyer failed to pay. The court treated the seller's actions as a conversion and deducted the value of the goods at the time of conversion from the balance due. In Peterson Mercury, Inc. v. Lombardo, 259 Minn. 281, 107 N.W.2d 221 (1961), a pre-Code case, the buyer refused to accept the seller's tender of conforming goods. The seller sued on a check which the buyer had given for the price but on which payment had been stopped. The goods had been sold by the seller prior to suit. The court held that the seller was not entitled to the price nor could he obtain that remedy under the guise of a suit on the check.

§ 176. Damages on Repudiation

Many of the problems facing a seller who desires to recover damages following a buyer's repudiation have already been discussed.[26] They were presented in connection with a buyer's action on repudiation by his seller, but the general Code section on repudiation (2–610) and the Code section on proof of market price when a repudiation case comes to trial before the date set for performance (2–723) apply irrespective of which party is the defaulter. Thus, many of the ideas already expanded have direct application when the buyer repudiates his contractual obligations. In summary, these ideas would be:

First, there is the problem of determining just when a buyer has "repudiated." This problem is both definitional and factual. The Code does not define repudiation, but this text has concluded that a repudiation occurs when the buyer has taken some action or inaction before he has received the seller's performance, signifying that he will not perform at the scheduled time.[27] After the seller has delivered or tendered delivery, the buyer can default by failing to accept or to pay the price when due—but he cannot "repudiate." Even within this context it may be difficult to determine, as a matter of fact, whether the words or acts of the buyer qualify as a repudiation or whether they are only a firm request for a substitute contract, made with the understanding that if the request is refused, the buyer will reluctantly accept and pay as required by the seller-buyer contract. This question calls for careful analysis of the legal impact of the activity of the buyer. Doubtful cases can be partially resolved by use of section 2–609. If a seller has reasonable grounds for insecurity, he need not deliver goods and trust to the future willingness of the buyer to accept and pay. He may demand adequate assurance of performance,[28] suspend "if commercially reasonable" any performance for which he has not received the agreed return, and treat a failure to give this assurance as a "repudiation." [29] This course of action will remove any ambiguity in the buyer's position, and in some cases open section 2–708 (1) damages.

Second, there is a problem of determining the date the seller's damages are to be measured. The answer given by section 2–708(1) appears to solve the problem. Damages, according to that section, are to be measured at the time for tender.[30] Therefore, if the contract

---

26. § 149 *supra*.

27. *Id.*

28. As to the meaning of "adequate assurance," see UCC § 2–609, Comment 4.

29. UCC § 2–609(4). If the buyer gives the necessary assurance, there is no repudiation and the seller must perform. The right to suspend exists only until the assurance is forthcoming. UCC § 2–609(1).

30. § 175 *supra*.

called for delivery on July 1 and the buyer repudiated on May 1, the important market price (according to section 2–708(1)) is the price on July 1.

However, section 2–610 inserts "a commercially reasonable time" during which an aggrieved seller can await performance, implying that if he waits longer, any damages which follow are attributable to the seller's lack of diligence rather than to the buyer's repudiation. Further, section 2–723 begins by providing:

> If an action based on anticipatory repudiation comes to trial before the time for performance with respect to some or all of the goods, any damages based on market price (Section 2–708 or Section 2–713) shall be determined according to the price of such goods prevailing at the time when the aggrieved party learned of the repudiation.

Thus, the Code presents several answers to the problem of when the seller's repudiation damages are to be measured. Section 2–708 selects the time for tender; section 2–610 suggests that the important date is the termination of a commercially reasonable time following the repudiation (which may be before tender was required); and section 2–723 states that, when the trial occurs before performance date, repudiation damages are to be measured at the time the seller learned of the repudiation.

Much this same problem occurred with the buyer's suit for damages based upon the seller's repudiation. This text there concluded that the differences between these Code sections was a result of oversight, not design.[31] The same conclusion is applicable to the seller's repudiation action. The reference in section 2–708(1) to repudiation was added without consideration as to how this addition would fit within other Code sections.[32] Amendment is needed to insure uniform results. In the meantime, a court faced with the problem of measuring a seller's repudiation damages in a fluctuating price market faces a statutory impasse which could be solved by referring to pre-Code decisions in the state involved [33] or, preferably, by seeking to promote

---

31. § 149 *supra*.

32. The 1952 version of UCC § 2–708 (1) contained no reference to repudiation—perhaps on the theory that a repudiation was one example of a non-acceptance of the goods. The language was revised in 1956 Recommendations of the Editorial Board of the Uniform Commercial Code 77.

33. *E. g.*, McJunkin Corp. v. North Carolina Natural Gas Corp., 300 F.2d 794 (4th Cir. 1961), *cert. denied* 371

U.S. 830, 83 S.Ct 43, 9 L.Ed.2d 68 (1962); Compania Engraw Commercial E. Indus. S.A. v. Schenley Distillers Corp., 181 F.2d 876 (9th Cir. 1950). Pre-Code law favored measuring the damages as of the date set for performance. See cases cited and discussion in 5 A. Corbin, Contracts § 1053 (1964). Cases are also collected in Comment, *A Suggested Revision of the Contract Doctrine of Anticipatory Repudiation*, 64 Yale L.J. 85, 91–99 (1954); Annot., 34 A.L.R. 114 (1925).

Code policies found within the several remedial sections. The Code's emphasis on resale as the seller's primary remedy, on compensation as the goal of all remedies, and on producing results which accord with commercial practices ought to result in measuring a seller's repudiation damages as of that date which gave the seller a commercially reasonable time following the buyer's repudiation to make an economical disposition of the goods. Until court decisions or statutory amendments are forthcoming, the only safe course for an aggrieved seller following a repudiation is to seek his remedy under section 2–706 (resale of the goods, where no reference is made to the time of tender), rather than under section 2–708(1).

§ 177. Recovery of Lost Profits

There are many sellers who are not compensated for their losses when they are awarded damages based upon either the market-price or resale-price formulas. These are the volume sellers who have a sufficient supply of goods available to them so that they could make as many sales as they are likely to obtain buyers. A wrongful rejection, a wrongful revocation of acceptance, or a repudiation by a buyer from one of these sellers does not free that seller to make a sale that he otherwise could not have made. Even if the buyer had performed, the seller would have been able to make his subsequent sale and would have had one more purchase price (the one from the buyer who defaulted) to help reimburse his costs and to contribute to his profits. Awarding that seller the unpaid contract price less either market or resale price will not place him in the same financial position that he would have occupied had there been no default. He has lost one sale and one profit which he would have made if the buyer had performed. Stated differently, the volume seller does not mitigate his lost profit when he makes a second sale—even of the same goods—that he would have made anyway.

This principle can be illustrated with the following example. Suppose an automobile dealer entered into a contract with a buyer for the sale of an automobile for $3,000. The dealer had other models like the one sold and could obtain still others from the manufacturer within a few days. The buyer either repudiated the contract or wrongfully rejected a conforming tender. One week later the dealer sold the same automobile to a third party for $3,000.

The resale-damage section (2–706) produces no recovery for the seller.[34] He resold the goods for the price set in the seller-buyer contract. Likewise, the market-price-damage section (2–708(1)) provides no recovery as long as the market price is measured in the

34. §§ 173–74 *supra.*

same retail market as was the contract price.[35] Nevertheless, this seller has suffered a substantial economic loss by the buyer's default. Had the buyer performed, the seller would have had the profits from two contracts; without the buyer's performance the seller has the profits from one contract. This is also true if the seller had made 50, 500, or 5,000 sales during the pertinent period. If the buyer had not defaulted, the seller would have had one more profit than he received. That lost profit is not compensated by other transactions entered into by this seller.

There are several ways to compensate such a seller. One could involve the use of the section 2–708(1) formula and the insertion of the wholesale market price as the subtrahend.[36] The Code, however, provides in section 2–708(2):

> If the measure of damages provided in subsection (1) is inadequate to put the seller in as good a position as performance would have done then the measure of damages is the profit (including reasonable overhead) which the seller would have made from full performance by the buyer, together with any incidental damages provided in this Article (Section 2–710), due allowance for costs reasonably incurred and due credit for payments or proceeds of resale.

Thus, whenever a seller can show that the market price formula would not compensate him for his losses, he can proceed to recover his lost profits. Further, such a seller could (and often should) forgo his resale remedy—which he may do by not giving the required notices— and request that his damages be measured under section 2–708.

The seller using section 2–708(2) is entitled to recover the *profit* he would have made from full performance by the buyer. "Profit" is not defined by the Code but the Comments indicate that it normally means the "list price less cost to the dealer or list price less manufacturing cost to the manufacturer."[37] The reference to list price was undoubtedly made on the assumption that the seller-buyer contract had been made at the list price of the goods. If the contract had

---

35. § 175 *supra*. The seller would be entitled to a damage recovery for the amount that his incidental damages exceeded the saved expenses. § 180 *infra*.

36. This solution was held erroneous in Charles St. Garage Co. v. Kaplan, 312 Mass. 624, 45 N.E.2d 928 (1942).

37. UCC § 2–708, Comment 2. That Comment adds that the profit may be recovered even though the venture is

new. This statement should prevent a court from confusing the UCC § 2–708(2) cases with those in which a buyer is seeking recovery of profits he claims he lost when he did not receive the goods from a defaulting seller. *E. g.*, Cramer v. Grand Rapids Show Case Co., 223 N.Y. 63, 119 N.E. 227 (1918); Comment, *Lost Profits as Contract Damages: Problems of Proof and Limitations on Recovery*, 65 Yale L.J. 992 (1956). § 153 *supra*.

established a different price from that listed on the goods or in some catalogue, the unpaid contract price should be used in the minuend to determine the seller's lost profit.

The entire unpaid contract price is, of course, not recoverable under section 2–708(2). From the unpaid contract price the seller must deduct the variable costs which he could have saved by reason of the default—that is, he must subtract those expenses which vary directly or proportionately with the amount of his production or sales and which he was not required to make because of the buyer's failure to perform.[38] In the example involving the sale of an automobile, the seller must deduct from the $3,000 unpaid contract price: (a) the amount the seller had to pay the manufacturer for the automobile (say $2,000); (b) any expense incurred by the seller in transporting the automobile from the manufacturer (say $150); and (c) all other expenses which vary with the number of automobiles handled (say $100). Variable expenses could include such items as undercoating and servicing the car on arrival at the dealer's place of business. These expenses were saved by the default because the seller will not be required to repeat them to make his second sale. A deduction of these assumed expenses leaves the seller with a recovery of $750 ($3,000 less $2,250).

Many sellers also have another kind of expense—one that does not vary with the number of sales or amount of goods produced. These expenses are usually called "overhead" and include such items as property taxes, heat, light, and administrative salaries. One less sale (or one additional sale) has no impact on the total overhead. Nevertheless, cost accountants divide the estimated yearly overhead of a business into the estimated yearly production or sales and attribute to each sale a portion of the total overhead expense. This procedure allows the seller to establish a selling price which is designed to produce sufficient income to pay the overhead and return a net profit.

Pre-Code courts disagreed as to whether a seller was also required to deduct the fixed overhead expense from the contract price to measure the amount of his recoverable profit from a defaulting buyer.[39]

---

38. See the definition of "variable cost" in E. Kohler, **A** Dictionary for Accountants 514 (3d ed. 1963).

39. The leading case denying recovery for overhead is A. Lenobel, Inc. v. Senif, 252 App.Div. 533, 300 N.Y.S. 226 (1937), *modified* 253 App.Div. 813, 1 N.Y.S.2d 1022 (1938). Some cases deny overhead recovery without discussion. *E. g.*, A. T. Klemens & Son v. Reber Plumbing & Heating Co., 139 Mont. 115, 360 P.2d 1005 (1961). Cases granting recovery include: Los Angeles Coin-O-Matic Laundries v. Harow, 195 Cal.App.2d 324, 15 Cal.Rptr. 693 (1961); Aerospace Electronics, Inc. v. Control Parts Corp., 183 So.2d 875 (Fla.Ct.App.1966); Louis M. Herman Co. v. Gallagher Elec. Co., 334 Mass. 652, 138 N.E.2d 120 (1956); Stewart v. Hansen, 62 Utah 281, 218 P. 959

The seller resisted the deduction for a very practical reason: the smaller the amount deducted from the unpaid contract price, the larger would be the final recovery. He has, however, several arguments which are more substantial, chief among which is this: a seller who has a sufficient source of goods to satisfy the likely demand and who probably could have made the subsequent sales even though the buyer had performed does not mitigate any of his overhead expenses through the subsequent sales. Had the buyer performed, the seller would have had all of his other contract prices plus the buyer's contract price to pay his overhead and to produce a net profit. Following the buyer's default, the seller cannot cut back on his overhead (if he could, the expense is a variable expense and should be deducted under principles already discussed) and the subsequent sales, which would have been made anyway, bear a larger proportion of the total overhead and produce a smaller net profit than the seller would have had with the buyer's performance. As one court pointed out:

> . . . Suppose a company has fixed overhead of $10,000 and engages in five similar transactions; then the receipts of each transaction would bear $2000 of overhead expense. If the company is now forced to spread this $10,000 over only four transactions, then the overhead expense per transaction will rise to $2500, significantly reducing the profitability of the four remaining transactions.[40]

The total amount of this significant reduction will always be the amount which the breached contract would have contributed to the total overhead—showing once again that overhead cannot be saved or mitigated by subsequent contracts.

The Code has resolved the disagreement among pre-Code decisions and has provided that a seller who is not compensated by the market-price formula can recover the "profit (including reasonable overhead) which the seller would have made from full performance." [41] Therefore, it appears that the argument made in this text has been accepted by the Code, and that a seller is entitled to recover from a defaulting buyer the unpaid contract price less the seller's variable costs saved by the breach.[42] There are two reasons for stating only that this "appears" to be the result of the Code.

(1923) ; Popp v. Yuenger, 229 Wis. 189, 282 N.W. 55 (1938). Several of these cases are discussed in Harris, *A Radical Restatement of the Law of Seller's Damages: Sales Act and Commercial Code Results Compared,* 18 Stan.L. Rev. 66 (1965). Annots., 3 A.L.R.3d 689 (1965) ; 24 A.L.R.2d 1008 (1952).

40. Vitex Mfg. Corp., Ltd. v. Caribtex Corp., 377 F.2d 795, 799 (3d Cir. 1967).

41. UCC § 2–708(2).

42. While this formula will properly resolve most of the cases, refinements are needed if the costs to the seller vary between the time of buyer's de-

First, the way the profit damage formula is written can cause serious mathematical problems. Does the Code mean that the seller first must prove his net profits and then show his fixed overhead attributable to this one sale? If so, the damage problem is needlessly complicated. The assignment of a certain amount of overhead to any one sale is an accountant's construct designed to give the seller a basis for determining the price to be charged for each item of goods so that the total receipts will pay the overhead and produce a net profit at the end of the year. There is nothing in the nature of any sale which compels a specific amount of overhead to be assigned to that sale, except as the management of the business determines. To argue this management decision in court needlessly complicates the trial—needlessly, because as already pointed out the same result can be obtained by deducting variable costs saved from the unpaid contract price without concern over what percentage of the damages will eventually be used to reimburse the seller for his overhead. In short, there is no reason to subtract overhead to find net profit and then to add that overhead back into the recovery to determine the seller's damages.[43]

Second, the Code reference to "reasonable overhead" is puzzling. Suppose the seller's overhead is unreasonably high. This means only that he will make less of a net profit than he would have made had his overhead been lower. Nevertheless, the seller has lost his net profit and, if he is to be compensated (that is, "placed in as good a position as performance would have done"), he is entitled to his net profit—whatever it might be. The same is true if this seller's overhead is unreasonably low. His net profit would have been greater than with a larger overhead; certainly this seller is not entitled to a bonus recovery through the addition of a *reasonable* overhead to his net profits. Perhaps the way to read the parenthetical phrase in section 2–708(2) is that the drafters meant to allow the seller recovery for any items which reasonably can be classified as overhead. This result is suggested by the Comments which effectively conclude that the

---

fault and the date the seller would have obtained goods to complete the subsequent contract. For example, if the wholesale price of automobiles increased from $2,000 to $2,200 and the retail price from $3,000 to $3,200 after the buyer defaulted, the sale to a subsequent purchaser produced a $1200 excess rather than the expected $1,000. This fact should be taken into account in *compensating* the seller. Comment, *Remedies for Total Breach of Contract Under the Uniform Re-*

vised Sales Act, 57 Yale L.J. 1360, 1370–76 (1948).

43. One of the best case discussions of this problem appears in Vitex Mfg. Corp., Ltd. v. Caribtex Corp., 377 F. 2d 795 (3d Cir. 1967) (citing Code). Other cases suggesting the textual analysis include F. A. Bartlett Tree Expert Co. v. Hartney, 308 Mass. 407, 32 N.E.2d 237 (1941); Kansas City Bridge Co. v. Kansas City Structural Steel Co., 317 S.W.2d 370 (Mo.1958).

correct measure of recovery for the volume seller is unpaid contract less variable costs saved.[44]

Applying these ideas to the example suggested at the beginning of this section, the automobile seller will recover $750 — $3,000 unpaid contract price less $2,250 in variable costs saved. These principles are also applicable to a manufacturer-seller when a buyer has repudiated prior to the time that the goods are completed. If the manufacturer decides to stop production, he has been saved the costs involved in further manufacture (price of material and cost of labor), and he has received the benefit of the salvage value of any work completed. These items (cost to complete and salvage value of work completed) must be subtracted from the unpaid contract price to produce the Code's measure of recovery.[45] The reference in section 2–708(2) to "proceeds of resale" must have been meant to apply to the resale of partially completed goods. If it is read to require reduction of damages by the full amount received on resale of completed goods, this subsection is nothing more than a restatement of section 2–706 and its main purpose of compensating the volume seller has been destroyed.

Section 2–708(2) applies only if the seller is not compensated by the usual market-price formula. It is of no benefit to the casual seller who has only one of the items sold, to the volume seller who does not have a sufficient supply or manufacturing capacity to meet his total demand, or to the seller who could not have interested the subsequent buyer had it not been for the default. In each of these situations the buyer's default made the second sale possible, and the second sale mitigates any profits lost from the first sale. Sections 2–706 and 2–708(1) compensate these sellers.

---

44. UCC § 2–708, Comment 2. Words like "reasonable" and "reasonably" are often added almost automatically by lawyers. They sound fair and just. Perhaps that happened here.

The seller is also entitled to incidental damages less expenses saved. UCC § 2–708(2). § 180 *infra*.

Seller normally bears the burden of proving that he could not make a substitute contract, Norwood Lumber Corp. v. McKean, 153 F.2d 753 (3d Cir. 1946), but a volume seller is often presumed to have no opportunity to mitigate his lost profits. Mt. Pleasant Stable Co. v. Steinberg, 238 Mass. 567, 131 N.E. 295 (1921). *See generally* 5 A. Corbin, Contracts §§ 1039, 1041 (1964).

45. There is a good discussion in Jessup & Moore Paper Co. v. Bryant Paper Co., 297 Pa. 483, 147 A. 519 (1929). In some contracts the buyer is given a privilege of selecting various sizes or qualities of goods at a variation in price. There is authority that this choice makes damages uncertain. Wilhelm Lubrication Co. v. Brattrud, 197 Minn. 626, 268 N.W. 634 (1936). Other courts have given the seller his least possible profit. *E. g.*, William Whitman & Co. v. Namquit Worsted Co., 206 F. 549 (D.R.I.1913), *aff'd* 221 F. 49 (5th Cir. 1915); E-Z Roll Hardware Mfg. Co. v. H & H Prods. & Finishing Corp., 4 UCC Rep. 1045 (N.Y. Sup.Ct.1968) (citing Code). Perhaps UCC § 2–204(3) will be used to help a court reach this result. Cases are collected in Annot., 106 A.L.R. 1284 (1937).

§ 178. Recovery of the Price

The limitations placed on the seller's remedy to recover the balance of the purchase price [46] made it a secondary remedy for the seller. A judgment for the price amounts to specific enforcement of the buyer's primary contractual obligation, and the Code continues the pre-Code reluctance to require specific performance of contracts for the sale of goods.[47]

There are good policy reasons to support the decision not to make the price action the principal remedy of an aggrieved seller. Price recovery can effectively force unwanted goods onto the buyer and require him either to dispose of them or to let them lie idle. An economic system ought not foster wasted goods; further, it is the seller, rather than the buyer, who is usually in the better position to resell the goods. The buyer is in the business of purchasing and has an office staff familiar with where goods like the ones involved can be *acquired*. The seller, on the other hand, has a sales force with the needed contacts to *dispose* of these goods to other purchasers. Thus, economic distribution of goods is usually fostered by restricting the situations in which the seller is allowed to force goods on the defaulting buyer.[48] Nevertheless, there are instances in which the seller is entitled to full price, and this remedy should be considered in determining the best course of action to pursue against a defaulting buyer.

The seller's action for price is covered by section 2–709. Two events must concur before the remedy is available. First, the buyer must commit the triggering event which opens the remedy and, second, the factual pattern must present at least one of the three situations detailed in the section. The triggering event occurs when "the buyer fails to pay the price as it becomes due." [49] This default is broader than the portion of section 2–703 which opens remedies on

Where there is no market for the completed product and the seller does not manufacture following repudiation, lost profits are the proper measure of recovery. Anchorage Centennial Dev. Co. v. Van Wormer & Rodrigues, Inc., 443 P.2d 596 (Alaska 1968). *See generally* Note, *Seller's Recovery When Buyer Repudiates Before Completion of Manufacture*, 99 U.Pa.L.Rev. 229 (1950). As to the seller's options when the buyer repudiates, see § 162 *supra*.

46. Although UCC § 2–709(1) states that the seller may recover "the price," courts will give the buyer credit for prepayments. Also, expenses saved by the seller should be deducted. § 180 *infra*.

47. § 139 *supra*.

48. There are instances in which the Code rule may have the opposite effect. When a distant buyer wrongfully rejects unwanted goods, his proximity to the goods may make him better able to dispose of them. This would depend on the nature of the goods, the distance between seller and buyer, the ease with which the defaulting buyer could resell the goods, and so on. 1955 N.Y. Law Rev. Comm'n (vol. 1) 565.

49. UCC § 2–709(1).

the buyer's failure "to make a payment due on or before delivery." Under section 2–709 the buyer's failure to pay may occur before, on, or after delivery. In fact, since the situation in which the seller is most apt to recover the price is that in which the buyer has accepted and retained the goods, often delivered on credit, the failure to make a payment due *after* delivery will be the typical triggering event opening section 2–709 to the seller.

The three situations in which the seller may recover the price are:

1. *Of goods accepted.*[50] A case clearly within section 2–709 is the one in which the seller has delivered goods to the buyer, the buyer has accepted and retained the goods, but the buyer has failed to make the agreed payments. The buyer has the goods and the contract obligates him to pay for them; the seller is entitled to performance of the buyer's promise to pay.

There will be some situations in which the seller has delivered goods to the buyer on unsecured credit and on the strength of the buyer's promise to pay a portion of the price at stated intervals—as, for example, where the buyer has promised to pay one-third of the price 30, 60, and 90 days after delivery. If the buyer fails to make the first or second payment, may the seller sue immediately for the entire price?

Unless the contract contains an acceleration clause (an agreement by the buyer that the entire price is due on the failure to make any one payment), section 2–709 would not be available to the seller. Section 2–709 is triggered only by a failure to pay *the price* as it becomes due—not by a failure to make *a payment* on the price.[51] Not until the buyer defaults in his obligation to pay the entire balance of the purchase price can the seller use section 2–709.[52] Although the Code does

---

50. "Acceptance" is defined in UCC § 2–606 and discussed in § 142 *supra*. Since the buyer has a right to inspect before acceptance, UCC § 2–513, seldom can this subsection of UCC § 2–709 be used to make the buyer liable for the price of goods still in the seller's possession.

51. Compare UCC § 2–703.

52. Pre-Code cases which refused to allow a seller to recover the price until the credit term had expired include Tatum v. Ackerman, 148 Cal. 357, 83 P. 151 (1905); Dudzik v. Degrenia, 48 R.I. 430, 138 A. 57 (1927). Some courts allowed a seller to recover the entire price although the credit period had not expired if the buyer had "repudiated" the contract. *E. g.,* Precision Dev. Co. v. Fast Bearing Co., 183 Md. 399, 37 A.2d 905 (1944), and cases cited therein. This text has argued that the failure to make a payment due after delivery is not a "repudiation" which will allow a seller to cancel and recover the goods. § 165 *supra*. That conclusion is not necessarily controlling when the seller is suing for the price and the possibility of a preference is not involved. Nevertheless, there will be difficulty in finding that a repudiation makes the *price* due, especially when the parties did not include an acceleration clause in their agreement.

not expressly give an aggrieved seller a remedy when the buyer fails to pay an installment due after delivery—unless it is the last installment—sections 1–103 and 1–106(2) can be used to allow recovery of all past-due installments. The section 1–106(2) "obligation" can be found in section 2–301.

The Code language requires only that the goods be "accepted." Therefore, a rejection—either rightful or wrongful—prevents the seller from recovering the price under this subsection.[53] However, a buyer may accept the goods and then revoke his acceptance, again either rightfully or wrongfully. May the seller recover the contract price on the theory that these goods have been "accepted" ?

If the revocation was rightful, the question is easily answered. Although acceptance bound the buyer to pay the contract price,[54] his rightful revocation indicates that the seller was in substantial default and that the buyer can recover "so much of the price as has been paid." [55] If a defaulting seller is allowed to use section 2–709 to recover the price of goods from the buyer whose acceptance was rightfully revoked, the buyer could demand its return under section 2–703—all of which means that the two amounts offset each other and that no section 2–709 recovery would be allowed the seller following a rightful revocation of acceptance.

If the revocation was wrongful, the answer is not so simple. In this instance the buyer is in default and has no damage remedy to offset the seller's price claim. Nevertheless, if the seller retakes the goods as the owner, he ought not also have a claim for their price under the "goods accepted" provision of section 2–709.[56] His remedy is under section 2–708. Of course, if the seller refuses the attempted wrongful revocation, the goods are still the buyer's and the seller may recover the price.

2. *Of conforming goods lost or damaged within a commercially reasonable time after risk of their loss has passed to the buyer.* It is important that the rules relating to recovery of full price be consistent with rules governing risk of loss. If the buyer bears the risk of loss, he ought to be liable to the seller for the price even though the goods are lost or damaged before the buyer has accepted them—else the conclusion that the buyer has the risk would be important only in those cases in which the price was paid in advance of shipment. Thus,

---

53. UCC § 2–401(4).

54. UCC § 2–607(1). The contract price must be paid even if the goods are defective. Columbia Novelty Co. v. Leslie Dawn, Inc., 6 UCC Rep. 679 (N.Y.Sup.Ct., App.T., 1969).

55. UCC § 2–711(1).

56. Friedman v. Pierce, 210 Mass. 419, 97 N.E.2d 82 (1912), and cases cited in § 175, note 25, *supra*.

in a shipment contract the due delivery of conforming goods to a carrier passes the risk of their loss to the buyer.[57] If the goods arrive and are accepted, the buyer is liable for the price because he "accepted" them. If the goods are lost or damaged in transit, the buyer is also liable for their price under this subsection. With lost or damaged goods the seller must prove that the risk of loss did pass, and this requires a showing (in a shipment contract) that the goods were conforming when tendered. The fact that the loss or damage prevented the buyer's inspection will not, however, free him of the price obligation. The buyer has a right to inspect before acceptance,[58] but not before the risk of loss passes to him.

This section requires that before price recovery is allowed, the loss or damage must occur *within a commercially reasonable time* after the buyer received the risk of loss. The probable meaning of this phrase has already been presented in connection with the risk of loss discussion.[59] It was there concluded that this phrase was included to make it clear that the risk of loss (in the sense of price liability) did not remain forever with a buyer who refused to accept a conforming tender. Thus, when a shipment has been wrongfully rejected at the buyer's city, the seller has a commercially reasonable time to dispose of those goods. If the seller waits a longer period of time, a later destruction or loss of the goods will not create a price liability in the buyer.

3. *Of goods identified to the contract if the seller is unable after reasonable effort to resell them at a reasonable price or the circumstances reasonably indicate that such efforts will be unavailing.* This provision was included to allow price recovery in those relatively rare instances in which the goods remain with the seller but are practically worthless. A buyer may have ordered an ornate set of silverware heavily embossed with his unique family crest or he may have agreed to purchase 50,000 specially designed commemorative medallions. If the goods have been identified to the contract,[60] the facts may indicate that the seller, even with his sales force and contacts, cannot dispose of these goods except for their salvage value. The Code allows this seller to recover the agreed price.[61] However, goods can normally be resold at a price substantially above their salvage value, and the normal situations call for damages under other Code sections already

---

57. UCC §§ 2–504, 2–509.

58. UCC § 2–513(1).

59. § 132 *supra.*

60. § 126 *supra.*

61. Walter Balfour & Co. v. Lizza & Sons, Inc., 6 UCC Rep. 649 (N.Y.Sup. Ct.1969) (specially manufactured goods); Jacobson v. Donnkenny, Inc., 4 UCC Rep. 850 (N.Y.Sup.Ct.1967) (goods that went out of style); Ludwig, Inc. v. Tobey, 28 Mass.App.Dec. 6 (1964) (altered goods).

discussed. The price remedy is not available to a seller solely because resale is difficult or the goods have to be resold at a discount.

These are the only three situations in which the seller is entitled to price. The fact that title may have passed to the buyer is no longer material.[62] An agreement expanding situations in which the buyer is liable for the price, although apparently valid under section 2–719, would probably fail as a penalty or as unconscionable.[63] However, if a seller sues for price when he is not entitled to it, his action is not dismissed but he will be awarded the appropriate damages under some other Code section.[64]

Section 2–709(2) protects the buyer in those instances in which the seller is entitled to the price but has retained the goods:

> Where the seller sues for the price he must hold for the buyer any goods which have been identified to the contract and are still in his control except that if resale becomes possible he may resell them at any time prior to the collection of the judgment. The net proceeds of any such resale must be credited to the buyer and payment of the judgment entitles him to any goods not resold.

This subsection should make the price remedy unattractive to most volume sellers (as defined in the prior section of this text) who remain in possession of the goods. If these sellers proceed under section 2–708, there is a high probability that they can recover their lost profits and not need to credit any amount received on resale of the goods.[65] On the other hand, if these sellers seek a price recovery under section 2–709, the "net proceeds" of the resale must be credited against the buyer's obligation. While it is possible to argue that the lost profit should be deducted from the resale price to obtain the "net proceeds," there is the danger that courts will read these words to mean the gross amount received on resale less the out-of-pocket expenses incurred.

§ 179. Recovery When Goods were Not Identified at Time of Buyer's Default

There are times when a buyer's default (usually in the form of a repudiation) occurs before the seller has completed manufacturing

---

62. This was the rule under Uniform Sales Act § 63. Some Code courts continue to talk in terms of passage of title. Conte v. Styli, 26 Mass.App. Dec. 73 (1963). This is incorrect. UCC § 2–709, Comment 6.

63. UCC §§ 2–302, 2–718(1). Denkin v. Sterner, 10 Pa.D. & C.2d 203 (C.P.1956).

64. UCC § 2–709(3).

65. § 177 *supra*.

the goods.[66] Such a seller must decide whether to stop or to complete their manufacture. This decision will turn in large measure on business considerations but could also be affected by the damages recoverable from the defaulting buyer.

If the seller stops manufacture before any expenditures have been made, he may recover damages under section 2–708. In a proper case those damages would be his lost profits—that is, the profit the seller would have made had the agreement been performed. That profit will be determined by subtracting his variable costs of completion from the contract price, thus allowing a recovery for the seller's overhead.[67] If some expenditures had been made by the seller before he learned of the buyer's breach, an allowance must be made for those expenditures.[68] If the manufacturing process produced a partial product which has a market (or even a salvage) value, that value will be deducted from the seller's recovery.[69] The result of this determination will be to place the seller in the same financial position as if the buyer would have performed and will protect the seller's expectation interest.[70]

The seller may, on the other hand, decide that it is preferable to continue production even though the buyer has defaulted. He may believe that the buyer will withdraw his repudiation, or that the loss will be minimized by completion of the goods, or that the operation of the remainder of his factory will be jeopardized if this production is terminated, or he may believe that he should continue production for any one of a number of reasons. If the seller's prophecies are accurate and the buyer withdraws his repudiation, accepting the goods, the buyer must pay the price of those goods just as if he had not attempted to repudiate. If the buyer fails to change his mind but if further production mitigates damages, the buyer will undoubtedly not complain about the reduction in his damages. However, the seller's prophecies may be inaccurate. The completion may enhance the damages which

---

66. If the manufacturing process had been completed at the time of default, the seller could identify the goods to the contract under UCC § 2–704(1) (a). His remedies would be those discussed in §§ 173–78 *supra*.

67. Vitex Mfg. Corp., Ltd. v. Caribtex Corp., 377 F.2d 795 (3d Cir. 1967); Perfecting Serv. Co. v. Product Dev. & Sales Co., 259 N.C. 400, 131 S.E.2d 9 (1963). Pre-Code courts disagreed as to when the manufacturer could recover lost profits and when he was limited to contract price less market value. Cases are digested in Annot., 44 A.L.R. 215, 250 (1926), s. 108 A.L.R.

1482, 1491 (1937). The Code rule is discussed in § 177 *supra*.

68. Allowing recovery for expenditures which could not be saved by the breach: Alexander H. Kerr & Co. v. Fooks, 145 F.Supp. 503 (W.D.Ark. 1956); Norton & Lamphere Constr. Co. v. Blow & Cote, Inc., 123 Vt. 130, 183 A.2d 230 (1962). Recovery for these expenditures will be allowed under the Code by virtue of UCC § 2–708 and the reference to UCC § 2–710.

69. UCC § 2–704(1) (b).

70. § 138 *supra*.

would have been suffered had the seller stopped his performance when the buyer repudiated. May the seller recover these enhanced damages?

The answer under the Uniform Sales Act was that he could not. That statute provided that the defaulting buyer would be liable to a completing seller "for no greater damages than the seller would have suffered if he did nothing towards carrying out the contract or the sale after receiving notice of the buyer's repudiation or countermand." [71] Such a rule, especially when combined with the doctrine of mitigation, required the seller to prophesy as to the future condition of the market. If he stopped production and prices went up, the doctrine of mitigation might limit him to the losses he would have suffered had he completed the manufacturing process; if he continued production and prices went down, the statutory limit on recovery prevented the seller from obtaining full compensation for his loss. In addition to requiring more of the seller than anyone knew at the time of making the decision regarding production, this rule confused the *duty* to complete manufacturing with the *privilege* of using reasonable business judgment to continue to produce the goods. It is one thing to say that the seller has no duty to finish the goods; it is quite another to say that he is not privileged to take such action.

These arguments need not be expanded because the Code has changed the approach to the completing seller's remedies. Section 2–704(2) provides:

> Where the goods are unfinished an aggrieved seller may in the exercise of reasonable commercial judgment for the purposes of avoiding loss and of effective realization either complete the manufacture and wholly identify the goods to the contract or cease manufacture and resell for scrap or salvage value or proceed in any other reasonable manner.

These words can cause construction difficulties. What is the meaning of "for the purposes of avoiding loss"? Does this phrase mean loss to the seller or loss to the buyer? What is meant by "effective realization"? Does this mean effective realization of the goods, the seller's factory, or something else? As with other parts of the Code, these words can be read so often as to become a meaningless blur of black ink on white paper.

They should not be read this way. The Code recognizes the dilemma facing the manufacturer when he receives a repudiation. It tells that manufacturer-seller to exercise reasonable commercial judg-

---

71. Uniform Sales Act § 64(4). Pre-Code cases are collected in 3 S. Williston, Sales § 589 (rev. ed. 1948).

ment in deciding whether to stop production and sell what he has for scrap or to go on manufacturing the goods.[72]   A part of that judgment should include a weighing of the losses which might follow—losses to the buyer and to the seller.[73]   Also a part of that judgment should be a determination of what will happen to the seller's labor force, his other contracts, his other buyers, and his reputation in the business community.   The judgment is a commercial one, and its reasonableness is to be measured by the facts which the seller had at the time he learned of the breach—not by facts which become apparent through hindsight.   Further, the "burden is on the buyer to show the commercially unreasonable nature of the seller's action in completing manufacture."[74]

If the seller does decide to complete the manufacture and if that judgment is commercially reasonable, he may identify the goods to the seller-buyer contract.   This would allow him to resell and recover damages under section 2–706.   In a proper case (one in which the goods turned out not to be readily resalable at a reasonable price) the seller could even recover the full price under the conditions of section 2–709.[75]   Finally, the seller could ignore either of these remedies and proceed under section 2–708 to recover his market value loss or his lost profits.

A seller who held finished goods at the time of the repudiation is also given the same privileges.   He may identify conforming goods to the seller-buyer contract after he learned of the breach and seek a remedy under one of the sections mentioned above.[76]

§ 180.   Incidental Damages and Expenses Saved

An award of damages measured by the resale or market price of the goods, by the seller's lost profit, or even by the full contract price will not always place the seller in the same financial position as full performance would have done.   The seller may have incurred extra expenses because of the default.   For example, the goods may have been wrongfully rejected at the buyer's city and have had to be returned to the seller for resale, or the goods may have required care until they were disposed of, or the seller may have had to pay a sec-

---

72. The same rule should be applied by analogy to a seller who is not a manufacturer but who must procure the goods from a third party to satisfy the seller-buyer contract.

73. The Comments emphasize the buyer's losses. UCC § 2–704, Comment 2.

74. UCC § 2–704, Comment 2.

75. For a pre-Code example of such a situation, see Bradford Novelty Co. v. Technomatic, Inc., 142 Conn. 166, 112 A.2d 214 (1955). For a Code case (but one in which the seller stopped production), see Anchorage Centennial Dev. Co. v. Van Wormer & Rodrigues, Inc., 443 P.2d 596 (Alaska 1968).

76. UCC § 2–704(1) (a).

ond commission in making the second sale, or any one of a number of other expenses may have been incurred because the buyer failed to perform his contractual obligations. These incidental damages are defined in section 2–710:

> Incidental damages to an aggrieved seller include any commercially reasonable charges, expenses or commissions incurred in stopping delivery, in the transportation, care and custody of goods after the buyer's breach, in connection with return or resale of the goods or otherwise resulting from the breach.

They are recoverable by virtue of specific reference in each of the various damage sections.[77]

There are some defaults which saved the seller certain expenses which he would have made had the buyer performed. One such default has already been discussed at length: the buyer who repudiated a contract with a manufacturer who stops production, saving labor and material costs.[78] The saved expenses must be deducted from the contract price to obtain the amount of the seller's recovery. A number of other situations are possible. If a seller of finished goods had agreed to pay the transportation charges to the buyer's city, a timely repudiation would save the seller from shipping the goods to the buyer —thus, saving the expense which the seller would have had to make had the buyer performed. Likewise, an early repudiation may also save the seller from having to pay a sales commission or the cost of putting the goods into some special condition ordered by the buyer. These savings must be taken into account in awarding damages to the seller.[79]

§ 181. Liquidated Damages and Penalties

This text has developed the general principles underlying the Code's allowance of liquidated damages and its general disallowance of penal damages.[80] That discussion will not be repeated except as those principles have application to a buyer's default.

---

77. UCC §§ 2–706, 2–708, 2–709. The seller is entitled to recover for extra transportation, storage, and legal expenses caused by the buyer's default. Procter & Gamble Distrib. Co. v. Lawrence Am. Field Warehousing Corp., 16 N.Y.2d 344, 266 N.Y.S.2d 785, 213 N.E.2d 873 (1965) (citing UCC § 2–710). Incidental damages were recoverable by the seller prior to the Code. Tankersley v. Cumberland Frozen Foods, Inc., 282 F.2d 636 (6th Cir. 1960).

78. § 179 *supra.*

79. UCC §§ 2–706, 2–708. No mention is made of deducting expenses saved in the suit for full price. UCC § 2–709. Nevertheless, saved expenses should be deducted in such a suit. Walter Balfour & Co. v. Lizza & Sons, 6 UCC Rep. 649 (N.Y.Sup.Ct.1969). *But see* Beco, Inc. v. Minnechaug Golf Course, Inc., 5 Conn.Cir. 444, 256 A.2d 522 (1968).

80. §§ 154–55 *supra.*

The pertinent section is 2–718(1) which provides that damages may be liquidated "but only at an amount which is reasonable in the light of the anticipated or actual harm caused by the breach, the difficulties of proof of loss, and the inconvenience or non-feasibility of otherwise obtaining an adequate remedy." Therefore, the parties can agree that, in the event of a default by the buyer, the seller is entitled to a stipulated sum as damages. If the sum selected meets the tests of section 2–718(1), that amount—and only that amount—is recoverable from the buyer.[81] The difficulty in meeting these tests is that if the sales transaction is one in which the seller must recover damages based upon either the market or resale price of the goods, the anticipated harm will probably be an amount which is subject to reasonably close estimation, and a damage provision which varies substantially from the actual harm will not be enforced.[82] The sales transaction may, however, be one in which the seller is entitled to his lost profits. These may be difficult to estimate in advance and difficult to prove after the default.[83] If so, a stipulated damage clause which is a reasonable pre-estimate of the anticipated or actual harm should be upheld.

There is one situation which presents a confusing Code solution. Suppose that the seller-buyer contract calls for a prepayment of a portion of the purchase price and provides that, in the event of a default by the buyer, the seller may retain the prepayment as liquidated damages.[84] That provision must meet the general requirements of section 2–718; thus, if the amount of the prepayment is not reasonable under the tests of section 2–718(1), it will be unenforceable. However, the measure of "reasonableness" when a down payment is involved could conceivably involve a determination of the amount which the seller could withhold from that down payment if there had been no

---

81. The Code defines liquidated damages but does not provide that they are recoverable in a separate suit by the buyer or seller. Conceivably, the only effect of the definition could be to provide the basis for a seller's deductions under UCC §§ 2–718(2) and (3). This limited reading should be rejected. The Code allows damages to be liquidated by "either party," thus covering a seller's default—which is not a part of UCC § 2–718(2). Further, the idea of recovering liquidated damages is so much a part of the common law that the omission of a remedy for UCC § 2–708(1) can be filled in by the common law and by UCC §§ 1–103 and 1–106(2).

82. Cf. 5 A. Corbin § 1064 (1964). Cases are collected in Annot., 11 A.L.R.2d 701, 713 (1950).

83. Sheffield-King Milling Co. v. Jacobs, 170 Wis. 389, 175 N.W. 796 (1920).

84. Protection of the seller is also attempted through disclaimers (§§ 86–88 *supra*) and through limitation of the buyer's remedies (§ 89 *supra*). As to the relationship between all of these devices and the conscionability requirement, see Dow Corning Corp. v. Capitol Aviation, Inc., 411 F.2d 622 (7th Cir. 1969).

stipulated damage clause. This is discussed elsewhere in this text,[85] where it is concluded that the Code probably allows a defaulting buyer restitution of his prepayments less (a) damages to the seller, and (b) a further sum which varies with the amount of the buyer's contractual obligations but does not exceed $500. Is this further sum to be considered by a court in determining whether the contractual provision allowing the seller to retain a down payment is "reasonable" under section 2–718(1)?

An argument can be made that this further sum should be considered. Without the clause the seller could have retained that amount in addition to his damages—if this is the way subsections (2) and (3) of section 2–718 are to be read. The inclusion of a liquidated damage clause which considers that amount ought not change the result. Indeed, striking the clause would only mean that the buyer could proceed under subsections (2) and (3), and recover his statutory penalty.

Nevertheless, the test of a liquidated damage clause is centered on anticipated or actual *harm*, not recovery. These will be the same (harm and recovery) except where the buyer is seeking restitution of his down payment, but since subsections (2) and (3) of the same section which establishes the right to liquidated damages deals with the prepayment problem, the more probable reading of section 2–718(1) is that the stipulated damage clause may not take account of the statutory deduction. The seller who receives a prepayment has a choice. He may either (a) retain his statutory deduction plus damages or (b) insert in the agreement a liquidated damage clause which measures the anticipated or actual *harm,* and retain that amount.

D. PROTECTION OF THE RESTITUTION INTEREST

§ 182. Introduction

The primary Code remedies concern themselves with defining the limits of protection to be given the aggrieved party's expectation interest—that is, they indicate the extent to which the nondefaulting party will be placed in the economic position he would have occupied had there been no default.[86] Partial analysis of the reliance interest is included in the two sections dealing with incidental damages, but the analysis is far from complete. For example, the section dealing with a seller's incidental damages contains no express mention of charges

85. § 184 *infra.* This section also discusses some problems of a liquidated damage clause which allows a seller to retain only a portion of the down payment.

86. The contractual interests of the parties to an agreement are outlined in § 138 *supra.*

incurred in transporting goods prior to breach (as might be borne by a seller who shipped goods, F.O.B. seller's city, only to have the buyer wrongfully reject the goods on arrival), relying instead on the general language which concludes that section. Further, the drafters did nothing to advance a solution of the difficult problem of the extent to which both parties' reliance interests merit protection when the contract has been discharged by some rule of law—as, for example, intervening impossibility.[87]

This text has presented the protection afforded the restitution interest following a breach by the other party to the contract. The buyer's right to a return of any prepayments on the price (on the seller's default) and the seller's right to a return of the goods (on the buyer's default or insolvency) are two examples of restitution protection already discussed.[88] This portion of the text does not repeat that discussion but centers on two other problems:

1. To what extent will a seller who is in default of his contractual obligations be protected for benefits transferred to the buyer?

2. To what extent will a buyer who is in default of his contractual obligations be protected for benefits transferred to the seller?

§ 183. Seller's Restitution Interest When Seller is in Default

With but few exceptions, the seller who is in substantial default but who has partially performed a contract of sale has long been allowed restitutionary recovery without concern over the quality of his default. The Uniform Sales Act contained three rules applicable to the defaulting seller who was seeking compensation. First, if the buyer accepted or retained a partial delivery knowing that the seller was not going to perform completely, the buyer was liable to pay at the contract rate.[89] Second, if the buyer used or disposed of a partial delivery before he knew that the seller was not going to perform completely, the buyer was not liable for more than the fair value to the buyer of the goods received.[90] Third, if the goods did not measure up to the warranted quality, the buyer could retain the goods paying the price and offsetting his damages.[91]

The Code continues the policy of allowing the defaulting seller recovery for goods accepted and retained by the buyer. Acceptance of the goods by the buyer entitles the seller to the contract price for the goods accepted.[92] The buyer may then offset his damages against

---

87. The problem is discussed in § 110 *supra* and in Comment, *Apportioning Loss After Discharge of a Burdensome Contract: A Statutory Solution,* 69 Yale L.J. 1054 (1960).

88. §§ 146, 160, and 163–72 *supra.*

89. Uniform Sales Act § 44(1).

90. *Id.*

91. Uniform Sales Act § 69(a).

92. UCC § 2–607(1).

the contract price, providing that he has perfected his right to damages. For example, he must have given the appropriate notice and not have waived any objection he might have as to the defects in the goods.[93] Damages will be figured pursuant to section 2–714,[94] and the formulas of that section are broad enough to allow a court to provide the defaulting seller with a recovery which is not in excess of the fair market value of the goods which the buyer accepted. Since the Code begins the seller's recovery with contract price, the amount awarded the defaulting seller will never be in excess of the contract price.

§ 184. Buyer's Restitution Interest When Buyer is in Default

A buyer who wrongfully refuses to accept or to pay for tendered goods is liable to his seller in damages. Those damages are computed under formulas designed to compensate the seller for the financial losses which were suffered by reason of the breach. No amount is added to punish the buyer for his failure to perform or to serve as a warning to others who may be contemplating default; nor is any amount added because the court believes sellers have some damages which are hard to prove. Indeed, unless the seller can prove his damages without resort to speculation, the buyer will be required to pay only nominal damages.[95]

It is strange how these principles are lost as soon as the buyer makes a substantial down payment prior to his default. If this prepayment was approximately equal to (or exceeded) the damages suffered, the seller is usually quite willing to retain the prepayment and forgo any damage action against the buyer. However, if the prepayment exceeded the seller's damages by any substantial amount, the buyer will most likely be interested in securing at least a partial return of what he paid. This is undoubtedly the fact which caused many common-law courts difficulty: the defaulting buyer was initiating legal action. How could he use his own neglect as a basis for a cause of action?

There are many answers to this question. Those same courts had no difficulty in awarding a defaulting seller damages based upon any benefits he transferred to an aggrieved buyer.[96] Certainly the "neglect" of the buyer calls for compensation, but there is nothing in the fact of prepayment which requires punishment. A buyer who has

---

93. UCC §§ 2–605, 2–607(3) (a). §§ 139–45 *supra.*

94. § 150 *supra.* For a discussion of the seller's restitution interest when the contract is not enforceable because of the statute of frauds, see § 29 *supra.*

95. The bases for the statements made in this textual paragraph were developed in §§ 173–78 *supra.*

96. § 183 *supra.*

made substantial payments on the price does not need some legal threat to make him perform; the simple economics of the situation will do that. Thus, the best answer to the question posed is that the buyer is not using his neglect as a basis of suit. He is bringing the action for the benefits he transferred to the seller. He is suing for the value of those benefits not because of, but in spite of, his neglect. The defaulting buyer should be made to compensate the seller for losses arising out of the default (including full protection of the seller's expectation interest), but the existence of a prepayment ought not be used as a reason to punish the buyer for default.

These general ideas can be made specific through the following hypothetical factual pattern:

Seller agreed to sell and Buyer to buy goods at an agreed price of $5,000. Buyer prepaid $2,000 and defaulted by committing one of the acts listed in section 2–703. Seller resold the goods for $4,200, incurring no incidental damages and saving no expenses because of the breach. The agreement contained no liquidated damage clause.

What the answer *ought* to be is not hard to state. The seller is entitled to the contract price for these goods; at the moment he has received $6,200 on a $5,000 contract, $2,000 of which came from the defaulting buyer; thus, the buyer should be entitled to a return of $1,200. This will compensate the seller without punishing the buyer. If the seller had also incurred $200 in incidental damages, those should be subtracted from the $1,200.

While some common-law cases reached this result,[97] the majority refused to grant the defaulting buyer any recovery,[98] often with colorful language about the impact which an allowance of restitution would have on the commercial world.[99] The Code rejected both of these positions and provided in section 2–718:

> (2) Where the seller justifiably withholds delivery of goods because of the buyer's breach, the buyer is entitled to

97. *E. g.*, Amtorg Trading Corp. v. Miehle Printing Press & Mfg. Co., 206 F.2d 103 (2d Cir. 1953); Michigan Yacht & Power Co. v. Busch, 143 F. 929 (6th Cir. 1906); Foster v. Warner, 42 Idaho 729, 249 P. 771 (1926); Stewart v. Moss, 30 Wash.2d 535, 192 P.2d 362 (1948).

98. *E. g.*, Tomboy Gold & Copper Co. v. Marks, 185 Cal. 336, 197 P. 94 (1921) (but compare Freedman v. Rector, Wardens & Vestrymen, 37 Cal.2d 16, 230 P.2d 629 (1951)); Thach v. Durham, 120 Colo. 253, 108 P.2d 1159

(1949); Reitano v. Fote, 50 So.2d 873 (Fla.1951); Notti v. Clark, 133 Mont. 263, 322 P.2d 112 (1958). *See generally* 3 S. Williston, Sales § 599m (rev. ed. 1948); Corman, *Restitution for Benefits Conferred by Party in Default Under Sales Contract*, 34 Texas L.Rev. 582 (1956); Talbott, *Restitution for the Defaulting Buyer*, 9 W.Res.L.Rev. 445 (1958). Annot., 11 A.L.R.2d 701 (1950).

99. Dluge v. Whiteson, 292 Pa. 334, 141 A. 230 (1928); Neis v. O'Brien, 12 Wash. 358, 41 P. 59 (1895).

restitution of any amount by which the sum of his payments exceeds

> (a) the amount to which the seller is entitled by virtue of terms liquidating the seller's damages in accordance with subsection (1), or
>
> (b) in the absence of such terms, twenty per cent of the value of the total performance for which the buyer is obligated under the contract or $500, whichever is smaller.
>
> (3) The buyer's right to restitution under subsection (2) is subject to offset to the extent that the seller establishes
>
> (a) a right to recover damages under the provisions of this Article other than subsection (1), and
>
> (b) the amount or value of any benefits received by the buyer directly or indirectly by reason of the contract.

In the hypothetical set out above the buyer will not lose his entire prepayment. Since there was no liquidated damage clause, the buyer is "entitled to restitution" in the amount of his prepayment less (a) the statutory twenty percent or (b) $500, whichever is smaller.[1] The $500 is the lesser amount; thus, the hypothetical buyer is entitled to restitution in the amount of $1,500.

Subsection (3) adds, however, that the "right to restitution"—the $1,500 [2]—is to be reduced by the amount of the seller's damages and the buyer's benefits. If some of the goods had been delivered to the buyer, the benefit measured by the contract price would be deducted from the $1,500. None had been delivered here; therefore, the only concern is with the seller's damages.

The seller in the hypothetical set out above has clearly suffered some damages; the problem is in determining their amount. The buyer's default left the seller with $4,200 worth of goods. Section 2–718(2) allows this seller to retain $500 of the buyer's down payment. Thus, the seller has received a total of $4,700 on a $5,000 contract and

---

1. It is possible to read UCC § 2–718 (2) (b) as placing the maximum deduction at twenty per cent of $500. This reading has been rejected because this amount would be fixed at $100 and, had the drafters intended a fixed amount to be the maximum recovery, the probabilities are that they would have stated that amount as a figure, not as a percentage.

2. Is this the meaning of "right to restitution" in UCC § 2–718(3)? Could it mean the right to the entire prepayments, not reduced by the liquidated damages or the statutory deduction? If so, perhaps an argument could be made that the seller has no "damages" except as they exceed the amount withheld under UCC § 2–718(2).

has suffered a $300 loss. That $300 loss should be deducted from the buyer's down payment, leaving the buyer with a recovery of $1,200.

The problem, however, is whether the Code allows the buyer to recover even this much. The above solution assumes that the statutory deduction (the twenty per cent or the $500, whichever is smaller) is to be considered in determining the amount of the seller's damages. The way in which sections 2–718(2) and (3) were drafted makes this assumption of doubtful validity. Subsection (2) provides for a statutory deduction of up to $500 without any showing of damages. Therefore, if the goods in the hypothetical had been worth $5,000, the seller would nevertheless have been able to retain $500 of the $2,000 prepayment even though the buyer's breach had caused the seller no damage. Is that $500 lost to the seller as the market price of the retained goods is worth less than the contract price?

Answering this question is difficult because the Code has mixed the policy of compensation expressed in sections 2–706 and 2–708 with what appears to be a penalty granted by section 2–718. An argument can be made that the statutory deduction is compensation to the seller rather than a penalty to the buyer. This argument rests on the idea that the seller has hidden losses from every defaulted contract, losses which are not compensated under market value formulas. There may have been a basis for this rationalization under prior law where, in some states, the seller could not recover for his overhead.[3] When the Code reversed these decisions and allowed the volume seller (the one most apt to have "hidden expenses") to recover his lost profits, there was no reason to give him an additional sum which is already compensated out of those profits. Equally important, if the drafters decided that all sellers have expenses which are not compensated by the usual damage formulas, recovery should have been allowed to sellers in all defaulted contracts—not just those in which the buyer has made a prepayment. Certainly the seller's handling of the buyer's check or cash has not increased his damages by twenty per cent of the contract price, up to $500.[4] The more reasonable explanation of section 2–718 is that it was an attempt to place the prepaying buyer in a better position than he occupied under many pre-Code decisions, but still leave the seller with some recovery which has nothing to do with compensation for losses.[5] Thus, the $500 remains with the seller without con-

3. § 177 supra.

4. See 5A A. Corbin, Contracts § 1122 (1964).

5. The 1952 draft of UCC § 2–718(2) was substantially different from the present version. The New York Law Revision Commission criticized the 1952 draft. 1955 N.Y. Law Rev. Comm'n (vol. 1) 703–06. Section 2–718 was revised in 1956, with the revision based in part on a New York statute. See N.Y. Laws 1952, ch. 823, § 1. There are excellent studies of the New York statute in 1952 N.Y. Law Rev.

cern over his damages and, the way subsections (2) and (3) are drafted, ought not be considered as compensation to the seller when his
Code damages are computed for the purpose of section 2–718(3).

The seller's damages arise either under section 2–706 or section
2–708. First, suppose that the hypothetical seller did not comply with
the resale requirements of section 2–706. His damages would be
measured by section 2–708—based either on lost profits or market
price. If the latter and if the court were to find that the market price
of the goods at the time and place for tender was $4,200, a literal
application of section 2–708 would produce no damages to be deducted
from the buyer's section 2–718(2) $1,500 restitution claim. The rea-
son is that the section 2–708 formula is *unpaid* contract price less
market price, and here the market price exceeds the amount due. Of
course, this buyer is not entitled to restitution of $1,500. His default
damaged the seller more than the $500 which section 2–718(2) allows
the seller to retain. The Code formulas can, however, be justified by
remembering that if the buyer were to receive a return of the $1,500,
the "unpaid" contract price would be increased to $4,500—and the
seller would then have at least $300 in section 2–708 damages ($4,500
unpaid contract minus $4,200 market price). The court should recog-
nize this interplay between the buyer's restitution claim and the
amount of the *unpaid* contract price for purpose of the section 2–708
damages and simply deduct the $300 from the $1,500 produced by
section 2–718(2)—leaving the buyer with a net recovery of $1,200.

Urging this result is tempting,[6] but it ignores the purpose of section 2–718: that of letting the seller retain up to $500 without a show-
ing of damages. If this buyer is allowed to recover $1,200, the seller
will end up with $800 from the defaulting buyer and $4,200 worth of
goods—or a total of $5,000 on a $5,000 contract. The extra $500
which is allowed by section 2–718(2) has been lost. To give effect to
both the compensation principle and section 2–718, this seller should
receive $5,500 from this transaction, a result which is reached by
ignoring the statutory deduction when damages are computed. This
can be accomplished by omitting the word "unpaid" in the section
2–708 formula, and by subtracting the market price of the goods from
the full contract price. Read this way, the seller has $800 in damages
($5,000 contract price less $4,200 market price) to be subtracted from

Comm'n 83 and in 1942 N.Y. Rev.
Comm'n 179. The Code differed from
the New York statute, causing some
of the problems referred to in the text
of this section.

6. This section concludes by suggesting that this way of reading UCC § 2–
718 reaches defensible results in many
factual patterns which do not fit easily
within UCC § 2–718. This reading
can be supported by concluding that
there are no UCC § 2–718(3)(a) "damages" unless the seller is not compensated after withholding the statutory
deduction.

the buyer's $1,500 right to restitution. The buyer's recovery would be $700, leaving the seller with $1,300 of the prepayment and $4,200 worth of goods. It is not urged that this is what the law *ought* to be if the statute could be rewritten; it is claimed only that this appears to be what the drafters had in mind when they wrote section 2–718.

Second, suppose that the seller did comply with section 2–706 when he resold the goods for $4,200. A literal application of the section 2–706 formula (which does not mention "unpaid" contract price) produces the $800 in damages. Although the seller could not recover this $800 in an affirmative action,[7] subtracting this amount from the buyer's restitution award results in a seller's net recovery of $5,500. The apparent policy of section 2–718 has been satisfied; the seller has been allowed to retain up to $500 of the prepayment without a showing of damages.

This analysis suggests that the word "unpaid" must be ignored in section 2–708 and not read into section 2–706 when the buyer is asking for protection of the restitution interest.[8] In the discussion of the seller's damages the opposite construction was urged: the word "unpaid" must be read into section 2–706 and left alone in section 2–708.[9] This difference is not caused by any change of mind between the times that these parts of the text were written; it results from attempting to put together two disparate policies—the policy of compensation expressed by the seller's basic remedies and the policy of allowing more than compensation expressed in section 2–718.

The problems discussed thus far can be solved after a fashion by referring to the supposed policies of section 2–718, but if the amount of the down payment is varied, solutions are even more doubtful. Suppose that the down payment had been only $500 in the hypothetical set out above. Can the seller retain the $500 under section 2–718(2) and (3), and later obtain a section 2–706 or 2–708 remedy—measuring his loss without considering the amount which he retained (as was suggested he could do when the prepayment was more substantial)? If the down payment was $700, the analysis suggested above allows the seller to retain the entire $700, but does he lose a part of his "damages" because he required a down payment which did not cover both the statutory deduction and the decrease in value? If the seller was fortunate and resold at above the seller-buyer contract

7. § 174 *supra*.

8. Notice that the buyer was not allowed to retain 20% of the goods, up to a value of $500, without payment

when the seller defaulted after delivery of some of the goods. § 183 *supra*.

9. § 174 *supra*.

price, is the "profit" on resale to be used to offset the statutory deduction? [10]

Real trouble arises if a liquidated damage clause is inserted in the hypothetical contract—the one with the $5,000 contract price, $2,000 down payment, and resale at $4,200. Suppose that the parties agreed that in the event of a buyer's default, the seller was allowed to retain $900 of the down payment as liquidated damages; suppose further that this agreement would be upheld under section 2–718(1).[11]

Applying the Code literally to these facts could produce amazing results. The buyer is entitled to a return of his $2,000 prepayment less the $900 liquidated damages. There is no further reduction for the statutory maximum of $500. However, section 2–718(3) provides that the buyer's "right to restitution" (the $1,100) is subject to offset to the extent that the seller establishes "a right to recover damages under the provisions of this Article other than subsection (1)." It makes sense to say that the seller cannot deduct his liquidated damages twice, but does the Code mean that this seller can now deduct his 2–706 or 2–708 damages? If so, the aggrieved seller will have both his liquidated damages *and* the damages which he can prove. Of course, this result can (and will) be obviated by concluding that the seller has no section 2–718(3) "damages" when the contract includes a liquidated damage clause, but the arrangement of section 2–718(2) and (3) makes this result questionable as a matter of construing statutory language. Also, it is exactly the result allowed when the statutory deduction is involved—that deduction was not considered in measuring the seller's "damages."

An attempt to apply the language of section 2–718 to the facts of many cases should show that the section, as drafted, comes close to being unworkable. One good thing about this section is that the $500 maximum is small enough to get lost in any substantial dispute.[12] A bad thing is that its principal impact will be with the smaller purchase which requires a down payment—usually a consumer buying consumer goods. If the volume seller retains the twenty percent portion (up to $500) of the down payment without pursuing his remedy for lost

---

10. Under UCC § 2–706(6) a seller is not "accountable" to the buyer for the resale profit, but this may mean net, not gross, profit. § 174 *supra*. The answers to the questions raised in the textual paragraph appear to turn on which party (seller or buyer) is taking affirmative action in the suit. When the seller seeks damages against a defaulting buyer, all prepayments are credited in the resulting judgment. When the defaulting buyer seeks resti- tution, only a portion of the prepay- ments are credited in the resulting judgment. This makes difficult a ra- tional interpretation of UCC §§ 2–706, 2–708, and 2–718.

11. §§ 154, 181 *supra*.

12. *E. g.*, Procter & Gamble Distrib. Co. v. Lawrence Am. Field Warehous- ing Corp., 16 N.Y.2d 344, 213 N.E.2d 873, 266 N.Y.S.2d 785 (1965).

profits, the results will approximate that which would be allowed anyway under section 2–708. It is when an attempt is made to reduce the buyer's recovery even further that problems arise.[13]

Sections 2–718(2) and (3) merit study by state legislatures, especially in view of recent legislation to aid consumers. Is there reason why a seller in small sales should be allowed to retain a portion of any prepayments without showing damages? Until the legislatures have considered this question, courts face a confusing statute which cannot be intelligently applied as written. Perhaps the best they can do in the harder cases is to recognize that the drafters did express a policy which favors allowing the buyer to recover his prepayments, but that some deduction should be made from those prepayments. Those deductions, in light of the principle of compensation and the statutory minimum, will be: (1) in all cases, any benefit received by the buyer; (2) in situations in which there is a liquidated damage clause, the amount stipulated by the parties; (3) in situations where there is no liquidated damage clause but in which the seller can prove damages, the amount of the damages; and (4) if the damages are less than the statutory deduction, twenty percent of the purchase price or $500, whichever is smaller.[14] This reading places a minimum on the seller's damages when a prepayment is involved, but will generally produce defensible results.

E. LIMITATION OF ACTIONS

§ 185. The Code's Statutory Period

In an effort to produce a uniform period of time within which actions must be brought on a contract for the sale of goods, section 2–725(1) provides:

> An action for breach of any contract for sale must be commenced within four years after the cause of action has accrued. By the original agreement the parties may reduce the period of limitations to not less than one year but may not extend it.

---

13. Many of the ideas in this section appear in Nordstrom, *Seller's Damages Following Resale Under Article Two of the Uniform Commercial Code*, 65 Mich.L.Rev. 1299 (1967). For a discussion of the buyer's restitution interest when the contract is not enforceable because of the statute of frauds, see § 29 *supra*.

14. If the down payment is in the form of goods (a trade-in), their reasonable value or resale proceeds—rather than the amount allowed on the trade-in—is considered as the payment for UCC § 2–718(2); but if the seller has notice of the buyer's default, the seller must follow UCC § 2–706 in making the resale. UCC § 2–718(4). Failure to follow UCC § 2–706 evidently prevents the seller from using the price on resale in determining the size of the prepayment.

If this attempt is successful, businessmen will be able to plan their record-keeping period—assured that they can destroy old records after four years.[15] Whether the attempt is successful will depend in large part on how courts answer two questions:

1.   Does the litigation present an action *for* breach of a *contract for sale*?   A contract for the sale of goods [16] (present or future) may be involved in the factual pattern, but the action may be "for" something other than its breach.   The statute clearly applies to suits by the seller for the price of goods [17] or for a deficiency following resale.[18] Likewise, the statute should be applicable to the seller's section 2–708 damage actions and to the buyer's claim that the seller did not transfer the warranted title, as well as to the buyer's suit for commercial losses following the seller's breach of the warranty of quality.   However, when the buyer sues for personal injuries arising out of a defect in sold goods, it is possible to classify the action as one "for" strict liability or negligence, thereby avoiding the Code's time period.   Some courts have reached this conclusion,[19] but the better decisions have held that the buyer's action is timely brought if commenced within the four-year period.[20]   Since tort statutes of limitations are sometimes shorter than four years, application of these statutes could leave the buyer liable for the price of goods without being able to offset any damages caused by a defect in those same goods.

A suit by the seller to recover the goods following discovery of the buyer's insolvency presents different considerations.   The Code requires a demand within ten days after receipt,[21] but does not expressly provide when the reclamation action must be begun.   However, if the demand is not followed up with reasonable diligence, a court could

---

15.   This purpose for a statute of limitations is presented in UCC § 2–725, Comment.

16.   See the definition of "contract for sale" in UCC § 2–106(1).

17.   Gimbel Bros., Inc. v. Cohen, 46 Pa. D. & C.2d 747 (C.P.1969).   There must be a sale of goods before UCC § 2–725 is applicable.   Warner Motors, Inc. v. Chrysler Motors Corp., 5 UCC Rep. 365 (U.S.Dist.Ct.E.D.Pa.1968);   Campana Pontiac, Inc. v. General Motors Corp., 46 Pa.D. & C.2d 486 (C.P.1969).   *But see* Gardiner v. Philadelphia Gas Works, 413 Pa. 415, 197 A.2d 612 (1964).

18.   Associates   Discount   Corp.   v. Palmer, 47 N.J. 183, 219 A.2d 858 (1966).

19.   *E. g.*, Abate v. Barkers of Wallingford, Inc., 27 Conn.Supp. 46, 229 A.2d 366 (1967);   Rosenau v. City of New Brunswick, 51 N.J. 130, 238 A.2d 169 (1968);   United States Fidelity & Guaranty Co. v. Truck & Concrete Equip. Co., 21 Ohio St.2d 244, 257 N.E.2d 380 (1970) (no privity).

20.   *E. g.*, Val Decker Packing Co. v. Corn Prods. Sales Co., 411 F.2d 850 (6th Cir. 1969);   Braser Co. v. Zuck Pail & Can Co., 6 UCC Rep. 511 (U.S. Dist.Ct.E.D.Tenn.1967);   Gardiner v. Philadelphia Gas Works, 413 Pa. 415, 197 A.2d 612 (1964).   The four-year period is applicable to a survival action.   Carney v. Barnett, 4 UCC Rep. 930 (U.S.Dist.Ct.E.D.Pa.1967).

21.   UCC § 2–702(2)—unless the seller made a written misrepresentation of his solvency.

find that there was no "demand" or that the demand was waived. Prompt action is needed in these cases so that other creditors will not be misled,[22] but even if the right to reclaim is lost by dilatory action, the seller has four years to pursue his claim for the price. To a lesser extent these same considerations apply to the buyer's specific performance action based upon the seller's insolvency.[23]

2. Was the litigation commenced within four years after the cause of action *accrued*? When a cause of action "accrues" is a legal conclusion—one which has caused considerable litigation under other statutes of limitations. In an effort to provide some certainty the Code adds:

> A cause of action accrues when the breach occurs, regardless of the aggrieved party's lack of knowledge of the breach. A breach of warranty occurs when tender of delivery is made, except that where a warranty explicitly extends to future performance of the goods and discovery of the breach must await the time of such performance the cause of action accrues when the breach is or should have been discovered.[24]

The result of these rules is that the time period begins to run at an early date—the time of breach, rather than the time of the discovery of the default. For example, the warranty of title is breached on delivery of the goods. The buyer has four years to discover the title defect and to commence his litigation against the seller, or he will lose his cause of action. If the title defect does not come to the buyer's attention until more than four years after delivery, the Code's statute of limitations bars any recovery from the seller for breach of the title warranty. The buyer's only hope is to be able to plead and prove some other cause of action—perhaps fraud—which has a longer statutory period.

These same rules apply to actions based upon a breach of the warranty of quality. The cause of action accrues on tender of delivery, irrespective of the buyer's lack of knowledge of the defect.[25] The single Code exception to this rule is the warranty which "explicit-

22. § 165 *supra*.

23. § 158 *supra*.

24. UCC § 2–725(2).

25. Val Decker Packing Co. v. Corn Prods. Sales Co., 411 F.2d 850 (6th Cir. 1969); Wolverine Ins. Co. v. Tower Iron Works, Inc., 370 F.2d 700 (1st Cir. 1966) (but Code statute of limitations is not applicable to negligence claim); Rufo v. Bastian-Blessing Co., 417 Pa. 107, 207 A.2d 823 (1965).

ly" extends to the future performance of the goods. Thus, if the seller warranted the goods for (say) two years, the four-year period does not begin until the buyer discovered or should have discovered the breach.[26]

The harshness of this portion of the Code's statute of limitations will probably cause some courts to classify the action as one other than for breach of a contract for sale. Defective goods may be purchased by a buyer, but their defect not show up for several years after the purchase. Should the seller escape liability for serious personal injuries because he makes goods which do not cause injury for at least four years? Reasonable minds can differ in answering this question. If the buyer wants longer protection, he could demand (and pay for) a warranty of the future performance of the goods. Had he received such a warranty, the cause of action would not have accrued on tender of delivery; his failure to protect himself should not cause courts to reclassify his cause of action to give him the protection he scorned. On the other hand, many buyers (especially consumers) do not purchase with an expectation of injury and do not think about default. The seller has placed his product on the market, inviting its purchase and use. The public deserves more protection than four years when the injury does not occur until long after the purchase. Thus will the arguments go, with courts reaching results which are hard to classify in any text.[27] This much can be predicted, however: the more rigid the statute of limitations, the more numerous will be the court-made exceptions to that statute.

§ 186.   Tolling—Termination of Suit

The Code's statute of limitation contains two other provisions designed to make it operate fairly. The first provides that the statute neither alters the law on tolling of the statute of limitation[28] nor applies to causes of action which have accrued before the Code became effective.[29] Thus, the pre-Code law relating to tolling will continue

---

26. Matlack, Inc. v. Butler Mfg. Co., 253 F.Supp. 972 (E.D.Pa.1966) (no warranty of future performance found in normal warranties); Rempe v. General Electric Co., 28 Conn.Supp. 160 (1969). For a construction of a warranty, see Perry v. Augustine, 37 Pa.D. & C.2d 416 (C.P.1965).

27. E. g., Hoeflich v. William S. Merrell Co., 288 F.Supp. 659 (E.D.Pa. 1967). The forum statute is to be applied in a choice of law case. Natale

v. Upjohn Co., 356 F.2d 590 (3d Cir. 1966).

28. UCC § 2–725(4). The statute is not tolled by seller's attempts to repair. Bobo v. Page Eng'r Co., 285 F.Supp. 664 (W.D.Pa.1967), aff'd 395 F.2d 991 (3d Cir. 1968).

29. UCC § 2–725(4). Tomble v. New York Central R. R. Co., 234 F.Supp. 101 (N.D.Ohio 1964).

even though the Code was adopted—a result which would undoubtedly have been supplied by the courts had it not been included by the drafters.

The second indicates what happens when the plaintiff has commenced an action within the four-year period, only to have it terminated too late to bring another suit within that same period:

> Where an action commenced within the time limited by subsection (1) is so terminated as to leave available a remedy by another action for the same breach such other action may be commenced after the expiration of the time limited and within six months after the termination of the first action unless the termination resulted from voluntary discontinuance or from dismissal for failure or neglect to prosecute.[30]

---

30. UCC § 2–725(3). Dismissal without prejudice for improper venue on motion of plaintiff is not a "voluntary discontinuance" within the meaning of the statute. D. & J. Leasing, Inc. v. Hercules Galion Prods. Co., 429 S.W. 2d 854 (Ky.1968).

•

TABLE OF CASES

References are to Pages

N

TABLE OF CITATIONS
TO THE
UNIFORM COMMERCIAL CODE

INDEX

References are to Pages

INDEX